Family Evaluation in Child Custody Mediation, Arbitration, and Litigation

Family Evaluation in Child Custody Mediation, Arbitration, and Litigation

RICHARD A. GARDNER, M.D.

Clinical Professor of Child Psychiatry
Columbia University
College of Physicians and Surgeons

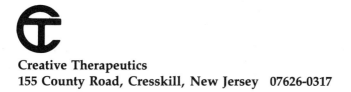

Creative Therapeutics
155 County Road, Cresskill, New Jersey   07626-0317

© 1989 by Creative Therapeutics
155 CountyRoad, Cresskill, New Jersey 07626-0317

Library of Congress Cataloging-in-Publication Data

Gardner, Richard A.
  Family evaluation in child custody mediation,
arbitration, and litigation.

  1. Custody of children—United States. 2. Forensic
psychiatry—United States. I. Title.
KF547.G38   1989   346.7301'7   89-17403
ISBN 0-933812-20-5   347.30617

PRINTED IN THE UNITED STATES OF AMERICA
10 9 8 7 6 5 4 3 2 1

To my late brother,
Ronald M. Gardner

And my parents,
Amelia and Irving Gardner

I was never ruined but twice —
once when I lost a lawsuit,
once when I won one.

Voltaire (1694-1778)

In all that is decent...in all that is just, the framers of our Constitution could never have intended that the "enjoyment of life" meant that if divorce came, it was to be attended by throwing the two unfortunates and their children into a judicial arena, with lawyers as their seconds, and have them tear and verbally slash at each other in a trial by emotional conflict that may go on in perpetuity. We have been humane enough to outlaw cockfights, dogfights and bullfights; and yet, we do nothing about the barbarism of divorce fighting, and trying to find ways to end it. We concern ourselves with cruelty to animals, and rightfully so, but we are unconcerned about the forced and intentionally perpetrated cruelty inflicted upon the emotionally distressed involved in divorce. We abhor police beating confessions out of alleged criminals, and yet we cheer and encourage lawyers to emotionally beat up and abuse two innocent people and their children, because their marriage has floundered. Somewhere along the line, our sense of values, decency, humanism and justice went off the track.

From a Petition for a Writ of Certiorari submitted to the Supreme Court of the United States of America by Cleveland, Ohio, attorney Sanford J. Berger on behalf of a divorced client's request for protection from cruel and unusual punishment (associated with penalties suffered in divorce litigation) as guaranteed by the Eighth Amendment of the United States Constitution.

Other Books by Richard A. Gardner

The Boys and Girls Book About Divorce

Therapeutic Communication with Children: The Mutual
    Storytelling Technique

Dr. Gardner's Stories About the Real World, Volume I

Dr. Gardner's Stories About the Real World, Volume II

Dr. Gardner's Fairy Tales for Today's Children

Understanding Children: A Parents Guide to Child Rearing

MBD: The Family Book About Minimal Brain Dysfunction

Psychotherapeutic Approaches to the Resistant Child

Psychotherapy with Children of Divorce

Dr. Gardner's Modern Fairy Tales

The Parents Book About Divorce

The Boys and Girls Book About One-Parent Families

The Objective Diagnosis of Minimal Brain Dysfunction

Dorothy and the Lizard of Oz

Dr. Gardner's Fables for Our Times

The Boys and Girls Book About Stepfamilies

Family Evaluation in Child Custody Litigation

Separation Anxiety Disorder: Psychodynamics
    and Psychotherapy

Child Custody Litigation: A Guide for Parents
    and Mental Health Professionals

The Psychotherapeutic Techniques of Richard A. Gardner

Hyperactivity, The So-Called Attention-Deficit Disorder,
    and The Group of MBD Syndromes

The Parental Alienation Syndrome and the Differentiation
    Between Fabricated and Genuine Child Sex Abuse

Psychotherapy with Adolescents

Psychotherapy of Psychogenic Learning Disabilities

CONTENTS

ACKNOWLEDGMENTS

I am deeply indebted to the following friends and professional colleagues who provided me with valuable recommendations for the first chapter of this book. Their input was particularly useful in the development of my three-phase proposal for resolving custody disputes without adversarial proceedings, but still within the structure of our legal system:

Sanford J. Berger, Esq., first lawyer to receive the Chief Justice Warren E. Burger Healer Award - for leadership in helping children of separation and divorce. October 23, 1987.

Arthur M. Berman, Esq., partner, Kirsh, Berman & Hoffenberg, Ltd., Chicago, Illinois.

Hon. Richard Y. Feder, Circuit Judge, 11th Judicial Circuit of Florida, Miami, Florida.

Eugene A. Friedberg, M.D., Assistant Clinical Professor of Psychiatry, Columbia University, College of Physicians and Surgeons, New York, New York.

Barbara Handschu, Esq., Vice-Chair, Family Law Section, New York State Bar Association.

Katherine Sweeney Hayden, Esq., partner, Boyar, Higgins & Hayden, Morristown, New Jersey.

John M. Haynes, Ph.D., President of Haynes Mediation

Associates, New York, New York and Huntington, New York and Founding President of the Academy of Family Mediators.

Harry Krop, Ph.D., Director, Community Behavioral Services, Gainesville, Florida.

Hugh McIsaac, Director, Family Court Services – Conciliation Court, Los Angeles, California.

Michael I. Sovern, Esq., President and formerly Dean of the Law School and Professor of Law, Columbia University, New York, New York.

It is important for the reader to appreciate that my listing these colleagues here does not necessarily mean that there was full agreement with and/or endorsement of every one of my opinions.

With regard to the editing of the manuscript I am deeply indebted to Robert Mulholland who dedicated himself to editing the manuscript. He provided useful suggestions and, at the same time, exhibited respect for my wishes regarding style, format, and content. I am also grateful for the editorial contributions of Frances S. Dubner and my wife, Patricia Lefevere Gardner.

My ever-loyal secretaries, once again, committed themselves enthusiastically to the typing of the manuscript in its various renditions. Donna L. La Tourette did the bulk of the work and provided valuable editorial comments as well. Linda E. Gould and Carol Gibbon, as before, dedicated themselves to the typing.

I am also grateful to Robert Tebbenhoff of Lind Graphics in Woodcliff Lake, New Jersey for his valuable contributions to the production of this book, from manuscript to final volume.

My greatest debt, however, is to the children of divorce who have taught me much over many years about the kinds of grief they can suffer. From their parents, as well, I have learned many things that are contained herein. Attorneys have also taught me a great deal about the adversary system, both its weaknesses and strengths (unfortunately, more of the former than the latter). My hope is that what I have learned from these sources will be put to good use in this book and will contribute to the prevention and alleviation of the sorrows of divorce ordeals in others.

INTRODUCTION

This book is an update and expansion of my *Family Evaluation in Child Custody Litigation*, first published in 1982. In the seven years since the publication of that book so much has happened in the field of child custody litigation that more than simply another reprinting of the original volume was warranted. Furthermore, subsequent experiences in the field have led me to modify and elaborate upon my earlier ideas. Probably the most important of these modifications is my introduction of the concept of the *parental alienation syndrome* and my increasing knowledge of the etiology, pathogenesis, manifestations, course, and treatment of this disorder. Although I have written about this disorder earlier (1985, 1986a, 1987a, 1987b) this is the first publication in which I present the breakdown of parental alienation syndrome families into three types—mild, moderate, and severe—and provide, as well, what I consider to be the best approaches to their treatment—both by the courts and mental health professionals. Another important development since the publication of the earlier volume has been the increasing frequency of false sex-abuse allegations in child custody disputes. These allegations have served to "heat up" such disputes and have complicated the evaluator's ability to assess parental capacity. Because I have dealt extensively with the differentiation between false and genuine sex-abuse allegations elsewhere (1987a) this issue will not be discussed to any depth in this volume.

One of the problems I had to deal with in the preparation of this update was that of terminology. The word *custody* has come into disrepute because of its implication of possession and possibly entrapment. The term *joint custody*, although implicitly egalitarian, still carries with it the burden of the implications of the word custody. For reasons to be elaborated upon in this book I generally prefer the term *residential and decision-making arrangement*. This term encompasses the two primary issues under consideration, namely, where the children shall be living at any particular time and who shall have the power to make decisions in major areas of concern to the children. *Shared parenting, parenting plan,* and *residential provisions* are terms that have also been utilized to circumvent the problems attendant to the use of the word custody. Interestingly, those who use these terms find themselves falling back on the word custody — conscious attempts to avoid it notwithstanding. A typical document (even legislative) begins with the new term and almost automatically reverts to the custody term because of the impracticality of the original term when it must be used in a wide variety of ways, e.g., as an adjective. Accordingly, at the risk of appearing to be old-fashioned and not in touch with the latest developments in this field I have decided to retain the word custody. I thereby circumvent the verbal gymnastics necessary to avoid the use of the word.

During the last few years even the word *divorce* has come into disrepute. Instead, the term *marital dissolution* is in vogue. I fail to understand what the objection is to the word divorce, and see nothing accomplished (but confusion) by substituting marital dissolution. Accordingly, I have had no problem using the word divorce throughout the course of this book.

Another term that warrants definition here is *mediation*. I use the word to refer to a process by which the examiner helps the parties resolve their custody dispute without litigation, lawyers, and courtroom proceedings. Mediation is sometimes referred to as a catalytic process, in which the mediator's primary purpose is to facilitate the parties' themselves resolving their conflict. I have no problem using the term in this way. However it is rare, in my experience, for the mediation to be so conducted. More often the mediator does provide input, guidelines, and even recommendations. Accordingly, I prefer to use the term in this more expanded way because, when I do mediate, I generally come forth with recommendations. Under these circumstances the mediation might justifiably be called nonbinding arbitration — especially when the parties at the outset have requested that the mediator provide specific recommendations for their consideration. This procedure, however, has to be sharply differentiated from binding arbitration in which the parties agree beforehand to accept the recommendations.

In some situations the mediation may be relatively simple and in-depth evaluation of parents and children not necessary. There are many mediations, however, in which such an extensive evaluation is warranted. In these more complex situations I generally conduct the kind of in-depth evaluation described in this book. Accordingly, the extensive custody evaluation described herein is applicable to both the litigation and mediation situations.

For reasons to be described in depth in Chapter One, in June 1988 I decided to remove myself entirely from custody and sex-abuse litigation. I am, however, continuing to mediate custody disputes, completely removed from adversarial proceedings and courtroom testimony. Accordingly, now I only use the intensive evaluation in the context of mediation. Examiners who are involved in courtroom litigation should, however, still find these procedures useful.

Also described in Chapter One is my three-phase proposal, which removes entirely the resolution of custody disputes from adversarial procedures and courtroom litigation. However, the procedures still utilize the services of both mental health professionals and attorneys. It is my hope that others in the field will proceed as I have and refuse to involve themselves in a process that has caused so much grief and psychopathology.

Following the introductory material presented in Chapter One I then present my views on examiners' serving as impartial evaluators, rather than as advocates. I then discuss in detail my provisions document (revision no. 36, the last) with numerous caveats for those who do not heed its many warnings. As the reader can readily appreciate, this seven-page document was not spun off the top of my head one night; rather, it represents the accumulation of many years of "plugging holes in the dike." The blood, sweat, and tears involved in the document's creation seep between the lines.

The next chapters are devoted to the details of interviewing the parents, individually and in joint interviews. The latter are crucial for examiners if they are to conduct properly a child custody evaluation. Next, I devote a chapter to the parental alienation syndrome, which examiners must understand if they are to examine properly the children involved in a custody dispute. Then I describe in detail the interview techniques I have found useful with children—with particular emphasis on the problems related to obtaining information about parental preference without necessarily asking the child to provide an open statement. Techniques for interviewing friends, stepparents, relatives, and the housekeeper are then described.

I then discuss in depth the techniques I utilize for making recommendations from the collected data. The next chapter focuses on evaluators' providing courtroom testimony, with many specific details which can help examiners deal with this often difficult situation. A chapter is devoted to advising judges on interviewing children. Although this chapter may not be crucial to the continuity of this book, the information is provided examiners because it can be helpful to them in the course of the litigation. Lawyers and judges themselves may find this chapter useful. The next chapter is devoted to mediation, the advantages of this method of dispute resolution over litigation, and the way in which the evaluative procedures described herein can be incorporated into the mediation process. The last chapter provides recommendations for change, especially in the education of lawyers and mental health professionals.

The response to this volume's predecessor was indeed gratifying. Many referred to it as the standard reference work in the field, and its utilization by mental health professionals and attorneys has been gratifying. I would like to believe that the book played a role in reducing the frequency with which mental health professionals were willing to serve as advocates ("hired guns") in custody litigation and made many in the field appreciative of the importance of mental health professionals as *impartial* examiners. It is my hope that this book will perpetuate these practices as well as promulgate the alternative three-phase method of custody dispute resolution proposed in it. My hope also is that it will increase evaluators' sensitivity to the parental alienation syndrome, especially with regard to the three types and the special therapeutic and legal approachesto their treatment.

Family Evaluation in
Child Custody Mediation,
Arbitration, and Litigation

⚖️ ONE

MY INVOLVEMENT IN CHILD CUSTODY LITIGATION: PAST, PRESENT, AND FUTURE

This book was originally planned as an expanded and updated second edition of my *Family Evaluation in Child Custody Litigation* (1982a). In the spring of 1988 I realized that much had happened in the six years since the publication of that book. In addition, the supply of the third printing was rapidly becoming depleted, providing yet another reason for considering an update. My plans were to spend time during the summer of 1988 preparing the revised edition. However, at approximately 3:00 p.m. on June 15, 1988 (a moment I consider a milestone in my life) I decided to stop taking on cases involving me in custody and/or sex-abuse litigation. (The incident which brought about this decision will be discussed subsequently.) Of course, I planned to continue my involvement providing services and testimony in those cases in which I was already involved, but I made the resolution that I would never again take on a *new* case.

Accordingly, I quit! Obviously, this decision had to have formidable implications for this book's functions and the nature and extent of its revision. The general principles of these modifications will be presented in this chapter and the details within the book itself. And, for reasons that will soon become apparent, even a change of title was warranted.

1

I recognize that my decision to leave the field of custody litigation probably comes as a surprise to readers who have become familiar with my work in this realm, but it should not come as a surprise to those who have involved themselves in providing such services. Every person has his (her) breaking point. I am not an exception to this principle. Of all the forms of litigation, custody litigation may very well be the most vicious. After all, the stakes are the highest: involved are one's most treasured possessions, one's children. Although litigants may certainly get viciously embroiled in disputes over issues such as money and property, I do not believe that such conflicts are likely to reach the levels of intensity that litigation over children inevitably produces. And if one then adds the additional rage and indignation generated when a sex-abuse allegation is added, the fury can reach fanatic and even psychotic levels. Therapists who involve themselves as impartial examiners (which I almost invariably had done) in such litigation are voluntarily placing themselves in a no-man's land between the warring parties. Even if they are willing to serve as advocates (a position I consider immoral), they are still placing themselves in the firing range of their adversaries. These were only a few of the factors that led to my decision to walk off the battlefield forever. At this point I will elaborate upon the sequence of events that ultimately resulted in my June 15, 1988 decision.

HOW I GOT INVOLVED IN CUSTODY LITIGATION

For most, life provides many surprises and unexpected experiences. We often get caught up in events in which we never anticipated we would become embroiled. I first began testifying in court in 1960. I was fulfilling a two-year military obligation as a psychiatrist at the United States Army Hospital in Frankfurt am Main, Germany. Early in my tour of duty, it became apparent that my commanding officer had no great affection for me; nor did I have significant love for him. I viewed him as having a "military mentality," and he viewed me as having an "Ivy League mentality." (I believe that these were quite accurate conclusions about one another.) But he was a colonel, and I a captain. This difference in rank provided him with an excellent opportunity for expressing his animosity toward me, which he did by selecting me for the less desirable assignments. And I had no option but to accept them. (As they say in the military, "orders is orders.") He considered providing court testimony to be the most repugnant of the many detestable jobs that one could have and so, not surprisingly, he assigned me these cases.

Considering his motivations, I initially assumed that the work would indeed be odious. Much to my surprise, I found legal work fascinating. Fundamental issues of human behavior were being dealt with and questions that have plagued the greatest thinkers over the span of history had to be addressed. One had to learn very quickly in order to appear as an "expert," only a few months out of residency. (The military has a way of making "experts" out of people quite quickly.) I evaluated soldiers who were being court-martialed and learned much of interest about military law. Furthermore, I had the unique experience of giving testimony in German civilian courts. Because military courts have no jurisdiction over wives and children, such dependents could only be tried in German civilian courts. However, these people were still entitled to military medical care, including psychiatric consultation and treatment. Included in such consultations were court evaluations. I found myself thereby testifying in German courts where I learned some fascinating things about European systems of adjudication. In order to save time I was often flown by helicopter to the various cities in Germany where I testified. As a fringe "benefit" en route, I would hang out the side hatch (supported well, of course, by safety belts) and take photos that I could not have otherwise obtained. I never let on to my commanding officer how thankful I was to him for having provided me with these experiences; had I done so I am certain he would have assigned me elsewhere (like winter maneuvers on the Czechoslovakian border).

In the mid-1960s (now out of the Army and in private practice), when the divorce rates started to climb, I once again became involved in lawsuits — primarily custody litigation. During that period no-fault divorce laws were being introduced. In most states they replaced the system whereby one had to prove that one's spouse was guilty of a marital crime such as infidelity, mental cruelty, etc. In many states this had had the effect of requiring people to involve themselves in adulterous behavior (or at least stage or claim "adultery") even if they had no desire whatsoever to do so. The new laws, though, only required the spouses to agree that they were incompatible and to live apart a prescribed period (usually one to two years, depending upon the state). Although the new no-fault laws or the easier grounds for divorce reduced the likelihood that people would have to litigate in order to get divorced, they did not reduce the frequency of litigating for money, property, and/or children.

In the 1970s things began to "steam up" in the field of custody litigation. Prior to that time women were generally viewed as the preferable parents under the *tender years presumption*. When men claimed that this presumption was intrinsically sexist, courts were sympathetic—thereby ushering in a new era of egalitarianism in custody disputes. Under the *best interests of the child philosophy*, courts were required to make custody decisions on the assessment of parenting capacity, ignoring the sex of the parent. Presumably such "sex-blind" decisions served the best interests of children. In fact, children then became open prey to both parents, each of whom claimed equal right to their custody. As a result we have witnessed an epidemic of custody litigation unlike that which has ever existed in the history of humankind. I too, over the years, became progressively more involved in such litigation.

WHY I GOT INVOLVED IN CUSTODY LITIGATION

As I look back, I ask myself the question: "How come, and why?" (We psychoanalysts are always asking questions like these.) There were other child psychiatrists who were not getting involved. When they smelled litigation (even over the telephone), they ran the other way. In fact, that was the usual reaction. I couldn't run the other way in the military, but I certainly had the freedom to refuse such referrals in my private practice. One factor related to my recognition that such involvement enhanced my expertise as a psychiatrist. Psychodynamic psychiatry (and, to an even greater extent, psychoanalysis) is probably the most speculative of all the allegedly scientific disciplines. In fact, it is reasonable to say that it is much more an art than a science. We spin off the most fantastic explanations for human behavior and often come to believe our own delusions. I learned in the military that courtroom experience could be a wonderful antidote to such professional morbidity. Good lawyers are schooled in separating fact from fantasy, evidence from speculation. In cross examination one must "stick with the facts." Observations and direct quotations carry weight. Speculations, fantasies, theories, and hearsay have no place in good testimony. Whatever regrets I may have in the future for having involved myself all these years in custody litigation, I will always consider this aspect of the experience to have been an extremely beneficial one for me (with regard to my professional competence, not my mental health).

Another motivating factor was money. When starting a private practice one generally is not as choosy regarding patient selection as one may be after the years progress and the practice grows. I usually could earn more going to court than I could in my office (and this is still the case). Testifying on a witness stand is a special skill and is generally a more demanding experience—thus the justification for charging a higher fee. At the time I decided to discontinue involvement in custody litigation I was deriving approximately 25 percent of my income from such participation. Obviously, this factor had to be taken into consideration when I made my decision, and there is no question that it made it more difficult to remove myself from providing such service. However, other factors were operative which outweighed this advantage.

Whereas in the early days I was somewhat fearful about testifying in court, as the years progressed and as my expertise grew I gradually reached the point where I found it an enjoyable game (as strange as that may seem). I often compared it to a fencing match. I learned the rules and I played rather well. I didn't even view it as a fencing match between equals; rather it was a match between a person with a longer sword and more protection (the lawyer) and a person with a shorter sword and less protection (the individual on the witness stand). The rules of cross-examination put the witness (even the so-called expert) in the weaker position. The witness is competing with an intrinsic handicap, built into the rules of the sport—which is what adversary litigation basically is (at least for the lawyers). Accordingly, when the witness wins it is an even greater victory. The cross-examining attorney was allowed to confine me to yes-no responses, select and focus on out-of-context material, and pose questions in a way that distorted and misrepresented my opinions. Getting across one's point under such circumstances was indeed a challenge, and I often felt that I was successful in accomplishing this. And this brought an ego-enhancing gratification to many of my court appearances.

As my knowledge and expertise grew, I became ever more relaxed and confident on the stand and realized that I was often providing impressive performances. (The courtroom scene is also a "spectator sport.") Furthermore, my books on custody litigation were becoming increasingly popular and often referred to as the "standards" and "classics" in the field. Throughout the country they were being quoted by lawyers and judges. Decisions derived from my publications and testimony occasionally cited these works as legal precedents. I was frequently invited to lecture to judges and lawyers throughout the United States and Canada. Obviously, this was extremely gratifying and I felt that it behooved me to enhance further my knowledge in order to ensure that my publications, lectures, and testimony maintained their position of high regard.

WHY I DECIDED TO QUIT THE
FIELD OF CUSTODY LITIGATION

Just as there were many reasons for involving myself, there were even more reasons for getting out while I was still alive. As I will explain, I am not saying this figuratively, but literally. The multiple factors operative in my making this decision had been percolating over the years with increasing intensity. The June 15, 1988 decision should be viewed as the point when the camel's back was broken by the final straw.

Dissatisfaction with the Adversary System As a Method for Resolving Custody Disputes

One reason for my quitting related to increasing dissatisfaction with the formidable limitations of the adversary system as a method for resolving disputes, especially custody disputes. As I have stated in numerous publications (e.g., 1982a, 1985, 1986a) the adversary system is perhaps the worst conceivable method for resolving a child-custody dispute. (I am not saying anything here about other kinds of disputes—only child-custody disputes. But this does not mean that I do not have serious reservations about its value in resolving other kinds of conflicts as well [1987a].) Elsewhere (1987a) I have discussed in detail the evolution of the system and how it perpetuates residua of its medieval origins in trial by battle (or champion), trial by ordeal (tolerance for pain, torture, etc.), and trial by wager (oath). Over the centuries, these methods of dispute resolution were (in England and its colonies) gradually replaced by and evolved into what we presently call the adversary system. The system is based on the theory that the best way of resolving a dispute is for both parties to present their arguments before a presumably impartial third party (or group). The impartial party may be a judge, a tribunal, or a jury. Each side is represented by an advocate (attorney) who is permitted to withhold from the impartial, to a reasonable degree, that information which might weaken its position if divulged, and each side is encouraged to present in full detail information that supports its contention. Out of this conflict of presentations the impartial party is presumably in the best position to determine who is telling the "truth" and then reach some decision regarding the dispute's resolution.

As the system is utilized today, champions are no longer hired knights, but lawyers. The ordeals are no longer the immersion of one's arm in a cauldron to see how quickly the lesion heals (God heals good, honest people quickly) or being thrown into the river to see if one sinks or floats (floaters—for a variety of perverse reasons—were generally considered guilty and sinkers innocent). Rather the ordeals today take the form of exposure to relentless litigious persecution, depletion of one's resources, and humiliating cross-examination in open court. The character witnesses ("compurgators") that testified in the Middle Ages in trial by wager have been replaced by one's friends and relatives who have no hesitancy committing perjury (nor are they punished for such) in our modern-day courts of law.

The system intensifies pre-existent psychopathology and causes psychiatric disorders even when they didn't exist previously. One could go through most of the psychogenic disorders described in DSM-III-R (American Psychiatric Association, 1987) and easily see how each of them can be intensified or produced by protracted courtroom litigation. Elsewhere (1986a) I have done just that, describing in detail the specific ways in which protracted custody litigation may bring about a wide variety of psychogenic disorders in parents and children. I have seen normal people become neurotic and neurotic people become psychotic, as a direct result of embroilment in adversarial proceedings associated with their divorces. A neighbor of mine, after two years of such involvement, died of a heart attack at the age of 43. There was no previous history of illness, cardiac or otherwise. A woman I evaluated in association with her custody dispute committed suicide two years after I had testified in court. I strongly recommended immediate transfer of the children back to her and requested that the court designate her the primary custodial parent. When I learned of her death (from a patient who was a neighbor of hers), I also found out that the court still had not made a custody decision. In order to lessen my own contribution to the perpetuation of this inhumane system for resolving divorce and custody disputes, I generally have served only as an impartial examiner, rather than as an advocate ("hired gun" or, less benevolently, "whore"). But I was still involving myself in the system.

The vast majority of parents involved in such litigation are to some extent being exploited by their attorneys. Although it is a legal form of exploitation, it is exploitation nevertheless. Rather than use *one* impartial person, who might help the individuals resolve their dispute quickly in a nonadversarial fashion, it requires *two* individuals who enhance and prolong the conflict, much to the financial benefit of the so-called advocates. The principle is well demonstrated by the story about the small town in which there was only one attorney who was planning to move elsewhere because he could not make a living. In order to discourage his departure, the townfolk brought in a second lawyer. The two of them then became rich.

Even though I was serving as an impartial, I was still serving within the system. It is an uncivilized and inhumane way of trying to resolve a custody dispute. A system originally designed to determine whether an accused party did indeed commit a crime is being utilized to decide which of two parents (often quite equal in parenting capacity) would better serve as the primary custodial parent for their children. The frustrations it inevitably causes the litigants are enormous and the sense of impotent rage that they inevitably feel is devastating. The system does not foster, and often does not even permit, the individuals to sit down together in a sane manner and attempt to resolve their differences by direct discussion in a free-flowing give and take fashion. Litigation is just the opposite of mediation, the more humane method for resolving disputes.

It may be of interest to the reader that the adversary system is primarily used in Great Britain and countries that were her former colonies (like the United States for example). The rest of the world has recognized its deficiencies and has little tolerance for it. Law students in the United States and Great Britain generally are presented with the system without being provided this information. Usually they uncritically accept adversarial litigation as the only (or optimum) way to resolve a conflict and rarely give consideration to alternative modes of dispute resolution (although these have recently been introduced in some United States law schools as part of the curriculum).

It was from the recognition of the system's deficiencies and the psychopathology that it caused that I made every attempt to serve as an impartial examiner, rather than as an advocate, in custody litigation. It was only after every reasonable attempt was made to serve as an impartial that I would even consider serving as an advocate. And then I would do so only when I had full conviction for the position of the party to be supported. But over the years I became increasingly guilty about even this level of participation. I too have taken the litigants' money, even though my role has generally served to shorten the litigation and reduce its cost. Although my involvement as an impartial examiner was designed to lessen and possibly prevent the development and/or perpetuation of psychopathology, I was still a contributor. Even though I was formally viewed by the court as an impartial examiner, after my findings became known I was usually considered to be the advocate of the person whose position I supported and was treated as such regarding courtroom procedures of examination. I was thereby still involving myself in the perpetuation of the litigation, even though I believed that my participation as an impartial served to shorten and, in some cases, even prevent courtroom litigation. Over the years I became increasingly appreciative of the fact that when I served as a mediator I was more likely to protect parents from the depravities of the adversary system, exploitation by attorneys, and the psychopathology that inevitably resulted from such exposure. Thus I decided to remove myself from courtroom litigation and to serve only as a mediator.

Ethical Considerations

I believe that ethics committees of mental health professional societies should consider involvement of its members in adversarial custody litigation (even as an impartial examiner) to be unethical. There is no question that individuals who voluntarily serve as advocates in such litigation—at the outset—are unethical. Coming to court and testifying that one parent would better serve as the primary custodial parent—without interviewing the other parent—is a despicable practice worthy of formidable condemnation. People who do this are truly selling their services as hired guns. They are providing ammunition for lawyers in their courtroom warfare and contributing thereby to the exploitation of the clients. They provide no useful service in that each side's advocate often cancels out the other's and thereby contributes to the formation and/or perpetuation of psychopathology. Such participation is patently unethical and, in my opinion, should be grounds for malpractice.

But what about serving as an impartial examiner? Should that also be considered unethical? One could argue that such an examiner is serving as an impartial, has evaluated both parents, and is not presumably serving as a hired gun. However, even when serving as an impartial, one is still voluntarily entering into and participating within a system that is psychologically detrimental to clients. Such service, therefore, violates the basic ethical tenets of the mental health professions. Such participation by physicians breaches their vow to subscribe to a fundamental tenet of the teachings of Hippocrates: *Primum, non nocere (Above all, do not harm.* Or, translated more loosely: *If you can't help patients get better, at least don't make them worse).* Professional societies should, however, encourage our participation as mediators and arbitrators. (I will elaborate on such participation later.) It has taken a long time for me to come to this realization, but as the years passed, I have been gradually brought to this point.

Client Rage

I introduce my next point anecdotally. In August 1985, I appeared as a guest on television's *The Phil Donahue Show.* I was talking about some of my modifications of children's fairy tales (1974, 1977a, 1980) and mentioned that I believe that many of the themes traditionally portrayed therein are psychologically detrimental, especially to women. The notion that a damsel in distress will be rescued by some handsome knight is a disservice to both sexes. It promulgates unhealthy dependency fantasies in females and unhealthy rescue fantasies in males. It is just the opposite of the kind of egalitarianism we are trying to bring about in modern society. I also spoke about the delusional factors operative in romantic love and how they interfere with more reasonable assessments of individuals. The women in the audience became progressively more upset over my comments. They accused me of trying to destroy cherished fantasies and insisted: "someday my prince will come." My responding explanations carried little weight, so great was their animosity. Their hostility crescendoed to the point where Mr. Donahue stated, "I think we're going to have to carry Dr. Gardner out of here on a stretcher."

After the show many friends asked me how I could sit there so calmly, while so many people were hysterically screaming at me. I had not given thought to this aspect of the program. But their questions interested me and, after giving the matter some thought, I responded, "I guess I'm used to this kind of thing. It's what I listen to all day. People are always yelling at me. People are always blaming me for things." I have come to appreciate that most often (but certainly not always) hysterical outbursts directed against me generally have less to do with anything I have done and much more to do with pathological factors operating within the head of the hysteric.

The blasts at me on the Donahue Show were like BBs or slingshot pebbles compared to the bombs detonated in custody litigation. But custody litigation represents the upper end of the continuum of anger to which therapists are subjected. Being a psychiatrist exposes one to an enormous amount of hostility. One is supposed to sit there, understand, be sympathetic and empathic, and analyze. It is a draining experience. My supervisors never warned me about how enervating it could be. Neither in residency nor in psychoanalytic training did they ever give me a hint about how exhausting the work could be and how the exposure to the rage of one's patients takes its psychological toll. Over the years I have found myself increasingly depleted at the end of a day. Although some of this fatigue, I am sure, relates to the aging process (I am 57 at this writing), I am convinced that more relates to the drainage of my energy caused by continual exposure to patients' hostility. I am still disappointed with and critical of my teachers and supervisors for never warning me of this danger of the field.

When young people, who are considering becoming psychotherapists, ask me for counseling, I inevitably advise them of this drawback. I say to them, "If you want to be an obstetrician, you have to resign yourself to getting up in the middle of the night. If you want to be a urologist, you're going to get urine on your hands. If you want to be a proctologist, you're going to get feces on your hands. If you want to be a psychiatrist or psychotherapist, you have to have very thick skin. You must be able to tolerate an enormous amount of rage being directed at you for things that you never did. You take a lot of blame when you're guiltless and innocent. You have to be able to tolerate a lot of screaming, crying, and grief. You have to develop a very thick skin if you are going to do this work properly." But the rage does not stop in the office. One gets maligned to one's colleagues, friends, and neighbors and sometimes one learns about the vilifications. Most often, explanations and correction of the distortions might involve a breach of confidentiality; so one just has to shut up. This too I have been able to accept.

Problems with Payment for my Services

Women's liberation and gender egalitarianism notwithstanding, men still have much more money than women. I am not claiming that this is justifiable, but it is the reality. Accordingly, in the vast majority of custody cases in which I have been involved, the fathers have either paid completely for all or the major portion of my fees. Although legislative statutes in recent years have generally required courts to be "sex blind" in custody determinations, the realities are that mothers, much more frequently than fathers, will win a custody case. This does not relate simply to "old fashioned" judges who subscribe to the traditional view that mothers are intrinsically the superior parent. Even the more egalitarian justices will often rule that the children would be better off remaining with the mother after using such criteria as relative strength of bonding, availability, and the children's preferences. In short, the father is usually the one who pays the money, and the mother is usually the one who is granted custody. Before this final decision is made, the father is likely to have to pay for a report that does not support his position and even pay a mental health professional to testify against him in court. Obviously, an examiner who believes that a father will fulfill financial obligations under these circumstances is naive. It is downright simpleminded to entertain such expectations. Anyone who is masochistic enough to enter the field and "trust" a person to pay for services involving testifying against him (her) in court will predictably gain gratification of these masochistic tendencies.

Because I am not a masochist (although it may be that I am one, after all, when one considers the fact that I have voluntarily involved myself in custody litigation), I have required an advance security deposit before agreeing to become involved. Over the years this deposit rose from $1000 to $2500. This related not only to inflation but also to progressively increasing reluctance by payers to fulfill their obligations to me. But this deposit was not the only mechanism I utilized for security. My provisions document (Appendix I) required the payer(s) to pay at the time that services were rendered and included a clause that I was entitled to discontinue services entirely after one week if payment was not forthcoming. Frequently I had to "remind" people that they were on the verge of defaulting and sometimes such reminders involved the threat that I would remove myself from the case and report my reasons for withdrawal to the presiding judge (with copies of my letter to the attorneys and clients). On occasion, even the security deposit did not provide proper protection against the formidable expenses incurred in a few days in court. Running after the clients to obtain my money was ego debasing. Whether one wants to view it as threatening or begging (or any combination of the two), the experience cannot but lower the examiner's feelings of self-worth. Although not to ask for the money might preserve one's self-esteem, the exercise of this option can lead to exploitation. The choice, then, basically boils down to that of being humiliated or being exploited. I have experienced both in the course of my work in custody litigation and now I want neither.

My Sense of Commitment

I suspect that, in some areas, I have an hypertrophied conscience. When I compare myself to most of the lawyers and judges who involve themselves in this kind of litigation, there is no question that, on the average, they have far less guilt over what is going on with their clients than do I. I have no hesitation in saying that some of these individuals are overt psychopaths. Many have absolutely no appreciation of the grief they are causing fellow human beings by extracting as much money as they can from clients, and then basically ignoring them when they run out of money. Although they may not formally be permitted to remove themselves from a case merely because a client no longer has any money, they in effect do so. I am not putting all attorneys into this category, only the majority of those whom I have encountered in this area.

With regard to judges, many I have encountered are uninterested, lazy, and uncommitted. I recognize that their caseloads often are quite large and that the demands being placed upon them may be enormous. Some rise to the challenge by dedicating themselves to doing the best they can under difficult circumstances. Others, however, basically "don't give a damn." I have seen judges sleeping in the courtroom while the lawyers are going through the motions of the trial, making believe that the judge is still awake. On the stand, I have seen judges reading newspapers and magazines in the course of the testimony and only I, sitting close to them, was able to observe what they were doing. Among my colleagues who do this kind of work, there is also a continuum regarding degree of commitment. There are people who will do an evaluation for a fixed fee (like $500 or a $1000) and promise the whole package—including courtroom testimony. Although this may serve to attract clients, there is no question that such a practice requires significant compromises regarding the kind of evaluation one can conduct. In order to make such an evaluation "cost effective" a limited number of interviews must be conducted, often precluding important individuals such as stepparents and even the children.

At the risk of being considered somewhat sanctimonious, I have too strong a sense of commitment to the people I serve to involve myself in watered-down and slipshod evaluations. I recognize that I may sound here like the Jewish mother in Philip Roth's book *Portnoy's Complaint* who stated that she had only *one* deficiency, namely, that she was "too good." Custody evaluations have always weighed heavily on me. I recognize and hope that the court will be giving serious consideration to my opinion and that the future course of a child's life may rest upon my conclusions. People have paid me only for the hours of formal work, i.e., interviewing, report preparation, court appearances, etc. I have not been paid for the hours of preoccupation, worry, soul-searching, and deliberation. I have not received fees for the tossing and turning at night and my inability to fall asleep. I have not been paid for the time I have spent worrying about some poor innocent child who is being kept in an unhealthy household because of the slowness of the legal process, the planned obstructionism of attorneys, and the various forms of parental psychopathology that have contributed to the misplacement of the child. The sense of urgency I have felt in many such situations has produced formidable frustration, with no possibility of hope or success that things would move more quickly and that a just decision be made regarding child placement.

Complaints to Ethics Committees and Malpractice Suits

It was the complaints to ethics committees and threats (and even institution of) malpractice suits that finally brought me to the point of removing myself entirely from custody litigation. It is extremely important for individuals who provide services in custody litigation to realize that they are voluntarily involving themselves with people who are not able to resolve their differences amicably in a civilized, humane fashion. Furthermore, in many cases their attorneys have tried to help them resolve their dispute through conferences and other humane forms of intervention. For such clients the involvement in custody litigation represents a failure of such efforts. In other cases, however, the attorneys have done just the opposite: they have discouraged and/or resisted such resolution conferences, recognizing that the more protracted the litigation the greater the fees generated. In both situations, when the parents come to the mental health examiner, they are likely to be deeply embroiled in vicious litigation, and the rage that has been so engendered is likely to be formidable. The likelihood that some of this will spill over onto or be directed toward the mental health examiner is quite high.

One would think that the examiner, who from the outset serves as an advocate, would be viewed as the "friend" of the litigant who originally engaged his (her) services. Often the demands and expectations of the litigants are so high that there is likely to be some disappointment with such an examiner— disappointment that fuels greater rage and cravings for retaliation. But it is when the mental health professional serves as an impartial examiner that he (she) becomes particularly vulnerable to the parents' animosity. The parent who is not supported is inevitably enraged because the impartial examiner's testimony will generally carry great weight in the courtroom. But even the supported parent may not consider the examiner to have gone far enough and so he (she) too becomes angry. And such parties are likely to bring their complaints to ethics committees or lawyers who will be happy to institute malpractice suits.

Whatever the degree of litigiosity the individuals may have had at the outset, there is no question that courtroom custody disputes increase litigiousness in the vast majority of people. The custody lawsuit becomes an end in itself wherein the aim is to win, regardless of the carnage, regardless of the destruction of the children in the process. Although the victory is inevitably a Pyrrhic one, this does not deter the individuals from fighting on. Litigious individuals do not generally stop with one case. Litigiosity is a disease. It is a compulsion that feeds on itself. It is a cancer that eats its way into the brain of the sufferer and causes others to suffer inordinately. There are parents whose lives have been literally wrecked by years of unrelentless litigation by a formerly loving spouse. Cancer only physically affects the individual who suffers with the disease. Litigation is a form of cancer that eats into the hearts and brains of others who become forced into the process.

Litigious people work on the principle: "If you don't like someone, sue!" Of course, poor people cannot indulge themselves in this folly. One must start with a reasonable amount of money. And, as long as the supply lasts, there will be those attorneys who will be happy to take the litigant's money. The most predictable cure for the disorder is poverty. When the individual runs out of money, lawyers are far less likely to take on the case. However, this principle does not hold for malpractice suits wherein the client does not have to pay a penny for the lawyer's services because the lawyer, if successful in the litigation, is entitled to recover about a third of the "take." Litigious people, mobilized by their rage, use the legal process as a weapon to wreak vengeance upon those who would thwart them or cause them discomfort. And mental health professionals, even those who serve as impartial examiners, are voluntarily involving themselves with litigious people and are setting themselves up to serve as targets for their litigiosity.

Often, the first step in the process is a complaint to the ethics committee of the examiner's professional society. In most cases this involves embarrassment in relation to one's colleagues, much time-consuming paperwork, and in many cases the hiring of a lawyer to represent oneself. It's not likely that one is going to get away with an attorney's bill for less than $1000. Generally the proceedings take about six months or longer. Even when one is completely innocent and exonerated, the whole process is an irritating and frustrating experience. And if one has really bungled, then there is the fear of repercussions, e.g., censure, probation, and loss of license. At this point I have been practicing psychiatry for over 31 years. During this period no *patient* has ever submitted a complaint about me to an ethics committee. By *patient* I refer here to an individual in therapy. I am not referring to people involved in custody litigation. These people are not patients; they are *litigants*. A patient is someone with whom the therapist is likely to have a warm relationship as the two work together to solve psychiatric problems. The litigant is an individual who wishes to use the therapist's expertise in the service of winning a case in court. Most often litigants extract as much as they can from the examiner, pay for the services, and then have no further use for him (her). With rare exception, it is a "cash and carry" operation with "no strings attached" and no deep emotional relationship. (On occasion, deeper relationships have formed—but this is unusual.) To the best of my recollection there have been four complaints submitted to ethics committees about me by such litigants. In all four situations I am certain that I did absolutely nothing unethical or inappropriate. In three cases the ethics committees agreed that there were no improprieties on my part and advised the complainer to that effect. In the fourth case the litigant withdrew the complaint because she appreciated that she would need my services subsequently in a malpractice suit (here justifiable) against a previous examiner.

However, it is the malpractice suit that gets you in the guts. As mentioned, complaints to an ethics committee (when the complaint has no justifiable basis) are a source of formidable irritation and frustration. A malpractice suit is a different story entirely. One can forget about it from time to time, but it intermittently causes a knot in the stomach that gnaws and gnaws. In over 30 years doing psychiatric treatment, no *patient* has ever initiated a malpractice suit against me. However, two *litigants* in custody evaluations have, and others have threatened (but not yet carried through with their threats). In one case the father started off with a suit for $750,000 and finally settled for $10,000 after 13 years. These cases drag on endlessly. Although I wanted to bring the whole matter to early closure, my attorney advised me that time was on my side and the longer we delayed, the greater the likelihood of events that might prove useful to me—events such as the death of the complainant or his acquisition of a disease that might destroy his brain and thereby render him incompetent. I was sympathetic to that eventuality; unfortunately (always the case) he continued to function adequately. Finally, the insurance company prevailed upon me to accept the $10,000 "token" amount in order to get the client off its back. I am certain that from the outset the client knew I had done nothing improper and was trying to exploit me. The insurance company decided it would be less expensive for them to pay the 10,000 bucks than to go to court. So the litigant took his money and ran. The second case is still pending and was only instituted, I strongly suspect, to remove me from the custody litigation. The parent recognized that with such a suit pending I could no longer serve as an objective, impartial examiner.

If the reader believes that one has to have a good case or a reasonable complaint in order to sue for malpractice then the reader is living in a delusional world. There is approximately one practicing lawyer for every 340 people in the United States. (I have obtained this ratio from the *American Bar Association* figures [1988] which indicate that in December 1987 there were 713,456 practicing lawyers in the United States and *United States Census Bureau* figures [1988] which indicate that the United States population in July 1987 was 243,400,000. [These were the latest figures available at the time of this writing in late 1988.]) Accordingly, there are many hungry lawyers in this country. No matter how absurd the complaint, no matter how frivolous and even psychotic it may be, there will always be a lawyer who will be happy to take the case. The client doesn't even have to put down a penny. Under the contingency system (with permissible cases, such as negligence) the lawyer gets about one-third of the award; the client pays nothing along the way. Most countries in the world consider the contingency system unconscionable and will have no part of it.

The "straw that broke the camel's back" on June 15, 1988 was yet another threat of a malpractice suit that came to me in a registered letter. An extremely angry, hysterical, and mildly paranoid woman, who was litigating for the custody of her children, threatened to sue me if I concluded that her husband would be the preferable custodial parent. The letter, although lengthy, did not point to a single thing I had done that could be considered to be improper or constitute malpractice. But such failure to provide evidence would not deter many attorneys from taking on the case. The letter made the decision for me. Even before I had finished reading it, I vowed that I would never again voluntarily involve myself in such litigation. Although I subsequently managed to assuage her rage and reduce the likelihood that she would carry through on her threat (I am still not sure that she won't), the decision was made and the vow will be kept.

Acquiring the Litigants' Psychopathology

Another factor operative in my decision to remove myself from the field of custody litigation relates to the risk of taking on one's patients' psychopathology. We therapists are basically putting out a sign which invites the craziest people to come to our offices. We are saying to prospective patients: "If your psychiatric problems alienate others, come in here and I will provide you with sympathy and empathy. If others find you odious and obnoxious, come to me and you will find acceptance. If you are a pariah and have not a friend in the world, come to me and I will be friendly toward you. No matter how vile and despicable the things you say, I will provide you with 'unconditional positive regard.' No matter how detestable your behavior I will try to help you understand what you are doing in order to make you a better human being." If one involves oneself many hours a day with crazy people, I cannot imagine some of the craziness not rubbing off on the therapist.

I recall as a resident taking relatives of newly admitted patients to visit the psychiatric ward. Most often, they expressed their concerns that exposure to patients on the ward might make their son (daughter) etc. sicker, not better. I was taught to reassure them that under the guidance of the staff this would not happen and that only good things could come of hospitalization. This was at best naive and at worst a lie. People do take on the traits of those around them, both healthy and pathological. We in psychiatry are not immune to this process. Spending many hours a day with psychologically sick people is likely to bring about psychopathology in the therapist. Involvement in custody litigation exposes one to even more severe psychopathology and increases, thereby, the risk of development of such pathology oneself. When envisioning this book I had the thought of placing on it a label: *Warning: Participating in custody litigation may be hazardous to your mental health!* I am quitting now because I still feel myself sane (although one cannot be objective about such things). I am making the assumption that as long as people keep reading my books and inviting me to lecture, that I am probably still sane. But I cannot speak for my prognosis if I spend yet another 30 years doing this work. Which brings me to another factor operative here. Although the reader may have first chuckled when I said another 30 years, this is not a totally impossible statement. At the time I write this, my father is almost 90 and my mother past 81. Both are in reasonably good health and still have their mental faculties. It is reasonable to assume that longevity is programmed into my genes. It is likely that I have many years ahead and I want them to be productive ones.

The risk here is not simply psychiatric deterioration. There is also the risk of somatic disorders derived from the enormous tensions related to such involvement. The stresses of litigation, the complaints to ethics committees, the spectre of more malpractice suits, the screaming, blaming, and ranting are bound to affect anyone. In the last few years I have increasingly conducted evaluations in other states. Generally, I fly in, check into a hotel room, and work at a marathon pace for 24-36 hours — taking out time only to sleep, eat, and go to the bathroom. I return subsequently to provide testimony in court. In one case recently the nonsupported lawyer threatened to have me picked up by the police at the airport and jailed for practicing medicine in his state without a license. This is the same lawyer who previously was a participant in inviting me to conduct an impartial evaluation in that state. I have reached the point where if I had a heart attack or a stroke I would not be surprised. Incidents such as this one have contributed significantly to my conclusion to leave the field.

The Sex-Abuse Contribution

In the last few years all of the above have been intensified significantly by the introduction of the sex-abuse allegation into custody litigation. Courts are traditionally slow and do not view with alarm parents' complaining about such indignities as failure to provide support payments, physical and mental cruelty, etc. Cases drag on for years, contributing enormously to ongoing frustration and rage. In the early 1980s many litigants (especially mothers) found that a sex-abuse allegation received quick action by the courts. (I am not saying that genuine sex abuse does not occur in the context of custody litigation, only that the sex abuse allegation has become a powerful weapon and many individuals have been falsely accused [1987a].) Sex-abuse allegations intensified even more the level of rage experienced by such litigants. The anger generated by protracted custody litigation is enormous. However, the hysteria and fury associated with a sex-abuse allegation may be unparalleled. The sexual exploitation of a child is viewed by our society as one of the most heinous crimes. Accordingly, the feelings of revulsion, indignation, and the desire to wreak vengeance become all-consuming.

Often, incompetent examiners, many of whom are zealots, conduct the evaluations. Some work on the preposterous principle that "children never lie." Some of these evaluators are women who were sexually abused themselves as children and still have not properly worked through their reactions to their trauma and exploitations. Many such individuals work as if they were operating under the influence of a lifelong vendetta in which all accused men must be sex abusers and there is no such thing as a fabricated allegation. Although I am basically in sympathy with the aims of the feminist movement, feminists (as is true of all groups) have their share of fanatics. Some of the latter have jumped on the sex-abuse bandwagon because it provides a predictable vehicle for venting hostility toward men. These individuals also subscribe strongly (and even fanatically) to the position that children never lie and that any allegation of sex abuse must be true. Many of the validators (a loaded title if there ever was one) fear losing their jobs if they conclude that too many of the investigated clients are innocent or the charges unsubstantiated. A whole power structure has grown up in which an army of prosecutors, detectives, investigators, and others rely on a continual stream of positive findings and convictions if they are to justify their ever-increasing demands for more funds from legislatures. If custody litigation is to be considered "a bag of worms" then sex-abuse litigation can only be considered "a bag of poisonous snakes."

Accordingly, the sense of impotent rage suffered by a person who is falsely accused of sex abuse can be enormous. One is never really found innocent after such an allegation. People's lives have been ruined by a charge of sex abuse. This new development hastened my decision to get out. The cesspool of sex-abuse litigation needs to be cleaned up. I leave that crusade to others, both in and out of the mental health professions. In the meantime, I'll devote my efforts to the crusade for mediation of custody disputes.

Concern About Personal Harm

And now to another factor that has contributed to my decision to withdraw from custody litigation. To elaborate: I am the middle of three sons born to my parents. My older brother died in an accident at the age of one (one year before I was born). Throughout my life I have known about Burton and, in ways irrelevant to this volume (but not to my psychoanalysis), he has clearly affected my life. In March 1985, my younger brother Ronald (age 52), was murdered by being shot twice in the head. A lawyer, he was killed in the parking lot outside The Bronx County Courthouse. He was clearly marked for the murder; his assailants waited for him all afternoon. They did not take a penny from him. The reason for his murder is still unknown to the family. The police have never found out what had happened. (But there have been over 5,000 murders in New York City since then, so how can one expect them to be thinking about who killed Ronald.) Most of my parents' friends have already died. Obviously, I am very important to them.

Since the murder of my brother I have absolutely refused to work with any patient—either within or without the context of custody litigation—who owns a handgun. In a recent custody case, near the end of the evaluation, I learned that the litigating father owned such a gun. Although no direct threats were made to me, it was not beyond the realm of possibility that it would be used on me. Anyone who becomes involved in custody litigation is in danger. The litigious process works people up to formidable levels of rage. The frustration is enormous. The resentment and hostility can reach psychotic proportions. Normal people may become neurotic, and neurotic people may become psychotic. The urge to murder must inevitably occur in many of the litigants. Although I know of no mental health professional who has been killed as a result of involvement in such litigation, I am convinced that such murders have taken place and I am getting out now while I am still alive.

It may be of interest to the reader that in my original draft this section ended with the above words *while I am still alive.* Between the time that I first dictated this material and the time of my review of the first draft, a litigant in one of the cases I was involved in killed his wife. Although initially shocked, I was not really surprised, so vicious was the litigation. I am convinced that this woman would be alive today if these people had not become involved in the adversary system as the first step toward resolving their custody dispute. The murder also lent confirmation to my decision to stop doing such evaluations in that I could not but think that the day might come when the gun might be pointed at me. There is no question that some of the nonsupported parents in custody litigation have harbored murderous rage toward me. So I repeat: "I am getting out now while I am still alive."

WHERE DO I GO FROM HERE?

But I am not leaving the field entirely. I believe that the talents and skills I have developed in this area can be profitably used in the context of mediation. I am not new to mediation. Over the years I have served in this capacity and am continuing to do so.

My involvement as a mediator has ranged from serving as a "pure" mediator (in which I have facilitated the parents' own resolution of the custody conflict) to conducting a thorough custody evaluation (as described in detail in this book) and using my findings as a point of departure to reach a mediated settlement. Generally, the parents are referred by lawyers who decide to remove the custody conflict from other areas of contention and recommend that I mediate the custody dispute. The same principles of evaluation are utilized as those used when I served as a court-appointed impartial examiner. I evaluate the parents and children in varying combinations, review records that have been submitted to me, come up with a recommendation, and present it to the parents as a point of departure for the mediation process. However, before agreeing to mediate a custody dispute I require the parents to sign in advance a statement (Appendix II) in which they pledge that under no circumstances will I be involved in their litigation. No report is prepared because it might ultimately find its way into the courtroom. There is no contact with lawyers, but I do agree to review legal documents. My conclusions and recommendations are given verbally and can be transmitted to the parents' attorneys and subsequently incorporated into the proper legal document.

An Alternative System for Resolving Child Custody Disputes

Mediation   I am not simply confining myself to doing mediation (and custody evaluations within that context). I am also devoting myself to promulgating (through lectures and writing) a three-stage system for the resolution of custody disputes. This method, although utilizing attorneys, would remove custody disputes *entirely* from adversarial proceedings. In the first stage, *mediation* would be required as the first step toward resolution of a child custody dispute. This is very much the situation in the state of California where the Conciliation Courts routinely attempt to mediate all custody disputes at the outset (H. McIsaac, 1984). In recent years many other states, as well, have introduced mandatory mediation before parents are permitted to embark upon adversarial litigation.

In the system I propose, parents could choose to mediate their dispute within or outside the court system. They could avail themselves of the services of psychiatrists, psychologists, social workers, lawyers, mediators, arbitrators, pastoral counselors, clergymen, and others qualified to conduct such evaluations — either privately or in clinics. Obviously, training programs and standards would have to be set up in order to ensure that only qualified mediators could be utilized at this stage. Crucial to the success of such mediation would be the reassurance that the content of the deliberations would, under no circumstances, be made available to outside individuals — such as lawyers, judges, etc. No written reports would be formulated and no verbal conversations between the mediator and lawyers would be permitted. And these provisos might be stipulated in a contract such as the aforementioned (Appendix II) which I utilize. Parents involved in a custody dispute would also be free to avail themselves of such services provided under the aegis of the court or court-designated mental health clinics. These would provide mediation services at a fee commensurate with the parents' financial situation. Again, there would be absolutely no transmission of the mediator's findings and recommendations to others — even to the legal system under whose authority the mediation might have operated. My hope is that such mediation would serve to resolve the vast majority of custody disputes.

The mediated parenting plan would be verbally communicated to the attorney preparing the separation agreement. Because divorce is still a legal matter (and probably will be for the foreseeable future), the services of an attorney would still be necessary. However, my hope is that other possible disputes related to the divorce would also be resolved by mediation. Whether or not the parents are successful in accomplishing this, the custody dispute (the focus of my three-step proposal) could not be dealt with — at any of the three levels — by proceedings within the adversary system.

Arbitration Panel   But mediation, like everything else in the world, is not without its drawbacks. All of us are fallible, all of us make mistakes, and the most skilled mediator is no exception. Mediation may break down for a variety of reasons, one of the most common of which is the refusal by one or both parties to provide full disclosure of finances. Or, each spouse may be so convinced of the other's ineptitude as a parent that the compromises necessitated by mediation may not be possible. Psychiatric problems may interfere with a parent's ability to make the necessary compromises. When mediation breaks down, most people today have no choice but to involve themselves in custody litigation. In the system I propose, the parents would then be required to submit their dispute to an *arbitration panel*, working within the court structure. I believe that the best panel to deal with such a dispute would be one consisting of two mental health professionals and one attorney. The panel members would be selected by the parents from a roster of properly qualified individuals provided by the court. (The training and experience requirements for such certification have yet to be determined.)

The mental health professionals on the panel would be expected to conduct the kind of custody evaluation described in this book. The lawyer would be involved in the legal aspects of the dispute and would draw up the panel's final decision in proper legal form. Like a judge, the panel (especially the lawyer) would have the power to subpoena medical records, request financial documents, etc. This power would be especially important when there is reluctance or refusal by one or both parties to disclose pertinent information. Most important, the parents would meet directly with the panel members. Although the discussion would be free and open, the panel would still have the authority to prevent the proceedings from degenerating into a free-for-all. By having three panelists there would be no chance of a tie vote. The majority decision will prevail. Obviously, a panel of three is less likely to be biased than an individual mediator or judge. Equally (if not more) important is the panel's data-collection process. Whereas the judge is confined to the constraints of the adversary method of data collection (gathering of evidence) the panel would be free to avail itself of the more flexible and far preferable procedures used by mental health professionals serving as impartial examiners.

The panel would be free to bring in any parties who might be helpful, and such parties could include attorneys to provide independent representation. However, such attorneys would (like all other participants) be required to involve themselves in free and open discussion. They would not be permitted to impose upon the proceedings courtroom procedures of inquiry, which constrain open discussion and could serve to hide information from the panel. For example, such an attorney might ask someone a question that could be answered by "yes" or "no." However, the respondent would be completely free to add the word "but" and then provide whatever qualifications and additions warranted to provide clarification. This would be a crucial difference between the panel's method of inquiry and that of the courtroom. Such independent representation might be especially useful, for example, for a passive wife who might not be able to hold her own against an overbearing husband. The panel, as well, would serve to protect such a person from being squelched and possibly exploited.

The mediated parenting plan would be verbally communicated to the attorney preparing the separation agreement. Because divorce is still a legal matter (and probably will be for the foreseeable future), the services of an attorney would still be necessary. However, my hope is that the other possible disputes related to the divorce would also be resolved by mediation. Whether or not the parents are successful in accomplishing this, the custody dispute (the focus of my three-step proposal) could not be dealt with—at any of the three levels—by proceedings within the adversary system.

Appeals Panel   The crucial question remains as to whether the findings and recommendations of the panel should be binding. On the one hand, one could argue that even three people could make a mistake (the nine member United States Supreme Court often has made what it subsequently came to realize were mistakes) and the parents should be free to enter into adversarial proceedings in order to appeal to a higher authority. On the other hand, one could argue that the process has to end somewhere and that such a panel, as the next step after mediation, is a good enough place to make final decisions in matters such as custody disputes.

At this point, I am in favor of a plan (again removed from adversarial proceedings) in which there would be the possibility of appeal to another panel of three individuals (again an attorney and two mental health professionals) who would have had significant experience in child custody mediation and arbitration. This panel would have the power to make a final decision. These panel members, as well, would be selected by the clients from a roster provided by the court. Many would be people who had served previously on arbitration panels. This *appeals panel* would involve itself in a two-step process of review. The first step would be similar to that of traditional courts of appeal wherein the members review the documents at the trial court level. At this stage they would have the power to refuse to consider the case further (like the power given to the United States Supreme Court) and then the findings of the arbitration panel would be final. The appeals panel might direct the arbitration panel to collect further data or reconsider its decision because of certain considerations. Or, after reviewing the arbitration panel's documents the appeals panel might consider another hearing warranted and could then hear the parties directly and conduct whatever evaluations were necessary. This could involve interviews as well as other forms of data collection similar to those conducted by the original arbitration panel. The appeals panel might even meet with the arbitration panel and the parents, all together. The appeals panel, as well, might choose to hear parties brought in by the parents, and such parties might include attorneys serving as advocates. However, once again, traditional courtroom procedures of examination would be replaced by open and free discussion (again moderated by the panel, to prevent deterioration of the proceedings). Whereas traditional courts of appeal allow lawyers only to provide testimony, the appeals panel would have the power to interview directly any and all parties it considered useful to hear. And the conclusion of this appeals panel would be final.

In order to discourage frivolous use of the appeals panel it would have to establish for itself the reputation of being quite stringent with regard to the possibility of changing the recommendations of the lower arbitration panel. In addition, litigious individuals would come to appreciate that they not only might not gain from such appeal, but that they might lose in that the panel might take away more than they might give. Another deterrent to the reflex appeal often seen in litigious people would be the panel's practice of reviewing the arbitration panel's records for the presence of perjury, slander, and libel. In all the years that I had been involved in divorce and custody litigation, there was hardly a case in which I did not see blatant examples of all of these practices. Yet, not once had anyone ever been prosecuted for these crimes. And not once had such behavior even been brought to the attention of the litigants by the court. If the appeals panel were to establish for itself the reputation of reviewing the arbitration panel's records for such behavior, this too could serve as a deterrent for reflex appeal by disgruntled parties.

It should be noted that the three-step procedure I have outlined above (mediation, arbitration panel, and appeals panel) does not involve adversarial proceedings at any level. The system would protect clients from the polarization and spiraling of animosity that frequently accompanies the utilization of adversarial procedures and contributes to the development and perpetuation of psychopathology. It replaces the cumbersome and inefficient method of evidence gathering used by the courts with the more flexible and efficient data-collection process used by mental health professionals. The parents would be given the opportunity to choose their own panel, protecting them thereby from the sense of impotence suffered by parents who are "stuck" with a judge who all recognize to be ill equipped to deal judiciously with custody conflicts. In short, they choose their own judges. By requiring decisions to be made by the majority of a three-member panel, the likelihood of bias is reduced. Last, and most important, it is a system that precludes any possibility of involvement in adversarial proceedings by people involved in a custody dispute. There would be no such forum for such individuals and the law would thereby protect them from involvement in a system that was never designed to deal with the question of who would serve as a better parent for children of divorce.

Due Process and Constitutional Rights   The system does not deprive the parents of any of their rights of due process guaranteed by the Constitution of the United States. They have the right to representation by counsel at both the arbitration and appeals levels. Nowhere in the Constitution is anyone (including lawyers) given the right to subject another individual to the frustrations and indignities of yes-no questions. (I have sometimes wondered whether yes-no questions deprive witnesses of their right to freedom of speech, guaranteed under the Bill of Rights.) The constitutional right of the accused to confront his (her) accuser is being protected. Even better, in this system the accuser is given the opportunity for direct confrontation with the accused without the utilization of intermediaries (adversary lawyers) and the restriction of courtroom procedures. Although individuals now have the opportunity for such direct confrontations in the courtroom if they represent themselves (pro se) this is not commonly done. In the system I propose the parents are essentially operating pro se. But even when they choose to bring in attorneys to represent them, the discussion will still be far freer than that found in the courtroom.

The constitutional right of a hearing before an impartial judge is being protected. Here, the parents not only have one judge but three (serving in a sense as a tribunal). And protection against bias is enhanced by the requirement that the majority vote will prevail. The requirement that two of the "judges" be mental health professionals is not only desirable for the purposes of the custody evaluation, but is in no way unconstitutional. Nowhere in the Constitution is anything said about the educational or professional requirements that need to be satisfied to serve as a judge. Last, the Constitution presumably guarantees a speedy trial. It requires a morbid expansion of the meaning of the word "speedy" to believe that this constitutional requirement of due process is being protected for the vast majority of litigants in custody disputes. This proposal is more likely to provide such speed, primarily because of the advantages of its method of data collection over that of traditional adversarial courtroom proceedings.

It is important for the reader to appreciate that this proposal is just that, a proposal. It outlines what I consider a reasonable approach to the resolution of custody disputes. I am not claiming that it is perfect and I suspect that if implemented it would probably warrant modification. Although the three-step procedure may appear cumbersome, there is no question that it would prove to be far more efficient and less expensive than adversarial proceedings. Although the plan is designed to protect disputing parents from injudicious judicial decisions, I suspect that the professionals involved in making the custody decisions, being human, will certainly make their share of mistakes. However, I believe that the number of people so harmed will be far less than the number inevitably traumatized by traditional adversary litigation. Although the three-step procedure is most relevant to custody disputes, I believe that the model lends itself well to being applied (with proper modifications) to other kinds of disputes as well.

THE RELEVANCE OF MY DECISION TO THIS BOOK

I mentioned at the outset that this book was originally planned as an update of my *Family Evaluation in Child Custody Litigation* (1982a). My recent decision to remove myself from direct involvement in custody litigation and my decision to utilize my talents and skills in the mediation area have necessitated certain modifications of the earlier book. It will still describe in detail techniques for conducting impartial custody evaluations within the adversary system. (The majority of people still work very much within it.) It will include, however, updated material reflecting much that I have learned since the 1982 publication. However, it also describes the utilization of the same techniques in the mediation/arbitration process. Mediation is clearly the saner, more civilized method for resolving custody disputes.

As the reader goes through this book he (she) will no doubt appreciate the blood and sweat that lie between most of its lines. I have learned many things in my life, but I believe that the things I have learned in this realm were learned in the most difficult and painful circumstances. I believe many of these lessons can be used by others to protect themselves from similar pains and indignities. I pass this information on to those who are more courageous than I, who have thicker skins than I, and who still have the guts to enter the battle. One suicide, one homicide, and one death by heart attack have been enough for me. I feel that I have contributed my share, have hung in far longer than most others, and am entitled to my peace. But by "peace" I do not mean vegetation. Rather, I mean removal from the adversarial battlefield and dedicating my efforts to finding a better method — such as the aforementioned proposal.

⚖️ TWO

THE IMPARTIAL EXAMINER VS. THE ADVOCATE

Throughout the course of this book I express deep criticisms of the adversary system. Although some of its tenets have been incorporated into the legal systems of other countries, the basic notion of polarizing people as a first step toward resolving their disputes is not generally respected in most parts of the world. The reader who is interested in a review of the historical development of the system may wish to read my chapter on this subject (1987a). The system has also been used in western society as a method for resolving divorce and custody disputes. With regard to custody disputes it was not generally needed throughout most of mankind's history because of the automatic assignment of children to their fathers. The notion that a mother could be the preferable custodial parent is very much a 20th century phenomenon. It has only been in the last 10-15 years that courts have taken an egalitarian view regarding gender considerations in custody disputes. And it has been in this recent period that the adversary system has been utilized to a degree not previously seen in mankind's history.

THE "HIRED GUN" EXAMINER

Adversarial proceedings are based on the principle that the best way of learning the "truth," when two parties have diametrically opposed positions, is for each to present his or her case before an impartial decision maker (a judge and/or jury). Each side is permitted to withhold (within certain guidelines and procedures) facts that might compromise its position and to present those that support it. The theory is that these opposing presentations provide impartial evaluators with the best opportunity for ascertaining the truth. The fact finder (whether it be a judge or jury) serves primarily in a neutral position. Although it originated in criminal proceedings, where the dispute is between a prosecutor and an accused person, it is also used in civil proceedings as well, where the dispute is between a plaintiff and a defendant.

The majority of attorneys in the United States consider the adversary system to be the best yet devised for dispute resolution. Consistent with this position they generally attempt to enlist the services of "experts" who come in and support their positions. Such attorneys are usually unreceptive to the notion of bringing in an impartial examiner, so much so that they may actually have difficulty conceiving of the idea. But even those who do recognize the value of the concept may be quite resistant to actually utilizing such a person because of the fear that he (she) may support their adversary's position. The attorney who is deeply committed to the adversary system and the examiner who serves only as an impartial may have great difficulty communicating with each other on the subject of custody litigation. I can best describe the problem with the following composite of many conversations I have had over the last 20 years:

I receive a telephone call from an attorney in which he begins: "Doctor Gardner, my name is Mr. So-and-So. I'm an attorney and was referred to you by Dr. So-and-So." The introduction is innocuous enough. It is with the next sentence that the trouble begins. It is usually a run-on sentence, with the second half being stated much more rapidly than the first: "I would like to know whether I can engage your services in testifying on behalf of my client who is involved in a custody conflict with her husband (the pace quickens here); however, Doctor, I want you to know that the best interests of the children are paramount."

To this I generally respond, "Suppose, after seeing your

client, I conclude that I cannot support with conviction her position and I decide that it would be in the best interests of the children for them to live with their father. Would you still use my testimony in court?"

The attorney then often answers in a confused and irritated manner: "Doctor, you can't be serious, suggesting that I use your testimony to support my adversary's client. Are you suggesting that I put you on the stand to testify on behalf of the other side?"

My response: "But I understood you to have said before that the best interests of the children were paramount. If that were truly the case, I would think you would welcome my testimony in order to do what is best for them. What you're telling me now suggests to me that supporting your client is really paramount!"

At this point the attorney may tell me (directly or indirectly) that it is clear that he has made a mistake in calling me and that the person who referred him to me wasn't aware of how ignorant I was of legal matters.

This attorney is essentially doing what he was taught in law school, namely, to support his client's position. He knows that psychiatrists are concerned with children's best interests and that the best way to ingratiate himself to one is to profess a similar commitment. However, the basic inconsistency in his comments quickly becomes apparent. One cannot commit oneself to support a client's claim for custody and *at the same time* state that the children's interests are paramount. At times it is in the children's best interests to live with the client whom the attorney is representing; and at times it is not. When the latter is the case the attorney must make a choice. Almost invariably that choice will be to support the client's claim, not the children's needs.

In addition, the attorney who is deeply committed to the adversary system may see nothing inappropriate in asking me to testify on behalf of his client *before I have even seen her*. I cannot be too critical of him here, because there are mental health professionals who will promise to provide such support before anyone has been seen. Such "hired gun" examiners are a disgrace to our profession. The attorney here is only a product of his system—a system based on respect for the adversarial process as a way of solving human problems. He is committed to the idea that "truth" emerges from conflict. And I am a product of my system—a system based on the premise that free and open inquiry is the best way to gather data for settling human conflicts.

Another way in which the attorney's and the mental health professional's orientations differ is well demonstrated by the following vignette:

Two clients (having no relationship with one another) have appointments to see an attorney. The first is a man. He has never previously been married and is presently married to a woman who has been divorced and who has two children. She has custody of the two children. He comes to the attorney to ask his advice regarding the advisability of adopting his stepchildren whose biological father has no interest in them and is receptive to the adoption. The attorney strongly discourages him from doing so, informing him that if this marriage were to end in a divorce, and if he were to have adopted the children, then he would have the obligation to provide for their support. However, if he does not adopt them, he would have no obligations for their support after a divorce, but their natural father might. Accordingly, the attorney strongly dissuades his client from going ahead with the plans for adoption.

The next client to see the same attorney is a woman. She has been divorced, has two children, and is now married for the second time to a man who has never been married before. She has custody of the two children. She has come to the attorney to ask his advice about her new husband adopting the children. Her former husband is receptive to the adoption. The lawyer advises her to proceed as rapidly as possible with the adoption plans. He tells her that once her new husband has adopted the children, he will be obligated to support them, even if this marriage ends in divorce. Furthermore, he warns her that if her new husband were not to adopt the children, he would have no obligation at all to provide for their support if there were to be a divorce.

In each case the attorney is seemingly protecting his client's best interests—especially if one considers monetary consider- ations to be paramount in determining what is in the best interests of children. At no point in his advice to these clients is there any consideration for the welfare of the children. His primary concern is the pocketbook of his clients. The decision whether or not to adopt should be based on a variety of considerations including the financial and the psychological effects on the parties concerned. Parenting is far more a psychological than a monetary phenomenon. The feelings and attitudes of the adoptive father, the reactions of the children (especially their feelings about being adopted and how this will affect their relationship with their natural father as well as their stepfather), and the reactions of the mother should all be taken into consideration. Although this lawyer may get an A+ from his law school professor, he would get an F− from this psychiatry professor.

Again, my point is that the lawyer's primary obligation is to serve the client, the parent who has enlisted his (her) services. At times, the parent's position may also be in the children's best interests; at times it may not. And the attorney is not likely to be able to make a reasonable judgment on this issue unless he (she) has information from the other parent and has explored the multiplicity of factors necessary to understand before one can decide if the client's position is reasonable and will truly serve the children. The adversary system does not permit the attorney himself (herself) to do this (the judge presumably does). The impartial examiner, however, has a court mandate to do so.

Mental health professionals who are foolish enough to testify on behalf of one parent−without having seen the other−invite serious criticism. I consider such "hired guns" (a less benevolent but more accurate term for these individuals is "whores") to be unethical and a disgrace to their profession. By playing into the hands of litigating attorneys, hired guns prolong the clients' grief and frustration. In order to help dissuade such individuals from appearing in this capacity and to contribute thereby to the general discouragement of this deplorable practice, I generally recommend that the attorney, whose position the testifying mental health professional is *not* supporting, conduct this type of cross-examination:

Attorney: Would you not agree, Doctor, that it is somewhat simplistic to categorize people as being either "good" or "bad" and that a more realistic view of people is to consider them to be mixtures of both assets and liabilities?

Mental Health Professional (mhp): Yes. (The mhp must say yes here. If he (she) does not, credibility is compromised because the statement is so patently true.)

Attorney: Do you agree, then, Doctor, that parents are no exception to this principle and that they too are mixtures of both "good" and "bad" qualities regarding their parental capacity?

Mhp: Yes. (Again, one has no choice but to answer yes.)

Attorney: Would you not agree, Doctor, that in ascertaining who is the better of two parents with regard to assuming custody, we are not trying to find out who is the "good" parent and who is the "bad" parent but who is the *better* of the two parents?

Mhp: Yes. (Again, the answer must be yes, even though he or she can now sense what is to follow.)

Attorney: Would you not agree also, Doctor, that in trying to determine who is the better of two parents it is preferable to see *both* if one is to determine most judiciously who is the *better* parent?

Mhp: Yes. (Obviously, if the mhp says no he (she) looks foolish.)

Attorney: Would you not go further and agree that an evaluation of parental preference is seriously compromised if both parents have not been seen?

Mhp: Yes. (Here again, it would be very difficult for the mhp to avoid a yes answer, even though he (she) recognizes that such a response weakens significantly his (her) position.)

Attorney: Doctor, have you conducted a psychiatric evaluation on Mrs. Jones?

Mhp: Yes.

Attorney: How many times have you seen Mrs. Jones?

Mhp: (The mhp states the number of interviews conducted with Mrs. Jones.)

Attorney: Can you tell us the exact dates of each of your interviews with her and the duration of each interview?

Mhp: (Mhp presents the dates of the interviews and the duration of each.)

Attorney: What was the total number of hours of interviewing?

Mhp: (Mhp states the total number of hours of interviewing.)

Attorney: Have you ever conducted an evaluation of Mr. Jones with regard to his parental capacity?

Mhp: No.

Attorney: To the best of your knowledge, is Mr. Jones in this courtroom today?

Mhp: Yes.

Attorney: Can you please point to the person whom you believe to be Mr. Jones.

Mhp: (Mhp points to the person believed to be Mr. Jones.)

Attorney: Is it possible that the individual at whom you are pointing is not Mr. Jones?

Mhp: Yes, it's possible.

Attorney: As I understand it, Doctor, you are here today to testify that Mrs. Jones is a better parent than Mr. Jones. Is that not correct, Doctor?

Mhp: Yes.

Attorney: And is it also not correct, Doctor, that you not only have never conducted an evaluation of Mr. Jones, but are not even certain whether he is actually the person you suspect him to be?

Mhp: Yes.

Attorney: In accordance with what you have said before about a custody evaluation being seriously compromised if both parties are not seen, would you not have to conclude that *your own* evaluation in this matter must be similarly suspect?

Mhp: (If the mhp answers no, testimony is compromised because of inconsistency and the attorney would do well to point this out. If the mhp hedges or responds that he (she) cannot answer yes or no, the testimony is similarly compromised and invites the attorney to point out the inconsistency. If the answer is yes [the more likely response], the attorney does well to respond as follows.)

Attorney (turning now to the judge): Your honor, because Dr. X has, by his (her) own admission, stated that his (her) testimony has been significantly compromised by the failure to evaluate Mr. Jones, I do not think anything useful can be obtained by further inquiry. Accordingly, I believe it would be a waste of the court's time to proceed further and I therefore have no further questions.

The cross-examining attorney does well to stop here. The attorney's adversary will already have questioned the examiner and is not likely to have any further questions. At this point the judge, of course, may ask further questions. However, the judge may feel compromised by such an inquiry because of the admission made by the evaluator that his (her) comments should not be taken seriously. If the nonsupported attorney wishes to proceed, however, in order to "rub salt into the examiner's wounds," my recommendation is that he or she focus on all hearsay statements made by Mrs. Jones about her husband. The attorney's main emphasis should be on the doctor's accepting as valid the criticisms of her husband made by Mrs. Jones. Even if the professional has not accepted as completely valid Mrs. Jones's allegations, the conclusions are likely to be based on the supposition that at least some of them are true (otherwise he or she would not be providing testimony in support of her position). Stopping at the earlier point would represent more of a denigration of the so-called expert's testimony than proceeding with a detailed inquiry into the report's contents. I believe that if more mental health professionals were exposed to such cross-examination, fewer would be willing to serve as advocates, and this would be a service to all parties concerned—the courts, the legal profession, the mental health professions, and the families themselves.

THE IMPARTIAL EXAMINER

The Impartial Examiner vs.
The Advocate Evaluation

Impartial examiners are in the best position to make a custody recommendation to the court. The impartial examiner has greater flexibility than the court to gather the most extensive and accurate information from both sides. He (she) is not constrained by courtroom procedures and adversarial practices which are inevitably complex, time-consuming, and provide the court with only selected information (lawyers' professions to the contrary notwithstanding). Accordingly, impartial examiners are in a unique position, and this is what makes them so valuable to the court despite the risk of bias. If they are to serve properly in this role, impartial examiners must have the court's support (preferably via a signed custody order) to interview the parents and children and to invite (they cannot require) others, such as stepparents, live-in parental surrogates, prospective stepparents, etc. – people who can provide them with meaningful information. The goal of these interviews is a statement regarding who is the *better* parent. Impartial examiners do this by comparing the parents' assets and liabilities as a parent. For example, in the section of the report where the evaluator summarizes the recommendations, he (she) might state: "Mr. R.'s liabilities as a parent far outweigh his assets; whereas Mrs. R.'s assets as a parent far outweigh her liabilities. Accordingly, I recommend that the court grant Mrs. R. primary custody of the children." Or "Both Mr. and Mrs. S. appear to be equally competent as parents. However, Mr. S.'s availability for parenting is compromised significantly by the fact that his work obligations allow him little flexibility with regard to taking care of the children after school, during school vacation periods, and at times of sickness. Mrs. S., as a homemaker, is much more available to the children. All of the other parenting liabilities that each parent exhibits do not appear to be significant. Accordingly, I suggest that the court allow Mrs. S. to continue to have primary custody of the children."

Until recently, courts relied more frequently on the testimony of advocates in custody conflicts than of others. Fortunately, in recent years, the value of the impartial examiner's testimony is being increasingly appreciated. L. S. Kubie (1964) was one of the earliest in the field of psychiatry to stress the importance of therapists serving as impartials, rather than as advocates. He would not testify in court in a custody conflict unless he was appointed by the judge as an impartial examiner. A. P. Derdeyn (1975) describes a custody case in which there was a parade of mental health professionals on either side; the effect of all their testimony was to cancel out one another's completely. He criticizes strongly the professionals in the case for having agreed at the outset to serve as advocates. He makes a strong plea for psychiatrists to serve only as impartial examiners. The canceling out of the adversary mental health professional's testimonies is a common occurrence. Accordingly, one can easily see what a waste of time and money is the utilization of such a parade of examiners. R. J. James (1978) is also a strong proponent of psychiatrists' serving only as impartial examiners and describes a number of examples of misguided recommendations that resulted when psychiatrists served only as advocates.

R. A. Solow and P. L. Adams (1977) are strong proponents of the psychiatrist as an impartial examiner rather than adversary. However, they suggest that both parents agree beforehand that the psychiatrist's recommendations shall be *binding*. I am in full agreement that the psychiatrist should serve as an impartial, but I am not in agreement that his (her) opinion should be binding. Such power places a heavy burden on the psychiatrist and assumes a degree of omniscience that we do not possess. Each parent should still have the opportunity to appeal the impartial's decision and have an attorney cross-examine him (her) in court. Solow and Adams go so far as to require the parents to sign a statement that they will consider the psychiatrist's recommendations binding. I suspect that such a procedure deprives parents of due process (specifically the right to representation in a court of law) and is therefore unconstitutional. M. G. Goldzband (1982) claims to be a strong proponent of the examiners being impartial. Although he informs both clients and attorneys that he will not automatically support the position of a parent being evaluated, many of his mock trials and case studies indicate that he has come to his conclusions after evaluating only one parent. Accordingly, I do not view such evaluations as impartial.

Some impartial examiners prefer to be viewed as advocates of the child or the children. This is consistent with the *best interests of the child presumption*—the guideline under which most courts have operated since the mid-1970s. I always preferred to view myself as someone who did not simply represent the child, but attempted to make a recommendation that took into consideration the best interests of *all* concerned—the child or children, the parents, and others who may have been involved. This involves a balancing of the needs of the various parties. It may involve compromises. To focus specifically on the best interests of the child (or children) may be too narrow a view in some cases. Such restriction may not give proper consideration to the needs of parents, and the effects of the decision on them and family subsystems, and may result in parental deprivation and/or psychological trauma. The term I would prefer to use is the *best interests of the family presumption*.

"Playing Judge" and "Playing God"

Critics of the impartial examiner concept argue that the mental health professional who places himself (herself) in such a position is "playing judge." I do not agree. I made it clear from the outset, to both parents and attorneys, that I fully appreciated that I am fallible and that my recommendation should be subject to courtroom scrutiny. I emphasized the fact that it is the judge, and not I, who has the power to make the final decision and that my contribution is best viewed as valuable input.

Another criticism of the impartial examiner is that he is "playing God." Critics claim that there is a grandiosity in placing oneself in this position. I believe that the impartial examiner is not "playing God" nearly so much as the judge. But *both* are playing God in the sense that they cannot help but be affected by their own biases and prejudices—no matter how hard they try for objectivity. The best that we can hope to obtain from the impartial examiner is the attempt to be impartial and neutral. We all have prejudices that stem from our childhood and subsequent experiences, and it is unreasonable to expect that the impartial examiner will be absolutely free from such contaminations to the inquiry. It is to be hoped that these biases will not play a significant role in the impartial's recommendation. The neutrality of the impartial is partially related to his (her) hoped-for objectivity and partially to the fact that he (she) has full access to both parties and has the opportunity to gain the relevant information from each. Each attorney gets a one-sided view. And the judge, because of the way in which material is presented in adversary proceedings, also gets filtered information. The *Group for the Advancement of Psychiatry* clearly recognizes the limitations of the filtered information supplied by each side to the judge. In their monograph on child custody (1980) they state:

The judge is ordinarily limited to the record before him, and it is difficult for him to compensate for the inadequacies of trial counsel or witnesses. Courts differ in their willingness to order staff investigations and reports to supplement the record, and facilities for such services also vary from court to court. Furthermore, if a judge has strong convictions about child rearing or a bias for or against a particular theory of child development, the facts available may be filtered through these preconceptions. Most judges strive to eliminate personal bias and to protect the best interests of children; nevertheless, in some instances, the judge's tacit convictions help shape the resulting decision.

It is because both the impartial examiner's and the judge's conclusions may be biased that I recommend that binding decisions (the mediator's recommendations are not binding) be made by a panel of three.

The Impartial Examiner's Values

The impartial examiner's own system of values inevitably will play a role in his or her decision making. In this regard there is little difference between the impartial's role as a court examiner and his or her role as a therapist. There are therapists who state that they strictly refrain from imposing their own values on their patients. I like to divide such therapists into two categories: 1) those who are lying and 2) those who are delusional and really believe what they are saying. Therapists in the latter category are at best naive and at worst simple-minded. I cannot conceive of a therapeutic program that does not involve some attempt on the therapist's part to convert the patient to his or her own way of viewing the world. A mother brings her son to the therapist because, although of high intelligence, he is doing poorly in school. The therapist agrees that this is a psychological problem and tries to help the child "reach his potential." Such a therapist is tacitly agreeing with the mother that educational pursuits are valuable. There are many in this world, however, who take a different position. Some parents are perfectly satisfied if their children reach the point of minimal competence with the "3 Rs." Others do not even see the need for such a degree of education and are satisfied with their children's growing up and living on welfare.

The therapist who believes that his male patient should resolve his Oedipus complex subscribes to the view that incest is undesirable. Although I share the therapist's opinion here, there are many societies in which this is not the case. The examples are legion. We hope that the values that therapists will be imposing on their patients will be ones that will serve the patients well. We hope that therapists will not impose maladaptive values on their patients and will be enough in touch with their own areas of distortion (more likely the case if they have been in analysis) that they can guard against such impositions. And this holds true whether the therapist is doing treatment or involving him- or herself in custody evaluations as an impartial examiner.

There are certain situations in which the therapist is likely to be at "high risk" for the imposition of biases in the custody evaluation. The therapist who has been involved personally in a custody battle, for his (her) own children, is not as likely to be as objective as the colleague who has not had the misfortune to be embroiled in such a conflict. The likelihood that such a therapist will identify irrationally or inappropriately with one of the parties is high. The likelihood that there will be similarities between the examiner's own experiences and that of one, or even both, of the clients is great. And such similarities are likely to evoke emotional responses that becloud objectivity.

Another situation likely to produce inappropriate emotional reactions in some evaluators is one involving adulterous behavior. If the examiner views such individuals as immoral, depraved, sinners, perverts, etc., he (she) is likely to lose objectivity and be biased against the parent who has been involved in the extramarital sex. In recent years courts have become increasingly appreciative of the fact that one's personal-private, voluntary sexual life is not generally related to parental capacity. There was a time when the adulterous mother (but interestingly not as often the father) was automatically considered "unfit" to be a parent. This is no longer the situation in most courts in the United States. The examiner who still subscribes to this view will be introducing what I consider to be an irrelevant consideration in most cases. Such therapists are compromised significantly in conducting meaningful custody evaluations.

The Impartial Examiner and
The Amicus Curiae

Some impartial examiners refer to themselves as an *amicus curiae* (*Latin:* friend of the court). Strictly speaking, the impartial examiner is not an amicus curiae. An amicus curiae is generally a group or organization, rather than an individual. The amicus curiae contributes information to the court to help the court make its decision. The impartial examiner does so as well. However, the amicus curiae usually has a specific position to support and the court knows this position from the outset. The impartial examiner starts clean, with no previous fixed notion regarding what recommendation he (she) will make to the court. In custody litigation the impartial examiner does not, from the outset, know which parent will be supported. A judge may invite a brief from an amicus curiae or the amicus curiae may ask the court if it wishes to receive a brief. The amicus curiae, then, will often play the role of an advocate; the impartial examiner does not start as an advocate, but may end up being viewed as one by the court.

An example of an amicus curiae would be the American Civil Liberties Union submitting a brief to a judge who is being asked to decide whether a neo-Nazi organization should be permitted to march in a demonstration. Other organizations might also wish to submit briefs, such as the Anti-Defamation League of the B'nai B'rith. Another example might be a situation in which a psychiatrist is being brought up on charges of malpractice or criminal conduct for not having revealed a patient's homicidal tendencies to a person the patient was planning to murder. The family of the murdered party might bring such a psychiatrist up on charges. The American Psychiatric Association might submit an amicus curiae brief to the court in such a situation. In short, the impartial examiner is an individual, whereas the amicus curiae is usually an organization. The impartial examiner begins as a neutral; the amicus curiae is often an advocate from the outset. Both, however, should be viewed as "friends of the court" in that both can be useful to the court in making its decision.

The Impartial Examiner and
The Guardian ad Litem

The *guardian ad litem* is generally an attorney who is appointed by the court to serve as guardian of the children, in order to act on their behalf in litigation. He (she) has free access to all information pertinent to the custody litigation and can present to the court information that either party may be interested in withholding. The guardian ad litem can initiate investigations (including psychiatric evaluations), introduce evidence, but generally does not cross-examine witnesses with regard to the custodial decision.

Although the guardian ad litem serves the children in a capacity similar to the way in which the parents' attorneys serve them, their functions are not entirely parallel. The guardian ad litem does not have the right to appeal, whereas the attorneys of the parents do. The guardian ad litem is paid by one or both parents. Because funds for attorneys are generally limited (except in cases of the wealthy), there is generally less money available to pay the fees of the guardian ad litem than there is for the parents' attorneys. Therefore, he (she) is likely to spend less time with the children than the parents' attorneys are spending with them. Thus, the children are not given the same degree of representation as the parents.

Although the guardian ad litem has access to information from both sides, I would consider it inappropriate for the impartial examiner to request significant amounts of verbal information from the guardian ad litem. First, he (she) is an attorney in the case, not a client. In addition, information obtained from the guardian ad litem must be considered hearsay, in that it was acquired from other sources or, at best, relates to his (her) (not the evaluator's) observations. Also, the examiner is being asked to provide his (her) *own* opinion, not one heavily weighted by information provided by the guardian ad litem. Although of limited value as a source of information, the guardian ad litem can be extremely valuable to the impartial evaluator *after* the submission of the final report. My experience had been that the guardian ad litem was generally supportive of my position. Since the guardian ad litem has the judge's "ear," so to speak, his (her) support can be invaluable. When I came in on the side of the mother, for example, the judge heard support for her position from her attorney and from me. If there was a guardian ad litem involved, and if he (she) agreed with my position (more often the case than not, in my experience), there were then three professionals supporting the mother's position (the mother's lawyer, the guardian ad litem, and me) and only one supporting the father (his own attorney). Recognizing this valuable role of the guardian ad litem, I was very pleased to learn that one had been appointed and would routinely invite the guardian ad litem to participate in the final conference with the attorneys and clients and send him or her a copy of my final recommendations.

CHOOSING AN IMPARTIAL EXAMINER

I believe that the ideal method of choosing the impartial examiner is for the parents themselves to agree upon the person and then recommend that individual to the court for its approval. The parents might make inquiry among friends, attorneys, physicians, psychiatrists, and others and then determine which name or names appears most frequently. They should inquire into the particular qualifications and experiences of the individuals under consideration. When the parents themselves have selected the impartial, and both have agreed without coercion to the choice, they are less likely to feel imposed upon by his (her) recommendations. Having confidence from the outset that the person has been a good choice, they are more likely to be receptive to his (her) recommendations. When such capacity to cooperate and communicate is present, the parents do well to consider mediation—the far less expensive and psychologically detrimental alternative (discussed at length in other parts of this book).

At any rate, when the impartial is agreed upon, the parents should then inform the attorneys of their choice and gain their approval. If all four have agreed, then the next step is verbally to invite the impartial, who must then decide whether to become involved. The examiner does well to have a contract delineating the provisions of his participation. In Chapter Three I present the document (Appendix I) I developed that proved useful. When all four agree to these provisions, one of the attorneys draws up a court order, has it approved by his (her) adversary, and it is submitted to the presiding judge for his (her) signature. It is very important for the impartial examiner to have the court order *before* beginning the evaluation process. Without such an order the examiner's position as an impartial may be compromised. Especially during the litigation this may prove to be the case, and the evaluator will then be sorry that he or she did not await full court sanction before proceeding.

It often happened that one party was very desirous of bringing me in as the impartial examiner and the other side refused. In earlier years I refused to involve myself unless both parties *voluntarily* agreed to invite my participation. I took this position because of my belief that a meaningful evaluation would not be possible with an individual who was not motivated to participate. Subsequently, an attorney strongly urged me to serve as an impartial in a situation where a reluctant party was being ordered to participate, but the other was willing to do so voluntarily. With reservations I agreed to conduct the evaluation. To my surprise, I found that there was no difference between the two parents with regard to the amount of censoring that they were exhibiting. I had come to expect a significant amount of censoring, even in parents who had come voluntarily and had assumed that censoring would be even greater in parents who were ordered by the court to involve themselves. I found that the level of censoring was so high in the voluntary parents that it was hard for the involuntary parents to exceed it. Accordingly, I changed my position and agreed to conduct evaluations under court order, regardless of the desire of the parties to appear. I found that it made little difference. In *both* cases there is a formidable amount of lying and censoring. I came to the point that all I needed to do was to get both bodies in the room and require them to return for as many interviews as I considered necessary.

An impartial examiner who frequently appears as an advocate is probably not a wise choice as an impartial. He or she is under suspicion of being someone who is a "hired gun" who will support whoever will pay the price. The parents should also be wary of someone who does evaluations in a short period, such as three or four sessions. Quick evaluations are likely to be compromised. Custody evaluations are very complex. Minimally, they involve interviews with the parents alone, interviews with the children, and interviews with various combinations of the family members. Often other interviews are desirable: one or two stepparents, a housekeeper, a prospective stepparent, a live-in parental surrogate, and so on. It is hard for me to imagine that such an evaluation can be done properly in three or four interviews.

Parents should be wary of using an individual who works for a fixed fee for all cases. One cannot tell in advance how protracted the litigation is going to be, how many interviews are going to be required, and whether or not court appearances are going to be necessary. The person who works for a fixed fee is likely to compromise his or her commitment and involvement if the case becomes complex and drawn out.

M. Lewis (1974) believes that it is unwise for the judge to appoint the impartial examiner. The main danger here is that the judge will appoint someone who shares his or her own biases. Unfortunately, I know a number of situations in which this has clearly been the case. This is especially the case in small communities with a limited number of mental health professionals available to provide such services. How often this occurs would be impossible to determine. Certain judges, however, may not agree to appoint the parents' choice, if they suspect that the parents' impartial will not support their own views. In cases like these, appeals to higher courts may be required if the parents are to get a fair hearing.

CONDITIONS UNDER WHICH I WOULD CONSIDER SERVING AS AN ADVOCATE

Sometimes the court will be willing to order a reluctant party to participate in a custody evaluation. At other times, the court will not support the request of the petitioning attorney for such an order. In such cases, there is no way to serve as an impartial. There is still the possibility, however, that one may serve as an advocate. But there were certain strict provisos that had to be satisfied before I was willing to consider serving in such capacity. I first required that the attorney of the parent who wished to enlist my support write a letter to his or her adversary requesting cooperation in bringing me in as an impartial. Following receipt of that letter of rejection I required the attorney to make a formal request of the court to order participation by the unreceptive party. Upon receipt of a written statement that the court had refused to issue such an order, I then agreed to consider involving myself as an advocate. I would then see the parent, with no promise beforehand that I would support his or her position. I promised, however, to come to some conclusion—within a few sessions—regarding whether I could provide support with conviction. If I could do so, then I proceeded with a more detailed inquiry. If I had no such conviction, I removed myself from the case. When I considered involvement to be warranted, I could do so without the fear that I would be subjected to the kind of cross examination described previously in which the impartial was made to look foolish because he or she was stating that one parent was *better* without having seen the other. A statement of these attempts in my report served to confirm that I had made every reasonable effort to involve both sides and I was thereby protected from questions by the opposing attorney designed to embarrass or compromise me.

When submitting reports in such circumstances, therefore, I made it clear that I had made every reasonable attempt to serve as an impartial, but that such attempts were not successful. I directly stated my awareness that my position was weakened by the fact that I did not have the opportunity to evaluate directly the other party, the party whose position I was not supporting. However, I made reference to powerful data (hospital reports, letters, etc.) that supported my conviction for coming in as an advocate. In short, I do not take the position that the evaluator should always insist upon involvement as an impartial. I am only saying that he (she) should make every reasonable effort to do so and should consider the possibility of serving as an advocate only after attempts to serve as an impartial have proved futile.

On occasion, a judge would refuse to formally appoint me the court's impartial examiner but would order the reluctant party to see me. Often a similar arrangement was ordered for the other side's advocate examiner, each advocate evaluating all parties in a kind of cross-over arrangement, i.e., mother is evaluated by father's advocate and father is examined by mother's advocate, with the children seeing both evaluators as well. However, in such a situation I was generally viewed by the court as an advocate of the inviting party. In such cases I made it clear to both the motivated and the reluctant party that I would not necessarily support the position of the party who initially engaged my services. In fact, I informed the reluctant party that I might ultimately support his (her) position and be willing to go to court and testify to my support. This was not only stated verbally but included in the provisions document (to be discussed in Chapter Three) that the inviting party, at least, was required to sign before I was willing to conduct the evaluation. I consider this to be a relatively innovative practice, and I generally recommend that both parents request that the other mental health professional in the case act similarly. Sometimes the other advocate mental health professional is receptive to this plan. However, inveterate "hired gun" mental health professionals generally are not. They maintain loyalty to the client to the end, regardless of how compelling the evidence that would warrant their changing their positions.

I consider my insistence on remaining impartial to be the most humane way to conduct the evaluation under these unfortunate circumstances. Otherwise the visiting party is exploited because the information provided is inevitably used against him (her) in court and there is no possibility that anything the person says will change the examiner's position. Unfortunately, crossover examinations have become quite common. I view them as court-ordered exploitation of clients. In the majority of cases it is a "no win situation" for the reluctant party. If the person refuses to participate the court views this as uncooperative and recalcitrant. The refusal will contribute to the judge's unreceptivity to that person's position. If the individual participates, everything that is revealed may be used as ammunition against that person. It is a deplorable practice. Accordingly, those who agree to serve in such capacity should do so in the way I have described. Although the court viewed me as an advocate, I did not conduct myself as one and sometimes actually came to court and testified on behalf of the "visiting" parent—much to the chagrin of the attorney who originally enlisted my services. The original attorney then found himself (herself) in a situation never taught about in law school. The attorney had to bring me in to testify as his (her) advocate; yet once on the stand I provided support for the adversary.

THE THERAPIST AS THERAPIST VS.
THE THERAPIST AS IMPARTIAL EXAMINER

An impartial evaluation will be seriously compromised if the impartial examiner has had any kind of involvement with the litigating parties prior to the initiation of the evaluation. Any previous contact at all will generally preclude true impartiality. The impartial must come in "clean," with no advance information that might conceivably "tip the scale" in one direction or another. The principle is similar to that which holds for judges who are expected to disqualify themselves from any litigation in which they have had some relationship with either party.

When the Therapist Is Treating
One of the Children at the
Time of Litigation

On a number of occasions, while a child has been in treatment, one (and on occasion both) of the parents has requested that I either serve as an impartial examiner or, more commonly, that I provide a recommendation to the court regarding who would be the preferable parent to have custody. In such situations it behooves therapists to explain to the parents that conducting such an evaluation and then providing testimony supporting one parent over the other will almost invariably jeopardize the child's treatment. Such testimony will cause the nonpreferred parent to harbor deep resentment against the therapist. The parents should be helped to appreciate that when a parent is significantly angry at a child's therapist, it is almost inevitably communicated to the child. Often the parent will express the resentment openly to the child. But even when attempts are made to hide the animosity, the child will sense the hostile feelings and will feel caught in the middle of a tug-of-war between parent and therapist. Such a situation will compromise the child's positive feelings toward the therapist—feelings crucial to have if therapy is to be meaningful. The child placed in the middle of such a conflict will, in the vast majority of cases, side with the parent's position. And the child must. The parents, despite their problems, are providing the child with food, clothing, shelter, and probably much more love and affection than the therapist is—even though the therapist professes interest, concern, and affection. I generally go further with such parents and tell them that I cannot stop them from requesting that I submit information to the court (I will elaborate on this point below), but if they do so there is a 99 + percent chance that the therapy will become practically worthless. If this happens they will have no one but themselves to blame. Therefore, I advise them to bring in another person to serve as impartial and "leave me out of it."

Borderline Situations Regarding the
Therapist's Role When Custody Litigation
Is Pending or Anticipated

The therapist should make sure to clarify his (her) role in any situation where there appears to be a question regarding this issue. In the initial telephone conversation, prior to the first appointment, the therapist may detect some confusion on the parent's part as to exactly what is being requested, that is, which role is being sought: therapist for the child, advocate for the caller, or impartial examiner. It is crucial that the therapist make clear to the caller that each of these is a *separate* role and they cannot be combined. It would be unwise for the therapist to invite the parent to discuss the matter in session, because if the decision is made to request that the examiner serve as an *impartial,* such participation will have been precluded by the earlier contact with one parent. If, however, both parents *together* wish to meet with the examiner to discuss beforehand his (her) involvement as an impartial examiner there will be no compromise and such appointment may prove useful in helping the parent decide which route to take and what role the therapist should have. However, if parents can cooperate enough to make such an appointment, they may be good candidates for mediation and this interview may serve as an excellent opportunity for discussing its advantages. If the parents decide to use me as a mediator then I require them to sign the mediation contract (Appendix II) before proceeding.

If the parents decide that therapy, and only therapy, is being requested, then an appointment can be made. However, even at that point, because the question of litigation has already been presented, the therapist should impress upon the parents that if there is a decision later to involve him (her) in litigation, the child's treatment would be seriously compromised, if not destroyed. Furthermore, I required parents who chose the therapeutic route at that point to sign a statement (Appendix IIII) that precludes my involvement in any custody/visitation litigation. I still use the document, even though the impartial examiner option is no longer available to them.

If the parent stated on the phone that he (she) was looking for an advocate, I informed the parent that I generally did not serve as an advocate and did everything reasonable to serve only as an impartial examiner in custody litigation. If the parent was willing to consider my participation as an impartial, I sent a copy of my provisions document (Appendix I) so that the parent would be in a better position to understand the rationale for my approach and the steps that had to be taken to bring about my participation.

At times a child will ostensibly be brought for treatment when actually a custody determination is desired. Sometimes parents may really believe that treatment is the only thing they want, or they may say that treatment is what they want, but will know that the custody consideration is also very much on their minds. They may withhold this at the beginning because they fear that the therapist will not want to be involved in the legal aspects of the case, or will refuse to take the child into treatment at all if an appearance in court is also being considered. The parents may know of the reluctance most therapists have over going to court, but may not appreciate the dangers that such appearances pose for therapy. They may consider our hesitation to stem from many factors unrelated to the desire to avoid the inevitable compromise of treatment that court involvement en- tails. (Of course, many therapists also avoid involvement in litigation because of the indignities and duplicities they may be exposed to.) The parents may have been turned down by a series of therapists who refused to get involved once they suspected that their services were being requested for the purposes of litigation. The parents may not realize that the therapist will, of course, be indignant about being forced to testify in a case that was initially presented without any reference to the litigation plans. Such resentment compromises the child's treatment. And this resentment beclouds the therapist's objectivity and may affect his or her custodial preference—specifically by the inevitable prejudice toward the parent who was dishonest.

When the litigation motive becomes disclosed after therapy has been instituted, I inform the parents that I cannot refuse their request that I provide information to the court. I inform them that they have the power to preclude my involvement, even if one or both attorneys are naive enough to request it. But they should know that such involvement on my part is likely to ruin their child's treatment, and they will only have themselves to blame.

Forced Involvement of the Child's Therapist in Custody Litigation

In spite of the above warnings, there are parents who will still insist that the therapist be involved. A parent may be so filled with rage and committed to vengeance as to be blind to the consequences of demanding the therapist's involvement in the litigation. Or the parent may have deep self-destructive tendencies which involve the children as well. When the therapist's services are so enlisted in the course of a treatment program, it is important for the therapist to make clear to the parents and the court that a formal custody evaluation has *not* been conducted and, therefore, one's contribution to the court regarding which of the two parents would be *preferable* for the children must be compromised. Nevertheless, the therapist may still be required to go to court—and may even be subpoenaed.

This legal point is best understood by utilizing an analogy to an automobile accident. A woman, for example, drives past the scene of an accident. She slows up, glances at the scene (just as dozens of others may be doing), and then drives on. It is possible that she may subsequently receive a subpoena to appear in court and provide information. In fact, to refuse to appear may place her in contempt of court and subject to punishment. Once in court she may be asked questions such as whether or not it was raining that day, whether the streets were slippery, whether she saw any bodies on the street, whether she saw any blood, how many people were lying on the ground, was it day or night, and how many cars were damaged. All these are questions that can be answered by any reasonably observant passerby. They do not require any expertise. Such a person would not be expected to answer questions like: "What was the length of the skid marks?" "About how many miles per hour was a particular car going prior to the impact?" "Were any of the participants inebriated?" "Did any of the automobiles show evidence of mechanical defects?" and "How deep were the treads on each side of the tires on each of the cars?" These questions can only be answered by experts after proper investigation.

A therapist who is treating a child and/or members of a family that subsequently become involved in custody litigation can generally serve only as a provider of facts, like the lay passerby in the aforementioned automobile accident example. Under such circumstances, the therapist can be asked questions like: "Did either of the parents use corporal punishment? If so, describe the method(s), frequency, etc." "Who, to the best of your knowledge, made the children breakfast each morning?" "What were the sleep patterns of each of the parents?" and "To the best of your knowledge, how many nights per week on the average did Mr. Jones not return to the home at all?" These questions, of course, provide information regarding parental capacity, but they do not specifically ask the therapist to make a direct statement regarding which of the two parents would be the preferable one to assume primary child-rearing responsibilities. The therapist who has only served as therapist and not as an impartial evaluator should not be asked the question: "Who would be the better parent to have custody of these children?" The primary focus of treatment was therapeutic, and the therapist has not conducted a formal evaluation to answer this question. In such cases the best answer is: "I cannot answer." However, the therapist may indeed have enough information to answer this question. If the therapist then *does* provide this information, he or she is most likely to destroy the child's treatment—if he or she has not done so already by having answered questions designed to make it obvious that one parent is preferable to the other.

An additional question that arises here is that of confidentiality. One parent may not be willing to allow the therapist to provide information when the other is very desirous of it (the therapist's protestations notwithstanding). States vary regarding what rights parents have under these circumstances. Some states deny privilege under the best interests of the child presumption. In these states a parent cannot prevent the therapist from revealing any and all information to the court that is pertinent to the child's welfare. The therapist, in such states, need not be fearful of a malpractice suit (at least on that point). In short, in these states, privilege is automatically waived by any party who actively contests child custody. There are other states, however, in which both parents must provide the therapist with their consent for him (her) to testify. If either parent refuses to give such consent the privilege must be honored. In such situations, the therapist may testify about the parent who has provided consent, but must strictly avoid making any comments about the parent who has not. Of course, the reluctant parent's position in the litigation is somewhat weakened by the failure to have provided release for the disclosure of the information. (People who plead the Fifth Amendment are rarely viewed as innocent and merely exercising their constitutional rights on principle.) In all the states I am familiar with (and I suspect in all the states) the consent of only one parent is enough to permit the examiner to provide information to third parties designated by the parent.

In order to avoid charges of unethical conduct or malpractice suits the therapist should consult an attorney on any question regarding laws that prevail in a particular state. This is not a situation in which one would want to get some quick free advice from one's lawyer brother-in-law or cousin. It is important to consult an attorney who is specifically knowledgeable in this area. Furthermore, one should seek the advice of one's malpractice insurance company. My experience has been that these companies are most receptive to such inquiries in that they much prefer to help their clients *before* the malpractice charges arise. In fact, I would go further and say that they are probably the best source of advice in such situations.

Besides the legal issues here, there is an ethical one. In states where a parent can invoke privilege and prevent a therapist from providing information, this particular ethical issue does not arise.

However, what about the state in which a parent is automatically considered to waive privilege under the best interests of the child presumption? When testifying in such situations, therapists are certainly obeying the law; however, they are not fulfilling their ethical obligations to respect the parents' confidentiality. If therapists decide that the ethical consideration is more important or compelling than the legal, then they are likely to find themselves in contempt of court. Under such threats, most comply with the law and justify their possibly unethical position with the arguments that they are law-abiding and doing what is in the best interests of the children. Those who cannot accept these justifications may choose to defy the law and suffer the consequences of their defiance. If the court wishes to invoke its power, these therapists can literally be put in jail. Although their professional societies may provide them with psychological support and even be willing to enter some cases as an amicus curiae, it is not likely that this support will be financial (although voluntary collections might be taken up). Therapists have little choice in such situations but to hire their own attorneys and assume the cost of such litigation (which may be enormous).

Some readers may be wondering at this point what I personally would have done were I in such a situation. Most of my experiences as an impartial examiner have been in two states, one of which holds that parents' privilege is lost in custody litigation and the other holds that privilege must be respected. Specifically, in the state of New Jersey (where I live and practice) the parents' privilege must be respected in custody litigation. However, in the state of New York (where I teach) a parent's privilege is not honored under the best interests of the child presumption. Accordingly, I had no ethical conflict with regard to my testifying in the state of New Jersey, because my failure to testify about one parent was in compliance with that parent's request and the law's support. Practically, my experience had been that the unreceptive New Jersey parent usually did not invoke privilege because of the recognition that such invocation might be viewed by the judge as a cover-up (and properly so) and thereby compromise that parent's position in the litigation. In contrast, in New York I did not have to concern myself with such impediments to my freedom to testify.

Up to this point I have focused on the situation in which the therapist is asked to testify while a child is in treatment and contact with the family is present and recent. There are times, however, when all contact with the family has been discontinued, for varying lengths of time, and the therapist's involvement is then sought or even ordered by court subpoena. Sometimes the situation is one in which the child was treated while the parents were married and the divorce decision came after the termination of contact with the therapist. The custody litigation, then, was generally not even remotely considered by the therapist during the course of the therapy. This may not deter parents, attorneys, and judges from inviting, and even ordering, a therapist to testify. Of course, the issue of compromising the child's treatment is not relevant. The legal and ethical issues regarding confidentiality, however, are still operative. My previous comments regarding whether or not to testify (the state laws, ethical issues, the malpractice threat, etc.) would still apply.

Exceptions to the Rule That Serving As Therapist and Impartial Examiner Is Risky and Injudicious

On occasion there may be an exception to the caveat that one cannot serve both as a therapist and an impartial examiner. This happened to me on one occasion when, five years after I had served as an impartial, the father asked me if I would treat his daughter. As is my practice—whether or not the parents are divorced—I try to involve both parents in the child's therapy, especially when the child is embroiled in the middle of the parental conflict. Such was the case in this situation. Because I had supported the father's position in the custody conflict, he was friendly toward me and I saw no problems from his side. I anticipated that there might be difficulties with his ex-wife's relationship with me, but she was in agreement with her former husband that I should treat their daughter. This was not simply a matter of "let bygones be bygones." Rather, I recalled that she basically did not want the children anyway. She was fighting for them because she could not allow herself to accept the fact that she really did not want to have custody. She therefore went through the motions of a custody dispute hoping (I believe even consciously) that she would lose (which she did). Accordingly, I had done her a service by recommending that her husband gain custody—thus the lack of animosity. In this case, I was able to serve as a therapist *after* the custody litigation had been completed.

There is another situation which may appear to be an exception to the rule that one cannot serve both as therapist and impartial examiner. One parent may be totally uninvolved, and even antagonistic, to the therapist. If legal and ethical considerations allow the therapist to provide testimony in support of the involved parent, the therapy will probably not be compromised any further than it has been by the noninvolvement of the hostile parent. No love has been lost by the therapist, because there was no love in the first place.

HYPOTHETICAL QUESTIONS

On occasion, I have received telephone calls from attorneys inviting me to answer hypothetical questions in custody litigation. Either my involvement as an impartial had not been requested or one side wished such involvement and the other refused. Generally, the invitation came from one side. Although the attorney initially may have denied that this was really a request for me to appear as an advocate, the failure of the other side to support my involvement as a provider of hypothetical information (the usual case) supported my supposition that I was basically being invited to serve as an advocate. Furthermore, the caller often wanted to know beforehand what my answers would be before making the final commitment for my appearance. He (she) agreed that if my responses were not to his (her) liking, my services would not be enlisted. Obviously, this is not the way one deals with an impartial examiner.

Although a provider of hypothetical answers may not be

formally designated an advocate, that person will certainly be treated as one in the court. In addition, ours is an inexact science and is more properly still viewed as an art. Answers to hypothetical questions are not likely to be as useful in our field as they may be in other disciplines and are likely to be a disservice to the court and the families involved. Every patient is different from every other patient. Every family is different from every other family. And every custody decision is based on factors peculiar to that particular family. The response to a hypothetical question must be general and the principle thereby promulgated to the court may not be applicable to the specific family under consideration. The result will be that the evaluator will have misled the court. Accordingly, in response to such requests I drew up a provisions document (Appendix IV) stipulating my requirements for providing answers to hypothetical questions. It basically requires the inviter to enlist the agreement of the adversary, and, if possible, the support of the court. Although I sent out many such documents, on only two occasions was I ever subsequently asked to provide answers to the inviter's hypothetical questions. The reason for this is obvious. The inviting party was basically looking for a hired gun (professions of a desire for my impartiality notwithstanding) and would not have brought me into court had my answers to the hypothetical questions not been supportive.

⚖️ THREE

THE PROVISIONS DOCUMENT FOR CUSTODY EVALUATIONS IN THE CONTEXT OF THE ADVERSARY SYSTEM.

INTRODUCTION

At the present time, there are few if any formal legal guidelines regulating the way in which a custody evaluation should be conducted. Therapists are totally free to refuse to involve ourselves in cases where there has been no previous contact. And even when involved, the courts and attorneys have little control over us regarding our methods of evaluation. Of course, once involved with patients—whether as therapists or as evaluators—we are obligated to give testimony in court, even when we may consider such testifying to be psychologically detrimental to a child's treatment.

Accordingly, methods for conducting custody evaluations are "open territory." Considering the burgeoning of such litigation, it is likely that certain procedures will become more commonly used than others. At this time, we in the mental health professions are the ones deciding how to conduct such evaluations. If we do not actively conduct them in the ways that we consider warranted, we may find ourselves submitting to rules, regulations, laws, and constraints that compromise us. If most members of the legal profession had their way, most of us would be involved as advocates. If all of us insisted that we would serve only as impartials (with rare and specific exceptions), they would have just two choices: 1) use us as impartials or 2) dispense with our services entirely. I am quite sure that the first alternative would be chosen by the overwhelming majority of the legal profession. They recognize our value, but we must insist that they take us on our terms. Otherwise, we risk doing our patients a terrible disservice as well as compromising our professional integrity.

There is an old bit of advice which states that if you want to do something that may not be acceptable to your superiors, it is sometimes preferable to go ahead and do it rather than ask for permission. The argument runs that if you ask for permission and are turned down, you will have no opportunity to pursue your course. However, if you don't ask permission, you may very well have your way and no one will ask any questions. One may be stopped, however, if the particular course comes to the attention of authorities and they order that the practice be discontinued.

I am not recommending this approach as a routine to justify an unconscionable act. I am only suggesting it in certain situations, when the course of action is a reasonable and humane one and when the individual suspects that superiors will be unreasonable in their refusals. And this is the course of action that I recommend mental health professionals *consider* taking when introducing new techniques in custody evaluations. The courts, although not strictly speaking our superiors, do have the potential to control us (by subpoena, for example), even though we deem compliance to be psychologically detrimental to our patients. On a number of occasions I found the aforementioned advice useful. I have not asked the court permission to introduce what I considered an atypical, but nevertheless justifiable, procedure in the course of my evaluation. At times such procedures have been met with raised eyebrows and incredulity, but I have not yet been put in jail nor have I even been told to cease and desist. At worst I was told that my services would not be enlisted if I insisted upon certain provisos. And even then, there were others who recognized how judicious my innovations were and continued to enlist my services.

THE PROVISIONS DOCUMENT

Up until the late 1970s I made verbal agreements with parents regarding the stipulations for my involvement in custody litigation. In retrospect, this was a serious error. I had no guidelines regarding how to conduct such evaluations and no one to tell me how seriously compromised an evaluation is likely to be if one does not lay down first—in writing—the stipulations and principles by which the evaluation is going to be conducted. I was never taught about custody evaluations in my residency training. Basically, I have had "on the job training." Even now, the field is a relatively open one, with few formal training programs.

The provisions document I describe in this chapter evolved during the last 10 years. Each stipulation was devised in an attempt to protect me from various kinds of traps, manipulations, grief, and malpractice suits. Over the years the document continued to grow as I found myself trying to "plug up new holes in the dike." In June of 1988, the month I stopped accepting invitations to do custody evaluations under court auspices, the document was in its 36th rendition. It averaged approximately three changes a year. I am convinced that had I continued to do such evaluations further updates would have been necessary. I am sure the reader will easily "read between the lines" and readily appreciate how much "blood, sweat, and tears" went into the formation of this document. The majority of attorneys and parents were not willing to agree to all of these provisions. Accordingly, I would send out approximately 25 documents for every one that was returned with a commitment to fulfill all its provisions. I recognize that I have had a reputation for being somewhat "hard-nosed" in my reluctance to become involved in custody litigation when these provisions were not satisfied. However, those in agreement with me that these stipulations were warranted found that they make sense and ensure a setting in which the optimum kind of evaluation can be conducted. The full document is reproduced as Appendix I. Here I will review it section by section and comment on the rationale for each of its provisions.

PROVISIONS FOR ACCEPTING AN INVITATION TO SERVE AS AN IMPARTIAL EXAMINER IN CUSTODY/VISITATION LITIGATION

Whenever possible, I make every reasonable attempt to serve as a court-appointed impartial examiner, rather than as an advocate, in custody/visitation litigation. In order to serve optimally in this capacity I must be free to avail myself of any and all information, from any source, that I consider pertinent and reasonable to have. In this way, I believe, I can serve best the interests of children and parents involved in such conflicts. Accordingly, before agreeing to serve in this capacity, the following conditions must be accepted by both parents and both attorneys:

1) The presiding judge will agree to appoint me impartial examiner to conduct an evaluation of the concerned parties.

It is not by pure chance that the judge's appointment of me (by name) is presented as stipulation number one. It puts in proper perspective the importance of this particular provision. As the first requirement of involvement as an impartial examiner, it gets across the message that I was going to serve as the court's appointee and no one else's. Examiners who informally agree to serve as impartials, without insisting upon a court order, may find themselves seriously compromised once they have come forth with their recommendations. The attorney whose position is not being supported is likely to "forget" the invitation and the judge, often having had no awareness of the arrangement, is not likely to view with respect the appearance of an impartial appointed in this way. In contrast, when the impartial examiner's services have been court appointed, the nonsupported attorney has no choice but to recognize the evaluation, and the judge is likely to have the highest respect for it. Also, without a formal court appointment the impartial examiner will not generally be allowed to send a report directly to the court nor "have the judge's ear" in certain special situations that may warrant direct communication with the court.

> 2) I will have available to interview all members of the immediate family—that is, the mother, father, and children—for as many interviews (individual and in any combination) as I consider warranted. In addition, I will have the freedom to invite any and all other parties whom I would consider possible sources of useful information. Generally, these will include such persons as present or prospective parental surrogates with whom either parent may be involved and the housekeeper.
>
> Usually, I do not interview a series of friends and relatives each of whom, from the outset, is particularly partial to one of the parents (but I reserve the right to invite such parties if I consider it warranted). The decision to interview such additional parties will be based solely on the potential value of their contributions to the data-collection process and not on whether one parent is represented by more such people than the other.

I cannot emphasize strongly enough the point that the joint interviews are the richest sources of information for the evaluator. Accordingly, a spouse who refuses to be evaluated in the same room as the other parent would not have been able to enlist my services as an impartial examiner. One does not ask a surgeon to perform an operation without a scalpel, nor will a competent surgeon agree to do so. The joint interview is the sharpest scalpel. Most interviews (single and joint) are with the parents and children. I consider the involvement of well-meaning friends and relatives to be reminiscent of the days before no-fault divorces when both parties would bring in a parade of such individuals to support their positions. They generally cancel one another out and are most often a waste of time and money. However, there are occasions when their comments may be useful. And a housekeeper, if she can be brought in, may be a valuable source of information. Unfortunately, she is often very fearful of revealing what she knows, recognizing that her position may be at risk.

A complaint frequently made by a nonsupported party after the presentation of my findings was that my evaluation was biased because I saw more friends and relatives of one party than the other. Attempts to impress upon the parties that it was the *quality* of the interviewees' comments, rather than the *quantity* of interviewees that was important to me, did not prove particularly convincing. And this point was often raised in court where a nonsupported attorney would ask me to name the number of people I interviewed on each side and try to use the fact that I interviewed fewer people supporting his (her) client to compromise my evaluation. Often, the fewer number resulted from the fewer people whom the nonsupported party could bring in for support. In order to protect myself from this absurd criticism, I made reference to the criteria for my selecting interviewees in the provisions document.

> 3) Information will be gathered primarily from the aforementioned clinical interviews. Although I do not routinely use formal psychological tests, in some evaluations I have found certain psychological tests to be useful. Accordingly, the parents shall agree to take any and all psychological tests that I consider helpful. In addition, they will agree to have one or more of the children take such tests if I consider them warranted. Some of these tests will be administered by me, but others by a psychologist of my choosing if I do not consider myself qualified to administer a particular psychological test.

I did not commonly utilize psychological tests. My findings and recommendations were based primarily on clinical interviews, my own observations, and statements made directly to me. These are the most powerful sources of information. Attorneys and judges (as well as lay persons) often have an exaggerated view of the value of psychological tests. Whereas clinical data are considered to be more subjective, these tests are often viewed as providing the "truth." This is not the case. A statement or an observation can be quite objective and provide much more information than projective material, which is subject to different interpretations by different examiners. Psychological tests are useful for obtaining an objective assessment of a child's intellectual level. Such information may help to assess the credibility of a child's statements. The older the child, and the more intelligent, the more seriously should the child's comments be taken. Only rarely did I use projective tests; they simply do not hold up well under astute cross examination. This is an important drawback to their utilization in litigation. It is not that I do not have the conviction for the value of these instruments in the hands of competent examiners, only that there is far more subjectivity to their interpretation than there is regarding whether or not a parent made a particular statement. The one situation in which I did use projective tests was when I suspected a parent might be psychotic and having delusions. Although clinical interviews provide definite ideas along these lines, a Rorschach Test can be most helpful, the risks in the courtroom notwithstanding.

> 4) In order to allow me the freedom of inquiry necessary for serving optimally families involved in custody/visitation litigation, the parents shall agree to a modification of the traditional rules of confidentiality. Specifically, I must be given the freedom to reveal to one party what has been told to me by the other (at my discretion) so that I will have full opportunity to explore all pertinent points with both parties. This does not mean that I will not respect certain privacies or that I will automatically reveal all information provided me—only that I reserve the right to make such revelations if I consider them warranted for the purpose of collecting the most meaningful data.

One cannot conduct a custody evaluation when important information must be withheld because a parent has not given the examiner permission to reveal certain material to another party. This provision ensured that I would have full opportunity to explore in depth every pertinent point. It also protected me from being in the position where one party provided me with information that he (she) did not wish me to reveal to the other. For example, a wife complained bitterly about her husband's drinking problem. Often, he would say absolutely nothing about this. This proviso enabled me to bring up the subject without waiting for him to do so himself. I was even free to introduce the subject with a comment like "Your wife has complained to me that you drink excessively. I'd like to hear about this from you." (The reader should note here that I have carefully refrained from accepting the wife's statement as valid. I merely opened the issue and invited his response to the allegation.)

In the course of the evaluation, a parent might tell me that there was an important issue that warranted disclosure, but the party feared that such revelation might compromise his or her legal position. In such cases, I would tell the parent that I do not automatically reveal everything said to me to the other party. However, I would not promise beforehand not to reveal the information; therefore, telling it to me involved a risk. I did not try to coerce the parent into providing the information. I did, however, inform the party that to the degree that I have all pertinent information, to that degree am I placed in the optimum position for making the most judicious custody recommendation. I left it to the parent to decide which was more important: the children's best interests or the legal situation.

A good example of this occurred with a father who told me that he had information that he was hesitant to reveal because he feared my divulging it might weaken his legal position. I presented him with the pros and cons and left it completely up to him to decide what he wanted to do. He decided to take the risk involved in telling me. He then revealed that he had a woman friend and that he had been having an affair with this woman prior to separation. He had no reason to believe that his wife knew anything about this relationship. In addition, he informed me that, even though separated, his lawyer had advised him not to reveal the relationship (past or present) to his wife until after the divorce became final. He also informed me that he planned to marry this woman soon after that. I told him that, from the psychological standpoint, there was probably nothing to be gained by revealing the nature of the past relationship to his wife. However, I also informed him that this involvement enhanced somewhat his chances of gaining custody because his work schedule was a heavy one and this woman was a homemaker. I explained to him that for the purposes of the evaluation it would be useful for me to interview her. Obviously, I could not include such information in my report without simultaneously divulging his "secret" to his wife. In this case I let the man decide whether or not he wished to disclose the information and told him that if he chose not to, I would not reveal what he had told me to his wife, either verbally or in my report. In a subsequent session the man told me that he had decided to reveal this woman's identity to his wife, because he decided that the advantages to be gained in the custody litigation far outweighed the drawbacks.

The vignette is presented as an example of how I used this special dispensation of the custody evaluation. As mentioned in the formal statement of this proviso, I did not automatically reveal information to other parties; I merely reserved the right to do so at my discretion. I certainly invited input from the parent whose information I might divulge; but I did not give that party veto power over my doing so. And I did not put direct pressure on people to reveal anything to me. I did, however, try to clarify for them the pros and cons of their doing so.

> 5) The parties shall agree to sign any and all releases necessary for me to obtain reports from others, e.g., psychiatrists, psychologists, social workers, teachers, school officials, pediatricians, hospitals (general and psychiatric), etc. This includes past records as well as reports from professionals who may be involved with any of the parties at the time of the litigation. Although I may choose not to request a particular report, I must have the freedom to request any and all such reports if I consider them useful sources of information.

Although there are many redundancies in this paragraph, they were placed there to ensure that there would be absolutely no interference with my obtaining any record that I considered useful for my evaluation. On occasion a parent was quite reluctant to provide such information. I generally insisted that the releases be signed in the first interview, before I had obtained a significant amount of substantive material. In this way, if a parent reneged, I would threaten to remove myself from the evaluation and write a letter to the presiding judge (with copies to the attorneys and the clients) that I would no longer conduct the evaluation because the party had refused to grant me permission to obtain certain documents. This was done at a point *before* I had obtained any substantive data, and so I could not be subpoenaed into court to provide testimony—because I had no information to provide.

When asked to sign releases in the first meeting, a parent may say, "Well, let me think about it and discuss it with my attorney; I'll get back to you. So why don't we just continue now." Examiners who comply with such a request are naive. It is not likely that an attorney is going to tell a client to sign these releases, even though stipulated in the provisions document. The examiner may then find him- or herself in the position of "running after" the parent to get the releases signed. Or, the examiner may have to convince the attorney that such releases were agreed upon in the provisions document. Such entreaties are frustrating and ego-debasing and will compromise the respect for the therapist that all concerned parties may previously have had. If the examiner continues to conduct the evaluation while appealing to the various parties to sign the release forms, substantive data will be obtained. If, then, the examiner decides to discontinue the evaluation because of the failure to sign the release(s) he or she may still be brought to court (sometimes by subpoena) and forced to provide data from an incomplete evaluation. And this can only be a disservice to the child(ren), family, and the court. All this trouble can be avoided by the examiner's insistence, early in the first interview, that the releases be signed at that point and refusal to continue the evaluation—at that point—if they are not signed.

Were my junior high school English teacher to have read this provision, she would have placed many red marks on my paper for redundancies. First, "any and all" is intrinsically redundant; any covers *all* and all covers *any*. But this is the way lawyers speak. Accordingly, if a particular source of information is not to be considered to fall under the category of *all*, then it might be justified to warrant placement under the category of *any*. Considering that *any and all* cover *everything*, one could argue that that there was no reason to delineate the various possible kinds of reports that I might wish to request. I included this list in order to reduce time wasted in justifying my request. By simply pointing directly to the source identified in this paragraph, I circumvented resistance and obstructionism. But even this list did not prove "perfect." One woman began to argue with me that a mental hospital was not the same as a psychiatric hospital and therefore I could not have permission to get a copy of the report of her hospitalization. I told her that I would not get into an argument with her as to whether or not a mental hospital was the same as a psychiatric hospital or different. I simply informed her that if she did not sign the release I would inform the judge of her lack of cooperation and let him make the decision about the definition of psychiatric hospital. (She signed the release.)

One could argue that the inclusion of *etc.* was also unnecessary considering the presence of the *e.g.* and the *any and all.* It was inserted just to be sure that in case a new kind of document was to be requested I would have justification for including it under *etc.* The reader would do well to be prepared for these kinds of picayune and time-wasting details when conducting such evaluations within the process of adversarial litigation.

It is important for the reader to appreciate also that written reports, although they may initially appear valuable, may not be particularly useful. The examiner should view them as containing hearsay information and so should not automatically consider them valid. To do so compromises the evaluation and opens up the evaluator for criticism during cross-examination. Therapists should use such information only as a point of departure in their direct inquiries with the parents. Even if one obtains a hospital record which states that a mother, for example, was committed with a diagnosis of paranoid schizophrenia, the information may not be particularly useful. The mother may have been grossly psychotic at the time of the hospitalization, but her present psychiatric status is much more important—although her past history is not totally irrelevant. As I will discuss subsequently, the therapist's own observations of the manifestations of psychopathology—rather than the *diagnostic* category—are the more important factors to be considered in the evaluation. Furthermore, schizophrenia does not necessarily compromise one's maternal capacity for all ages of children. Lastly, the extent of the father's psychopathology in this case—especially with regard to symptoms that compromise his paternal capacity—must be weighed against the mother's before coming to any conclusions regarding parental preference. When one considers these additional factors, the hospital report becomes less meaningful.

I generally did not request reports from therapists who had a meaningful relationship with a parent at the time of the custody evaluation. If such a therapist were to provide information that could compromise the parent's position in the custody litigation, it was likely to have a detrimental effect on the therapist-patient relationship. I was less reluctant to request such information from past therapists, especially if the relationship was not a particularly deep one.

My experience had been that about 20-25 percent of all requests for such information are never responded to. I think this is related to the fear the recipients had of involving themselves in the litigation. On other occasions I suspected that the recipient of my letter wanted to protect one party from a divulgence that might compromise his (her) position in the litigation. Such "protectionism," although often benevolently motivated, is usually misguided. It generally stemmed from some prejudicial preference for one parent over the other, without having had the full opportunity to evaluate both sides. Whatever the motivation of the nonresponder, I never saw fit to press the issue with further letters or any kind of coercive maneuver. As mentioned, such information is generally of low value and serves best as a point of departure for the evaluator's own inquiries.

> 6) My fee for conducting a custody evaluation is $150 per hour of my time. Time spent in interviewing as well as time expended in report preparation, dictation, telephone conversations, responses to letters (regardless of which side submits them), court preparation, and any other time invested in association with the evaluation will also be billed at the $150 per hour rate. My fee for court and

deposition appearances is $200 per hour while in court and $120 per hour travel time to and from my office. During the data-collection phase of the evaluation, payments shall be made at the time services are rendered. Payments for the final conference at which my findings and recommendations are presented (item #9 below), the court report, and my court appearance shall be made in advance—in accordance with estimates provided prior to the rendering of these services.

Prior to the initial interview (with both parents together) the payer(s) will deposit with me a check (in my name) for $2,500. This shall be deposited in the Northern Valley-Englewood Savings and Loan Association branch in Cresskill, New Jersey, in my name, in a day-to-day interest bearing account. This money, with accrued interest (taxable to the payer), shall be returned *after* a final decision has been made regarding custody/visitation and after I have received a letter from *both* of the attorneys that my services are no longer being enlisted.

This payment is a security deposit. It will not serve as an advance retainer, in that the aforementioned fees will not be drawn against it, unless there has been a failure to pay my fees. It also serves to reassure the nonpayer that my objectivity will not be compromised by the fear that if I do not support the paying party, my fee will not be paid.

The average total cost for an evaluation is generally in the $3,000-$6,000 range. Although this figure may initially appear high, it is generally far less costly than protracted litigation. If as a result of the evaluation the litigation is shortened (often the case) or the parties decide not to litigate further over custody/visitation (also a common occurrence), then the net savings may be signifi-cant. It is very difficult, if not impossible, to predict the cost of a particular evaluation because I cannot know beforehand how many interviews will be warranted and whether or not I will be asked to testify in court.

Clearly, my evaluations were expensive and were not avail-able to indigent individuals. However, all the other provisions can certainly be utilized in a low-cost clinic setting. The security deposit was especially reassuring to the party not paying for the evaluation. Usually this was the mother and her fears that I might be biased against her—because her husband was paying my bills—were often relieved by this provision. But this security deposit was not only for the mother, it was for me as well. The likelihood that one (and even both) of the parents would end up being extremely angry at me was quite high. After all, their most cherished possessions, the children, were at stake. In the most common situation, the father was the one paying the bills and the mother the one to whom I was more likely to recommend primary custody. This was in line with my belief that custody should be awarded to that parent (regardless of sex) with whom the child has established the stronger, healthy psychological bond. And that parent (regardless of sex) who was the primary caretaker during the earliest years of the child's life is more likely to be the one with whom the child has developed the stronger, healthy psychological bond. In our society—women's involvement in the workplace notwithstanding—mothers, much more often than fathers, have assumed the primary care of their children during the formative years. The application of this important principle often tipped the balance in the mothers' favor, although certainly many other factors were operative—especially when there was a long gap between the infancy period and the time of the custody dispute. (I will discuss this issue in greater detail in Chapter Nine.)

The rage engendered by my decision most often resulted in sudden professions of inability and/or refusal to pay my bills. Up to that point most parents somehow found the money to pay punctually. Such reneging generally presented no problem. I would mosey over to the bank across the street—whistling all the way—and withdraw the appropriate amount. The reader will note that although the *parents'* money was being deposited in the account, the account was in *my* name. Accordingly, there was absolutely no problem withdrawing the money. I took great care, however, not to draw one cent more than was owed me—lest I be justifiably criticized as borrowing, taking, or even stealing the parents' money. The reader will note also that although the account was in my name, the interest reported to the government was that of the parents. In recent years banks have been required to report interest on banking accounts to the Internal Revenue Service in order to ensure that individuals will pay taxes on this income. The reader may consider this a little picayune on my part, considering the small amount of interest that appears to be involved. However, when one considers that these cases last an average of three to four years and that I have 15 to 20 bankbooks in my office at any point, the interest accrued can be formidable and I see no reason why I should pay income taxes for these parents, most of whom end up being furious at me anyway, even those whose position I supported. Setting up the accounts in this way is quite easily accomplished. One merely indicates, when opening up the account, that the account is in the therapist's name *for* Mr. John Doe (the parent). Most banks are familiar with this procedure, and use it routinely for attorneys who set up escrow accounts in this manner.

The reader may have noted that I indicated that I would be expected to be paid for "responses to letters (regardless of which side submits them)." This provision came about because one party would, on occasion, insist that he (she) was not responsible for paying for my time expended in responding to letters and other documents submitted by the other parent. Although one could argue that this was a justifiable position, one could also argue that such letters were a necessary part of the evaluation, that they were often time-consuming to prepare, and that I was entitled to be paid for preparing and reviewing them. Rather than involve myself directly in a discussion with the two parties regarding who has the obligation to pay for such letters, my provisions document stipulates that they be paid for like any other service provided for in the contract and at whatever fraction stipulated therein.

A recent addition was the requirement that payments for the final conference at which my findings and recommendations were presented to the clients and attorneys, as well as all subsequent fees, be made in advance in accordance with estimates provided prior to the rendering of these services. My reason for inserting this requirement related to the unfortunate experience that once my conclusions became known to the payer (and this generally took place at the time of the final conference) reneging and refusal to pay became common if the payer was not supported by me. I recognize that mine is a very "hard-nosed" approach, but my only defense is that if I did not do this I would often have difficulty collecting payment. My choice, as mentioned, had been to be either humiliated or exploited. I much preferred to be demeaned than to be exploited. This requirement was a direct outgrowth of the predictable experience that *most people will resist strongly the demand that they pay money for someone who is going to court to testify against them.* The examiner who does not appreciate this phenomenon should not be involved in conducting custody evaluations.

> On occasion, I am invited to conduct evaluations in cities at varying distances from Cresskill, New Jersey. This generally entails situations in which there is a choice between my traveling to the family's location and all interviewees traveling to New Jersey and acquiring temporary accommodations in the area of my office. Although I prefer that the evaluation take place in my office, I have on occasion agreed to conduct the evaluation elsewhere. However, my fees for such evaluations are higher than for those conducted in my office and are determined by the distance I have to travel and the time I am being asked to be away from my office. My fee schedule for such distant evaluations is available on request.

On occasion I conducted evaluations at sites at great distance from the New York-New Jersey area. Usually, these were conducted in hotels in which one room would serve as my consultation room and another as my waiting room. In order to ensure privacy I preferred that the rooms be across the hall from one another. These were often marathon evaluations. I would arrive in the late afternoon or early evening and soon thereafter conduct the first few hours of my interviews, generally with the parents alone. The next day I would interview the children and parents in varying combinations. I would also interview other parties who might be involved in the evaluation. Near the end of the second day, and at times not until the third, I would complete the data-collection process. I would then take an hour or two alone to review my material and come up with a recommendation. I would then meet with the clients and their attorneys to inform them of my conclusions and recommendations. As the reader can well imagine these were exhausting experiences, with time out only to eat, sleep, and go to the bathroom. I would then return to New Jersey, formulate my report, and send it to the court, the clients, and their attorneys. I would then return at a subsequent time to provide testimony in court.

Appendix V details my fees for providing such evaluations. Clearly, only those who were in a strong financial position could afford such an evaluation. It was generally more expensive to have me conduct the evaluation at the distant site than for the parents and children to come to New Jersey and be evaluated in my office. However, the latter option would generally preclude my meeting with the attorneys as well as interviewing directly other individuals who might have been able to provide me with useful information, but whose input did not warrant the expense of a trip to New Jersey. The reader may note that I required not only an advance security deposit but payment in advance for each trip, by certified or bank check. This unfortunate practice was necessitated by disgruntled individuals canceling large checks once they learned that my findings did not support their position. I was not comfortable with this requirement and found it somewhat demeaning. However, as stated before (and as I will state again), I much prefer to be demeaned than to be exploited if my choice is restricted to these alternatives only (often the case in custody evaluations).

> 7) Both attorneys are invited to send to me any material that they consider useful to me.

The examiner should read these documents with a certain degree of incredulity. They often contain significant amounts of hearsay information, which would compromise the evaluation significantly if accepted as facts. The evaluator must appreciate that many attorneys who write these documents recognize that their clients may be exaggerating and even fabricating, but they consider themselves to be serving their client's cause by recording their often specious complaints. Other attorneys naively accept as valid their clients' allegations, so convincingly are they presented.

Even if the parent has not exaggerated, the attorney can generally be relied upon to do so. Many attorneys do not seem to appreciate that the more adjectives one utilizes to modify a noun, the weaker the noun becomes. Some of the allegations appear "canned." One gets the feeling that if a mother, for example, tells her attorney that her husband beat her on one or two occasions, this appears in the affidavit as an extended paragraph in which are included "cruel and inhumane punishment," "mental cruelty," "sadism," and references to various other horrendous indignities. The therapist does well to take such hyperbole with a grain of salt and to recognize that they are typical legal maneuvers designed, in part, to improve one side's position over the other in the legal conflict as well as to impress the client with the lawyer's pugnacity.

In all the years I did custody evaluations, I never heard of anyone being charged with libel for including lies in these reports or being brought up on charges of perjury for lying in court. The ancient practice of trial by wager (which originally involved a pledge that one was telling the truth) was based on the theory that people genuinely felt there would be repercussions in the hereafter if they were to lie under oath. But those were ancient, simpler times. There is hardly a human being today (at least in the segment of the population involved in custody litigation) who has any fear that there will be any consequences (either in this life or in the hereafter) for stating under oath the most preposterous lies.

These allegations and counterallegations, however, may serve as useful points of departure for inquiry with the parents, and these documents often bring up issues that were not previously covered in the interviews. In earlier years I used to review all these documents myself, earmarking important points for discussion with the parents. More recently, I found a far more efficient method that was also far less expensive for the parents. Specifically, I invited the parents to review the material and earmark those points that they considered important to focus on. This was done on their time, not mine. In joint sessions, we would go over these points. Most of the documents, especially the court documents, presented primarily one person's opinion without direct opportunity for rebuttal. In the days when I read all these documents myself, I found myself hunting for the rebuttal arguments in the other party's documents. When I began reviewing these papers in joint meetings, the process was made much more efficient as each party was available to comment immediately on the other's allegations.

> 8) After receiving 1) the court order signed by the presiding judge, 2) the signed statements (page 8) from both parties signifying agreement to the conditions of the evaluation, and 3) the $2,500 deposit, I will notify both parties that I am available to proceed with the evaluation as rapidly as is feasible. I generally cannot promise to meet a specific deadline because I cannot know in advance how many interviews will be required, nor can I predict how flexible the parties will be regarding availability for appointments I offer.

An examiner is foolish to proceed before *all* of these items are obtained. If the evaluation has started and all have not been obtained, the examiner may find himself (herself) in the position of appealing for the missing material. This not only compromises the dignity of the examiner but will compromise significantly the evaluator's ability to conduct the examination properly. The reader will note that I must have a court order *signed* by the presiding judge. I am convinced that most readers probably read item #1 without appreciating the full significance of the word *signed*. Most often, the court order is drawn up by one of the attorneys, reviewed by the other, and when both are in agreement with its contents, it is sent on to the presiding judge for signature.

Many years ago I had a very sobering experience in association with such a court order. Specifically, the attorney had sent me a batch of material on the top of which was a face letter indicating that attached was the court order and, indeed, it was attached. Also included were the provisions documents and the security deposit. Accordingly, I proceeded with the evaluation. When presenting my findings and recommendations to the parents and attorneys I learned, to my amazement, that the court order was never signed and that I was therefore not operating as a court-appointed impartial examiner. The slimy shyster who had put that one over on me represented the nonsupported parent and literally laughed in my face. And the attorney of the client whose position I supported was extremely upset by the fact that he had been deceived. Under these circumstances I could not send my report to the presiding judge and came to court simply as an advocate—a far weaker position. It was a bitter lesson but, as I am sure the reader appreciates, I never let that happen to me again. But this is only an isolated example of lawyers' trickery. Most of the provisions contained in this document were derived from similar experiences.

It is important that the evaluator read carefully that section of the court order that pertains to the examiner's involvement (there are usually other provisions in it relating to issues such as finances, etc.). One does well to insist that the exact request be spelled out clearly. An order that merely states that the evaluator should conduct an examination is usually not satisfactory. Such a statement does not define exactly what is the purpose of the evaluation. It will provide a nonsupported attorney with an opportunity to claim that the evaluator was not asked to perform a particular function, such as to conduct a custody evaluation. Accordingly, one should insist that the court order define exactly what the evaluator is being asked to do, e.g., provide recommendations regarding who would better serve as the primary custodial parent and what kind of visitation arrangement is warranted. In some cases there may be a question of whether the child was sexually abused. If the examiner has any question, he (she) does well to send the order back to the court, with copies to both attorneys, with a face letter requesting a specific statement indicating exactly what the court is asking the examiner to do.

It is foolhardy for an examiner to promise adherence to a deadline. Generally, it behooves one party to prolong the proceedings because time is generally on the side of the party who has custody of the children. Children, like the rest of us, resist change and the longer they remain with one parent (even the more deficient one) the more likely that they are going to resist living primarily with the other. And such resistance may be revealed to the examiner, the attorneys, and the judge. Even when both parents are eager to proceed as rapidly as possible, there are usually other interferences that slow down the progress of the evaluation. These include illnesses, vacations, business problems, and attorney's unavailability to attend an early meeting for the presentation of the findings and recommendations. All of these are completely beyond the examiner's control, making it even more risky to agree to a deadline. In all the years I conducted custody evaluations I cannot recall one case in which we proceeded as rapidly as I had hoped. Accordingly, when a deadline was presented, I stated very clearly that I was making no promises regarding my ability to meet it and, most often, I was not able to do so. And this was invariably the result of delays on the part of a client, one or both attorneys, and the court. I cannot recall one case in which my own scheduling and availability slowed things up. Most often the slowness was regrettable because the children suffered as a result of the prolongation of the litigation, even if they were in the home that I ultimately suggested they remain in. Although such prolongation is harmful to them (and their parents as well) more harm might be done by an examiner's rushing through an evaluation.

9) Upon completion of my evaluation—and prior to the preparation of my final report—I generally meet with both parents together and present them my findings and recommendations. This gives them the opportunity to correct any distortions they believe I may have and/or alter my opinion before it becomes finalized in my report. In addition, it saves the parents from the unnecessary and prolonged tensions associated with wondering what my findings are.

Both attorneys are invited to attend this conference. However, this invitation should be considered withdrawn if only one attorney wishes to attend because the presence of only one attorney would obviously place the nonrepresented parent in a compromised position. When a guardian ad litem has been appointed by the court, he or she will also be invited to attend this conference. Before accepting this invitation attorneys should appreciate that the discussion will be completely free and open.

Accordingly, during this conference it would be improper for an attorney in any way whatsoever to restrict or discourage the client from answering questions or participating in the discussion. On occasion, the litigants have used this conference as a forum for resolving their custody/visitation dispute and avoiding thereby the formidable expense and psychological trauma of courtroom litigation. After this conference the final report is prepared and sent simultaneously to the court, attorneys, and parents.

The meeting with the attorneys was a more recent development. In earlier years I did not engage in this practice. I thought about it, but feared that judges might be resentful and consider my conducting such a meeting as an attempt to usurp their position. After deliberating about whether I should conduct such meetings, I decided to ask legal audiences (consisting of judges and lawyers) what their feelings would be. The consensus was that "judges need all the help they can get" and that such meetings—held by a competent examiner—would generally be welcome. In addition, some expressed the hope that litigation might be avoided and thereby contribute to the reduction of cluttered court calendars. The reader will note my use of the word *some* in the previous sentence. There is no question that there were *others* who were not so happy about my attempts to resolve the dispute because of the obvious loss of income for them that such resolution would entail. And even those who supported my resolving the conflict at that point did not necessarily do so out of the most humanitarian instincts. Rather, many attorneys appreciate that by the time clients are ready to go to court, they have generally been depleted of funds and so the attorney, at that point, can express the noble wish that the case be settled out of court. My experience has been that lawyers of rich people are far less receptive to the notion of settling out of court than lawyers of poor people. Lawyers of poor people, however, are required ethically to "hang in there" to the end even though remuneration by that point may be questionable.

This can be a most valuable conference. It is not only useful for the parents, in that it gives them a last-minute opportunity to change the examiner's opinion before it's finalized in the written report, but it gives them the opportunity to have their attorneys participate in this conference as well. It was rare for an attorney to refuse to attend. Some did so because they were genuinely desirous of trying to avoid courtroom litigation. Others, I am certain, had no intention of utilizing the meeting for this purpose but recognized that direct contact with me put them in a better position to examine me on the witness stand. (Every military man knows that it is important to "know your enemy.") But this principle works both ways and my meeting with the attorneys put me in a better position to deal with them when in court.

Sometimes, the nonsupported party's attorney was convinced by my recommendations and encouraged the client to accept them. At other times, the attorney strongly resisted resolution (whether out of conviction that I was wrong or from the belief that he or she must support the client, no matter what) and would then start the wheels rolling for further litigation. Often, such an attorney would then attempt to bring in an adversary mental health professional whose evaluation, however, was compromised significantly by the fact that the parent whom I supported had nothing to gain by cooperation.

The insertion of the warning that it is improper for attorneys to squelch discussion in that meeting was also a recent development. This clause resulted from a number of experiences in which, in the middle of an open and free discussion, an attorney would suddenly turn to the client and say: "Don't answer that question." The inclusion of this statement enabled me to pull out the provisions document and point directly to this proviso and confront the attorney who was now breaking the contract. On occasion, I said to such an attorney: "When I'm in your house, I have to follow your rules. When I'm on your witness stand, I have to go by the rules of the courtroom. This is my house, and as long as you're in my house, you will follow my rules. You advised your client to sign this document which specifically precludes your interference in free and open discussion in this office. I would appreciate your refraining from advising your client to break the contract which he signed under your direction." Although such comments did not generally engender affection for me, they did have the effect of allowing free discussion.

In the course of these meetings with the clients and attorneys, I would attempt to bring about a resolution of the dispute. This was most often done when the meeting appeared to be approaching the end and when some final decision had to be made regarding whether or not we would go to court. Sometimes, I encouraged separate, private meetings—in which each attorney would meet alone with the client—outside of the consultation room. These meetings were only encouraged when I had the feeling that the attorneys were indeed trying to bring about a resolution. Otherwise, private, separate meetings only polarized the clients further.

There is a fringe benefit to the therapist in discussing the findings and recommendations with the parents prior to writing the final report—a benefit that I had not anticipated when I decided to introduce this procedure into my evaluation. Specifically, it helps the therapist avoid placing errors in the written report, errors that crept in in spite of the evaluator's attempts to be meticulous. I rarely found these to be major. However, minor errors are the ones the cross-examining attorneys will focus upon if they do not think they will be successful in refuting major arguments. The therapist may have thought that a particular relative was a sister when, in fact, she was a sister-in-law. The age of a significant person may be incorrect or a time duration miscalculated. The year in which the evaluator states a particular event occurred may be off slightly. In the interview in which the findings and recommendations are presented the parents often correct these minor errors, the nonsupported party thus unwittingly contributing (admittedly in a very small way) to the strengthening of the other parent's position. At times, in the preparation of this presentation, I had not been clear myself regarding some of the small points. This interview provided me with a good opportunity to ask questions for clarification.

10) After this conference I strictly refrain from any further communication with either parent or any other party involved in the evaluation. However, I am willing to discuss any aspect of the case with *both* attorneys at the same time, either personally or by conference telephone call. Such communication may occur at any time from the end of the aforementioned conference to the end of the trial. This practice enables me to continue to provide input to the attorneys regarding what I consider to be in the children's best interests. And this may be especially important during the trial. At that time, in order to preserve my status as impartial, any discussions I may have with an attorney and/or parent is only conducted under circumstances in which the adversary attorney and/or parent is invited to participate.

It is important to have such closure because the litigating parties may go on endlessly trying to get the examiner to appreciate how injudicious his or her recommendation was. The door must be left open, however, for new developments that may take place after the report has been submitted. Requiring that both attorneys be party to such input lessens the likelihood that frivolous and inconsequential material will then be presented to the examiner. The provision also describes what I consider to be a useful departure from strict court routine. Specifically, if while under cross-examination by an adversary attorney, I am inhibited from providing information to the court that I consider important to present, I will, when I leave the stand, advise the attorney whose position I support that I wish to be asked certain questions when I return to the stand, However, in order to preserve my status as impartial, I invite the adversary attorney to witness and even participate in the discussion. Needless to say, this invitation has never been refused. Both parents also are invited to participate in and/or witness this discussion. It is important for the reader to appreciate that my practice here is a complete departure from traditional courtroom procedures. I am convinced that had I asked anyone's permission to do this I would have been refused. I just decided to do it and hoped that no one would raise an objection. No one ever did.

Because there is often a significant time gap between the

submission of the report and the trial, the likelihood of new developments may be great in certain cases. For such cases the following provision was included.

> 11) When there has been a significant passage of time between the submission of my report and the trial date, I will generally invite the primary participating parties for an interview update prior to my court appearance. This conference enables me to acquaint myself with developments that succeeded my report and ensures that my presentation in court will include the most recent information. All significant adult participants will be invited to this meeting and on occasion one or more of the children (especially teenagers). This conference will be held as long as at least one party wishes to attend.

My experience was that the party whose position had not been supported generally chose not to attend this conference. However, the information provided by the supported party was generally most useful and added weight to my evaluation and depth to my conclusions. This practice especially enhanced my position when adversary examiners (most often previously engaged "hired guns") had not utilized this practice. Sometimes their reports were one to two years old. Accordingly, no matter how powerful their arguments, they entered the courtroom in a weakened position because they did not have updated material. Examiners who do not routinely conduct such update interviews are compromising themselves by exposing themselves to a serious criticism of their testimony.

The nonsupported party often did not attend this meeting, usually on the advice of attorneys, who felt there was nothing to gain and everything to lose by input at that point. This was a serious error, because at times the meeting provided new information which warranted significant alteration of my original findings. Many things can happen in a year or two, so much so that the modifications might even involve my reversing my conclusions. The failure of the previously unsupported party to attend this conference might have robbed that party of the opportunity to provide the kind of input that could bring about this change. Attorneys reflexly advising their clients not to attend this conference deprived them of this important opportunity.

> My experience has been that conducting the evaluation in the manner described above provides me with the optimum conditions for providing the court with a thorough and objective recommendation.

This paragraph is really not essential, but was included to "soften" the impact of the formal stipulations and to help impress upon the reader their importance. The provisions described above refer to the "pure" situation in which there is general agreement by both parties that I should be brought in as the impartial examiner and the judge orders me to serve in this capacity. Paragraph 12 deals with special situations in which a court will agree to order me to serve, but not formally designate me the court's impartial examiner.

> 12) Often one party will invite my services as an impartial examiner and the other will refuse to participate voluntarily. On occasion, the inviting party has then requested that the court appoint me impartial examiner and order the reluctant side to participate. Generally, there are three ways in which courts respond to this request:
> A. The court responds affirmatively and appoints me the impartial examiner. In such cases I then proceed in accordance with the above provisions (#1-#11).
> B. The court is not willing to formally designate me its appointed impartial examiner, but rather orders the reluctant side to cooperate in interviews with me as if I were the advocate of the initiator. (This usually occurs when the presiding judge orders both parents to be evaluated by each one's selected adversary examiner.) In such cases, I still do not view myself to be serving automatically as the advocate of the initiating party. Rather, I make it understood to all concerned that I will proceed as closely as possible with the type of evaluation I conduct when serving as impartial examiner—*even to the point of testifying in court as an advocate of the initially reluctant party.* In that eventuality, if the initially reluctant party requests a court appearance, that party will be responsible for my fees (item 6) beyond the point at which my

final report has been sent to the court, attorneys, and the clients. The party who initially invited me, however, will still have the obligation to pay for my report, whether or not it supports that party's position. I believe that this plan ensures my input to the court regarding what I consider to be in the children's best interests and precludes my serving merely as a hired advocate.

C. The court refuses to order my participation, but recognizes the right of the inviting party to enlist my involvement as an advocate. In such cases I proceed in accordance with provision 13.

This provision was a recent addition to my provisions document and stemmed from my appreciation that parties who have been ordered by the court to cooperate with adversary mental health professionals are often being exploited, and I consider it unethical and immoral to be party to such exploitation. I do not use the word exploitation lightly here. It is common practice for judges to order each parent to be interviewed by the other parent's (the adversary) mental health professional in order to produce "balance." Parents who are forced into such interviews know from the outset that they have nothing to gain and everything to lose by exposing themselves. They know that the chances of changing the examiner's position is practically nil because of his or her hired-gun status. I believe that examiners who agree to such interviews are bastardizing their roles and are a disgrace to our profession. Therefore, I refused to be party to such utilization by the court. Accordingly, I informed both parties, at the outset, that I would be conducting the evaluation as much as possible as if I were an impartial examiner and made absolutely no promises beforehand that I would support the party who originally enlisted my services.

I required the parent who has enlisted my services to sign the provisions document and I gave a copy of it to the spouse as well as to his (her) attorney. I could not require the spouse to sign the document, but I informed him (her) that I would be operating as much as possible under its provisions.

The reader will note that, in those circumstances in which I decided to support the "visitor," I required that party to pay for my services for testifying, i.e., services performed after the submission of my report to the court. I considered this only fair. It is bad enough when the nonsupported party has to pay an impartial examiner to testify on behalf of the other side. I considered it "cruel and inhumane punishment" to ask a parent to pay for the services of someone who was initially hired as an advocate to testify in court on behalf of the adversary. However, I required the initiator to pay for the report even though it may not have supported his or her position. Although reluctant to pay for such a report, someone had to do so, and it was most reasonable to require the initiator to do so. I considered it risky to have a provision requiring the visitor to do so, especially because the visitor was not generally signing any contract. If I had not required the initiator to pay for this report, I might have ended up being required by the court to prepare one without being paid for it.

SERVING AS AN ADVOCATE

13A) On occasion, I am willing to *consider* serving as an advocate in custody/visitation litigation. However, such participation will only be considered after evidence has been submitted to me that: 1) the nonparticipating side has been invited to participate and has refused and 2) the court has refused to order such involvement. If I do then suspect that the participating party's position merits my consideration, I would be willing to interview that party with no promise beforehand that I will support his or her position. On occasion I have seen fit to support the participating party's position, because it was obvious to me that the children's needs would be served best by my advocacy and/or not to do so would have deprived them of sorely needed assistance. On other occasions I have concluded that I could not serve with conviction as an advocate of the requesting party and so have refused further services to the client.

B) If I do decide to serve as an advocate, I ask for the standard $2500 security deposit, which is dealt with as described in item #6. Furthermore, if in the course of my evaluation in which I am serving as an advocate, the nonparticipating party decides belatedly to participate I will, at that point, no longer consider myself automatically committed to serve as an advocate for the original party. Rather, I will conduct the evaluation, as far as possible, in accordance with the provisions for my serving as an impartial examiner—even to the point of testifying in support of the belated participant. Before interviewing the belated participant, however, all parties will have to agree upon any possible modifications of the fee-paying arrangement that may be warranted.

This provision (#13), as well as the previous one (#12), served well to assure clients and attorneys that I indeed did everything possible to serve as an impartial. The examiner is well advised to do everything to establish a reputation for being totally unavailable to serve as a "hired gun." Provisions such as these are in the service of this goal.

I have read the above, discussed the provisions with my attorney, and agree to participate in the evaluation procedures delineated above. I agree to pay _____% of the $2,500 advance security deposit and _____% of the fees in accordance with the aforementioned payment schedules. I recognize the possibility that Dr. Gardner may *not* ultimately support my position in the litigation. Nevertheless, I will still fulfill my obligation to pay _____% of his fees. I appreciate that this may entail the payment of fees associated with his preparing reports that do not support my position and even testifying in court in support of my adversary (with the exception of the situation in which items 12B and 13B are operative).

Date:_____   _____

                                                    Parent's Signature

Revision No. 36

This last statement makes it quite clear that one of the parties may actually have to pay me to testify in court for the other side. Although this is implied at the outset, stating it twice here at the end of the document, lessens the likelihood that people will blot out from memory the possibility that this eventuality may come to pass. It is important for the examiner to emphasize this point because people are not famous for their desire to pay someone to go to court to testify against them. Accordingly, they may conveniently forget this important provision in the contract.

Furthermore, each party is usually 100 percent convinced that theirs is the correct position and may not entertain the possibility that the other side may prevail. This too can reduce the likelihood that this item in the document will be properly processed.

CONCLUDING COMMENTS

I am sure that the reader will consider these provisions hard-nosed and rigid. I can only say that they became so over the years as new situations developed. Those willing to subscribe to them generally were reassured that they were obtaining a fair, objective, and impartial evaluation. The reader does well to compare these provisions with those that I require to be satisfied before agreeing to mediate a custody/visitation dispute (Appendix II). These will be discussed in Chapter Twelve.

⚖️ FOUR
THE INITIAL INTERVIEW
WITH THE PARENTS

INTRODUCTION

When conducting custody evaluations in the context of *mediation* I utilize the same procedures, with minor differences, used in custody litigation evaluations. Although I no longer conduct custody evaluations for litigation, I do so for mediation. I therefore use the present tense when describing such procedures. In my initial interview with parents who were litigating, I would often spend significant time in the first interview reviewing the custody provisions document and involving myself in other considerations pertinent to the litigation. Obviously, the mediation custody evaluation does not require such focus. However, the inquiries regarding the marriage, reasons for the dispute, etc. (which are also covered in the first interview) are identical in both types of evaluation. When past tense is used, therefore, the material generally refers to procedures pertinent only to custody litigation, procedures I no longer utilize; when the present tense is used, the material refers to practices that I am still using, whether or not they had derivatives in the earlier custody evaluations conducted with litigating parents.

Usually I require the parents to be present together for the initial interview. In fact, I consider it injudicious to start the evaluation with one party alone, and subsequently interview the second, because I want to establish from the outset my impartiality and the notion that both parties are going to be treated equally and fairly. A parent who is seen alone first might be viewed by the other party as the preferred one. When the second parent is then interviewed, he (she) may justifiably wonder what misinformation provided by the first party has to be corrected, disclaimed, etc. This cannot but contaminate the evaluation at the outset. I generally do not have the children come for this first interview because they may prove to be a distraction. This is in contrast to my usual procedure in therapy in which I set up a two-hour evaluative session, during which I see the parents and the child in varying combinations as warranted (1986b). In the therapeutic evaluation, I generally do not view the children's so-called interferences as distractions from the work at hand. The children's interruptions almost invariably enable me to observe interactions which are a useful source of information about the family. In contrast, in the custody evaluation, the amount of "administrative work" that has to be done is significant. This is especially true when the parents are litigating. It may consume an hour, and even more, of the initial two-hour interview. The children then may very well become a distraction, especially if they are young, because the material being discussed will be of no interest to them and generally not understandable. Furthermore, the detailed discussion of the custody dispute is likely to prove upsetting and even psychologically detrimental to the children.

THE INITIAL TELEPHONE CALL

Generally, one of four parties (the parents and attorneys) called initially to invite my participation in custody litigation. On rare occasion, a judge would call to inquire about my involvement. I would generally inform the caller that I did not usually serve as an advocate and inquire whether the caller was interested in enlisting my services as an impartial examiner. If there was some receptivity to this proposal, I would send a copy of the provisions document (Appendix I). I generally made it a point not to permit the caller to provide me with substantive data, lest I compromise my position as impartial examiner. In the conversation I might mention that there was still the possibility of my coming in as an advocate. However, as described in detail in the provisions document, the caller would have to make every reasonable attempt to enlist my services first as an impartial. On occasion, the caller (especially if an attorney) would hesitate to communicate to the other side the request that I be brought in as an impartial because of the fear that if the adversary spouse and/or attorney refused to agree that I be brought in as an impartial—and I did then see the client to consider serving as an advocate and then refused such participation—the adversary side might make inquiries. If the adversary side learned (from the children, for example) that I had conducted interviews and then refused to serve as an advocate, such refusal could then be brought to the attention of the court and weaken the caller's position. In response I generally informed such callers that they would have to take this risk but if, indeed, the caller's position was a strong one, the parent could enter the consultation with a sense of optimism that I would ultimately support that party's position. But such conversations were generally rare.

Callers receptive to considering my involvement as an impartial examiner in their custody litigation would be sent a packet of information, which included the provisions document. In such cases the conversation generally closed with my informing the caller that I would set up the initial appointment with both parents after I had received four documents: the signed court order designating me the impartial examiner, the two provisions documents (one signed by each parent), and the security deposit check.

Since June 1988, such callers have been informed that I no longer involve myself in adversary litigation, but only do mediation. Some have been receptive to the mediation alternative, but such receptivity has been uncommon because most of the callers (both in the past and the present) are so embroiled in litigation that they are beyond the capacity to consider seriously the mediation option. Some, however, have called with the expressed purpose of engaging my services for mediation. In such cases the mediation document is sent and the caller notified that when I receive the signed pledges from both parties, I will be in contact with them to set up the initial appointment. This is the practice I utilize now that I have confined myself to mediation only.

PRELIMINARY COMMENTS TO THE PARENTS

Whether the parents are litigating or mediating, it is preferable for them to be seen together in the first interview. This practice provides the parents with the experience that the examiner is "starting fresh" with both. As mentioned, if the parties are interviewed separately, the person who is seen second may consider himself (herself) to have an "uphill fight" in order to dispel anticipated misrepresentations and fabrications provided by the person who was interviewed first. It is preferable that evaluators have practically no information about the family prior to the first interview. Examiners know, of course, that the parents are disputing for custody of one or more children. Ideally, they should have received so little information that they may not even know the number of children involved. Such "ignorance" may be reassuring to the parents because it lessens suspicions that the examiner has been provided with advance information.

I usually begin the joint session by expressing my full appreciation of how difficult this evaluation will be for them and emphasize that I will do my utmost to make it as painless as possible. Similarly, I express my appreciation that the evaluation may be especially difficult for the children, but again I will try to be as sympathetic and understanding as I can. Although these introductory comments are not likely to lessen significantly the psychological toll of the evaluation, they may play some role in this regard. Knowing that I am sympathetic to their plight and empathetic with the painful feelings they are suffering at this point can be helpful in reducing (admittedly to a small degree) their pains and frustrations. Such comments also have the fringe benefit of contributing to the parents' forming a good relationship with me – the circumstances of their involvement with me not-withstanding.

In my training I was taught that the ideal way to begin any psychiatric interview was to use the open-ended approach. Specifically, therapists were advised to limit themselves at the outset to an introductory comment that was nonspecific, yet catalytic and facilitative of comments to be made by the patient. Traditional openings included: "So what brings you to the hospital?" "Let me hear what the trouble is." and "So tell me, what's on your mind?" Although questions and statements such as these are uncontaminated by specifics provided by the examiner, they are not without their drawbacks. Specifically, they are posed at the time when they are least likely to be answered directly and honestly. The patient comes to the initial interview extremely anxious and especially fearful that the therapist will be alienated by what is being revealed. The situation is particularly anxiety provoking because the patient is so dependent (already) on the therapist for help in the alleviation of presenting difficulties. In fact, these open-ended questions are the most anxiety provoking possible in a situation in which the patient is already quite tense. The likelihood, then, of receiving meaningful and completely honest responses is significantly reduced. The drawbacks of such questions, therefore, far outweigh their advantages at this point. I much prefer to ask a series of simple, factual questions – questions that I know the patient can readily answer – in the initial phase of the interview. These may only take a few minutes, but they can be extremely anxiety alleviating. With each "right answer" the patient feels more comfortable and five or ten minutes later, after these basic data have been obtained, little if anything has been contaminated. But a "different" patient is now answering the open-ended questions. After this decompression of the anxiety, there is a far greater likelihood that meaningful answers will be obtained.

Recognizing that parents coming for a custody evaluation, although not patients, are just as likely to be extremely anxious, I will at this early point ask basic data questions for my records.

From each parent I obtain his (her) name, home address and telephone number, date of birth, occupation, and business address and telephone number. I then get the names of the attorneys, their addresses, and telephone numbers. I then list the name, age, birth date, school, and grade of each child. I find out whether anyone else is living in the household, especially someone whom I might interview. Most often I plan to interview other household members, especially full-time housekeepers. (As will be discussed, the full-time housekeeper can be an extremely valuable source of information and is often an untapped source of information in child psychiatric evaluations.) I ask for the date of the marriage, the date of separation, and the dates and duration of previous marriages. I then ask if either party is involved significantly with another person, especially someone with whom either parent is living or whom either is planning to marry. These individuals, as well, are important persons to interview.

The basic-data questions are posed in both the litigation and mediation situation. When conducting evaluations for litigating parents I would add further comments designed to discourage them from proceeding with adversarial proceedings. I strongly advised them that the best thing they could do for themselves and their children would be to try to resolve the custody dispute themselves and avoid the psychologically draining and expensive evaluation they were about to embark upon. I tried to impress upon them that they know their children better than anyone else, that their children are theirs, and that their fate rests now in their hands. I tried to get them to appreciate that any *reasonable* custody arrangement would generally be approved by their attorneys and the court. I tried to impress upon them, as well, how psychologically detrimental custody litigation can be—to children and parents. I advised them that going to court is risky business and that judges are not famous for the judiciousness of their custody decisions. I reminded them that I, too, am not infallible and that there is no recommendation which I have ever made that would be uniformly agreed to by all professional people. I reminded them, what they knew already, that my opinion will carry heavy weight in the court and that their involving themselves with me is also risky business.

By the time parents reached me—with court order, two provisions documents, and an advance security deposit—they were so deeply embroiled in the litigious process that they were most often incapable of hearing my warning. Accordingly, I never had the experience of parents responding then that they would like to interrupt proceedings at that point in order to give further consideration to what I had said. There were a few, however, who did switch to the mediation track after a few interviews—when it became obvious that they were not so far apart from one another that I could not be of service as a mediator. In those cases a letter was sent to the judge (with copies to the attorneys and the clients) that the parents had decided to utilize my services as a mediator and were removing the custody dispute from litigation. But such situations were rare. Most were driven to proceed with the litigation.

I also advised litigating parents to take my final recommendations very seriously, i.e., those I would ultimately be making at the end of my evaluation. I told them that my experience had been that the nonpreferred party and his (her) attorney often reflexly talked about bringing in another psychiatrist or thought of other ways to refute my final recommendations. I explained to them that they had every right to do so and that I considered it part of my obligation to appear in court to defend my position. However, I also recommended that they consider the alternative possibility, namely, that my recommendations might be judicious and they might do themselves and the children a great service by discontinuing the custody litigation at that point. I am pleased to say that there were many parents who did just that at the time of the completion of my evaluation. Sometimes even the attorney of the nonsupported parent convinced that parent of the advisability of my recommendations.

Also at the initial session, I generally impress upon the parents that I have no preconceived notion regarding who would be the better parent for their child(ren). I emphasize that this will not be an evaluation in which I am going to conclude that one party is the "good" parent and the other the "bad" one. Rather, the usual situation is one in which both parents are relatively good, capable, and deeply involved and the question is who would be the *better* parent to have primary custody of the children, i.e., who has fewer liabilities and greater assets regarding the assumption of the role of custodian.

REVIEW OF THE PROVISIONS DOCUMENT

In this section I discuss the details of my review of the provisions document (Appendix I) signed by litigating parents. Although mediating parents sign a much simpler document (Appendix II), some of the provisions of the litigation document are also pertinent to the mediation process. Accordingly, this section devotes itself primarily to the litigation situation and therefore I will use primarily the past tense. However, when the item under consideration is also pertinent to the mediation evaluation I will use the present tense because I am still utilizing the procedure.

Although the litigation provisos had been reviewed by the attorneys and signed by the parents, I found it useful to review them in detail during the initial interview. This served to clarify in detail all the provisions, clear up any misconceptions the parents may have had (not uncommon, in spite of my attempts to make them clear), as well as to ensure that there would be no problems in their implementation (the parents' signatures notwithstanding). As will be elaborated upon below, the most common areas of "misunderstanding" were related to the fees and the signing of the permission slips. And such misunderstandings are much more common in litigation than in mediation.

The Parties to be Interviewed

For both litigating and mediating parents I make a list of all the parties to be interviewed and discuss problems that may arise regarding exactly who will and who will not be involved in the evaluation.

The Parents I inform the parents that the next sessions will involve my seeing each of them individually. I try to help them appreciate that the best thing they can do for their children is to be open and honest with me regarding all aspects of the inquiry. I try to impress upon them that to the degree they withhold information from me they compromise my ability to make a judicious decision. If, as they usually claim, they really have their children's best interests at heart, they will give me *all* the information I need to help them in this regard. It is a rare parent who follows this advice. Each generally believes that he (she) is the better parent and is not going to really leave such an important decision to me, a stranger. Such certainty is generally greater for litigating parents than for those who choose mediation. Often the only reason litigating parents were talking to me was that the court required them to do so. Accordingly, the censoring was usually great and the advice unheeded—professions of agreement and promises of compliance notwithstanding. But I made the statement anyway in the hope that some of it might be heard.

I then inform them that I plan to conduct the evaluation in such a way that when it is completed neither party should be able to justifiably say: "He never gave me a chance to tell him that." Unfortunately, there were a few situations in custody litigation in which I was not able to fulfill that promise. One or both of the parents were so embroiled in the litigious process that they could literally go on for years—working over the same material and adding ever more details. In those situations I had to interrupt the evaluation and inform the parents in a very firm manner that I had collected enough data, that we had gone far beyond the usual number of meetings, and that there was nothing new that I needed to complete the data-collection process. I advised them, as well, that when I met with the attorneys I would hear them out if they were in disagreement with me. Generally, the attorneys as well agreed with me and saw no purpose for lengthening what was already an exhausting and unnecessarily lengthy data-collection process.

I also inform the parents that I will be starting each interview with an open question in which I invite them to tell me anything they feel is important for me to know. As will be discussed in detail in the next chapter, the structured questions come only after each parent has exhausted all possible spontaneous comments and statements. The word *exhausted* is applicable here because the amount of information that each party has to give me is often extensive. However, I do not wish to go on endlessly with people who are very verbose and might ramble on for weeks with seemingly endless repetitions. I advise the parents that following my individual interviews with them I will be conducting a series of interviews with the two of them together. During the individual interviews I generally get different opinions regarding many issues, and the later joint experiences with them help me clarify to some degree (but never completely) the conflicting renditions.

The Children   I tell the parents also that I will be interviewing each of the children. The nature of my contacts with them vary with their ages. It is not likely that I will do much individual interviewing with a very young child of one or two, although I generally see such a child along with the parents and make observations. I routinely involve older children (from about three and up) in varying depths of psychiatric evaluation, depending upon their ages and degrees of cooperation. Generally, I conduct two to three interviews with children above the age of four or five. I inform parents that I plan to conduct a family interview as well.

Other Interviewees   Most often I interview other individuals. I may want to interview a housekeeper who has been or will be significantly involved in the care of the children. I recognize that the parent with whom the housekeeper lives, and even the other parent, may be very reluctant to permit such an interview — and the housekeeper herself generally is not overjoyed at the prospect. She must be told in advance that the information she will be giving me will be used at my discretion and I cannot promise her that some of it may not get back to the mother and father. It is only ethical to provide her with this information because of the possibility that she may be compromising her relationship with her employer(s). A housekeeper, by the way, may be a very valuable source of information for the child therapist and it is rare that we have an opportunity to avail ourselves of the information that she can provide. She hears the family's squabbles. Sometimes, she lives for little but learning about what's going on in the family, and her main topic of conversation with other housekeepers may concern what is happening in their employers' households. On those occasions when I have had the opportunity to interview housekeepers, and when they have been forthright with me at the encouragement of the parents, I have learned many valuable things about the family. Most often housekeepers are quite timid when speaking with the therapist. They may have never been in a therapist's office and may be awed and frightened. On occasion, having one (or even both) employers present at the beginning can help the housekeeper relax; however, their presence may make her tighten up even more. Because of the extreme anxiety many housekeepers suffer during such interviews, I generally confine myself to one interview.

If there are grandparents who will play a significant role in the lives of the children, I may request an interview with them, both singly and together. Plans may include their taking care of the children during the day or a parent's moving back into their home. There may be some reluctance on the grandparents' part to being interviewed, but the therapist should advise them that their failure to participate may weaken the position of the parent who wishes to enlist their aid in caring for the children. (Again, this is an unfortunate way of getting someone to agree to a psychiatric interview, but it is common and often necessary in custody evaluations.)

There are times when one, or possibly both, of the parents may be involved with another person who may be a potential marriage partner or someone with whom the children will be living. For example, a wife may have met another man with whom she plans to live, and may hope to have the children live with her. She may claim that this will be a good environment for the children because they will have a new relationship with another male. The examiner should not get involved in the moral question of whether or not these people plan to get married. Rather, he (she) should simply try to decide whether this man will provide a good environment for the children and be a good surrogate father to help the children compensate for the absence of their natural father from the home. Accordingly, this man should be invited *by the mother* to participate in the evaluation. (I do not invite such "third parties" myself, because I consider it to be intrusive and bordering on the unethical.) If he hesitates to come, the wife should be informed that my ability to conduct the evaluation is being compromised and her position is being weakened. In fact, this is the general response I have to those who do not wish to cooperate in the evaluation. Although such "motivation-enhancing" threats may make a mockery of the psychiatric interview, the therapist is often reduced to having to make them in custody evaluations. My experience has been that potential parent surrogates in this category rarely refuse to involve themselves in the evaluation. In contrast, they are generally quite eager to participate.

I then ask the parents to suggest any *other* parties who might be sources of information for me. I inform them that I am receptive to their suggestions and will give serious consideration to objections by the nonrecommending parent. I advise them, at the same time, that I reserve the right to make the final decision regarding whether or not such a person will be *invited* to participate. I emphasize the word invited because I do not have the power to force anyone to participate in the evaluation. Even when I conducted custody evaluations for litigation, I generally was not given power by the court to interview anyone other than the parents and children. I will not give one party veto power over the other regarding extending such an invitation. I will, however, listen with receptivity to any objections to the proposed interview. Generally, I do not interview a parade of friends and relatives whom each side can collect for the purposes of evaluation. These testimonials elicited from selected friends and relatives generally balance one another out, are likely to be highly biased and exaggerated, and are therefore of little value. For example, if the wife proposes a certain individual and the husband claims that he would be very unhappy if I were to interview that person, I allow each party to provide reasons and then make the final decision myself. Also, I do not make the first telephone call to invite the proposed individual to participate in the evaluation; rather, I ask the parent to invite that party to call my office for an appointment. To call such a person is somewhat unethical in that physicians should not be calling up strangers for appointments. Furthermore, the party may be far less enthusiastic about the interview than the parent who proposed the name. Having the parent request the party to call my office for an interview lessens the likelihood of this kind of embarrassment for both the proposed participant and the examiner. At this point I make a list of all the parties to be interviewed. This includes not only the family members, but others who have been recommended and whom I have agreed warrant an invitation.

Confidentiality

When parties are involved in a mediation evaluation I generally do not need any kind of signed statement regarding confidentiality. They are generally in agreement that the information they provide me must be available to the spouse and that all data provided by third parties becomes part of the common flow of information. In contrast, in the litigation evaluation one *must* have *written* permission for such revelations. Not to do so is a serious error. Accordingly, such release is placed in my provisions document (Appendix I). In the initial meeting I reviewed this stipulation with the parents. Sometimes I actually read it verbatim. I emphasized the point that I would not necessarily reveal such information, but that I *reserved the right to do so*. I impressed upon them, again, the importance of their being honest with me in spite of this provision. I told them, as well, that I appreciated that what was revealed might weaken one's position in court; but this might be the price they had to pay for the benefit of an impartial and objective evaluation. I tried to get across the notion that there had to be an open pool of information available to me and that I had to have the freedom to communicate with all the concerned parties and not be constrained by a confidentiality obligation. I tried to impress upon them that this was only possible if my hands were not tied by the restriction of being unable to reveal any information.

I fully recognized that this provision resulted in some (if not many) parents' withholding important information. I appreciated, as well, that many had probably been briefed by their attorneys regarding what to reveal and what to withhold. I recognized that without this provision more information might have come my way. However, without it I would have been significantly restricted regarding my flexibility. Accordingly, I believe its advantages outweigh its disadvantages for the purposes of a custody evaluation.

In the mediation evaluation I also inform the parents about this modification of the traditional confidentiality, but I usually have little difficulty gaining their cooperation. Parents who have problems with this provision are generally not candidates for mediation. Mediation requires complete honesty. This is not to say that I always reveal all information during the mediation process. Each party is still entitled to certain privacies, especially privacies that are not directly relevant to the question of the ultimate parenting plan.

The Signing of the Release Forms

When mediating a custody dispute, the evaluator generally has no problem obtaining signatures for the release of reports. However, getting such permission slips signed was a common problem with litigating parents. Here it is extremely important that the examiner obtain such permissions *early* in the initial interview—before substantive data has been collected. If a parent reneges at that point and refuses to sign the permission slip, then the examiner can threaten to discontinue the evaluation with the justification that the parent is not fulfilling his (her) obligations under the provisions document. If the interview breaks down because of the parent's refusal, then the examiner cannot be brought to court to testify because no substantive data has been collected by that point. If the examiner continues on with the data-collection process – pending a decision regarding the signing of the provisions slip (with or without attorney involvement) – then a serious mistake will have been made. The examiner will then have substantive data and may even be brought into court and asked to give partial conclusions, which is obviously a serious compromise of the evaluation.

When meeting with the parents I list the possible sources of information from other professionals. This includes therapists and counselors, both past and present. However, I generally try to avoid contacting therapists who are treating either of the parents at the time of the evaluation. Writing a report to me can often compromise treatment if the therapist provides information that may be detrimental to the patient's position in the litigation. Also, my experience has been that therapists seeing only one of the parents are usually biased toward their patients. The "mutual admiration society" formed in therapy often beclouds therapists' objectivity. However, on a few occasions, in very difficult cases, I have requested information from such therapists. I have, however, no reservations about getting reports from past therapists. Whether one communicates with a past or present therapist, it is important that the report be in writing. Folksy telephone conversations have no place in custody evaluations, especially when done in the context of litigation. One wants to have a written report because the material contained therein may become an issue in the courtroom litigation. Clearly, a written statement leaves little to be questioned regarding whether or not a particular statement was made. If the therapy involved joint counseling, permission from both parents must be obtained. A sample letter requesting such information in the context of litigation is reproduced in Appendix VI. This is accompanied by a standard printed medical release form, which, of course, is signed by the parent(s). When conducting mediation evaluations, I generally request the parents to write letters themselves soliciting this information. I usually have no trouble enlisting their cooperation. Parents who do not cooperate in my obtaining such information are not likely to be candidates for the mediation evaluation.

The reader may have wondered why my request in custody litigation is in written form and the request in the mediation evaluation is made verbally to the parents, who are then requested to write the appropriate letters. This difference in procedure is not without its reasons. In the mediation evaluation I want to do everything possible to avoid any written material coming to the attention of third parties: attorneys, courts, or otherwise. Although a letter from me requesting information is certainly not a source of information about what has transpired in the mediation, it does give the impression that other written statements might emerge from the procedure. Furthermore, my sending out such letters might be construed as an abrogation of the original mediation contract in which it clearly states that no written information of *any* kind will be forthcoming. A letter requesting information is basically a written statement. In contrast, the request for information letter sent in the context of a custody evaluation provides a clear statement to the recipient that the information so provided will be revealed to attorneys and the court—with all the implications of such revelation (including the request to testify in court). The person being asked to provide information under these circumstances is entitled to know the implications of the request. Furthermore, writing a letter provides me with the opportunity to ask specific questions, especially regarding child-rearing capacity. A parental request may not include this and other questions that the examiner may have.

I recognize fully that, in the context of custody litigation, such information is considered hearsay. However, these reports can provide me with useful points of departure for my inquiries. The issues raised in them may not have arisen in the course of the evaluation, and it is in this way that they can be most useful. In addition, they will often lend support and/or credibility to allegations made by one party and refuted by the other. When conducting custody evaluations in association with litigation, the examiner is then in a better position to make comments in thewritten report such as: "Although I cannot be completely certain that Mr. Smith is telling the truth with regard to his allegation that his wife abuses alcohol, the weight of the evidence certainly supports his contention. For example, Dr. X, in his report dated..." In mediation evaluations also the material contained in these reports can serve as points of departure for the evaluator's inquiries. Although the legal issue of hearsay is not applicable, the examiner still does well to consider such information hearsay pending verification in the course of the evaluation.

Discussion of the Financial Arrangements

Parties who come for mediation generally understand quite well the financial arrangements and there are usually no problems related to its implementation. This is in direct contrast to parties involved in custody litigation. Even though my policy is clearly spelled out in the provisions document, the examiner does well to review the policy carefully—early in the first interview. The reason here is the same as that proposed for discussing the signing of the release forms early in the initial interview. It is at this point that the examiner is in the most powerful position to interrupt the meeting—pending a clarification of the difficulty. Interrupting then presents no particular complications because the examiner has not yet collected substantive data. To allow a difference to be unresolved—pending further thought and possible discussion with an attorney—is to potentially compromise the total evaluation. It may result in an ongoing conflict between the evaluator and the parent and this cannot but undermine the evaluation.

Accordingly, for parents who were litigating, I reviewed in detail the payment procedures as described in the provisions document. I generally did this by reading that section verbatim and inviting inquiry at any point of misunderstanding. Even though clearly spelled out in the written document, misinterpretations and misunderstandings often remained. I explained that the previously received security deposit had been placed in a bank account, in my name, within a day or so of its receipt. I informed them, as well, that the bank would be reporting the accrued interest to the Internal Revenue Service and that the parent would be the one responsible for paying taxes on this interest. I informed them that this money (with accrued interest) would be returned *after* a decision had been made regarding custody and *after* I had received a letter from *both* attorneys informing me that my services were no longer being enlisted. It is an error for an examiner to return this deposit after receiving a letter from only *one* attorney. The other attorney may have every intention of going back to court, appealing, or doing nothing at that point (pending further developments). And that attorney will have every right to bring the evaluator back into the litigation. This is another situation that warrants the examiner's being hard-nosed.

Such a deposit serves two purposes: 1) It protects the examiner from disappointed payers expressing their hostility by not paying the bill (a very common occurrence) and 2) It serves as reassurance to nonpayers that evaluators will not be "hired guns" and that their objectivity will not be compromised by the fear that if they ultimately support the nonpayer the payer will not fulfill his (her) financial obligation. As the reader might suspect, this stringent policy was the result of many unfortunate experiences. There is obviously a distrust element here that could compromise a treatment relationship. However, we are not dealing here with psychotherapy. We are dealing with *clients*, not *patients*. The drawbacks of such distrust are more than outweighed by the freedom from contamination that the examiner can enjoy when such a payment program is a proviso of involvement in the litigation. Furthermore, the examiner must appreciate that we are living in a world that is becoming increasingly sociopathic.

Although litigating parents are more likely to renege than those who are mediating, reneging may also be seen in mediation. In both cases a disappointed party may become quite hostile and withholding funds is one of the most convenient and effective methods of expressing one's animosity. To date, I have not required mediating parents to provide me with an advance security deposit. I only request that they pay at the time services are rendered. This has usually proved satisfactory. I would not, however, utilize a payment policy in which I was paid at the end of the month. This may work well with patients with whom there is an ongoing relationship. But it is risky when conducting mediation because a disgruntled party may discontinue and, once again, express resentment by default in payment.

The way in which the parent deals with his (her) financial obligations to the examiner can provide information that may be useful in the custody evaluation. Irresponsibility in this realm is much more likely to reveal itself in the evaluation associated with litigation than the one associated with mediation. In the former, the expenses are much greater and the animosity usually formidable. In the latter, the expenses are much less and the acrimony is generally at a lower level. If the payer reneges on financial obligations, even though these have been clearly spelled out by the examiner at the outset, it may reflect generally upon the parent's honesty and sense of commitment.

Even after the aforementioned presentation of the fee program, both in the written document and in the first interview, a litigating (not likely a mediating) parent may feign ignorance of the "rules" of payment. Although one could not use this specific area of "ignorance" or attempt to renege as a strong argument against recommending custody, it should lead the examiner into other areas of nonfulfillment of obligations. Often the recalcitrant party's spouse will be happy to provide information in this realm that can serve as a point of departure for inquiry. In addition, one might consider such failure to reflect an attempt (either conscious or unconscious) to lose in the custody dispute in spite of professions to the contrary. In the course of the evaluation parents are generally quite interested in creating a good impression with the examiner, up to the point where the final recommendation is revealed. Generally, the payer who is strongly motivated for gaining custody is wise enough to know that reneging on the payment is going to irritate the evaluator and recognizes that this may compromise his (her) position.

Documents from Attorneys

In both mediation and litigation evaluations, the examiner does well to review previous legal documents. In mediation it is preferable that the parents themselves, rather than their attorneys, provide this material. This is the safer course and gets across the message that there will be absolutely no contact whatsoever between the mediator and the attorneys and even one-way transfer of information (attorney to mediator) is not acceptable. In contrast, in litigation such one-way communication—at that point—does not generally present any problems. In litigation I advised the parents to ask their attorneys to send any material that the lawyer suspected might be of use to me. This included the various affidavits, certifications, depositions, and other documents pertinent to the separation, divorce, and custody litigation.

I generally told the litigating parents that it was unwise for their attorneys to be communicating with me directly and that ideally I should have absolutely no direct contact at all with either of the attorneys—except during the meeting in which I presented my findings and, of course, during my appearance in court. Those attorneys who did attempt to communicate with me directly most often hoped to press their client's position and otherwise "tip the scales." In such cases I informed the lawyers that this kind of intervention was inappropriate and that I would make no mention of it in my report if it was discontinued. This statement usually sufficed to "help them remember" not to call me again. At other times I advised such callers to place their comments in a letter with a copy sent to the other attorney and the judge. This, too, served to discourage such calls. This is another example of the extra clout that an impartial examiner has. Examiners serving as advocates, even advocates who see both parties, do not have such direct input to the judge and could not make such a request regarding letters sent to them.

The material in such documents must not be taken too seriously. It is frequently replete with hyperbole. (Many lawyers seem to work on the principle that the more adjectives there are in a sentence the stronger it becomes; writers and psychologists know better.) Furthermore, the information contained in such documents will be considered hearsay by the court if the therapist presents it. Accordingly, evaluators compromise their credibility by doing so. Impartial examiners do best, for both legal and psychiatric reasons, to confine their testimony to their own observations.

Sometimes I do not receive the pertinent affidavits, pleadings, etc. On occasion this is due to laxity on the part of the attorney (a not uncommon problem in divorce litigation). On other occasions, the parent does not transmit the request to the attorney. A good attorney, one who is "on top of things," will send this material automatically, especially because the request had already been made in the provisions document, which the client had already discussed with the lawyer. If, after the initial session, the attorney still has not sent the material, the client is invited by me to remind the lawyer. I do not, however, pursue the matter further. I consider two reminders enough in most situations. It is rare that I will "bug" a patient for this material. The failure to provide it is a parental deficiency, although generally not a strong one in my deliberations. The examiner should also appreciate that sometimes the failure to provide this material relates to the lawyer's and/or the client's appreciation that it will weaken that side's position, much more than strengthen it.

Discussion of the Final Recommendations

When parents are mediating I inform them that, following the data-collection process, I will review my material and provide them with my findings and recommendations. I advise them that this will be an open-ended meeting and may take a few hours. When evaluating litigating parents, they were generally pleased to learn from my provisions document that my final written report would not be prepared until they had an opportunity for input. Most parents were pleased about my strong suggestion that their attorneys participate in this conference. Those parents who hesitated to invite their attorneys generally did so because of the financial implications. Most often, attorneys were receptive to participation in this meeting, but I did receive occasional refusals. Generally, these were the hard-nosed types, those who were extremely committed to the adversary system and took the position: "I only speak to my adversary in court." I advised parents, in the initial interview, to emphasize to their attorneys the importance of attending this meeting and told them to relate to their lawyers my belief that even if I were not ultimately to support a particular attorney's position, lawyers were still in a better position to cross-examine me in court if they had the opportunity to meet with me beforehand and find out what kind of a person I am. I believe that this communication enhanced the motivation of some attorneys to attend. It basically communicates the message: "The more information you have about your enemy, the better the chance you'll be able to defeat him (her)." Of course, this advice worked both ways and so I too welcomed the opportunity to meet beforehand with the attorneys.

I informed litigating parents that following this final interview I would have absolutely no further contact with them (unless, of course, I saw them in court). I impressed upon them that during the course of the evaluation I would be giving each one every opportunity to provide me with all information considered appropriate. However, I told them also that I would not go on endlessly hearing the various allegations and counterallegations after I had reached the point (the final meeting) when I believed that no further information would tip the balance significantly. I recognized that events might subsequently take place that warrant a reconsideration of my final recommendations. Under such circumstances they had to work through their attorneys in order to set up the reevaluation meeting. I reviewed with them the stipulation in my provisions document that indicated that if there were a significant passage of time between the final recommendations meeting and my appearance in court (most often the case) I would conduct an update meeting in which they would still have the opportunity to attempt to alter my position and that this sometimes did occur.

The parents were generally pleased to learn that I would not write my final report without discussing with them first my recommendations and my reasons for making them. They usually welcomed the opportunity to discuss them with me, correct any errors I may have had, and be given the opportunity to refute what they considered to be distortions or misguided conclusions. Although it was extremely rare for me to completely reverse my major recommendations by that time, minor alterations in the recommendations have resulted from such discussions. The meeting provided them with a sense of power in a situation in which they basically felt impotent. It was anxiety alleviating in that it shortened the period during which they were kept wondering what my final recommendations would be. Although some judges and attorneys were not happy with this step in my procedure, I have deep conviction for its benefits. Evaluators who allow themselves to be talked into dispensing with it (with some legal rationalization for doing so) will be doing the parents a terrible disservice in that they will be contributing to the psychopathological reactions that are so frequently (if not inevitably) caused by protracted custody litigation (1986b).

When discussing the final meeting with the attorneys and litigating parents I once again impressed upon them the importance of their avoiding courtroom litigation. I informed them that at the time of the presentation of my final recommendations, I would once again advise them to come to some agreement on their own, rather than submit the decision to the judge. I also tried to impress upon the parents that what would be best for the child would ultimately be best for them as well. The child who is correctly placed will be a happier child, a less frightened child, and will therefore be a greater source of pleasure to both parents. As L. Despert (1953) says: "In the long run the parent who follows a wise course (regarding custody) is rewarded by a better relationship with the child and greater peace with himself." This advice also usually fell on deaf ears—so certain was each of the parents that he (she) would be the preferable one to have primary custody. A woman may hate her husband so much that she cannot imagine that her children might do better living with such a wretch. And similarly, the enraged man may not be able to conceive of the possibility that his wife can make an adequate mother for his children.

I suggested to litigating parents that they be receptive to my final recommendations and consider going along with them — rather than resort to courtroom litigation to resolve their conflict. I impressed upon them, as well, that they had every right to bring me to court to be cross-examined. I informed them that I considered it my obligation to make such appearances and that this was especially the case because I, like all human beings, am fallible.

Before closing this phase of the interview (for both litigating and mediating parents) the examiner does well to ask them if they have any questions about anything that has transpired thus far. Of course, they may have asked many questions already, but this final invitation is made to ensure that they are completely clear about the format. Such discussion also has the fringe benefit of reducing anxieties about the evaluation. The more information one has about a feared situation, the less tense one is likely to be. Part of the fear that we have of the unknown relates to our ignorance.

INITIATION OF THE
DATA-GATHERING PROCESS

The above discussion of the basic procedures for litigating parents generally took about an hour. I then had about an hour to devote to a joint interview for data collection. Obviously, when parents mediate there is no lengthy provisions document and so much more of the two-hour initial interview can be devoted to data collection of substantive material related to the evaluation. Accordingly, my discussion at this point refers not only to the procedure I used when evaluating litigating parents, but is the procedure I also use in mediation evaluations.

I usually begin by asking the parents about the reasons for the separation. I will generally throw the question out without directing my attention to either parent. At times, the more assertive and/or talkative one will respond very quickly, before the other parent has had a chance to answer. After one parent has given reasons for the separation, I will then ask the other to comment on what has been said. Often there is even disagreement here about what the major problems were. Then I ask the other parent to present what he (she) believes to have been the marital difficulties, whether or not they coincide with the first presenter's rendition. It is extremely important for the evaluator not to assume automatically that either parent's rendition is the more accurate one. There are exceptions, however, in cases such as alcoholism. Alcoholics typically deny the extent of their drinking (even to themselves) and are well known for their capacity to rationalize. But even here, one should not divulge which parent's rendition seems more credible. In fact, throughout the course of the evaluation, the examiner must be extremely careful not to reveal "which way the wind is blowing" or which party's rendition appears more credible. Such a revelation can seriously compromise the evaluation. It will reduce the freedom with which nonpreferred parties will reveal themselves. After such a statement of potential preference, both parties could justifiably complain that all subsequent meetings were unnecessary, and that an added and unnecessary expense was incurred. The examiner could respond that further inquiry was still needed in order to support or refute the initial impression, but this may not be particularly convincing. And such complaints are likely to come up in the courtroom, much to the embarrassment of the examiner.

I do not go into great detail at this point regarding the various areas of contention in the marital conflict. I merely want to learn about the major issues. And I do not explore a point to the depth where I am firmly convinced which of the two opinions is more likely to be valid. It is in the subsequent interviews that I attempt to do this (to the degree possible in the course of a few interviews). It is important for the examiner to appreciate that a custody evaluation (whether done in the context of litigation or mediation) is not therapy. One explores to the depth that one needs to in order to come to some conclusion regarding parental capacity. In therapy the exploration is far deeper because one wants the data for the purposes of alleviating psychopathology. Examiners who do not make this distinction will cause unnecessary lengthening of the evaluative procedure, contribute to the development of potential psychopathology, and certainly add further expense. Furthermore, examiners who believe that it behooves them to provide therapy in the context of the evaluation are compromising both processes. (In Chapter Three I discussed this issue in greater detail.)

I then inquire about each parent's reasons for requesting primary custody. This question follows the one about marital conflicts because the reasons for seeking primary custody are often based on complaints about the other spouse. Accordingly, one's knowledge of the marital difficulties helps the evaluator understand better the reasons for requesting custody. I ask each parent to comment *briefly* on the other's reasons. I do not ask each parent to comment *in depth* on the other's allegations. Again, I want to deal with the main issues here, not with all the details. I will be obtaining these in subsequent interviews. Nor do I reveal any inkling I may have regarding which parent's complaints are more likely to be valid. In the next chapter I will describe some of the specious reasons parents may have for seeking custody. It is in the initial inquiry that one may start to learn about these.

I have often found that the parent whose position I ultimately do not support presents at this early point far weaker criticisms of the spouse than the parent whose position I do finally support. For example, in one case, a mother was strongly critical of her husband because of his limited involvement in the home with her and the children—throughout the course of their married life. She stated that on the average, he would return home at 11:30-12:00 in the evening and even on weekends would often be away from the home in order to attend to his business. The children had, at a very early age, given up on their father as a source of support, guidance, etc. The father's primary complaint about the mother was that she was "overprotective." After further inquiry I concluded that she was in no way overprotective and that what her husband was calling overprotective maneuvers

were merely the usual manifestations of deep parental involvement. There was no evidence that the mother was trying to
infantilize the children, indulge them, or otherwise pamper them.

In another case, the mother was a chronic alcoholic, and over
the years the three children had joined with their father in
searching for hidden bottles of alcohol that their mother con-
cealed in various places in the home. The mother would drink
until 4:00 or 5:00 in the morning and then sleep throughout the
day. When the children came home from school she was still
sleeping. The mother's primary complaints about the father were
that he did not take the children to enough museums, plays,
concerts, and other cultural activities. The father was a very
involved parent and preferred to take his children to movies,
rodeos, circuses, and sporting events. The mother was not
particularly sophisticated in the cultural realm, and the father's
somewhat reduced interest in such activities could not be considered a deficiency—considering all the recreational and enriching
activities he did engage in with the children.

Before closing the interview, I generally ask what visitation
schedule each parent would propose for the other if he (she) were
to gain custody. Healthy parents generally recognize the importance of the other's having some meaningful contact. The parent
who would remove entirely (or almost entirely) the other party's
opportunities for visitation with the children is generally exhibiting signs of deficiency (with the rare exception, of course, of the
situation in which there is obvious and blatant abuse, neglect, or
other severely detrimental exposures).

Sometimes I may not be able to accomplish all of the above
in the initial two-hour interview. This is especially the case for the
litigation evaluation. Sometimes, the discussion of the people to
be interviewed becomes prolonged by lengthy arguments regarding whether or not a particular individual shall be seen. Sometimes "clarification" regarding the financial arrangements becomes time consuming. On occasion, problems arise over the
signing of the various permission slips and those individuals
whom the examiner shall be contacting. Under these circumstances, there is not enough time available for the aforementioned

substantive inquiry regarding reasons for the separation, reasons for requesting primary custody, and proposed visitation arrangements. Under these circumstances these matters need to be focused on in subsequent interviews with the parents.

⚖ FIVE
INTERVIEWS WITH
THE PARENTS

This chapter will detail the techniques I use to evaluate each parent's *parental* capacity. The same interviewing techniques may be used with parents in both mediation and litigation evaluations. The presentation is lengthy, and it would be unrealistic to expect any examiner to utilize every technique or pose every question in the evaluation of a particular parent. I myself have certainly not done so. I have, however, used all the questions and methods presented here at one time or another. My purpose is to present as much information as possible in the hope that the examiner will find much that may prove useful.

RECORD KEEPING

At the outset, I have found it useful to prepare a separate question sheet for each member of the family. These sheets are labeled: questions for father, questions for mother, questions for Bob, questions for Jane, etc. When interviewing mother, for example, I place next to the sheet of paper on which I am recording information about her, the question sheets for father and each of the children. Then, when the mother makes a questionable allegation about any of the other parties, I make an entry on the appropriate question sheet for one of the other parties to use as a reference in a subsequent interview with that party. This procedure makes the data-collection process very efficient and avoids lost time searching for particular comments one party made about another in a previous interview. It also has the fringe benefit of making my presentation and report preparation more efficient and comprehensive.

For example, during the initial interview, a father may describe a significant alcoholic problem of the mother's. I make a short note on his general data-collection sheet (not his question sheet): "Mother has a drinking problem?" Rather than making any further notes on the father's general data-collection sheet, I will note on the mother's question sheet the details of the father's allegations: the times of the day when the mother drinks, the particular kinds of alcohol she consumes, the amounts, the specific effects of the alcohol on her behavior, and any other information that may help me learn about the true extent of her alleged alcoholism. In addition, I list similar information on the sheets of questions to be asked of the children. If the father has also reported that the mother has encouraged a teenage daughter to join her in her drinking, I will make a note of that on the daughter's question sheet as well. I then leave ample space below the entries for responses by each party during subsequent sessions. The examiner does well not to be too credulous regarding what any party says about the other. When conducting custody and mediation evaluations, one quickly comes to appreciate how differently two individuals can interpret the same event. One's anticipations and desires play an important role in how one is going to interpret the meaning of an event. This point is well demonstrated by an old anecdote:

> The story is told of a rabbi who dies and finds himself in the hereafter. However, he's not sure whether he's in heaven or hell. He's not feeling very much pleasure; so he concludes that he's probably not in heaven. However, he's not feeling very much pain either; so he decides he's probably not in hell. As he wanders about trying to determine where he is, he suddenly sees walking toward him from the distance none other than Rabbi Abraham

Cohen, his mentor from the Talmudic Academy, dead now these thirty years. The rabbi remembered well that Cohen had the reputation of being one of the most pious, dedicated, and humane men ever to grace this planet.

Happily and excitedly the rabbi races toward his old mentor. As he gets closer, he sees that standing by the old man's side is a young, beautiful, and voluptuous woman – obviously the old rabbi's companion. Gleefully the two men embrace one another and with tears rolling down his cheeks, the rabbi tells his old teacher how happy he is to see him and then joyfully says, "It's obvious to me, Rabbi Cohen, that if *you* are here, this must be *heaven*. A more pious, dedicated, and noble individual never set foot on earth. And it's obvious also, Rabbi, that this beautiful, voluptuous, and gorgeous woman is God's reward to you for the good deeds you did while on earth."

To which the old mentor replies, "Rabbi, I'm sorry to have to tell you that number one, this is *not heaven*, this is *hell!* And, number two, this beautiful, gorgeous, voluptuous woman is *not* God's reward to me. *I am her punishment!*"

The moral of this story, of course, is: with the same data, two observers can come to entirely different conclusions regarding the meaning of a particular event. The story provides an important lesson that is not only applicable to custody evaluations but to other aspects of clinical psychiatry as well. And the aforementioned recording system enables the examiner to efficiently collect data from all parties and assess most judiciously conflicting interpretations of the same events.

Another procedure I have found useful in the data-collection process relates to the affidavits, certifications, and other documents submitted by the parents. As mentioned, I usually use these as points of departure for discussion during joint interviews. Most often, these interviews are conducted with both parents, without any other parties. In earlier years I myself would go through the voluminous material submitted to me by the clients and earmark those points that I considered important to discuss with both parents together in joint interviews. In more recent years I have used what I consider to be a less time-consuming method (at least for me), which is also less costly for the parents. Specifically, I let *them* review the voluminous material and I instruct *them* to earmark those issues which they consider important to bring up as points of departure for conversations in joint interview. Not only is this method more efficient, but the parents generally know better than I exactly which points would serve well for the purposes of the evaluation.

The joint interviews are usually the primary source of information and usually comprise the most time-consuming part of the evaluation. It is in this setting that the parents have the opportunity to respond directly to the various allegations included in their documents. It is a far more efficient system than that utilized by the lawyers and the courtroom. The parents are given the opportunity for a direct and immediate response to an allegation, without any loss of time or frustration. Furthermore, if information from a third party is warranted, it often can be enlisted immediately. For example, the mother and father may have a difference of opinion regarding an event that took place in the presence of a third party. In such situations I will ask the parents if they have any objection to my calling the third party. Most often neither will object. However, if I sense any reluctance on the part of either parent, I will immediately suspect that that parent is hiding something or has less commitment to the input by that third party. In the courtroom, it may cost hundreds of dollars (and even more) and many hours to accomplish what I can within a few minutes in the office with such a telephone call.

In order to facilitate the organization of data from subsequent documents I will generally place a parent's response verbatim in the surrounding margins. However, if the response is lengthy, I will assign a code letter next to the paragraph of the allegation (the letter "A" for example) and on an attached sheet, write the response next to the code letter "A." And I do this similarly for items "B," "C," etc. The response sheets are stapled directly to the page on which the allegation appears. All submitted documents that have been responded to and on which notations have been made are placed in a separate file for data that has already been collected. I use the original file for the collection of data that is present and future. The way in which all this material is then collated and organized will be described in Chapter Nine.

It is extremely important for examiners conducting evaluations in association with litigation to keep very meticulous records regarding who was interviewed, on what day, at exactly what time (e.g. 9:30 a.m.-10:30 a.m.) and the fee for each of these sessions. Attorneys may ask for this information under cross-examination when they do not have a strong basis for criticism of the content of the report. It is one of the maneuvers attorneys may use when "fishing around" in the hope that something might be found to compromise the testimony of the impartial examiner. When mediating, it is far less important to keep such meticulous data regarding time of day, etc.

Examiners do well to get across the notion that their files are open at all times to both parents. Although the parents may have trouble reading the evaluator's handwriting, and although it is unlikely that they are going to spend precious session time looking through the examiner's notes, the very principle is reassuring. It gets across the message that the examiner has absolutely no secrets from the parents. Furthermore, in litigated evaluations this policy can serve the examiner well in the courtroom. Attorneys, with justification, become very suspicious of material that is hidden from them or even material that they suspect the examiner is trying to withhold. That's the kind of stuff they immediately go after. By taking a blasé and relaxed attitude about either attorneys' examining the examiner's notes, an up-front decompression of such inquiry can be accomplished and the attorney generally drops the whole thing completely. In the service of this principle, the examiner should advise each parent to provide copies to the spouse of any material given to the examiner. And, if these are not provided directly, the examiner will do so, if warranted. In this way, also, the general principle of full disclosure is promulgated.

SPECIOUS MOTIVATIONS FOR ATTEMPTING TO GAIN PRIMARY CUSTODY

It is important for the examiner to appreciate that the motives parents have for requesting primary custody may not simply stem from love and affection for the children. Often there are much more mundane considerations. The examiner should be aware of this at the outset and should bear this possibility in mind throughout the evaluation—parental professions of love for the children and their fervor to gain custody notwithstanding. People will fight as hard for the reasons given below as they will for love.

The Bargaining Maneuver

Prior to the mid-1970s, if a father told his lawyer that his wife's demands were exorbitant and that he was going to retaliate by asking for custody of the children—and then back down on his demand if the wife would reduce hers—the lawyer would discourage such manipulation by advising the father that he had no grounds for such litigation and that it would not be taken seriously by the other side. At that time, only the most obvious and deep-seated deficiencies of the mother could cause her to lose custody—defects such as chronic alcoholism, prostitution, gross neglect of the children, severe and obvious promiscuous behavior, drug addiction, overt psychosis (especially with hospitalizations), and other blatant impairments in the mother's capacity to care for the children. Because such gross deficiencies were relatively uncommon, fathers rarely sued for custody from the appreciation that their cases were often hopeless.

It was only in the mid-1970s that courts began to adhere to the principle that the sex of the parent should not be a consideration in determining parental preference in custody disputes. Since then, gross negligence or severe incapacitation for parenting has not been necessary to prove in order to gain custody. Rather, the court is asked to grant custody to that parent— regardless of sex—who is better able to provide love, affection, protection, guidance, and other necessities for the children.

At the present time a father may receive no discouragement from his attorney regarding the use of a custody litigation threat as a bargaining maneuver. In fact, he may even be encouraged to do so. I sometimes use the term bargaining *chip* in such situations because of the implication that the children so utilized are being viewed as practically worthless objects, of little intrinsic value. Their value here is only symbolic, but nevertheless it is real. Such a father may know from the outset that he is not going to press the custody conflict to the point where the final decision will be made. Rather, he will use his custody demand as a weapon, as a bargaining maneuver in the negotiations. He may then finally "give up" on the custody fight when he gets concessions from his wife on such matters as alimony and support payments. A parent who is engaging in this practice is not likely to admit so to the examiner conducting the custody evaluation in association with litigation. (This is just one example of the kind of duplicity that the examiner can expect in such evaluations.) Parents involved in a mediation evaluation are far less likely to utilize this maneuver, but it will occasionally be found.

The therapist should appreciate that such a course represents a deficiency in parental capacity. It is a manifestation of the parent's considering personal financial gain to be more important than the children's psychological well-being. Custody litigation is invariably traumatic to children—pulled as they are between parents, lawyers, and other adults. Parents whose desire for personal gain is so great that they are blind to these effects on the children reveal a serious defect in parental capacity. This insensitivity to the children's welfare should be considered one of the arguments against that parent's being granted primary custody.

Financial Gain

Prior to the mid-1970s, the mother was generally given custody of the children, and she remained in the house or apartment while the father moved elsewhere. The basic rationale for this arrangement was the appreciation that children need constancy of environment, and allowing the custodial parent to remain in the home ensured such continuity. The children could then remain in familiar surroundings, not only with regard to their home, but in relation to their neighborhood, friends, school, and teachers. Furthermore, the noncustodial parent (usually the father) was required to provide his former wife with alimony and support. Basically, with the children came the house and support money. In addition, it usually costs more money to support children in another home than one's own. Now fathers have greater opportunities for gaining custody. Many envision their remaining in the house with the children and their wives leaving the home. This would result in their spending less on the children's support because, if successful in winning the custody battle, they would be living with the children. In short, the person who wins the children, may also win the house, may not have to suffer the psychological traumas associated with relocation, and can save support money as well. The examiner does well to recognize this important motivating factor of many parents who are seeking custody—whether through litigation or mediation.

Vengeance

The new egalitarian laws allow a parent to wreak vengeance in a way not previously possible. What better way is there for a disgruntled parent to retaliate for indignities suffered in the course of a marital and divorce conflict than to take away the children—the other parent's most treasured possessions. As mentioned, this is one of the reasons why custody litigation is so vicious. And this is the first time in the history of Western civilization that the parents "start even" when they decide to fight over the children. Adversarial proceedings provide such vengeful parents with a powerful weapon. This is one of the important reasons why I am so critical of the method. One is far less likely to see the vengeance motive in parents who are mediating; but even then this factor must not be discarded completely.

Guilt Reduction

Prior to the mid-1970s, a father might say to a child, "If there was any chance in the world of my gaining custody, I would fight for it. I would go to the Supreme Court if I had to. But my lawyer tells me that I don't stand a chance of getting custody of you children. He tells me that mothers almost automatically get the children." Such fathers can no longer use this argument. From the outset they are viewed equally by the court with regard to their potential for parental capacity.

A father, for example, who never particularly distinguished himself as a devoted parent, may profess great love for the children at the time of separation and fight viciously for custody. Such a parent, either consciously or unconsciously, may not even wish to be granted custody. What he really wants is to put up a good fight so he can convince himself and others that he really loves his children. Such a parent may do many things during the evaluation to ensure that he loses the custody battle. Most parents are especially careful to spend maximum time with the children during the time of a custody evaluation and litigation in order to impress all concerned with their devotion. Parents who basically wish to lose custody may be oblivious to this common maneuver. Or they may choose a lawyer who is obviously incompetent or neglectful of them. Here the aim may not simply be that of losing the children, but sustaining other losses and disadvantages as well. Such parents are secretly relieved when they are not granted custody, and detecting early this basic desire to lose makes the evaluator's job much easier.

Mothers, as well, may fight for custody in an attempt to assuage guilt. Mothers are supposed to be strongly maternal. In fact, the two words are often used synonymously. But *motherhood* is a biological state, as is *maternity*. However, not all who experience maternity are maternal. For every mother who actually kills her child there are dozens who would like to (not simply occasionally, but on an ongoing basis). There are many mothers who are secretly happy when a child dies, because their goal of having gotten rid of the child has been realized without their suffering any guilt, public rejection, and/or punishment for having killed it. Many mothers cannot admit to themselves and/or others that they would much prefer that their husbands take the children. Accordingly, they may "go through the motions" of a custody fight and hope all the while that they lose. At least then they can say to themselves (and to others) that they have put up a good fight, and they can blame the judge (and even the impartial examiner) for their losing the children. Such mothers are not likely to admit to the evaluator their wish to lose. It therefore behooves the examiner to try to ascertain whether or not such is the situation. For some, mediation is the less expensive way to "lose." For others, unfortunately, they may have to go through the motions of litigation in order to put on a "good show" for themselves and others.

An incident from a litigation evaluation some years ago provides an excellent example of this phenomenon. I was evaluating an English woman who was married to an American. My view of her was that she preferred more to lead a jet-set life than to stay at home taking care of her children, ages one, three, and five. I strongly suspected that she was "going through the motions" of the custody litigation because she could not admit to herself that she really did not wish to have the children. In an interview that took place in early December, she asked me what I thought of her going back to England during the Christmas-New Year's holidays. It was one of those rare occasions that I decided to "change hats" and be a child therapist advising a parent rather than an impartial evaluator collecting information. Accordingly, I told her that I thought it would be unwise, considering how upsetting the separation and litigation already had been to the children. To this she responded that she was definitely going anyway, because she just couldn't tolerate the idea of not being in England during the Christmas-New Year's season. This is the answer I expected to receive when I switched roles. I do not know whether it was conscious or unconscious, but I do know that at some level she wanted to do things that would compromise significantly her position in the custody conflict.

Other Pathological Reasons for Trying to Gain Custody

There are various kinds of pathological interactions that parents may have with children that may result in their fighting for custody. A parent, for example, may be extremely dependent on a child (especially a teenager) and may view loss of custody with fear of intolerable loneliness. A sadistic parent may need the child as a scapegoat. An overprotective mother may view the child as the main way in which she can prove herself an adequate person. The child is not viewed as an individual who must be helped to become more independent. Rather, every attempt is made to prevent such independence and keep the child at an infantile, dependent level of functioning. A father with considerable hostile feelings toward society at large may need a child to act out his hostility. He may have good enough judgment to appreciate the consequences of such acting out, but his child may not. Accordingly, the youngster serves as a perfect vehicle for the expression of the father's antagonism toward the world. The examiner does well to consider these pathological forms of relationships with children and recognize that the loss of the child may be an extremely anxiety-provoking prospect for such a parent.

A very moralistic and/or religious parent may claim that the other parent should not have custody of the children because of "sexual promiscuity." The examiner may find that what is labeled "promiscuity" is the normal private involvement in heterosexual activity that a separated or divorced parent today commonly engages in. In these situations, one should ask such complaining parents to specify the effects they suspect the other parent's private sexual behavior is going to have on the children. Such a parent may be hard put to provide specific responses, other than to make comments along the lines that the children will identify with the parent's promiscuity and will grow up to engage in similar perversions themselves and will therefore be punished by God. Although there are certainly parents who believe with deep conviction that such will be the case, the examiner must appreciate that there are many for whom such moralistic-religious convictions are espoused in the service of vengeance and used as a rationalization for depriving the other parent of the children. Sometimes, the complaining parent was never particularly religious and the "conversion" came right after learning of the former spouse's new relationship.

On occasion a parent, more commonly a mother, will

threaten suicide if the child chooses the father. In less extreme cases, the mother will communicate to the child that she will psychologically decompensate, become severely depressed, or exhibit other terrible untoward psychological reactions if the child expresses preference for the father. This is clearly a negative on the mother's part in the custody/visitation evaluation. It is not a reason for the examiner to decide that the child should stay with the mother.

The Attorney's Role in Specious Custody Demands

The attorney may appreciate that the client does not deserve custody, but will nevertheless vigorously support the client's demand. The lawyer may welcome the use of the custody issue as a weapon in the litigation in the hope that pressing this issue will gain concessions in other areas. Using as a rationalization the lawyer's obligation to support the client's position, the attorney may serve as a useful weapon for the parent who wishes to use the custody issue to wreak vengeance, assuage guilt, or extract other concessions. And, of course, there are always the financial considerations. Lawyers can earn significant amounts of money from custody litigation and the richer the client and the more prolonged the litigation, the more money there is to be made. This factor also is likely to support a client's specious commitment to the process of litigating for a child's custody.

However, more benevolent considerations are operative on occasion. The attorney may recognize that the client needs the custody litigation in order to assuage guilt over a basic desire not to have custody. In such cases the lawyer may harbor the hope that the exposure of the client's parental deficiencies in open court will help the parent gain insight into the fact that he or she will be the less desirable custodian. The lawyer may also support the client's demand with future considerations in mind. Although recognizing that the client is presently the less desirable parent, the lawyer may appreciate that future changes may improve the client's capacity or diminish the other spouse's parental ability.

Having on the court records that the client has fought for the child may enhance the parent's chances of gaining custody in the future. And the information obtained in the earlier trial may be useful and supportive in such future litigation. A client who has never fought for the children in the past, when he or she had the opportunity to do so, is less likely to gain custody in the future. However, there is the risk to the client that such litigation may place on the court records information that would weaken the parent's case in subsequent litigation, and this may cause the lawyer to be less enthusiastic about the parent pressing the custody issue.

Occasionally a parent will justify cruelty, exploitation, or other forms of unconscionable behavior by claiming that the attorney has recommended such and that the parent is only complying with the attorney's advice. The examiner does well to consider such statements as rationalizations. For example, one father, who was married to a wealthy woman, was not only asking for alimony, but custody of the children and support of them as well. He claimed that under state laws of equitable distribution he was entitled to alimony because he was the financially poorer parent. In addition, he claimed that there was nothing inappropriate about his requesting support—if he were to gain custody—because state laws allowed this. He exhibited no loss of masculine pride as he spoke of his "rights," and he used his attorney's advice regarding what he was entitled to under the law as a rationalization for exploitation. His past life revealed other evidences of his manipulation of others for his personal gain. I considered this father's interest in gaining custody of the children to serve the goal of exploitation of the mother, in that if he were to gain custody he would have more of an excuse to exploit her for her money via child support payments. In such cases the examiner must be careful about using terms like "exploiter" in the report unless this can be demonstrated clearly. The examiner can, however, get across this point by quoting the mother's comments that her husband is trying to exploit her and then either saying nothing or making a comment that her view appears reasonable to the evaluator. This more cautious approach was the one I used here. I was able to get across the message without *my* using the term *exploiter*—thereby protecting myself from questions under cross-examination like: "Have you personally interviewed those persons whom you claim Mr. H. allegedly exploited in the past?" and "Isn't it difficult, if not impossible, to differentiate between taking what is rightfully due us and exploitation?"

Concluding Comments

In the course of the evaluation, especially of the parents, the evaluator does well to be alerted to the possible presence of these specious factors that may be operative in the parent's desire to have primary custody of the children. When present, they must be put on the scale when weighing each parent's assets and liabilities regarding custodial capacity. The examiner must be wary, however, of jumping to the conclusion that such factors may be operative and assuming that they are present on the basis of hunches and feelings. Rather, such suspicions must be followed up and supported by hard data (direct observations or supporting statements made by the parents) if one is justifiably to include them in one's final report and courtroom testimony. In the mediation evaluation, these factors should be discussed openly and attempts be made to resolve them because they may contaminate the arrangement being proposed.

**THE PROBLEM OF PARENTAL LYING
IN THE CUSTODY EVALUATION**

In both litigation and mediation evaluations, one is likely to observe parental lying. However, lying is much more common when litigation is taking place, especially because the parent is likely to be programmed and tutored by the attorney regarding what lies to provide—either by omission or commission. In certain respects mental health professionals tend to be more naive than lawyers with regard to believing a patient's statements. Generally, the therapist expects the patient to be truthful. We are certainly trained to be dubious about what our patients tell us, and our antennae should ever be out sensing for deceptions. But the kinds of deceits that we are most acute in detecting are self-deceptions—things that our patients are trying to hide from themselves. We are quite sensitive to such forms of self-deception as reaction formation, rationalization, and denial. We are also sensitive to the kinds of self-deceptions involved in the formation of many psychopathological symptoms such as phobias, obsessions, compulsions, and paranoia. In all of these there is an element of the unconscious attempt to suppress and repress unacceptable thoughts and feelings. But patients most often do not consciously deceive us. They recognize that it behooves them to reveal things that may be difficult and even embarrassing to talk about because they appreciate that such revelations are vital if the therapist is to be helpful.

Lawyers, however, more frequently deal with clients who are consciously untruthful with them, and they routinely assume that their adversaries' clients will be so. Having some experience with duplicity, they may be more astute than the therapist in detecting it. Policemen, judges, and those who work in penal institutions are also more sensitive to conscious duplicity than we are. Accordingly, therapists are handicapped somewhat in the ability to evaluate patients involved in legal proceedings. For example, when we evaluate a parent in a custody determination the parent generally (either consciously or unconsciously) withholds information that might be detrimental to his or her cause. Our expectation of honesty and our inexperience with conscious deliberate deceit may significantly compromise our efficacy here. Furthermore, parents litigating for custody of their children are bound to distort the truth to a significant degree. Each is likely to exaggerate the other's deficits and downplay the other's assets. Traditionally, the parent will make "mountains out of molehills" with regard to the spouse's liabilities. And this is another kind of duplicity that custody evaluators inevitably have to deal with. Although litigating parents are far more likely to be deceitful than those who are mediating, one certainly may see duplicity in parents who are mediating. Whereas in the former situation the deceit is more likely to be conscious and deliberate, in the latter it is more likely to be unconscious and the product of a variety of self-deceptive mechanisms.

As I will discuss in greater detail in various parts of this book, the joint interview can be extremely valuable in "smoking out" fabrications. Proponents of the adversary system consider it one of the best (if not the best) method for finding out who is telling "the truth." They claim that the kinds of confrontations provided in the open courtroom allow the two sides to directly expose one another, as well as to the judge and jury, their opinions and out of this presentation of opposing views "the truth" will then emerge. Although the method is certainly an advance over the previous Inquisitorial system in which accused persons often did not have the opportunity to confront their accusers, it has certain obvious deficiencies which limit the system's capacity to find out what is "the truth." One of its deficiencies is that the confrontation is not a natural one, but rather one in which the two parties confront one another through their intermediaries: the attorneys.

This procedure interferes significantly with the acquisition of the kinds of data that mental health evaluators can obtain in their offices, data which can be more important than the actual statements made by the parties. For example, a mother may claim that one of the reasons her husband spent so little time with the children was that he was out gallivanting with a whole string of women. In response to this allegation the father may deny infidelity and respond, "Doctor, she doesn't know what she's talking about. She just keeps imagining things. Business requires me to stay out very late, sometimes till 2:00 or 3:00 in the morning, at meetings where I can't get in touch with her." To this the wife may respond, "Doctor, I've lived with that man for 18 years and I know him inside out. When he's lying he has that shit-eating grin on his face, just the expression you're seeing right now." In response to the confrontation the husband begins to blush, stutter, and ramble. Although such responses might be obtained on the witness stand, they are far less likely to be elicited because of the time-lag between the confrontation and the response, the opportunity to formally prepare a response, and the transmission of many of the communications through intermediaries. This loss of spontaneity reduces the likelihood that one will obtain "the truth" in the courtroom.

In another case a wife complained that her husband had been unfaithful to her on numerous occasions. He flatly denied that this was the case and stated, "She's always looking for trouble. She's just got a vivid imagination." The woman then asked her husband to explain the presence of a condom in her car, after she had let her husband use it during a weekend when she was off on a business trip. His reply, "I lent the car to my brother, and you know he sells condoms."

To which the wife replied, "Oh, your brother sells *used* condoms?" At which point the husband said, "There you are, just trying to make trouble again. I don't know how it got there. Maybe he took a girlfriend in the car."

The wife then replied, "And how do you explain the used condom I found behind the couch in our living room? Was that your brother's too?"

The husband's reply, "Doctor, she's always trying to make trouble. As I told you, she's got a vivid imagination."

I leave it to the reader to decide which person's version here sounds more credible. What is important to my discussion, is the value of direct face-to-face interchanges in "smoking out" the truth, interchanges that are not possible in adversarial courtroom proceedings.

Furthermore, the adversary system strictly prohibits the accuser from directly cross-examining the accused. When one is dealing with domestic situations, in which the accuser and the accused are spouses, their knowledge of one another is far superior to that of any attorney and/or judge—no matter how brilliant and no matter how skilled in the law. Letting them "have it out with one another" is more likely to bring about responses that will enable the evaluator to determine what is "the truth." Even though there are situations in which things may get out of hand, and in which the individuals may become quite emotional, these do not warrant examiners' depriving themselves of this valuable source of information. There may even be situations in which one might have to protect the individuals from one another, such as by the use of a steel-perforated screen or thick glass separation, but this should not preclude conducting such interviews.

In joint interviews one has the immediate opportunity to telephone, without any delay, other individuals who might be able to provide important information regarding which parent is telling the truth. The judge cannot do this; an impartial evaluator can do so readily. It might take weeks or months to bring in this third party to provide testimony and even then one might not be successful because of the reluctance on the part of the third party to "get involved." However, a telephone call made by one of the spouses is much more likely to elicit the third party's comments during a brief conversation over the telephone. It is very much different from appearing on a witness stand in a courtroom. And the spouse who lies and is being potentially "smoked out" by such a call is not likely to resist strongly because of the knowledge that such resistance implies guilt, shame, or some kind of cover-up that will compromise that party's position in the custody evaluation. There is no lawyer involved to "protect" the client's rights and to justify thereby cover-ups and the perpetuation of the fabrication.

I recall one situation in which the mother claimed that the father had a problem with petty thievery and described how he prided himself on how much food he could steal from supermarkets and other items from a wide variety of stores. I asked the mother how many times, to the best of her knowledge, her husband had involved himself in such thievery. (The reader will note here, as I will repeat many times throughout this book, the importance of trying to get numbers and frequency in association with custody visitation/allegations.) The mother replied, "I really don't know how many times, but I'm sure it's been in the hundreds." The father denied any such behavior. The mother then stated that he would often do this with a certain friend, George. Again, the father denied that this was the case. I then asked them if they would have any hesitation over my calling

George. Both agreed that I could do so immediately; however, the father did so with a slight but definite tone of hesitation. I asked them whom they preferred to make the call and the father agreed that he would let the mother do so. I suspected again that this related to some reluctance on his part to put through the call, but I was pleased to have the mother make it in that there would be less chance of her communicating any messages to George regarding cover-up of the father's activities.

I instructed the mother to call George and merely tell him that she was in my office and that a custody evaluation was being conducted. I asked her to ask George to speak with me, without giving him any further information. Once on the phone I told George who I was and informed him that I was conducting the evaluation under court order and that he should understand that any information he provided me could be transmitted to any of the involved parties and used in any way whatsoever in the course of the litigation. He agreed to speak with me. I then simply asked him if he had any information about any possible stealing habits on the part of either of the parents. George immediately described the same pattern of stealing presented by the mother. I asked George if he would be willing to come to a court of law and describe under oath what he had just told me. He stated that he would, although he was most reluctant to get involved. The father suddenly "remembered" that perhaps on one or two occasions he had stolen items, but denied that the problem was as serious as George and his wife had described. When I asked George how many times he himself had actually observed the father engaged in thievery, he said, "I'm ashamed to admit it, but I myself must have gone with him 20 or 30 times. He told me that he had done it hundreds of times, but I never saw him do it other than the times I was with him. But he was proud of what he was doing and I believed him when he said he had done it hundreds of times."

Family interviews, as well, can be extremely valuable in finding out who is telling "the truth." After all, the children live in the home and are direct observers to what is going on. Although they may initially express some reluctance to involve themselves in such confrontational interviews, my experience has been that they generally do so and as the interview moves along they eventually become more relaxed. Such interviews also help the evaluator learn something about the reality behind exaggerations. The children's input is likely to give the examiner a more accurate picture of exaggerated criticisms. However, if a parental alienation syndrome is present (this will be discussed in greater detail in Chapter Six), then the children's exaggerations may make it even more difficult to ascertain "the truth."

THE VALUE OF THE CLASSICAL PSYCHOANALYTIC APPROACH IN THE EARLY PHASES OF INTERVIEWING THE PARENTS

I generally explain to the parents that I will be conducting a psychiatric evaluation of them as if they were voluntarily coming to me for consultation or therapy. Although I am not a strong subscriber to many of the theories and techniques espoused by the classical psychoanalytical school, I am psychoanalytically trained and believe there are certainly aspects of that approach that, when used judiciously, have great merit. Such is the case for the early phases of the interviews with the parents.

I will generally begin each of the early sessions, both in litigation and mediation, with a question such as: "Is there anything you have on your mind that you'd like to tell me?" It is rare for a parent in a custody evaluation to respond in the negative. Most often each of the parents has many things to tell me and each can go on for hours elaborating on the various deficiencies of the spouse and the ways in which granting custody to the other party would be a terrible mistake and extremely detrimental to the children. The therapist should not feel rushed to get to more standard questions that I will soon be presenting; rather, he or she should appreciate that this open invitation to the parent to speak freely may provide the most important information. In this early phase of my interviews I want the parent to "roll," to pour forth a steady stream of information with little or no interruption by me.

Catalyzing this outpouring serves a number of useful functions in the custody evaluation. It provides detailed information about the various marital complaints and alleged deficiencies exhibited by the other parent. The structured or specific question might not direct itself to the particular issues that carry the greatest emotional charge at that point. Accordingly, such a question might deprive the interviewer of the most vital information. It is a good principle of psychotherapy that the issues with the greatest degree of emotional charge are the best "handles" for the therapist to "grab onto" in that they are most likely to lead to the more significant problems. Another value of this approach relates to the nonjudgmental factor. By passively taking in all the information and strictly refraining from revealing any reactions — especially the negative ones — the examiner is likely to be viewed by the parent as being completely sympathetic to what is being said. The complete absence of a negative response is interpreted as positive agreement and support. The evaluator is thereby viewed as being on that parent's side. In such a setting the parent is more likely to reveal deficiencies. In short, the evaluator comes to be viewed as a trusted friend who is in basic agreement with most, if not all, of the complaints. Presumably, such a friend is not going to let the revelations of a few deficiencies affect the basic positive regard. Alternatively, the therapist who expresses disapprobation — ever so slightly — will be viewed as the "enemy" and the patient is likely to "clam up" and reveal few, if any, of the deficiencies that are important for the therapist to learn about. (As I will elaborate subsequently, the parent's own statements about his or her deficiencies are among the most important information the evaluator attempts to acquire.)

I do not wish to give the impression that I remain absolutely silent in the face of this outpouring. I do interrupt, at times, to be sure that I am jotting down accurate information on the data collection sheet of the parent being interviewed, as well as on the aforementioned pages of questions to be asked of the other parties. In addition, if a parent is repetitious (often the case) I will politely interrupt and remind him (her) that we do have certain time limitations, that I understand the main point, and that we would do better to go on to other issues. If such interruptions are properly executed, the parent is not likely to object out of the realization that the examiner is trying to save time and money (and, of course, the payer is particularly appreciative of the latter consideration).

On occasion I will interview a parent who has very little to say. He (she) briefly enumerates the major complaints and after a few minutes "runs dry." On the one hand, such failure to "roll" could be viewed as a positive personality trait. The individual quickly "gets to the point" and doesn't waste time with repetition and elaborations that add nothing new. On the other hand, one could argue that there is little emotional charge behind the complaints and the individual is not particularly pained by them. I consider the latter explanation to be the more likely, i.e., the parent who does not fight very hard is revealing a parental deficiency. And this should be taken into consideration in the total assessment.

My experience has been that the average parent needs one or two hours (in custody evaluations I find it more efficient to conduct full-hour sessions, rather than the 45- to 50-minute sessions I set up in treatment) of rolling before "running out of steam." Once that has happened, it indicates to me that I have gained the optimum benefit from this phase of the interviews and I can then proceed to the more structured aspects.

THE PARENT QUESTIONNAIRE
ABOUT THE CHILDREN

Whether or not we have completed the outpouring process by the end of the first interview, I often give the parent a copy of my questionnaire which requests information about the children. One copy of the questionnaire is given to each parent for each child. This questionnaire, reproduced in its entirety in Appendix VII, is one that I prepared originally for diagnostic/therapeutic purposes. I routinely send it to parents of all children prior to the initial consultation. I have found this questionnaire useful in the custody evaluation as well. The ostensible purpose is to give the examiner information about the children that is of psychiatric significance. However, of equal (if not more) importance is the information it provides about the parent who is filling out the questionnaire. Because each parent fills out a questionnaire about each child, one can compare the parents' responses. Because they are not likely to be collaborating on filling out the questionnaire (as do parents who are living together), we learn something about each parent's knowledge of the child. This is especially true with regard to such information as developmental milestones, school performance, and past history. Less knowledgeable parents will reveal their ignorance on the questionnaire. They are not likely to be asking the spouse for help—as is the case when parents are married and filling out together a single questionnaire. And such parents, of course, "lose points" in the evaluation. Furthermore, one should try to get some idea about the dedication that the parent exhibited in filling out the form. A hastily done, slipshod, haphazard approach says something about the parent's commitment to the child. In addition, it may reveal ambivalence about actually winning custody. Doing a sloppy job is one way to manifest (either consciously or unconsciously) one's basic desire not to gain custody.

For example, on page four of the questionnaire the parent is asked to list the ages at which the child reached each of 20 important milestones (sat without support, walked without assistance, recognized colors, etc.). The instructions also advise parents who do not recall the exact time at which the particular milestone occurred, to merely check off whether it occurred early, at the usual time, or late. One mother (who was litigating for the custody of her two children) recalled 19 of the 20 items accurately with regard to being able to provide the exact time (to the nearest month). Only one item was checked in the early, usual time, or late column. Her husband, however, could not check any of the items in the exact-date column and checked all items in the second column. The same was true for the other child's questionnaire. Another parent never returned the questionnaire at all. I generally make it a practice not to remind the parent to return it and consider the failure to do so as a manifestation of parental deficiency. It is likely that the same lax attitude is exhibited in other aspects of the parent's relationship with the children. It indicates that other things take higher priority than the needs and interests of the children. On occasion, I suspect that failure to return the questionnaire is done (again either consciously or unconsciously) because the parent does not wish to reveal ignorance of the child's life. Or, such failure might reflect the parent's desire not to gain custody, protestations to the contrary notwithstanding.

INDICATIONS OF PARENTAL CAPACITY FROM THE PAST HISTORY

Introduction

I begin the more structured phase of the interview with each parent along the lines of the traditional history-taking. I cover typical questions regarding the interviewee's parents, relationships with them, siblings, relationships with siblings, education at all levels (academic and social aspects), peer relationships, jobs, etc. However, there are certain aspects of the routine evaluation that I particularly emphasize, namely, those that relate to parental capacity.

It is important for the examiner to appreciate that the information gained from the background history is *not* of the highest priority in the custody evaluation, its great importance in psychoanalytic treatment notwithstanding. First, one is much more convincing when focusing on assets and liabilities that exist at the time of the evaluation and in the period immediately antedating it. Also, to argue that a particular childhood experience produced a specific adult behavioral pattern is the kind of speculation (and it *is* a speculation, as much as we may not wish to admit it) that cross-examining attorneys love to seize upon: "Isn't it *possible*, doctor, for a woman to be a good mother even though she was cruelly treated, abused, and neglected by her own mother in childhood?" The answer to this question obviously must be *yes*. But the attorney is not likely to give the examiner the opportunity to speak about its unlikelihood. One might argue, then, that the examiner should not be wasting time in this area. My response is that it is not a complete waste of time in that it does provide information (even though it may not be included in the final report) that can help the examiner come to a conclusion regarding parental capacity. It is information that is placed on the scales that weigh assets against liabilities. It should be viewed as backup verification of the stronger arguments presented in the report—arguments related to the examiner's direct observations and statements made by the parties involved.

For ease of presentation, I will focus on the mother as the interviewee. On occasion, I will make direct reference to the father. However, most of the topics should be covered, to the degree applicable, in the father's evaluation as well. No particular item should be viewed as being of overriding significance; all are taken together in making the decision. Each question and issue focused on is not rated positive or negative simply on the basis of a short answer. Rather, the question serves as a point of departure from which one should try to gain information about the degree of parental capacity that the response reveals. In order to facilitate open discussion, the questions are not of the type that can be answered yes or no; rather, they stimulate more revealing answers.

Relationships Between the Parents and Grandparents

The examiner should find out about the parents' relationships with their own parents, i.e., with the children's grandparents. One tends to be the same kind of parent that one's parents were. If the maternal grandmother, for example, was a very unmaternal person, if she was somewhat neglectful of or uninterested in her children, the likelihood that the mother herself will be compromised in this area is high. This is especially the case if the maternal grandmother physically abused the mother. Though not invariably so, one must consider the possibility because the mother is likely to incorporate the children's grandmother's deficient model. Similarly for the father: if his relationship with his father was poor, he is likely to be compromised in his paternal capacity—but again, not invariably. One wants to get information, as well, about the mother's relationship with her father, i.e., the children's maternal grandfather. A woman's relationship with her father is the model for her subsequent relationships with other men, both in the dating and marriage periods. The nature of a poor relationship between the mother and the maternal grandfather may provide information about the mother's relationship with her husband. And similar principles operate with regard to the father's relationship with his mother, i.e., the children's paternal grandmother.

Games Played in Childhood

Recent reduction in sexual stereotypes notwithstanding, I believe that little girls today are still playing "house" more than little boys. Mothers now being evaluated are still likely to have grown up at a time when "house" was even more typically a girl's game. The same is true with regard to doll play. Accordingly, I ask the mother: "What were your favorite games as a girl?" If she describes games like "house," I consider that a positive response regarding her maternal capacity. If she doesn't mention that game specifically, I will ask what her feelings were about playing it. I inquire about her feelings when playing with dolls and how old she was when she stopped. Liking doll play throughout a few years of childhood is positive information. I ask what her feelings were about helping her mother cook and do other work around her home. This does not preclude my inquiring into extradomestic activities and interests. I believe that both of these areas should be evaluated, but the homemaking interests and identifications are an important factor to be considered in determining custody. If she hated it, or *her* mother had hated it, and she most often did it begrudgingly, then this would be a negative factor. Although it is unrealistic to expect a child or an adult to relish housework, a certain degree of enjoyment is usually had by many, if not most, girls as they bake cakes, help set the table, and assist in other household activities.

Again, recent diminution in gender stereotypes notwith-standing, boys are still much more involved in sports than girls. Although girls are certainly becoming more involved, sports are still primarily a masculine activity for the vast majority of children. A father who was involved in sports in his own childhood is more likely to involve his own son(s) in such activities. Parents who were more involved in intellectual-type games as children are subsequently more likely to involve their own children in such games. Parents who had few friends as children and had few involvements with peers are likely to become remote from their own children because they have not acquired a repertoire of activities with which to relate to their offspring.

Pets

Children almost invariably enjoy playing with pets. In fact, the child who does not enjoy pets probably has some kind of psychological problem. Pets serve many important functions for the child. Children readily identify with them because of the great similarity between the way the pet and the child are treated. Both are dependent on some more competent figure for sustenance and both thrive on tenderness and affection. Much can be learned from children by discussing the fantasies they have when playing with their pets. Although the child may, at times, relate to a pet as a peer, more commonly the child-pet relationship is similar to the parent-child relationship. As C. Kestenbaum and S. Underwood (1979) have pointed out, interest in pets in childhood is positively related to strong parental capacity in adulthood. Many children gain their first parental-type experiences in their relationship with their pets.

Babysitting

I ask the parents what their feelings were about helping care for younger children or babysitting. Sometimes this can be a chore that the child will resist, especially when it is coerced or exploitive. However, such activities provide an opportunity for parental expression that I believe the child has the capacity to enjoy—even at ages as young as four to five. A. Freud and D. T. Burlingham (1944a and 1944b) described well how children, when separated from their parents, will often assume the role of parental surrogate toward younger children. If a parent has experienced such gratifications, and recalls them with more pleasure than pain, it is an argument in favor of a strong parental interest and capacity.

Previous Marriages

I will ask about previous marriages. I am interested in learning about the reasons for the breakup of each previous marriage, particularly as they relate to child-rearing capacity. For example, if a divorce was the result of failure of a parent to assume childcare obligations, maltreatment of the children, neglect of them, or abuse, such patterns may repeat themselves in the custody evaluation presently being conducted. Even accusations by the former spouse to this effect should be looked into carefully with questions asked about any possible justification for the allegation. On occasion I have even spoken on the telephone to an ex-spouse in order to clarify a particular point that was relevant to the custody evaluation under consideration. Of course, such former spouses are often reluctant to involve themselves, but I have, on occasion, found receptive individuals whose input was useful. I am also interested in each present parent's involvement with children from previous marriages. Most often children from previous marriages are not under consideration in a custody dispute, but remain with the parent who had them at the time of the marriage that is now being dissolved. If, however, children from previous marriages are living with others, I want to know the nature of the relationship between the parent being evaluated and the children who are living elsewhere. Also, I am interested in the present relationship with stepchildren from previous marriages. Typically, the relationship between a stepparent and a stepchild is a tenuous one and most often it fizzles out completely after the separation— promises of ongoing involvement notwithstanding. Accordingly, a nonexistent relationship with a stepchild from a previous marriage is not of significance in an evaluation. If, however, a parent has a good ongoing relationship with such a stepchild, then it represents a strong statement of parental capacity. However, such a situation is rare in my experience. In contrast, if a parent has a very poor relationship with a natural child from a previous marriage, especially one in which there is a nonexistent relationship, then this speaks poorly for that parent's prognosis with regard to the child(ren) of this marriage. It is a strong negative on the evaluator's "score sheet."

Plans About Children at the Time of the Marriage

I ask the parents how many children they envisioned having before they got married. I consider an answer of none or one to be a negative response. (Clearly, the parent who has no children is not coming to me for a custody evaluation. However, a parent may have *planned* to have none and an accidental pregnancy has taken place.) I generally consider a response of two to five or six evidence of strong parental capacity. However, if the parents actually have more than seven or eight children, they show, in my opinion, suggestive manifestations of parental inadequacy. Prior to the last half century, this was not the case. If one wanted four children, one might have to have had eight because of the high infant and childhood death rate. This is not the case at this time in Western society. I believe that parents *today* who have seven, eight, or more children show little respect for the individual needs of children and I lose some respect for such ostensible parental capacity. In such large families children get lost in the crowd and suffer from various deprivations. Even when religious conviction is given as a reason for such a large family, I still hold that it reflects an impairment in parental capacity.

I will also ask: "At the time of your marriage, how long did you plan to wait before having your first child?" If the couple did not take into consideration their resources and just went right ahead, this would be a negative. If they waited a reasonable time because there were reality factors that may have caused them to hold off, even factors like wanting to get to know one another better or having a few years of freedom before having children, I would consider the response positive. If, however, there were many years of ambivalence or procrastination, this would be a negative. One does well to go into the question of whether each of the children was planned or accidental and, of course, the planned child does speak for greater parental interest.

The Pregnancy

A healthy mother has adequate prenatal care and a healthy father is also concerned about this. The failure to be involved in such care is a definite negative, social and economic factors notwithstanding. Even the poorest families have access to clinics where such care is provided. The mother's attitude about her body changes associated with the pregnancy can also give a clue about maternal capacity. If the mother considered herself ugly, rather than beautiful, it is a compromise. The healthy woman is not ashamed of the body changes associated with pregnancy; in fact, she is genuinely proud of them. However, it is reasonable that she may not be pleased with facial changes and edema. Similarly, the father who finds his wife repulsive when pregnant is demonstrating an impairment in paternal capacity. The healthy father is not "turned off" by his pregnant wife's physical changes. Again, when there is significant edema, especially of the face, one might modify this position to some degree.

One might ask: "During the pregnancy was there any preference that the child be of a particular sex?" A standard answer here is that the parent had no preference. If, however, the therapist poses the question differently: "Most parents usually have a secret preference, even though they may not feel comfortable expressing it. Did you have such a secret preference?" a more honest answer may be provided. Beginning with "Most parents usually have a secret preference" gives some sanction to express what might previously have been considered an unacceptable response. If there was strong and unjustifiable bias in one direction, this would be a negative factor. This might manifest itself in the parent's having chosen a name for just one sex.

Breast-feeding

Breast-feeding should be discussed. There are those who consider this to be the most important criterion for determining a mother's maternal capacity. I believe this is unfortunate. It is probably true that on a statistical basis, on studies of thousands of women in Western society, the breast-feeding mother would probably prove to be more maternal than the nonbreast-feeding mother. However, there are unmaternal women who will breast-feed because they have learned a little psychology and have been taught to equate it with femininity and maternal capacity. They will use it as a way of denying basic deficiencies in this area and think that merely by performing this act they are proving themselves highly maternal. Therefore, one must be cautious about the significance of the answers to this question; nevertheless it should be asked. The milk drying up after a short period of time could reflect some impairment of maternal capacity. The mother's tension with the child, an unconscious desire not to feed it, and other psychological factors could cause reduction and even total resorption of breast milk. However, physical factors might also be operative. But we do not know enough about breast functioning to be able to say in many cases that it was definitely maternal deficiency that caused the breast glands to stop secreting milk. The father's attitude about his wife's breast-feeding should also be explored. Husbands who view it as "animal" or "primitive" are likely to be less paternal than those who are very desirous of their wife's breast-feeding. Again, those who read psychology and psychiatry books may learn the "right" answer to this question, so the examiner must be cautious before coming to any specific conclusions.

Postpartum Depression

The mother's suffering a postpartum depression following the birth of one or more of the children is an argument against strong parental capacity. Such depressions usually involve deep feelings of dissatisfaction with the maternal role, often preoccupations of a frightening sort involving hostility toward the child, and impulses to throw the child out of the window or kill it. Although these obsessions are frightening and often ego-alien, they still reflect unconscious hostile impulses pressing for expression – impulses that are likely to detract from the mother's healthy involvement with her children.

This book is being written at a time when the pendulum has shifted significantly toward biological explanations for various psychopathological phenomena. A biological explanation for depression is very much in vogue. Although I am in agreement that there are drugs that can reduce depression symptomatically, I am not convinced that all depressions are biological in etiology. I believe that in manic-depressive psychosis, the biological factors are probably extremely important. However, I am less convinced about a basic biological cause for many other types of depression and my incredulity extends to postpartum depression as well. One cannot deny that there are massive metabolic changes occurring in the pregnant woman, both during the pregnancy and after the delivery. I am, however, dubious that such changes are of importance in bringing about postpartum depression.

Adoption

When a custody evaluation is being conducted with parents who have adopted their children, one should inquire about the reasons why the parents adopted. Considering our present state of knowledge, I think it premature to conclude that a sterility problem on the part of either parent is necessarily psychogenic. In some cases the argument for psychogenesis seems plausible; in others both organic and psychogenic factors appear to be operating; and in others the organic factor(s) may be the more important. In many cases, however, one cannot be certain as to the cause.

Accordingly, it would be a disservice to an adopting parent to conclude, as some psychiatrists might, that the sterility probably had a psychogenic basis. Prior to the adoption it is likely that the parents spent years trying to conceive. When this failed they may have made the rounds among gynecologists, endocrinologists, and other sterility specialists. Such consultations may have involved an endless series of expensive and sometimes painful examinations, tests, and even operative procedures. Years may have been spent meticulously making temperature charts to determine the most fertile period and numerous theories may have been followed as to the best method of conceiving. Finally, when all failed, the parents may have gone through significant ordeals with adoption agencies or other sources before finally being given a child. Such a pursuit is testimony to the strong parental interests of such people, and it is therefore a terrible disservice to automatically dismiss the sterility as psychogenic. In fact, I would go further and say that if they have embarked on this pilgrimage, I would consider it evidence of strong parental capacity.

Memory Impairments

If, in the process of obtaining the parent's past history, one finds that the parent's recollection of important past events is significantly impaired, one should try to find out the reason for such memory lapses. Unless there is obvious evidence for borderline intelligence, mental deficiency, schizophrenia, or organic brain syndrome, the cause is likely to be psychogenic. Extremely anxious individuals are likely to have memory lapses because tension distracts them from recollections they would otherwise have. Often disorganization is associated with such chronic anxiety.

Less important than the failure to recall important events from the past is whether such anxiety/disorganization is interfering with the parent's capacity to take care of the children at the time of the evaluation. If such is the case, then this would obviously be a parental deficiency. Organizational capacity is not generally considered when one is trying to evaluate a parent's capabilities. However, it is an extremely important factor to consider when assessing parental functioning. Not only does the disorganized parent deprive the child of many needs, but such a parent also creates anxieties in the child because of the unpredictability of the environment.

The Presence of the Spouse
In an Individual Interview

My usual practice has been to interview a parent alone when getting information about past history. However, on occasion, I have found it useful to have the spouse sit in on such interviews because I can often get valuable information. For example, a parent generally lacks objectivity regarding the description of his or her own parents (the children's grandparents). A spouse can often provide useful information about these people (the spouse's in-laws). I recognize that there is often an acrimonious relationship between a parent and the in-laws and that this factor may compromise objectivity somewhat. However, when both parents together present their views, one can often obtain an accurate picture—usually somewhere in the middle. There are drawbacks, however, to having a spouse present in an individual interview devoted to collecting information about past history. The presence of another party may compromise the interviewee's freedom to be completely honest. Even the best marriages have some areas which are not spoken about to the other party. Accordingly, I do not routinely bring each spouse in on the other's individual interviews devoted to collecting data about past history. However, in the joint interview with both parents together I may very well bring up subjects from the individual interviews that warrant joint discussion, subjects that might be clarified by getting input from the spouse.

EVALUATION OF PARENTAL CAPACITY
FROM THE RECENT HISTORY
AND PRESENT FUNCTIONING

The Super-parent

It is quite common for parents (especially less adequate ones), at the time when they learn that the custody evaluation will take place, to suddenly become "super-parents." Such parents appreciate that the examiner is going to make inquiries regarding parental capacity and in anticipation of the evaluation may start being a better parent than they ever were before. The other parent will usually describe this to the examiner. And the children too will often notice the difference (unless they are very young). One does well to try to detail these changes and, if possible, get the "transformed" parent's admission (to whatever degree possible) that this indeed occurred. Obviously, the parent whose belated involvement coincides with an impending custody evaluation is certainly less parental than the one who has exhibited ongoing commitment prior to the possibility of there being litigation over custody.

The Parents' Description of the Children

In this phase of the evaluation, I find a useful question to be: "Describe each of your children to me." One wishes to determine whether the parent's description is heavily loaded with negatives such as excessive complaints, derision, and comments that would be ego deflating were the child to hear. One wants, however, not only to focus on negative distortions but positive distortions as well. I believe that the healthy parent distorts somewhat in the positive direction, tends to ignore deficiencies, and views the child as having more assets than the nonparent might observe. To a degree I think this is healthy and a sign of strong parental capacity. We need this extra ego enhancement to serve as a buffer against the undeserved criticism and denigration all of us receive at times. I believe that the child with a parent who is completely objective regarding his (her) assets and liabilities loses the extra support and denial of deficiencies that are vital (to a reasonable degree) to healthy growth and development. However, one must be sure that the parent is not denying deficits to a pathological degree or exaggerating assets to the point where the child is not confronted with liabilities.

If, in response to the aforementioned general question about the children, the parent has not focused on specific examples the therapist should elicit such particulars. One can ask such questions as: "Tell me each of your child's assets and liabilities, his or her strong points and weak points." Or one might ask, "What are the things about each of your children that you like and that you dislike?" If a parent cannot think of significant assets, this is a parental liability. One way in which this manifests itself is the parent's immediate description of a liability. When the examiner again asks the parent to describe *assets,* the parent shifts quickly back to liabilities. A parent might consider a child's refusal to eat what is prepared to be a liability. On further inquiry, the examiner learns that power struggles over eating are related to the parent's inflexibility in allowing the child a reasonable amount of choice before the preparation of a particular food. A related example would be the child whose refusal to practice a musical instrument is described as a liability. The child's wish not to play the instrument is not given reasonable consideration. The problem here is much more that of the parent than of the child. A parent might consider a liability a child's interest in watching an occasional violent movie on television. The parents who protect their children from the so-called detrimental effects of *occasional* exposure to such fare are, in my opinion, only seemingly benevolent and only ostensibly concerned with their children's best interests. I view such an attitude, especially when rigidly enforced, as a manifestation of overprotection: "I would never let *my* child see such a film." And like other types of overprotection, it generally relates more to hostility, manipulation, and insensitivity than it does to love. Elsewhere (Gardner, 1988a) I have elaborated on my views about the effects on children of watching violent programs on television.

The order in which the parent discusses the children may also provide useful information. This is especially the case if the order of presentation is not in accordance with the chronological ages (oldest to youngest or youngest to oldest). The child who is favored may be selected first for presentation and much more detail given about that child than the others. Favoritism of one child over the others is generally a parental defect. The nonfavored children, then, will feel like "second class citizens." And the favored child generally does not feel too happy either with regard to the favoritism. I suspect that such a child senses, at some level, that the parent who places a child in a secondary position is not as strongly parental as one who doesn't. Less favored children generally feel rejected, and the favored child is likely to reason: "If he (she) can reject my sibling(s), she can probably reject me also."

The parent who answers the question "Describe each of your children" with an emphasis on physical characteristics (especially when there is no particular quality worthy of such emphasis) may be doing so in order to avoid touching on psychological issues. These are individuals who are extremely threatened by discussion and revelation of personal, psychological, or emotional factors in human relationships. They are much more comfortable with the concrete. Such an inhibition (seen in extreme form in schizophrenia) is a definite parental liability. This kind of parent serves as a model for the development of such inhibitions in the children and contributes, thereby, to the development of various forms of psychopathology in them. I recall evaluating a father, a physicist, who was litigating for the custody of his children. He was just about incapable of discussing any issue in which emotions might arise. He was a tight, tense, monotonous kind of person who at best would be diagnosed as obsessive-compulsive, but who was more likely a borderline psychotic. (He exhibited no evidences at all of overtly psychotic symptomatology.) He confined himself to physical descriptions of the children and, although I invited him to discuss their personalities in each of three interviews, he found it just about impossible to do so. He stated, "I was never good at talking about emotional things. They confuse me. I don't understand them. I'm much better talking about things I can see, touch, and measure. I guess that's why I became a physicist." In this particular case I recommended that the mother have custody. One important (but certainly not the only) reason for my decision was this significant liability in the father's personality. At no point in the report did I use such terms as "obsessive-compulsive" or "borderline psychotic." (As I will discuss subsequently, the examiner does well to avoid use of diagnostic terminology.)

Rather, I described the aforementioned personality traits and, in addition, noted verbatim the father's own statements regarding these inhibitions. As I repeatedly state in this book, such direct observations and quotations are the most powerful data for supporting the examiner's position in custody litigation and mediation.

The Parents' Description of Their Own Parenting Assets and Liabilities

Whereas in the above section, information about parental capacity is elicited via questions focusing on the children, the questions discussed in this section tend to elicit such information from the parents' discussing their own parenting assets and liabilities. Here, one requests that the parents talk about their own parenting qualities and then discuss the spouse's. One might approach this subject by beginning: "No one is perfect. Everyone has both assets and liabilities, both good points and bad points. With regard to parenting, what do you consider your assets and what do you consider your liabilities?" The question is so worded that it makes it acceptable to describe one's own deficits. In fact, it is so posed that the parent who is inclined to deny any liabilities would find it difficult to do so because such a statement would suggest atypicality.

Most people equate atypicality with unacceptability. A parent involved in a custody evaluation does not generally wish to risk such a designation. Accordingly, most parents are likely to answer this question with a revelation of deficiencies. This is a very important principle in posing questions in the custody evaluation. The general message one wants to get across is: "Everybody exhibits such and such, from time to time. Under what circumstances do you exhibit these qualities?" "Such and such" is generally an undesirable quality which the parent would ordinarily not wish to admit. However, phrased in a context in which the quality is presented as a universal phenomenon, the parent is far less likely to deny sharing this deficit with the rest of humanity.

In assessing the responses to this question, one must attempt to ascertain whether the particular liability is truly one. Most often there is a continuum from the normal to the abnormal, and it may be very difficult, at times, to determine whether or not the parent exhibits the particular deficit to a degree that would be considered pathological. For example, a mother may say that she screams too much at the children. Healthy mothers should *at times* be screaming at their children. A softly worded request will often not work. The blood-curdling shriek has much more clout. Children, very early, differentiate between these two types of parental demands. They generally feel that they can ignore with impunity the type-1 demand. With the type-2, however, they recognize that the parent "means business" and they'd better snap to attention and get moving. Only by getting further information about the *frequency* of the type-2 demands, whether or not they work, whether the children respond most often or ignore them, whether there is follow-through, etc., can one determine if there is a parental deficit in this area. Often the children's input will help the examiner determine whether the particular pattern is indeed a deficiency.

Sometimes a parent will confirm a deficiency described by the spouse or children. For example, one father complained that his wife was more interested in breeding dogs for shows than raising the children. He described numerous weekend absences when she was involved in dog shows. The children, as well, complained that they thought that their mother loved dogs more than she loved them. In response to the personal assets/liabilities question, this mother responded, "I guess I'm into dogs too much. But you know, German shepherds are beautiful animals. But they take a tremendous amount of work. They're not like kids who can grow up by themselves. They're basically still animals." Another mother stated, "I'm just not the mother type. To me, a mother is a cow. She's a tit, nothing more. Maybe I never should have had children. I resented every minute in the house when they were very young. My husband was good about it. He would let me go out a lot, so I wouldn't go crazy. When I was with them, I used to scream too much. I was on top of them for every little thing. I guess it was because I was so frustrated because I had to take care of them. If we could have afforded a full-time maid, they would have been better off and I would have been happier. But, you know, he's no 'father of the year' either. . . ." Another way of posing this question is: "In the course of each of your children's growth and development, what do you consider to be the best things you've done for them?" And "In the course of each of your children's growth and development, what do you consider to be the greatest mistakes you've made?"

Sometimes parents will proudly present what they consider to be a parental asset and not realize that a liability is being described. Quoting such statements provides the most compelling arguments in support of the evaluator's recommendations and is the best protection against the compromises caused by the inclusion of hearsay information. For example, one father described with pride what a moral and ethical life he lived, so much so that he was appointed a deacon of his church. He made it very clear to me that such appointment was only possible after an extensive investigation into his lifestyle and personal practices. He then went on to discuss his views on the use of profanity in the home and the various punishments his children received after he had learned that they had used foul language. These included being deprived of television for three weeks, being confined to their rooms with suppers of bread and water for two weeks, and not being allowed to have friends in the house for a month. He spoke about these punishments with pride and was amazed that I viewed them as parental deficits in my final report.

The examiner should ask the parents' opinion about what the spouse thinks of them with regard to parental capacity. Useful questions are: "What comments has your husband (wife) made about the way you handle the children?" "What does he (she) consider to be your strong points with regard to child rearing?" "What does he (she) consider to be your weak points regarding child rearing?" Some of these criticisms will probably have been mentioned in the initial interview. It is in this phase of the evaluation that one should go into them in depth. Another question that might provide information about the parents' view of their own assets and liabilities with regard to child rearing is: "How would you describe your relationship with each of your children?"

There is another question that I have mixed feelings about, but which can occasionally be useful: "If the judge decided upon a split custody arrangement, that is, one in which the children would be divided between you and your husband, and told you that the decision would be yours regarding the split, what would you do?" One could say that this is an unfair question and that it is extremely unlikely that any judge would do such a thing. Decisions made with a "gun at one's head" are not necessarily the same as those one would make in a freer atmosphere. However, the answer can, on occasion, provide useful information. It is especially useful if the therapist is considering the split custody arrangement. One mother answered: "I've always been better with my daughter than my son. Although I love Jim very much, I often don't know what's going on inside his head. Sara and I are on the same wave-length. I guess I'd choose Sara, but it would tear my heart out if I had to lose Jim. As I told you, I never had tremendous criticisms of Mike as a father, until he met that whore, Gail. . . ." In this case, I ultimately recommended the split custody arrangement with the mother taking her daughter and the father taking the son.

Inquiries Relevant to Child-Rearing Practices in the Infancy-Toddler Period

Responses to Babbling and Cooing   A crucial element in the child's learning to talk is parental feedback. When the child first babbles and coos, it is crucial that there be environmental response. Otherwise, the verbalizations (as primitive as they are) will not be reinforced and it is unlikely that the child will then proceed to more advanced levels of speech. One should inquire into parental feedback to the child's verbalizations from the earliest months of life. The parent who justifies nonresponse with rationalizations such as "it's just babble" or "it was just baby talk and didn't mean a thing" exhibits a parental deficit.

Cuddling   A most valuable question is: "Are (were) your children the kind who liked to come into your bed in the morning, especially on weekends and holidays?" I believe that the psychologically healthy child likes to do this—at least up to the age of five or six (and often even until the pre-pubertal period). Parents with strong maternal and paternal capacity enjoy such morning cuddling immensely. I assume that all children enjoy such cuddling, and a child described as not enjoying it usually reflects the discouragement of one or both parents. If on weekends (I am not saying during the work-week) the parents most often prefer their sleep, don't like the kicking, or find it uncomfortable, a deficit in their parental capacity is strongly suggested. I consider this one of the most valuable questions in the evaluation, and it warrants full discussion.

The reader will note the question is posed in the nonthreatening manner previously described. It suggests that there are two kinds of children: those who like to come into the bed and cuddle in the morning and those who do not. In a sense, this is true. Severely retarded, autistic, and schizophrenic children probably aren't interested in climbing into their parents' bed in the morning. I assume, however, that other children are strongly desirous of such activities and if they are disinclined, it is because their parents have been so. The question implies that the desire arises within the child, and if it is not present it is just a manifestation of common, normal variation and a defect in the parent is not suggested. Accordingly, the parent need not feel embarrassed, guilty, or atypical when answering in the negative.

A number of mothers have reported to me that they have refrained from cuddling with and lying down in bed with their sons after they reach the age of two to three because they had been warned that the boys would develop Oedipus complexes. First, I think that this is very unfortunate and misguided advice by the person who dispensed it. The Oedipal theory is, as the name states, only a *theory*. To recommend that a mother not cuddle with her son after the age of two to three—because he might develop an Oedipus complex—is most unfortunate advice. Such compliance deprives the child of important biological gratifications. The theory holds that such cutaneous stimulation is a sexual act that can induce exaggerated attachment to the mother, inordinate rivalry with the father, and castration anxiety (the father will castrate the boy for his incestuous designs on his mother). Physical contact and sexual seductivity are not necessarily the same. (I am in full agreement that it is psychologically deleterious for a mother to sexually stimulate her son—regardless of his age.) I believe that healthy mothers do not take such misguided warnings seriously, and they continue to cuddle their children—even their sons. Mothers who do subscribe to such advice are probably receptive to it because it provides them with a rationale for removal from physical contact. I believe that we certainly should reduce the amount of physical contact with our children as they get older, but there should be no age at which there is absolutely none. Even when they become adults, embraces are important and healthy. Elsewhere (1986b) I discuss in detail my views on the Oedipus complex.

Another factor in the bed situation that warrants inquiry is that of the parents' own enjoyment of cuddling. If the parents have separate beds it is likely that their desire for cutaneous gratification is small. If the parents don't like to cuddle with one another, it is not likely (but still possible) that they will want to cuddle with their children. Separate beds can, therefore, be an argument against strong parental capacity—but this criterion must be used with caution, because there are exceptions, e.g., severe snoring and marked restlessness.

I ask the mother what kinds of feelings she has when she sees someone else's new baby. If the mother likes cuddling new babies, gets a heartwarming response when doing so, and spontaneously describes such enjoyment, this would be a positive factor. Or I might ask specifically: "Are you the kind of woman who likes to cuddle babies?" Again, the question is so worded that it implies that there are two kinds of women: those who like cuddling babies and those who don't. I ask the question in a way that attempts to imply that I would be equally receptive to a positive or negative response and that neither is preferable to the other. I will also ask fathers this same question. However, the failure of a father to react with a heartwarming response to someone else's newborn baby is not necessarily a parental defect. As I have discussed in detail elsewhere (1988a) I consider females to be superior to males with regard to their genetically programmed parental instincts. Although environmental factors may certainly modify these propensities, they are still powerful. Because of this belief I would not penalize a father who does not respond with the desire to hold an infant not related to him. Consequently, I consider fathers who do respond warmly to babies to demonstrate strong parental capacity and they do get "credit" in my evaluation.

Recreational Activities   I generally inquire into the amount of time the parent spends with the child in recreational and other activities not strictly crucial to child rearing. Does the mother, in addition to preparing meals and taking care of the house, set aside time to sit alone with the children, read books, and play with them? Admittedly, this is not easy for some mothers, especially when there are many children, and for most parents these activities may be a little boring—at times very boring. There is a limit to the number of children's stories that the average adult can tolerate. But the healthy parent enjoys them to some extent, primarily because of the pleasure the child derives. One does well to get specific information about the nature of the interaction between parent and child during the reading activity. Does the child sit on the parent's lap while being read to? Is there cuddling? At bedtime, is the child lulled into sleep with stories? Afterwards, does the parent lie down and cuddle with the child to help him or her fall asleep? If done, these are obviously positive factors.

Similarly, I inquire into the father's involvement with the children when he is not at work, especially with regard to such activities as reading, sports, and doing mutually enjoyable things together. One must take into account that the father, after a full-day's work, may have limited capacity for such involvement. However, his fatigue notwithstanding, most healthy, involved fathers do find gratification from such activities and will give them high priority.

I often ask the question: "What things do you like doing *most* with the children?" If the parent has difficulty answering this question and cannot think of something he or she likes doing most, it reflects negatively. Then I ask: "What things do you like doing *least* with the children?" If the parent denies there is anything that he or she doesn't like doing, that there is so much love and affection that *everything* done with the children is enjoyed (including getting up at three in the morning and changing the diapers), then the examiner knows that the parent is being deceptive. Evaluators should then be somewhat incredulous of answers to other questions and take this duplicity into account when making the final recommendation.

In the context of this question, as well as many others, the examiner should direct attention to parental *patience*. Raising children can be a very frustrating endeavor at times, but devoted parents generally exhibit a degree of patience with their own children that others do not. The devoted parent has the patience to shop for their clothing, bathe them, help them with their homework, teach them, and engage in games that might not be completely stimulating. The involved parent has a toleration for dialogue with the child that others would find boring.

The Child's Illnesses The examiner does well to inquire about parental involvement in the child's illnesses. How upset does each parent get when the child is ill? What priority does illness take for each of the parents? Which parent takes the child to the pediatrician? One must, of course, consider work obligations before making judgments on this question. In the traditional household, the mother is generally much more available than the father to involve herself in the children's illnesses. However, this does not preclude active interest by the father (calls from business or office, visits to the doctor with the child in off hours, and spending time with a sick child after work). Work commitments do not preclude psychological involvement and concern.

Nightmares A useful area of inquiry is a child's nightmares. Most children, especially between the ages of three and nine, have nightmares on occasion. Only when they are severely anxiety provoking and frequent (more than three or four times a week) would I consider them to be pathological. In the context of discussing the nightmare, I will ask a number of questions related to their frequency, content, whether the child awakens the parents, and what is said to the child in response to them. For the purposes of the custody evaluation, I am less interested in the *content* of the nightmares (they are most often stereotyped: a monster, menacing form, etc.) than I am in the person whom the child calls and what is said to the child about them. I want to learn which parent more frequently is called and which parent more commonly responds. I am also interested in the degree of warmth and sensitivity exhibited in the attempt to console and reassure the child. I will also ask the child questions that can provide me with information in this area.

Craving for More Children

If the parent has had all the children that were planned, I ask whether there are still occasional cravings for yet another child. This question is especially useful when the parent is reaching the end of the child-bearing period. The healthy parent generally has such feelings and it is even normal to describe the squelching of such feelings because of their impracticality. It is healthy for a parent to have some lingering feelings of wanting more children after the family is complete. When it is no longer possible or practical to have more children, then these fantasies are gratified through anticipation of grandparenthood. If one elicits these, it speaks for strong parental involvement.

Availability

A father who works full time, or a mother who works full time, is not likely to assume optimally both the obligations of breadwinning and child rearing. The parent who has more time available for the children has an edge over the other in a custody evaluation. Although this may be considered by some to be "unfair," it is nevertheless a reality that must be considered in the custody evaluation. Of course, *quality* as well as *quantity* of the time with the children must be taken into consideration. But even here the parent with the full-time job is likely to be compromised because one parent who is exhausted after a full-day's work is not in a good position to provide optimum parenting. This is probably one of the main drawbacks for fathers trying to gain primary custody of their children, especially when the mother is a homemaker. Although *quality* of parenting must certainly be taken into consideration in all cases, a mother's greater availability is a strong point in her favor when there is a custody conflict in a traditional household.

Often, a working parent will propose one or more surrogates who are (or will be) providing care in their absence. The most common situation in a custody evaluation is the one in which the mother is a homemaker and the father the breadwinner. Recognizing that he must provide parenting figures during his absence he will generally propose caretakers. The quality of care provided by these surrogates must be examined carefully, especially with regard to how they compare with the biological mother.

One father, whom I considered to be the less preferable parent for a variety of reasons related to his personality, was clearly in the less desirable position in the custody evaluation. His ex-wife was home all day, whereas he had a full-time job as an architect. There were two daughters involved, ages seven and nine. He lived in a large apartment house with a swimming pool. His plans were to have the two girls come home from school each day and be taken care of by a group of high school and college girls who worked as lifeguards at the swimming pool. They would rotate their baby-sitting days with their lifeguard duties. He provided me with the names, addresses, and telephone numbers of each of the girls (there were five) and insisted that each one was highly maternal (he had interviewed them himself) and promised to be available for at least a few years.

In my report I described how I considered the plan an impractical one for a number of reasons. I suspected that these teenagers could not be relied upon to dedicate themselves to the care of the children in a predictable fashion. In addition, I considered it extremely unlikely that these girls would be available over a period of years, considering the usual turnover of such positions. One year later, when the case came to trial (a common time lapse), *none* of the five girls was still working at the swimming pool. The plan that this man had submitted to strengthen his case was basically a poor one and, as I had predicted, it was not likely to succeed. In court he "lost points" because of his obvious impracticality. This case provides an excellent example of a man who was "hoist on his own petard." This is an old phrase, not frequently heard these days. A *petard* was a thick iron engine of war that was filled with gun powder and fastened to gates, barricades, etc., in order to blow them up or, in the case of walls, blow holes in them. The engineer who devised and built such instruments was often directly involved in hoisting and placing the device in the most strategic place and then igniting it. The danger in their use was that the engineer who fired the petard would be blown up by the explosion of his own instrument. The term "hoist with his own petard" has come to mean caught in one's own trap or defeated by one's own plot. On occasion, in the course of a custody evaluation, a parent will make a statement, present a plan, or exhibit some kind of behavior thought to reflect well on his (her) parenting capacity. However, without realizing it, the parent is really compromising his (her) position. The parent is motivated to discuss the issue with the examiner from the belief that it is an asset. Such a parent will have thereby, as the old expression goes, been "hoist with his (her) own petard."

Disciplinary Techniques

This is an important area of inquiry from which one can learn much about parental capacity. Again, the questions are best posed in a non-accusatory way and one does well to begin with general questions on the subject and then proceed with more specific ones. A good general opening is: "Most parents have some problems in the upbringing of their children. What problems have you had with yours?" Again, saying "most parents have some problems" gives the parent sanction to discuss those that the child may have as well as parental disciplinary and punitive techniques. Without such acceptability to respond with a description of difficulties, the mother in a custody evaluation would tend to deny them. Depending upon the nature of the problems and how the parent handled them, one tries to learn something about parental capacity. It is important, when inquiring about disciplinary measures, techniques, etc. for the evaluator to attempt to *quantify* the data by getting approximate numbers. One wants to know *how often* a child exhibits a certain form of behavior and *how often* the parent administers disciplinary or punitive measures. Of course, parents do not "keep score" regarding such issues, but examiners must get some idea about frequency, duration, etc. if they are to be in a good position to assess whether such encounters fall within the normal range. Of course, we do not have actual "normative data" regarding how often children require the utilization of disciplinary measures. But examiners must have some criteria and guidelines on this issue if they are to make statements about whether the frequency of punishment is normal or abnormal. And this principle is applicable to other aspects of a custody evaluation such as the frequency that one drinks, beats one's spouse, stays out beyond midnight, etc. Parents may sometimes find such inquiries irritating and resist providing numbers, but the examiner does well to persist, because it is only in this way that one is going to get an accurate idea regarding whether or not the frequency of utilization of disciplinary and punitive measures is in the typical or atypical range.

One can learn still more about the parent-child relationship with the question: "What things do you find you have to punish the children for?" Notice again how the question is posed: "things. . .*you* have to punish the children for." The implication is that punishment is appropriate, that all parents punish their children at times, and the only question is how often the parent is forced to administer punishment. The implication also is that the parent does it only because he (she) gets backed into a corner.

I do not agree with those who believe that in a healthy

household one need not resort to discipline and punishment. (The proponents of this view have either not had children or, if they have had, could not possibly have been truly involved with them.) There are times to punish and discipline a child and implementation of such measures does not necessarily reflect negatively on parental capacity. (In fact, the failure to do so might very well be considered a parental deficiency.) One should learn about the kinds of punishment utilized, the severity, and whether there was cruelty involved. I might say here that spanking, in my opinion, is not necessarily a cruel punishment. There are times and places when, used judiciously and benevolently, it has a place. My personal view is that it should be used mainly in the two-to-four-year period, that the pain inflicted should be primarily psychological, that the site is best confined to the backside, and that it be the punishment of last (not first) resort. Because of the view generally held by laymen that therapists deplore spanking, one does best to load the question with a high degree of sanction: "How often do you find you have to spank the children?" or "Most parents find that at times they have to spank their children. How has this been the case with you?" Such license is especially important for parents who are being evaluated in custody litigation, because they are ever on the alert to censor information that may be detrimental to their legal position.

Another useful question: "Who do you think is generally more effective in getting the children to behave, you or your husband (wife)?" When evaluating the response, one should appreciate that *effectiveness* does not only mean getting results, but utilizing methods that do so in the most humane and reasonable way. The cruel and insensitive parent may get results much more frequently than the "softer" one, but obviously the latter parent's approach is preferable.

If the aforementioned general questions do not provide the examiner with significant information, more specific questions should be used. However, these too must be carefully posed in order to avoid an accusatory implication. Of particular value in this regard is a questionnaire designed by A. Gardner, et al. (1980) (Appendix VIII). Although designed for research purposes, some of the questions from this protocol are useful in the evaluation of maternal and paternal capacity. For each question the parent is asked how he or she would handle the situation in which the child has exhibited a particular type of undesirable behavior. Following the parent's response, the interviewer requests a second method if the first doesn't work, and again a third if the second didn't work as well.

The questions are of particular value because they depict situations in which all parents find themselves with their children, and there is no single "right" response. The questions may put the parent "on the spot," but the answers can be very revealing. Often the first response will be a stereotyped one that the parent suspects is the anticipated "correct" answer. The second and third choice reactions are then likely to be more revealing and useful. It is often difficult for the parent to know exactly what kind of a response would reflect parental deficiency. The instrument is analogous to the Rorschach Test with regard to the examinee's ignorance of the significance of an answer. Of course, the parent is in a slightly better position with regard to understanding the significance of a response to questions here than to Rorschach responses, but there is still a significant element of doubt.

For example, question 10 asks "_____ has broken a very important possession of yours. When you're asking for an explanation, he (she) denies having done it. You know he (she) is lying. What would you do?" The parent may respond, "I'd tell him that if he tells me the truth I won't punish him." This is a common response and the parent may believe that the examiner is impressed here with the parent's benevolence and good sense. However, such a parent may not appreciate that this method of handling lying encourages further lies because the parent is not providing meaningful deterrents to their repetition. The child is essentially being taught that all one need do is confess that one has lied and there are no repercussions. No social system could possibly survive if judges were not to impose restrictions or inflict punishments if the alleged criminals were to confess.

Question 11: "_____ refuses to go to bed when you

tell him (her) to. What would you do?" A parent may respond with a restrictive or punitive answer such as "I tell him that he can't watch television tomorrow if he doesn't go to sleep or that he doesn't get ice cream tomorrow if he doesn't go to sleep." Although such an answer might be reasonable after the third attempt during the same evening, the healthier parent tries to lure the child to bed, and then to sleep, by such seductive activities as reading, cuddling in bed together, listening to soft music, singing lullabies together, etc.

Question 16: "You are in a store. _____ reaches up on the counter, takes something, hides it in his (her) pocket, and walks away. What would you do?" The healthy parent, in my opinion, takes the child back to the store and either gets the child to return it to the owner or returns it to the owner in the child's presence. In either case, the child is made to suffer a certain amount of embarrassment over the transgression. The parent who merely returns the object, without informing the storekeeper of the theft, is depriving the child of an important learning experience. Such a parent is teaching a child that such transgressions are without significant repercussions. To punish the child in a reasonable way for the theft is certainly an acceptable punitive measure. However, it is preferable that the person upon whom the "crime" has been perpetrated be involved directly with the child while he (she) is being required to make amends.

I recently had occasion to use the scale in a very effective way. Two parents were litigating for the custody of an eight-year-old boy. The father claimed that the mother was significantly impaired in her child-rearing capacities because of cerebral impairment. The mother suffered brain injury at the age of 15 in an automobile accident. She claimed that there were no residual cognitive problems, although she admitted to the obvious mild left hemiparesis that persisted. The father claimed that one of the manifestations of her brain injury was her inability to deal with situations in a complex fashion and her tendency to persist with the first option proposed by others or provided by her. I administered the A. Gardner protocol to both parents. The instrument demonstrated beautifully the mother's impairment in this area.

For the first question of each item she was able to give a response that was sometimes reasonable and sometimes not. However, when it came to answering the second and third questions— regarding what she would do *then* if plan A did not work, and then what she would do if plan B did not work—she found it almost impossible to come up with different options. In contrast, not only were the father's first responses more appropriate than his wife's, but he was able to draw from a much larger repertoire of subsequent options. The verbatim statements provided by each parent proved to be very valuable in the courtroom and played an important role in the judge's deciding to designate the father as the primary custodial parent.

Many of the questions in the A. Gardner protocol are generally referable to the two-to-five-year-old child. There are other questions I have formulated that I have found useful for older children. As is true for the A. Gardner protocol, I try to get one or two alternatives, if the first suggested response doesn't work. Each question essentially asks parents how they would deal with a particular childhood problem. They are all problems for which there is no single good answer. One basically wants to know whether the parent will handle the situation malevolently or benevolently, reasonably or irrationally. Some sample questions:

What's the best way for a parent to handle a child's temper tantrums?

What would you do if your child cheated while playing a game with you?

What do you do with a child who sucks his (her) thumb?

How do you handle a child who uses profanity to a parent?

What do you do with a child who uses profanity in front of a parent, profanity that is not directed toward the parent?

How do you handle the situation when a child refuses to finish supper?

What's the best thing to do when a parent catches a child involved in sex play with a neighbor's child?

How do you handle children's fighting, especially when it becomes fierce?

What do you do when a child steals and then lies about having stolen?

What's the best thing to do when a child refuses to do homework?

What's the best way to handle a child who refuses to do household chores, such as taking out the garbage or making the bed?

What is the best thing for parents to do if they find out that their 14- or 15-year-old daughter is pregnant?

For each of these questions, the examiner might wish to make it more personal and direct the question to the parent's actual experiences in handling his (her) particular child with regard to the aforementioned problems. Sometimes the direct reference to the parent's own child is useful. On other occasions, such a direct reference may not be applicable. In such cases, the general speculation on how the parent would handle the situation, if he (she) were to have a child who did such a thing, can also provide valuable information. If the parent responds with a statement like "My child would never do such a thing" or "I've never had any such experiences," the examiner should encourage the parent to *speculate.* Some of the responses that are generally inappropriate (and thereby reflect negatively on parental capacity) would include: failure to punish, when punishment is warranted; bribing; excessively harsh punishments; prolonged isolations; prolonged withdrawal of affection; prolonged ignoring of the child; excessive reliance on reasoning and getting the child to understand; empty threats; and, delegating the power to punish to another person. Responses that generally suggest good parental functioning include: distracting the child; short-term withdrawal of privileges; short-term isolation; short-term withdrawal of affection; parental expression of disappointment; a short explanation which attempts to help the child understand; firm command; reasonable threat, especially when there is a high likelihood of follow-through; and recognition of praise and reward as useful preventive measures. The reader who is interested in a detailed description of the disciplinary techniques that I consider preferable for younger children, might wish to refer to the Reward, Discipline, and Punishment chapter of my book on child-rearing practices (Gardner, 1973a). In my *Psychotherapy with*

Adolescents (1988a) I describe disciplinary and punitive measures that I consider warranted for youngsters in that age bracket.

Encouragement of Healthy Peer Relationships

One should ask about each parent's receptivity to the child's involvement with friends. A parent's attitude toward the children's having friends in the home can provide significant information about parental capacity. The healthy parent recognizes the importance of such visits and is willing to tolerate the discomforts attendant to them. The healthy parent recognizes that noise, mess, discomfort, disruption, fighting, and other annoyances are a small price to pay for the advantages accrued to the child by having friends. One father stated, "The house is no place for children to play. Kids just make a mess. Also, I don't like kids on my lawn because it kills the grass. Kids should play in the street where they belong." This response, of course, is quite revealing of this parent's significant deficiencies as a father. Furniture and grass to him are far more important than his child's psychological development. One mother responded to the question about friends in the house with this response: "My parents never let me have friends in the house. They always wanted it very quiet and were afraid that things would be broken. I promised myself that I would never treat my children that way, and I haven't. I always welcome their friends and treat them very nicely—even when it's trouble. I can't ever remember sending a friend out of the house." The children corroborated their mother's statement.

The examiner does well to inquire about birthday parties. An impaired parent hesitates to make them because of the mess and trouble. If the parents are living separately at the time of the evaluation (the usual case) one does well to find out how they deal with birthday parties. Some parents will make two parties, one at each home. This is a perfectly acceptable plan and does not generally reflect any deficiencies on the part of each parent. In fact, such a plan generally reflects positively on both with regard to parental capacity. If, however, the children's friends are all in one neighborhood (usually the mother's) then an inquiry into the father's participation in the birthday party can be useful. If, for example, the father wishes to come to the marital home in order to attend the party, and the mother refuses, then it is likely that she is revealing a parental deficiency. Unless she can provide compelling evidence that the father will disrupt the party, or in other ways be a detrimental influence, her rejection of him for this occasion is a deficiency on her part. It suggests that her rage at him is so great and her desire to wreak vengeance on him so formidable that she is blinding herself to the benefits to be derived by the child from the father's presence at this important event.

In recent years people have been making videotapes of such parties. Some parents bring in these tapes for the examiner to view in order to support their position in the custody conflict. Or the parent might bring videotapes to prove parental capacity during visitation. I generally discourage examiners from spending significant time viewing such tapes. Clearly, the parent who brings them is going to select just those tapes that reflect well on that parent and the other parent could similarly provide such tapes. Considering the time and expense expended in viewing them, they generally are a waste of time for the examiner and a waste of money for the parents. If, however, a parent provides a tape that gives compelling evidence that a certain deficiency is present, then, of course, such a tape could be extremely valuable. Whereas in earlier years courts were somewhat unreceptive to the introduction of audiotapes (because of the potential for altering) they have been more receptive to videotapes because they are more difficult to alter.

The examiner should inquire about what efforts the parents make to bring the children to others, especially in situations where they may not be readily available. For example, if the child lives in a neighborhood where there are few if any playmates, one should ask about what efforts each parent has made to bring the children to distant friends and make appointments for them. Of course, in most traditional homes, the mother has far more opportunity for such transport than the father. One mother in this situation stated that she would love to have her child visit other homes, but she was afraid to drive, which resulted in the child's visiting far less than he might have otherwise. This mother's driving phobia was only one manifestation of a generalized dependency problem on her husband, and it was only one of the many ways in which her psychological problems were compromising her child's growth and development. Overprotective parents will often consider their children "too young" to visit the homes of others, at ages when other parents feel quite comfortable with such arrangements.

It is useful to inquire into the friendships that the parents themselves have, both as a couple and individually. The parent who has no social relationships is likely to be impaired as a parent. One could argue that there are parents who are so involved with their children that their failure to have friends provides them with more opportunity for time with their children. However, I believe that the person who cannot relate meaningfully to other adults has significant personality problems and that these are likely to affect one's child-rearing capacity. One cannot serve as a good model for children if one cannot relate to adults, because the ultimate aim of child rearing is to help the child become an independent functioning adult who can relate well to other adults. In addition, the particular personality problems that compromise the parent's capacity to relate to other adults are also likely to be filtered down to the children. For example, the parent who is distrustful (not necessarily paranoid) is likely to communicate this quality to the children. The parent who is anxious in social situations is basically communicating the message that there is something to be afraid of in one's relationships with others. Accordingly, a detailed inquiry into the reasons why the parent does not have social relationships can very quickly bear on the issue of parental capacity. Asking questions about what each parent does on Saturday night is a good starting point for this inquiry.

Attitudes Toward Children's Use of Profanity

The parent's attitude regarding the children's using profanity can provide important information related to parental capacity. I believe that profanity is one of humanity's greatest inventions. Of the various ways with which an individual can express hostility, what could be more innocuous than using certain words that the society has designated for this purpose? To the best of my knowledge, there is no language that does not have such words. There is no question that they play an important civilizing role. It is reasonable to speculate that without them people would have to resort to more damaging ways of expressing their resentments. This basic concept is epitomized in the old aphorism: "Sticks and stones may break my bones, but names will never harm me."

The healthy parent generally recognizes the basic validity of what I have just said and will not be particularly punitive when the children's profanity is confined to the street with their friends. The healthy parent, as well, will generally react negatively to the child's use of profanity in the home, especially when it is directed toward the parents. However, such a parent will differentiate between words and deeds and is much more likely to discipline the latter than the former. A certain amount of reasonable castigation for the use of profanity against a parent is a norm in our society ("How dare you speak that way to your mother!"). I think this is justified in that such disapprobation helps preserve such words' utilization as an innocuous hostile weapon. It is a social contribution of the highest order and each parent should play his (her) role in this important contribution to the perpetuation of civilized society. Seemingly liberal parents—with a strong commitment to the principle of egalitarianism between parents and children—lose sight of this obvious benefit of parental disapproval of profanity. In fact, I often say that the person who invented dirty words should have received the primitive equivalent of a Nobel Peace Prize. To allow the free use of these words would soon cause them to lose their clout as aggressive vehicles and the child might then have to resort to genuinely harmful methods of hostile expression.

I generally open the topic with the question: "What do you think about children using profanity?" With the aforementioned guidelines, the parental response can be put in perspective. One father answered, "Those words make me sick to my stomach. They make me vomit. I can't believe it when my son uses them. I tell him he's a bum, an ignoramus, and that he's a good-for-nothing. But even that doesn't stop him." I considered this response to reflect an extremely punitive attitude. This was only one way in which he was contributing to his son's severe self-esteem problem. Such denigration for the use of profanity was clearly unwarranted and reflected a definite parental deficit.

A mother once answered about her son, "It's good for him to get anger out of his system. So when he gets angry and uses dirty words, I encourage him to tell me more." This mother, although seemingly "enlightened" and "modern," was doing her son a disservice. She was not making her social contribution to the perpetuation of the "sanctity" of profanity. In addition, she was not helping her child adjust well in a world that does not subscribe to her position. Accordingly, she was contributing to her child's being viewed as atypical and subjected to unnecessary and avoidable ridicule. Both of these parents exhibited parental deficiencies with regard to the use of profanity. One was far too rigid and the other far too free. As is true with most things, the moderate position is generally the preferable.

Commitment to the Educational Process

The parents should be evaluated regarding their commitment to the educational process. In our modern technological society a good education is crucial. A central element in the child's commitment to and motivation for education is the parents' *genuine* commitment, not their *professed* commitment (Gardner, 1990, in press). The vast majority of parents will claim that they are very interested in their children's doing well in school. But the degree to which they will involve themselves in the child's education varies greatly. I am not referring here simply to physical involvement, but to psychological as well. A girl, for example, comes home from kindergarten and proudly demonstrates to her father that she has learned how to write her name. One father responds: "Don't bother me now, I'm watching the ballgame. Would you please get me another beer." Another responds: "This is terrific! Does your mother know? I'm going to hang this on the refrigerator and we'll show grandma and grandpa when they come on Sunday." One wants to learn about each parent's receptivity to helping the child with homework. The children themselves often give valuable information in this area. The parents who essentially do the homework for their children, to protect them from receiving a low grade, are generally doing more harm than good. Such parents are probably overprotective in other areas as well. The parent who is always fighting with the child while "helping" with the homework is probably doing the child a disservice.

We all gain a certain amount of vicarious gratification through our children. Our children can serve to compensate for deficiencies and failures that we ourselves may have suffered. A reasonable amount of this need for gratification through our children is normal and healthy. It provides them with support and encouragement for their own growth and development and contributes, thereby, to the perpetuation and enhancement of civilized society. In fact, I often say that if not for this phenomenon we might all still be living in caves. However, when it becomes an obsession with the parent then the pressures and coercions are unhealthy.

In addition to an inquiry into the parents' involvement in the formal academic program, one does well to learn about involvement in other aspects of the school situation. I cannot overemphasize the importance of an inquiry into this area. One wants to know about attendance during "open-school week." The parent who is "too busy" is insensitive to the importance of this school visit to the child. One should also ask about conferences with the teacher. It is unfortunate, but most teachers state that generally only one parent (usually the mother) attends such conferences even though the teacher may be willing to accommodate a father by coming in very early in the morning. The most important school activities about which to make inquiries are school plays, dances, concerts, and other artistic performances. Children often work many weeks in their preparation and they are extremely important to the child. Attendance at such activities should be high priority for the parents. The examiner does well to take the firm position that there are very few acceptable "excuses" for not attending them. A few areas are highly sensitive indicators of general parental capacity and attendance at school performances is one of them. In fact, I do not recall a parent who was uninterested in attending such performances to be ultimately the one whom I recommended for primary custody of the children. This is not to say that such a defect should automatically deprive a parent of the examiner's recommendation. (If that were the case, then all we would have to do would be to ask this one question.) I am only saying that this particular interest is, in my experience, highly correlated with parental capacity.

Interest in Enrichment

The healthy, involved parent is not only interested in the child's academic and social life, but is interested in enriching the child as well. By enrichment I refer to the wide variety of experiences that could make a child more interesting, both to himself (herself) and others. One should inquire into parental involvement in such activities as music lessons, dance, visits to museums, visits to historical sites and other places of interest, and involvement in sports. One must be careful to differentiate between the parent who encourages these activities out of duty, with little commitment or conviction, and the one who has a genuine interest in and enjoyment of these pursuits. The examiner should inquire as to whether the child is being coerced into lessons as opposed to being facilitated and encouraged. Of course, many of these activities are expensive and not available to all. However, even the poorest children can avail themselves of many of them if the parents are willing to take the trouble to find out which facilities in the community will make them available.

I am a strong proponent of the summer camp experience for children. In the earlier years of childhood (approximately five to seven) I strongly recommend day-camp experiences and in the later years (eight through thirteen) I suggest sleep-away camp. It is an ideal way for children to take their first steps toward independence. In a sense, we are teaching our children to become independent of us from the earliest years of life. Sleeping over at a friend's house is another important step in this direction and summer camp also serves this purpose. The fun and games serve to assuage and distract the child from separation anxieties. Dependency on parents can be shifted to dependency on the counselor and other camp administrators. And this serves as a transition from dependency on the parents to full independence. There are parents who rationalize not sending their children by claiming that those who do so are neglectful and are using the summer camp as a way of getting rid of their children. Although this certainly may be the case, it need not be. Although parents can certainly enjoy the vacation from the children that summer camp allows, the sleep-away camp experience can be extremely salutary for children. Committed parents are willing to make reasonable sacrifices for it because they appreciate its importance.

Children Talk

We have come a long way from the Victorian tradition of the after-dinner conversation in which the men retire to talk business and politics, and the women separately discuss their children and homes. I think, however, that there are residua of this tradition in modern society and that healthy women still like to talk about their children with other women. I ask the mother if she enjoys talking about her children with other mothers. The woman who says, "I prefer talking to the men. I have enough of children all day long" may be healthy, but she may also be reflecting some deficiency in her maternal capacity. In our society, new job opportunities for women notwithstanding, more men are still deeply committed to and spend more time with their jobs or businesses than women. Accordingly, they generally have significantly more investment in the extra-domestic world than their wives. The healthy man, however, still enjoys spending some time talking about his children. However, not to be interested in doing this, as much as his wife, should not be viewed as a defect at this time.

Wallet and Purse Pictures of the Children

In the initial session with the parents I generally ask them if they have any pictures of the children. This question is preferably asked in the first session when I have the greatest justification for asking to see such pictures. I might even provide a rationale with a comment regarding the fact that it would facilitate my talking about the children if I could see a picture or two. Although this is certainly a fringe benefit of the request, my main reason is far more important. The involved parent generally carries such pictures and will speak of the children with pride when showing them. Accordingly, carrying such a picture in a wallet or purse weighs in the parent's favor; whereas failure to do so might be considered a negative—but certainly not strongly so. If a picture is produced, one tries to get a sense of the amount of pride the parent has when showing it. One may make a positive comment in order to elicit such a response in the modest, for example: "They're very good looking children." One then observes whether there is a reaction of pride and beaming. The parent who looks at the examiner with a blank stare after such a comment does not know the pride experience (but that parent is not likely to have a picture anyway).

Dreams About the Children

I ask about dreams the parent may have had about each of the children. I must emphasize that this is not a very accurate source of information, considering our present state of ignorance regarding the meaning of dreams. It is often very difficult to understand the meaning of a dream of a person who is in analysis. It is even more difficult to be certain about the meaning of a dream of a person who is almost a stranger. If the mother has repetitious dreams in which the child is dying, or falling out of a window, or having an accident, the chances are that this reflects unconscious hostility. *Occasional* dreams and preoccupations of the aforementioned type are within the norm, in my opinion, and should not be considered a negative factor in determining parental capacity. I must warn the examiner here that even if the parent falls into the category of having dreams that are considered reflective of low parental capacity, one should be extremely cautious regarding including this finding in a court report. As I will discuss in detail in subsequent sections of this book, using information based on projective techniques is extremely risky in custody evaluations, especially when giving testimony in court. Dream interpretation is very much in this category. The examiner may wish to use this information to confirm other conclusions, but should be very careful about including dream interpretations as a major argument in reaching conclusions.

Parental Psychopatholgy

The examiner should evaluate, to some degree, for the presence of psychopathology not directly related to parental capacity. Many forms of psychiatric disturbance can interfere with parental capacity. These include anxiety, hysteria, depression (with or without elation), obsessive-compulsivity, hypochondriasis, and of course, various kinds of psychotic states. I must warn evaluators here that they should not (I repeat *not*) include a diagnosis in any written report of any of the people interviewed in a custody evaluation associated with litigation. Basically, the court is asking who is the preferable parent. It is not likely that a diagnostic label is going to add a significant amount of information here. Is the schizophrenic a better or worse parent than a psychopath? Is the hysteric a better or worse parent than an obsessive-compulsive? These are absurd questions. In addition to comparative diagnoses being of little value, they open the examiner to criticism. For example, the cross-examining attorney might ask the examiner to define the word *schizophrenia*. Following the presentation of the definition, the attorney may produce a standard psychiatric dictionary. The attorney may then ask the examiner if he (she) recognizes that particular dictionary as one of the authoritative texts in the field. The likelihood is that the examiner will say *yes*. The lawyer will then read the definition of schizophrenia provided by that volume. Even if the examiner were to be an internationally famous authority on the subject, and even though the definition in the dictionary might have been written by a librarian, the court is likely to view the written definition as having greater validity than the examiner's verbal one. (After all, everyone knows that things in print are more likely to be true than things that are said!) Accordingly, there is much to lose, and little if anything to gain, by using diagnostic labels.

Such displays in the courtroom make a mockery of psychiatry. I often say that "God forgot to read DSM-III-R before he put human beings down on earth." Not even the most astute diagnosticians are likely to agree about which diagnostic label best fits a particular person. Accordingly, providing diagnoses only opens up a can of worms in the courtroom and the examiner does well not to provide attorneys with this time-consuming and wasteful ploy in their adversary games. If I am asked on the stand what a person's diagnosis is, I will refuse to answer the question and claim that it is not relevant to this evaluation. If given an opportunity to explain (sometimes I am and sometimes not) I will speak about how symptoms, behavioral patterns, and a variety of other behavioral manifestations are the criteria on which I decide who is the preferable parent. I describe how diagnostic labels do not provide significant information in this regard and can be a waste of time to focus on in the courtroom. Accordingly, my refusal to provide a diagnosis is in the service of courtroom efficiency. And even when conducting a mediation evaluation, diagnostic labels may be misleading and obfuscating. They may divert all participants into discussions that are a waste of time and money.

The examiner should describe those symptoms and behavioral manifestations that interfere with parental capacity—regardless of the diagnostic disorder of which they are a manifestation. For example, in one report I stated, "A family interview was conducted with the Smith family on September 23, 1978. As the parents and the two girls entered the room, Jane (age 3) tripped on the threshold. She fell down and began to cry. She quickly got up, however, and ran to her father and put her head in his lap. As she sobbed he caressed her head and made reassuring comments such as 'Don't worry baby, everything will be all right' and 'Daddy will kiss it and make it all better.' Following a few such kisses and caresses Jane stopped crying, but remained sitting next to her father while her head rested against his arm. While this was going on Mrs. Smith sat staring into space, seemingly oblivious to what was going on. This observation tends to confirm Mr. Smith's allegation that, when he leaves his home in the morning, his wife is sitting in the living room watching television and when he returns at the end of the day, she is still in the same position, with no evidence that the house has been taken care of or the children supervised to any significant degree." As I am sure the reader can appreciate, such descriptions have far more clout than the diagnostic term schizophrenia. It is very difficult, if not impossible, for a cross-examining attorney to do anything with such a statement. This attorney will just have to let it rest as one of the strong negatives against his (her) client and hunt for other issues on which to focus.

Another example of the superiority of the substantive description over the diagnostic label: "In each of my three individual interviews with Mrs. S. and in each of the two family interviews she rambled, at times to the point of incoherence. In response to a question she would often start on the topic, but then quickly verbalize a series of loose associations that became increasingly unrelated to the issue under discussion. In each of the individual interviews she asked the examiner whether the conversation was being tape recorded. I informed her that I never tape record without permission. She insisted that I place my tape recorder in front of her, without an inserted cassette, so that she could be reassured that I was not deceiving her. Even after I did this, she searched under the chairs and couch in order to reassure herself that I was still not taping the conversations with a hidden tape recorder. I consider her rambling to the point of incoherence to represent a grave problem in her communication with her husband and her children, and this was demonstrated many times over in the family interviews. Her suspiciousness is likely to engender in her children a similar attitude toward others, and this will interfere with their interpersonal relationships." At no point did I refer to this woman as a paranoid schizophrenic, which she clearly was. To do so would have invited unnecessary and time-wasting questions in the courtroom.

Others have come forth with the same caveat. D. B. Saxe (1975), for example, warns against the use of diagnoses in custody proceedings and discusses how misleading they can be and how they may complicate rather than elucidate the issues under consideration. He points out how the use of such diagnoses as *schizophrenia* or *psychosis* may mislead a naive court into believing that these disorders are invariably associated with inability to function as a parent. D. L. Bazelon (1974), a well-known judge, deplores the psychiatrist's penchant for diagnostic labeling and describes how it can narrow options for patients once they have been put into a particular niche by a diagnosis.

Involvement with Grandparents

A healthy parent recognizes the importance of the children's having good relationships with their grandparents. Child therapists do not give the relationships between grandparents and grandchildren the attention they deserve. Although parents will, on occasion, idealize their children, grandparents are much more likely to do so. They have fewer of the irritating and frustrating experiences that compromise such idealization. The enhanced positive regard that grandparents have for their grandchildren contributes to building the children's self-esteem. In addition, it serves to help them tolerate and more effectively deal with the inevitable criticisms (sometimes undeserved) and rejections (often unwarranted) that all of us suffer, as children and as adults.

Accordingly, grandparents serve as an important buffer. A strongly parental parent will recognize this and do everything to foster good relationships with the grandparents, even after divorce. Inquiry about the grandparents should not only be conducted with the parents, but with the children as well. The children should be asked about the grandparents in an attempt to ascertain which ones are the more involved and have better relationships with the children. In addition, one can often learn from the children which parent makes greater efforts to foster good relationships between grandparents and the children. Of course, there are some grandparents who are strongly parental and others who are not. One must therefore try to learn whether a poor relationship between a grandparent and a grandchild is due to grandparental defect or parental discouragement of the relationship (or both). It is important for the examiner to appreciate that I am not presenting this as a strong point in the evaluation, merely one that should be taken into consideration.

I believe that the better parent usually has better parents himself (herself). This should not be surprising. Healthier grandparents are going to produce healthier children, so the preferable parent in the custody evaluation is more likely to have more highly parental parents than the nonpreferred parent. It has been my experience that in the large majority of the custodial cases in which I have been involved, the parent I ultimately recommended to have primary custody has had more parental parents than the nonpreferred parent.

Most often the grandparents will support their own children, i.e., the mother's parents support her and the father's parents support him. On occasion, however, a grandparent will support the son- or daughter-in-law over his (her) own child. When this occurs the examiner has very powerful data in the evaluation. If a grandparent believes that a son- or daughter-in-law would provide better care for the grandchildren than his (her) own son or daughter then a strong statement is being made. For example, one grandparent stated, "Doctor, I love my son very much. However, as much as I love him, I don't believe that it would be better for my grandchildren for them to live with him. It's much better for them to live with my daughter-in-law. This divorce is tearing my heart out. If the children end up living most of the time with him it's just going to cause more trouble. He just doesn't know how to take care of the children as well as she does." Grandparents who take such a position must override the inevitable biases in support of their own child that are likely to operate in life and in custody conflicts as well. Generally, merely including the grandparental statement in one's report is enough to have an important effect on the court's deliberations. On occasion, however, it may be necessary for the grandparents to appear in court. I am generally reluctant to advise such an appearance because of the obvious loyalty conflicts. Even though the nonsupported child-parent is aware of the grandparental preference for the son- or daughter-in-law, testifying in court adds an additional loyalty conflict for the grandparents which should be avoided, if possible.

Visitation and Parental Capacity

For simplicity of presentation, I will generally refer to the father as the visiting parent and the mother as the custodial parent. Even though we are living at a time when fathers are gaining custody more frequently than in the past, mothers are still the primary custodial parents in the vast majority of households. The reader should appreciate, however, that when I refer to the father as the visiting parent, the issues discussed will be valid for visiting mothers as well, unless otherwise specified.

It is useful to ask each parent what visitation schedule he (she) would provide for the other if granted primary custody. The healthy parent recognizes the importance of reasonably ample visitation time for the other parent. The parent who recommends an insignificant amount of visitation (when there is no justification for such) reveals a parental defect. If, however, there is a reasonable risk of abuse then, of course, restricted and even supervised visitations may be warranted. And it is the examiner's job to assess the degree of such risk and to make appropriate visitation recommendations in such cases. Parents who are blinded by rage may often express their animosity by preferring an inordinately restricted visitation arrangement. They are so angry that they have to blind themselves to the potentially detrimental effects on the children of their stringent visitation schedule.

In a war, it is a generally accepted practice to place guards at one's borders and to be suspicious of any strangers who may try to cross them. Specifically, one usually wants to prevent spies and saboteurs from entering one's country and occupied territories. One wants to protect oneself from those who would carry out information to the enemy. In addition, one wants to protect oneself from those who would enter with the intent of destruction. In the war called Divorce, we have a unique situation with regard to those who may cross the border. Whereas the enemies (the parents) have little or no access to one another's territory, the children have free access without being interrogated or searched. In fact, they are most often literally "met with open arms." They serve thereby as convenient spies and saboteurs if either one or both parents wishes to use them as such. And they often are so used.

The two most important issues about which parents wish to gain information are money and sex. The father wants to know if mother's support money is indeed being spent on the children or squandered frivolously. The mother is interested in knowing if the father is squandering money on dates and other "indulgences" while claiming that his funds available for alimony and support are extremely limited. Although both parents may be extremely antagonistic toward one another, there is most often residual affection and sexual attraction. Accordingly, although separated or divorced, there may still be significant jealousy regarding involvement with new sexual partners. The curiosity associated with such jealousy can be satisfied by information provided by the children. Some parents, although not actively trying to extract such data from the children, may find it impossible to avoid hearing about these matters. Johnny returns from a weekend visit with his father and speaks glowingly to his mother about Fran: "Dad's new girl friend, Fran, is terrific. She makes the best pizzas I ever ate and her Hamburger Helper is terrific. And you should see the beautiful gold watch Dad bought her. It has jewels and everything!" During a weekend visit, Jimmy excitedly tells his father about Dan, his mother's new friend, who has moved into the home: "Dan's a great guy. He's a lot of fun to be with. Because he doesn't work, he has lots of time to play ball with me when I come home from school." There are few parents who could restrain themselves from indulging their curiosity further in such circumstances.

Accordingly, when trying to assess whether a parent is utilizing the children as spies, one does well to try to determine whether it is an active process or a passive one, whether the children are being "briefed" and "debriefed," or whether the parents are more in the category of the passive recipient of the inevitable information that will come their way. It may be difficult for the examiner to ascertain exactly in which category a particular parent lies, but it is worthwhile to attempt to do so. Sometimes inquiry of the children can help in the assessment of this issue.

Using the children to perpetrate "inside jobs" behind the enemy lines is quite tempting. Mother calls father and, in a state of impotent frustration, begs him to speak to the boys in order to use his authority to get them to stop maltreating her and to be more cooperative. Father responds: "They're all yours, baby. You asked me to leave the house. I didn't want to go. You can't have it both ways. You're on your own, kid" (hangs up). Such a father is so desirous of vengeful gratification that he is blinding himself to the effects of such vengeance on his children. He is so pleased with the opportunity they are providing him to wreak vengeance on his former wife, that he does not seem to appreciate that by abrogating his authority, he is contributing to the development of behavior problems in his children. They need his conscience to help them form theirs, and this is especially the case in the situation where the mother appears to have some impairment in exerting her authority. Although this mother's inability to control her children is a parental impairment, their father's active utilization of them as weapons against his former wife is a greater impairment. In one case I was involved in a father got his

10-year-old boy to secretly tape record his mother's telephone conversations with her attorney and man friend. Although the court would not permit the tapes to be brought in as evidence, the information so gained proved very valuable to the father in his litigation.

Although a rigid visitation schedule is often outlined in the separation agreement, a certain amount of parental flexibility is still necessary for the well being of the children. The evaluator should try to determine each parent's degree of flexibility with regard to the visitation schedule. The parent who rigidly subscribes to it may be doing so as a way of thwarting the other and is probably not giving proper attention to the needs of the children. This is illustrated in statements such as, "The divorce decree says you get them Fridays at 6:00 p.m. I don't give a damn what you'll be late for, you're not getting them one second before that. And if you don't have them back here by 6:00 p.m. on Saturday, I'm going to call my lawyer about stopping you from seeing the kids." A mother who interferes with the visitation, either covertly or overtly, is less sensitive to the children's needs for a good relationship with their father and is thereby compromised in her parental capacity. Such a mother may "forget" to have the children ready and so may thereby thwart the father. On other occasions she may "forget" to bring them home, and he may be kept waiting for them for an indeterminate amount of time—much to his frustration. There are some mothers who will retaliate for their husband's failure to fulfill financial obligations by withholding visitation. Sometimes courts will support such withholding. Although I am not justifying a man's not fulfilling his financial obligations to his wife and children, this is not a justifiable retaliation. I am fully sympathetic with the privations that such withholding of money can entail. However, to use the children as weapons in this conflict will inevitably cause them psychological distress. It is a tempting but injudicious and misguided method of getting vengeance. Requesting the court to garnishee the father's salary or attach his property is a far more reasonable course and is not likely to have detrimental effects on the children.

Soon after the separation the father usually visits with the children alone. However, he may start to combine dating with visitation. This may not be a manifestation of any insensitivity or neglect, but rather the result of the limited free time he has available. Symbolic of what happens on such occasions is the shifting of the children from the front to the back seat of the car. Previously they sat in the front with him and engaged in active conversation. Now they may find themselves in the back watching the father engage in lively conversation with his date. This can be very painful to them, and the sensitive father is careful to include the children as much as possible when he does combine a date with the visitation. Generally, the father does well to reserve such combined visits for involvements with an important person. If there is a "parade" of dates, a new person for each visit, this is likely to be detrimental to the children. Elsewhere (1977b, 1979b) I have described in detail what I consider to be the detrimental effects of children's being exposed to a parent's parade of dates.

Many fathers, especially in the period immediately following the separation, will indulge their children significantly during visitation. Visits then may consist of an endless round of entertainment and recreational activities. Homework may be neglected as well as household chores and the normal routine of everyday living. Often, guilt alleviation is the primary motivation. On occasion, such a father may be trying to compensate for feelings of parental inadequacy produced by the divorce. In addition, the father may be trying to compete with the mother for the children's affection by proving that he is the better parent. Whatever the motivations, such a practice is detrimental to the children. It is indulgent and does not provide them with the proper balance of activities—the pleasant *and* the unpleasant, work *and* play. And when there is a custody conflict, additional motives may be operative, e.g., bribing the children into choosing the father as the preferable parent. The examiner should be aware of all of these factors that may contribute to the "good guy" father syndrome, especially when he was previously not particularly attentive and involved.

J. S. Wallerstein and J. B. Kelly (1980) make the following statement about the visiting father:

> Men who could bend to the complex logistics of the visiting; who could deal with the anger of the women and the capriciousness of the child without withdrawing; who could overcome their own depression, jealousy, and guilt; and could involve the children in their planning; who could walk a middle ground between totally rearranging their schedule and not changing their schedule at all; and who felt less stressed and freer to parent, were predominantly among those who continued to visit regularly and frequently.

Although this represents an ideal, and there are probably few who could live up to it entirely, it does outline the criteria by which one might evaluate the visiting father (or mother).

Child Snatching or Abduction

In child custody conflicts between parents, the term *child snatching* or *child abduction* is often used in preference to kidnaping because, until recently, parents could not be charged with kidnaping their own children. Because a parent could not be charged with kidnaping his (her) own child, the law essentially permitted it (P. W. Beck, 1977). Probably the most common situation in which we see the phenomenon of child snatching is one in which a separated or divorced parent wishes to wreak vengeance on a former spouse by depriving him (her) of the most treasured possessions, the children. Another motive is protection of the children from what the abductor believes to be the terrible privations and abuses that would be perpetrated upon the children if they were to remain in the former spouse's home.

In the United States, a special and unusual situation prevails with regard to abduction of one's own child. It was the position of the founding fathers that the individual states should legislate issues relevant to personal, private, and family matters and that the federal government should concern itself with issues that are more national and international in nature. This principle has certainly served us well. It was based, in part, on the recognition that there are regional differences with regard to family issues and that if these were legislated from a central government injudicious and harmful laws might be passed—laws that might be relevant to certain sections of the country, but not to others. Divorce laws have traditionally been considered to be in this category, that is, a family matter that should be under the jurisdiction of each state. Accordingly, we are at present in a situation where there are 50 different sets of laws in 50 different states. Although there are certainly similarities in state laws, there are many differences as well. One of the effects of this situation has been that the crossing of state lines places one in an entirely new jurisdiction, enabling one to escape from consequences that would have to be faced if one were to have remained in the original state. Litigating across state lines is traditionally difficult, time consuming, and expensive—so much so that for many individuals it can serve as a protection from any consequences of wrongdoing.

Until recently, a parent could take a child across state lines and be immune from prosecution. The parent from whom the children had been abducted was relatively impotent. There was little an aggrieved parent could do if the snatching parent remained in a different state. The greater the distance, the less was the likelihood of effective legal action being taken, even if the kidnaper and the child were located. On occasion, the abandoned parent could abduct the children back or engage the services of others to perform this task. In recent years, states have been recognizing and enforcing decisions in other states in regard to custody. Many have followed the model of the *Uniform Child Custody Jurisdiction Act* which requires judges to recognize and enforce the custody decisions of courts in other states. In addition, it requires that child custody litigation "take place ordinarily in the state in which the child and his family have the closest connection and where significant evidence concerning his care, protection, training, and personal relationships is most readily available, and that courts decline the exercise of jurisdiction when the child and his family have a closer connection with another state." It gives states the power to deter abductions and other unilateral removals of children undertaken to obtain custody awards. It allows states to modify custody decrees of another state in order to diminish jurisdictional competition and conflict and to avoid relitigation of custody decisions of other states.

In addition, in 1980 Congress also passed the *Parental Kidnaping Prevention Act* (PL96-611). Under this law the Federal Bureau of Investigation can be brought in on child snatching cases once arrest warrants have been issued. Accordingly, the child-snatching parent is now considered to be perpetrating a punishable crime and the FBI can be invited to pursue such a parent across state lines. There is little question that the new law deters some parents who are planning to kidnap their children.

It is important to appreciate that the child-snatching parent is not necessarily the one who should automatically lose custody of the children. It is certainly the case that the child snatcher is being insensitive to the children's needs for intensive involvement with the other parent. And this is certainly a negative in the custody evaluation. However, our court system is not famous for the judiciousness of custody decisions and many have been ill-advised. The child snatcher, then, may be rescuing the children from an extremely detrimental environment, the gravity of which the court may not have appreciated. In evaluating such parents, the fact of child snatching is certainly a negative. However, one must also consider each parent's qualities as a parent. In addition, one must take into consideration the desires of the children with the full recognition that their preferences may be related to their having lived a significant period with the child snatcher. Sometimes all of these factors will balance out in favor of the parent with whom the children lived prior to their abduction. At other times, they will balance out in favor of the child snatcher. I have had two experiences in which I considered the child snatcher to be the less preferable parent in terms of parental capacity. However, the children had lived so long with that parent (partially as a result of court delay) and were so committed to the abducting parent that my ultimate recommendation was that the children be allowed to remain living with the child snatcher. My main point here is that the examiner must have great flexibility in such cases and not automatically assume that the child snatcher is the less preferable parent. In addition, the examiner must appreciate that there are times when the children's desires are so strong and that the trauma of being removed would be so great for them that one may end up recommending that they stay with the parent who is intrinsically the less desirable one.

The most extreme example of this kind of situation is the one in which the children live with a paranoid parent. I recall one situation in which the children were living with a paranoid schizophrenic mother. She viewed her ex-husband as the incarnation of all the evil that ever existed in human history. The children were exposed to a constant barrage of vilification of their father. They, in a kind of *folie à deux* relationship with their mother, developed the same delusions. At the very sight of their father, they panicked and resisted going with him—believing that if they did so they would probably be murdered. Although a paranoid schizophrenic, this mother was functioning adequately in many areas. There was no reason to believe that she could be committed to a hospital and she was certainly not going to admit herself voluntarily. Her paranoid delusional system appeared to involve primarily her ex-husband. Here, I recommended that the children be allowed to remain living with their mother. I suggested to the father that he intermittently try to communicate with the children (via letter, messages through third party intermediaries, etc.) in the hope that as time passed the children might ultimately come to see him in a more reasonable light. Although the children in this case were not actually abducted, the vignette demonstrates the principle that the examiner may, on occasion, recommend that the children remain in the custody of the nonpreferable parent because their long-term removal from that parent would make it psychologically traumatic for them. Children who are abducted may have to be dealt with similarly.

I recall one case in which a judge awarded custody to a father because the mother had had an affair. Although the father did not claim that the mother had significant parenting deficiencies, he was so incensed by her infidelity that he used his gaining primary custody of the children as a tool for revenge. At the time of the trial the father claimed that he would hire a housekeeper to take care of the children if he were awarded custody. In the ensuing months there were a series of housekeepers, most of whom were neglectful and negligent. At times, the children were left unattended when the father would go to work and a housekeeper would not show up. The mother was aware of the situation and appealed to the court for reconsideration. Because her finances were limited and because the court was unreceptive, she found herself impotent and watched her children deteriorate. She therefore decided to kidnap the children. She took them to another state, and it took the father almost a year to find her. At that time he again instituted litigation in order to retrieve his children.

I was invited to conduct an evaluation as an impartial examiner. My conclusion was that the mother was a superior parent and that her kidnaping was justified. The trial judge was unreceptive to my recommendation and unconvinced. He claimed that the mother was a criminal because she had flaunted the law, and he spoke at length about the fact that society cannot survive under anarchy. He awarded custody to the father. Fortunately, the case was brought to appeal and the appeals court overturned the trial court's decision and awarded primary custody to the mother. This case demonstrates well how a parent cannot rely upon the courts to provide "justice" and kidnaping children, in certain situations, may be in their best interests.

It is my hope that courts will act more quickly with regard to implementing the provisions of these important acts. My experience has been that there is still much "forum shopping" as attorneys encourage their clients to stall, spend significant time on the question of which state has proper jurisdiction, and therefore questioning which state has the right to override the jurisdiction of other states. It is only via quick resolution of these problems and fast action by the courts that the children will be placed in the optimum environment. The greater the stalling, the greater the likelihood the children will remain in the home of the abducting parent, whether justified or not, whether in their best interests or not.

Homosexuality and Parental Capacity

The Question of the Etiology of Homosexuality   Now to the difficult and controversial subject of homosexuality. No one can say that he or she knows with certainty the etiology of homosexuality. Some claim it is a normal variation in the human repertoire. Others consider it a definite form of psychopathology. Still others hold that both genetic and psychological environmental factors may be operative to varying degrees and that individuals differ regarding the contribution of each of these factors. The subject, unfortunately, often generates strong emotional reactions that are likely to becloud objectivity. For example, if in a conference on the etiology of schizophrenia, an authority believes personally that it is organic in etiology, even those who disagree are not likely to get too heated in their refutations. Similarly, those who claim the disorder to be psychogenic are not likely to raise the blood pressures of those who disagree with them. Last, those who claim it results from a combination of both organic and psychogenic factors are not likely to be vilified by those who disagree. Similar calmness is seen when one talks about organicity vs. psychogenicity for such disorders as migraine headaches, ulcerative colitis, peptic ulcers, hypertension, etc.

But if one says publicly in the 1980s that homosexuality is a psychological disorder, the speaker may be pelted with rocks and, if well known, may be the subject of public demonstrations, angry editorials in newspapers, and heated diatribes. Even in university and academic settings, where differences of opinion are presumably given equal opportunity for expression, those who hold that homosexuality is a psychological disorder may find themselves ostracized. I believe that such intense emotional reactions may be related to reaction formation on the part of those who respond with such strong feelings. Certainly, their anger and condemnation are the hallmark of reaction formation and suggest that it is psychologically threatening for many to accept the possibility that homosexuality may be psychogenic. (Similarly, it may be psychologically threatening to some to consider it organic.)

The position taken by most mental health professionals in the 1970s and 1980s is that homosexuality is a normal human variation and not a form of psychopathology. This is not my view. I recognize that my position on this point is atypical and unpopular; it is nevertheless my belief. To elaborate: I consider there to be a continuum with strong heterosexuality on one end and strong homosexuality on the other. No individual, no matter how strongly heterosexual, is free from homosexual tendencies. Similarly, no homosexual individual, no matter how strongly homosexual, is free from heterosexual inclinations. All individuals, therefore, are at some point between the two ends of this continuum. Although homosexuality is seen in lower animals, it generally manifests itself when heterosexual outlets are not available or as a transient phenomenon. To assume that there are human beings in whom it is the inborn preferential orientation requires the assumption that mankind has departed markedly from the evolutionary pattern. In addition, one must then believe in the existence of a human sexual variant without the goal of direct or indirect species procreation. Although such variants are seen in lower animals they are not, to the best of my knowledge, found in animals that have more recently developed on the evolutionary scale.

I believe that the person who is an *obligatory* homosexual, who cannot or who has no desire to function heterosexually (especially when such opportunities are available), is suffering with a psychiatric disorder that is primarily, if not exclusively, environmentally induced—although there still may be a small genetic (or constitutional) contributing factor. Such an individual has a problem that might readily be classified in many cases as a kind of phobia or inhibition. These individuals are so fearful of or inhibited from functioning sexually with members of the opposite sex that they *cannot* do so, even when opportunities are available and the heterosexual partner is desirous of such an involvement. I will discuss in the next section what I consider to be the more common factors that contribute to the development of an obligatory homosexual orientation. Such an individual might be viewed as similar to the person with other kinds of phobias, such as agoraphobia or claustrophobia. There may very well be a genetic predisposition to such phobias in that the individual has a very low threshold for elicitation of the flight reaction. Environmental factors that engender fear and flight responses become superimposed upon this genetically determined foundation and the clinical phobia manifests itself. The fact that a genetic component may be operative in homosexuality does not warrant our declassifying the phenomenon from the list of psychiatric disorders. And this is what has happened with homosexuality. I believe that political factors, much more than psychiatric, have played a role in its removal from the list of disorders.

My views are less firm with regard to the possible psychopathology of people who are bisexual or are non-obligatory homosexuals. Such individuals appear to work on the principle: If it feels good I'll do it — regardless of the sex of my partner. Such persons may enjoy homosexual activities, even when heterosexual opportunities are available. Although I am less firm in my belief that bisexuals are suffering with psychopathology, I suspect that many (but not necessarily all) are. Lastly, because of the homosexual potential in even the strongest heterosexuals, I would not consider pathological a rare homosexual act engaged in by a heterosexual person. This would especially be the case when heterosexual opportunity is not available. The inborn homosexual *capacity* allows for homosexual gratification in a heterosexual when heterosexual gratification is not available. It provides a vehicle for the release of pent-up sexual tensions in a situation where such release would be difficult or impossible. Accordingly, homosexuality serves a function in certain situations. As an alternative mode of sexual release one could even argue that it is superior to masturbation because it involves human interaction rather than narcissistic self-gratification.

It is important for the reader to appreciate that I am not

claiming to know with certainty that the above theory is correct. It is the view I hold at this time on the basis of my present understanding of human sexual behavior. It behooves examiners to have an opinion on this issue if they are to be providing recommendations regarding the treatment of people who present with homosexual urges and are considering treatment. One cannot wait for all the information to come in (it may take hundreds of years). A mother brings a four-year-old boy for consultation because he is preoccupied with dressing in her clothing and has been exhibiting effeminate gestures. One therapist might take the position that the child's behavior is normal and/or the child is an individual who is genetically programmed to be homosexual. Accordingly, that therapist would not recommend treatment. Another therapist might consider the child to be exhibiting pathological manifestations and would recommend therapy. (I consider myself to be in the latter category.) A 14-year-old boy asks his parents to bring him to therapy because of homosexual preoccupations. One therapist may consider the boy's thoughts to be inevitable concomitants of a normal homosexual variation and might treat the youngster to help him to become more comfortable with his homosexuality. Another therapist (include me again in this group) considers the boy to be exhibiting pathological manifestations and recommends treatment for the alleviation of the homosexual tendencies. Obviously, the position the therapist takes in each of these situations may have an important effect on the total course of these youngsters' future lives. Accordingly, we *must* make recommendations, recognizing that they have been made on the basis of *hypotheses* regarding the etiology and significance of homosexuality.

Although I believe that the obligatory homosexual is suffering with a psychiatric disorder, this should not be interpreted to mean that I believe that an obligatory homosexual (or any other kind of homosexual for that matter) should be deprived of his or her civil rights. One's private sexual life should not be a factor in determining job opportunities, career choice, and so on. If a homosexual's proclivities interfere with job functioning, then that must be taken into consideration. But this same principle holds with heterosexuals. If a homosexual man has a job as an elementary teacher and encourages homosexual activities among his students, then one should limit his opportunities for such inculcation. But the same principle holds if a heterosexual teacher were to engage in similar behavior.

In addition, I consider the average male obligatory homosexual to be suffering with more psychological difficulties than the average female obligatory homosexual. This may come as a surprising statement to many readers, and I have not seen anything in the literature supporting such a statement. What I say here is my own opinion supported, I believe, by these arguments: With rare exception, the primary sexual object for both males and females is the mother. She has carried the child within her own body for nine months, has suffered the pains of its delivery, and has the capacity to feed it from her own body (although she may not choose to do so). The average healthy father, no matter how deeply involved with his yet unborn infant, is not as likely to have as strong a tie with the *newborn* child as the average healthy mother.

In our society, where the mother is still the primary caretaking parent in most families (recent changes in the pattern notwithstanding), the earliest primary attachment for infants of both sexes is the mother. In the normal development of the boy, he transfers his affection from his mother to girlfriends and ultimately to other adult females. The progression is a relatively smooth one for the average healthy boy and does not involve the kind of shift required of the female. The girl, in contrast, must transfer her sexual involvement from a female (her mother) to male figures: boyfriends and then adult males. It is reasonable to assume that residua of the attraction to the mother are likely to be present at subsequent levels of development. One confirmation of such residual attraction is the fact that many more heterosexual women are physically attracted to the naked female body than heterosexual men are to the naked male body. Many more heterosexual women purchase magazines depicting naked women than heterosexual men purchase magazines depicting naked men. (The latter are primarily purchased by homosexual males.) For a woman to become a lesbian involves a fixation at an earlier level of development: the level at which she was attracted to her primary sexual object, the mother. Her subsequent lovers are in the same mold, so to speak, and are readily understandable. Blocked from heterosexual gratification by internal psychological and/or external situational factors, it is reasonable that she may remain fixated at or regress to an earlier level—but along the track of sexual attraction to a female.

The male homosexual, in contrast, has a much more complex course toward his resultant homosexual orientation. He must abrogate mother and all her derivative surrogates. He must shift toward an intense sexual involvement with a father surrogate without any continuity with his previous psychobiological track. The psychological processes involved in such a path are complex and extremely powerful. The distortions of thinking necessary to effect such a transfer are profound. It is for these reasons that I consider the obligatory male homosexual to have deeper psychopathology than the obligatory female homosexual. Elsewhere (1988a) I have described in detail what I consider to be the more important psychodynamic factors that contribute to the development of homosexuality in both men and women.

Custody Considerations for the Homosexual Parent   A parent's homosexuality, although a manifestation of psychopathology (in this examiner's opinion), should not in itself be a reason for depriving that parent of custody. It should merely be one factor considered in the decision. It may be an extremely important one, or it may be of little significance. It is important for the examiner to appreciate that removal of the children from a homosexual parent can deprive them of valuable experiences. Homosexuality per se need not make a parent incapable of providing children with most of the benefits of parenthood. Homosexuality need not impair parental capacity. There are many male homosexuals who make very good parents—oriented as they are toward maternal functioning. Although such men may contribute to a boy's becoming homosexual by serving as a model for such an orientation, they do not often exhibit the punitive rejecting attitude toward their sons that may contribute to boys' becoming homosexual. There is this compromising identification factor, therefore, a factor that may contribute to the son's becoming homosexual; but it is not generally that great that I would suggest that the homosexual father automatically be deprived of visitation and custody rights to which he might otherwise be entitled. Similarly, with the lesbian mother, her homosexuality should not in itself be a reason for depriving her of custody and visitation rights that she might otherwise be granted, even though I believe that her sexual orientation might be a negative factor in making the decision. I would consider it along with other factors, both positive and negative, in making a recommendation.

In custody evaluations involving homosexual parents, I try to determine whether the parent is trying (either overtly or covertly) to raise the child to become homosexual. It can be done overtly with the parent stating directly that he (she) wants the child to be homosexual. (This, by the way, is rare, in my experience. Most homosexuals I have encountered, if they are to be directly honest, would prefer that their children be heterosexual. Although they claim that they say this because their children's lives would be easier in a society that discriminates so terribly against homosexuals, I believe that it is also stated from the deep appreciation that the homosexual way of life is less potentially gratifying—their professions to the contrary notwithstanding.) More commonly, the homosexual parent encourages homosexuality in the children more covertly, with comments such as "I'll tell my children that I have no particular preference regarding whether they become homo- or heterosexual." Healthy parents, in my opinion, do have a preference—and strongly so. They want their children to be heterosexual—have no doubts about it—and shudder at the possibility that a child might become homosexual. This has less to do with the social stigma that the homosexual suffers (which, fortunately, is lessening) and more with the appreciation that such a way of life is more likely to be unrewarding and painful than a heterosexual existence – as is true of all life patterns that are associated with psychological disturbance.

Although a homosexual parent provides, in my opinion, an unhealthy model for sexual identification, this fact should not in itself be a reason for depriving such a parent of primary custody if the child is above the age of three or four and exhibits definite heterosexual orientation. By that time the child's sexual orientation is fairly well established and is not likely to be altered – unless there has been unusual and prolonged indoctrination into homosexual attitudes and behavior and/or ongoing exposure to environmental factors that can contribute to the development of homosexuality. When involved in custody evaluations of homosexual parents, I examine carefully each child's sexual orientation and look for signs and symptoms of homosexuality and sexual identification problems – both present and potential. For boys, the signs of a potential homosexual problem would include the *frequent* desire to put on the mother's make-up and to wear her shoes, underwear, and other articles of clothing; a preference for the role of mother in playing "house"; and a marked preference for playing with girls rather than boys. These criteria are especially valid when they have taken on an obsessive or compulsive quality. Present uncertainty about traditional male and female roles notwithstanding, I still hold that these criteria are valid. I would recommend that a homosexual father of such a child not be granted primary custody, unless there were other very powerful counterbalancing considerations. There are also less definite manifestations of a homosexual problem in the male. If a boy exhibits traditionally effeminate gestures and intonations and is *often* called "sissy" or "fag" by his peers, I suspect a potential homosexual problem. Some "momma's boys" may be revealing the kind of attachment seen in the homosexual. Although tomboyishness may reflect a homosexual problem in the girl, it is not a very valuable criterion, especially in more recent years, when girls' involvement in traditional male activities is becoming more common, happily so, in my opinion.

During the prepubertal and pubertal periods special problems may arise that can affect my recommendations regarding custody and visitation. If a homosexual father, for example, is frequently bringing his 13-year-old son together with his homosexual friends, he is providing the boy with a detrimental exposure. Even though there may be no overt invitations to sexual involvement, such a boy is often quite attractive to homosexual men and their feelings toward him will be subtly appreciated by him. A boy of this age normally exhibits a certain amount of homosexual interest. The setting therefore cannot but be a titillating and seductive one for all concerned. Even if the boy exhibits no evidence of homosexual orientation, the atmosphere is bound to be a charged one for him. Although it may not result in his becoming homosexual, it can add to the sexual anxieties and confusions that he will normally have during this period. Accordingly, I would consider such exposures an argument against granting such a father primary custody. I would certainly, however, encourage visitation, but would recommend that such exposures not be permitted during the visiting times.

If a homosexual parent is reasonably private about the homosexuality, is not trying to induce homosexuality in the children or expose them to sexual activities, and if the children are above the age of four and show no evidence of homosexuality or of sexual orientation disturbance, then I would not consider the parent's homosexuality a reason for disqualifying him (her) as the primary custodial parent. Nor would I recommend that there be any reduction or restriction of visitation rights. Although the homosexuality, in itself, would be viewed as a negative in my considerations, if the above criteria are satisfied, it becomes a small one.

The question of what recommendations to make regarding custody for a homosexual parent who is living with a homosexual partner is a more difficult one. Those who argue that homosexuality is not a psychiatric disturbance would compare such a relationship with a heterosexual one and argue that the same criteria should hold with regard to the granting of primary custody. If the court would grant primary custody to a mother who lives with a man to whom she is not married, and if it would grant custody to a father who is not married to the woman with whom he is living (and courts commonly do so today in both of these situations), then, they would argue, the court should not discriminate against the parent who lives with someone of the same sex. I am in agreement with the more liberal criteria that courts have recently been using with regard to the granting of custody to a parent who is living with but not married to a heterosexual partner. Because I believe that homosexuality is most likely a psychiatric disorder, I do not equate heterosexual with homosexual exposure.

I believe that a child who lives in a home in which both "parents" are of the same sex is being unduly exposed to an unhealthy psychological environment. The situation is very different from the one in which the homosexual parent does not live with anyone and keeps his or her homosexual life apart from the children. When the parent lives with a homosexual partner, there is an exposure to homosexuality of such great intensity that it is likely to affect the children. I do not believe that the effect is so great that it could reverse the sexual identity of children over four who have already established a heterosexual identity and orientation. Rather, I believe that such exposure could create confusions, anxieties, and compromises in sex role identification that might otherwise not have developed. In addition, as mentioned above, in the adolescent period the titillations engendered in such a situation could not but cause the adolescent significant anxieties. Accordingly, I consider such an arrangement to be a strong negative in weighing the pros and cons for recommending custody. Just as the heterosexual parent who exposes the children to a parade of lovers is, I believe, providing a detrimental exposure, a homosexual parent who frequently brings a partner or series of partners into the home—whether to sleep over or not—similarly compromises the parental role. Like all the other criteria I use, no one of these is overriding. I might still recommend custody for such a parent if other factors were present that counterbalanced this one.

When providing recommendations regarding visitation and custody rights for a homosexual parent, the guideline that I use is this: The greater the degree to which the child is exposed to a homosexual environment, the greater should be the restrictions imposed to protect the child from the detrimental effects of such exposure. Homosexuality in itself should not be a reason for reducing a parent's visitation or custody rights. But when there is exposure to homosexuality and imposition of it, one should consider limiting such a parent's privileges.

Joan's case provides an example of the kind of situation in which I recommended that a lesbian mother not be given custody of her child and that there be a curtailment of her visitation rights. Joan was 13 years old when her parents separated because of her mother's homosexuality. She was an only child. At around the time of the separation Joan's mother became a gay activist. Originally the mother was given custody of Joan, and she moved into an apartment house where there were many other homosexuals who were involved in the Gay Liberation Movement. Joan's mother became increasingly swept up in her political activities, fighting for the civil rights of homosexuals. So involved was she in these activities that she had little meaningful time left over for Joan. Many homosexuals visited the home, where meetings often took place. The apartment was flooded with literature and pamphlets supporting the gay cause. In addition, many homosexual magazines were strewn about the apartment, magazines with pictures depicting various kinds of homosexual activities. On occasion the mother would bring Joan along to gay activist marches and demonstrations and encourage her to hand out leaflets in support of the movement. She took a strictly neutral attitude regarding Joan's future sexual orientation. She denied that Joan had ever been invited into sexual encounters with any of her friends. She claimed that although Joan was a little young for such experiences she would have no objection to her having homosexual experiences by her mid-teens if this was her preference.

Joan's father instituted legal proceedings in order to gain custody of his daughter. As the result of my examination of Joan and both parents, I supported his request. Although Joan showed no evidence for a homosexual orientation at that time, I concluded that the intensive exposure to the homosexual environment was sexually titillating and confusing to Joan, but that it was not likely that she would become a lesbian. I considered her mother's intensive involvement in her political activities to be depriving Joan of the amount of attention and affection she warranted. This had nothing to do with the nature of her mother's activities. (In fact, I was in full sympathy with her mother's political activities, believing as I do that there is absolutely no justification for depriving a homosexual of his or her civil rights merely because of the presence of this disorder.) Even if the mother had been involved in activities having nothing to do with homosexuality, her obsessive involvement in a cause resulted in her neglecting Joan. The court agreed with my recommendation and Joan's father was granted primary custody. The court followed my recommendation that the mother be granted liberal visitation privileges. However, she was not allowed to involve the child in her gay liberation activities or bring her to the apartment where she was living, because of the intensive exposure Joan had there to the homosexual environment.

Before closing this discussion of homosexuality, I wish to emphasize again that I make no claims that my opinion that the obligative homosexual has a psychiatric disorder is "right." I only claim that it appears to me to be the most reasonable conclusion I can come to from my knowledge of and experiences with people who are homosexual. The recommendations I make regarding custody and visitation for the homosexual parent are based on this presumption. Evaluators who do not share my view, and I recognize that they are numerous (although I am not alone either), will, of course, make very different recommendations.

JOINT INTERVIEWS

Here I will focus on joint interviews with both parents together. In Chapter Seven I will discuss two types of joint interviews with the children: 1) Interviews in which the parent is seen alone with each child separately and 2) Family interviews in which both parents together are seen with one or more children. The joint interviews are generally the richest source of information in a custody evaluation. Accordingly, they are clearly mandated in the litigation provisions document, in case a parent might resist such encounters. It is here that the examiner can do something that is not possible for the courts to accomplish under the adversary system. At no point in adversary proceedings are the two persons brought into the same room and allowed to have a direct active interchange with one another. The artificial setting of the court-room, where each party is heard independently—and there may be hours, days, or even weeks between each party's appearance—deprives the data collectors of important information. When a parent lies in court, the spouse is impotent to say or do anything at that moment. Doing or saying anything at such times exposes the parent to the risk of being considered in contempt of court. In contrast, in the joint interview confronting the liar is immediately possible. It is in this active interchange that the examiner may be in a better position to decide what is the "truth." In the joint interview the evaluator has the opportunity to telephone and even bring in other parties who may have been witness to the events under consideration. Here too one is at an advantage over the court regarding finding out what really occurred.

In adversary proceedings when one side brings up an important allegation, the other is given time to "prepare a response." Such preparation is cooly accomplished and designed to withhold or downplay data that compromises the respondent's position. In the joint interview no time may be allowed for a response to a compromising confrontation. Under such circum-stances one is more likely to learn the true response of the accused party. Again, the impartial examiner can do this as a matter of routine; the court may never be in a position to accomplish this.

It is important for the examiner to appreciate that the joint interviews are more important than the sessions in which the individuals are interviewed alone. This is especially the case for the interviews with the adults. In the individual interviews each parent makes statements about the other. These are justifiably called *allegations* by the attorneys. In the joint interview, one has an opportunity to hear the refutations directly (as opposed to their being communicated through a third party—the examiner) as well as observe the interplay between the accuser and the accused. Out of this interplay may come some consensus or even an admission. These admissions and mutually agreed upon statements are the most powerful aspects of the examiner's conclusions and recommendations. The allegations, however, are usually of little or no informational value if they are denied or refuted. The examiner may personally believe that one party's position has much greater credibility than the other's. However, examiners do best not to utilize such hunches in making their final conclusions and recommendations. Rather, they are on much safer grounds if they confine themselves to issues in which a party is clearly supported by statements of admission and/or direct observations of deficiency by the evaluator. One of the biggest mistakes an examiner can make is to accept as valid one party's allegation. If done in a litigation report, the opposing attorney is likely to recognize this weakness and may cause the evaluator embarrassment under cross-examination in court.

As mentioned, mutually agreed-upon statements and admissions are the kinds of things one wants to focus on in the joint sessions. For example, the mother may state that the father is late for 90 percent of his visitations and that the average lateness is two hours. If the father denies completely that he is ever late, one may not be able to come to any specific conclusions regarding this issue (unless one has some corroboration from the children). If the children are too young or unreliable, then one can do nothing with this information even though one may suspect that the mother is probably telling the truth. If, however, the father does admit to such lateness, but to a lesser degree, then one has more valid data. For example, if the father says that he was late only half the time and that the average lateness was one to one-and-a-half hours, he is admitting a deficiency. In one's final report one can give both parents' accounts and then state that even if Mr. Jones' version is true, it still represents a compromise of his paternal capacity. I cannot impress upon the reader strongly enough the power of this kind of statement in the custody report. A statement made by the deficient party him- or herself is more convincing than any other source of data.

The joint interviews can also be therapeutic for the parents. Often, by the time an impartial examiner is brought on the scene, their animosity has built up to such proportions that they come to view each other as despicable individuals, the incarnation of all the evils that ever existed in the history of the human race. Having a *living experience with one another*—over the course of a few sessions—may help to dispel some of the delusions and distortions that may have built up. For many months, and even years, they may have communicated only via lawyers and this failure to have direct experience with one another may contribute to the formation and perpetuation of their distorted views of one another. D.W. Cantor and E.A. Drake (1983) and M.B. Isaacs et al. (1986) are also strong proponents of joint interviews in custody evaluations and provide useful illustrative examples.

THE QUESTION OF PROVIDING ADVICE TO PARENTS IN THE COURSE OF THE EVALUATION

In the course of the evaluation, examiners should make every reasonable attempt to restrict themselves to the primary goal: collecting data in the service of making the best possible custody recommendation. The combination of therapy and data collection in a custody evaluation is a poor one. Therapy, among other things, involves providing advice. When one provides advice there is the risk of producing anxiety and alienation of the parent—and such feelings can contaminate unnecessarily the evaluation. Such advice may give the parent a hint as to "which way the wind is blowing," because it may imply: "You are doing things wrong and this is the right way to do them." Although transferential reactions are bound to arise in the most conservative evaluations, once the examiner starts doing therapy the likelihood of such responses occurring increases immeasurably. All kinds of feelings may then come forth: anger, fear, sexual attraction, and so on. These may be very useful to investigate in therapy, but they are not only less useful to investigate in the custody evaluation, they may actually compromise it. On the one hand, one could argue that such data are also in the realm of what the examiner should be interested in. On the other hand, they are generally of less value than the kinds of "facts" one is searching for, and they may contribute to a wide variety of criticisms and accusations that parents may communicate to their attorneys. They may provide attorneys with "ammunition" in court if they are sophisticated enough to appreciate that the examiner is involving him- or herself in therapy.

Accordingly, the best and safest position for the examiner to take is that of the strictly neutral data collector who is ever asking questions. This does not mean that the examiner must be an automaton or a data-collecting computer. The evaluator can be human, sensitive, and benevolent in the inquiry. Examiners can still be sympathetic to the parents' plights and the pains they are suffering in the course of the evaluation. The evaluator can be sympathetic to the fact that "old wounds" are being opened and are intensifying the psychological trauma of the divorce and custody conflict.

These warnings notwithstanding, I do on occasion provide minor bits of advice in the course of the evaluation. Sometimes the parents' responses provide me with useful information. For example, on a few occasions, a mother has refused to let the children visit their father as long as a new woman friend was present. This is especially the case when the woman friend would sleep over in the father's bedroom in the course of the visitation. In those cases in which I considered such visits therapeutically advisable for the children (and one must be judicious here), I commented to the mother that I considered her position psychologically inappropriate and that she was not acting in the best interests of the children. I described how such a position could deprive the children of important contact with their father. Many such mothers use moral principles and religious teachings to justify what is really vengeful acting out on their parts. (Most of these women were not particularly religious prior to the time the father met the new woman friend.) Their rage at the thought of the father's being with another woman was so great that they were willing to sacrifice their children's visitation benefits in the service of hurting the father and/or interfering with his new liaison. Some ignored my advice and rigidly held to their position—contributing thereby to their children's being deprived of freer involvement with their father. Others were willing to modify their position from the recognition that my explanation was a reasonable one. In short, the advice was given *en passant,* and the reactions provided useful data in the custody evaluation.

To reiterate, evaluators do well to restrict themselves to providing advice on rare occasions only—and then only to a limited degree. Under no circumstances should they become involved in an ongoing therapeutic experience in the course of the custody evaluation. In Chapter Two I discussed in greater detail my reasons for this caveat.

CONCLUDING COMMENTS

My general approach is to make every attempt to conduct the evaluation as rapidly as possible. My main reason for doing this is that the longer the evaluation, the greater the likelihood both parents and children will be psychologically traumatized. Although the time expended in conducting the evaluation is generally short compared to the time the parents are involved in litigation, any lag contributes to the psychopathology derived from the prolongation of the litigation. In spite of my attempts to conduct the evaluation as quickly as possible, it was most often the case that things dragged out. One of the reasons for this related to the fact that time is on the side of the custodial parent. That parent recognizes that the longer the delay the greater the likelihood the children will express a preference for remaining in that parent's home, regardless of how deficient the parent may be. Accordingly, such parents find a wide variety of excuses for not accepting appointments and breaking them. This delay, however, is not without its potential advantages. The longer the evaluation, the greater the likelihood "things will happen." By this I am referring to unanticipated events that may provide the examiner with useful information that might not otherwise have been obtained if everyone agreed to proceed as rapidly as possible. The awareness of this may help lessen the frustration of the examiner who, in his (her) commitment to the children, is making every reasonable attempt to proceed rapidly with the evaluation.

I recall one evaluation which began in the summer. The usual procrastinations resulted in the evaluation extending into the fall. Now it so happened that in that particular year Columbus Day and Yom Kippur fell on the same day. A visitation arrangement had been carefully planned two years previously. The parents were to alternate major jewish holidays as well as major national holidays. In that year the father was assigned to have the child on Yom Kippur and the mother to have the child on Columbus Day. No one had anticipated – neither the lawyers, nor the parents, nor the judge who had signed the order – that in that particular year both holidays fell on the same day. In mid-September, when this "flaw" in the agreement became apparent, each parent initially claimed that he (she) had priority. The father claimed that he would take the dispute to the Supreme Court if necessary to win his case. The mother, although initially tempted to take the matter to court, came to appreciate that the expense and psychological toll of such litigation was not worth the issue. She backed down, let the father take the children to synagogue on Yom Kippur (to repent for his sins) and she spent a lonelier (but psychologically healthier and financially richer) Columbus Day. (The major loss, of course, on this double holiday for all adherents to the Judeo-Christian faith were the lawyers who lost out on a wonderful opportunity to extract a few more bucks from these people.) Had everybody cooperated during the course of the summer I would never have been witness to this conflict and would not have learned how litigious the father was and how much more reasonable was the mother.

When an evaluation begins in the fall, one certainly hopes to finish it by the Christmas season. However, examiners should not feel discouraged if the evaluation extends into that period. It is on Christmas Day, especially, that one may observe the most fanatic adherence to church worship and celebration, even among those who previously considered themselves agnostics and even atheists. Visit any family court the day before Christmas and one is likely to see a horde of divorcing people who fanatically subscribe to the importance of their sharing Christmas with their children. In compliance with their strong adherence to this Christian holiday, they will do everything in their power to denigrate, humiliate, and financially deplete their soon-to-be ex-spouses. Among the common war cries: "On this point, I have absolutely no flexibility. There is no way I will ever agree to be away from my children on Christmas." "He'll get the children on Christmas over my dead body!" and "If you want the children on Christmas Day, I have only one thing to say to you, Buster, and that's 'Drop dead!'" Even attempts to compromise may prove futile. One family decided to compromise by having the children spend Christmas Eve with father and Christmas Day with mother. However, they actually went to court because they could not decide between themselves when Christmas Eve began: "12:01 a.m. on December 24th, 12:00 noon on December 24th, sundown (approximately 5:00 p.m.) on December 24th or at some point later in the evening, such as when church services began. Each parent gave over a thousand dollars to their Jewish lawyers to get a Jewish judge to make this decision for them. Again, had the evaluation not been extended into the season of peace on earth and good will to all mankind, I would not have had the opportunity to learn about these qualities in the parents.

My primary purpose in this chapter has been to present to the examiner a compendium of the questions and techniques that I have found useful for evaluating parental capacity by interviewing the parents, singly and in combination. As mentioned, it would be unreasonable to expect the evaluator to use all these methods and questions with any particular parent(s). The examiner will not generally need all of these questions and methods of data collection to come to a conclusion. It is well to utilize those questions and techniques that show promise of providing the most meaningful information, to exclude questions that provide little promise for gaining useful or new data, and to discontinue the interviews when enough information has become available to draw meaningful conclusions and recommendations.

⚖ SIX
THE PARENTAL ALIENATION SYNDROME

INTRODUCTION

Examiners who evaluate families involved in custody disputes should be familiar with the etiology, pathogenesis, and manifestations of a disorder which I have referred to as the *parental alienation syndrome*. The evaluator who is not familiar with this disturbance will be compromised in conducting an adequate custody evaluation. In fact, a lack of familiarity with this disorder may result in the examiner's taking at face value the children's comments—with the result that an injudicious and even psychologically detrimental recommendation may be made. Accordingly, I devote a chapter to a discussion of this disorder before proceeding with the chapter on the interviews with the children.

Prior to the early 1980s, I certainly saw children whom I considered to have been brainwashed by one parent against the other. However, since that period I have seen—with even increasing frequency—a disorder that I rarely saw previously. This disorder arose primarily in children who had been involved in protracted custody litigation. It is now so common that I see manifestations of it in about 90 percent of children who have been involved in custody conflicts. Because of its increasing frequency and the fact that a typical picture is observed—different from simple brainwashing—I believe a special designation is warranted. Accordingly, I have termed this disorder the *parental alienation syndrome*.

I have introduced this term to refer to a disturbance in which children are preoccupied with deprecation and criticism of a parent—denigration that is unjustified and/or exaggerated. The notion that such children are merely "brainwashed" is narrow. The term *brainwashing* implies that one parent is systematically and consciously programming the child to denigrate the other. The concept of the parental alienation syndrome includes the brainwashing component, but is much more comprehensive. It includes not only conscious but subconscious and unconscious factors within the programming parent that contribute to the child's alienation from the other. Furthermore (and this is extremely important), it includes factors that arise within the child— independent of the parental contributions—that play a role in the development of the syndrome. In addition, situational factors may contribute, i.e., factors that exist in the family and the environment that may play a role in bringing about the disorder.

There are two important reasons for the recent dramatic increase in the prevalence of this syndrome. First, since the mid-to-late 1970s, courts have generally taken the position that the tender years presumption (that mothers are intrinsically superior to fathers as parents) is sexist and that custodial determinations should be made on criteria relating directly to parenting capacity, independent of a parent's sex. This concept became known as the *best interests of the child presumption*. Second, in the late 1970s and early 1980s the joint custodial arrangement became increasingly popular. The notion that one parent be designated the *sole* custodian and the other the *visitor* was considered inegalitarian; joint custody promised a more equal division of time with the children and of decision-making powers. Both of these developments have had the effect of making children's custodial arrangements far more unpredictable and precarious. As a result, parents are more frequently brainwashing their children in order to ensure "victory" in custody/visitation litigation. And the children themselves have joined forces with the preferred parent in order to preserve what they consider to be the most desirable arrangement, without the appreciation that in some cases primary custody by the denigrated parent might be in their best interests.

These changes have placed women at a disadvantage in custody disputes. Under the tender years presumption, mothers were secure in the knowledge that fathers had to prove compellingly significant deficiencies in their wives' parenting capacity before they could even hope to wrest custody of the children. Under the best interests of the child presumption, especially when the sex-blind doctrine was used in its implementation, mothers' positions became less secure. And, with the subsequent popularization of the joint custodial concept, their positions became even more precarious. Accordingly, mothers have been more likely than fathers to attempt to alienate their children against fathers in order to strengthen their position in custody/visitation conflicts. And, for reasons to be elaborated upon, children have been supporting their mothers much more than their fathers, providing thereby their own contributions to the parental alienation syndrome.

Because of this clinically observed difference, namely, that mothers are more likely than fathers to be the alienators ("brainwashers"), I will, for simplicity of presentation, refer more frequently to the mother as the preferred or "loved" parent and the father as the rejected or "hated" parent. I place the words *loved* and *hated* in quotes because there is still much love for the so-called hated parent and much hostility toward the allegedly loved one. This does not preclude my observation that on occasion (in about 10 percent of cases) it is the father who is the preferred parent and the mother the despised one. It would be an error for the reader to conclude that the designation of the mother as the preferred parent and the father as the hated one represents sexist bias on my part. Rather, it is merely a reflection of my own observations and experiences as well as others who work in the field. It also would be an error for the reader to conclude that my belief that mothers, more often than fathers, are the active contributors to the brainwashing components necessarily implies condemnation of these women. Actually, as I will discuss later, I am in sympathy with most of these mothers and believe that they have been "shortchanged" by the aforementioned recent developments.

In this chapter I will first describe the most common manifestations of the parental alienation syndrome. I will then describe the factors that I consider to be operative in bringing about the disorder. I divide such contributing factors into four categories: 1) brainwashing (conscious programming), 2) subconscious and unconscious programming, 3) the child's contributions, and 4) situational factors. In Chapters Nine and Thirteen I will discuss approaches to the prevention and treatment of this disorder.

THE MANIFESTATIONS OF THE
PARENTAL ALIENATION SYNDROME

Typically the child is obsessed with "hatred" of a parent. (As mentioned, the word *hatred* is placed in quotes because, as will be discussed, there are still many tender and loving feelings felt toward the allegedly despised parent that are not permitted expression.) These children speak of the parent with every vilification and profanity in their vocabulary—without embarrassment or guilt. The denigration of the parent often has the quality of a litany. After only minimal prompting by a lawyer, judge, probation officer, mental health professional, or other person involved in the litigation, the record will be turned on and a command performance provided. Not only is there a rehearsed quality to the speech, but one often hears phraseology that is not commonly used by the child. Many expressions are identical to those used by the "loved" parent. (Again, the word *loved* is placed in quotations because hostility toward that parent may similarly be unexpressed.) Typical examples: "He harasses us." "He sexually molested me." "His new girlfriend is a whore."

Even years after they have taken place, the child may justify the alienation with memories of minor altercations experienced in the relationship with the hated parent. These are usually trivial and are experiences that most children quickly forget, e.g., "He always used to speak very loud when he told me to brush my teeth." "He used to tell me to get his things a lot." "She used to say to me 'Don't interrupt.' " "He used to make a lot of noise when he chewed at the table." When these children are asked to give more compelling reasons for the hatred, they are unable to provide them. Frequently, the loved parent will agree with the child that these professed reasons justify the ongoing animosity.

The professions of hatred are most intense when the children and the loved parent are in the presence of the alienated one. However, when the child is alone with the allegedly hated parent, he or she may exhibit anything from hatred, to neutrality, to expressions of affection. When these children are alone with the hated parent, they may let their guard down and start to enjoy themselves. Then, almost as if they have realized that they are doing something "wrong," they will suddenly stiffen up and resume their expressions of withdrawal and animosity.

Another maneuver commonly seen in this situation is the child's claiming affection for the parent spoken to and hatred of the other and asking the loved parent to swear not to reveal the confessions to the other parent. And the same statements are made to the other parent with a similar extraction of a promise that the divulgences not be revealed to the absent parent. In this way these children "cover their tracks" and thereby avoid the disclosure of their schemes. Such children may find family interviews with therapists extremely anxiety provoking because of the fear that their manipulations and maneuvers will be divulged. The loved parent's proximity plays an important role regarding what the child will say to the hated one. The closer the loved parent, when the child is with the hated one, the greater the likelihood the hated parent will be denigrated. When seen alone in consultation, the child is likely to modify the litany in accordance with which parent is in the waiting room. Judges, lawyers, and mental health professionals who interview such children should recognize this important phenomenon.

The hatred of the parent often extends to include that parent's complete extended family. Cousins, aunts, uncles, and

230 THE PARENTAL ALIENATION SYNDROME

grandparents—with whom the child previously may have had loving relationships—are now viewed as similarly obnoxious. Grandparents, who previously had a loving and tender relationship with the child, now find themselves suddenly and inexplicably rejected. The child has no guilt over such rejection nor does the loved parent. Greeting cards are not reciprocated. Presents sent to the home are refused, remain unopened, or even destroyed (generally in the presence of the loved parent). When the hated parent's relatives call on the telephone, the child will respond with angry vilifications or quickly hang up on the caller. (These responses are more likely to occur if the loved parent is within hearing distance of the conversation.) With regard to the hatred of the relatives, the child is even less capable of providing justifications for the animosity. The rage of these children is so great that they become completely oblivious to the privations they are causing themselves. Again, the loved parent is typically unconcerned with the untoward psychological effects on the child of this rejection of the network of relatives who previously provided important psychological gratifications.

In family conferences, in which the children are seen together with both the loved and hated parent, the children reflexly take the position of the loved parent—sometimes even before the other has had the opportunity to present his (her) side of the argument. Even the loved parent may not present the argument as forcefully as the supporting child. These children may even refuse to accept evidence that is obvious proof of the hated parent's position. For example, one boy's mother claimed that her husband was giving her absolutely no money at all. When the father showed the boy canceled checks, signed by him and endorsed by the mother, the boy claimed that they were "forged." One girl claimed, after the death of her maternal grandfather from cancer, that it was her father who had murdered him. Although the mother herself considered the accusation preposterous, the child still persisted with the accusation. Commonly these children will accept as 100 percent valid the allegations of the loved parent against the hated one. One boy's mother claimed that her husband had beaten her on numerous occasions. The child presented this as one of the reasons why he hated his father. The father denied that he had ever laid a finger on the mother; in contrast, he claimed that the mother on a number of occasions had struck him. When I asked the child if he had even *seen* his father hit his mother, he claimed that he had not, but that he believed his mother and insisted she would never lie to him. In this situation, as a result of an exhaustive evaluation, I concluded that the father's rendition was far more likely to have been valid.

Another symptom of the parental alienation syndrome is complete lack of ambivalence. All human relationships are ambivalent, and parent-child relationships are no exception. The concept of "mixed feelings" has no place in these children's scheme of things. The hated parent is "all bad" and the loved parent is "all good." Most children (normals as well as those with a wide variety of psychiatric problems), when asked to list both good and bad things about each parent, will generally be able to do so. When children with parental alienation syndrome are asked to provide the same lists, they will typically recite a long list of criticisms of the hated parent, but will not be able to think of one positive or redeeming personality trait. In contrast, they will provide only positive qualities for the preferred parent and claim to be unable to think of even one trait they dislike. The hated parent may have been deeply dedicated to the child's upbringing, and a strong bond may have been created over many years. The hated parent may produce photos that demonstrate clearly a joyful and deep relationship in which there was significant affection, tenderness, and mutual pleasure. But the memory of all these experiences appears to have been obliterated. When these children are shown photos of enjoyable events with the hated parent, they usually rationalize the experiences as having been forgotten, nonexistent, or feigned: "I really hated being with him then; I just smiled in the picture because he made me. He said he'd hit me if I didn't smile." "She used to beat me to make me go to the zoo with her." This element of complete lack of ambivalence is a typical manifestation of the parental alienation syndrome and should make one dubious about the validity of the professed animosity.

The child may exhibit a guiltless disregard for the feelings of the hated parent. There will be a complete absence of gratitude for gifts, support payments, and other manifestations of the hated parent's continued involvement and affection. Often these children will want to be certain the alienated parent continues to provide support payments, but at the same time adamantly refuse to visit. Commonly they will say that they *never* want to see the hated parent again, or not until their late teens or early twenties. To such a child I might say: "So you want your father to continue paying for all your food, clothing, rent, and education—even private high school and college—and yet you still don't want to see him at all, ever again. Is that right?" Such a child might respond: "That's right. He doesn't deserve to see me. He's mean and paying all that money is a good punishment for him."

Those who have never seen such children may consider this description a caricature. Those who have seen them will recognize the description immediately, although some children may not manifest all the symptoms. The parental alienation syndrome is becoming increasingly common, and there is good reason to predict that it will become even more prevalent if the recommendations presented in Chapters One and Thirteen are not implemented.

FACTORS THAT CONTRIBUTE TO THE DEVELOPMENT OF THE PARENTAL ALIENATION SYNDROME

As mentioned, the parental alienation syndrome should not be viewed simply as due to *brainwashing*—the act of systematic programming of the child by one parent against the other, in a consciously planned endeavor. This is only one of four factors, each of which I will discuss separately.

Brainwashing

The brainwashing factor may be present to varying degrees. In some cases it may be minimal or even absent, and the disturbance results from one or more of the other contributing factors. More often, however, it is one of the predominant factors. I confine the word brainwashing to *conscious* acts of programming the child against the other parent. Most often the brainwashing is overt and obvious to the sensitive and astute examiner. The loved parent embarks upon an unrelenting campaign of denigration that may last for years. A mother, for example, whose divorce was the result of marital problems that contributed to her husband's seeking the affection of another woman, may continually vilify the father to her children with such terms as "adulterer," "philanderer," and "abandoner." Similarly, she may refer to the father's new woman friend as a "slut," "whore," and "home breaker." No attention is given to the problems in the marriage, especially this mother's problem(s), that may have contributed to the new involvement.

At times the criticisms may even be delusional, but the child is brought to believe entirely the validity of the accusations. The child may thereby come to view the hated parent as the incarnation of evil. A father, for example, may develop the delusion that his wife has been unfaithful to him and may even divorce her without any specific evidence for an affair. Innocent conversations with strange men are viewed as "proof" of her infidelity, and the children may come to view their mother as an adulteress. Often the infrequency of visits or lack of contact with the hated parent facilitates the child's accepting completely the loved parent's criticisms. There is little or no opportunity to correct the distortions by actual experiences.

A common form of criticism of the father is to complain about how little money he is giving. I am not referring here to situations in which the divorce has brought about some predictable privation. The healthy mother in such a situation recognizes that she and the children will not enjoy the same financial flexibility that they had prior to the separation. I am referring here to the use of the financial restrictions in the service of deprecating the father. A mother may complain so much about her financial restrictions that she will lead the children to believe that they may actually go without food, clothing, shelter, and that they may very well freeze and/or starve to death. I have seen cases in which extremely wealthy women utilized this maneuver, women who have been left with so much money that they will be comfortable for the rest of their lives. They may be spending thousands of dollars on extravagances, and yet the children may come to believe that because of their father's stinginess they are constantly on the verge of starvation.

There are mothers who, when talking to the children about their husbands having left the home, will make such statements as, "Your father's abandoned us." In most cases the father has left the mother and has not lost any affection for the children. Lumping the children together with herself (by using the word "us" rather than "me") promulgates the notion that they too have been rejected. In this way the mother contributes to the children's view of the father as reprehensible. The father in such situations may attempt (often unsuccessfully) to reassure the children that he has left the mother and not them, that he no longer loves the mother, but he still loves them.

Another way of brainwashing is to exaggerate a parent's minor psychological problems. The parent who may have drunk a little extra alcohol on occasion will gradually become spoken of as "an alcoholic." And the parent who may have experimented occasionally with drugs comes to be viewed as "a drug addict." Even though the accusing parent may have joined with the former spouse in such experimentation with drugs, the vilified parent is given the epithet. The deprecated parent might then be described in quite "colorful" terms: "He was dead drunk that night and he was literally out cold on the floor. We had to drag him to the car and dump him in the back seat." "The man was so stoned that he didn't have the faintest idea where he was and what he was doing." Often denial by the accused parent proves futile, especially if the accuser can provide concrete evidence such as a pipe used to smoke pot or a collection of bottles of liquor (which may be no more than the average person has in one's home anyway).

There are parents who are quite creative in their brainwashing maneuvers. A father calls the home to speak to his son. The mother answers the telephone and happens to be in the son's room at the time. The father simply asks if he can speak with his son. The mother (with the boy right next to her) says nothing. Again, the father asks to speak with his son. More silence (during which the son is unable to hear his father's pleas for a response). Finally, the mother responds: "I'm glad he can't hear what you're saying right now" or "If he heard what you just said, I'm sure he would never speak with you again." When the father finally speaks with the boy and explains that he had said absolutely nothing that was critical, the boy may be incredulous. The result is that the father becomes very fearful of calling his son, lest he again be trapped in this way. A related maneuver is for the mother to say to the calling father (after a long period of stony silence during which the boy is within earshot of the mother and the father has made an innocuous statement): "That's *your* opinion. In *my* opinion he's a *very fine* boy." The implication here is that the father has made some scathing criticism and that the mother is defending the child.

Another mother greets her husband at the front door while their daughter is upstairs awaiting her father's visitation. Although the conversation is calm and unemotional, the mother suddenly dashes to the corner of the room, buries her head in her arms, and while cowering in the corner screams out, "No, no, no. don't hit me again." The girl comes running into the living room, and although she did not actually observe her father hit her mother, she believes her mother's claim that her father had just pulled himself back from beating her when he heard the girl coming down the stairs.

Selected use of pictures can also be used in the brainwashing process. There is hardly a child who hasn't at some time or other refused to be in a family picture. There is hardly a family who hasn't had the experience of cajoling the child to join them in the photograph. In many families a picture of the crying child will be taken, with a fond memory of the situation, the child's crying notwithstanding. Such a picture may be used by a brainwashing parent to convince the child that the other parent caused the child's grief and tears. The parent who is collecting evidence for litigation may be very quick to take pictures that could be interpreted as proof of the other parent's hostility toward the child. The healthy parent will argue with a child, scream once in a while, and make threatening gestures. If these can be caught on the camera they are considered to be good evidence for the parent's sadistic behavior toward the child.

Sarcasm is another way of getting across the message that the father is an undesirable character. A mother might say, "Isn't that wonderful, he's taking you to a ballgame." Although the words themselves are innocent enough, and might very well apply in a benevolent or noncharged situation, the sarcastic tonal quality says just the opposite. It implies: "After all these years he's finally gotten around to taking you to a ballgame" or "He really considers himself a big sport for parting with the few bucks he's spending to take you to a ballgame." Another mother says, in a singsong way, "Well, here he is again, your good ol' Daddy-O." Another says to her daughter, "So, the knight-in-shining-armor took his damsel to the movies." These comments are powerful forms of deprecation. If a therapist were to attempt to point out to such a mother how undermining these comments are, she might respond that she was "only kidding" and accuse the therapist of not having a good sense of humor.

A common maneuver used by these mothers is to instruct their children to tell their father that they are not at home when he calls. Or, they will tell them to give excuses like "She's in the bathroom" or "She's in the shower." These children are not only being taught to be deceitful, but they are being used as accomplices in the war between the parents. Of pertinence here is the message that the father is not an individual who is worthy of being treated with honesty and respect. Furthermore, there is the implication that he has objectionable qualities that warrant his being lied to and rejected. One mother told her children not to reveal the name and location of the day camp they were attending, and the children dutifully submitted to their mother's demand. When questioned in family session as to why she gave her children these instructions, she could only come up with a series of weak rationalizations: "He'll go to the camp and make trouble," "He'll embarrass them when he visits," and "I just get the feeling that it's not good for them for their father to know where they're going to camp." I knew the husband well enough to know that there was absolutely no justification for these concerns. Clearly, this mother was using the children as accomplices in her war and they were submitting.

There are a wide variety of other ways in which a mother may contribute to the children's alienation against their father. She may not forward to him copies of school reports. The implication here is that he is not interested in such material and that any comments he may make about them will be of little value to the child. Many go further and obstruct the father's attempt to obtain such material and may even inform the school that they, as the custodial parent, have every right to prevent the school from transmitting such material. She may refuse to allow the father to join with her in teacher's conferences and this may require the teacher to set up two separate meetings. When asked why she refuses to allow him to join her, the mother will often provide weak answers such as, "He'll disrupt the meeting," "I need all the time for myself," and "I just don't want to be in the same room with that man and that should be enough of an explanation." Of course, such mothers will have difficulties with school plays, concerts, and other presentations which are only given once. She may place the children in a very difficult position by stating that if the father attends she will not. Again, the implication is that even if the father is in the same auditorium with her, unpleasant and even terrible things are going to happen. And this position may be taken with regard to confirmations, Bar Mitzvahs, graduations, and family events to which both parents may be invited. These refusals also transmit the message that the father is somehow a noxious individual whose presence at any of these affairs is likely to ruin them.

A common way in which a parent will contribute to the alienation is to label as "harassment" the attempts by the hated parent to make contact with the children. The alienated parent expresses interest by telephone calls, attempts at visitation, the sending of presents, etc. These are termed "harassment" by the mother, and the children themselves come to view such overtures in the same vein. In frustration the father increases efforts in these areas, thereby increasing the likelihood that his attempts will be viewed as nuisances. A vicious cycle ensues in which the denigrated father increases his efforts, thereby increasing the likelihood that the approaches will be viewed as harassments. When such fathers call, the mother may respond with a quick statement which seemingly justifies hanging up on him immediately, without giving him any chance to respond or communicate with the children. Some of the more common putoffs utilized: "They're busy," "They're just ready to eat," "They're eating," "They're not done eating yet," "They're watching TV," "They're doing their homework and can't be disturbed," "They're playing with friends," and "They're getting ready to go to sleep." The father never seems to call at the right time. No matter what the children are doing, it serves as an excuse not to interrupt them. Every activity takes priority over speaking with the father. Related to this view of the calls as harassments, a mother may say to a calling father (with the child within earshot): "If you keep up this pressure to see him we're going to have one of those teen-age suicides on our hands." If this is said enough times the child then learns that this is a good way to avoid seeing his father. The next step then is for the child to threaten suicide if the father attempts to visit, to which the mother can then say to the father: "He keeps saying that he'll kill himself if he has to visit with you. Look what you've driven him to."

Subtle and Often Unconscious Parental Programming

The aforementioned attempts to denigrate a parent are conscious and deliberate. The brainwashing parent is well aware of what he (she) is doing. There are, however, other ways of programming children that can be equally if not more effective, but which do not involve the parent's actually recognizing what is going on. In this way the parent can profess innocence of brainwashing propensities. The motivations and mechanisms here are either unconscious (completely unavailable to conscious awareness) or subconscious (not easily available to conscious awareness).

There are many ways in which a parent may subtly and often unconsciously contribute to the alienation. A parent may profess to be a strong subscriber to the common advice: "Never criticize the other parent to the child." A mother may use this advice with comments such as: "There are things I could say about your father that would make your hair stand on end, but I'm not the kind of a person who criticizes a parent to his children." Such a comment engenders far more fear, distrust, and even hatred than would the presentation of an actual list of the father's alleged defects. A mother insists that the father park his car at a specific distance from the home and honk the horn, rather than ring the doorbell. She is implicitly saying to the child: "The person in that car is a dangerous and/or undesirable individual, someone whom I would not want to ring the doorbell of my house, let alone enter— even to say hello."

The parent who expresses neutrality regarding visitation ("I respect her decision regarding whether or not she wishes to visit with her father") is essentially communicating criticism of the father. The healthy parent appreciates how vital is the children's ongoing involvement with the noncustodial parent and encourages visitation, even when the child is "not in the mood." The healthy parent does not accept inconsequential and frivolous reasons for not visiting. Under the guise of neutrality, such a parent can engender and foster alienation. The "neutrality" essentially communicates to the child the message that the noncustodial parent cannot provide enough affection, attention, and other desirable input to make a missed visitation a loss of any consequence. Such a parent fails to appreciate that neutrality is as much a position in a conflict as overt support of either side.

Related to the neutrality maneuver is the parent who repeatedly insists that *the child* be the one to make the decision regarding visitation. Such a parent hammers away at the child with this principle. The child generally knows that the parent basically does not want the visitation, and so the child then professes the strong opinion that he or she does not wish to visit. Such a mother might say, after the child refuses: "I respect your strength in standing up for your rights." I once saw a mother in this category who went further and said, "If you don't want to visit with him, you can count on my full support. If we have to go to court to defend you we'll do it. I'm not going to let him push you around. You have your right to say no, and you can count on me to defend you." In extreme cases I have seen mothers who will actually hire an attorney to "protect" the child from this so-called coercing father who is insisting on visitation. Such mothers will give their children the impression that they would go to the Supreme Court if necessary in order to support them in "their" decision not to visit. And the more vociferous and determined the mothers become, the more adamant the children become in their refusal—refusal based not on the genuine desire not to see the father, but refusal based on the fear of not complying with their mothers' wish that they not visit. The mother and children then build together a stone wall of resistance against the father's overtures for involvement with the children.

One separated father calls, the mother answers, exchanges a few amenities, and then calls the child to the phone. Another mother answers and curtly says to the child, "It's your *father*" and stiffly gives the phone to the child—conveying the message that the caller is not a former husband, but a person who is so objectionable that the mother would not want in any way to be associated with him. The implication is that the caller is a possession of the child and is in no way related to her.

One mother encourages her child to visit with the father by saying, "You have to go see your father. If you don't he'll take us to court." Nothing is mentioned about the positive benefits to be derived by the child from seeing the father. The only reason to go is for them to protect *themselves* (". . .he'll take us to court") from the father's litigation. One mother, who had agreed to involve herself in court-appointed therapy in order to bring about a rapprochement between her two daughters and their father, told me early in the first session that her main purpose was to bring about such reconciliation. However, about ten minutes later she told me that she felt it was her obligation to help support her daughters' decisions not to see their father. In this case, there was absolutely no good reason for their not seeing their father, except that they were complying with their mother's subconscious wishes that they not do so.

There are mothers who use the "guilt trip" approach to programming their children against their husbands. For example, when the child wants to visit with the father during the scheduled visitation period, the mother might say, "How can you leave your poor old mother?" Not only is the child made to feel guilty about abandoning the mother, but in the ensuing discussion the father is also portrayed as an individual with little or no sensitivity to the mother's feelings. He has not only abandoned this poor helpless mother, but is now luring the children away, thereby increasing her loneliness. He comes to be viewed by the children as insensitive and cruel. The children then, by exaggerating any of the father's weaknesses or deficiencies, can justify their not visiting with him and thereby lessen the guilt they feel over the abandonment of their mother.

The mother who moves to a distant city or state is essentially communicating to the children that distance from the father is not a consequential consideration. It is sometimes done with the implication that they are moving to bring about a cessation of the harassment and other indignities that they suffer while living close to the father. I am not referring here to situations in which such a move might be to the mother's benefit with regard to job opportunities or remarriage. Rather, I am referring to situations in which there is absolutely no reason for the move, other than to put distance between the children and their father. Sometimes parents will even litigate in order to gain permission to leave the state. However, the ostensible reasons are often unconvincing; the basic reason is to bring about a cessation of the parent-child relationship.

Another subtle maneuver commonly utilized by brainwashing parents relates to the psychological mechanism of doing and undoing. An example of this would be an individual who makes a racial slur, recognizes that the other person has been offended, and then retracts the statement by saying, "Oh, I didn't really mean it" or "I was only fooling." In the vast majority of cases the person so criticized does not "get the joke," the smiles and acceptance of the apology notwithstanding. Doing and undoing is not the same as never having done anything at all. A mother might angrily say, "*What* do you *mean* you're going to your father's house?" This may then be followed immediately with the statement, "Oh, what am I saying? That's wrong. I shouldn't have said that. I shouldn't discourage you from seeing your father. Forget I said that. Of course, it's okay for you to go to your father's house." The initial statement and the retraction, all taken together, are not the same as undiluted and unambivalent encouragement. The child gets the message that a strong part of the mother does not want the visitation. Some mothers may make such derogatory comments and then, when confronted with them later, claim that they were said at a time of extreme duress and that they were really not meant. One mother threatened her husband, as he left the home, "If you leave this marriage I vow to God that you'll never see your children again." She said this to her husband in front of their four children. In subsequent custody litigation she first denied to me that she had ever made the statement. When, however, in family session her husband and four children "refreshed her memory," she reluctantly admitted that she had made the statement. She then gave as her excuse that she was quite upset when her husband was leaving and she was thereby not responsible for her comment. She explained at length how, when people are upset, they will say all kinds of things that they don't really mean. Again, doing and undoing is not the same as never having done at all—and the children, at some level, recognize this.

One father, the owner of a large trucking company, dealt effectively with tough and often brutal truckers, union chiefs, and even underworld Mafia figures. He considered carrying a gun to be crucial for his survival as well as that of his company. A gun was viewed as standard professional equipment, like a doctor's stethoscope. He described numerous encounters with violent gangland figures. His fearlessness in these situations was remarkable. Yet, this same man claimed total impotence with regard to convincing his somewhat underweight and scrawny ten-year-old daughter to visit his former wife. His professions of helplessness were often quite convincing to his friends and relatives, and even when I pointed out to him the disparity between his ability to impose his opinion on people at work as compared to his home, he still claimed that he had absolutely no power over his child: "Doctor, I can't do a thing with her!"

One could argue that such subtle programming is extremely common in the divorce situation. I cannot deny this. However, in the parental alienation syndrome the child is *obsessed* with resentment above and beyond what might be expected in the usual divorce. It is the extent and depth of the alienation that differentiates the parental alienation syndrome from the mild alienation that is engendered in many divorces. In addition, there are other factors operative in producing the parental alienation syndrome that are not present in the common type of divorce programming—the most important of which are the presence of custody litigation and the threat of disruption of a strong parent-child (usually mother-child) bond.

Although the mothers in these situations may have a variety of motivations for programming their children against their fathers, the most common one relates to the old saying: "Hell hath no fury like a woman scorned." Actually, the original statement of William Congreve was: "Heaven has no rage, like love to hatred turned. Nor hell a fury, like a woman scorn'd" (*The Mourning Bride*, III, viii). Because these mothers are separated, and cannot retaliate directly against their husbands, they wreak vengeance by attempting to deprive their former spouses of their most treasured possessions, the children. And the brainwashing program is an attempt to achieve this goal. One of the reasons why such brainwashing is less common in fathers is that they, more often than mothers, have the opportunity to find new partners. Less frustrated, they are less angry and less in need of getting revenge.

It is important for the reader to appreciate that these mothers are far less loving of their children than their actions would suggest to the naive observer. Ostensibly, all their attempts to protect the child from harm by the dreaded parent are made in the service of their love of their children. Actually, the truly loving parent appreciates the importance of the noncustodial parent to the children and, with the rare exception of the genuinely abusing parent, facilitates all meaningful contact between the children and their father. These campaigns of denigration are not in the children's best interests and are in themselves manifestations of parental deficiency. Moreover, these mothers exhibit the mechanism of reaction formation, in that their obsessive love of their children is often a cover-up for their underlying hostility. People who need to prove to themselves continuously that they *love* are often fighting underlying feelings of hate. On a few occasions, I have observed dramatic examples of this in my custody evaluations. In the midst of what could only be considered to be violent custodial conflicts—in which both parties were swept up in all-consuming anger—the mother would suddenly state that she was giving up the custody conflict and handing the child over to the father.

In one such case, in the middle of a very heated session, the mother suddenly stated to the father: "Okay, if you want him that bad, take him." When I asked the mother if she was certain that this was her decision, she replied in the affirmative. I reemphasized that the implication of her statement was that the custody litigation should be discontinued and that I would therefore be writing a letter to the judge informing him that my services were no longer being enlisted because the mother had decided voluntarily to turn custody over to the father. At this point the mother's second husband leaned over and asked her if she appreciated the implications of what she was saying. After two or three "jolts" by her new husband, the mother appeared to "sober up again" and stated, "Oh, I guess I didn't realize what I was saying. Of course, I love him very much." She then turned to her son and hugged him closely, but without any genuine expression of affection on her face. I believe that what happened here was an inexplicable relaxation of internal censorship that keeps unconscious processes relegated out of conscious awareness. My statement and that of her new husband served to "put things back in place" and she then proceeded with the litigation as viciously as ever. In short, we see another motivation for the obsessive affection that these mothers exhibit toward their children—an underlying rejection. And when these mothers "win," they not only win custody, but they win total alienation of their children from the hated spouse. The victory here results in psychological destruction of the children which, I believe, is what they basically want anyway. And they are dimly aware that their unrelenting litigation, indoctrination, and alienation will bring this about. In Chapter Nine I will discuss additional psychodynamic factors operative in these mothers, especially as they relate to the therapeutic approaches and the ways in which the courts should deal with them.

Factors Arising Within the Child

Here, I refer to the factors that initially involve no active contribution on the part of the loved parent, conscious or unconscious, blatant or subtle. These are factors that originate within the child. Of course, a parent may use the child's contribution to promote the alienation, but it originates from psychopathological factors within the child.

The most important contributing factor relates to the fact that the child's basic psychological bond with the loved parent is stronger than with the hated parent. The campaign, then, is an attempt to maintain that tie, the disruption of which is threatened by the litigation. The aforementioned maneuvers utilized by mothers are also an attempt to maintain the integrity of this bond. (This point will be discussed in greater detail in Chapter Nine.)

It is important also for the reader to appreciate that the weapons children use to support the mother's position are often naive and simplistic. Children lack the adult sophistication to provide themselves with credible and meaningful ammunition. Accordingly, to the outside observer the reasons given for the alienation will often seem frivolous. Unfortunately, the mother who welcomes the expression of such resentments and complaints will be gullible and accept with relish the most preposterous complaints. Unfortunately, attorneys and even judges are sometimes taken in by these children and do not frequently enough ask themselves the question: "Is this a justifiable reason for the child's never wanting to see the father again?" The inconsequential nature of the complaints and their absurdity are the hallmarks of the child's contribution to the development of the parental alienation syndrome.

Related to the aforementioned desire on the child's part to maintain the psychological bond with the preferred parent (usually the mother) is the fear of disruption of that bond. And there is also the fear of alienating the preferred parent. The hated parent is only ostensibly hated; there is still much love. But the loved parent is feared much more than loved. And it is this factor, more than any other, that contributes to the various symptoms discussed in this section. Generally, the fear is that of losing the love of the preferred parent. In the usual situation it is the father who has left the home. He has thereby provided for himself the reputation of being the rejecter and abandoner. No matter how justified his leaving the home, the children will generally view him as an abandoner. Most often the children subscribe to the dictum: "If you (father) really loved us you would tolerate the indignities and pains you suffer in your relationship with our mother." Having already been abandoned by one parent, the children are not going to risk abandonment by the second. Accordingly, they fear expressing resentment to the remaining parent (usually the mother) and will often reflexly take her position in any conflict with the father. This fear of the loss of mother's love is the most important factor in the development of the symptoms that I describe in this chapter. The parental alienation syndrome, however, provides a vehicle for expression of the anger felt toward the father because of his abandonment. This expression of resentment is supported by the mother, both overtly and covertly. It is part of the maneuver by which the children become willing weapons in the mother's hands, weapons that enable her to gratify her hostility through them.

A common factor that contributes to the obsessive hatred of the father is the utilization of the reaction formation mechanism.

Obsessive hatred is often a thin disguise for deep love. This is especially the case when there is absolutely no reason to justify the preoccupation with the hated person's defects. True rejection is neutrality, when there is little if any thought of the person. The opposite of love is not hate, but indifference. Each time these children think about how much they hate their fathers, they are still thinking about them. Although the visual imagery may involve alienating fantasies, their fathers are still very much on their minds. The love, however, is expressed as hate in order to assuage the guilt they would feel about overt expression of affection for their fathers, especially in their mothers' presence. This guilt is often coupled with the aforementioned fear of their mothers' rejection if such expressions of affection for their fathers were to manifest themselves. One boy, when alone with me, stated: "I'm bad for wanting to visit with my father." This was a clear statement of guilt over his wish to visit with his father, his professions of hatred notwithstanding. This child was not born with the idea that it is bad to want to be with his father. Rather, he was programmed by his mother to be guilty over such thoughts and feelings.

Oedipal factors are sometimes operative in the alienation. A girl who has a seductive and romanticized relationship with her father (sometimes abetted by the father himself) may find his involvement with a new woman particularly painful. Whereas visitations may have gone somewhat smoothly prior to the father's new relationship, following the new involvement there may be a rapid deterioration in the girl's relationship with her father. Such a girl may say to her father: "You've got to choose between me and her." In such situations there may be no hope of a warm and meaningful relationship between the father's new woman friend and his daughter. Sometimes the mothers of such girls will support the animosity in that it serves well their desire for vengeance. Elsewhere, (1986b) I describe in detail my views of the Oedipus complex.

There are situations in which factors operate with the result that the child will opt to support the parent with whom there is a weaker psychological bond or an unhealthy psychological bond.

For example, a paranoid mother may be so successful in programming her child against the father that the child will take on her paranoid delusions. In such cases the child may exhibit morbid fear at the prospect of the father's coming to the home—lest the terrible consequences predicted by the mother be realized. Such children may even hide in closets and under the bed when the father comes to the home and visitation under such circumstances may be impossible.

Many of these children proudly state that their decision to reject their fathers is their own. They deny any contribution from their mothers. And the mothers often support this vehemently. In fact, the mothers will often state that they want the child to visit with the father and recognize the importance of such involvement. Yet, such a mother's every act indicates otherwise. Such children appreciate that, by stating that the decision is their own, they assuage mother's guilt and protect her from criticism. Such professions of independent thinking are supported by the mother, who will often praise these children for being the kinds of people who have a mind of their own and are forthright and brave enough to express overtly their opinions. As mentioned, in extreme cases such mothers will hire lawyers for the children and go to court in order to support what is ostensibly the child's own decision not to visit. The realities are that, with the exception of situations in which the father is indeed abusive, there is no good reason for a child's not wanting to have at least some contact with a father. Children are not born with genes that program them to reject a father. Such hatred and rejection are environmentally induced, and the most likely person to have brought about the alienation is the mother.

Situational Factors

Often situational factors are conducive to the development of the disorder. By situational factors, I refer to external events that contribute to the development of the parental alienation syndrome—factors that abet the internal psychological processes in the parents and in the child. Most parents in a custody conflict know that time is on the side of the custodial parent. They appreciate that the longer the child remains with a particular parent, the greater the likelihood the child will resist moving to the home of the other. Even adults find change of domicile to be anxiety provoking. One way for a child to deal with this fear is to denigrate the noncustodial parent with criticisms that justify the child's remaining in the custodial home. For example, a mother dies and the maternal grandparents take over care of the child. Although at first the father may welcome their involvement, there are many cases on record of the maternal grandparents then litigating for the custody of the child. The child may then develop formidable resentments against the father in order to ensure that he or she will remain with the grandparents, the people whom the child has come to view as the preferable parents.

In one case I was involved with, two girls developed this disorder after their mother, with whom they were living, met a man who lived in Colorado. The mother then decided to move there with the two girls. The father brought the mother to court in an attempt to restrain her from moving out of the state of New Jersey with the children. Whereas previously there had been a good relationship with their father, the girls gradually developed increasing hatred of him, as their mother became progressively more deeply embroiled in the litigation. It was clear that the disorder would not have arisen had the mother not met a man who lived in Colorado, a man whom she wished to marry.

A common situation in which the child will develop complaints about the hated parent is one in which the child has observed a sibling being treated harshly and even being rejected for expressing affection for the hated parent. One boy I treated repeatedly observed his mother castigating his sister for her expressions of affection for their father. The sister was older and could withstand better the mother's vociferous denigration of her. The boy, however, was frightened by his mother's outbursts of rage toward his sister and was adamant in his refusal to see his father, claiming that he hated him, but only giving inconsequential reasons for his hostility. In this way he protected himself from his mother's animosity toward him. We see here clearly how his hatred of his father stemmed not so much from alienating qualities within the father, but from fear of the loss of his mother's affection.

One girl observed her mother making terrible threats to her older brother: "If you go to court and tell the judge that you want to live with your father, I'll have you put away as a psychotic. I'll have the child authorities put you away. You're crazy if you want to live with him." In this case the father was an unusually good parent, and the mother suffered with a moderately severe psychiatric disturbance. The older brother was strong enough to overtly express his preference for living with the father and appreciated that the mother had no power to unilaterally and perfunctorily have him incarcerated in a mental hospital. The younger sister, however, believed that this was a possibility and therefore told the judge that she wanted to live with her mother. Again, it was fear, not love of the mother, that brought about the child's professions of preference.

One boy repeatedly observed his father sadistically and mercilessly beating his mother. In order to protect himself from similar maltreatment, the boy professed deep affection for his father and hatred of his mother. The professions of love here stemmed from fear rather than from genuine feelings of affection. This phenomenon is generally referred to as "identification with the aggressor." It is based on the principle: "If you can't beat 'em, join 'em." Those who were knowledgeable about the father's brutal treatment of the mother expressed amazement that the child was obsessed with hatred of his mother and love of his father, and they were unable to understand why the boy kept pleading for the opportunity to live with his father. Another factor that may be operative in such situations is the child's model of what a loving relationship should be like. Love is viewed as manifesting itself by hostile interaction. Father demonstrates his "affection" for mother here by beating her. In order to be sure of obtaining this "love," the child opted to live with the hostile parent. This mechanism, of course, is central to *masochism* (C. Thompson, 1959; R. A. Gardner, 1970, 1973a).

One 13-year-old girl's mother died in an automobile accident during the course of her parents' custody litigation. Specifically, she was killed en route home from a visit to her lawyer. Even prior to her mother's death, the girl had identified with and supported her mother's position and viewed her father as an abandoner. Her mother was supported in this regard by the maternal grandmother as well. At the time of the mother's death the girl manifested what I have described elsewhere (1979a) as an "instantaneous identification" with her dead mother. This is one of the ways in which children (and even adults) may deal with the death of a parent. It is as if they are saying: "My parent isn't dead; he or she now resides within my own body." In the context of such immediate identification the child takes on many of the dead parent's personality traits, often almost overnight. And this is what occurred in this case. There was a very rapid maturational process in which the girl acquired many of the mannerisms of her mother. As part of this process she intensified her hatred of her father and even accused him of having caused the death of her mother: "If you hadn't treated my mother so badly, there wouldn't have been a breakup of the marriage, she wouldn't have had to go visit with her lawyer, and she wouldn't have been killed on the way home from his office." Although there were many other factors involved in her obsessive hatred and rejection of her father, this identification factor was an important one. Prior to her mother's death she had grudgingly and intermittently seen her father; after the death there was a total cessation of visitation. Interestingly, this identification process was supported by the maternal grandmother, who began to view the girl as the rein-carnation of her dead daughter. And in the service of this process she supported the girl in her rejection of her father.

CONCLUDING COMMENTS

In this chapter I have focused primarily on the manifestations of the parental alienation syndrome and described contributing factors from four areas: 1) brainwashing, 2) subtle and often unconscious programming, 3) the child's contributions, and 4) situational factors. The main emphasis has been to describe the phenomenon of the parental alienation syndrome, but not to delve significantly into its underlying psychodynamics. Later in this book I will discuss in greater depth certain aspects of the programmer's psychodynamics, especially as they relate to therapeutic approaches and the ways in which the courts can deal with parents who contribute to the development and perpetuation of their children's parental alienation syndromes.

Lawyers and judges often ask examiners involved in custody evaluations whether a particular child has or has not been "brainwashed." Frequently, under cross-examination, they will request a yes or no answer. Under these circumstances I generally respond: "I cannot answer yes or no." To answer simply yes, I would only be providing a partially correct response and this would be a disservice to the brainwashing mother. The yes or no response does not give me the opportunity to describe the more complex factors, especially those originating within the child and the situation. Examiners are often asked, "With which parent does the child have a psychological bond?" Again, I usually refuse to answer this question. If I am given an opportunity to elaborate, I state that there is rarely a situation in which a child has a psychological bond with one parent and not with the other. Generally, the child has psychological bonds with both parents. What one really wants to know in custody evaluations is the parent with whom the child has the *stronger and/or healthier* psychological bond. And, if a stepparent is under consideration, one wants to know about the strength and nature of the psychological bond with the stepparent, as compared with each of the natural parents. The psychological bond consideration will be discussed in greater detail in subsequent chapters.

⚖️ SEVEN
EVALUATION OF THE CHILDREN

THE PROBLEM OF THE CHILD'S CREDIBILITY

Evaluating the child in a custody dispute presents examiners with one of their greatest challenges. The primary difficulty relates to children's credibility (or lack of it) and the criteria that children may utilize to support their positions. For example, a six-year-old boy might say, "I want to live with my daddy. My mommy is mean. She makes me get up every day to go to school and she makes me turn off the TV to go to sleep early because she says there's school the next day. My father is nicer. When I visit him on weekends he doesn't make me go to sleep early and he doesn't make me get up in the morning to go to school. I want to live with my father." Although no competent examiner would use such a statement as a reason for recommending that this child live with his father, the statement is a good example of the reasoning processes that might be utilized by the child to determine parental preference.

Another problem that faces the examiner is that children tend to be fickle and change their preferences from day to day. Their memories are shorter than adults' and they may utilize their most recent experiences as the primary criteria with which they make their preference. On different days the examiner may get different answers. In addition, because children's reasons are so superficial, they are likely to change their minds as well. Because of the fickleness of children, I often suggest that they be seen twice. One may get an entirely different story in each of the two interviews. If the child gives the same information in two successive interviews, it is to be taken more seriously.

Children caught in the middle of warring parents often take the position of whichever parent they are with at the specific time. And this may even be carried over into the interview. When the father is sitting in the waiting room, the child may profess a preference to live with him. On another day, when the mother is in the waiting room, she is presented as the preferred parent. In a similar manner, each parent may tell the examiner that the child has told him (her) that he (she) is the preferred parent. The parents are being honest here, but they are often unaware that the child has given the opposite story to the other party. This phenomenon is so common that examiners should expect it to be present in the vast majority of children who are involved in custody evaluations (with the exception of those who suffer with the parental alienation syndrome described in Chapter Six).

J. S. Wallerstein and J. B. Kelly (1980) hold that, prior to adolescence, children's preferences regarding parental choice should not be taken too seriously. They were particularly impressed from their studies over the intense hostility that children from the fourth to sixth grades (ages nine through eleven) exhibit in association with their parents' divorce. The children are angry at the parent whom they hold to be responsible (regardless of the accuracy of their blame). They are willing to take sides and involve themselves as weapons in the parental conflict. They tend to split the parents into the "good parent" and the "bad parent." In adolescence they may be sorry for their impassioned responses. Such anger makes these children's preferences suspect. This anger may be so great that it will persist into adulthood (J.S. Wallerstein and S. Blakeslee, 1989a, 1989b). Although this examiner has certainly seen many children who exhibit hostility toward the parent whom they consider to be at fault, there are others who will prefer to live with that parent. Many of these children appear to be operating in accordance with the mechanism of *identification with the aggressor* in which they basically follow the principle: "If you can't beat 'em, join 'em." Their preference is based on fear of being on the losing side in what they consider to be an unequal battle. In order to protect themselves, they join the more powerful party and this becomes their primary criterion for deciding parental preference. This is clearly not a healthy criterion, especially in situations where the preferred parent exhibits overt sadistic behavior.

When considering children's input into the custody decision, the question is often asked: "At what age should a child's opinion be taken seriously regarding parental choice in custody conflicts?" I am in agreement with D. M. Siegel and S. Hurley (1977) that there is no such age. Every child is different. There are some children who will give important information at very young ages and there are others who at much older ages are not to be relied upon. Each child must be evaluated separately regarding competence to provide useful information. Accordingly, no arbitrary age standard should be utilized, but rather the mental development of the child should be assessed. It has been this examiner's experience that verbalizations made by children under the ages of four or five have little credibility. One should, however, give weight to one's observations of such children's interactions with each parent. One wants to observe for such things as cuddling, affectionate expressions, glances, gestures, and the general level of tension and anxiety of each parent when with the children. At the other extreme, in the adolescent period, one should generally give great weight to what the youngster has to say. Siegel and Hurley describe a number of cases in which the courts have given great weight to the adolescent's preference. However, courts are often impotent to do anything but comply with an adolescent who does not wish to live with the assigned custodial parent if the noncustodial parent is receptive to taking the child in. In the middle period, between ages six and twelve, there is a gradual progression of increasing credibility as the child gets older.

The following vignette demonstrates well how careful the

examiner should be with regard to a child's statement of preference:

Sarah was seven years old at the time of the evaluation. She and her five-year-old brother were caught in the middle of vicious custody litigation. Sarah was an extremely bright and articulate child and could carry on a conversation with the examiner in a convincing fashion. She seemed to have no need to provide information through indirect channels such as projective play. In the first interview she stated quite openly and directly that she wished to live with her father. She enumerated a long list of reasons for her preference, including her belief that her father was much more patient with her, could read stories to her at length, would sit on the floor and play with her, would take her to the zoo and other places her mother was disinclined to visit, and was much more cuddly with her physically. In her second interview with me, as well, Sarah spoke at length about her preference to live with her father.

My evaluation of the parents revealed them to be, with minor exceptions, both dedicated and committed parents. Sarah's mother denied that she was deficient in the areas that Sarah had described. However, her father stated that his observations of the mother matched those of Sarah. As the evaluation proceeded, I became increasingly closer to the conclusion that the mother was indeed a dedicated and good mother and that the father, although also an involved parent, could not provide Sarah and her brother with the attention that the mother could because of his full-time work as an architect. The mother, in contrast, was not employed outside the home and was totally available for the children. However, Sarah's descriptions of her preference made me uneasy about making a final decision to recommend that her mother have primary custody of the two children.

Sarah and her younger brother were being seen in therapy by a psychologist. In addition, the mother was also being counseled by him with regard to helping the children deal with the divorce and litigation. The psychologist only saw the father on one occasion. My original decision was not to get information from the psychologist, in accordance with my policy of hesitating to involve therapists who are seeing the parents or children at the time of my evaluation. I do not wish to put them in the position of possibly compromising the child's treatment by providing information to the court that might strengthen one parent's position over the other. However, in this case, because of my indecisiveness, I decided to get a report from the psychologist. To my surprise, he reported that Sarah had repeatedly told him in interviews that she wished to live with her *mother* and had given many convincing arguments for this decision. In addition, Sarah told her therapist that she had told me, as well, that she wanted to live with her mother. Incredulous, I called the psychologist in order to confirm this and he indeed stated that at no point had Sarah ever veered from her fixed position that she wanted to live with her mother and had told him that she had definitely told me that she did not want to live with her father.

In a joint interview with the parents, I presented this information to them to see if their comments could clarify what was going on. Each parent immediately offered an explanation. The father stated that Sarah really wanted to live with him and had told him so. However, it was clear to him that Sarah was telling her therapist that she preferred her mother because she considered the therapist to be her mother's friend (the father had little contact with him) and believed (correctly) that her preference would be transmitted to her mother through the therapist. He considered Sarah to be afraid to tell her own therapist her true feelings lest she appear disloyal to her mother, whom she assumed would be party to the preferences stated to her therapist. He concluded that Sarah was therefore fearful of expressing her true preference for him. However, he believed that she was stating her true preference to me because she appreciated the importance of my role in the custody evaluation.

Sarah's mother, in contrast, stated that Sarah viewed me as her father's confidant. Sarah was aware that her father was paying me and that her mother was paying the psychologist. She suspected that Sarah assumed that everything she told me would be transmitted to her father, just as everything she told the psychologist would be transmitted to her mother. She viewed each professional as the ally of the payer and considered each to be serving as the vehicle for the transmission of just that information she suspected each parent wanted to hear. And this was the reason she had professed so strongly to me her preference for her father.

Both explanations seemed plausible. Although the parents certainly solved the dilemma of Sarah's providing two different renditions of her custodial choice, the problem of what Sarah's *real* preference was could not be determined. Accordingly, I discounted her stated preferences entirely (both those made to me and to her therapist) and based my final recommendation on other factors related to the family situation. In this case, I recommended that the mother have primary custody (my original inclination, as described above), but recommended very liberal visitation with her father, whom I also saw to be an excellent parent.

This vignette demonstrates well the importance of the examiner being cautious with regard to giving great credence to a child's statement about parental preference. It also demonstrates the importance of the joint interview. Had I not thrown this dilemma out to the parents, and asked their opinions and explanations, I probably would not have solved the problem and resolved the conflict. Their input was crucial in enabling me to understand what was going on with Sarah.

CONFIDENTIALITY IN THE INTERVIEWS WITH CHILDREN

Whereas I tell both parents at the outset that I must be free to use my judgment with regard to respecting their confidentiality, and that I insist upon the freedom of divulgence if it will serve the purposes of the evaluation, such "courtesies" are not generally extended to the child. Specifically, I do not routinely tell children, from the outset, that what they tell me may, at my discretion, be revealed to their parents. Rather, I say nothing at all about confidentiality and divulge what I consider appropriate. However, if the child does ask me whether I will reveal to the parents what I am told, I respond that I may very well do so if I think it is important, and I make no promises about what I will or will not reveal. However, I also advise children to tell me what they wish me to withhold and I will give their requests serious consideration. The main difference between my approach to children and parents is that for children I do not bring up the issue of confidentiality, but I do so with the adults.

One could argue that this policy is deceitful to children and that they have the right to know in advance that disclosures may be made. My response to such criticism is that I approach the situation in a manner similar to the one I use in my therapeutic work. There, I have found it most useful *not* to bring up the confidentiality issue and attempt to establish the general pattern that all information is put into the common pool for consideration by all interested parties. I want to promulgate an atmosphere of open communication. Bringing up the confidentiality issue tends to squelch revelations and thereby compromise treatment. It is my hope that this approach will help children and parents communicate better with one another as important issues are brought forth. The drawbacks of divulgence are, I believe, far outweighed by the therapeutic benefits of the open-pool-of-communication policy. Carrying this policy over to the custody evaluation, it is far better for the child to tell the parental preference openly than to hide in fear with regard to its disclosure. Usually, the parental repercussions for such preference will not be as punitive as the child anticipates. Furthermore, the divulgences may serve as a point of departure for discussion in family interviews. These conversations not only serve data-collection purposes, but can have a therapeutic fringe benefit as well.

The nonpreferred parent usually knows anyway his (her) status in the child's mind. Over the many years in which I have been doing custody evaluations, I have not found my confidentiality policy to be a problem for the vast majority of the children I have interviewed. (Nor is it a problem in therapy.) Children generally expect me to reveal what they tell me to their parents. Even though children in a custody evaluation may have been initially hesitant to reveal parental preference, they recognize that their divulgences are important if they are to do everything for themselves to live with the parent of their preference. Elsewhere (1986b) I discuss in detail my views on confidentiality in the evaluation and treatment of children.

It is a common practice for judges to interview children in their chambers and try to elicit from them information regarding their custodial preference. Judges are basically not trained to conduct such difficult interviews. Nor do they generally have the time to gain the important information in the more relaxed and nonthreatening way that is desirable (and even necessary) for gaining meaningful data. Accordingly, their interviews are often inept—their professions of sensitivity to the child notwithstanding. It is not uncommon for judges to promise children that their confidences will be respected and that their preferences will not be communicated to their parents. However, my experience has been that judges will often reveal such preferences, completely oblivious to their promises. Often what the children have said becomes part of the court record. This is obviously a disservice to them. It can be disillusioning and can contribute to their feelings of distrust of authority.

Moreover, when the judge sees the child in chambers and does not reveal what is said to the attorneys and to the parents, the parents are being deprived of information that may have been vital to the decision. This, in my opinion, is unfair to them and, I suspect, could be proved illegal in that a decision has been made without their being given all the information that contributed to it. The child may provide the judge with false information, which the parents have had no opportunity to refute, and the judge's decision may have been based heavily on these errors (D. M. Selby, 1973). Elsewhere (1987b) I elaborate on the issue of judges interviewing children in custody disputes. Furthermore, in Chapter Eleven I will also focus on this issue.

INTERVIEWING THE CHILD

Introduction

As mentioned, this may be the most challenging and difficult part of the evaluation. Some of the techniques I will present are standard; others I have developed over the years in order to deal with the special problems the examiner has in interviewing children involved in custody litigation. The evaluator wants to gather information about the child's thoughts and feelings about each of the parents, especially as they relate to that parent's parental capacity. In addition, the evaluator is interested in the child's preference. Obviously the latter question is not one that the examiner should be posing early in the interviews. Because it is the most anxiety-provoking question and the one that most children may not initially wish to discuss (they may not wish to discuss it at all), it is best left to the end in most evaluations. Accordingly, I will describe in this section how I proceed from questions that are seemingly remote from this issue to those that get closer to it. Finally, for the child who is willing to discuss parental preference directly—my experience has been that most children I see are ultimately willing to do so—I will discuss the specific ways in which I broach this subject.

In my training in the late 1950s I was taught that the best question with which to begin an interview was the open-ended one: "So what brings you to the hospital?" "Tell me, what are the problems?" and "So what's on your mind?" Such questions have the advantage of providing answers that are "uncontaminated" by any of the examiner's specific questions or comments that may elicit particular associations. As reasonable as this approach may seem, it has definite drawbacks. The most important of these is the fact that such open-ended questions are being posed at the most injudicious time. When patients are new to the therapeutic situation, it is most likely that they will be quite anxious. And when people are anxious they are not likely to process information in the most accurate way. They are more likely to misinterpret, distort, and be defensive. Accordingly, the answers one receives at such times are likely to be unreliable.

In contrast, if one begins with specific questions to which the patient is likely to provide ready answers, anxiety levels are bound to be reduced. General questions pertaining to name, address, age, school, occupation, and so on, only take a few minutes to ask. Getting the "right" answers makes the patient more comfortable. After a few minutes of such "structured" questions, an entirely different patient is available for answering the more anxiety-provoking, unstructured questions such as "What brings you to see me?" And this principle is useful in the custody evaluation as well, especially when interviewing children.

Accordingly, I will generally begin with the child by asking specific questions about name, age, birth date, grade level, school, teacher, and siblings. In the course of the interview itself, I proceed from the more concrete and less anxiety-provoking questions to the more general and higher anxiety-level questions — roughly in accordance with the sequence provided in the ensuing pages. And I leave to the end the most difficult question, that is, the question of specific parental preference. In fact, with some patients I may decide *not* to ask that specific question, because I recognize that the child may not wish to answer it and/or because I already have received my answer in less direct, but nevertheless useful, ways. After obtaining the name-and-address type data I may, in some cases, ask the child if he (she) understands the purpose of the evaluation. Older children generally do; younger children (under five or six) generally do not. If the child's response suggests a belief that I make the final decision, I will correct this misunderstanding and inform the child that my job is to advise the judge and that *the judge makes the final decision.*

Inquiry About the Physical Aspects
Of the Home and Neighborhood

In the realm of concrete questions, questions about the physical characteristics of the home may provide useful information about parental capacity. The child may find focusing on the concrete aspects of each of the parent's homes less anxiety provoking than talking about the parents themselves. However, in the course of such description the child may provide important information about the parents. One could pose the question: "Tell me about your house" or "Describe your home." One could then follow up with questions like: "Tell me things about your house that you like" and "Tell me things about your house that you don't like." In addition to eliciting a description of the home in which the child lives, one should also ask about the home that the child visits.

It is important for the therapist to appreciate that many children may state a preference for living with the parent with the larger home, especially if that home has more space and play equipment. Obviously, this should not be an important consideration in the custody recommendation. It is the parent, not the woodwork, that is going to play the most important role in the child's growth and development. A child, for example, might say, "I want to go live with my father because he has a swimming pool." In such circumstances, one does well to ask the child, "Would you still want to go live with your father if he didn't have a swimming pool?" One does well to remove, one by one, all the concrete and material items that attract the child in order to focus more clearly on the personality qualities that are the crucial elements in the evaluation.

A question I have found useful to ask a child is: "What would you do if your father moved into the house where your mother is now living and your mother moved into the house where your father is now living?" This helps the examiner differentiate between choices made on the basis of home, neighborhood, friends, school environment, and familiarity and those based on the personality of the parent. Children who respond that they would stay in the same home, regardless of which parent lived there, reveal that parental emotional ties are less strong than the ties to school, neighborhood, and friends. However, children who state that they would want to go with the parent who moves, are basically stating that the bond with the parent who moves is probably quite strong, and this consideration is being given preference over the aforementioned "externals."

Some Questions About Siblings as a Source Of Information About Parental Capacity

Asking children to discuss their siblings often provides information about the parents, without the children necessarily recognizing that they are providing such data. Again, this is an area of inquiry which is not directed specifically toward the child being interviewed and so it is less anxiety provoking than the more direct inquiries to be discussed subsequently.

One might ask the child how each of the parents gets along

with each of the siblings. Many children are much freer complaining about how a particular parent treats siblings than discussing how that parent treats them. An older child might be asked about a parent's involvement with a younger sibling, especially a baby. Questions about who changes the diapers, who makes breakfast, or who likes to cuddle more with the baby can provide useful information about which of the two is the more strongly parental.

Even more revealing information can be obtained when the child is asked to discuss each of the other siblings' preferences with regard to which parent the sibling would like to live with. When answering this question children need not describe their own preferences, but significant information may be obtained about the parents. If Mary, for example, says that her brother Jimmy wants to live with their mother, the examiner might ask, "Why does Jimmy want to live with your mother?" One can go further and ask Mary what she thinks about Jimmy's preference. Again, Mary is not being asked specifically to say anything about her own preference. One six-year-old boy, who stated at the outset that he would never tell me his preference, was quick to add that his brother definitely wanted to live with their father. He then told me again how he had no strong preference, except that he did not wish, under any circumstances, to be separated from his brother and then described at great length how close they were, how much they had in common, and how much fun it was to be with his brother. He then sadly described how terrible it would be if he were to be separated from his brother, especially if they were to live in different places.

After extracting as much information as possible about sibling preferences and the child's feelings about them, one might broach the subject of where the child being interviewed wants to live. However, if the examiner senses that this issue would be too anxiety provoking for the child, this direct question should be avoided.

Information About Parental Capacity
Derived from a Discussion of Visitation

It is helpful to get specific and concrete details about visitation times. Older children will often be able to give such information, but even younger children can provide much useful data. When discussing visitation the examiner should try to assess how excited the children are in anticipation of a forthcoming visit. One must be cautious here, however, because weekend visitations are still more fun than going to school, doing household chores, and adhering to the regular routines of the custodial parent's household. Questioning the children about the reasons for wanting to visit can also provide useful information about the nature of the relationship with the noncustodial parent. One tries to differentiate between visiting for gifts, indulgences, or freedom from obligation and visiting for human warmth and deep relationship gratification.

The examiner should try to get information about the visiting parent's punctuality and reliability. Does the parent show up on time? Does the parent show up at all, after having made an appointment? Has the child expressed resentment over such lateness or failure to appear? Is the child fearful of expressing such anger? Or, if expressed, has this proved useful? Was the noncustodial parent frequently late before the initiation of the custody evaluation, and is that parent suddenly proving to be punctual? The child's comments about such deficiencies in the noncustodial parent may differ from the visiting parent's rendition, but both opinions should be recorded. Better yet, if the visiting parent admits to such deficiencies, then, for reasons given previously, important information will have been obtained.

The examiner should inquire whether the child wants to go on the visit. If the child wishes to, one should learn the reasons why. Is the child happy to be free from the custodial parent's reasonable restrictions? Or, is the child happy to be free of the custodial parent's pathological interactions with the child? Children who state that they do not want to visit and provide reasons such as fatigue, nonspecific illness, "too much homework," or "I just don't feel like going," are likely to be rationalizing their basic wish not to be with the visiting parent. Such children are usually fearful of expressing overtly their real reasons and so resort to the aforementioned excuses. One can learn much by asking the child about the details of the visitation: what is done, who is present, where they go, etc. A child, for example, might describe a father who brings along every transient date, thereby fulfilling two obligations at the same time. Does the visiting parent drop the children off at the home of a third party and then pursue other interests? Does the parent cross-examine the children on visitation days to extract information that might serve as useful ammunition in the evaluation? Is there overindulgence (usually for the purpose of guilt assuagement or rivalry with the custodial parent)?

If the child is not visiting with the noncustodial parent at all during the time of the evaluation, the examiner does well (if the situation warrants it and if there is little or no risk) to suggest that the child be given a trial of visitations with that parent. These visits will provide such children with actual living experiences upon which to base the thoughts, feelings, and reactions given to the evaluator. It also provides the examiner with better data for coming to conclusions about the relationship with the noncustodial parent. If the child reacts negatively, one should not immediately assume that the experience was a detrimental one. Changes are anxiety provoking for all of us, and especially for children. The duration of trial visitations may not have been long enough to allow the child to overcome initial anxieties. As will be discussed in Chapter Twelve, one of the advantages of the mediation evaluation is that it enables the examiner to recommend trials over time, an experience that the litigation examiner may not be able to provide. I am in agreement with J. Goldstein, A. Freud, and A. J. Solnit (1973), that such trials may do more harm than good in situations where, for example, a foster child, who has been living with the foster parents for many years, is moved into the home of biological parents, who have belatedly decided they want him (her) returned. This is more likely to be traumatic than the situation I have described above, in which the transfer is from one known parent to another.

It may sometimes be possible to recommend, during the course of the evaluation, that the child actually live with the other parent on a trial basis. This would be done in situations in which the child expresses strong preference for the transfer and/or the examiner believes that such an experience might provide useful data in the evaluation. Rather than just theorize about what it *might* be like living with the other parent, the child will then have firsthand experiences to assist in making a more judicious choice. If the evaluation is long enough to reasonably provide such an opportunity, the information then given by the child is likely to have much greater credibility. Unfortunately, most evaluations are not long enough for this. In addition, school involvement and work situations often make such a trial difficult. However, when the therapist does have the opportunity to make such a recommendation he or she should do so. Of course, these trials are much more reasonably and feasibly accomplished in the mediation evaluation in which there are no court pressures and where accommodations can be made in a much more relaxed and natural fashion.

**Information About Parental Capacity
Derived from the Child's Comments
About the Parents**

Discussion of the Divorce   I will often ask the child why his or her parents are getting a divorce. If the child has not been told, this represents a deficit on the part of both parents. The healthy parent appreciates the importance of providing the children with reasonable information about the divorce. The parent who gives rationalizations for not providing such information ("He's too young." "They wouldn't understand." "It would only upset her more.") are compromised in their parental capacity. One must be careful, however, to verify with the parents that the child has not indeed been told. There are many children who will say that they were told nothing when, in fact, they were given detailed explanations. If one of the parents has been providing information, and the other not, then the provider is exhibiting what I would consider to be better parenting.

If the child does provide the reasons, one may get information about parental capacity in the context of such a discussion. For example, if a girl says that her mother no longer wishes to live with her father because her father has been "very mean" to her and the other children, I will ask the child to describe the kinds of mean things. I am particularly interested in the child's own observations regarding the justification for her mother's allegations. If the "meanness" includes, for example, vilifying and beating the mother, and the child has directly observed such behavior, this would represent a very significant parental deficiency. Other examples: "My mother couldn't stand my father's drinking any more. She said he would come home, start drinking right after supper and by 9:00 he was sound asleep." "My father said my mother was more interested in going to the country club and taking vacations than being with the children." For these and similar allegations the examiner does well to get the child's own observations and opinions regarding the validity of the complaints. Of course, in interview with the parents (individually and jointly) these comments are important to follow up in order to ascertain their validity or lack of it.

Asking children about their specific reactions, thoughts, and feelings about the breakup of the parents' marriage may provide information about parental preference. One girl said, "I'm glad my father's not living in the house any more. He was always starting fights with my mother and he was always picking on me and my brother. It's really quiet in the house, now that he's gone. I don't even miss him. Last week I missed him a little bit, but then I thought about all the mean things he did to us and then I stopped missing him." This child had not been directly asked which parent she preferred to live with. However, she clearly stated her preference in the context of her response.

The more common response to the question of the child's reactions to the separation is that of sorrow about the parents' having split up. In addition, most children (at least in the early phases of the separation) will wish that the absent parent will once again return to the home. Children generally take the position that if the departing parent truly loved them, that parent would stay in the home and suffer through the wretched marital relationship. Not being able to project themselves into the position of the suffering parent, they can only consider how the separation affects them. In such cases, the question about their feelings and reactions to the breakup may give little information about parental preference or parental capacity.

In the context of the explanation about the causes of the separation, the child may reveal the parent who is believed to have been at greater "fault." Elaboration of this issue may give the examiner important information regarding custodial preference. The more detailed the inquiry, the greater the likelihood the examiner will obtain such information. It is important, however, for the evaluator to appreciate that the parent who has left the home is often viewed as the one who was responsible for the marital breakup. That parent is often seen as the "abandoner," regardless of how justifiable the departure may have been. Some children view the parent who has remained in the home as having driven out the other one, no matter how justifiable the ejection. These children may view the custodial parent as the worse of the two and the one who was "at fault." Accordingly, such information about who was to blame must be put into context and considered with other data. In fact, every bit of information collected in the custody evaluation (especially as provided by the children) must be viewed as part of the larger picture. Serious errors can result if the therapist places too much weight on one bit of data, no matter how compelling.

Children of divorce are most often angry over the separation. It is only in those cases where the departure of one of the parents has been a relief for the child and decompressed the psychologically traumatic situation that the child will view the separation positively. Although some children suppress the anger they feel over the divorce, many act it out. Many direct such hostility more freely toward the custodial parent, in most cases the mother. It is as if the child reasons: "I'd better be careful about expressing my anger to my father. He's already left the home. If I tell him how angry I am, I may see even less of him. In fact, I may never even see him again. I'd better be careful. My mother, in contrast, has proved herself to be loyal. She hasn't left the house. She's a safer target for my hostility. I know she'll be loyal to me no matter what I do." Such children may expound at length about all the indignities they suffer at mother's hands: being made to get up early in the morning to go to school, being pressured into eating breakfast, suffering television restrictions, bedtime curfews, and so on. The mother may describe passive-aggressive and uncooperative behavior at home. The father, however, may describe model behavior. In such cases, the examiner should be extremely careful before deciding that the parent toward whom the child is expressing the greater amount of anger is, indeed, the less preferable one. The mere fact that the child is more hostile toward one parent should not, in itself, be a reason for recommending against that parent. One must attempt to ascertain the causes of the hostility—and whether or not it is justifiable—before coming to any conclusions regarding parental preference.

Description of the Typical Day   It is useful to ask the child to describe in detail exactly what happens on a typical day, from arising in the morning until bedtime. I generally refer to these criteria for ascertaining parental preference as "grandma's criteria" (1986a). These are the parent-child experiences that grandma would consider to be manifestations of parental capacity if her ghost were free to roam the house and then report her findings to the examiner. Most grandmas do not have PhDs in child psychology or the equivalent advanced training and therefore have not been contaminated by the presumably more sophisticated and sensitive criteria that we professionals pride ourselves on utilizing. Grandma would focus on the parental behaviors that indicate affection. And one can get information in these areas directly from the children as well as from the parents. One can lead the child along here and ask specific questions; however, it is preferable to start with a general question like: "I'd like you to tell me about your whole day, from the time you get up in the morning until the time you go to bed at night." After the child has given this description, the evaluator should then proceed with more specific questions. The spontaneous responses, unsolicited by the evaluator, are the more meaningful. For example, in answer to the original general question one boy stated, "Before my daddy left the house, he always used to wake me up because my mommy slept late. He always gave me my breakfast because my mommy didn't want to be waked up in the morning. Now that he's gone my mommy sometimes forgets and I've been late for school a lot." Such a response obviously gives much meaningful information about this mother's maternal capacity. However, if such specifics were not provided in the child's general description, the examiner might ask questions like: "Do you wake up yourself in the morning or does someone wake you up?" "Who wakes you up?" "Who helps you get dressed?" The main purpose of these questions is to learn about the child's depth of involvement with each of the parents and each parent's commitment to the child's rearing.

The questions should cover the wide variety of experiences the child has during the day. Because they will usually be posed at a time when the parents are already separated, the examiner should direct the child to the time *prior* to the parents' separation. It is important to appreciate that a parent who was involved in a particular activity is not automatically the one who was most desirous of such involvement. It may be that the other parent was reasonably not available. For example, if a father's job required him to leave the home before the children awakened, it is unreasonable to penalize him if the mother was always the one to wake up the children. In fact, in the traditional household, the mother will generally have been the one involved in many of the daily activities with the child. Therefore, it may always have been the mother, for example, who greeted the children when they returned home from school, simply because the father was, with rare exception, working.

It is in the evening, however, when both parents are generally available, that one can make the best comparisons. One might ask about the homework situation: "When both of your parents were living together, who helped you with your homework at night?" One should determine not only which parent was more involved, but the children's feelings about the nature of the parent's involvement. One wants to know whether doing homework with the child was accomplished smoothly or whether there were typically power struggles, tears, fits, tantrums, threats, and other manifestations of a poor relationship. One child stated, "I never wanted my father to help me with my homework because he was always screaming at me. My mother had much more patience." In the inquiry one tries to determine whether a parent is doing the homework in an overprotective way, i.e., doing it *for* the child, rather than *helping* the child learn *how* to do the homework. Besides homework, one wants to inquire about recreational activities with the child during the evening. The working father who rarely spends such time with the child is generally compromised. Similarly, if such a father spends every evening with paperwork, this is also a parental deficiency, even though his work or business may have warranted such extra obligations. The healthy father knows his priorities with regard to profession vs. child rearing.

A particularly useful area to explore is the bedtime scene. The strongly involved parent enjoys sitting with the child at bedtime and reading bedtime stories. I am not claiming that all healthy parents will invariably love reading these stories endlessly, only that they will derive enough pleasure from them to make it a common activity. In addition, the examiner should try to determine whether the parent enjoys cuddling with the child while engaged in reading such stories. The strongly involved parent will also enjoy lying down with the child and cuddling as well. There are parents who will refrain from such cuddling practices (especially with opposite-sexed children) because they have been told that this will give the child an "Oedipus complex." The parent who follows such advice (often given by professionals such as psychiatrists and psychologists) may be complying with it to rationalize noninvolvement. The healthy parent does not take such advice seriously, the qualifications of the "expert" notwithstanding. The wise parent appreciates the difference between occasional cuddling and sexual stimulation—the former need not be associated with the latter. The examiner should also inquire about what happens when the child wakes up in the middle of the night with nightmares. Who comes to console the child? To which parent does the child turn for reassurance and consolation? Which parent has traditionally taken the child to the emergency room or the doctor's office when there have been nighttime accidents and/or other medical emergencies? One should inquire about typical weekends prior to the separation. What was done? Who initiated recreational activities with the children? Who went with them? Who was more patient with the children while engaged in these activities? Who was willing to go to more inconvenience in order to involve the children in them?

I have often found it useful to ask parents to submit to me a list of questions that I should ask the children. Invariably, each parent will include in that list questions which, if answered according to parental expectations, will reflect badly on the spouse. Many of these questions can be incorporated into the series of questions about the typical day. This procedure lessens the likelihood that the children will sense that they are being presented with questions that are going to focus specifically on areas that will evoke loyalty conflicts.

As mentioned, it is important to make every attempt to ascertain what the situation was prior to the separation, and especially prior to the initiation of custody evaluation. It is quite common for parents to become "super-parents" when a custody conflict is brewing. In addition, it is important to get parental responses and comments (from both sides) regarding each of the children's descriptions of the parents — especially those that reflect negatively on parental capacity. The examiner who does not do this may justifiably be criticized for accepting the description of a young child as valid. It is in the joint interviews, especially, that one has the opportunity for parental input into the child's descriptions. When the parent admits that the child's criticism is valid, one is provided with very powerful information.

Direct Description of the Parents   When asking direct questions to the child regarding the parents, my aim is to obtain concrete descriptions of parental assets and liabilities, without asking specifically which parent the child would prefer to live with. Of course, the information obtained relates directly to parental preference. Again, I start with general questions before proceeding to more specific ones. I might ask: "Tell me about your mother" or "Describe your father." These are far better questions than: "Do you love your mother?" "Does your father love you?" or "Who loves you more, your mother or your father?" The latter group of questions will provide yes or no answers or one-word responses. The former will generally elicit descriptive, concrete information that is much more valuable for the purposes of the custody evaluation. One should get the child to try to provide elaborations and examples in order to elicit as much information as possible. One can then proceed with questions like: "Everybody is a mixture of both good and bad parts. No one is perfect. Tell me some good things about your mother." When one has exhausted this possibility, the therapist should go on with questions like: "As I have said before, everybody is a mixture of both good and bad parts. Tell me some bad things about your mother. What things about your mother don't you like?" A similar inquiry should then be pursued with regard to the father. Another question in this category might be: "What's the best thing you can say about your mother (father)?" "What's the worst thing you can say about your mother (father)?" One must try to get the child to elaborate upon simple, short answers in order to get as much mileage as possible out of the responses.

Then, a similar inquiry should be pursued with regard to other significant adults who may be involved in the child's upbringing, e.g., a stepparent or a friend with whom a parent is living. It is important to get information about these individuals to the degree that they may be serving as parental surrogates. In the course of such an inquiry the examiner should get details about the duration of these involvements. Of course, younger children are less likely to be able to provide accurate information about the passage of time. In the joint sessions, however, one can get parental input into this issue. Clearly, the parental surrogate who has enjoyed a longer salutary relationship with the child is going to be in a stronger position for custody than the person whose more meaningful involvement is of more recent origin (a common situation in custody evaluations). This is an important area of inquiry because it is common for a father to present a new woman friend as being equal to the mother in child-rearing capacity. He may be so blinded by his rage that he fails to appreciate that his new involvement, even if a highly maternal woman, is not likely to have developed a psychological bond with the children that is a fraction of the strength of that which exists with the mother.

The evaluator must appreciate that what the child may consider a "bad" quality on a parent's part may indeed be an asset. For example, if a child says, "My father makes me turn off the television set in order to go to sleep," and if the sleep time is a reasonable one, this "criticism" is actually an asset and a point of credit to the father in the evaluation. Obviously, the father who lets a child stay up late watching television (especially on school nights) is compromising his paternal capacity.

I have found it useful to ask children whether, prior to the separation, their parents slept in one bed or two separate beds. If the parents slept in separate beds, I will ask the children whose bed they went into when they would crawl into a parent's bed in the morning to cuddle. Or, if the parents slept in the same bed, I will ask on whose side they would more frequently enter in order to cuddle. I sometimes go further and ask, "If you were in the middle, between your mother and father, with whom did you cuddle the most when you were younger?" If there was no bed entering and cuddling at all, both parents were probably deficient in this area. The healthy parent enjoys such cuddling experiences and welcomes the child's involvement, especially on weekends and holidays. The child who is not "interested" is one who has been rejected from such involvement and has "gotten the message" that overtures for such cuddling are unacceptable.

Questions About Friends   I have found useful an inquiry into each parent's attitudes toward the children's friends. The healthy involved parent is very respectful of the importance of friends and tries to encourage friendships from the earliest years of life. The devoted parent is willing to tolerate some of the discomforts, noise, mess, and fighting that is usually entailed when visitors come to the house. The committed parent recognizes that these inconveniences are a small price to pay for the important advantages to the child in having friends and relating well to others. The parent who does not appreciate this is definitely compromised. Accordingly, I will ask the child about each parent's attitudes toward having friends in the home. One child answered, "When my father's home, he never lets me have my friends in the house. He says they make too much noise and so he can't sleep or watch television. When he's not at home, my mother lets the kids come in and play. But she usually makes them go home before my father gets home because he'll get very angry and make a fuss. I think she's scared of him." Although this mother's fear of her husband and her compliance with his wishes is a deficiency, she clearly recognized, far more than her husband, the importance of the child's having friends. I consider a parent's failure to appreciate the importance of friendships to be a significant deficiency.

In addition to inquiring about each parent's receptivity to having friends visit the children, one should inquire about the interest the parent has in bringing the children to visit friends elsewhere. The evaluator should try to determine who makes efforts to bring the children in contact with others and how extensive these efforts are. Of course, the mother, usually being at home more, is more likely to be available for this. On the weekends, however, when both parents are usually home, one may get a better idea regarding which parent is more receptive and willing to be inconvenienced for the children's involvement with peers. Here again, one must appreciate that the father may feel more obligated to extend himself on weekends because the mother assumed this obligation throughout the week. In such situations, one gets little information about relative parental capacity. An important point here is that the healthy parent recognizes the importance of involvements with friends and is willing to facilitate such involvements.

It can sometimes be useful to ask the children what their *friends* think of each of the parents. Sometimes children will be freer to express parental negative qualities through the vehicle of a companion than to do so themselves. Sometimes the comments of friends will corroborate what the child has said. For example, the child of an alcoholic mother said, "My friends don't want to come to the house. My mother never wears nice clothes. She's always wearing that same old dress, and she's usually cranky. She's not nice to them. And they say that she's mean and that she's a mess." Another child said, "My friends like to come to the house when my mother's there, but they don't like to come to the house when my father's there. My father's always kicking them out and saying that they make too much noise. My mother doesn't seem to mind them. Kids will come to the house and say, 'Is your father home yet?' They just don't want to come to the house when he's there." Because friends' comments are not generally made directly to the examiner, they should be used with caution. Strictly speaking, they are hearsay. Nevertheless, they are useful information to have as supporting quotations.

The question is sometimes asked whether there is a particular age at which a child's opinion regarding parental preference can be given credibility. I do not believe that there is any such cut-off point. Younger children, of course, are less credible than older ones and the more intelligent the child, the greater the likelihood his (her) reasons will be valid. When giving credence to a child's preference, the examiner may wish to have an intelligence test administered. This can often provide information about how seriously a child's preference should be taken. For example, if a six-year-old child's IQ indicates that he is functioning in the nine-year level, this would be important information to include in any statement about how much credence should be given to the child's stated preference. If the *Wechsler Intelligence Scale for Children-Revised (WISC-R)* (D. Wechsler, 1974) is utilized, one might wish to look particularly at the Comprehension and Picture Arrangement subtests, both of which are sensitive to the child's social judgment capacity and common sense. If time and money do not permit the administration of the WISC-R, I have found the *Slosson Intelligence Test* (R. L. Slosson, 1961) to be useful. Whereas the services of a trained psychologist are generally necessary to administer the WISC-R, most mental health professionals are qualified to administer the Slosson. As will be elaborated upon subsequently, I do not recommend projective tests such as the Rorschach or the TAT in the custody evaluation.

With rare exception, an intelligence test is the only formal psychological test I consider warranted in a custody evaluation. (Later in this chapter I will elaborate on this point.)

Direct Questions About Parental Preference   All of the above approaches, although providing key information about parental capacity, are designed to studiously avoid placing children in the position of directly stating their parental preferences. For children who do not wish to state such preference, the examiner will generally have a significant amount of information provided by the above questions. For children who are willing to state a preference, the above questions can help ease the child into the discussion. They serve to desensitize the child to the issue and thereby make it easier to discuss this sensitive area. But even here, I may not directly "get to the point." Rather, I may ease into the issue by posing questions that may be less anxiety provoking.

Types of questions that can ease children into discussing parental preference are those that encourage discussion of others or general principles: "With which parent is it best for a boy (girl) to live, the mother or the father?" Here the examiner is not asking specifically with whom the child would like to live, but is asking a general question about children. This type of question makes it easier for children to reveal themselves because they are speaking about "third parties." In addition, many children, after discussing the general question of parental preference, will begin to talk about their own preferences. Although there is a projective element in this question, it is far more understandable to the court than the more traditional projectives that tap deeper layers of the unconscious. I will, on occasion, use this kind of material in my report whereas, as will be discussed later in this chapter, I would hesitate to use the "deeper" types of projective material.

Another way of talking about "third parties" is to ask a series of questions about the preferable custodial parent for boys and girls of various ages. For example, when interviewing a seven-year-old boy, one might ask the following series of questions: "With which parent should a one-year-old baby live, the mother or the father? Why?" "With which parent should a three-year-old boy live, the mother or the father? Why?" One can then repeat this question for a five-year-old, six-year-old, seven-year-old, and so on. One can then ask the same boy the same series of questions, but this time with regard to a little girl. In interviewing a girl, one could similarly present the series, first with one sex and then with the other. My experience has been that when one gets to the age of the child being interviewed, children will generally shift into a discussion of themselves. This not only provides the examiner with a direct statement about parental preference, but it avoids the possible (but small) risks of using projective material.

Another useful way of getting the child to reveal parental preference, without directly asking, is to pose what the legal profession refers to as "hypothetical questions." The best ones I have found useful for this phase of the custody evaluation are those which begin: "If the judge said. . .," "If the judge decided. . .," and "If the judge asked you. . . ." This is a particularly useful phrase when introducing various "touchy" questions. For example, "If the judge asked your brother whom he would wish to live with, what would be his answer?" "When the judge asks you which parent you wish to live with, what are you going to answer?" "Whom do you think the judge is going to decide to give custody, your mother or your father?" and "Whom do you think the judge is going to think is the better parent, your mother or your father?" These questions are often less threatening for children to answer than a direct one about their preference.

Another way of avoiding the request for an overt preference is to use questions that relate to each parent's stated preference: "Why does your father want you to live with him?" "Why does your mother want you to live with her?" "Why does your mother think that she's a better parent than your father?" and "Why does your father think that he's a better parent than your mother?" The child should then be asked whether he (she) agrees or disagrees with the parental reasons. Here again, such inquiry often leads directly into the child's own statement of parental preference. Sometimes a child will actually state that the parent's motive is vengeance, keeping the house, or saving money by gaining custody. Here, however, one must be careful to differentiate between the child who is parroting a parental statement and the one who has a genuine understanding of and conviction for the reason being given. At times, of course, such differentiation may be difficult, if not impossible.

All of the above indirect questions not only serve to protect the child from the feelings of anxiety and disloyalty associated with stating a direct preference, but serve to desensitize the child and prepare the way for a possible direct statement. It is the direct statement that is the most powerful and the strongest in the face of cross-examination. My experience has been that about 80 to 90 percent of all the children I have seen in custody evaluations were ultimately willing to give me a direct statement. In such cases I do not simply stop the inquiry after a statement of preference. Rather, I ask the child to elaborate at length the reasons for the preference. I take careful notes during such elaborations. I then make every attempt to encourage the child to state these reasons in a joint interview with both parents. Although some children are too fragile and fearful of such confrontation, my experience has been that most are willing to do this. In fact, the "revelation" usually comes as no surprise to both parents in that they generally know each child's preference prior to the initiation of the evaluation. I do not put great pressure on children to state their preferences and reasons in the joint session, but encourage them to do so. This encouragement is only partially done for the purposes of the evaluation. It is also done for its fringe therapeutic benefit, because I believe that open communication of these issues is the best way to reduce the problems that invariably arise when they are not discussed openly. In the joint interviews one has the opportunity to correct distortions that the child may have as well as to get statements of admission of deficiency from the nonpreferred parent. The children's statements and parental responses provide important information for my final recommendations. And this is especially true in the litigation evaluation when these comments become incorporated into the report to the court.

Earlier in this chapter I presented a discussion of sibling

preferences and how these can contribute to understanding a child's own preferences as well as parental capacity. Once the child has stated a preference, the examiner may use "sibling questions" to get even further information, especially if there is some confusion regarding what the child really wants. One can often get additional information in such situations with questions like: "You say you want to live with your father and that you want your brother to live with your father also. If the judge said that your brother must live with your mother, but that you could choose to live with either your mother or your father, what would you do then?" If the child still wants to live with the father, even though it means separation from the brother, it is a strong statement of preference for the father, because the child is willing to give up the fraternal relationship in order to live with him. In contrast, if the child switches preferences and no longer wishes to go with the father but rather to live with the mother and brother, we learn something about the weakness of the child's attachment to the father. There is also some implication here that the maternal option was not that weak in the first place.

Even children who adamantly refuse to express a preference throughout the course of my interviews will often give me significant information about their preferences. At times the preference will be "slipped in" as the child leaves the final interview. It is as if the child did not wish to leave the consultation room without giving some indication of preference—lest he (she) be assigned to the "wrong" parent. In such cases the child might make a statement like: "I don't care who I live with, but I don't mind living with my mother." Or "I don't want to make either one of my parents feel bad, so I'm not going to say who I want to live with. But, if the judge makes me live with my mother, I'll do it." Sometimes the child, in the closing minutes of the evaluation, will make a statement that one parent is "a teeny-weeny, little bit better." It is important for the examiner to appreciate that the child may want the examiner or the judge to take the "blame" for making the decision. In this way the child may be freed of guilt feelings over disloyalty and safe from the feared retaliation from the nonpreferred parent. The child will then be able to say to the nonpreferred parent, "I really wanted to go with you, but that (expletive) Doctor Gardner told the judge that I should live with Mommy (Daddy)." Examiners do well to allow themselves to be used for such purposes.

GRANDPARENTS

One does well to try to find out about each of the parent's commitment to involving the children with the grandparents. The healthy parent recognizes the importance of children's relationships with their grandparents, relationships that we in the mental health professions do not generally appreciate fully. The adoration that grandparents often have of their grandchildren can be very esteem-enhancing for the children. They can serve as a buffer against the unwarranted criticisms that children (as well as the rest of us) inevitably receive in life. One should try to find out from the children who calls the grandparents, who invites them to visit, and who seems to be proud of the children's accomplishments vis-à-vis the grandparents.

In some situations the grandparents may be serving either directly or indirectly as parental surrogates. This is direct when, for example, a mother may move back into her own parents' home with her children. In such cases, the examiner should interview the maternal grandparents. In other cases the grandparents may serve indirectly as parental surrogates, especially during visitation. Unfortunately, it is often the case that after a divorce children become estranged from the grandparents on the side of the noncustodial parent. An inquiry into the children's relationships with each of the grandparents can provide information about the two extended family settings which the evaluator is trying to compare. Although the primary persons being compared are the parents, comparison of the grandparents warrants the evaluator's consideration—even if these parties are not interviewed directly. An inquiry (with the children and the parents) into the children's relationships with each of these persons provides useful information in the evaluation. The parent who would provide the children with the most meaningful involvement with the grandparents—especially with the preferable grandparents (if such is the situation)—gets "extra points" in the custody evaluation. However, this "edge" should not be given great weight in that it is of much less importance than qualities possessed by the parents themselves. An additional reason for making such an inquiry is that healthy grandparents are likely to produce healthier children and the preferred parent is more likely to have healthier and more parental parents than the nonpreferred parent.

A good way to start such an inquiry is with the concrete. One might ask the child to list each of the grandparents and to tell what name is used when referring to each one. Then the evaluator might proceed with a more specific inquiry into each grandparent's assets and liabilities. One can use such questions as: "What are the things about your grandmother (grandfather) that you like the best?" "What are the things about your grandfather (grandmother) that you don't like?" One should try to get information about the frequency of visits with each of the grandparents. Other questions should be asked like: "Which one likes to hug you the most?" "Who is most proud of the things you do?" and "Who seems to enjoy being with you the most?" At times I have asked the child to list all the grandparents in order of preference: "Put on the top of the list the name of the grandparent you like the most and then put at the bottom of the list the name of the grandparent you like the least. Then put in the middle the names of the others."

THE GUARDIAN AD LITEM

In some cases a guardian ad litem may have been appointed by the court. To date I have had few direct contacts with a guardian ad litem during my evaluation. This is probably preferable in that information so provided might be considered hearsay and, in addition, he (she) might justifiably be criticized by one of the parents for trying to influence the impartial evaluator. However, the children's comments about their relationship with the guardian ad litem may provide some useful information in the custody evaluation. For example, three children I was evaluating in a custody conflict referred to the guardian ad litem as *their* lawyer. Their view was that he truly represented them and that they could go to him with their complaints. The youngest boy stated, "My father hasn't sent me my allowance this week. I'm going to call my lawyer!" Here, the guardian ad litem was certainly playing an important role in this child's life. The boy's reference to his involvement with *his* lawyer provided information about the father with regard to the latter's reliability in sending his son's allowance. Of course, I did not automatically assume that the father did not send the allowance. I spoke with the father, in a joint session with the boy, and invited his input on this matter. He admitted that he had been defaulting in this regard, stating that he was quite busy and had forgotten. In addition, he denied having received any of the messages the boy left with the father's secretary "reminding him" to send the allowance. As mentioned, open admissions of deficiencies are the most powerful tools the examiner can use in the custody evaluation.

THE JUDICIOUS USE OF SELECTED PROJECTIVE MATERIAL

Dreams

As I have already mentioned on a few occasions, the examiner should be extremely cautious about using projective material in the custody evaluation. One does well to compare such data to dreams. Most would agree that dreams, per se, are of little diagnostic significance. The dream of the healthiest person utilizes the logic of the psychotic. In the dream there is a bona fide break with reality in which we actually believe that our dream experiences are occurring. In fact, one useful way of understanding the psychotic state is to consider it a dream in the waking state. Even the healthiest person will have dreams that are not significantly different from the dreams of the psychotic. Accordingly, not only are dreams of little, if any, diagnostic significance, but they are not well correlated with clinical behavior.

Dreams do, however, *at times* provide us with useful *psychodynamic* (as opposed to diagnostic [labeling]) information. They can tell us something about *why* a person is behaving in a particular way. This is especially the case if we have the opportunity to elicit the free associations of the dreamer and to utilize his (her) assistance in analyzing the dream. In short, then, the dream has great potential for telling us something about *why* a person is thinking and acting in a particular way, but it is of little, if any, value in providing us with information about depth of psychopathology and degree of impairment in the real world. Accordingly, it is of little value in telling us something about such functions as parental capacity. I am not stating that it is of absolutely no value in this regard. If a mother, for example, describes repetitious dreams of murdering one or more of her children, there is the *possibility* that she may be harboring homicidal impulses toward her progeny. However, the dream may have nothing to do with such impulses. The children, as extensions of herself, may very well symbolize qualities of her own that she may wish to get rid of. One must know the patient well and have full opportunity for analytic work (generally over a long period) before one is in a good position to come to definite conclusions about a dream's meaning. And even then one could only state what is the most probable interpretation. And one should be even more cautious about the interpretation of children's dreams. This is especially the case because children are not as cognitively capable of analyzing them and their capacity to provide meaningful free associations is often limited. One certainly could not get up in a court of law and say that there is definite "proof" about the meaning of a particular dream, even a repetitious one. Elsewhere (1986b, 1988a) I have discussed my views on dream analysis in detail.

The Rorschach Test

The Rorschach Test (H. Rorschach, 1921) is one of the most widely used and respected projective tests. One does well to view the projections facilitated by the inkblots to have much in common with the dream. Like dream interpretation, there is a wide variety of opinion among psychologists about the meaning of these projections. I agree with those who hold that they can provide useful information, in many cases, about underlying psychodynamics. *The Rorschach Test* is probably a better source of information about *diagnosis* than the dream. However, it certainly has drawbacks in this regard. (But *diagnosis*, as has already been mentioned, is of little value in the custody evaluation.) And as far as a predictor of behavior *The Rorschach*, like the dream, leaves much to be desired. I am not claiming that it has no value in this regard; I am only claiming that it is of little value because of the highly speculative nature of the predictions and the correlations between Rorschach response and clinical behavior. Accordingly, it is of questionable value in the custody evaluation in which we are trying to learn something about parental capacity. As I described above for the dream, repetitious Rorschach responses in which there is, for example, a high frequency of sadistic and even murderous impulses toward children does not necessarily mean that the adult wishes to torture or kill his (her) own children. Such projections might relate to feelings about such aspects of one's self (as just one possible alternative explanation).

The Thematic Apperception Test and Other Projective Tests

The Thematic Apperception Test (H. Murray, 1936) is another widely used projective test. Here the patient is presented with a series of pictures and asked to create a story that is suggested by them. Although the pictures are designed to be nonspecific, they certainly restrict and contaminate fantasies. L. Bellak and S. S. Bellak (1949) subsequently developed the *Children's Apperception Test (CAT)*, which follows the same principles. However, the pictures, although again nonspecific, tend to elicit fantasies that are more relevant to the lives of children. I view these tests to have definite value in providing the examiner with psychodynamic material. They have less value (but are not of no value at all) in providing diagnostic information in terms of the specific diagnostic category in which the patients' problems may best be described. However, conclusions about parental capacity derived from these cards are highly speculative and are not likely to hold up well in court. E. S. Schneidman's *Make-A-Picture Story Test (MAPS)* (1948) has certain advantages over the TAT and CAT in that the patient is presented with a series of scenes (in which there are no figures, either human or animal) and an assortment of human and animal figurines. Patients are asked to create their *own* pictures. The stories obtained thereby are less contaminated by the external facilitating stimuli and are more truly revealing of underlying psychological processes. However, I have the same reservations about the MAPS as I have with the aforementioned projective tests with regard to their value in legal proceedings. J. N. Buck (1946) introduced the *House-Tree-Person Test* in which the child's drawing provides useful psychodynamic information. One not only analyzes the drawings per se, but the fantasies the child creates around the drawings. Subsequently, K. Mackover (1949) published her techniques which follow similar principles for analyzing children's drawings. Buck's and Mackover's contributions have been the subject of significant controversy, and there is no question that a high degree of speculation is involved in making interpretations in these two tests. Nevertheless, there is also no question that these are useful instruments for learning something about psychodynamics, are less useful with regard to diagnostic information, and are of little value in the courtroom. They are also of limited value in the mediation evaluation because of their subjectivity. Even in the mediation evaluation one does far better to utilize direct quotations, observations, and other "hard facts."

Projective Tests in Court

The way in which the utilization of projective material can compromise an examiner's position in court is well demonstrated by this vignette. A six-year-old boy, in the course of the custody evaluation, is given a piece of drawing paper and crayons. He is invited to draw anything he wants and then to tell a story about what he has drawn. This is standard procedure in child diagnosis and treatment. The child draws a house and then draws a man in the middle of the house. The man is drawn in black crayon and as the boy fills in the human outline (again with black) there is a vigorous and intense quality to his work. He then takes a red crayon and says, "The whole house is burning down and so is the man." Again, there is a frenetic quality to his work as he covers the whole drawing with red lines. He then says, "The whole house is burned down. Everything is ashes. Even the man is ashes." The child is then asked how the house caught on fire. The reply, "The boy's friend, who lives next door, burnt it down. He was angry at the man who lived in the house. He didn't like him because he was mean."

Most examiners would agree that the drawing and its associated story reveal that the child is extremely angry at his father. Depicting his father as completely black, and drawing him frenetically, suggest that the child views his father as a fearful and ominous figure, as anxiety-provoking and dangerous. Most would agree, as well, that the friend next door is merely a convenient device, an alter ego, for assuaging guilt over his hostility. It is not *he* who kills his father, but his friend (his alter ego) next door. His hostility toward his father is being released through a drawing in which he totally destroys the father by burning him to death.

Now let us imagine the situation in which the evaluator has included the above material in the report and considers the child's massive hostility toward his father as one argument (among many) for recommending that the mother be given custody of the child. The husband's attorney, during cross-examination, could ask the examiner to show the court the picture and explain its supposed meaning. Following this presentation, the attorney could ask the following questions, to which only yes-no answers could be required:

> *Attorney:* "Is it possible, Doctor, that this child watched television before drawing this picture, either on the same day or one or two days previously?"
> *Examiner:* "Yes."

The examiner has no choice but to answer yes. A "no" response essentially says that there is absolutely *no* possibility that this child watched television over a three-day period. Even if there is no television set in the home, there would still be the possibility that he watched in another child's home. The attorney then continues.

> *Attorney:* "Is it possible, Doctor, that the child observed a program in which a building burned?"
> *Examiner:* "Yes."

Again, the examiner has little choice but to answer yes, because to say that there was *no* such possibility is absurd. This is especially the case because most news programs routinely describe the major fires of the day. The attorney then proceeds.

> *Attorney:* "Is it possible, Doctor, that such a program depicted people being injured and even killed in such a fire?"
> *Examiner:* "Yes."

Once again, the examiner has to answer yes to preserve credibility.

> *Attorney:* "Is it possible, Doctor, that the picture that you've just shown us was suggested by his watching such a television program, a program in which a fire was described, a program in which people were burned to death in the fire?"
> *Examiner:* "Yes."

If the examiner tries to follow the one-word response with an explanation, the attorney will likely interrupt and instruct the testifier to confine responses to yes or no. This is likely to frustrate the examiner because of the deep-seated conviction that such environmental suggestions play a small role, at best, in producing such pictures and fantasies. The examiner firmly believes that it is the internal pressure of psychodynamically meaningful material, rather than external suggestive stimuli, that play the most important role in creating such fantasies in the child. But a skilled lawyer will not permit the testifier to provide this explanation. Even if the examiner were permitted to give it (and sometimes the judge might ask for it), the attorney could still extract a statement that such an explanation is "theory" and not "fact." And the attorney could then proceed with further inquiry designed to weaken the explanation:

> *Attorney:* "Is it possible, Doctor, that your explanation is incorrect?"
> *Examiner:* "Yes."

If the examiner claims that there is absolutely no possibility that the explanation is incorrect, the examiner compromises credibility. So, once again, the examiner has no choice but to answer in the affirmative. The examiner has no choice but to agree that the explanation may be incorrect and there may be no opportunity to elaborate and explain that the possibility of being incorrect is extremely low, that well-established psychological principles would highly support such an explanation, and so on.

An astute attorney (especially one who consulted a knowledgeable and experienced psychologist or psychiatrist) might proceed as follows:

> *Attorney:* "In the course of your practice, Doctor, have you ever treated children who have been exposed to psychological traumas such as divorce, accidents, injuries, hospitalizations, and death of a parent?"

To this question, the examiner almost has no choice but to say yes. To a negative response, the attorney might justifiably ask about how long the "expert" has been in practice and what kind of patients have been seen. Assuming then that the answer will be yes the attorney will then continue.

> *Attorney:* "Is it not true that children who are exposed to such traumas deal with them via reiteration because such reiteration

contributes to the desensitization process. In other words, each time the child thinks about the trauma, talks about it, and emotes to it, the youngster experiences some relief from the psychological pain associated with the trauma?"

Again, the examiner has no choice but to say yes. To answer in the negative would compromise significantly the examiner's credibility and degree of competence because the statement is a well known principle in child therapy. Assuming, therefore, that the answer is again affirmative, the attorney might continue:

> *Attorney:* "Isn't it possible, then, that this child was upset by watching a television program in which people were killed in a fire and attempted to deal with the untoward psychological reactions by a desensitization process?"

Again, it behooves the examiner to say yes or else risk a loss of credibility. The attorney then continues:

> *Attorney:* "Isn't it true, Doctor, that children commonly use their self-created drawings and associated stories as a vehicle for such desensitization?"

Again, the examiner almost has no choice but to answer in the affirmative for the same reason. The attorney then continues:

> *Attorney:* "Isn't it possible, Doctor, that this child's picture then was the result of an attempt to desensitize himself to his strong emotional reactions evoked by watching this scary program?"

It is likely again that the examiner will have to say yes. The attorney may then continue:

> *Attorney:* "Accordingly, Doctor, by your own admission you have agreed that an alternative explanation is perfectly credible and fits in with well-known psychological principles."

Again, the examiner has almost no choice but to agree with the attorney that there is a credible alternative to the examiner's explanation—an alternative that has nothing to do with parental capacity.

The lawyer whose position the examiner is supporting may provide an opportunity for a presentation of the rationale for the explanation. But it is important for the evaluator to appreciate that the judge may be extremely unsophisticated when it comes to understanding such psychological processes. And the cross-examining attorney may fully convince such a judge that the expert's interpretations are totally speculative creations, not worthy of consideration. In order to avoid such compromises of one's position, the evaluator should avoid the use of such projective material. In fact, I would go further and suggest that they not even be elicited for the evaluator's own personal information. Once in the files, there is always the possibility that the drawings and notes will be brought before the court. The opposing attorney may ask to look at the evaluator's files (which the competent examiner should bring to the court). If the pictures are found, the attorney may not only ask for the explanations but, in addition, ask the evaluator why they were not included in the report. There is no good explanation. The real answer would have to be that the evaluator wanted to avoid the kind of misguided and misleading interchanges that the revelation of such material might involve. The cross-examining attorney might encourage the evaluator's providing such an explanation because it involves the assumption that the judge is naive with regard to understanding psychological processes. Although, unfortunately, this is often the case, it is obviously injudicious for the evaluator to question the judge's intelligence or competence. Accordingly, the safest procedure is not to elicit such projective material at all and rely on more objective information that is far less likely to cause embarrassment in court—information that will be understood by even the most psychologically naive judge.

All evaluators who use self-created drawings and associated stories have had the experience that parents will state that the examiner's explanations are not valid and that the story comes from a recent television program or experience. In earlier years I tended to go along with the traditional explanation that the parents were trying to deny a painful reality and that the child's selection of a particular television program or experience was of little importance. More important was the child's selection of that material because it lent itself well to utilization and incorporation in the child's psychological processes. In more recent years I have come to agree more with the parents than those who taught me the aforementioned explanation. I have found that the vast majority of children (especially younger ones) were "lifting" their stories from public media and personal experiences. I do still obtain idiosyncratic material, but the contamination with external stimuli has been formidable. Accordingly, in recent years, I have brought the parents in to invite their input regarding the child's self-created stories elicited when administering the Draw-a-Person Test, Draw-a-Family Test, and many freely-drawn pictures around which children spin fantasies. Such experiences just add support to the aforementioned warning against the use of these pictures and stories in the courtroom, or even in mediation evaluations.

It would be an error for the reader to conclude that I consider such self-created stories to be of no value whatsoever. This would be a *reductio ad absurdum* of my statement. In the therapeutic situation, when one has an opportunity for ongoing elicitation of stories and close work with parents, then one is more likely to be able to differentiate stories that have been externally contaminated from those that are truly idiosyncratic. The former are of limited psychotherapeutic value; the latter serve well for use in the mutual storytelling technique (1971) and its derivative games (1986b, 1988b). There are judges who will frequently, if not routinely, order psychological tests on both parents and/or children. As mentioned, this is a manifestation of the judge's naiveté. It reflects the court's view (promulgated by mental health professionals) that these tests are "objective" and that they provide information that is much more accurate than clinical observations. The judge here has probably been duped into the belief that there is something more objective and scientific about an instrument such as *The Rorschach Test* than the clinical interview. Such a request is probably also related to the judge's belief that these tests are more efficient and can get to the "roots" of personality problems more efficaciously than clinical interviews. There is no question that psychological tests can often provide much extra information in an expeditious way. But it is very unlikely that they are of greater value than clinical interviews in custody evaluations. Accordingly, examiners who cooperate in such cases by complying with court dictates are doing their patients and the court a disservice. Unfortunately, such utilization of these tests is widespread and contributes, thereby, to each party's bringing in a parade of professionals to provide different explanations for the same projective data.

In spite of my strong criticism of the use of projective materials in the custody evaluation, I do not refrain from their use entirely. There are a few projective techniques that I do utilize, but I am careful to do so only as a vehicle for obtaining more objective and "hard" data. In short, I utilize instruments that allow themselves to be *points of departure* for the obtaining of overt statements that can be more useful in a custody evaluation. For example, I described above the series of questions that I will often ask a child about where would be the best place for a one-year-old child to live, in the mother's home or in the father's home. I then proceed with asking the same questions for children of older ages. Ultimately I hope the child will shift into a discussion of his (her) own situation. The earlier responses are of little value in the custody evaluation; the later ones can be very useful.

The projective instruments that I will now describe are in the latter category. Although they do not tap the deeper unconscious material obtained from instruments such as *The Rorschach* and TAT, they do provide a vehicle for obtaining objective responses that may be very useful in the custody/visitation evaluation.

The Talking, Feeling, and Doing Game

The author's *Talking, Feeling, and Doing Game* (1973b) was designed primarily to elicit meaningful psychodynamic material from children who are resistant to talking directly about their problems or revealing their psychodynamics through play fantasy. The game has proved useful, however, as an additional therapeutic modality for those who are freer to reveal themselves as well.

In this game each player in turn throws the dice and moves the playing piece along a path of colored squares (Figure 7-1). Depending upon which color the piece lands on, the player can respond to the question or directions on the card, after which a reward chip is given. As their names imply, the Talking Cards elicit material of a cognitive nature; the Feeling Cards attempt to evoke emotional responses; and the Doing Cards encourage physical expression. None of the cards attempt to obtain responses that would be as anxiety provoking as free fantasy expression or the relating of self-created stories. The cards range from the low anxiety provoking ("What is your address?" "What present would you like to get for your next birthday?" "Make believe you're blowing out the candles on your birthday cake." "Make a funny sound with your mouth. If you spit, you don't get a chip.") that just about any child can answer and thereby get involved in the game, to the moderately higher anxiety provoking ("Someone passes you a note, what does it say?" "Make up a message for a Chinese fortune cookie." "Suppose two people were talking about you and they didn't know you were listening. What do you think you would hear them saying?" "What's the worst thing a child can say to his mother?" "A boy has something on his mind that he's afraid to tell his father. What is it that he's scared to talk about?" "Everybody in the class was laughing at a girl. What had happened?" "All the girls in the class were invited to a birthday party except one. How did she feel? Why wasn't she invited?").

The playing piece may also land on "Go Forward" and "Go Backward" squares, as well as on squares directing the player to spin the spinner (which can result in gaining or losing chips or squares on the playing path). These elements of the game do not generally bring about revelation of specific psychodynamic mate-

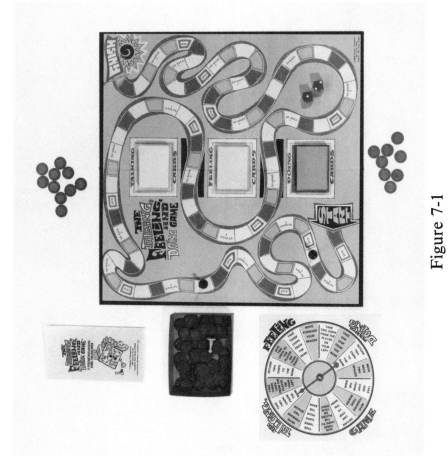

Figure 7-1

rial; rather, they enhance the child's involvement in the game and thereby reduce resistances to the therapeutic activity.

Some of the cards ask the child to talk directly about himself (herself) ("Tell something about your mother that gets you angry."); others request information about "third parties" ("A boy was scared to make a telephone call. What was he afraid of?"). In response to the first category of cards, children are likely to talk directly about themselves. In response to the second category, the examiner can often shift from a discussion of third parties to a discussion of the children themselves.

Many of the questions provide information that can be useful in the custody/visitation evaluation. For example: "A boy has something on his mind that he's afraid to tell his father. What is it that he's scared to talk about?" "A girl is ashamed to tell her mother about something. What is it?" "What is the worst thing a parent can do to a child?" "What do you think about a boy who curses at his father?" "Act out what you would do if you found that you had magic powers." "Tell about something scary that once happened to you." "What's the worst thing that ever happened to you?" "What is the most important thing that can make a family happy?" "When was the last time you cried? What did you cry about?" "Name three things that could make a person angry." "Tell about a time when your feelings were hurt." "Was there ever a person whom you wished to be dead? If so, who was that person? Why did you wish the person to be dead?" "What is the worst problem a person can have? Why?" "Make believe that you were told that any three wishes you made would come true. What would you wish for?" "People are a mixture of both good and bad, that is, everyone has good and bad parts. Say something good about someone you don't like." "Of all the places in the world, where would you like to live the most? Why?" "If you became mayor of your city, what would you do to change things?" "Tell something about your father that gets you angry." These are typical questions and, as the reader can appreciate, they may give the examiner information about the child's feelings toward the parents that might not otherwise be so readily obtainable. The board-game structure and token reinforcement facilitate the child's revealing this vital material.

For the purposes of the custody evaluation, it is crucial that the examiner select from the child's responses those statements that are directly relevant to the parents themselves, rather than indirect reference via discussion of third parties and people in general. The former kind of information is very valuable in the examiner's testimony; the latter is risky to use in that it opens the examiner to criticism under cross-examination and may compromise credibility. Elsewhere (1986b) I describe in detail the utilization of this game.

Verbal Projective Questions

A traditional verbal projective question that children are often asked is what animal they would choose to be if they had to be so transformed and why. N. Kritzberg (1966) has elaborated this type of question into a more comprehensive series of verbal projective questions that he has found useful in gaining psychodynamic information from both adults and children. For the purposes of the custody evaluation, I have found some of the children's questions to be particularly useful as points of departure for discussions that may provide useful information. I generally start by asking the child the question: "If you had to be changed into an animal—any animal in the whole world—which animal would you choose?" Then I will ask why the child has chosen that particular animal. After I have extracted as much information as I can from the response, I go on with second and third choices and the reasons why. Then I ask: "Of all the animals in the world, which animal would you not want to be? Why?" Again, I request second and third choices. The same series of questions is then repeated, but this time I ask the child what object, that is, what nonliving thing the child would choose to be if he (she) had to be so transformed. Again, I ask for first, second, and third choices, both positive and negative and the reasons for each choice.

Generally, one isolated response is not as useful as a trend in which there is the same theme repeated in various forms. For example, if the child chooses animals that are described as getting a lot of attention and care, I might suspect that the child is suffering some emotional deprivation. If I can then get the child to shift into a discussion of the parents and the issue of deprivation in the relationship with them, I may have some meaningful material for my report (in litigation) or my presentation of recommendations (in litigation and mediation). If I cannot accomplish this, I will not speculate about the deprivational element (at least not from data provided by these particular questions).

Actually, the aforementioned animal and object questions are merely lead-ins to the more important ones regarding the parents. Specifically, I will ask the child "If your mother had to be turned into an animal, what animal would be a good one for her to turn into? What animal would be like her? What animal suits her personality? Why?" I then elicit first, second, and third choices, both positive and negative and the reasons for each choice. I then ask a similar series of questions about which animal would suit (and which would not suit) the father's personality. I then proceed with: "If your mother had to be turned into an object, something that isn't alive, what would be a good object to turn her into? What object would be like her? Why?" Again, three choices are elicited, with the reasons, and similar questions are presented for the father. This is a very valuable form of inquiry. In a nonthreatening way it provides answers to the therapist's questions as to how the child really feels about the parents. Furthermore, it is fun for children and most involve themselves enthusiastically. It generally is not difficult to get children to elaborate upon their feelings about the parent after the animal or the object has been selected. Using this projective information in this way, the examiner can obtain direct information without having to resort to the kinds of speculations one often utilizes when describing information derived from projective instruments. Elsewhere (1986b) I have described this technique in greater detail.

Sentence Completion Tests

Sentence completion tests are another form of projective test often included in the psychologist's diagnostic battery. Used judiciously these can be of value in the custody evaluation, as long as the examiner makes sure to translate the responses into direct conscious awareness of the child's own situation. As is true of *The Talking, Feeling, and Doing Game,* some of the questions ask for general responses and others make direct reference to the child's own feelings and situation. The *Holsopple-Miale Sentence Completion Test* (1954) is one of the more commonly used such tests. The questions in this instrument that I have found most useful are:

> Children are usually certain that. . .
> The hardest decisions. . .
> Fathers should learn that. . .
> The most pleasant dreams. . .
> One can repair the damage caused by. . .
> The nicest thing about being a child. . .
> If only people knew how much. . .
> To be a good liar one must. . .
> A mother is more likely than a father to. . .
> A father is more likely than a mother to. . .

The questions that I usually add when administering these questions to children being evaluated in custody/visitation evaluation are:

> There would be fewer divorces if. . .
> The best of fathers may forget that. . .
> Mothers should learn that. . .
> I wish that. . .
> The worst thing that could happen to a family is. . .
> The best kinds of homes are the ones that. . .
> Mothers often. . .
> Fathers often. . .

Again, only when the child's responses can be directed into particular statements about each of the parents should the information elicited here be used.

INTERVIEWS WITH THE PARENTS

The Family Interview

Family interviews are a valuable source of information in a custody/visitation evaluation. Much data can be derived from the interactions among the various family members. If a family interview can be compared to an individual interview it can truly be said that the whole is greater than the sum of its parts. Verbalizations, gesturing, and all forms of interaction should be studiously observed during these interviews. It is important to appreciate that the parents may try to "put on an act." Accordingly, it behooves the examiner to try to differentiate between playacting and genuine, spontaneous expressions and involvement. However, children—and the younger they are the more truly this can be said—are not going to be able to playact very well, nor will the younger ones even try. Children's naiveté make them poor liars. Accordingly, they can provide valuable input when one is trying to learn "the truth." It is also important to appreciate that the situation is an extremely artificial one and that the parents, especially, are likely to be quite guarded. The tensions and anxieties engendered by the situation are likely to compromise parental spontaneity and relaxation.

The examiner should try to observe how much a child is involved with the mother as compared with the father. Generally, in the first interview children may be afraid of the therapist, who is a stranger, and may try to cuddle a parent, hide their heads in a parent's lap, and/or exhibit other maneuvers which serve to enlist the parent's aid in assuaging anxiety. It is important to note which parent is preferred for such anxiety alleviation. If the parent is caressing and responsive, and if the child sinks comfortably into the parent's lap or arms, this is a positive sign. If the parent tends to freeze or stiffen in response, this is definitely a negative. Excessive criticism of the child—"Don't touch that," "Go away from there," etc.—is usually a reflection of some impairment. It is often useful for the evaluator to compliment the child and observe and compare the parents' reactions (just as was done when the child's picture was shown). If the parent responds with pride, this is a positive sign; if not, it is a definite negative.

The way in which the family interview can provide important information was described by the aforementioned case of the schizophrenic mother who stared into space when her child tripped at the threshold. Another example is well demonstrated by my interview with Mr. and Mrs. R and their two daughters, Brenda (age 7) and Marie (age 5). (I present this in the way I described it in the final court report in order to provide the reader with the format that I consider most effective for such observations.)

On January 7, 1981 a family session was held. When I entered the waiting room to invite the family to my office, Mrs. R was sitting on one side of a partition which partially divides the waiting room, and Mr. R and the two girls were sitting on the other side. There were enough seats on both sides of the partition to accommodate any arrangement. Although it is reasonable that Mr. and Mrs. R might not wish to sit together (divorced people often seat themselves on opposite sides of this partition), the girls chose to sit with their father. Although this is not presented as a major point, it does have some significance with regard to the children's preference.

The family members were seen in the following sequence: First, Brenda was seen alone. I usually see older children first because they are less likely to be reluctant to go in the room alone with the evaluator. Once the younger ones have the experience that nothing terrible is going on, it is easier for them to follow suit. Generally, when I come back into the waiting room, after the completion of my time alone with the older child, I will say to the younger one, "Now it's your turn." Because the younger child is familiar with this concept, and because there have probably been many occasions in which the younger child has had to suffer the frustrations of waiting for a turn, the child generally reacts positively to the invitation and goes off alone with me. Accordingly, I then interviewed Marie alone. While Marie was sitting in the consultation room, I stepped out into the waiting room and invited Mr. and Mrs. R and Brenda to join us. When Mrs. R entered the room, she sat down in the chair next to the one in which Marie had already been sitting. Mr. R and Brenda sat on a couch opposite to the two chairs which were occupied by Mrs. R and Marie. As soon as Mrs. R sat down next to Marie, Marie got up and walked across the room to the couch in order to sit next to her father. Again the voluntary seating arrangement revealed the children's preference: the two girls with their father sitting on the couch together and Mrs. R sitting alone on the opposite side of the room.

Such behavior by the children should not necessarily bring the examiner to the conclusion that the recommendation should be made that these children live primarily with their father. One can see a similar picture in children suffering with a parental alienation syndrome (Chapter Six). I am only presenting this vignette to demonstrate that family interviews can provide important data when one is considering the issue of parental preference.

The family interviews may be traumatic to some children because they often involve the child's stating a preference for one parent over the other. The examiner does well not to pressure children to make such a choice. However, my experience has been that many children will express their preferences during the course of the individual interviews, after they have developed a relationship with the examiner. In contrast, in the family interview most children are hesitant to reveal their preferences and may become quite anxious at those points in the family interview when such divulgences might be warranted. This potential untoward effect of the family interview notwithstanding, the family diagnostic interviews may also be therapeutic. They provide a forum for communication among all parties that may never have been present. And this breakthrough may carry over beyond the interview, much to the benefit of all family members. If a parent is denying the children's preference the family interview may provide the children with the opportunity to state their preference—sometimes for the first time. This can sometimes be more easily accomplished in the interview because the presence of the examiner provides the children with the implied protection from the anticipated horrendous parental responses. They may then have the *living experience* that the terrible consequences are not forthcoming. This then makes it easier for them to be with the nonpreferred parent following the interview.

Sometimes the family interview consumes completely the allotted time. On other occasions, however, time permits individual interviews in which one parent and child can be seen together. In such situations, I may say to *one* of the children (usually the oldest), "I'm finished now seeing you with *both* of your parents. Now, I want to see you with *one* of your parents. First I'll see you with one parent, and then with the other parent. Which parent do you want to start with, your mother or your father?" The child's choice may give me information about which parent the child is most comfortable with. However, it also may give me information about a parental alienation syndrome. Other data collected during the course of the examination should help the examiner determine which of these two situations is present in any particular case. I will then tell the other children that they will also have a turn for individual meetings with each parent alone.

Parent-Child Interviews

When conducting the interview with the child and parent alone, I generally begin by sitting silently while observing them. I either say absolutely nothing or make some very vague comment like, "I won't be saying anything now; I leave it to the two of you to decide what you want to do and say." Most often the parent is quite tense in this situation but it provides very useful information. The tension is increased by the examiner's taking careful notes about what is going on, but this should not be a reason for not conducting such an interview. The parent who is comfortable with the child is likely to think of things to do and stir up active and ongoing conversations and interactions. The parent who is less comfortable with the child is less likely to do this. Sometimes a parent will spontaneously bring along toys and other objects to serve as points of departure for the two of them in their interactions. Sometimes the parent does not bring in such materials. I say nothing beforehand regarding whether or not such materials should be brought in and make a note in either case as to what was done. Most often, the parent does not come so supplied. The more involved parent is likely to be more creative with regard to what to do with the child in the "partial vacuum" that I have created. Such a parent may direct the child to pictures on the walls, or actual therapeutic toys that I have on my shelf in the office. This is a very important type of interview and I recommend it highly. It provides excellent information about parental capacity.

CONCLUDING COMMENTS

I have presented much more material than one would reasonably want to include in the evaluation of any child. As mentioned, my purpose in this chapter has been to provide examiners with a wealth of material from which they might draw when conducting custody evaluations. Many examiners rely heavily on projective material. I hope the reader will agree that the use of such material in the custody evaluation is risky and that it may seriously compromise the evaluator's testimony. Some examiners may find it difficult to refrain from using these instruments. Therefore, I have provided a variety of techniques for eliciting nonprojective material. Another aim has been to demonstrate how rich a source of information children can be in custody evaluations, their youth notwithstanding. Evaluating this information, however, presents the examiner with a formidable challenge. I have sought to assist examiners in assessing optimally this valuable source of information.

⚖️ EIGHT
INFORMATION FROM
OTHER SOURCES

INTRODUCTION

Information from the sources discussed in this chapter is generally less valuable than that obtained from the parents and children. However, it can serve to corroborate what has been obtained in the interviews with the primary family members. In addition, it may open up areas of inquiry not previously explored, although much of this data must be considered hearsay and subject to all the dangers of utilizing such information in one's testimony. Whereas the parents and children *must* be seen in order to conduct an impartial evaluation, these individuals cannot be required by the examiner to be interviewed.

Accordingly, in my statement of provisions for involving myself in custody litigation (Chapter Three), I speak only of my right to *invite* such individuals to see me. The invitations are best extended through the parents because direct invitations could justifiably be considered by the recipient to be intrusive, coercive, and even unethical (especially for the physician). Furthermore, a parent may state that a particular individual is quite interested in speaking with me and yet, if I were to call that person, I might learn that just the opposite is the case and that the party has absolutely no desire to "get involved." Examiners do well, therefore, to protect themselves from such embarrassment and unnecessary complications by requiring the parents themselves to inform the prospective informants that they should make the initial contact with the evaluator.

The degree of receptivity of each of the parents to extend such invitations is often very revealing of that parent's true commitment to be open and honest in the inquiry. And this should be taken into consideration when discussing with the parents the extending of these invitations. Hesitation, delays, and rationalizations for not agreeing to invite a particular party are best viewed as attempts to prevent the disclosure of information that would be damaging to the recalcitrant parent. As mentioned in the discussion of the provisos (Chapter Three), I generally take a conservative position regarding interviewing the assortment of friends and relatives that each parent may wish me to see. The testimonials generally cancel one another out because each has been selected to support the particular parent's position. Also, I do not allow one parent to veto the other parent's request that I see a particular person. I do, however, hear both sides out and reserve the right to make the final decision regarding whether the invitation should be extended.

On occasion parents will start "keeping score" regarding the number of informants the evaluator sees from each side. Or, each spouse will try to "balance out" the interviews, e.g., "Well, if you're going to see her sister, then you should see my brother." The determinant in such cases has little if anything to do with the quality of the information that the informant can provide; rather it relates to an attempt to be "even" regarding the number of people so interviewed. And in court an attorney might very well point out to the examiner that one side's interviewees far exceeded the other. Accordingly, in order to protect myself from this absurd criticism, I make it clear both in the provisions document as well as during my initial interviews with the parents that I am concerned with the *quality* of each interviewees' potential contribution rather than the *quantity* of individuals interviewed.

THE HOUSEKEEPER

Preliminary Considerations

Of all the interviewees, the housekeeper can probably provide more useful information than any other person. She lives in the home, is party to what goes on, and may spend more of her time thinking about what happens between her employers than many other aspects of her life. She is often a surrogate parent and plays an important role in the children's growth and development. If this is the case, the question as to whether or not she will be involved in the children's upbringing is an important one, and the kind of person she is—especially with regard to her maternal capacity—is an important consideration for the examiner.

Unfortunately, the housekeeper may be very hesitant to divulge information about the family, fearing she may compromise her relationship with one or both employers. In addition, she may never have been in a psychiatrist's (or other mental health professional's) office before. She may be petrified over the prospect of seeing such an evaluator, may believe that her mind can be read, or she may just be generally fearful of authority. It is likely that the examiner has become an even more formidable figure to her because of what she has heard regarding the evaluation. Also, she may appreciate that each parent has placed the examiner in a position of great power.

It is important for the evaluator to advise the parents that the housekeeper be told, at the time the invitation is extended, that the examiner must have the freedom to reveal to her employers, at his (her) discretion, any information the housekeeper provides in the interview. It is only ethical to do this. However, such a statement is likely to increase her fears. Sometimes her resistances to revealing information can be overcome by suggesting that the parents impress upon her that if she really loves the children she will provide information openly and honestly. Some may consider this approach "low" and that stooping to guilt evocation as a method of getting the housekeeper to come is beneath the dignity of the evaluator. My answer to this criticism is that I have found the housekeeper a very valuable source of information and that it genuinely is in the children's best interests for her to see me. Although the approach is not a commonly accepted one in psychoanalytic interviewing, the communication is basically valid, and I have not lost any sleep over utilizing it.

The housekeeper's anxieties can be further assuaged by the parents' assuring her that she does not have to tell me anything she does not wish to and that I will not coerce her into speaking about any topic which she expresses definite reluctance to discuss. They should also advise her that it might be detrimental to the children if she lies to me. (Unfortunately, this warning has not discouraged many from providing me with the most absurd fabrications.) They are also advised to tell her that, at my discretion, I must have the freedom to reveal (or not to reveal) what she says to me about the parents and children. However, they should impress upon her that I will not necessarily reveal everything and that I will not automatically be a channel of communication between her and the parents.

It is important for the examiner to appreciate that in the common situation, where the housekeeper is living with the mother, she is more likely to side with the mother in order to preserve a good relationship with her. This situation also gives the mother more opportunity to "brainwash" the housekeeper and instill in her the fear that if she provides information that compromises the mother's position, her job may be in jeopardy.

The Interview with the Housekeeper

At the beginning of the interview I do everything possible to try to make the housekeeper more comfortable. I recognize that she is probably more anxious than the majority of people I interview in my office. I generally will begin with a simple everyday interchange about things like whether she had difficulty finding the office, the weather, and so on. These interchanges may serve to make the atmosphere a more familiar one and are, thereby, anxiety alleviating. As is true of most, if not all, psychiatric interviews it is best to start with "basic statistical data" questions, rather than open anxiety-provoking ones. (Borrowing from military terminology, I call these "name, rank, and serial number.") I generally will ask the housekeeper her name, address (if not live-in), and telephone number. I inquire into her marital status. I get other information such as date of birth, and, if applicable, how long she has been in the United States. I find out the date on which she began her employment with the parents being evaluated and the hours of employment. All these questions are usually answered quite readily and serve to reduce anxiety.

I then ask the housekeeper what she understands to be the purposes of the interview. If there are any distortions I clarify these. When we both know exactly what my purpose is, I then tell her that it is important for her to appreciate that I reserve the right, at my discretion, to reveal to other parties involved in the evaluation (her employers, their attorneys, and the judge) any information that she has imparted to me. However, I am quick to add that I do not necessarily do this. I impress upon her that I appreciate her position and that she may, with justification, fear that her job may be in jeopardy, or her relationship with one of the parents significantly compromised, if she is too critical of either of them. I tell her that out of respect for her position, I will be very judicious regarding what I reveal and that I will not necessarily divulge what she says. In fact, I promise her that I will make every effort not to do so. I have found that I can often keep this promise and actually protect the housekeeper by getting one of the parents to make the same statement or criticism that was initially suggested to me by her. For example, the housekeeper may bring up a criticism about a father that was not previously brought forth. If I can get the mother to make a statement about this criticism I can protect the housekeeper and need not reveal her to have been the original source of information. However, there are occasions on which I need her corroboration to emphasize the point.

I will then ask the housekeeper what plans she has for herself after the separation or divorce. Is she planning to remain with her present employer, switch to the other parent, or leave the employment of the family entirely? In the context of her answer, she may provide me with useful information about whom she considers to be the preferable parent. She may say that she is willing to work for whichever parent is granted primary custody. She may, however, state that she would only work for one parent and not the other. In giving the reasons why, she may focus on the parent's qualities as an employer or she may focus on the parent's qualities as a parent. The latter information is generally useful and the former may be as well.

Sometimes getting information from the housekeeper is like "pulling teeth." It may be necessary for the examiner to make statements and ask her to respond with a yes or a no. Although this approach is not in the highest psychoanalytic tradition, it may be the only way to get meaningful information from a tight-lipped or fearful housekeeper. One must surmise what she is trying to say and recognize that she is being ultracautious. As was described in my discussion of interviewing the parents and children, it is generally preferable to proceed from the low anxiety-provoking to the high anxiety-provoking questions. The yes-no questions are in accordance with this principle. Also, I will often ask the housekeeper to tell me the parental preference of each of the children. By talking about the *children's* preferences I may learn something about the housekeeper's opinion regarding the preferable parent. I focus on each child separately and ask the housekeeper to comment on the child's statements. Through the quotes of the child's comments, the housekeeper may be able to express her own opinion without fear of being considered disloyal.

Often carefully chosen specific questions can be less anxiety provoking and more revealing than open-ended general ones. I have found particularly useful certain questions related to the home situation prior to the separation: "Who prepared breakfast in the morning?" "Who changed the diapers?" "Who got up in the middle of the night when the children cried?" "Who more frequently sat on the floor and played with them?" "Who spent longer times playing with them?" "Who had greater patience?" "Who could engage the children in talk for longer periods?" "Who sang songs more often with them?" "Who enjoyed more reading books with them?" Similar specific questions can provide information about the visiting parent's habits, especially with regard to punctuality and reliability.

I then go into the more general questions, the more anxiety-provoking ones. I might ask the housekeeper to describe her employer. I might then say, "No one is perfect. Everyone is a mixture of both strong points and weak points. Tell me about Mrs. Jones' strong points." Then I will ask about weak points and ask similar questions about the father. In the context of such inquiry, the housekeeper may make comments that bear on parental capacity without being aware of it. Typical comments in this category made by the hesitant housekeeper: "She's really trying," "She's now spending a lot more time with the kids," and "No one is perfect." These comments can be points of departure for exploration in which one focuses primarily on the positive and then hopes to gain some information about the negatives in the context of the discussion.

The housekeeper is more likely to lie than other interviewees in the custody evaluation. However, she is more likely to do so in a primitive fashion because she is often less well educated. These factors may enable the examiner to get information from her when she doesn't realize that she is providing it. For example, I once asked a housekeeper, "What can you tell me about Mrs. Smith with regard to her taking care of the children?" She replied, "She's doing better now than before she was in the hospital last September." By focusing on the areas in which she was now doing better (the positives) I was able to learn something about the negatives. The housekeeper thought she was supplying me with useful positive information and thereby not criticizing her employer. However, she did not realize that, in the process of doing so, she was providing me with criticisms as well. A housekeeper may not wish to make a direct comment or openly express parental preference. However, she might make a comment like "I don't want to say which parent would be better for the children. However, children are best off with their mothers." In this way she does not openly express her disloyalty but, by a general comment, provides her opinion. Another housekeeper stated, "Mr. Brown will have something against me if I say what's on my mind." The housekeeper did not make a similar statement about Mrs. Brown. The simple statement clearly indicated to me who her parental preference was.

For most housekeepers my experience has been that covering up is the name of the game. I have had housekeepers who have claimed that both parents are 100 percent perfect with regard to their parenting capacity and that in all the years of employment they never saw *one* defect, *one* example of compromise in parenting capacity. No matter how incredulous my response, no matter how dubiously I expressed my belief that in all these years she must have observed at least *one* deficiency, these housekeepers would "stick to their guns." I once had a housekeeper who claimed that she went to bed at 8:30 p.m., immediately after putting the children to sleep, and entered into a deep slumber until the time that she awakened the next morning. She denied hearing the fighting, the sounds of the furniture and dishes being thrown, the physical encounters between the parents, the children crying in response to these altercations, and even police sirens as they approached the house. Again, when I expressed incredulity, she firmly claimed that she sleeps very deeply. Another responded to each question with "All I want is that everyone should be happy." When I tried to explain to her that this could never be the case and that, with regard to divorce problems, we have to try to find out which is the lesser of the various painful options, she replied in parrot-like fashion, "All I want is that everyone should be happy!" Needless to say, I did not devote much time to interviews with these housekeepers, recognizing that I was defeated before beginning.

During one evaluation, after I had interviewed the housekeeper (who was brought by the mother), I received a telephone call from the father. He told me that he had spoken to the housekeeper after the interview and it was clear to him that she had not been completely candid with me. He arranged for her to call me on a subsequent day to give me the "true story." In the course of the telephone conversation with the housekeeper it became clear that she was only making the call to protect herself from the father's anger if she had refused to do so. She would not (and probably could not) directly say all of this; I could only surmise it from the fact that she had no information to provide me and spoke generally about how difficult her position was and how she did not wish to alienate either parent. I then asked her some very specific questions:

> *Gardner:* "Am I correct in saying that you have no new information to give me at this point?"
>
> *Housekeeper:* "Yes."
>
> *Gardner:* "As you were talking, I began thinking that you really didn't want to make this call, but that you only did so in order not to get Mr. G. angry at you. Is that correct?"
>
> *Housekeeper:* "Yes."
>
> *Gardner:* "Am I correct in believing that you still feel that Mrs. G. would make the better parent at this time and that you didn't want to tell Mr. G. that this is your opinion?"
>
> *Housekeeper:* "Yes."
>
> *Gardner:* "So you really still believe that the children will be better off living with Mrs. G., but you don't want to let Mr. G. know that this is what you believe?"
>
> *Housekeeper:* "Yes, that's right."
>
> *Gardner:* "And you're only making this telephone call so that he'll 'get off your back.'"
>
> *Housekeeper:* "Yes, but please don't tell him that."
>
> *Gardner:* "As I told you, I can't promise anything regarding what I will reveal. However, I will try very hard not to tell anyone about this part of our conversation."
>
> *Housekeeper:* "Thank you very much. You're a *nice* man!"

In this case I was successful in not having to reveal all the details of this conversation. The information that the housekeeper had given me supported other observations of mine that the father was a coercive and manipulative person who had little guilt over using people for his own ends. I was able to quote certain comments made by the housekeeper that were useful. Of course, had I been cross-examined on the witness stand with regard to every detail of the conversation, both in my notes and what I could recall, I would have had to reveal the above interchange.

LIVE-IN FRIENDS, POTENTIAL STEPPARENTS, AND STEPPARENTS AS PARENTAL SURROGATES

Most custody litigation takes place before there has been a remarriage. Often, the custody decision is included in the divorce decree and so stepparents, in the literal sense of the word, are not usually involved. However, "third parties" often appear on the scene in the form of lovers, live-in friends, and potential stepparents. The parent who is involved with such a person may have an advantage in the custody conflict in that there is at least the promise of a two-parent home—generally considered to be more desirable than a one-parent home. Although the new party may have had a longstanding relationship with a parent, usually he (she) has had only a minimal relationship with the children at the time of the custody conflict.

Because these third parties are presented as parental surrogates (either present or potential), it behooves the examiner to interview them. However, the examiner should appreciate that this person is almost invariably prejudiced against the alienated parent and will present a highly one-sided view, often parroting that of the parent with whom he (she) is involved. There may have been little, if any, direct contact with the parent being denigrated, but this does not prevent a detailed description of the alienated party's deficiencies. Examiners who include such data in their reports are risking the criticism of having introduced hearsay material. Such third parties will often profess great affection for the children. The children, however, most often do not reciprocate. When one compares the depth of involvement between the surrogate parent (at this stage) and the natural parent, the differences are often vast. Although the surrogate may certainly serve as a "second body" in the home, he (she) is often just that and little more with regard to the capacity to provide dedicated attention and deep affection. Accordingly, the examiner should be careful about giving too much weight to the parent who presents such a third party at the time of the custody/visitation evaluation. However, when the evaluation takes place a significant time after the separation there may have been a deep relationship formed with such a third party. Then, of course, the above caveats are not applicable.

It is important for the examiner to appreciate that even when one of the parents is remarried, the relationship between stepparents and stepchildren is notoriously a bad one. As I have discussed elsewhere (1984, 1986b), the view that stepmothers are mean and evil is not simply derived from fairy tales. Rather, fairy tales reflect the ubiquitous antagonism that children traditionally have toward stepparents. And this antagonism does not necessarily arise within the children, with the stepparents being the innocent recipients of the children's animosity. Rather, it is the frequent failure on the stepparents' part to have developed deep-seated loving relationships with the children that engenders the children's anger. I am not suggesting that this is necessarily the result of a deficiency on the stepparents' part. Rather, it seems to be the natural state of affairs and it would be hard to imagine the situation to be otherwise.

There is truth to the ancient aphorism that "blood is thicker than water." The natural mother has carried the child in her own body for nine months, has suffered the pains of its delivery, and has the capacity to feed the child from her own body (even though she may not choose to do so). Most fathers are genuinely concerned with and psychologically involved in the growth of their children in utero. And both parents generally share (to varying degrees) the child's upbringing: its joys, tribulations, gratifications, and disappointments. The stepparent appears on the scene after the "rival" has had many years of investment with the child. The natural parent, then, has a formidable advantage over the newcomer with regard to parenting and psychological involvement with the children. Often the newcomer is absolutely no match for the real parent in these areas and the only thing that can be said in his (her) behalf is that there will be a "body" in the home that may potentially prove to be a genuine parental surrogate. The tenuous involvement of stepparents with their stepchildren (protestations to the contrary notwithstanding) is well demonstrated by the low survival rate of stepparent-stepchildren relationships following the dissolution of second and subsequent marriages. Although a stepparent at the time of the break-up of the stepfamily may profess the desire for an ongoing relationship with the stepchildren, such continuity is rarely realized. In short, then, lovers and other strangers should be interviewed, but what they say should not be taken too seriously. What they say about the alienated spouse is likely to be highly biased and the love and/or affection they profess for the children is not likely to have a deep basis. However, two bodies are better than one when it comes to assuming the many responsibilities involved in rearing children. Accordingly, the third party should still have a role to play in the custody evaluation.

GRANDPARENTS

The role of grandparents is generally not given the attention it deserves in child psychotherapy. The parent whose own parents are deeply involved with the children has extra "credit," and it is one of the arguments (admittedly small) for recommending custody. However, it is a far less important criterion than the parent's own personality characteristics and involvement with the children. Grandparents can make an important contribution to a child's feeling of self-worth. Healthy grandparents idealize their grandchildren and such idealization is important to get in childhood as a buffer against all the unwarranted criticisms that one inevitably receives in life.

As discussed in Chapter Seven, I attempt to elicit information from the children about their relationships with their grandparents. In addition, I will ask the parents about the grandparents' relationships with the children. I am particularly interested in the proximity of the grandparents, because this may play an important role in their availability to serve in emergencies, as well as to provide surrogate parenting. Although parents embroiled in custody disputes will often provide different opinions on a number of issues, my experience has been that they are generally in agreement regarding the depth of involvement of the various grandparents.

If a mother- or father-in-law supports a son- or daughter-in-law as the preferable custodial parent over the parent who is the natural son or daughter, this is a very powerful argument in favor of the son- or daughter-in-law. For example, if a mother-in-law is described as preferring her son-in-law over her own daughter, the evaluator should interview this woman directly. Because of the expected preference of parents for their own children, there are usually overwhelming compromises in parental capacity that would warrant a grandparent's preferring a son- or daughter-in-law over a natural child. Getting this information from the parents is not nearly as valuable as a direct quote from the grandparent. One grandmother once said to me, "There's no question about it, my daughter has a terrible drinking problem. Her husband was telling you the truth when he said he and the children had to go around the house searching for hidden bottles. Last year, after my husband's heart attack, we stayed in the house for about a month. I used to help them look for the hidden bottles. Although she's my daughter, and I love her very much, my son-in-law is right. She's in no condition to take care of the children. She's my daughter and I love her very much, but I feel sorry for her. She needs help, but she won't get it. She won't even admit that she has a drinking problem." The statement, in itself, was a very powerful one. However, coming from the mother's own mother, it was even more impressive and was a heavy argument in favor of the father.

THE PEDIATRICIAN

It is common for a mother to go to a pediatrician and ask for a letter which states that she is a good mother and should have custody of her children. Such a letter is practically worthless to the court and to an evaluator. Pediatricians know that if such a request is declined, they might alienate and even lose a patient. There are few who are so noble and/or sophisticated that they would say that they cannot be of service or that they would be willing to provide a similar letter to the father in that their experiences with him (although less) have been just as favorable.

In short, the impartial evaluator does well to give little if any weight to such letters and put them in the same category as testimonies by friends of each of the parents.

There are occasional situations, however, in which a pediatrician's letter might prove useful. I am referring to letters in which the pediatrician provides confirmation that one parent is clearly superior to the other. An example would be a family in which the pediatrician is willing to state that he has never seen the father throughout the course of the children's lives, even in emergencies, night visits, etc. Another example would be the situation in which the letter confirms the mother's allegation that the father has refused to follow through with medical advice. However, my experience has been that such letters are rare because pediatricians generally prefer not to write letters in order not to alienate the nonpreferred parent and thereby compromise their relationships with the criticized parent.

TEACHERS AND PRINCIPALS

In general, teachers' comments can be very useful in psychiatric evaluations of children. An elementary school teacher spends five to six hours a day with a child and has many important observations that can be useful to the child therapist. The information the teacher provides about the child's academic performance and behavior is an important contribution to the diagnostic process and is also useful in ascertaining the child's progress while in treatment.

Unfortunately, such information is of little value in custody litigation. If the child is doing well in school, it may very well be the result of both parents having contributed to the child's healthy development. If the child is doing poorly, in either the behavioral or academic area, it may reflect psychopathology. However, this information per se does not tell us *which* parent was more responsible for such psychopathology. Moreover, teachers tend to be very fearful of involving themselves in parental divorce, especially when litigation is involved. They traditionally fear alienating parents and may not wish to "take sides." My experience has been that many teachers and school personnel have not been straightforward enough to state directly that they don't wish to be involved. Rather, they may paint pretty pictures of the child's classroom situation, denying that there have been any problems at all. Or, they may speak in the particular educational euphemisms that are in vogue.

On occasion, a teacher may confirm a parent's statement that one parent has been actively involved in the child's schooling, has typically appeared at teachers' conferences, at school plays, etc., and the other has not. If a letter can be obtained which will confirm this, it can be useful in corroborating parental statements regarding school involvement. It is important that the examiner obtain statements in written form (even though this request may produce even more reluctance to cooperate by the teacher or school administrator). Otherwise, the information is more likely to be considered hearsay. And, as mentioned, hearsay information is not only of little value in court, but its inclusion is likely to compromise the examiner's report or testimony. And even in the mediation evaluation it can reasonably be objected to by the nonsupported party.

REPORTS FROM HOSPITALS AND OTHER MENTAL HEALTH PROFESSIONALS

I routinely get permission to request reports from hospitals. As stated, it is a proviso of my involvement that the parents agree in advance to sign releases that facilitate my obtaining such material. Hospital reports are often useful to confirm allegations of suicidal attempts, drug overdoses, and child abuse. They also provide useful information about the depth of pathology when hospitalization was required. With regard to the latter type of information, the therapist should not fall into the trap of assuming that past psychopathology and/or hospitalization(s) should automatically deprive a parent of custody. It is the *present* parenting status that is most important. The hospital documents can be very powerful sources of information, and it is not likely that an opposing attorney will try to refute them. Nevertheless, such information is still, strictly speaking, hearsay in that the examiner has not observed directly the difficulties described therein. Corroborating statements by the parties concerned can strengthen the value of these already important and convincing documents.

It is also important for the evaluator to make a sharp differentiation between commitments and voluntary admissions. If a person is committed it usually indicates serious psychopathology. In contrast, voluntary hospitalizations need not necessarily reflect serious psychiatric disturbance. Evaluators must appreciate that private hospitals are often lucrative businesses and the doctors working therein (often part owners of the hospital) encourage hospitalization because of the money to be made from such patients. They will often utilize what I consider frivolous and superficial criteria for recommending hospitalization. Not surprisingly, patients so admitted generally get "cured" at around the time their insurance runs out. Elsewhere (1988a) I have discussed in detail my views on hospitalization, with particular focus on the private psychiatric hospital.

With regard to requesting information from therapists, I recommend that the evaluator divide them into two categories, present therapists and past therapists. I generally do not ask for reports from therapists who are treating patients at the time of the evaluation, especially if the treatment is analytically oriented or psychoanalytic. This may involve the therapist's providing information about the patient that may compromise the patient's position in the custody/visitation evaluation. Although such information may be in the best interests of the child, it may also compromise significantly the relationship between the parent and the therapist. Such compromised therapy might result in the child's losing out in the long run, in that the parent then experiences less adequate and less efficient treatment and becomes a less adequate parent. This is another reason why strict and narrow adherence to the *best interests of the child doctrine* may not always end up to be in the child's best interests. I prefer to be guided by what is in the best interests of *all* parties concerned and try to balance the various interests.

I have less trouble with requests for information from past therapists. This is especially the case when there is little if any likelihood that the parent will be returning to that therapist. Appendix VI shows a typical letter that I sent to such therapists. The reader will note that I described myself as having been "invited" to serve as an impartial, even though the court termed such an invitation an "order." I did this in order not to be party to the notion that people such as myself, with no previous involvement in a family, can be ordered to conduct a custody evaluation. I also made it clear that the court is requesting my "recommendations." This helped dispel the notion that the impartial examiner's decision is the final one. In the second paragraph I requested the therapist to focus specifically on the parental capacity of each of the parents. Sometimes a therapist did not wish to commit to such a comparison and, instead, provided me with a wealth of information about the various problems dealt with in treatment. I emphasized that I wanted a written report. As mentioned, this is no place for "folksy" telephone conversations. The examiner does not want to be in a position of being accused of having misquoted the verbal report. This just opens up an area of inquiry and possible compromise under cross-examination that can be completely avoided. Unfortunately, therapists all too often were afraid or hesitated to commit themselves in such a responding letter. All too often, my letter was completely ignored. In such situations I did not repeatedly request a response. I sometimes asked the parent(s) to "remind" the previous therapist to respond. If there was still no response, I made a note of it in my final report so that the judge could subpoena the therapist if the law of the state permitted such action and if the judge wished to pursue the matter. In mediation evaluations I generally ask the parents to request the reports themselves. This usually results in a report. I generally do not write a letter because, as mentioned, it could easily be interpreted as an abrogation of my commitment not to involve myself in any letter writing and/or communication with third parties regarding the mediation.

REPORTS FROM ATTORNEYS

I usually ask both parents to ask their attorneys to forward any material that they and/or their attorneys think will be of interest or value to me. Generally, these include pleadings, affidavits, depositions, certifications, etc. I have sometimes found that the party with the stronger case is very quick to respond to this request, whereas the party in the weaker position responds slowly or not at all. In short, the party with the stronger arguments is very happy to send me all kinds of supporting evidence. The party in the weaker position senses this and recognizes that there is not much to be gained by my reading his (her) complaints or refutations.

I wish to emphasize here again that it would be foolish (and even self-destructive) for the examiner to quote these documents verbatim. These reports are infamous for the exaggerations and distortions they contain. When one compares the statements made by one party with those made by the other, it is hard to believe that the same people are being described. Hyperbole is invariably present, as each party believes that his (her) position will be strengthened by it. The threat of perjury seems not to deter either party from introducing the crassest duplicities. Little guilt is felt over including the most humiliating and denigrating allegations. The attorneys themselves often translate their clients' statements into stock phrases and even paragraphs. It is common for a noun to be preceded by a whole string of adjectives, the writer believing that such adjectives strengthen the argument. The examiner, therefore, can only use the information contained in these documents as points of departure for direct inquiry with the parties concerned. Examiners can justifiably be criticized for using this hearsay information in their litigation reports. Similarly, in mediation the examiner should use the material only as a departure point for mutual inquiry and not conclude that the statements contained in these documents are valid.

In my previous edition of this book, *Family Evaluation in Child Custody Litigation* (1982a) (pages 209-210), I described a somewhat complex system that I utilized for reading these reports and recording the important data with which I wish to confront each parent. In more recent years I have utilized what I consider to be a far more efficient system. I used this system in recent litigation cases and still use it for mediation evaluations. Specifically, I ask each parent to pore through the material that they wish to present to me and to earmark those points that they believe will be most useful for me to focus on. Then, rather than spend the time reading this directly (often a formidable task), I review this material in joint sessions with both parents together. In this way I have the opportunity to obtain direct response for each allegation from the parent who is being accused of the impropriety. Although this adds to the number of interviews conducted, it generally results in the evaluation costing less because I myself spend less time reviewing documents between sessions. Furthermore, the parents know better than I which issues are important to zero in on and which issues can conveniently be skipped.

INTERVIEWING FRIENDS
AND ASSORTED RELATIVES

R. A. Solow and P. L. Adams (1977) recommend interviewing friends of the parents. I have not found this to be useful. Generally, each parent is able to come up with a list of friends and relatives who can be relied upon to support, in the most glowing terms, each party's position. Early in my career I was naive enough to see such individuals. I subsequently concluded that most came well rehearsed and were not above lying in the service of what they considered to be the more noble end of supporting the parent they favored. I found also that the comments of these friends and relatives tended to cancel one another out and the interviews therefore were a waste of time. Wealthy people can afford to bring a parade of such individuals to the courtroom. The examiner, however, should not be party to such shenanigans, even if the parent can well afford to pay for it. I am not stating that one should uniformly refuse to see such individuals; I am only suggesting that the examiner recognize that such interviews are more likely to be a waste of time, with rare exception.

THE PROBATION REPORT

Often a judge will order an investigation by the local probation agency. Generally, this involves a visit to one or both homes, as well as interviews with the parents and sometimes the children. Generally, a probation officer is not a psychiatrist or psychologist. Some are social workers and others have less formal training. It behooves the probation officer to make a specific recommendation to the court regarding custody. On occasion, however, I have seen a probation report in which the probation officer has provided a wealth of information and then not come forth with a specific recommendation. This, in my opinion, is an abrogation of responsibility. (It would similarly be an impartial examiner's abrogation of responsibility to avoid making a specific recommendation regarding which is the preferable parent.)

In the past I have on occasion been told that I should not have the probation report available to me. In recent years I have made this a proviso of my involvement in that it would compromise my provision that I must have *all* information available to me. The people who enlist my services will have to trust that I will not be swayed by an individual report, whether it be the probation officer's or anyone else's. Like all other reports, the examiner should view this one as hearsay. However, there may be information therein that may serve to lead one to direct inquiry with the parents and children. Often, the probation officer will have spent much time getting details of the past history. As mentioned, such information is not of the highest priority in the custody evaluation (although it should be taken).

What is more important in the probation report is the home visit. Most psychiatrists (including this examiner) do not routinely include home visits as part of the custody evaluation. Actually, there is a strong argument for making such visits. However, they are often very time consuming and costly and so they are not frequently made by psychiatrists and clinical psychologists. The probation officer, however, is very likely to visit one or both homes and describe these in some detail in his (her) report. Such information is of some value to the examiner. On those rare occasions when I have conducted home visits (usually after very strong requests on the part of one or both spouses), I have not found them extremely valuable. Generally, the parents are not sure how to treat me. On the one hand, their inclination is to treat me as a guest, offer me coffee, cake, and even a drink. On the other hand, they recognize that I am not a guest and that such traditionally social overtures may not be appropriate. Generally, they are quite ill at ease and there is a somewhat artificial and playacting quality to what transpires. In contrast, the children are generally more spontaneous, take me to their rooms, show me their toys, etc. Invariably, the house is impeccable and I usually have the feeling that great pains have been taken to clean up all messes before my arrival. Considering the extra expense involved in my conducting such visits and considering the paucity of additional information that they can provide in custody evaluations, I generally discourage them.

My overall experience has been that the probation report is of value in my evaluation but not crucial, and I have conducted many evaluations without having one available. M. G. Goldzband (1980) recommends that the psychiatrist and probation officer freely communicate with one another. I am in disagreement with this in that there is a risk of undue influence. The probation officer, like the guardian ad litem, although neutral, should not, in my opinion, be discussing the evaluation with the impartial examiner. Reading the probation officer's report provides the examiner with input of information. Discussing the case with the probation officer opens the examiner to the criticism of being influenced by another professional. I am in agreement with Goldzband, however, regarding his view that if there are differences of opinion between a probation officer and the evaluator these should be aired in court and not personally between the two.

ANSWERING MACHINES

Answering machines are becoming increasingly popular. I personally am pleased about this development because I have long considered them extremely valuable instruments. They are a wonderful time-saving device in that one need not repeatedly call an individual, but merely leave a message and await a return. Whereas years ago many people were quite reluctant to use them, such resistance appears to be lessening. Previously, many were offended by them, considered them impersonal, and refused to leave messages on them. I believe that there are fewer such individuals at this point. There were others who were so petrified over creating a message that they refused to use the instruments. These people also are lessening their anxieties.

Occasionally, the message an individual creates for an answering machine can provide the examiner with useful information. Most often, the messages are standard and stereotyped and provide little data for the custody evaluation. However, the more atypical and idiosyncratic the message is, the more revealing it will be of the individual's personality. For example, I once did a custody evaluation in which the father was a building contractor. On one occasion I called his home in order to change an appointment. In the course of his message he stated (while chuckling): "If I don't call you back, keep trying. Don't give up. You'll ultimately get through to me." Aside from the effects that such a response must have had on his business, there was no question that it was an important statement regarding his sensitivity to other people's feelings and his concept of human relationships. He manifested the same insensitivity in his relationships with his wife and children. His basic position with his family was that if people loved him they would show their affection by suffering a variety of inconveniences on his behalf. He once actually said to me, "My dogs come to me." His telephone machine message (which I recorded verbatim) was another example of this personality deficiency.

Probably my most dramatic example of important information obtained from an answering machine occurred in the early 1970s. A mother claimed that her husband, with whom her 14-year-old son was living, was basically an adolescent himself and that he had taken on "hippie" personality traits. She believed, thereby, that he was not serving as a healthy model for their son, especially because the boy was living with the father. She claimed that the father was afraid to accept the fact that he was an adult and wanted to live the lifestyle of an adolescent. The father claimed that this was just another example of the mother's delusional state and that there was absolutely no truth to her allegation. Up until the time I called the father's house, I could not come to any conclusion on this particular point. However, an occasion arose which warranted my calling the father (again to change an appointment). The answering machine message began with rock music, which lasted about 30 seconds. After this introduction, the father's voice came on (with the rock music now lowered to background levels): "You lucky cats have hooked into Bob and Jack's pad. If any of you cool cats want to speak with us. . . ." The message clearly confirmed the mother's allegation. I recorded it verbatim and included it in my final report.

SPECIAL CONSULTANTS

On rare occasions I have seen fit to bring in a special consultant who has an area of competence or expertise that I do not possess. The situation was one that warranted the person actually participating in a joint interview with me. I recall one case in which the custody of an interracial child was being litigated. The father was black and the mother was white. My basic view of the father was that he would not have been the preferable parent. He exhibited a number of personality deficiencies which would have made him a poor father model. In contrast, I observed no such deficiencies in the mother. The mother, however, was pressuring me to recommend an extremely stringent visitation arrangement. Both parents politicized the evaluation. The father made it known to me that if I did not support his position he could only conclude that I was prejudiced against blacks and that his attorney would be prepared to demonstrate this in court. The mother claimed that if I did not support her position that I was clearly being sexist and that her attorney would demonstrate this in court.

Before I communicated to the parents my preliminary impressions (stated above), I decided that I would invite in a consultant who could address herself to the custodial issue and who could circumvent the problems related to the politicization of the evaluation. Specifically, I had a colleague, a black woman who was a social worker, whose opinion I highly regarded. I told the parents that I wanted to have her join us in a joint interview to discuss the custody issue and that I would give her no information beforehand regarding any of the issues that we were focusing on. I told them that her input, as a black person, would be useful regarding the presence or absence of racial prejudice on my part and that as a woman she could be useful regarding the possible issue of my sexism. Both parents happily agreed to her participation. (I might say here that even if they had not agreed I would have brought her in under the "any and all" powers granted to me by the provisions document.) Accordingly, my colleague joined us "cold" and at the end of two hours—completely independent of any input from me—came to the same conclusions toward which I was heading, namely, that the mother was a far superior parent than the father, but that her restricted visitation plan was too stringent. Her comments took the wind out of both of their sails and the prejudice and sexism issues never came up in court.

⚖️ NINE
THE FINAL
RECOMMENDATIONS

INTRODUCTION

Examiners conducting custody evaluations may feel that the burden placed upon them in making such crucial recommendations is formidable. This may be especially true in situations that are not clear-cut. Potential guilt over making injudicious and possibly injurious recommendations can be assuaged if examiners remind themselves that the final decisions are still not theirs alone. Many people will have an opportunity to contribute their opinions, and although the judge will generally take an impartial examiner's opinion seriously, he (she) is not required to do so. Furthermore, although one hopes the custody decision will be final (in order to provide the children with the most stable and predictable environment possible under the circumstances), new information and life changes may arise that may justify a reconsideration of the court's decision. Accordingly, if a decision has been an injudicious one, there are still possibilities for its rectification. Last, examiners' burdens will be reduced if they can say to themselves after completing their custody evaluations that they have been dedicated to the task, have conducted their inquiries with integrity and fairness, and have made every reasonable attempt to provide the best possible recommendations. This is all the court asks of the examiners; and it is all the evaluators should ask of themselves.

As mentioned in the document outlining provisions for my involvement (Appendix I), my usual procedure was to present my findings and recommendations to the parents and their attorneys prior to the preparation of my final report to the court. This serves the purpose of shortening the period of anxiety between the final interview and submission of the report. The parents, therefore, are the first ones to learn of the decision and are spared the anxiety they would have suffered had they been required to wait (often 6 to 18 months) to learn it from the judge. There was a time, prior to about 10 years ago, when some judges in my area objected to my discussing my findings and recommendations with the clients themselves and wanted me instead to submit my report directly to them. I absolutely refused to involve myself under such a restriction. We are living at a time when people have every right to access to their medical records. Accordingly, I believe that such judges' position might even be illegal. Parents are entitled to know of the evaluator's findings and recommendations prior to their being communicated to the court, especially to give them the opportunity to discuss them in detail with the examiner and even try to change his (her) opinion. Providing the parents with the opportunity to have input at this point lessens their feelings of impotence, which are generally quite great in the course of custody litigation. In this chapter I first discuss reviewing one's material and preparing the final recommendations to the parents. Specific emphasis will be given to the factors that I give weight to when making the custody recommendation. Then I will discuss the presentation of findings to the parents and their attorneys and the ways in which such presentation is utilized in the preparation of the final report. Finally, I will discuss the details of the preparation of the final written report.

MAKING THE CUSTODY RECOMMENDATION

Preliminary Considerations

Making a custody recommendation involves some prediction into the future. Because we are not omniscient and because accurate predictions are impossible, we must extrapolate from the information we have and hope that our extrapolations will be judicious. Furthermore, most litigating families settle down after the final decision and reveal less pathology than they may have during the course of the evaluation. The greater the experience the examiner has with the family, the more intense the evaluation, the greater the likelihood the prediction will be a judicious one. One of the advantages of mediation is that if the mediator's recommendations prove to be injudicious the family can easily return for a follow-up evaluation in order to discuss a modification of the original proposals. This is far less readily accomplished in traditional custody litigation.

It behooves mental health professionals who serve as impartial examiners to do everything possible to come ultimately to a specific recommendation regarding who is the better parent. This usually involves weighing the assets and liabilities of each parent and ascertaining which parent's assets more outweigh the liabilities. Even if the comparison appears to be a very close one, it still behooves the examiner to make a specific recommendation regarding who would serve better as primary custodial parent. I am in agreement with A. P. Derdeyn (1976) that the impartial evaluator must commit himself (herself) to providing an opinion. I am in agreement with him, as well, that not to do so is an abrogation of the evaluator's responsibility. The clear-cut cases are usually the easiest ones for the court to decide. It is the more difficult ones—the ones in which the parents appear to be equally well qualified—that impartial examiners are often invited to contribute. I have seen reports from court-appointed examiners who have concluded that both parents are equally well qualified and that the court should make the final decision. This is a "cop-out." No two people are equal and a *decision must be made.*

No matter how many hairs have to be split in the process of doing so, we mental health professionals are in the best position to conduct the kind of sophisticated evaluation required in certain custody conflicts. And the examiner who, as a basic principle, never makes a recommendation, but only provides the court with information and elucidation, is seriously defaulting on what I consider an obligation to the court. Perhaps the time will come when I will be totally stymied, when I will find it impossible to make a recommendation. Although I have been involved in a number of cases in which deciding on parental preference has been very difficult, I have to date always come through with a specific recommendation. My hope is that I will always be able to do so, even though now only in the context of mediation.

In the course of the evaluation, one may become quite confused. When speaking with the mother, the examiner may feel quite confident that she deserves to be designated the primary custodial parent. The indignities she describes herself to have suffered at the hands of her husband and the neglect that he has exhibited toward the children appear to be formidable. Then, during the interview with the father, the examiner may wonder how he could have been naive enough to consider, even for one moment, recommending primary custody for the mother. The father provides convincing arguments that the mother's view of the situation is entirely distorted, possibly even to the point of paranoia. And so, back and forth the arguments go—producing in the therapist mounting confusion and ambivalence. Generally, the joint interviews, as well as input from the children, help the examiner determine which of the two versions is closer to the "truth."

Actually, my best evaluations have been those in which I have experienced the most confusion and ambivalence. In such cases, I have had to be "on my toes" and have been therefore highly motivated to extract as much information as possible from all concerned parties. This indecisiveness has sharpened my inquiry and contributed to my ultimately formulating the most comprehensive and convincing evaluation.

It is important for the examiner to appreciate that just as one element in obsessive love is reaction formation to unacceptable hostility, so excessive hatred (as witnessed in divorce conflicts) can serve, in part, as reaction formation to underlying, lingering affectionate feelings. It is unreasonable to believe that two people who have been living together for a number of years, and who have reared together one or more children, do not still have residual feelings of affection and even love. They may have to deny these to enable themselves to separate successfully. They may have to exaggerate the hateful feelings to provide themselves with the strength to sever the marital bond. Because such exaggerations and distortions are the rule, rather than the exception, the evaluator must be ever alert to this element during the interviews.

On occasion, it becomes apparent very early in the evaluation which parent is likely to be supported. The evaluator should not immediately interrupt the evaluation in such cases, but should still conduct a full evaluation and collect whatever information is necessary to support adequately this early conclusion. One does not want to be in the position of not having done a complete evaluation. The parents too are entitled to at least full history taking and reasonable collection of data because of the small possibility that new information may arise that would change the examiner's initial conclusion.

J. Goldstein et al. (1973) use the term "least detrimental alternative" to refer to the kinds of decisions that have to be made in custody evaluations. It is a situation in which there is no "good" or "bad" disposition for the child, but rather a choice between two undesirable alternatives. And it is our job to try to ascertain which is the less detrimental. Accepting the situation as one in which there is absolutely no happy solution can lessen somewhat the examiner's burden. I have a mild criticism of J. Goldstein, both grammatical and substantive. The word *alternative*, when strictly defined, refers to a decision between *two* choices. Properly speaking, one cannot choose one of three alternatives. J. Goldstein would have done better to use "least detrimental option" because most often there are more than two choices regarding the various kinds of plans that one must take into consideration when making a custody recommendation.

The method I have found most useful for formulating my final recommendation is to dictate (into a hand machine) material from my basic notes under four categories: the mother's assets as a parent, the mother's liabilities as a parent, the father's assets as a parent, and the father's liabilities as a parent. I simply go through my notes—from beginning to end—and dictate pertinent material under each category. My secretary sets up four categories on the word processor: *Mrs. Mary Jones' Assets as a Parent and Arguments Supporting Her Position in the Custody Dispute, Mrs. Mary Jones' Liabilities as a Parent and Arguments Against Her Position in the Custody Dispute, Mr. John Jones' Assets as a Parent and Arguments Supporting His Position in the Custody Dispute,* and *Mr. John Jones' Liabilities as a Parent and Arguments Against His Position in the Custody Dispute.* Within each of these four large categories subcategories may be inserted such as Availability, Psychological Bonding with the Child(ren), Commitment to the Child's (Children's) Education, Involvement in School Extra-curricular Activities, etc. As I go through my notes, from beginning to end, I instruct her to insert the particular data into the appropriate category. Although these four categories are the primary ones for determining parental preference, she also places information in other categories into which I place data in the course of my reviewing the material. These include a category for basic statistical data about each of the parties interviewed: name, age, occupation, and the date(s) of interview. A category describing the history of the marriage and the marital difficulties is included, as well as separate categories for each of the nonparent individuals interviewed such as the children, stepparents, etc. However, the bulk of the data is included in the four main categories concerning parental assets and liabilities. No attempt is made at that point to organize material within a category or subcategory; rather, this is done at the time of the preparation of the final report, between the meeting with the parents and attorneys and submission of the final written report to the court.

The material as formulated above is used as a guideline in the presentation of findings to the parents and their attorneys. During this presentation I would jot down corrections of any errors that may have crept in (thereby protecting myself from possible error and embarrassment in court). I would also ask questions to fill in minor data that might not have been previously obtained.

Factors to Consider When Making the Custody Recommendation

Of course, the most important factors to consider are the parental capacities of the mother and father. By organizing each parent's assets and liabilities in accordance with the aforementioned plan, the examiner should be able to come to some definite conclusion regarding the custody issue. In Chapters Three through Eight I have provided guidelines for collecting and assessing the most important kinds of data to be included under these four categories. One cannot make up a specific score sheet in which one gives an objective assessment of assets and liabilities. Rather, the best one can do is subjectively weigh these factors and attempt to ascertain which parent has fewer liabilities compared to assets. Although the comparison of parental capacities is the most important factor in coming to one's conclusions, other considerations must also be made. I will discuss the most important of these.

The Tender Years Presumption   As I have discussed in detail elsewhere (1987a), prior to the mid-19th century fathers were generally the preferred parent. One cannot say that fathers were the preferred parent in custody disputes, because there were few such disputes. Fathers were the "rightful" owners of their children; mothers had no education, sources of income, or legal rights. A practice that subsequently came to be called the *tender years presumption* appeared in the middle of the 19th century. It was based on the notion that one should not wrest a suckling child away from its mother's breast. There was some feeling that psychological damage might be caused by such separation during these tender years. However, once the child was weaned (usually by age three to four in the 19th century), the mother's input was then no longer considered vital. Children were then transferred to their fathers, their rightful parent anyway.

As the result of the women's liberation movement, advances in psychology, child labor laws, and other social changes, women became increasingly considered the preferential parent. By the mid-1920s, laws were passed in most states giving mothers equal rights to fathers regarding custodial preference. However, during the next fifty years mothers were generally favored in custody conflicts. From the 1920s to the 1970s, custody was generally given to the father only if he could prove conclusively that the mother was unfit. To do this, the father would have to demonstrate the mother's incapacitation, gross neglect of the children, or obvious maltreatment of them. In order to prove this, he would have to demonstrate that she was, for example, a chronic alcoholic, a prostitute, or grossly promiscuous. Or he would have to provide compelling evidence of significant incapacitation in child-rearing capacity. This preference for mothers was a reflection of the court's working under the tender years presumption.

In the early 1970s a "backlash" movement by fathers arose in which they claimed that the tender years doctrine was "sexist," discriminated against fathers, and did not provide them with equal protection under the law—as guaranteed by the 14th amendment of the United States Constitution (*Watts* vs. *Watts*, 1973). Courts then began to appreciate that many mothers, although not grossly negligent, were not the better parents for children to live with. Accordingly, since the mid-1970s courts have been granting custody to fathers without their having to prove their wives to be grossly negligent or incapacitated as child rearers. However, in spite of this trend the percentage of fathers who are being given custody is still quite small.

The Best Interests of the Child Principle   Since the 1970s, most courts have been operating under the best interests of the child doctrine. This doctrine is generally considered to have been laid down by Justice Benjamin Cardozo in 1925 in the case of *Finlay* vs. *Finlay*. There Cardozo stated that the judge "does not proceed upon the theory that the petitioner, whether father or mother, has a cause for action against the other or indeed against anyone. He acts as *parens patriae* to do what is best for the interests of the child." It took approximately 50 years for the best interests of the child doctrine to become widely subscribed to. However, during this 50-year period the tender years presumption was the primary one utilized in custody disputes. The tender years doctrine is viewed today as discriminating against men and not providing them with equal protection under the law. It is also viewed as being in conflict with the best interests of the child doctrine, which is now the predominant guideline for jurists.

Although most psychiatrists and attorneys today subscribe to the best interests of the child philosophy, it has never been clearly defined. An attempt to define the term has been made by the State of Michigan's *Progressive Child Custody Act* of 1970, which provides ten specific criteria for determining just what a child's best interests are. Although those who drafted these criteria were attempting to provide specific guidelines for defining just what factors should be considered when ascertaining what are the best interests of the child, I do not believe that they have succeeded. I consider the guidelines to be so vague, ill defined, and so all encompassing, that they have little value for the impartial evaluator. For example, consideration 1: "the love, affection, and other emotional ties existing between the competing parties and the child." Item 2: "the capacity and disposition of competing parties to give the child love, affection, and guidance and to continue to educate and raise the child in his religion and creed, if any." And item 6: "the moral fitness of the competing parties."

Although E. P. Benedek (1972) states that the Michigan Criteria for Custody provide very useful and specific guidelines, I have not found them useful because they are not specific enough. I am in agreement with P. W. Beck (1977) who states, "the courts have found it (the best interests of the child doctrine) impossible to operationalize this standard, which at worst has been called meaningless and at best inexact. In reality it offers the judge no substantial guidance. Although he may sincerely believe he is acting in the best interests of the child, he may be influenced by his biases and prejudices." Another factor that makes the doctrine meaningless is that *everyone* subscribes to it, everyone waves the banner of the best interests of the child as they enter the battlefield. The parents and the lawyers on both sides invoke it like belligerents praying to the same God for victory. And even the judge feels compelled to genuflect to the doctrine in his (her) ruling. And every argument, no matter how biased or preposterous, is used to justify its implementation.

In this book I have provided criteria by which the mental health professional can "operationalize" the inquiry that brings about a recommendation regarding what would be in the best interests of the child. However, the best interests of the child doctrine may be somewhat narrow. I much prefer to view myself as making recommendations regarding what would be in the *best interests of the family.* To focus narrowly on what may be in the best interests of the child may result in the examiner's not giving proper attention to the psychological effects of the placement on one or both parents. Making a recommendation that might be significantly deleterious to a parent might ultimately be to the detriment of the child. Accordingly, I attempt to make my recommendations in accordance with "the best interests of the family presumption." The *Group for the Advancement of Psychiatry*'s monograph on divorce and child custody (1980) also makes this point. The group recommends that custody recommendations not be based simply on what is in the best interests of the child, but on what is in the best interests of the family. However, as I will discuss in detail below, I also subscribe to the utilization of what I refer to as the *Stronger, Healthy Psychological Bond Presumption.*

The Concept of the Psychological Parent   In the past, biological parents were automatically given preference over adoptive, step-, and foster parents. Such preference was given in accordance with the "blood is thicker than water" concept. In recent years, courts have been much more impressed with the psychological tie as being as important as, if not more important than, the biological. *Beyond the Best Interests of the Child* (J. Goldstein et al., 1973) was an important contribution that emphasized this point and played a role in shifting the general attitude of the courts in the United States. Prior to that time (and, unfortunately, to some extent today) the legal profession was deeply wedded to the concept that the biological parent should be given priority over anyone else in custody conflicts.

Goldstein discusses the psychological tie vs. the biological tie in the context of a number of possible situations in which adults are fighting for the custody of children: foster parent vs. biological parent, adoptive parent vs. biological parent, etc. The emphasis on the psychological tie has resulted in a certain amount of distortion of this concept (not, I believe, promulgated by the authors) that there is one parent with whom the child has a psychological tie and another parent with whom the child does not. Unfortunately, their emphasis on *the* psychological parent has contributed to this notion. As a result other persons have thereby been precluded from sharing the status of psychological parent. In their publication on divorce and child custody, the *Group for the Advancement of Psychiatry* (GAP) (1980) takes issue with the notion that the child has only one psychological parent. I am in agreement with the GAP's assertion that children develop multiple attachments to a host of figures, each of whom may have the position of psychological parent. We do well to attempt to evaluate the *depth* and *extent* of psychological parenting that is provided by the various adults with whom the child is involved. Most often we do well to give priority to the parent who is the strongest psychological parent and recognize that there are others who share this position to a lesser degree. These other persons may have psychological and/or biological ties with the child. Also we must not lose sight of the fact that the psychological bond must be a *healthy* one. We are not dealing here with a situation in which *any* psychological bond will do, but rather we are comparing the depth of what might be a few psychological bonds and the nature of each is important to consider.

I once served as impartial expert in a custody conflict in which some of the aforementioned points were well demonstrated. Both parents were remarried and their only child, a nine-year-old boy, was living with his mother. The child had a very deep and warm relationship with his stepfather. In fact, I considered it to be a better relationship than the one that he had with his natural father, who had frequently been cruel to him. The boy was openly antagonistic to his natural father and stated that he wished to remain living with his mother and stepfather. In spite of this antagonism toward his father, there was no question that some warm and tender feelings still persisted and that the child was still capable of having enjoyable times with him and his new wife during visitation periods. I supported the mother's position that the child should remain living with her. I also recommended liberal visitation with the father.

In cross-examination, the father's attorney continued to ask me *which one* of the two fathers, the natural father *or* the stepfather, was truly *"the* psychological father." I persistently responded that I could not choose one or the other. When the mother's attorney gave me an opportunity to elaborate on this point, I explained that the question of which man was the psychological father was not a reasonable one because *both* were psychological fathers. In this particular situation the child was ambivalent in his relationships with both fathers. In his relationship with his stepfather, the loving affectionate feelings outweighed the hostile; in his relationship with his natural father, the opposite was the case. Ambivalence toward his biological father notwithstanding, there was still a deep psychological involvement. This child had "two" psychological fathers and it was an oversimplification to assume that he should have only one.

J. Goldstein et al. also emphasize the importance of continuity in the formation of the psychological tie and the detrimental effects of its disruption. The examiner should consider this factor when making a custody recommendation. Unfortunately, there are times when the continuity factor may result in an initially less desirable parent becoming designated the preferential custodial parent. This is sometimes the case in the kidnaping situation when the less desirable parent (the kidnaper) may have spent enough time with the child to become the preferable parent because of the detrimental effects of disruption of continuity.

The Stronger, Healthy Psychological Bond Presumption During the last few years, in association with my increasing involvement in child custody litigation, I have often had the thought that perhaps we should not have dispensed with the tender years presumption. If we are to consider the greatest good for the greatest number, I believe we probably would have done better to retain it. Of course, there would have been some children who would then have remained with the less preferable parent; however, many more children would have been spared the psychological traumas attendant to the implementation of the best interests of the child doctrine and the widespread enthusiasm for the joint custodial concept. There is no question that custody litigation has increased dramatically since the mid-1970s and there is no question, as well, that this increase has been the direct result of these two recent developments.

What should we do then? Go back to the old system? I think not. I believe that there is a middle path that should prove useful. To elaborate: First, the displacement of the tender years presumption with the best interests of the child philosophy was initiated primarily by men who claimed that the tender years presumption was intrinsically "sexist" because women are not necessarily preferable parents by virtue of the fact that they are female. State legislatures and the courts agreed. As a result, the best interests of the child doctrine has been uniformly equated with the notion that custody determinations should be "sex blind." Considerable difficulty has been caused, I believe, by fusing these two concepts. *It is extremely important that they be considered separately.* Everyone claims to be in support of doing what is in the best interests of the children. Everyone waves that banner: each parent, each attorney, the mental health professionals who testify, and certainly the judge. No one claims to be against children's best interests. The situation is analogous to the position politicians take with regard to their support for widows, orphans, the handicapped, and the poor. All politicians wave that banner. Even the suggestion that a politician might not be in strong support of these unfortunates would be met with denial, professions of incredulity, and righteous indignation.

With regard to all those who claim that the best interests of the child is their paramount consideration, one could argue that a wide variety of possible custodial arrangements could serve children's best interests. One could argue that automatic placement with the father serves their best interests, and this was certainly the case up until the early 20th century. Or one could claim that automatic preference for the mother serves the children best, and this was the case from the mid-1920s to the mid-1970s. One could argue that placing them with grandparents, uncles, aunts, or in foster homes, adoption agencies, or residential cottages might serve children's best interests. At this time, the prevailing notion is that sex-blind custody evaluations automatically serve children's best interests. Although it may be an unpopular thing to say in the late 1980s, I do not believe that sex-blind custody decisions necessarily serve the best interests of children. Somehow, the acceptance of the concept that fathers can be as paternal as mothers can be maternal was immediately linked with the concept that such egalitarianism serves the best interests of children. I do not accept this assumption of gender equality in child-rearing capacity and would go further and state that the younger the child, the less the likelihood that this assumption is valid. It follows then that I do not believe that sex-blind custody evaluations and decisions serve the best interests of children. I recognize that this is an unpopular position to take in the late 1980s, that it might appear to be very undemocratic and even sexist of me (here with the prejudice being against men), but it is the opinion that I have. My hope is that the reader will read on with some degree of receptivity and will come to the same conclusion.

To elaborate: No one can deny that men and women are different biologically. No one can deny, either, that it is the woman who bears the child and has within her the power to feed it with her own body (although she may choose not to do so). I believe that this biological difference cannot be disassociated from certain psychological factors that result in mothers' being more likely to be superior to fathers in their capacity to involve themselves with the newborn infant at the time of its birth. After all, it is the mother who carries the baby in her body for nine months. It is she who is continually aware of its presence. It is she who feels its kicks and its movements. It is she who is ever reminded of the pregnancy by formidable changes in her body and by the various symptomatic reminders of the pregnancy: nausea, vomiting, fatigue, discomfort during sleep, etc. Even the most dedicated fathers cannot have these experiences and the attendant strong psychological ties that they engender. The mother, as well, must suffer the pains of the infant's delivery. Even though the father may be present at the time of birth and an active participant in the process, the experience is still very much the mother's. And, as mentioned, it is the mother who may very well have the breast-feeding experience, something the father is not capable of enjoying. All these factors create a much higher likelihood that the mother—at the time of birth—will have a stronger psychological tie with the infant than will the father. This "up-front" programming places her in a superior position with regard to psychological bonding with the newborn infant at the time of birth. I believe that most individuals would agree that, if parents decided to separate at the time of birth and both were reasonably equal with regard to parenting capacity, the mother would be the preferable parent.

Some might argue that even if the aforementioned specula-tions are valid, the superiority stops at the time of birth and men are thereafter equal to women with regard to parenting capacity. Even here I am dubious. It is reasonable to assume that during the course of evolution there was a selective survival of women who were highly motivated child rearers on a genetic basis. Such women were more likely to seek men for the purposes of impregnation and more likely to be sought by men who desired children. Similarly, there was selective propagation of men who were skilled providers of food, clothing, shelter, and protection of women and children. Such men were more likely to be sought by women with high child-rearing drives. This assumption, of course, is based on the theory that there are genetic factors involved in such behavior. Women with weaker child-rearing drives were less likely to procreate, and men with less family provider and protective capacities were also at a disadvantage with regard to transmitting their genes to their progeny. They were less attractive to females as mates because they were less likely to fulfill these functions so vital to species survival. As weaker protectors they were less likely to survive in warfare and in fighting to protect their families from enemies.

Accordingly, although it may be the unpopular thing to say at the time of this writing (1988), I believe that the average woman today is more likely to be genetically programmed for child-rearing functions than the average man. Even if this speculation is true, one could argue that we are less beholden to our instincts than lower animals and that environmental influences enable us to modify these more primitive drives. I do not deny this, but agree only up to a point. There are limitations to which environment can modify heredity, especially in the short period of approximately 10-15 years since the tender years presumption was generally considered to be sexist. Environment modifies heredity primarily (and many would say exclusively) by the slow process of selective survival of those variants that are particularly capable of adapting to a specific environment. Accordingly, I believe that these genetic factors are still strong enough in today's parents to be given serious consideration when making custody decisions.

It would appear from the aforementioned comments that I am on the verge of recommending that we go back to the tender years presumption. This is not completely the case. *What I am recommending is that we give preference in custody disputes to the parent (regardless of sex) who has provided the greatest degree of healthy, child-rearing input during the children's formative years.* Because mothers today are still more often the primary child-rearing parents, more mothers would be given parental preference in custody disputes adjudicated under this principle. If, however, in spite of the mother's superiority at the time of birth, it was the father who was the primary caretaker—especially during the early years of life—such a father might very well serve better as the preferable primary custodial parent. This presumption, too, is essentially sex blind (satisfying thereby present-day demands for gender egalitarianism) because it allows for the possibility that a father's input may outweigh the mother's in the formative years, even though he starts at a disadvantage. It utilizes primarily the *psychological bond* with the child as the primary consideration in custody evaluations. I would add, however, the important consideration that the longer the time span between infancy and the time of the custody evaluation and decision, the greater the likelihood that environmental factors will modify (strengthen or weaken) the psychological bonds that the child had with each parent during the earliest years.

I refer to this as the stronger, *healthy* psychological bond presumption, which, I believe, is the one that would serve the best interests of the child. It is important for the reader to appreciate that the parent who had the greater involvement with the child during infancy is the one more likely to have the stronger psychological bond. However, if the early parenting was not "good," then the bond that develops might be pathological. Accordingly, I am not referring here to any kind of psychological bond at all, but a *healthy* psychological bond. It is not a situation in which *any* psychological bond at all will do. A paranoid mother, who has so programmed her son that he too has developed paranoid feelings about his father, may have a strong psychological bond with her son, stronger than that which he has with his father. But this *folie à deux* is certainly not a healthy one and its presence is a strong argument for recommending the father as the primary custodial parent. It is for this reason that I refer to the presumption as the stronger, healthy psychological bond presumption. To clarify my position on these principles, I will first present a vignette that will serve as a basis for my subsequent comments.

Let us envision a situation in which a couple has one child, a boy. During the first four years of the child's life, the mother remains at home as the primary child rearer and the father is out of the house during the day as the breadwinner. When the child is four the mother takes a full-time job. During the day the child attends a nursery school and then stays with a woman in the neighborhood who cares for the children of working parents. At the end of the workday and over weekends both parents are involved equally in caring for the child. And the same situation prevails when the child enters elementary school. When the child is seven the parents decide to separate. Each parent wants primary custody. The father claims that during the three years prior to the separation, he was as involved as the mother in the child's upbringing. And the mother does not deny this. The father's position is that the court should make its decision solely on the basis of parenting capacity—especially as demonstrated in the most recent three years of the child's life—and claims that any custody decision taking his gender into consideration is "sexist" and is an abrogation of his civil rights.

In the course of the litigation the child develops typical symptoms of the parental alienation syndrome (Chapter Six). He becomes obsessed with hatred of his father, denies any benevolent involvement with him at any point in his life, and creates absurd scenarios to justify his animosity. In contrast, his mother becomes viewed by the boy as faultless and all-loving. I believe that in this situation the child's psychological bond is stronger with the mother, and the symptoms of alienation are created by him in an attempt to maintain that bond. Because the child's earliest involvement was stronger with the mother, residua of that tie are expressing themselves at the age of seven. If the father had been the primary caretaker during the first four years of the boy's life, and if then both mother and father shared equally in child-rearing involvement, I would predict that the child would develop symptoms of alienation from the mother, the parent with whom the psychological tie is weaker. Under such circumstances, I would recommend the father be designated the primary custodial parent.

In summary, the stronger, healthy psychological bond presumption is best stated as a three-step process:

1)Preference should be given to that parent (regardless of sex) with whom the child has developed the stronger, healthy psychological bond.

2)That parent (regardless of sex) who was the primary caretaker during the earliest years of the child's life is more likely to have developed the stronger, healthy psychological bond.

3)The longer the time-lag between the earliest years and the time of the custody evaluation or decision, the greater the likelihood other factors will operate that may tip the balance in either direction regarding parental capacity.

The Child's Gender as a Custody Consideration   Although it is not usually implemented, there are some who believe that boys should live with their fathers and girls with their mothers. Proponents of this view emphasize the importance of modeling and identification with the same-sex parent as an important developmental consideration. Although I am in agreement that such modeling is important, those who subscribe to this position are not giving proper attention to the importance of learning how to deal with and relate to members of the opposite sex during the formative years. Children need to be intimate with members of both sexes and this opportunity is compromised for the child who grows up in a single-parent home. It is difficult, if not impossible, to say which of these two factors is more important to consider when recommending placement for a child in a custody dispute. More specifically, if a girl lives with her mother she enjoys the modeling advantage, but is deprived of learning how to live with a man. If she lives with her father, modeling with her mother is compromised, but she experiences the benefits of relating more deeply with a male. Until we know more about these two processes the principle of placing a child (especially an older one) with the parent of the same sex must be subscribed to with caution.

Some classical psychoanalysts hold that boys should live with their fathers and girls with their mothers in order to avoid oedipal problems. They believe that a boy's living alone with his mother is likely to result in his believing that he has won the oedipal conflict and has been successful in driving his father out of the house. A similar argument is made against a girl's living with her father. As I have described elsewhere (1968, 1971, 1973a), I believe that those problems generally referred to as oedipal have their roots in emotional deprivations during the first two to three years of life and have a breadth and depth that go beyond mere sexual and possessive desires. Such problems, therefore, are not likely to be alleviated by the somewhat simple maneuver of having a child live with a same-sex parent.

In the adolescent period one also hears the same aphorism: a boy should live with his father and a girl should live with her mother. Here, the sexual implications are more obvious in that the subscribers to this dictum want to protect adolescents from being overstimulated by living together with an opposite-sex parent. Others, however, claim that it is important for the adolescent to live with the parent of the opposite sex in order to have this last opportunity to learn how to live with an opposite-sex person before finding his (her) own mate. Those who disagree would argue that this places the adolescent in a sexually stimulating situation. I do not generally subscribe to either of these dicta. Rather, I believe that other factors—relating to parenting capacity independent of sex—should be the primary considerations. If, however, there is parental seductivity, then I might very well take this factor into consideration (as one among many) in making my recommendation. Also, one must take into consideration sibling bonding and the psychological effects of splitting children of opposite sex in order to subscribe to the aforementioned dictum.

It is also important for the examiner to appreciate that the decision may often be made by the adolescent—independent of the examiner's (and even the judge's) opinion. Adolescents usually have very strong opinions regarding whom they would like to live with, and the court often recognizes its impotence when ordering adolescents to live where they do not wish to. (This is especially true if the noncustodial parent is receptive to the adolescent's living with him [her].) Accordingly, I will give great weight to an adolescent's expressed preference and use it as an important criterion for making a recommendation. However, there are often complications. The adolescent's wishes may be ill-advised and inappropriate. The desired parent may not be receptive to having the youngster. Each case must be evaluated on its own merits. One guideline that should be given serious consideration is that the adolescent's preferences should be taken more seriously than those of younger children. To make gender, per se, an important consideration is generally ill advised. It is sometimes invoked in order to lessen the burden of the examiner or judge and to oversimplify what is generally a very complex consideration.

Parental Sexual Behavior as a Custody Consideration   In past years the sexual behavior of the mother, and to a lesser extent of the father, was an important consideration for courts when determining primary custody. Although adultery by *either* spouse was (and still is) generally considered grounds for divorce, adultery by the mother (but, interestingly, not generally by the father) was considered justification for not granting her custody. The courts would often consider the mother's sexual life in great detail: if she was having extramarital sexual experiences – even after the separation and even though she was not bringing her sexual partner(s) into the home – her maternal capacity would be questioned. The fact that she was having sexual experiences – even one sexual experience before the divorce was final – was in itself evidence to the court of her unfitness as a mother.

Most examiners today consider this to have been a very moralistic and punitive attitude for courts to take, and courts in recent years have been much more liberal with regard to using sexual behavior as a criterion for determining primary custody. However, it would be a mistake to give no consideration at all to the sexual activities of a parent. If a separated parent with temporary custody were, for example, to bring into the home a series of lovers and sleep with them overnight (even without direct exposure of the children to the sexual activities), I would consider this behavior potentially deleterious to the children and an argument against such a parent obtaining primary custody. It is not on moral grounds but on the basis of purely clinical considerations that I believe such behavior to compromise a parent's capacity. It is the *parade* of many individuals through the parent's bedroom that can be psychologically detrimental to the child.

A boy, for example, whose mother invites a series of men to sleep over with her is likely to conclude that just about every man in the world shares intimacies with his mother from which he has been singled out for exception. Such an atmosphere cannot but produce in him resentments toward both his mother and the men who share her bed. Even though the child has had no opportunity to observe the sexual activity, he still feels resentful. And the sexual excitation that such encounters may produce in him can cause added frustration and resentment. A girl living with a father who similarly exposes her to numerous sexual partners is likely to react similarly. Counterbalancing considerations, of course, might still result in my recommending that such a parent keep the children. Each consideration I describe must be weighted in relation to others; no single one should be taken in isolation and/or used as the sole deciding factor.

If a mother were to bring a man friend into the home to live, I would not necessarily consider this a reason for recommending that she be deprived of custody of her children. In fact, if the children had a good relationship with this man an argument could be given for her to have primary custody of the children. She would then be providing them with a father surrogate in compensation for their father's absence. The children can maintain a good relationship with their father *and* with the mother's live-in friend; one need not preclude the other. If such a mother, however, were to enlist the aid of the children in keeping from their father the fact that a man friend was living in the home, then, of course, this would be detrimental to them. Asking them to be party to a conspiracy of silence places an unnecessary burden on them in addition to that which they are already bearing in association with the divorce. Similar considerations would hold for a man living with a woman friend.

An adolescent girl whose mother has a whole series of affairs and who communicates this to her daughter, either overtly or covertly, is likely to behave similarly as she models herself after her mother. She comes to subscribe to the view that the greater the number of lovers, the more attractive she is. The youngster is not likely to gain appreciation of the value of more continual and deeper relationships. In addition, her awareness of her mother's activities can be very titillating—as she is stimulated to fantasize exactly what her mother is doing—and this can contribute to her desire to gain similar gratifications herself. She may then begin to compete with her mother. Sometimes such competition is confined to boys her own age; at times she may seek older men and even her mother's lovers. Similarly, if an adolescent girl lives with a father who exposes her to a series of affairs, a variety of psychological problems is likely to result. In both of these situations the parental sexual life is directly affecting the children in a detrimental way and would be a negative consideration in the custody evaluation. If a father or stepfather were seductive with a girl, or a mother or stepmother were seductive with a boy, such behavior would be an argument for the youngster's living in the other home. Elsewhere (1976, 1979c), I have elaborated on these issues.

Availability   Availability is an extremely important consideration in a custody evaluation. A mother who is primarily a homemaker has a definite advantage over a father who is primarily the breadwinner. And if this has been the situation for the children throughout the course of their lives, her advantage is even stronger. Under these circumstances the likelihood is that the children will have developed a stronger psychological bond with the mother than with the father. If both are reasonably good parents, it is likely that the bond with both parents will be healthy, but the healthy psychological bond with the mother will be stronger than that which they have with the father. Under these circumstances fathers may claim that this consideration is "unfair." A working father may have been quite devoted to his children and have spent every penny of his earnings for his family's welfare. One could argue back and forth regarding whether this is fair or not, but the primary consideration in custody evaluations is not what is fair to the parent but what is in the best interests of the children. As stated, I believe that the children's best interests are served when they live primarily with the parent with whom they have developed the strongest healthy psychological bond. It matters not to the children that the bread and milk they are being fed was paid for by the father. What does matter to them (and the younger they are the more valid this is) is who is placing the food in their mouth and who is most often available to provide them with food when they are hungry.

A father in this position may present a new woman friend who herself is a homemaker. In the course of the custody dispute he may claim that the mother, who at this point may not have a man friend, is no more available than his new woman friend, and therefore the consideration of availability has been thereby equalized. Any examiner who gets taken in by this argument should consider doing other kinds of work. In the vast majority of situations the biological mother is going to be far superior to this newcomer, even though the latter may have won a mother of the year award. Although both may be equally available regarding the number of hours per day they can devote to the children's upbringing, the biological mother's tie with the children is very likely to be significantly stronger than that of this newcomer. Most often they just cannot be compared. It would require significant deficiencies on the biological mother's part for me to view the newcomer as superior.

Involvement with the Child's School Activities　In preceding chapters I have described many criteria that the examiner should consider when making a custody recommendation. It is not my purpose in this section to review all of them, but only the most important. One most worthy of significant emphasis is the parents' involvement in the child's educational program, both the curricular and extracurricular aspects. It is important for the examiner to find out the nature of such involvement *prior* to the onset of the custody dispute. To focus primarily on such involvement after the onset of the conflict may give the evaluator a false impression about the depth of such involvement. For example, a father who was previously negligent in this area may suddenly exhibit intense interest in the children's academic life from the recognition that the examiner is going to be asking questions about such interest.

Accordingly, the examiner should inquire about attendance at teacher conferences and PTA meetings. Involvement in helping the child with homework is also important. Of particular importance is involvement in the child's extracurricular activities such as school theatrical performances, concerts, recitals, and sports events. The healthy parent enjoys these activities immensely and swells with pride as the child performs. The parent who is uninterested in these activities, who gets little if any pleasure from them, exhibits a weakness in the parenting bond. It is a very important differentiating criterion and the examiner who ignores it is compromising the evaluation.

Appreciation of the Spouse's Importance to the Children
The healthy parent recognizes the importance of input by the spouse, the divorce animosities notwithstanding. The failure to appreciate the importance of such involvement is a parental deficit and is an important consideration in evaluating parental capacity. Generally, in my first interview with the parents alone, I ask each what visitation arrangement he (she) would propose for the other if designated the primary custodial parent by the court. There are parents at that point who may make such comments as, "Doctor, if I had my way they'd have no contact at all with him" and "I think one Sunday afternoon a month, for about four hours, would be enough." Unless the other parent exhibits serious deficiencies—such as physical, sexual, or severe emotional abuse of the children—such a stringent visitation program is not only unnecessary but to enforce it would be detrimental to the children. Under these circumstances, parents who propose such a program are likely to be so blinded by rage that they fail to appreciate the importance of input by the other parent. At times, a parent will inwardly crave such a stringent visitation program but recognize that expressing such a wish will compromise that parent's position in the custody evaluation.

Accordingly, the parent may profess a more liberal program, but do so without much conviction. Under such circumstances the other parent may retort that the professed liberal program is a lie, being made for the examiner's benefit, that on repeated occasions a more restrictive program was spoken of. The other parent may provide many examples of such formidable restriction of visitation that the statement is patently hypocritical.

More important than the statements that parents make about what kind of visitation program they would want is their actual behavior regarding visitation during the course of the evaluation. A good evaluation generally takes a few weeks, during which time there are likely to be a number of visitations. Inquiry into what goes on during each of them is an important source of information for the evaluator. One should be particularly interested in cancellations for frivolous reasons, latenesses, refusal to allow the children to go with manifestly weak rationalizations, discouraging the children from going, and the utilization of the wide variety of alienating mechanisms which produce a parental alienation syndrome.

Financial Considerations   In most evaluations a mother will complain that the father is not providing her with an adequate amount of money. In response, the father will often complain that his wife is trying to exploit and even ruin him through financial pressure. The mother may complain that the privations she suffers as a result of her husband's withholding of funds is directly depriving the children. The husband may respond that, although his gross income is large, his expenses and debts are even larger and that he is living on the brink of poverty in spite of his ostensible wealth. The wife may claim that her husband is using various ploys and maneuvers, both legal and illegal, to hide money and that his stated earnings are only a fraction of his true income. Examiners do well to avoid coming to any conclusions regarding the validity of either party's allegations in such conflicts over finances. They should make every attempt to confine themselves narrowly to psychological considerations when formulating their conclusions. It is quite risky for mental health evaluators to come to conclusions regarding finances and legal issues, because these are generally beyond the examiners' area of competence and may significantly compromise their evaluations. Such naiveté by the examiner will readily be recognized by attorneys and may be one of the first areas focused on under cross-examination in court. These extra-psychological issues will be considered by the judge and those trained in such matters. Examiners do best to view themselves as providing only part of the data under consideration—that data which relate to their area of expertise.

The examiner should not fall into the trap of giving preference to the parent who has more money or more attractive facilities for the child. Although these factors must be taken into consideration, the most important factor is the relationship between the parent and the child (under the stronger, healthy psychological bond presumption). Although the child who is living at a bare subsistence level is not as likely to grow up as healthily as the one who is above these circumstances, there is little evidence that poorer children (at least those who are being provided with a reasonable amount of the basic necessities) grow up any healthier or sicker than richer children. It is the *relationship* between parent and child that counts, not the luxuriousness of the home in which the relationship exists.

The Remarried vs. The Single Parent   The parent who has remarried (or is living with someone) has an edge over the single parent in custody litigation. This is the result of the simple fact that two caretaking adults can provide a child with twice as much care as one. Of course, the *quality* of the care must also be assessed. Quantity certainly counts, but quality counts more. It is better to live with one deeply devoted parent than two who have compromised involvements.

This principle can be especially unfair to a mother who, having suffered the loss of her husband, now finds that upon his remarriage she is placed at a disadvantage in the custody conflict. She may find that she has little choice but to combine the roles of mother and breadwinner. And now, she may suffer the additional burden of risking losing her child because her remarried husband can provide more time than she. However, one must take into consideration the fact that a stepmother's involvement rarely matches that of a natural mother and so the aforementioned mother may still not be at a significant disadvantage. In such a situation one must look carefully into the number of hours that each of the three parties has available for the children as well as the depth of commitment. Of special importance here is the question of adult availability during emergencies. One must compare each household with regard to what provisions have been made for caring for children at the time of illness, accident, and other situations that require immediate adult attention.

There are certain similarities between a situation in which a parent kidnaps a child and one in which a parent moves with the child to another state, often for the purpose of remarriage. The situations are similar in that the parent with the child is making the move without the permission of the other parent. In addition, the move is generally considered illegal. The difference, of course, is that in the kidnaping case, the kidnaper strictly attempts to avoid any communication with the other parent. In the out-of-state move, there is generally communication and the whereabouts of the child are known.

In some states there are laws prohibiting the custodial parent from moving outside the state without the permission of the noncustodial parent and/or the court. However, such laws have little "bite" in that there are generally no particular punitive measures automatically enforced, measures such as loss of custody of the child. They do, however, provide the "abandoned" parent with easy access to the legal system to take some action. As is true for the kidnaping situation, time is very much on the side of the parent who has the child, regardless of the legality of the custodianship. That parent can generally rely on court delays with the full knowledge that the longer the child is with the custodial parent the greater the likelihood the child will develop a relationship and prefer to remain there. The evaluator must be primarily interested in what is in the best interests of the child and should not automatically assume that the parent who moves out of the state is the worse parent. The illegal act should certainly be taken into consideration as a compromise in parental capacity. If, however, it is an isolated defect, and is not just one manifestation of a pattern of duplicity and other forms of dishonesty, then it should not carry overriding weight.

A mother, for example, may have an opportunity for a new marriage to someone with whom she has formed a deep relationship. Her fiancé may live at some distance and a marriage may require a move. She may recognize that the relocation will compromise her child's relationship with her former husband. However, she must also think of herself and her own future. In such situations she may choose to marry and move with the full recognition that her child's relationship with the father will be compromised. I cannot say that such a decision is necessarily pathological. The older the woman is at the time, the more reasonable the decision may be. A mother who turns down an opportunity to remarry, because it necessarily involves a move to a distant place, may become so resentful and bitter over the restriction that her maternal capacity will be impaired and the child will suffer. Accordingly, considering all factors, the child's best interests may still be served by the move. This is another example illustrating the weakness of a narrow interpretation of the best interests of the child principle, and it is one of the reasons why I prefer the best interests of the family doctrine.

One could argue (as might the noncustodial parent's attorney) that the parent who has moved out of the state has broken the law and should therefore lose custody. Adherence to this position could result in the child's suffering for the "crime" of its parent, in that the parent who moves may still be the preferable one. Accordingly, I would not support automatic deprivation of custody for such a parent. However, that parent should not totally escape some kind of repercussion. The parent might be required to bear the expenses of visitations and be the one to bring the child to the noncustodial parent. The latter has been inconvenienced enough by the removal of the child to the distant location and should not be made to bear additional discomforts or privations attendant to traveling long distances for visitation. In addition, financial payments made by the noncustodial to the custodial parent might also be reduced (as long as the child does not necessarily suffer) as part of the "price to pay" for having broken the law and deprived the noncustodial parent of an active role in the child-rearing process. If a mother, for example, moves out of the state in order to marry a man whose work necessitates her relocating, the father who remains behind will automatically no longer have to pay alimony because of his ex-wife's remarriage. In addition, the court should consider reducing support payments as a "penalty" that the wife should pay for having deprived the father of active involvement in the child-rearing process and for the discomforts attendant to the more infrequent visitations that such a move entails. If the wife's new husband can afford it, the court might even consider cutting off support payments entirely. Of course, one would not want to implement this action if the child is caused significant privation. Without such repercussions the laws become meaningless as a deterrent to such moves.

When a Parental Alienation Syndrome Is Present   Families in which the children exhibit manifestations of the parental alienation syndrome can be divided into three categories: severe, moderate, and mild. Although there is actually a continuum, and many cases do not fit neatly into one of these categories, the differentiation is still useful—especially with regard to the therapeutic approaches. In each of the three categories not only are the children different, but the mothers as well. It is extremely important that evaluators determine the proper category if they are to provide the most judicious recommendations. In each category I will discuss the mothers, the children, and the appropriate therapeutic approaches. I will use the mother as the example of the preferred parent as this is so in the majority of cases; however, the same considerations apply to the father when he is the favored parent.

I wish to emphasize at this point that in many cases the therapy of these families is not possible without court support. Only the court has the power to order these mothers to stop their manipulations and maneuvering. And it is only the court that has the power to place the children in whichever home would best suit their needs at the particular time. Therapists who embark upon the treatment of such families without such court backing are not likely to be successful. I cannot emphasize this point strongly enough.

Severe Cases of the Parental Alienation Syndrome   The *mothers* of these children are often fanatic. They will use every mechanism at their disposal (legal and illegal) to prevent visitation. They are obsessed with antagonism toward their husbands. In many cases they are paranoid. Sometimes the paranoid thoughts and feelings about the husband are isolated to him alone; in other cases this paranoia is just one example of many types of paranoid thinking. Often the paranoia did not exhibit itself prior to the breakup of the marriage and may be a manifestation of the psychiatric deterioration that frequently is seen in the context of divorce disputes, especially custody disputes (1986a). Central to the paranoid mechanism is projection. These mothers see in their husbands many noxious qualities that actually exist within themselves. By projecting these unacceptable qualities onto their husbands they can consider themselves innocent victims. When a sex-abuse allegation becomes part of the package (1987a), they may be projecting their own sexual inclinations onto him. In the service of this goal they exaggerate and distort any comment the child makes that might justify the accusation. And this is not difficult to do because children normally will entertain sexual fantasies, often of the most bizarre form. I am in agreement with Freud (1905) that children are "polymorphous perverse" and they thereby provide these mothers with an ample supply of material to serve as nuclei for their projections and accusations.

Such mothers do not respond to logic, confrontations with reality, or appeals to reason. They will readily believe the most preposterous scenarios. Skilled mental health examiners who claim that there is no evidence for the accusation are dismissed as being against them, or as being paid off by the husband. And this is typical of paranoid thinking: it does not respond to logic and any confrontation that might shake the system is rationalized into the paranoid scenario. Even a court decision that the father is not guilty of the mother's allegations does not alter her beliefs or reduce her commitment to her scenarios of denigration. Energizing the rage is the "hell hath no fury like a woman scorned" phenomenon.

The *children* of these mothers are similarly fanatic. They have joined together with her in a *folie à deux* relationship in which they share her paranoid fantasies about the father. They may become panic-stricken over the prospect of visiting with their father. Their blood-curdling shrieks, panicked states, and hostility may be so severe that visitation is impossible. If placed in the father's home they may run away, become paralyzed with morbid fear, or be so destructive that removal becomes warranted. Unlike children in the moderate and mild categories, their panic and hostility may not be reduced in the father's home, even when separated for significant periods.

With regard to the *therapeutic approaches* in this category, traditional therapy for the mother is most often not possible. She is totally unreceptive to treatment and will consider a therapist who believes that her delusions are not warranted to be joining in with her husband. He thereby becomes incorporated into the paranoid system. A court order that she enter into treatment is futile. Judges are often naive with regard to their belief that one can order a person into treatment. This is an extension of their general view of the world that ordering people around is the best way to accomplish something. Most judges are aware that they cannot order an impotent husband to have an erection or a frigid wife to have an orgasm. Yet, they somehow believe that one can order someone to have conviction for and commitment to therapy. Accordingly, the evaluator does well to discourage the court from such a misguided order.

Therapy for the children, as well, is most often not possible *while the children are still living in the mother's home.* No matter how many times a week they are seen, the therapeutic exposure represents only a small fraction of the total amount of time of exposure to the mother's denigrations of the father. There is a sick psychological bond here between the mother and children that is not going to be changed by therapy as long as the children remain living with the mother. While still in the mother's home the children are going to be exposed continually to the bombardment of denigration and other influences (overt and covert) that contribute to the perpetuation of the syndrome.

Accordingly, the first step toward treatment is *removal* of the children from the mother's home and placement in the home of the father, the allegedly hated parent. This may not be accomplished easily and the court might have to threaten sanctions and even jail if the mother does not comply. Following this transfer there must be a period of decompression and debriefing in which the mother has no opportunity at all for input to the children. The hope here is to give the children the opportunity to re-establish the relationship with the alienated father, without significant contamination of the process by the brainwashing mother. Even telephone calls must be strictly prohibited for at least a few weeks, and perhaps longer. Then, according to the therapist's judgment, slowly increasing contacts with the mother may be initiated, starting with monitored telephone calls. The danger here, however, is that these will be used as opportunities for programming the children.

Therefore, this period of slow and judicious renewal of contact between the children and the brainwashing parent must be monitored carefully so as to prevent a recurrence of the disorder. In some cases this may be successful, especially if the mother can see her way clear to entering into meaningful therapy (not often the case for mothers in this category). In these cases the children might ultimately be returned to the mother. However, if she still continues to alienate the children it may be necessary to assign primary custody to the father and allow a frequency of visitation that will be limited enough to protect them from significant reprogramming. In extreme cases, one may have to sever the children entirely from the mother for many months or even years. In such cases the children will at least be living with one parent who is healthy. The children will then be in a position to derive the benefits of placement with the father, continuing hostile attitudes toward him notwithstanding. However, my experience has been that in such cases the animosity toward the father gradually becomes reduced. In contrast, if the court is naive enough to allow the children to remain living with such a disturbed mother, then it is likely that there will be lifelong alienation from the father.

With regard to the individual therapeutic work with the *fathers,* my comments here refer to those fathers who have been good fathers, who have been significantly involved with their children, and in no way deserve the animosity being vented upon them. The first step is to explain to them what is happening to their children and help them not to take so seriously the children's professions of hatred. The fathers must be helped to appreciate that a strong, healthy psychological bond has been formed with their children during their formative years and that the children's allegations of hatred are generally a facade. Accordingly, the fathers must be helped to develop a "thick skin." Some fathers become quite discouraged and think seriously about removing themselves entirely from their children, so pained are they by the rejections. Many will even have been given advice (sometimes by well-meaning therapists) to "respect" the children's desires not to see them. This is a grave mistake. Such removal will generally be detrimental to the children. The fathers must be encouraged to keep reaching out, keep telling the children how much they care for them, and divert the children's attention when they are involved in the denigration. At times, it is useful to encourage such fathers to say such things as: "You don't have to talk that way with me now, your mother's not around" and "I don't believe a word of what you're saying. You know and I know that we love one another deeply and that we've had great times together in the past and will have more great times in the future." As mentioned, in some cases permanent residence with the father may be the only viable option. In other cases varying degrees of visitation with the mother may be reasonable, and in some cases ultimate return to the mother (with liberal visitation to the father) may be possible.

Moderate Cases of the Parental Alienation Syndrome   The *mothers* of children in this category are not as fanatic as those in the more severe category, but are more disturbed than those in the mild category (who may not have a psychiatric disturbance). In these cases the rage-of-the-rejected-woman factor is more important than the paranoid projection contribution. They are able to make some differentiation between allegations that are preposterous and those that are not. There is still, however, a campaign of denigration and a significant desire to withhold the children from the father as a vengeance maneuver. They will find a wide variety of excuses to interfere with or circumvent visitation. They may be unreceptive to complying with court orders; however, they will often comply under great pressure, threats of sanctions and/or transfer of custody, etc. These mothers are less likely to be paranoid than those in the severe category. When a sex-abuse allegation is brought into the parental alienation syndrome, they will be able to differentiate between the children's preposterous claims and those that may have some validity. Whereas the mothers in the severe category have a sick psychological bond with the children (often a paranoid one), the mothers of children in this category are more likely to have a healthy psychological bond that is being compromised by their rage. The mothers in this category are more likely to have been good child rearers prior to the divorce. In contrast, the mothers in the severe category, even though not significantly disturbed prior to the separation, often have exhibited formidable impairments in child-rearing capacity prior to the separation. It is for these reasons that the mothers in the moderate category can most often be allowed to remain the primary custodial parent and the combined efforts of the court and the therapist may be successful in enabling the children to resume normal visitation with the father.

The *children* in this category are less fanatic in their vilification of the father than those in the severe category, but more than those in the mild category. They, too, have their campaigns of deprecation of the father, but are much more likely to give up their scenarios when alone with him, especially for long periods.

Once removed entirely from their mother's purview, the children generally quiet down, relax their guard, and involve themselves benevolently with their father. A younger child may often need the support of an older one to keep the campaign going. Under such circumstances the older child is serving as a mother surrogate during visitation. The primary motive for the children's scenarios is to maintain the healthy psychological bond with the mother.

With regard to the *therapy* for these families it is important that *one* therapist be utilized. This is not a situation in which mother should have her therapist, father his therapist, and the children their own. Such a therapeutic program, although seemingly respectful of each party's individual needs, is not likely to work for the treatment of families in which the children exhibit a parental alienation syndrome. Such fractionization reduces communication, sets up antagonistic subsystems within the family, and is thereby likely to intensify and promulgate the pathological interactions which contribute to the parental alienation syndrome. It is also important that the therapist be court ordered and have direct input to the judge. This can often be facilitated by the utilization of a guardian ad litem or a child advocate, who has the opportunity for direct communication with the court. The mother must know that any obstructionism on her part will be immediately reported to the judge, either by the therapist or through the guardian ad litem or child advocate. The court must be willing to impose sanctions such as fines or jail. The threat of loss of primary custody can also help such mothers "remember to cooperate."

If the mother has her own therapist a mutual admiration society may develop in which the therapist (consciously or unconsciously) becomes the mother's champion in the fight. Women in this category have a way of selecting therapists who will support their antagonism toward the father. Most often, the mother chooses a *woman* as a therapist—especially a woman who is herself antagonistic toward men. Typically, the mother's therapist has little, if any, contact with the father and so does not have the opportunity to hear his side of the story. When they do meet with him they typically will be hostile and unsympathetic. Accordingly, the mother and the therapist often develop a folie à deux relationship. Although the court may not wish to stop the mother from seeing this therapist, it does well to prohibit the children from being "treated" by her (as mentioned, rarely a man). Even if the court were to order the mother's therapist to stop treating her, it is likely that she would find another person who would support her position. And this is another reason why I generally do not recommend that the court order a cessation of the mother's treatment with the therapist with whom she is pathologically involved.

The court should order the mother to see the court's therapist, even though her cooperation is not likely to be significant and even though she may be influenced significantly by her own therapist. The court's therapist must have a thick skin and be able to tolerate the shrieks and claims of maltreatment that these children will provide. Doing what children profess they want is not always the same as doing what is best for them. Therapists of the persuasion that they must "respect" their child patients and accede to their wishes, will be doing these children a terrible disservice. These same therapists would not "respect" a child's wish not to have a polio shot, yet they will respect the child's wish not to see a father who shows no significant evidence for abuse, maltreatment, neglect, etc. The therapist does well to recall that prior to the separation the children were likely to have had a good, strong relationship with the father and that strong psychological ties must still be present. The therapist should view the children's professed animosity as superficial and as designed to ingratiate themselves to the mother. To take the allegations of maltreatment seriously is a terrible disservice to these children. It may contribute to an entrenchment of the parental alienation syndrome and may result in years of, if not lifelong, alienation.

Similarly, when a fabricated (as opposed to bona fide) sex-abuse allegation has been introduced, and if the therapist is convinced that it is false, then he (she) does well not to dwell on these allegations. Typically, over time such false allegations become elaborated and new allegations arise when the earlier ones do not work (1987a). It is antitherapeutic to listen to these. Rather, it is therapeutic to say, "That didn't happen! So let's go on and talk about *real* things like your next visit with your father." The therapist must appreciate that the children *need* him to serve as an excuse for visiting with the father. When "forced" to visit with the father they can say to the mother that the therapist is mean, cruel, etc. and that they really do not want to see the father, but the therapist "makes them." And the judge should appreciate that he (she) too can serve this function for the children. With a court order, they can say to their mother, "I really hate my father, but that stupid judge is making me see him."

The therapist must also appreciate that older children may promulgate the mother's programming down to younger ones. And the older children are especially likely to do this during visits with the father. The mother thereby relies on her accomplice to "work over" the younger ones when in the enemy camp (the father's house). These older children may even mastermind "inside jobs" in the father's house. Accordingly, a "divide and conquer" approach sometimes is warranted. This is best accomplished by requiring the children to visit separately—or at least separate from the older sibling programmers—until they all have had the living experience (including the mother) that the terrible consequences of being alone with the father were not realized. For example, an older sister may be programming her two younger brothers into believing that the father is dangerous and/or noxious, when they themselves exhibit only mild manifestations of a parental alienation syndrome. When they visit with the father and relax their guard she may quickly remind them about the indignities they are likely to suffer under such circumstances. Structuring the visitations so that the sister visits separately from her brothers (at least for a time) is the most effective way of dealing with this kind of problem. This is a good example of an important aspect of the therapy of these families, namely, that less is done via the attempt to get people to gain insight and much more is accomplished by structuring situations and providing individuals with actual experiences.

Transition periods, that is the points when the children are transferred from mother to father, may be especially difficult for children with parental alienation syndrome. It is then (when both parents and the children are together) that the loyalty conflicts become most intense and the symptoms most severe. Accordingly, it is not a good idea to have the father pick up the children at the mother's home. In that setting—with the mother directly observing the children—they are most likely to resist going with their father and will predictably gain their mother's support (overt or covert) for their resistance. Alternative transitional arrangements must therefore be devised, arrangements that do not place the children in a situation in which they are with mother and father at the same time.

A good transition place is the therapist's office. The mother brings the children, spends some time with them and the therapist, and then goes home, leaving the children alone with the therapist. Subsequently the father comes, spends some time with the children and the therapist, and then takes them to his home. Or a truly impartial intermediary, with whom the children have a good relationship, can pick the children up at the mother's home and bring them to the father's home. A therapist, guardian ad litem, or child advocate can serve in this role.

Once the court has made a final decision that the children shall remain living with their mother, then the children are able to dispense with their scenarios of deprecation. This is a very important point. The children develop their campaigns of denigration in the desire to maintain the psychological bond with the mother. The custody litigation has threatened a disruption of this bond. Once the court has ruled that the children shall remain living primarily with their mother, they can relax and allow themselves to enjoy a more benevolent relationship with their father. In short, the court's order obviates the need for the symptoms and so they can be dispensed with.

I have been involved in a number of cases in which mothers in this category would suddenly decide that they wanted to move to another state. They suddenly become "homesick," after many years of comfortable adjustment in the state in which the children were raised. Some suddenly decided that they wanted to remove themselves (and children, of course) from the scene of the custody conflict (including the whole state) and "start all over" and/or "find themselves" at some remote place. A few claimed better job opportunities in another state. It would be an error for the examiner to take these arguments seriously. Rather, the court should be advised to inform the mother that she is free to leave the state at any time she wishes; however, she should understand that if she does so it will *not* be with the children. And such a position can be included in the evaluator's recommendations.

Whereas mothers in the severe category are not likely to be candidates for treatment, some mothers in the moderate category may indeed involve themselves meaningfully in the therapeutic process. I believe it is preferable for the court-ordered family therapist to work with the mother in dealing with her underlying problems. However, working with a separate therapist—who does not support her distortions—may be useful. It is crucial that the mother's therapist not be in the aforementioned category of person (more often a woman) who joins with the mother in her delusions about the father. Sometimes a central element in the mother's rage is the fact that the father has established a new relationship and she has not done so. Her jealousy is a contributing factor to her program of wreaking vengeance on her former husband by attempting to deprive him of his children, his most treasured possessions. Another factor that often contributes to the campaign of animosity is the mother's desire to maintain a relationship with her former husband. The tumultuous activity guarantees ongoing involvement, accusation and counteraccusation, attack and counterattack, and so on. Most people, when confronted with a choice between total abandonment and hostile involvement, would choose the acrimonious relationship. And these mothers demonstrate this point well. To the degree that one can help her "pick up the pieces of her life" and form new involvements and interests, one is likely to reduce the rage. The most therapeutic experience such a woman can have is meeting a new man with whom she becomes deeply involved and forming a strong relationship.

The therapeutic approaches to the fathers in this category are similar to those utilized with fathers in the first category. One must explain to them what is happening and help them "thicken their skins." They must be helped not to take so seriously the children's vilifications. They must be helped to divert them to healthier interchanges and not dwell on whether a particular allegation is true or false. They must be helped to provide the children with healthy living experiences—which are the most effective antidotes to the delusions regarding his noxious and/or dangerous qualities.

When working individually with the children they must be discouraged from "buttering up" each parent and saying to each what they think that one wants to hear at the moment, regardless of the consequences. The therapist should express his incredulity over the children's vilification of the father. They should not take seriously the children's false allegations and quickly move on to other subjects. However, following visits with the father, they should emphasize to the children that their view of their father as an ogre was not realized during the visitation. In family sessions the therapist should "smoke out" the lies. This is much more likely to be done in family sessions than in individual sessions. The therapist does well to appreciate that as long as the litigation goes on direct work with the children will be difficult and complete alleviation of symptoms may not be possible. Accordingly, in communications to the judge the therapist should be ever reminding him (her) of the fact that the longer the litigation goes on the less the likelihood the treatment will be successful.

The therapist does well to try to find some healthy "insider" on the mother's side of the family. Sometimes the mother's mother and/or father can serve in this capacity. On occasion it might be the mother's brother or sister. Here, one is looking for a person who is aware that the mother is "going too far" with regard to the animosity that she has toward her husband and is fostering the children's alienation from him. If a good relationship existed between the father's parents and the mother's parents prior to the separation, the therapist might prevail upon the father's parents to speak with the mother's parents. Sometimes family meetings in which all four grandparents are present—with the mother and father—can be useful in this regard. The mother's mother can be a very powerful therapeutic ally if the therapist is able to enlist her services. I cannot emphasize strongly enough the importance of the therapist's attempting to find such an ally on the mother's side of the family. That individual can sometimes bring the mother to her senses and effectively prevail upon her to "loosen up" and appreciate how detrimental her maneuvers are to her children. Many parties who are appreciative of the mother's injudicious behavior take the position of "not wanting to get involved." The therapist does well to attempt to have access to such people and to impress upon them that their neutrality may be a terrible disservice to the children. I have no problem eliciting guilt in such individuals if it will serve the purpose of facilitating their involvement in the therapeutic process.

Not all therapists are suited to work with such families. As mentioned, they must have "thick skins" to tolerate the children's antics as they claim that they are being exposed to terrible traumas and indignities in their fathers' homes. They must also be people who are comfortable with taking a somewhat dictatorial position. And this is especially important in their relationship with the mothers of these children. The therapist must appreciate that more of the therapy relates to manipulating and structuring situations than providing people with insight. To the degree that the therapist can provide people with living experiences, to that degree will false perceptions be altered. Therapists with a strong orientation toward psychoanalytic inquiry are generally not qualified to conduct such treatment. I am a psychoanalyst myself and involve most of my adult patients in psychoanalytic therapy. However, when a parental alienation syndrome is present the therapeutic approach must *first* involve a significant degree of people manipulation (usually by court order) and structure before one can sit down and talk meaningfully with the parties involved. Moreover, therapists who accept as valid the patient's wishes (whether child or adult) and consider it therapeutically contraindicated to pressure or coerce a patient are also not candidates to serve such families. I too consider myself sensitive to the needs of my patients. As mentioned, doing what the patient *wants* and doing what the patient *needs* may be two entirely different things. It is for this reason that the courts play such an important role in the treatment of families in which a parental alienation syndrome is present. Without the therapist's having the court's power to bring about the various manipulations and structural changes, the therapy is not likely to be possible.

Mild Cases of the Parental Alienation Syndrome   The *mothers* of children in this category generally have a healthy psychological bond with the children. These mothers may recognize that gender egalitarianism in custody disputes is a disservice to children, but are healthy enough not to involve themselves in significant degrees of courtroom litigation in order to gain primary custody. These mothers recognize that alienation from the father is not in the best interests of their children and are willing to take a more conciliatory approach to the father's requests. They either go along with a joint custodial compromise or even allow (albeit reluctantly) the father to have sole custody with their having a liberal visitation program. Although these mothers believe it would be in the best interests of the children to remain with them, they recognize that protracted litigation is going to cause all family members to suffer more grief than an injudicious custody arrangement, namely, one in which the father has more involvement (either sole or joint custody) than they consider warranted. However, we may still see some manifestations of programming in these mothers in order to strengthen their positions. There is no paranoia here, but there is anger and there may be some desire for vengeance. The motive for programming the children, however, is less likely to be vengeance than it is merely to entrench their positions in an inegalitarian situation. Of the three categories of mothers, these mothers have generally been the most dedicated ones during the earliest years of their children's lives and have thereby developed the strongest and healthiest psychological bonds with them.

The *children* in this category also develop their own scenarios, again with the slight prodding of the mother. Here the children's primary motive is to strengthen the mother's position in the custody dispute in order to maintain the stronger healthy psychological bond that they have with their mothers. These are the children who are most likely to be ambivalent about visitation and are most free to express affection for their fathers, even in their mothers' presence.

With regard to *therapy*, in most cases therapy is *not* necessary. What these children need is a final court order confirming that they will remain living primarily with their mother and there will be no threat of their being transferred to their father. This usually brings about a "cure" of the parental alienation syndrome. If the children need therapy it is for other things, possibly related to the divorce animosities.

Concluding Comments Regarding Recommendations for Families in which a Parental Alienation Syndrome Is Present   My purpose in this section has been to provide mental health practitioners with guidelines for advising courts on how to deal with parental alienation children and their families. As mentioned, without proper placement of the child (for which a court order may be necessary), treatment may be futile. In the majority of cases of parental alienation syndrome, it is the mother who is favored and the father who is denigrated. However, there are certainly situations in which the mother is deprecated and the father favored. For simplicity of presentation, and because mothers are more often the favored parent, I have used her as the example of the preferred parent – but recognize that in some cases it is the father who is preferred and the one who may be programming the child and it is the mother who is the despised parent. In such cases the fathers should be divided into the aforementioned categories and given the same considerations as described for mothers.

I recognize that the division of these families into three categories is somewhat artificial. In reality, we have a continuum from very severe cases to very mild cases. However, the distinctions are valid and extremely important if one is to make proper therapeutic recommendations. It is especially vital for the examiner to make every attempt to differentiate between mothers in category one (severe) and those in category two (moderate). The former mothers are often so disturbed that custody should be transferred. The latter mothers, their antics notwithstanding, generally still serve better as the primary custodial parent.

Last, a special comment about the guardian ad litem. In most of the custody evaluations I conducted, I found the guardian ad litem to be useful. He (she) could generally be relied upon to assist in obtaining documents that a parent might have been hesitant to provide or to enlist the court's assistance in getting reluctant parents to cooperate in the evaluation. The guardian ad litem can be a powerful ally for therapists treating families in which a parental alienation syndrome is present. However, there is a definite risk in recommending that the court appoint such a person. A guardian ad litem who is not familiar with the causes, manifestations, and proper treatment of children with parental alienation syndrome may prove a definite impediment in the course of treatment. The guardian ad litem generally takes pride in supporting the children's needs. Unfortunately, many are naive and reflexively support the children's positions. They may not appreciate that they are thereby promulgating the pathology. Some have great difficulty supporting coercive maneuvers (such as insisting that the children visit with a father who they profess they hate) because it goes so much against their traditional orientation to clients in which they often automatically align themselves with their client's cause. For guardians ad litem to effectively work with families of parental alienation syndrome children, they must accommodate themselves to this new orientation toward their clients. Accordingly, evaluators do well, when recommending a guardian ad litem, to impress upon the court the importance of securing an individual who is knowledgeable about the special approaches necessary to utilize when working with these families.

Considerations Not Included in One's Presentation and Report   In particularly difficult evaluations I will sometimes utilize methods of inquiry that are somewhat untraditional but useful. I may, for example, try to form a mental image of the children's lives in each of the two situations. I try to gain a feeling for what it would be like living with each of the parents (and other adults who may be involved) and try to determine the reasons for any preferences I may have. Although I could not include in my court report my "feelings" and "hunches," I still try to understand my *reasons* for coming to this preference. These reasons could be included in the report. Similarly, I sometimes try to project myself into the future and envision the lifestyles in each of the homes in two, five, and even ten years. There are, after all, many feelings we get about interviewees which, although not fully conscious, nevertheless affect us deeply. One way to tap such impressions is to allow one's mind to wander and try to get a feeling for each situation during such reverie states. In the twilight state between sleep and waking (or between being awake and asleep), one is in an excellent position to get in touch with such thoughts and feelings. We are less absorbed in reality yet are still awake enough to appreciate mental imagery that enters our conscious awareness. Again, only through derivative objective self-questioning can one record in the report the particular reasons for the conclusions gained in these dreamlike states.

Another way in which I sometimes gain useful information is to ask my wife what she would do if she were in my position as impartial examiner. Without revealing the identities of the individuals involved, I present the major issues under consideration—especially those that are giving me trouble in making my decision. As a man, I recognize that I may be viewing the situation from a narrow vantage point. I recognize that I cannot be without my biases and prejudices. My wife can provide me with the female point of view. Obviously, I cannot include the conclusions of such discussions in my report insofar as to quote my wife, but I certainly can include the information gained from such conversations. Similarly, I have on occasion posed crucial questions to friends. For example, when having dinner with another couple I might present an important conflictive area in an evaluation without revealing the identity of the family. I could not, of course, state in my report: "When discussing this custody problem with my friends, Bob and Mary, they suggested that. . . ." However, they may certainly come up with some good ideas which may affect my decision.

Custody Recommendations and Predicting the Future
Often, if not always, a custody recommendation involves a certain amount of prediction regarding what will happen in the future. The evaluator is basically saying that one parent will provide a better home than the other in the near future. Sometimes such extrapolations are justifiable, because past behavior is likely to persist. There are situations, however, in which the future unknowns are so significant and important that an immediate recommendation cannot justifiably be made. In such situations a tentative recommendation might be offered, subject to review and re-evaluation (preferably by the same examiner) at some future point—such as six months or one year.

For example, I once served as an impartial examiner in a case in which there was a three-year-old girl over whom the parents were fighting for custody. My evaluation revealed that the parents appeared to be relatively equal with regard to their assets versus their liabilities. Both had been involved in the child-rearing process and so, as best I could determine, the child's psychological bond with each was about the same. At the time of the evaluation, each parent had been remarried about two months. Both had quickly remarried following the divorce. It was immediately after the remarriages that the custody conflict began. In accordance with my usual procedure, I also evaluated the new stepparents. Here too, the assets versus the liabilities seemed to balance. The child, however, had lived with the mother during the four-month period between the time the father moved out of the house and the time of my evaluation. During that period the father's single status and full-time job made him an unlikely candidate for custodial parent. Now that he had a new wife who was fully available as a homemaker, he considered himself to be in a much better position to demand custody. At the time of the evaluation both stepparents were relatively unknown to the child, although they were not complete strangers to her.

In this case I decided to recommend no particular decision be made regarding custody at that point. Rather, I suggested that the child alternate two- to three-week periods of residence at each of the two homes over a six-month period, after which time the custody issue would be re-evaluated. It was only then, I believed, that one could be in a position to assess adequately the child's adjustment in each of the two situations as well as get information about the kinds of relationships that would have developed with each of the stepparents. With practically no past experience in these relationships, there was nothing from which to extrapolate to predict the future course of these relationships. The argument that such alternating residence would be psychologically detrimental to a three-year-old child is not necessarily valid. Although such transfers are certainly not desirable, I am not convinced that they are detrimental to the majority of three year olds. More important than the domicile in which the child lives are the personalities of the people with whom the child is living. It is not the woodwork, but the human beings who count in terms of whether the child will develop healthily. If the caretaking figures are warm and loving, the detrimental effects of residence change are likely to be small, if nonexistent.

The presiding judge considered my recommendation reasonable and ordered its implementation. When seen again after six months, I had much more information to help me make a judicious recommendation. The stepfather appeared to be far less paternal than the stepmother was maternal. In addition, the deficiencies that were originally described in the natural mother became much more blatant over the six-month period. The father's deficiencies, in contrast, appeared to be reduced during the six-month period. Considering all these factors I recommended that the father have primary custody of the child and the mother have liberal visitation. The court supported this recommendation.

It is important for the reader to appreciate that the aforementioned case is not typical. The examiner should make every attempt to make a recommendation that should be viewed as permanent, subject to change only if there are extenuating circumstances or significant change of situation. Scheduling a follow-up evaluation only prolongs the litigation and its attendant detrimental psychological effects. These drawbacks and caveats notwithstanding, the examiner should consider a plan of the aforementioned type in selected cases.

Before closing this section on the factors to consider when making the custody recommendation, it is important for the reader to appreciate that I have focused here on only the most important factors for the evaluator to take into consideration. In earlier chapters (Three - Eight) I have provided additional criteria that the examiner might utilize.

The Various Kinds of Custodial Arrangements

Introduction   Before making a final decision regarding which would be the preferable custodial arrangement, the examiner must be familiar with the various kinds presently utilized. It is important for the individuals involved to be certain that they are thinking about the same plans when the various terms are used. My experience has been that a common source of disagreement among people involved in custody disputes (clients, lawyers, mental health professionals, etc.) has stemmed not so much from the fact that they are basically in disagreement on the issues per se, but from their failure to have defined specifically what they mean by important terms that are being utilized. This situation certainly prevails in discussions about custodial arrangements—so much so that I most frequently ask the party with whom I am conversing to define specifically what he (she) means by a particular term before I allow the discussion to continue. Most often, the other person's concept of a particular custodial term may be significantly at variance with my own. This is not to imply that the other person is wrong. No word or term has an intrinsic meaning. There are no tablets in heaven on which definitions are inscribed. Only social convention dictates the meaning of a particular word, and even then definitions change over time. Such semantic differences are often of little consequence. However, in discussions over child custody the implications may be formidable. And, when litigation ensues and the discussants are attorneys and judges, an additional expense may be incurred that may run into thousands of dollars. Whereas this is generally to the benefit of the attorneys, it is to the obvious disadvantage of the clients.

Here I discuss the common custodial arrangements and define what I mean by each of them. Generally, my definition is one of the prevailing ones—I am not coining any new terms or redefining old ones. To do so might only add to the widespread confusion. I will then elaborate on the joint custodial arrangement in that it is the one that is enjoying significant popularity at this time. Finally, I will discuss in detail my belief that we would do well to dispense with *all* custodial terms entirely and focus on the substantive factors that are central to each of them.

Sole (or Primary) Custody   When we speak of one parent having custody and the other having visitation privileges (the traditional arrangement), we are generally referring to the *sole custody* arrangement. More recently, the term *primary custody* has come into vogue in replacement for the term sole custody. I am in agreement that the implication of the word primary is a little less harsh because it implies a lesser degree of power and constriction. In practice, however, the person who has sole custody generally must allow the children to visit, with the net result that the two arrangements are basically the same. Accordingly, I use the terms interchangeably. As discussed below, there are many arrangements that are labeled joint custodial, but which are absolutely no different from the traditional sole custodial arrangements designated previously. I will discuss in detail below the joint custodial arrangement. Here I focus on what is generally referred to as the sole custodial arrangement.

Primary custody is the most common type of custodial arrangement. The parent with whom the child lives makes most of the minor decisions regarding his (her) life, although both parents usually participate in such major decisions as education, religious training, medical care, and vacations. Usually a fairly specific schedule of visitation is included in the separation agreement and divorce decree. Ideally, this schedule should serve as a guideline if the parents are flexible enough to agree to alter it as conditions warrant. Such flexibility requires a reasonable degree of cooperation and good communication between the parents. The traditional visitation schedule is basically unnatural, because it cannot take into consideration the unpredictable circumstances of life as well as the vicissitudes of the desires of the various individuals involved. When working at its best the sole custodial arrangement blends into a joint custodial pattern (to be discussed below).

When the parents have demonstrated an inability to cooperate significantly with one another, the sole custodial arrangement may be the best available, its rigidities notwithstanding. In fact, its specificity now becomes an asset in that it spells out very clearly what each parent's rights are with regard to the children. It leaves less room for argument as each parent can threaten to enforce through the court what had been mutually agreed upon by both parties and/or what had been ordered by the court.

The primary custodial arrangement is the most common one that I recommended in my services as an impartial examiner. As will be discussed in detail below, the joint custodial arrangement (very much in vogue at this time) is not likely to be an option for people who have gone to the point of utilizing the court to help them resolve their conflict over custody. Such parents have not demonstrated the capacity to cooperate enough to warrant their being considered good candidates for a joint custodial arrangement. And their communicating through attorneys is a statement of their inability to communicate well directly— an important criterion to be satisfied if one is to be a candidate for joint custody. Such parents usually need the rigidity of the sole custody decree. In deciding which of the two parents would be the better sole custodian, one factor that should be considered is each parent's receptivity regarding giving the other parent access to the children. I am in agreement with the position of the *Group for the Advancement of Psychiatry* (1980) that the very possessive parent, the parent who is going to discourage the child from visitation, is likely to deprive the child of important input from the estranged spouse. The healthier parent, divorce antagonisms notwithstanding, recognizes the importance of the continuing tie with both parents. The examiner does well to treat this factor as an important one when the sole custodial arrangement is under consideration.

Split Custody   In this arrangement the children are divided between the two parents. One or more children live permanently with the mother and one or more live with the father. Most agree that there are many good arguments for attempting to keep the children together. And I am in agreement that this is most often, but not invariably, the case. The children can provide support for one another and a sense of continuity of the family in spite of the parental breakup. As A. Freud and D. Burlingham (1944a, 1944b) have well demonstrated, children isolated from their parents tend to form surrogate families in which the older take on parental roles and thereby serve as substitute parents for the younger. Although the authors studied children separated from their parents during the London Blitz, their findings are relevant to children of divorce. An older brother can serve as a father surrogate and an older sister as a mother substitute.

Although the arguments for keeping the children together are compelling, the examiner should not adhere rigidly to the position that it is *always* important to keep the children together. The examiner should appreciate that there is no completely satisfactory solution to custodial problems when there is a divorce. Every option has its drawbacks. Whatever solution the examiner may suggest, someone is likely to be unhappy. One advantage of the split custodial arrangement is that each parent has an opportunity to live with one or more of the children. Such division of the children can at least give the parents the feeling that "half a loaf is better than none." However, this consideration should only be one factor when recommending a split custodial arrangement. Its drawback of loss of sibling camaraderie and family cohesiveness must not be underestimated.

When considering the pros and cons of the split custodial arrangement, the examiner might compare the following two situations. In one, there are two children, boys ages four and five. They are very close friends, have much in common, and the younger one admires the older one—almost to the point of idolization. Although they occasionally fight, they are basically inseparable. Most will agree that separating such boys would be psychologically detrimental. Consider, in contrast, the situation in which there is a 13-year-old boy and a 15-year-old girl. Each leads a separate life at this point. The girl is deeply involved with her friends, and the boy with his. They have occasional squabbles, but for the most part go their own ways. If this boy is close to his father and the girl is close to her mother, then a split custodial arrangement might not be detrimental, and, in fact, might be the most salutary of the various options.

I recall one situation in which a mother of two children, a boy and a girl, stated to me, "My father died when I was one. I grew up with my mother and my two older sisters. To me males were like strangers from another planet. I still know nothing about them and can't relate to them. I do know one thing about them, however, and that's that I hate them all." Unfortunately, her husband and even her son were no exceptions to this formidable hatred of men. Her boy was openly neglected and used as a scapegoat, and her husband was openly scorned. With regard to her daughter she said, "I can understand my daughter. We're on the same wavelength. I know what makes her tick. She's the apple of my eye." In spite of this rejection and sadistic attitude toward her son, she still wanted custody so as not to "split the children up." I recommended that the son live with his father and the daughter with her mother. The court agreed. In this case, I did not have the feeling that the mother's own attorney basically supported her position—even though he ostensibly did so.

I recall another situation in which a split custody arrangement appeared to be the most judicious. In this case, the parents consulted me for mediation and wanted to do everything to avoid custody litigation. (Children would be far better off if there were more parents like this.) The father was a native Australian and the mother was from Denmark. They had met while studying in the United States. When they married, they both felt that they could live comfortably in the United States for the rest of their lives. Unfortunately, after ten years and two children (a boy and a girl), they both came to the sad conclusion that they still remained deeply homesick for their native countries and could not adjust to living in the United States. Although their relationship was still a relatively good one, the pains they suffered over being away from their families compromised significantly their potential for marital happiness. The daughter was then eight and the son six. Both parents were relatively healthy and stable people, and I could find no significant differences between them with regard to parental capacity. Both were deeply involved with and loving of the children and the prospect of living without either one was deeply painful. The children also were psychologically healthy.

In this case I recommended that the daughter return to Denmark with her mother and that the son return to Australia with his father. The relationships were such that this seemed to be the more reasonable arrangement. I recommended that every attempt be made to maintain meaningful contact between parents and children. I suggested that there not only be frequent letters, but occasional telephone calls (admittedly expensive) and, when possible, direct visits. Even while making this recommendation I recognized that the likelihood of there being an ongoing relationship between both children would be small. I recognized that the recommendation might mean that the children would never see one another again and that early attempts at following my suggestions were not likely to be perpetuated. Under the circumstances, however, I believe that it was the best for this family. It followed the principle of "half a loaf is better than none." The split custodial arrangement is only one example of the many compromises that divorced people must make, both with regard to themselves and to their children. There are no perfect solutions to most of the problems that confront divorced parents. The split custody arrangement is merely one of the more obvious examples of this unfortunate fact. In Chapter Twelve I discuss this case in greater detail.

Divided (or Alternating) Custody   The divided custody arrangement is sometimes referred to as alternating custody. Accordingly, I will use these terms interchangeably. This is a relatively unusual arrangement. Here, the children spend approximately half the time with one parent and half the time with the other. It is also called *shared custody*. Each parent generally has reciprocal visitation privileges. I have had limited experience with divided custody. Generally, it is most workable when the two homes are in the same school district. Otherwise, it involves twice yearly upheavals from both school and neighborhood—a situation that most would consider educationally and psychologically detrimental. I once saw a situation in which the mother lived on the East Coast and the father on the West Coast. The three children spent one year living with their mother and one year living with their father. Not surprisingly, all three suffered with an assortment of moderately severe psychiatric problems. Some of these were caused by their involvement in the divorce hostilities, but the divided custodial arrangement was clearly an additional psychological burden for them. Although I have stated previously that frequent transfers back and forth are not necessarily psychologically damaging and that the people with whom the child resides in each home are the more important factors, the situation described here is one in which the transfers were of such a nature as to be psychologically detrimental. Short-distance transfers between two homes, especially in the same school district, are not likely to be detrimental. Here the transfer involved a total disruption of lifestyle, a removal from friends, and the necessity of formidable readjustment.

I have had two cases in which the shared custodial arrangement took rather unique forms. In one case the children remained living in the same house permanently. For six months of the year the mother lived in the home and for six months the father lived in the house. In another situation the father remarried and then brought his new wife into the home during his half-year residence. Of course, this arrangement insured continuity of neighborhood, schooling, and friends. The discontinuity of parental figures in the home did not appear to exert a significantly detrimental effect in these two cases, because the relationships of the children with *both parents* were good ones. These families demonstrate well the principle that it is the *relationship* with both parents that is the most important factor that determines whether or not the children will exhibit psychopathology. The divorce per se need not cause psychiatric disturbance and even a somewhat atypical custodial arrangement need not be detrimental. If there is healthy input from parents, the frustrations of the custodial arrangement can usually be handled.

Joint Custody   In recent years the term *joint custody* has become popular. Although there are often differences of opinion regarding the correct definition of all the custodial terms, there is probably much more disagreement regarding the meaning of joint custody. When I use the term joint custody, I envision a custodial arrangement that attempts to approximate as closely as possible the flexibility in the original two-parent home. In such an arrangement both parents have equal rights and responsibilities for their children's upbringing, and neither party's rights are superior. Neither parent is designated as the sole or primary custodial parent. Central to the concept is that there is *no structured visitation schedule:* the children *live* in *both* homes (I. Ricci, 1980). They do not *live* in one home and *visit* the other. This distinction separates joint custody from traditional custodial arrangements and, when successful, offers many advantages to both children and parents. Psychologically, joint custody is probably the healthiest and most desirable of the various custodial plans available to divorced parents and their children. As a result, it has become quite popular—perhaps too popular (as will be discussed later in this chapter).

There are some who use the term joint custody to refer to an arrangement in which there *is* a structured visitation schedule. Often, the arrangement turns out to be one of the traditional custodial arrangements, but is given the name joint custody to provide a specious sense of egalitarianism between the parents— when there is in fact none or very little. Those who call *sole*

custody *joint* custody in order to protect the ego of the nonpreferred parent are naive. Judges and lawyers, especially, do this
frequently. They fail to appreciate that we are what we *are*, not
what people *call* us.

Since the middle-to-late 1970s we have witnessed a marked
upsurge in the frequency with which the joint custodial arrangement is being recommended. In fact, at this time the arrangement
is very much in vogue. One factor in the recent popularity of joint
custody has been the changing concept of the role of fathers in the
child-rearing process. As long as mothers were deemed the
preferable parent, joint custody was not considered seriously. In
the 1970s, when a parent's gender became a less important factor
in custody decisions, the joint custody option became a more
viable one. The popularity of the joint custodial concept has
reached the point where in many states judges are required to
order a joint custodial arrangement for all divorcing parents—
unless there are compelling reasons for another arrangement. As
will be discussed below, I think more harm than good will come
from such laws.

Advantages of Joint Custody   Joint custody provides children with certain distinct benefits. First, of all the custodial
arrangements it most closely approximates that of the original
marital household. Artificial schedules, often unrelated to mo-
mentary desires and the vicissitudes of life, are not utilized. Like
the household that existed prior to the divorce, there is a freer
flow of involvement with both parents. Children suffer less of a
sense of impotence in the joint custody arrangement in that they
have some input into what happens to them (of course, the older
the child the greater the participation). There is, of course, the
danger that the child will try to use the greater flexibility of the
joint custodial arrangement to manipulate the parents, avoid
responsibilities, and express hostility. A common way in which
this is done is for the child to say, "If you don't stop making me
do such and such, I'm going to go to my mother's (father's)
house." Healthy parents, of course, do not acquiesce reflexively to
such a command and still exert veto power over the child. They

take with serious consideration the child's wishes, but certainly utilize their own adult judgment as well. Healthy parents do not allow the children to use their input as a way of fleeing from working through difficulties. They do, however, recognize that at times transfer to the other home can be a useful way of decompressing conflict-laden situations.

One of the advantages of the joint custodial arrangement is that each of the parents is protected against the terrible sense of loss that comes with the sole custodial arrangement—in which the noncustodial parent feels extraneous, expendable, or an outcast. Neither parent's self-esteem is lowered as much as is the case when sole custody is granted. When sole custody has been decreed, the parent who loses not only loses the children, but self-esteem as well. He (less often she) has been judged the *worse,* or at least, the *less adequate* parent. And such designation has been made by a court—often after serious and prolonged deliberation. But even when the decision has been impetuous and not well thought out by the judge, the parent who loses custody cannot but feel this double loss, that is, children plus self-esteem. The reader should note that what I say here about the ego-debasing effect on the visiting parent in the sole custodial arrangement is not inconsistent with my previous statements about the efficacy of a new label (joint custody, for example) in enhancing self-worth. The sole custodial arrangement is intrinsically ego-debasing. The feeling often is that the primary parent has gotten "the cake" and that the visiting parent is merely "groveling for the crumbs."

The joint custodial arrangement can protect parents from such an ego-debasing experience and is therefore tempting to recommend. However, this should not be a primary consideration. In fact, I could easily argue that it should not be a consideration at all in that the decision should be based on what is in the children's best interests, not what is in the parents'. However, if a parent is psychologically fragile and a sole custodial decision would risk significant psychological deterioration, then the children might suffer from such a parent's decompensation. Accordingly, I would not dismiss this factor entirely as a consideration even though one could argue that the need of the parent (to maintain psychological stability) is being given priority over the need of the children (to be in the best possible home). This is one of those dilemmas to which there is no good answer (like so many of the other important problems in life). My only response here is that parental self-esteem should be brought into consideration only on those rare occasions when warranted. This is in accordance with my position that custody recommendations should be based on what is in the best interest of the family.

Another advantage of joint custody is that it avoids an element of the sole custody situation that is likely to engender controversy. Specifically, in sole custody arrangements one parent is placed in a position of authority over the other and this is bound to produce resentment. Joint custody obviates this difficulty (O. J. Coogler, 1977). Another aspect of the joint custodial arrangement that may reduce hostility is the noncustodial parent's greater opportunity to be with the children. There is thereby less frustration and less hostility to be vented on the custodial parent. Still another fringe benefit of the arrangement is realized when the noncustodial parent is the primary supporter. A father, for example, who has a joint custodial arrangement may be more motivated to contribute to the support of the child(ren) than when he is a visiting noncustodial parent.

Joint custody also avoids the problem of discrimination between the sexes in that the court does not have to award the child to either the father or the mother. In addition, the arrangement allows the child to see the father assuming traditional female roles of housekeeping and child rearing. The children's mother, too, may have to assume work functions outside the home. The children, then, come to view both parents in a more balanced way—each assuming both domestic and extra-domestic responsibilities. The situation increases the likelihood that the children will be comfortable in both of these roles when they become older.

Joint custody reduces the possibility of the father's being viewed as the "good guy," the bearer of gifts, and the director of recreation who takes the children to circuses and rodeos, etc. In such a situation the mother may come to be viewed as the "bad guy," the one who requires the children to do their homework, makes them turn off the television set in order to go to bed, imposes discipline, etc. In joint custody both parents share both roles (V. Eder, 1979).

Disadvantages of Joint Custody   I am in full agreement with attorneys H. H. Foster and D. J. Freed (1978) who state, "A joint custody award may be a judicial 'cop-out' in order to avoid complex and difficult fact-finding." It is certainly easier for a judge to award joint custody than to consider all the mind-boggling facts often presented in a custody conflict. Such judges may rationalize avoidance of the problem by considering themselves advanced thinkers who are up to date with modern trends. Such thinking may be enforced by reference to statutes that require the judge to award joint custody unless there are compelling reasons for considering an alternative.

The drawback here is that automatic or too frequent granting of joint custody may do children much more harm than good. The arrangement increases the chances that the children will be used as weapons or spies in the parental conflict. There are no restraints on the parents in the joint custody arrangement to keep them from utilizing their children in this manner. Children then become like ropes in a tug-of-war. They are in a no-man's land in which they are "up for grabs" by either parent. Obviously, in such situations the children may suffer formidable psychological damage. Although the sole custodial arrangement cannot protect children completely from such use, it certainly reduces the opportunities for the parents to involve their children in such maneuvers. Sole custody lessens the likelihood of arguments over when the children shall go to whose home, when they shall come home, etc. Automatic award of joint custody does not take into consideration the logistics of school attendance, and thus it can cause problems in the educational realm.

S. Abrahms (1979) points out that joint custody is likely to be more expensive than sole custody. Each parent must maintain full facilities for the children in both homes. This often includes extra rooms, clothes, toys, bikes, facilities for sleepover friends, etc. This consideration, however, should be a minor one for the examiner in considering the joint custodial arrangement. Parental personality factors and many other aspects of both parents' life situations should be given much more importance.

A common criticism of the joint custodial arrangement is that it can produce confusion in the child who is shuttled back and forth between different homes in which he (she) is exposed to different lifestyles, rules, disciplinary measures, parenting styles, and even socioeconomic milieu. In addition, its critics claim that it is invariably associated with an unpredictability and lack of environmental continuity that cannot but be detrimental. I believe that these drawbacks are most relevant for much younger children, especially those under the age of three or four. Above that age, however, I believe that most children can accommodate well to the arrangement and need not suffer from confusion over lack of continuity. However, more important than frequent transfers as a cause of psychological stress are the parenting qualities of the mother and father. If the parents are indeed providing optimum parenting then the drawbacks of frequent transfer are reduced significantly. Even if a young child experiences some mild degree of psychological harm from such environmental discontinuity, this disadvantage is generally more than outweighed by the advantage of the child's having access to both parents in a less structured and less artificial arrangement than is found in sole custody. This is just another example of the realities of divorce: because there is no perfect or happy solution, one must choose the least detrimental from the various deleterious options.

In recent years some new terms have been introduced in the attempt to clarify joint custodial rights and privileges as well as reduce the opprobrium of the sole custodial label. In order to accomplish this, the terms *physical custody* and *legal custody* have been introduced. Physical custody relates to the parent with whom the children live primarily. Legal custody refers to decision-making powers. Accordingly, a mother may be granted physical custody and both parents given joint legal custody. Basically, what is being said here is that the children shall live primarily with the mother, have visitations with the father, and that both parents shall participate in important decisions such as education, medical care, and religious training. This still sounds like the old sole custodial arrangement to me. It is nothing more than playing with words. But people will spend thousands of dollars in legal fees and hundreds of hours fighting for these labels. (Later in this chapter I will discuss further labels in custodial arrangements.)

Criteria for Recommending Joint Custody   Joint custody is viable only when these provisions are satisfied:

1. Both parents are *reasonably and equally capable* of assuming the responsibilities of child rearing. When there is a significant disparity between the parents in this area, another custodial arrangement should be considered. Considerations of availability and psychological stability are important here. When the father is the traditional breadwinner and the mother the homemaker a joint custodial arrangement may not be viable. Furthermore, if one parent suffers with a significant psychiatric disorder, the healthier parent cannot be reasonably expected to acquiesce to the irrational decisions of the more unstable one.

2. The parents must have demonstrated their capacity to *cooperate* reasonably and meaningfully in matters pertaining to raising their children. They must show the ability to *communicate* well and be willing to compromise when necessary to insure the viability of the arrangement. The key words here are *cooperation* and *communication*.

3. The children's moving from home to home should not disrupt their school situation.

Recommending joint custody requires a certain amount of foresight. Although the first and third provisions may be satisfied by many parents involved in custody disputes that go to litigation, the second is not likely to be. The greater the friction and hostility, the less the likelihood that the second provision will be satisfied. Litigating parents have proven themselves to be deficient in their ability to cooperate, otherwise they would not be going to court to attempt to resolve their dispute. And litigating parents are not likely to be communicating well either, otherwise they would not be resorting to attorneys to communicate for them.

Because the animosity between parents may be greatest at the time of their divorce, that often is not a good time to recommend a joint custodial arrangement. Also, if both parents are fighting for primary custody, they probably are poor candidates for joint custody — a compromise that may appear attractive. Unless one can reasonably predict that the hostilities will die down and cooperation will increase, joint custody should not be recommended. This problem can be prevented to some degree by making joint custodial arrangements temporary, and finalizing them only after the parents have had an opportunity to demonstrate that they truly can handle it. As mentioned, this arrangement results in a prolongation of the litigation and its attendant psychological sequelae.

E. P. Benedek and R. S. Benedek (1979) suggest that the following criteria must be satisfied before a viable joint custody arrangement be recommended:

1. Both parents have a clear understanding of what joint custody involves and have the desire for such an arrangement.

2. The parents have the psychological flexibility and maturity to make the sacrifices and compromises necessary for the arrangement to work.

3. Both parents exhibit strong parental capacity.

4. The parents can cooperate significantly well with one another.

5. The parents live close enough to one another so that the travel arrangements do not become cumbersome or unrealistic.

As can be seen, the Benedek and Benedek criteria are basically the same as this author's. Unfortunately, courts are not giving the attention to these criteria that they deserve, and the joint custodial arrangement is too freely being recommended.

People Who Are Poor Candidates for Joint Custody   Parents who cannot communicate well with one another are poor candidates for the joint custodial arrangement. During the custody evaluation, particularly in a joint session, the examiner has an excellent opportunity to observe how the parents communicate.

The evaluator should not only observe how the parents are communicating in his (her) presence but obtain information about their communicative capacity from others involved in the evaluation.

The adversary system may actually reduce parents' capacity to qualify for the joint custodial arrangement. It may worsen parental communication because messages are often relayed through intermediaries—the attorneys. Responses are often delayed and the chances of inaccuracy increase. Furthermore, the adversary system tends to polarize parents even further and thereby reduces the likelihood of their cooperating with one another. Attorneys do well, therefore, to schedule conferences at which both parents and attorneys together try to reduce animosities and work out marital difficulties in a nonadversarial setting. Mediation (Chapter Twelve) may increase the likelihood that a joint custodial arrangement will be viable.

As mentioned, parents who are in active conflict (especially those who are embroiled in custody litigation) are not likely to be good candidates for joint custody. One might argue that a joint custodial arrangement would reduce such parental fighting in that it would remove one of the issues of conflict. In the sole custodial arrangement one parent has significant control over the child-rearing process whereas the other is relatively impotent. In the joint custodial arrangement, both have equal powers over the children. However, my experience has been that when litigating parents are given a joint custodial arrangement the children are more frequently used as weapons in the fighting rather than reducing this likelihood. Accordingly, it increases rather than reduces the animosity.

There are some who hold that the evaluator should ascertain whether the areas of conflict are confined to the marital realm and whether there is basically agreement about child rearing. In such cases, they believe that the joint custodial arrangement can still be a viable one in that the parents have been able to separate their marital problems from conflicts over parenting. Although theoretically there may be such people, I have not seen any to date. Generally those who come to the point of custody litigation are involved in an all-out war which includes criticisms of the other party both as a marriage partner and as a child rearer. In fact, if there were no criticisms over child rearing, the parents would not be litigating for custody. Accordingly, we are still left with the basic conclusion that people who are involved in custody litigation are unlikely candidates for a joint custody recommendation.

On occasion, one will see a situation in which one parent wants joint custody and the other sole custody. Here it is likely they are fighting over how much time and control each will have of the child. On inquiry, one may learn that the parent who ostensibly is litigating for joint custody, basically wants sole custody and is using the joint custodial label as a cover-up. An inquiry into the details of the proposed "joint custodial arrangement" will often reveal the true intent of this parent. Under the rubric of joint custody the parent may include a stringent visitation arrangement and significant restriction of decision-making powers for the other party. But even if this is not the case, the fact that the parents are litigating is in itself a reason to conclude that the joint custodial arrangement likely will not work. M. G. Goldzband (1980) is also firmly of the opinion that parents involved in a custody dispute are not likely to be able to handle a joint custodial arrangement. He too does not consider this a reasonable recommendation to be made frequently by the impartial evaluator.

The reasons for desiring joint custody must be assessed. The mother, for example, may welcome the joint custodial arrangement because it gives the father more time with the children and leaves her with less responsibility for their upbringing. Sometimes vengeance may be a motive. A father, for example, may recognize the mother to be the preferable parent and realize that if he were to fight for sole custody he would not be likely to win. However, if he tries to gain joint custody he may be successful, and this may serve him well as a way of wreaking vengeance on his wife. By gaining joint custody he may be able to deprive the mother of some of the time with the children that she might ordinarily have under the sole custody arrangement. Just as one wants to look into the motivations, one also should consider the unmotivated parent. Joint custody should not be imposed on a parent who does not really want it (such as is the situation in many states where the judge is required to order it unless there are compelling reasons for considering an alternative). The likelihood that the unmotivated parent is going to assume the degree of responsibility entailed in the joint custodial arrangement is small. Accordingly, the plan may be doomed to failure.

Some parents will request joint custody in order to reduce guilt. A parent may not want the degree of involvement required in a joint custodial arrangement but will request it in order not to appear (both to himself [herself] and others) as undesirous of having the children as much as possible. The increasing prevalence of the joint custodial arrangement makes such parents feel even more guilty if they do not request it. Child rearing which stems from guilt rather than love is not likely to be very effective (A. Salius, 1979). For two parents who constantly shift to each other the responsibility for raising their children, joint custody may seem an easy way out. Under a strict visitation schedule in a sole custody arrangement there is a greater obligation to assume parental duties by both the custodial and noncustodial parents. Joint custody provides flexibility for parents' copping out.

Joint custody is commonly requested (and even granted) as a compromise. It may appear to be a reasonable course, but this is a poor reason for recommending it. In such situations, instead of the parents having a *joint custodial arrangement,* they have a *no custodial arrangement.* Neither parent has power or control, and the children find themselves in a no-man's land, exposed to the crossfire of the parents. The likelihood of the children's developing psychopathology in such situations approaches the 100 percent level.

The lifestyles of the parents must also be considered. Parents with significantly different lifestyles are not likely to be good candidates for a joint custodial arrangement. A father, for example, may be an adherent of the view of traditional roles of male and female: the male the breadwinner and the female the housekeeper. It may be very difficult for such a man to assume household and child-rearing responsibilities merely by being awarded joint custody. He must prove himself capable of the shift before being seriously considered a candidate for these responsibilities. Also, equal exposure of the children to dramatically different lifestyles is likely to be confusing, and the examiner does well to consider this factor. The examiner's own values are likely to contaminate such assessment. This handicap notwithstanding, the effort must be made to ascertain what specific aspects of each lifestyle might be detrimental. The less detrimental lifestyle will then be recognized as preferable and the sole custodial arrangement for the preferred parent will be recommended.

One must also consider availability in assessing parents as possible candidates for joint custody. This involves a flexibility of scheduling that may not be possible for a parent with a full-time job, especially a job that requires the parent's continual presence. In most school systems, there are only about 180 school days per year, and there are few full-time jobs in which an employee has the freedom to work only 180 days. In addition, there are the emergencies that inevitably take parents away from their chores and duties. A joint custodial arrangement requires both parents to have significant flexibility in this regard if it is to be viable.

The Prognosis of Joint Custody   A court-ordered custodial arrangement invariably involves a certain element of future prediction. In the joint custodial arrangement, however, this factor is crucial. Even though litigating parents are generally not candidates for this arrangement, courts have seen fit to order it anyway. To do so is based on the assumption that hostilities will be reduced, passions will die down, and cooperation will increase. Obviously, this is not always the case. But even when it is, other factors may jeopardize a smoothly running joint custodial arrangement. A parent who takes a job with increased responsibility or travel may no longer have the flexibility necessary for joint custody. And if one parent moves out of the school district or far from the children's private school, joint custody may become impractical. I generally recommend that the divorce decree stipulate that the custodial arrangement will no longer apply if one parent moves a significant distance away. In fact, there are divorce decrees which stipulate that if a parent moves out of a certain radius that parent will lose custody of the children, whether it be under a sole, joint, or other custodial arrangement.

A smoothly running joint custodial arrangement may run into difficulty when one of the parents remarries. This parent then has many more obligations (especially if there are stepchildren on the scene) and may not be able to handle so easily the responsibilities of joint custody. A stepparent may "gum up the works" by not being receptive to all the cooperation with the ex-spouse that is entailed in the joint custodial arrangement. And if both parents remarry, the risk of the joint custodial arrangement breaking down is even greater.

Parents who appear capable of cooperating and communicating well at the time of their divorce may later find their relationship deteriorates, precluding then a successful joint custodial arrangement. Divorced mothers generally are in a more vulnerable position than divorced fathers in regard to picking up the pieces of their lives. Fathers usually have greater opportunities to remarry and still have more earning power, the advances of the feminist movement notwithstanding. As a result, divorced mothers may become increasingly frustrated with their lives. The resentment engendered by the disparity between the mother's own life and that of the father may reduce communication and cooperation between the parents—compromising thereby the joint custodial arrangement.

Parents whose joint custody arrangement is getting into difficulty do well to seek counseling. A mediation service for couples in the joint custody situation might very well be useful. If these services are not utilized or available, it is possible that the couple will have to resort to litigation as a last attempt to resolve their conflict.

Yet despite all the threats to its success, joint custody, approximating as it does the original marital situation, is the most desirable and psychologically healthy of the various custodial plans that have been proposed thus far. When it works, it can protect the children better than any of the other plans from the psychological damage a divorce often causes.

Currently, the arrangement is much in vogue. It has a reputation of being egalitarian, nonsexist, and benevolent. Unfortunately, joint custody is being indiscriminately recommended for people who are extremely poor candidates for it. The criteria presented here should help define more specifically which families may profit from the arrangement and which may not. The reader interested in further information about joint custody may wish to refer to publications of *The Association of Family Conciliation Courts* (1979), J. Folberg (1984), and the author (1982b). D. W. Cantor and E. A. Drake (1983) provide a useful description of the various custodial arrangements.

Arguments for Dispensing Entirely with the Practice of Naming the Custodial Arrangement

As discussed, the term joint custody is variously defined, not only by state statutes but by attorneys, mental health professionals, and clients. Therefore, an element of confusion has been introduced—confusion that has resulted in unnecessary litigation and time wasted on irrelevancies. The result has been further expense and psychological trauma to parents, most often avoidable.

Often, the conflicts are semantic ones. The parties involved in discussing a potential joint custodial arrangement may each have a different concept of the meaning of the term—a situation that will predictably cause confusion and waste of time. Or attorneys will haggle over the definition of the term and/or whether a particular client's custodial arrangement warrants the designation. In such conflicts the parties become sidetracked onto issues that may be basically irrelevant to the decision. Furthermore, as mentioned, what has traditionally been called *sole custody* may be given the name of *joint custody* because of the belief that such designation will protect the unfavored party from feelings of lowered self-worth. This misuse of the term may introduce further confusion, especially in those who are reviewing the court rulings and possibly even using such rulings as established precedents. In other instances, *joint custody* is essentially *no custody,* and what was designed to provide children with a flexible visitation program ends with their being in a no-man's land, equally available as weapons and/or spies to both of their warring parents.

The problem may be further complicated by the term *joint custody* itself. In a sense, *joint custody* is oxymoronic, self-contradictory. The word custody implies entrapment, possession, and restraint. The word *joint* connotes cooperation and flexibility of movement. When older children are involved, the joint custodial arrangement includes taking into consideration their wishes in any decision making. Accordingly, there is an internal contradiction in the term *joint custody,* especially when it applies to older children. Last, there are parents who *fight* for joint custody. If people are indeed *litigating* for joint custody, they are generally not likely to be candidates for it.

I believe that the aforementioned problems concerning the joint custodial arrangement could be obviated in a relatively simple way. The semantic problem could be eliminated by strictly avoiding the utilization of *any* of the commonly used terms to refer to the various custodial arrangements previously described. Rather, I would recommend that all arrangements be subsumed under a general rubric such as: *residential and decision-making arrangement.* This is essentially what we are concerning ourselves with anyway. We want to decide where the children should be at any particular time and what powers each parent shall have. All of the terms used at present are attempts to define a particular arrangement for the children's residence, visitation, and parental decision-making powers. The use of this general term (or one like it) would enable us to avoid the time and energy wasted in arguing over which type of custodial arrangement would be most applicable to a particular family. Rather, we should focus on the *substantive* considerations that are relevant to the particular family.

One has to ascertain whether the parents are equally capable of parenting and equally available to assume parental obligations. One must determine whether they have demonstrated the capacity to cooperate well with one another and to communicate successfully. One has to ask about the feasibility of the children moving freely back and forth between the two residences, while attending the same school. When these issues have been explored, an evaluator should consider the question of whether or not the parents need a court-imposed schedule or whether they can be relied upon to utilize successfully a nonscheduled arrangement. Generally, people who are equally capable as parents and who can communicate and cooperate can be trusted to a nonscheduled arrangement for visitation and place of residence. Those who cannot may need a court-ordered schedule.

The next question relates to decision-making powers. Are both parents relatively equal with regard to decision-making capacity? If not generally equal, are there some areas in which one parent should be given priority? To simply designate one parent as the only one to make primary decisions may not fit in well with the reality of the situation. Of course, considerations of cooperation and communication must also be attended to when deciding about decision-making powers. Last, one must look into the children's school situation and ascertain whether the two parents' residences are so situated that they would allow for attendance at one school while flexibly alternating between the two homes.

When all these issues have been explored, a suitable program should be formulated. I would recommend that attempts to compare it to one of the traditional arrangements are not only a waste of time, but may be detrimental to the whole process. The only name given should be *residential and decision-making arrangement* or an equally suitable name. This name circumvents the problems resulting from the use of the aforementioned traditional terms and directs attention to the substantive issues. It has the fringe benefit of reducing the likelihood of litigation because one cannot readily fight for it. One may choose to fight for sole custody, split custody, etc. But one is far less likely to fight for a residential and decision-making arrangement because one has it already. Without the win or lose element, without the opportunity for wrestling something from the spouse, the impetus to fight is reduced (but not completely removed, because one could still litigate for a particular kind of residential and decision-making arrangement).

I am recommending this idea primarily because it will reduce time and energy expended on irrelevant issues in litigation and protect parents thereby from unnecessary expense and psychological trauma. I am not recommending this plan to protect the self-esteem of the parent who was traditionally designated the noncustodial parent or the one who has "lost" the custody battle. Self-esteem is far too complex an issue to be affected significantly by this relatively minor factor. The plan encourages our focusing on the concrete issues—rather than on abstractions which are often irrelevant and meaningless.

I recognize that the proposal to drop entirely any special name for the custodial arrangement comes at a time when most state legislatures have devoted significant time and energy to considerations around the joint custodial concept. It is reasonable to say that tens of thousands of hours, and maybe more, have been spent by mental health professionals and members of the legal profession defining the term *joint custody* and then incorporating such definitions into statutes. The implications of my comments here are that most of this has been a waste of time. That should not be a reason, however, to refrain from modifying these statutes. This will not be the first time in history that laws have been passed that quickly proved to be injudicious.

In recent years, from the recognition of the drawbacks of the joint custodial label, the term *parenting plan* has come into vogue. In fact, in some states the term has been incorporated into statutes. Subsumed under this rubric is information about the time the children will spend in each of the households, whether scheduled or nonscheduled, and what each parent's decision-making powers will be. I have a slight preference for my term *residential and decision-making arrangement* because it specifies exactly what areas will be focused on. However, the term parenting plan is certainly better than joint custody. Within the parenting plan arrangement each parent's *parenting time* is defined. This too serves to circumvent the problems around the use of the term custody, with its implication of entrapment. However, it is extremely difficult to avoid using the term custody entirely. Anyone who has tried to speak about the subject, write on it, or incorporate its concepts into statutes finds himself (herself) falling back on the word. To studiously avoid its utilization requires all kinds of semantic gymnastics that serve to compromise communication and reduce the smooth flow of what is being said or written. Accordingly, at this point, I believe we do best to continue using the word custody, its intrinsic drawbacks notwithstanding. At any rate, I believe that people are what they are, not what they are labeled. And, even more important, from the children's point of view it matters not what the court or a state law labels a parent, but what the parent's relationship is with the children.

Visitation Considerations

The court is generally not significantly interested in the impartial evaluator's specific recommendations regarding visitation. It usually makes a distinction between an impartial providing information that may be useful to the court in general and the examiner making recommendations regarding such specifics as the visitation scheduling. The particulars of the visitation schedule are generally worked out among the clients, the lawyers, and the judge. The parents, especially, know their particular needs and life situations far better than the professionals involved, and the nitty-gritty details of the visitation schedule are best worked out by them, with the attorneys attempting to resolve differences when warranted.

However, the attorneys and court may ask the impartial for advice regarding basic principles of visitation, and this may be taken seriously by the court and incorporated into the final plan. For example, one may recommend that a father be given primary custody but that the mother be granted very liberal visitation privileges. This is a general recommendation; the particulars can be worked out by the parties. Or, the examiner may advise that a few shorter experiences may be better than a longer one. In order to demonstrate the rationale behind this recommendation, it is useful to compare visitation with the frequency of psychotherapeutic sessions. If a patient has one session a week, he (she) may bring in a dream as old as six days. It is generally quite difficult to analyze such a dream because the events that contributed to it may be blurred in memory. However, if a patient has two sessions a week, no dream can be more than three days old (assuming the sessions are evenly spaced), and the analysis of such a dream becomes more meaningful because the events that have contributed to it are more readily recalled. Accordingly, twice-a-week therapy is not just twice as good as once-a-week therapy but significantly more effective (although one cannot reasonably quantify it).

Similarly, events that occurred six days prior to a session may be quite "stale" and the emotional reactions surrounding the events are likely to have been dissipated. This is less likely to be the case when an event is two to three days old. In the same way, shorter and more frequent visitations are preferable to fewer and longer ones. This is the kind of general information that the court can find useful. However, the examiner tends to trivialize and demean his role if he gets involved in the petty particulars of the visitation scheduling, such as whether the father should pick up the children at 5:00 p.m. or 6:00 p.m. on Saturdays, or exactly when on December 24th Christmas Eve should be considered to start (12:01 a.m., 12 noon, 6:p.m. [sundown]). I am not suggesting that evaluators should *never* be involved in the particulars of the visitation schedule. In fact, there are times when the court may specifically request such a recommendation. Most often, however, such involvement is unwarranted and unnecessary.

The evaluator should be wary of recommending a visitation arrangement that compromises significantly the children's opportunities for involvement with the noncustodial parent. It is important to recognize the significant role of the noncustodial parent as a source of identification and as a way of learning how to relate to people of that sex. Only when the noncustodial parent is exposing the child to severe psychological and/or physical abuse should there be special restrictions placed on visitation. When a noncustodial parent exhibits mild to moderate deficiencies that are detrimental, there is often a tendency to "protect" the child from such exposures. For example, if a father is routinely late or unreliable, parents (and sometimes the court) will prohibit visitation in order to protect the child from the anxieties and disappointments associated with such behavior. This is an error. The child should be helped to express to the deficient parent the thoughts and feelings resulting from the parent's behavior in the hope that some change will be effected. If this fails, the child should be helped to engage in other activities and not "hang in there" waiting expectantly for that which may not occur. These living experiences are much more likely to help the child deal with the visiting parent's deficiencies than artificial cessation of visitation entirely. In such cases, the unreliable parent is likely to seize upon the rationalization: "You know I'd be here every day of the week if I could, but your mother (father) hates me so that she (he) got the judge to stop me from seeing you entirely." The custodial parent then becomes the "bad guy" and the visiting parent the innocent one who is being unjustifiably persecuted. The principle of providing living experiences with a parent who exhibits mild to moderate (but not severe) deficiencies is an important one therapeutically that can be justifiably included in the impartial's recommendations.

The evaluator must appreciate that the visitation schedule is less important than the nature of the relationships the child has with each of the parents who are visited. M. B. Isaacs (1988) in her study of visitation schedules concluded that the stability of visitation is more predictive of child adjustment than the frequency of the visits.

Placement Outside Either Home

When both parents exhibit significant deficiencies, some examiners give serious consideration to recommending to the court that the children be taken away from both parents as one possible solution to the problem. They take the position that since both parents are significantly defective the children will be better off in a foster home or in a residential treatment center. Although certain situations warrant such a recommendation, I personally am very loath to suggest it. Only when there are *severe* deficiencies manifested by *both* parents should this be considered.

The examiner should appreciate that parents who are involved in a custody conflict, their deficits notwithstanding, are still demonstrating strong parental interest, by virtue of their willingness to expend the time and money attendant to such litigation. The evaluator must appreciate that healthy, loving forces are still operative when parents are in the midst of a custody conflict and that basic affection for the children is probably still present—despite the previously discussed specious reasons for demanding custody. It is very unlikely that a total stranger is going to provide such a depth of involvement and affection. As deficient as the parents may seem to the examiner, they may be far better for the children than a stranger. An examiner who is going to recommend a foster home, should get a significant amount of information about the prospective foster parents. Ideally, this should involve interviewing these people.

When asked the question about foster homes I will often say, "If you want me to tell you whether these children would be better off with foster parents, as compared to their biological parents, you are going to have to let me interview *Mr. and Mrs. Foster.*" Without comparing the three (there are now three options: the mother, the father, and the foster home) one is in no position to make any statement about which is the preferable. Merely to say that the child should not be in either home but should be in "a foster home," without knowing anything about the foster home, is similar to saying that the child is better off with the mother without having seen the father. The basic principle of this book is that custody recommendations involve the examiner's comparing the mother with the father and this cannot be meaningfully done without seeing both. When one introduces a third option (a foster home) one must evaluate the people concerned in order to make a judicious recommendation. The same holds true if one is going to recommend the home of a relative. Residential treatment centers should only be recommended when the child's problems (not the parents') result in severe psychopathology. The treatment center should not be viewed as a dumping ground but rather as a place for providing the child with a psychotherapeutic environment. Again, the evaluator should have specific knowledge of the institution before recommending it. Elsewhere (1988a) I present my views on the indications and contraindications for placement in a residential treatment center.

The Final Decision

During the data-collection process I generally do not try to think about what my final recommendations will be. Rather, I devote myself to the data-collection process and recognize that thinking about who I will finally decide would be the preferable parent could be a distraction that might compromise the efficacy of my efforts. I try to avoid thinking about the final decision until all the data has been dictated into the material that I will use for my presentation. When the print-out of this material is given to me I then review it carefully in order to come up with my final conclusions and recommendations. I am sometimes surprised when I receive this material from my secretary. Specifically, I may not have realized in the course of the data-collection process how many criticisms I had to make about a particular party. Accordingly, the section devoted to the liabilities of one parent may be many times more lengthy than that devoted to the other. And the assets of that parent may be quite small compared to those of the other. Under those circumstances the conclusions almost "jump out of the pages" and leave the examiner with little ambivalence about what recommendation to make. On other occasions careful perusal of the material and thoughtful consideration to the various criteria are necessary if one is to come up with a judicious decision. It is important for the examiner to appreciate that one is not simply concerned with the *quantity* of the assets and liabilities but the *quality* as well. Both must be given serious consideration. Otherwise, one's secretary could make the decision by merely determining the amount of data devoted to each of the four categories and simply report this to the evaluator. In formulating arguments the examiner does well to separate hearsay information from direct observations and quotations. This is not only useful for enhancing credibility but is an excellent discipline in its own right. Psychiatrists tend not to make this differentiation, especially those who are analytically oriented and are concerned with fantasy, often more than with reality. In the courtroom the opposite is the case. Fantasy is not only given little credibility, but examiners who mention it to support their position are likely to compromise significantly their credibility.

Mention has been made of the injudiciousness of examiners' providing diagnoses in custody evaluations. In line with what I have said (Chapter Five), a diagnosis should not be placed in these preliminary notes, and certainly not in the final report. There are examiners who will not provide any particular parental preference, but merely tell the court that both parents are qualified. This is a cop-out. Even in situations when the parents are relatively equal, it behooves the examiner to express an opinion regarding which is the better parent in order that the court may be in the optimum position for making its decision. Although the parents may be close in their capacity to rear the children, a 50/50 split of time and obligations for parental involvement may not be possible. It is in such situations (quite common) that the examiner must come forth with a preference, no matter how slight. A. L. McGarry (1986) holds that clinicians, experts as they are in psychopathology, take a justifiable position when they decline to provide a custody recommendation when neither of the parents exhibits any psychopathology. I am in strong disagreement with this position. We are not simply diagnosticians. We are also familiar with psychodynamics, both normal and abnormal. Our interviewing techniques are superior to those of the attorneys with regard to picking up data that is important to consider when evaluating parents for parental capacity. Examiners who subscribe to McGarry's position should not agree to undertake a custody evaluation. If they do so, and if they finally conclude that neither parent is superior and that the court should decide, they are likely to engender considerable animosity in the parents and attorneys and warrant criticism by all concerned parties, including the court.

PRESENTING THE FINDINGS AND RECOMMENDATIONS TO THE PARENTS AND ATTORNEYS

In Chapter Three I discussed the evolution of my practice of inviting the attorneys to participate in the conference with the parents. My experience had been that it was rare for an attorney to decline this invitation. And those who came but attempted to take control, obstruct, or otherwise compromise the free flow of discussion were prevented from doing so by the restrictions placed upon them in the provisions document, signed by their clients under their supervision. But such obstructionists were rare; most often the attorneys were receptive to the meeting and cooperated. The good ones appreciated that their getting to meet me personally could be useful to them in court in that, as any military man knows, the more one knows about the enemy the better one's position will be on the battlefield. A. L. McGarry (1986) discourages such interviews because they might be painful for the parent who is not considered the preferred one by the examiner. I believe this to be a very poor reason for not conducting such interviews. The advantages of having input into the final decision, shortening the anxieties associated with waiting, and having one's attorney present at the time of the presentation, far outweigh this minor disadvantage. Furthermore, the nonpreferred parent is going to learn in court of the examiner's opinion. Accordingly, the protection that McGarry considers desirable is basically nonexistent.

I generally did not begin this meeting until all four parties were present, i.e., both parents and *both* attorneys. If only one attorney was present I would not begin the meeting because a parent would then be in the room with me without proper representation. If one attorney called in and was going to be considerably late I would begin the meeting with the two parents, leaving in the waiting room the attorney who came earlier. He (she) generally appreciated the judiciousness of this procedure.

As soon as both parents and both attorneys were seated I immediately stated, without any introduction or explanatory comments, which parent I was recommending. I might say, while looking at the father: "Mr. Jones, I'm going to recommend to the judge that you have primary custody of the children." I then quickly turned to the other parent and stated, "However, I'm going to recommend that the judge give you, Mrs. Jones, liberal visitation rights." I consider this the most humane approach to providing the parents with the decision. They are invariably quite anxious about the decision and preliminary build-ups and other preparatory explanations only increase their anxiety. *After* the statement had been made, I generally paused in order to allow for immediate reactions. Generally, the preferred parent responded with a sigh of relief and some glee. The nonpreferred parent was usually irate and upset. I then told the nonpreferred parent that one of the purposes of this interview was to provide him (her) with the opportunity to attempt to change my opinion. I also stated (as I did previously) that the final decision was not mine but the judge's. I also advised the nonpreferred parent that I considered it my role to appear in court and to testify in order to defend and explain my recommendations. In fact, I went further and told that parent that I welcomed the opportunity to defend my position under cross-examination in that I am not infallible and nonpreferred parents have a right to bring me to court to defend my position.

I generally set up a three- to four-hour segment for the meeting with the parents and the attorneys. Most often I conducted between 10 and 20 interviews in the course of my evaluation and reviewing the material was not likely to be accomplished in a one- or two-hour meeting. On a number of occasions three to four hours did not prove to be enough time and we had to have another meeting, often of the same duration. Although the reader may consider such lengthy meetings to be excessive, I can only say that we are dealing here with very complex problems, the children's whole future lives are at stake, and one does all parties a disservice by working under time constraints.

I then repeated the recommendation made to the parents in the initial interview, namely, that they still had the opportunity to resolve the differences between themselves and not resort to lengthy and psychologically devastating courtroom litigation. I tried to impress upon them once again that the custody of their children still lay within their hands and that any reasonable decision that they agreed upon was not likely to be rejected by their attorneys (who are best viewed as their advisors and employees, rather than their masters) or the judge. I warned them that the judge is a human being, has his (her) own prejudices, and that often injudicious recommendations are thereby made. I emphasized that now *they* had the control; once they go to court they place control in the hands of a stranger. I pointed out to them that they and the children had already suffered significant psychological pain over being embroiled in the litigation and that what they had suffered thus far was small compared to what they would experience if they went to court.

On a few occasions the parents were receptive to my suggestion and were able to resolve their custody conflict in the confines of my office, or with one or two further meetings. On those occasions the attorney's input was important. If he (she) was basically in support of resolution and compromise, then it was more likely to take place. Sometimes the attorneys would impress upon their clients that the impartial examiner often carries great weight with the court and they are now coming in at a significant disadvantage. I also had a number of experiences in which the attorneys, after receiving my report, encouraged the nonsupported parent to go along with the recommendation. Or a judge would meet with the attorneys in chambers and encourage the attorney of the nonsupported parent to encourage his (her) client to comply.

Early in the presentation it is advisable for the examiner to state (if appropriate) the belief that both parents are dedicated, interested, and qualified; that the recommendation is based on a careful weighing of the assets and liabilities of each; and that the person whom the evaluator is recommending to have custody is the one who has fewer liabilities and more assets for child rearing. The parent who loses the children is likely to feel labeled *totally* deficient as a parent. Emphasizing these points may serve to lessen the likelihood that the nonpreferred parent will continue to harbor this ego-debasing self-concept.

Before presenting the specific reasons for my recommendation, I again told the parents that the interview had three purposes: 1) to tell them my findings at the earliest possible time so that they are protected from the terrible anxieties and tensions associated with not knowing what they are; 2) to give them the opportunity to correct any distortions in my findings; and, 3) to provide them the opportunity to change my opinion. This lessened their sense of impotence and provided them with an open forum for expressing their opinions. In the courtroom situation they are forced to swallow their rage and suffer terrible frustration as each observes the other making statements that he (she) believes to be total lies—fabrications designed to mislead the court. As mentioned, my presentation also had a fourth purpose (a hidden agenda), namely, providing me with the opportunity to correct minor distortions that may have crept into my notes, errors that the cross-examining attorney was generally happy to seize upon in the attempt to compromise my credibility.

I then told the parents that I was going to present my findings from the preliminary notes that would be used in the preparation of my final report. I told them that I had divided the presentation into four categories: 1) the father's assets as a parent, 2) the father's liabilities as a parent, 3) the mother's assets as a parent, and 4) the mother's liabilities as a parent. I would then describe the rationale for my having made a particular recommendation by presenting in detail all the data that fell within each of these four categories and then balancing these four areas of consideration to ascertain which parent would be preferable. I also informed them that I would be presenting information from other parties, especially related to the custody issue. I reminded them that the session would be an open-ended one and that I welcomed their interrupting me to correct any distortions they believed I had. I urged them to express their differences during this session because, as indicated in my statement of provisions, I would have absolutely no contact with either of them between the time of this meeting and my possible appearance in court. Again, I reminded them that I did not want them to leave the evaluation with the feeling that I had not provided both with the opportunity to give me any pertinent information.

As the reader may well imagine, such meetings were often tumultuous. Crying, pleading, accusations of incompetence on my part, and deep regret over having agreed to become involved in the evaluation were common. Sometimes, prior to the completion of the evaluation, one (or both) of the parents had been advised by counsel that the aid of other professionals would be enlisted if my recommendation did not support the particular client's position. Although the nonsupported parent might then find some solace in the prospect of bringing in another professional, such comfort was generally naive because it did not behoove the supported party to cooperate in or agree to an evaluation by an additional impartial. Also, the court was not likely to order yet another evaluation by an impartial examiner, considering the intensity and length of my own. Accordingly, the new professional was then left in the position of serving as an advocate, a very weak position to be in—especially when following the testimony of an impartial.

In the course of the presentation the examiner does well to appreciate that anything that he (she) may say in that meeting may be quoted in the courtroom on the stand. In the year or two prior to my discontinuing involvement in custody litigation I offered to videotape these meetings. Generally, the clients and attorneys were receptive. I was very enthusiastic about this practice because it left no question regarding what I did say and what I did not say. And my hope was that, in some cases, after the clients reviewed the tape they might then decide to resolve their differences. Although the videotapes never served this purpose, I still maintained the hope that they would. Whether these meetings are videotaped or not, examiners do well to be extremely careful not to say anything that might cause subsequent embarrassment or a compromise in the strength of their testimony. For example, in the relatively relaxed atmosphere of such a meeting, the evaluator might say something like "You must have had a screw loose in your head to do something like that" or "That was a crazy thing to do." I use such terms in work with patients *with whom I have an ongoing relationship* and with people who know that my basic motivation is benevolent. This is consistent with the principle "it's not what you say, but how you say it" that will determine a person's reaction to an unpleasant or painful confrontation. However, as mentioned earlier in this book, the people we are dealing with in custody litigation are not *patients;* they are *clients* (and even worse, they are *litigants*). On the stand an attorney might then ask the examiner, "Did you ever under any circumstances call my client 'crazy'?" or "Did you ever say to my client that he has 'a screw loose' in his head?" The examiner will not be given the opportunity to explain that the motives were basically benevolent when these statements were made. Accordingly, it is best to be careful about utilizing such terminology.

One of the important advantages of meeting with the clients and the attorneys is that it provides the parents with a certain degree of protection from injudicious decisions. The nonsupported parent's attorney may very well bring up some very important points to which the examiner did not give proper consideration. We evaluators are certainly not omniscient and we make our mistakes. On rare occasion I did indeed change or modify my position as a result of these meetings. Certainly, the examiner does better to make these changes prior to the submission of the written report rather than afterward. The input of the attorneys here is somewhat similar to the kind of input I potentially find useful in the proposed arbitration and appeals panels described in Chapters One and Thirteen. Specifically, in both situations the attorneys are expected to involve themselves in open and free discussion, rather than imposing courtroom constraints of cross-examination and the confining of people to yes-no responses.

In the course of the evaluation, the examiner is likely to find many manifestations of psychopathology in each of the parents.

As described earlier, being embroiled in custody litigation is a predictable way of producing such psychopathology and/or exacerbating pre-existing psychiatric disorders. Examiners should be extremely cautious with regard to recommending therapy. They might wish to do this in the final interview because of a moral obligation to suggest treatment that the parent may not realize is needed. However, when recommending treatment verbally in the final interview, the evaluator does well to make the suggestion passively and cautiously. The principles here are not very different from those that are applicable to the situation in which, in the course of evaluating a child, I observe psychopathology in a parent. The parent has brought the child for treatment and expects a specific recommendation regarding whether the child should have therapy. Although parents may expect and usually welcome some counseling for themselves, regarding how to deal with and help the child, they may have no insight that they themselves have psychological problems and thereby will not be motivated for treatment. Similarly, parents who come for a custody evaluation are not seeking to know whether they need treatment. In the custody evaluation they may be more receptive to the examiner's statement about the children's needing treatment, so this can be stated more directly as a fringe consideration of the evaluation.

With regard to the parents, if I did believe that therapy was warranted, I did not come out directly and say so to either parent in a direct confrontation. Rather, I considered it preferable to approach the matter with a question such as: "You told me many things about yourself which suggest that you recognize that you have psychological problems. Am I correct?" If the parent agreed, then I continued, "Have you ever considered going into treatment?" This was a good point of departure for exploring the possibility. The examiner should appreciate that if a person goes into treatment because he (she) has been talked or coerced into it, it is not likely that the experience will be a meaningful or productive one. The examiner should recognize also that treatment can only be meaningful (for an adult) if there is *insight* into the fact that one has problems and *motivation* to do something about them. If the parent appears ambivalent or lacking in insight to a significant degree, then the examiner might recommend a few consultations and attempts at therapy to "see what it's like." If the parent is receptive to pursuing this recommendation, *it is inappropriate for the impartial examiner to recommend himself (herself) or to accept an offer from the parent to assume that role.* This would be a serious breach of the role of impartial examiner. When treating an adult the therapist does well to do everything possible to have a good relationship with the nearest of kin who are not the primary patients. And this not only includes present spouses, but former spouses as well who may still be involved with the patient. Having testified in court against the spouse cannot but compromise significantly that relationship, if not prevent entirely a good one ever being formed at all. Accordingly, those who offer or agree to take into treatment parents who are litigating for custody are seriously compromising their roles. It suggests opportunism and exploitation, rationalized as helping a sick person.

Another risk of making a recommendation in the report that a particular person go into treatment is that the court might use it coercively and require a parent to do so. Some judges, lawyers, and courts tend to be very dictatorial and ordering people into therapy is consistent with this philosophy. Members of the legal profession do not often appreciate that meaningful treatment cannot be mandated, that without motivation and insight it is likely to be a farce. Accordingly, impartial examiners who believe that a parent needs treatment do well to indicate in their final reports that the subject was broached with the parent and treatment refused. A few comments might then be made about the importance of insight and motivation for viable therapy. Most important here is a statement discouraging the court from ordering a reluctant party into therapy.

Over the years, I found these meetings with the clients and the attorneys to be extremely valuable. Whereas I was initially reluctant to even recommend them, they progressively became more useful and members of the legal profession became increasingly enthusiastic about them. In fact, prior to my discontinuing conducting such evaluations, judges were ordering reluctant attorneys to attend. Most of the experiences I had were good ones, and even many of those attorneys whom I did not support agreed that the meetings were useful. The main benefit came from my having the opportunity to change the mind of the attorney of the nonsupported client. No matter how adamant such attorneys were in support of their clients, the meetings served to lessen their often reflex conviction for their clients' positions. The only bad experiences I had were with those attorneys who were somewhat hard-nosed in their commitment to adversarial proceedings. These were the people who worked on the principle that they only speak to their adversary in court. These were the people who felt that it behooved them to be pugilists at every point and never to take off that mask. These were the people who I had to remind that the provisions document specifically precluded their conducting cross-examinations and imposing courtroom procedures on the meeting. It was my beneficial experiences with this kind of meeting that resulted in my recommending it as a potential part of the arbitration panel's work (as discussed in Chapters One and Thirteen).

THE FINAL WRITTEN REPORT

Introductory Material

My general format was to begin with the report's title: PSYCHIATRIC CUSTODY EVALUATION. Because the report might be buried in a pile of complaints, affidavits, certifications, and other documents, this lets the reader know exactly what is contained in the document. Next, I indicated the date on which the full report was sent to the court, the attorneys, and the parents. Then I indicated the name and address of the judge. This let all readers know that it is a direct communication between the impartial examiner and the judge. Next I indicated the particular case to which the report related by stating: 1) the names of the litigants, e.g., Parker vs. Parker and 2) the Docket Number, e.g., M-2753-81. It is extremely important that the examiner include the docket number. This is what the court clerk will look at when filing the report. Court calendars are so tight and the number of cases so great that it is unlikely that the judge is going to read immediately the examiner's report. Rather, it will be filed until the time the case comes before the judge, which may be a few months to a year after the report is submitted. (This was my experience in the New York-New Jersey area. It may be different elsewhere.) I cannot emphasize strongly enough the importance of placing the docket number in a conspicuous place on the first sheet of the report, as well as on any other correspondence with the court. Without it there is the risk that the report will be unfiled or misfiled. (This happened to one of my reports, so I speak from bitter experience.)

I then addressed the judge directly as if writing a letter: Dear Judge Smith. My introductory paragraph usually followed this format:

> This report is submitted in compliance with your court order dated February 26, 1988 requesting that I conduct an evaluation of the Parker family in order to provide the court with recommendations that would be useful to it in deciding which of the Parker parents should have primary custody of their children, Thomas and Elizabeth.

The paragraph indicates the evaluation is submitted in compliance with a court order—once again affirming my position as an impartial examiner who serves the court. It makes it clear that I am merely providing recommendations that would be useful to the court in helping the *court decide* which of the parents would be the preferable one to assume primary custody. This makes it clear to all concerned that it is the court's final decision. In many cases it is judicious if the examiner quotes exactly what the court order states regarding the request being made of the impartial examiner, e.g., "This report is submitted in compliance with your court order dated April 22, 1986 in which you state: 'Doctor Richard A. Gardner shall evaluate the parties in order to advise the court regarding a custody and visitation arrangement that would be in the best interests of the children.' " This serves to protect the examiner from legal nit-picking that may take place if the report includes material not specifically requested by the court order.

Dates of the Interviews and the People Interviewed

I introduced this section with a statement: "My findings and recommendations are based on interviews conducted as itemized below:" I then listed the date of each interview, the person(s) seen, the duration of each interview, and the *total* number of hours of interviewing. I then added the date and duration of the meeting in which the findings and recommendations were discussed with the parents and their attorneys.

Basic Data About Each of the Parties Interviewed

I then gave a mere skeleton description of each of the parties. This includes the age, occupation, residence, and the people with whom the party is living. In this section I listed all of the parties interviewed. Generally, this included each parent, each of the children, and individuals such as stepparents, live-in friends, grandparents, a housekeeper, or anyone else interviewed in the course of the evaluation. I also presented at this point the code initials I used for that party throughout the course of the report. This makes reading and writing the report more efficient. I might add here that I have seen a number of reports in which the examiner refers to the parents by first name. I consider this improper and some parents, with justification, might consider the practice demeaning. After all, the examiner is probably referred to as Dr. X by the parents, so the parents should be referred to as Mr. and Mrs. Y. A typical description at this point would be: "Mr. Henry Johnson (hereafter referred to as Mr. HJ), age 43, lives alone in Belmont, N.J. He is an accountant employed by the Star Employment Agency in Rockville, N.J."

With regard to the children I had no problem referring to

them by first name in that this practice, in our society, is not generally considered offensive. Accordingly, for a child my statement might read: "Jennifer Smith (hereafter referred to as Jennifer), age 6, is in the first grade at the Holy Virgin School in Graceland, N.J. She lives primarily with her mother but visits with her father in accordance with the temporary court-ordered schedule."

Summary of Conclusions and Recommendations

A short statement then followed in which I summarized my final recommendation(s). Just as in the interview, in which I presented my findings and recommendations, I began with a short statement of my conclusions in the report as well. Whereas in the interview with the parents its purpose was to lessen parental anxiety, here it lessened the reader's curiosity and helped the reader avoid hunting at the end of the report for the final recommendations. A typical statement:

> It is my opinion that Mrs. Mary Marino should be granted primary custody of both children. However, Mr. John Marino should be given a liberal visitation schedule, formulated by the attorneys with the approval of the court. My reasons for coming to this conclusion are elaborated below. Although much information was obtained in the course of the evaluation, only those items specifically pertinent to the custody consideration will be included in this report.

This statement covered me for a possible question by a cross-examining attorney as to why a particular bit of information may not have been included. This is easy to do because the most voluminous report will never include all the possible data that might be considered relevant. Actually, there are degrees of pertinence and I made it clear that I was presenting only the information that I considered most pertinent. However, because my reports were so comprehensive (often 60-70 pages) it was not common for this criticism to be directed toward me.

This is only one example of an extremely important consideration for examiners when writing their reports. Specifically, examiners should frequently be thinking about the cross-examining attorney interrogating them on the stand. The good attorney will scrupulously examine the report and look for any loophole — even a word — that might represent a weakness. Sometimes a poorly chosen word may be enough to provide the opposing attorney with ammunition in the attempt to discredit the evaluator. It is not that the attorney will expect the examiner's entire testimony to fail by pointing out one such defect, but the more such deficiencies, the weaker the valid parts of the report will appear to be. For example, in one report in which I described a mother's extreme ambivalence about her marriage I wrote, "She has left her house countless times in the last few years, only to return after a few days or weeks." Her lawyer picked up on the word *countless* and asked with incredulity and associated histrionics if that was indeed the case: "You mean to say, Doctor," he asked in utter disbelief, "she left the house so many times that it would be absolutely impossible to count them?" Actually, the number of such episodes was about ten to fifteen, but I did not consider it important to spend time calculating the specific number. I had to admit it was an ill-chosen word and he managed to get some mileage from this "defect" in my report. Opposing attorneys will find flaws that do not in fact exist; the examiner should not provide them with real ones as well.

Background Information
Pertinent to the Issue of Custody

At this point I presented background information, particularly pertinent to the custody evaluation. Generally this involved the age and place of birth of each of the parents, and important vital statistics such as the age at which the parent came to the United States (if foreign born), dates of previous marriages, and previous occupation(s). As mentioned in my discussion of the parental evaluation (Chapter Five), I recommend getting some background history of each parent, but do not consider this a vital part of the custody evaluation. I am not saying that such information is totally inconsequential; only that for the purposes of the custody evaluation it is low priority information. It is high priority if one is doing psychotherapy or psychoanalysis. For the purposes of the custody evaluation one is much more interested in the immediate past and the present.

I then indicated the date of the present marriage, the date(s) of separation, and the reasons for the separation. Here, I would quote directly from the statements made by each of the parents. Such a quotation may occupy a page or two for each parent. I did *not* go into a detailed description of the various denials and counter-accusations. Rather, I made a simple statement like "Mr. MT states that the majority of the aforementioned allegations of his wife are false, with the exception of the drinking problem which he readily admits to. However, he claims that even there she is exaggerating the extent of his alcohol consumption." It is particularly important to include here allegations that relate to child rearing. For example, "Mrs. RT claims that one of the many reasons she asked for a separation was her husband's 'incessant berating of the children.' She claims that he would frequently call John 'a stupid moron' or 'the village idiot.' " I would then make a statement about whether or not the parents are divorced and make comments about remarriage. Included here would be the names of stepparents (usually listed already in the aforementioned list of parties interviewed) as well as children from other marriages who may be living in the home, grandparents who are involved with the children, and any other data important to the custody evaluation. However, only skeleton material is provided here because the examiner is conducting a custody evaluation, not a full psychiatric evaluation. This section, then, provides the reader with a concise statement of the present status of the family.

The Description of Each Parent's Assets and Liabilities with Regard to Parenting Capacity

A report that presents one parent as having only assets and the other as having only liabilities is not likely to have much credibility. The evaluator's primary goal in the custody evaluation should be to attempt to assess each parent's assets and liabilities in the parental role. Consistent with this goal, the mode of presentation that I prefer is one in which each parent's assets and liabilities are listed separately in four separate sections:

> Mrs. Mary Jones' Assets as a Parent and Arguments Supporting Her Position in the Custody Dispute
> Mrs. Mary Jones' Liabilities as a Parent and Arguments Against Her Position in the Custody Dispute
> Mr. John Jones' Assets as a Parent and Arguments Supporting His Position in the Custody Dispute
> Mr. John Jones' Liabilities as Parent and Arguments Against His Position in the Custody Dispute

Then, a discussion in each of the four sections may be presented in which an attempt is made to assess the importance of the various parenting qualities in such a way that the arguments for preferring one parent over the other are convincing. In the preparation of these four sections, I used material prepared for the presentation to the parents and attorneys. I found it useful to take these basic data and literally cut the sheets into strips on each of which is some statement about a parental asset or liability. (Having the material typed on one side of the paper only is an obvious prerequisite to this procedure.) Whereas in the presentation to the parents these were stated in a somewhat randomized fashion (as dictated in the preparation of that presentation), here I organized them into some meaningful subcategories and sequences. Specifically, I tried to place the slips of paper into piles — each of which represented a specific asset or liability. For example, there might be a stack of slips about a mother's duplicity, a father's drinking problem, a mother's frequent and unexplained absences from the home, a father's neglect of the children, visitation practices, etc. Within each category I arranged the slips in some meaningful sequence, such as chronology or importance. I then dictated directly from these slips of paper. Of course, each examiner will develop his (her) own method. I only present here the one that I found most effective after having tried others, and I recommend it for the reader's consideration.

In the course of writing the report the examiner should avoid the use of hyperbole. Overstatement and "overkill" generally weaken rather than strengthen a report. As a college freshman, I recall an English professor telling the class, "The adjective is the enemy of the noun." The statement has relevance to the final report. The more adjectives one uses to modify a noun, the weaker the statement becomes. Although the reader of the report may not be aware of this, he (she) is likely to respond negatively, either consciously or unconsciously, to overkill. D. Lambuth (1923), one of Dartmouth's most revered English professors, often said: "If you're going to hit a nail, hit it on the head." There is great wisdom in this statement and it is useful for the examiner to remember it when writing a custody evaluation.

It is a good idea to place in the final report defenses or arguments against anticipated refutations. It places on the record the reasonable refutation that the examiner may not be given the opportunity to provide on the stand. In essence, it punctures the balloon before the cross-examining attorney has a chance to blow it up. For example, a mother once complained that it was a sign of serious parental deficiency on her husband's part to have brought their 12- and 14-year-old boys to his attorney in order to make statements and sign affidavits criticizing her. She somewhat condescendingly stated that she would never do such a terrible thing to her children. Although I am in agreement that there are times when utilizing the children in such capacity can be psychologically detrimental to them, it is not always the case. In this situation, the children were strongly desirous of living with their father because their mother entertained a parade of lovers in the home. Although she did not actually have sexual relations in front of the children, they were exposed to a series of men friends sleeping overnight with her. The mother, however, flatly denied having lovers in the home. The children were the only witnesses to this and the father needed their testimony to support his position. They welcomed the opportunity to provide testimony because of their strong desire to live with their father. In this case, I did not view the father's bringing the children to his attorney to be a sign of parental deficiency (as the mother would have wished me to believe). Rather, I viewed it as a manifestation of his affection for his children and his desire to do everything reasonable and possible to remove them from their mother, who, in my opinion, was clearly the less effective parent.

Accordingly, in this situation, I quoted the mother's criticism of her husband and then stated my own opinion that in this case it was justifiable for the husband to have the boys interviewed by his attorney. I described them as relatively healthy and stable and quite capable of handling the situation in the lawyer's office. I stated that I did not consider the experience to have been psychologically traumatic to them. And I went further and stated that I considered it a psychologically salutary experience in that it provided them with a sense of power in a situation in which most children generally feel impotent. Not surprisingly, the mother's attorney asked me no questions about this alleged deficiency of the husband.

Examiners should base their strongest arguments on deficiencies about which *both* parents agree. In such situations the nonsupported attorney will not be able to provide a meaningful refutation because his (her) own client has agreed that the deficit exists. For example, a father may complain that his wife stays up drinking all night and, when the children return from school the next day, she is still sleeping in bed 90 percent of the afternoons. The wife may deny the drinking, but may agree that she is a "night person" and therefore needs much sleep during the day. She may claim that she is only asleep on 50 percent of the afternoons when the children arrive home. In such circumstances, the examiner should quote each parent's statement. He then might state: "Even if Mrs. Jones' more conservative estimate is valid, it still represents a deficiency in maternal capacity in that she is not available for her children half of the days on their return home from school." These deficiencies, on which both parents agree, are very powerful arguments and are extremely difficult, if not impossible, for an attorney to refute in cross-examination.

The previously discussed advice to avoid the use of diagnostic terms can extend, at times, to labels that may be generally viewed as signifying pathology. For example, one may even get in trouble using a term like *alcoholism*. As is true for most disorders, there is a continuum between the normal and the pathological—and there is often no sharp cutoff point between the two. For example, most people at times become obsessed with or "hooked" on an idea. It is within the normal range of human behavior to become so preoccupied, on occasion, and to have difficulty "unhooking" oneself. Where this degree of normal proclivity for preoccupation ends and the pathological degree begins—the degree that would justifiably be called an obsessional disorder—is very difficult to define. Accordingly, if one refers to a parent as an "alcoholic" the opposing attorney may ask the examiner to define alcoholism, to state exactly how one diagnoses it, and how much alcohol one must consume in order to be so diagnosed. There are people who can consume huge amounts of alcohol and exhibit no interference in functioning, and there are others who, after very small amounts, become incapacitated. The alcohol ingestion becomes a "problem" when it interferes with functioning in significant areas of life, e.g., work, family relationships, social relationships, etc. Accordingly, one does well to describe the incapacitation that is caused by the alcohol and avoid terms such as alcoholism or alcohol abuse. This may appear to be a very fine distinction to the examiner, but it is the kind of thing that an attorney might want to seize upon in cross-examination. By focusing on the behavioral difficulties that are described to result from alcohol ingestion, one presents a stronger picture. Otherwise, the examiner exposes himself (herself) to being asked to define terms like alcoholism or alcohol abuse and to define the so-called "point" where normal alcohol ingestion ends and pathological ingestion begins. One may, however, quote the interviewees who used such terms. By doing so, one "plants seeds" and gets across the message to the court.

I have found this "seed planting" principle to be useful to follow in the custody evaluation. Occasionally, the examiner will have very strong suspicions about an undesirable personality trait manifested by a parent, but will not have enough bona fide evidence to make a definite statement about this trait. One way to get such a statement "into the record" and, thereby, plant a seed in the judge's mind is to quote a party who makes the particular criticism. For example, in one case a husband, who was suing for custody of the children, was in a far less stable financial situation than his wife. Under recently passed equitable distribution laws in New Jersey, the assets of the marriage are divided equally between the partners, regardless of sex. Under these laws, a husband can conceivably receive alimony from his former wife and, if the children are living with him, support payments for them as well. Under such circumstances it is even possible for him to remain in the house, especially if it is in the children's best interests to remain there with the custodial parent (the usual case). The examiner might have the tendency to be biased against the husband in such circumstances because it is so untraditional an arrangement and can easily be viewed as exploitation on his part. In this particular case, I was convinced that the husband was exploitive and that his desire for this arrangement was just one manifestation of this defect. However, I could not use his claims for custody and child support as confirmation because he was operating with the blessings of state law and could claim, through his attorney, bias on my part. What I did here was to quote a number of the wife's statements in which she accused her husband of being exploitative. These were statements made to me in his presence. In this way, I was able to introduce the notion without actually claiming that I was supportive of the wife's position.

As mentioned, in the presentation of assets and liabilities, one should strictly confine oneself to direct quotes. These provide the most powerful arguments. In addition, one does well to describe direct observations. It is not likely that the cross-examining attorney is going to accuse the evaluator of duplicity. This is especially the case if the observation took place in a family setting in which the examiner's observation was shared by other persons. These quotations and observations are at the heart of the report and are the most important material contained therein.

Comments on the Children and Other Parties

Following the presentation of parental assets and liabilities I provided a section devoted to each of the children, quoting each one's comments, especially as they related to the custody evaluation. Whereas the comments made by the parents are self-explanatory and may not require explanations and elaborations, this is not the case for the children's comments. For example, a seven-year-old might say, "I want to live with my daddy. He's nice. My mommy's mean. When I see him on weekends he lets me watch as much television as I want, takes me to fun places like circuses and rodeos, and doesn't make me do homework. My mom is mean. She makes me do homework and makes me turn off the television to go to sleep." Obviously, this child's criteria for parental preference should not be given significant weight in making the final custodial recommendation. Children suffering with a parental alienation syndrome are likely to flood the examiner with a barrage of reasons to justify their choosing to live with their mothers. Although many of these should be quoted, it is important to note that they are manifestations of a parental alienation syndrome and must be assessed within the context of that disorder.

I then provided information about other parties interviewed, especially stepparents, a housekeeper, and on occasion, grandparents. Here again direct quotations and observations provide the most compelling support.

Comments on the Reports of Other Examiners

In many cases reports of other examiners were provided. The evaluator does well to read these carefully and to comment on them, both with regard to areas of agreement and areas of disagreement. The sharpest criticism should be reserved for those evaluators who make custody recommendations without evaluating *both* parents. Furthermore, I am extremely critical of evaluators who do not conduct joint interviews—my richest source of information in a custody evaluation. On occasion, a previous examiner would come to a conclusion based on what I considered to be erroneous information. Review of that report gave me an opportunity to provide input about this error to the court.

Early in my work in custody evaluation I was somewhat hesitant to comment on the reports of previous examiners. I suspected that I might be criticized for having gone beyond the confines of what a report should include. However, there were really no precedents regarding what should be in reports and the field is still, in many ways, open territory regarding how to conduct an evaluation and what to include in a report. There were a few cases in which it was clear to me that my comments would provide a definite service to the court because of what I considered to be egregious errors made by previous examiners. The report provided me with an excellent vehicle for bringing these to the attention of the judge. My experience has been that my earlier hesitations were not justified. I have not once had the experience in which an attorney criticized me on the stand for having commented on the reports of other examiners. Accordingly, I strongly recommend that evaluators devote a section of their report (preferably at the end) to a discussion of the findings of previous examiners.

Conclusions and Recommendations

I summarized my conclusions in a section entitled *Conclusions and Recommendations*. There I restated my final conclusions regarding custodial preference and outlined some of the main arguments for them. In this summary one does well to make reference to those assets and liabilities that have been well demonstrated and/or confirmed in the course of the evaluation. However, one might also want to refer to character traits which the examiner suspects strongly are present, but has no compelling evidence to support conclusively. In such cases one can make a statement such as: "If the court accepts as true Mr. X's allegation that his wife consumes, on the average, one-fifth of a gallon of whiskey a day, then I would consider this an argument against her receiving custody of the children." Examiners should use other statements which indicate that they consider certain allegations likely, or very likely, but should not commit themselves to 100 percent acceptance. A typical statement in this category: "The weight of the evidence strongly suggests that Mrs. X's and the children's description of the father's visitation pattern is more likely than Mr. X's rendition. Specifically, the weight of the evidence supports their claim that during the last three years Mr. X has visited the children on the average of once a month and that such visitations were unannounced in over 90 percent of the cases. Mr. X's claim of visiting on the average of once every ten days appears, to this examiner, to be the less credible version—considering his inability to describe in specific detail the times of such visitations and the experiences he alleges to have had with the children during such visits. Mrs. X and the children claim that Mr. X is 'lying.' Mr. X claims that Mrs. X and the children are involved in a 'conspiracy' against him. Although I am not 100 percent certain, I believe that the weight of the evidence suggests that Mrs. X's and the children's rendition is closer to the truth. If the court agrees with me, then I would consider this an important factor in recommending that Mrs. X maintain custody of the children."

Consistent with my position not to provide diagnoses in my report, I made a statement in this section about my failure to provide a diagnosis. I would usually make a comment along these lines: "I believe it would be injudicious on the court's part to devote itself to inquiries regarding the specific diagnoses of each of the parents. Most often such diagnoses do not shed light on the primary issues confronting the court, namely, parental assets and liabilities. Furthermore, different examiners are likely to provide different diagnoses and even the most competent examiners may have differences of opinion—such is the nature of the art/science of psychology and psychiatry. Accordingly, I would consider it a waste of the court's time to provide diagnoses and have therefore omitted them from this report." This statement protected me from the kind of cross-examination I might have been subjected to if I simply omitted the diagnosis without providing an explanation. Were one to do so the cross-examining attorney might ask me, "Doctor, isn't it unusual not to have a diagnosis in a psychiatric report?" This kind of advance protection from anticipated criticisms can prove quite useful in strengthening one's report.

I would generally make a statement as well about my failure

to give a name to the custody/visitation arrangement. I often made a comment along these lines: "The court may note that I have not given any *name* to the custody/visitation arrangement recommended here. This was purposely done because it is my belief that deliberations over the name of the arrangement are often wasteful of time and money. I believe I have answered the court's request that I provide information about parenting capacity as well as who shall be designated the primary custodial parent, who shall have primary decision-making powers in each of the important areas, and where the children shall live at any particular point. Accordingly, I have provided what should best be referred to as a residential and decision-making arrangement." This too protects me from an incredulous attorney asking me in the courtroom, "Isn't it unusual, Doctor, for an examiner not to give a name in a report to the custodial arrangement?" Again, my comment provided advance protection from what the attorney might have enjoyed exposing in court as a deficiency in the report.

In this section, as well, I might comment about one or both parents having psychiatric difficulties and the advisability of treatment. If, however, a parent exhibited no interest or motivation for therapy, I would emphasize to the court the futility of ordering treatment for such a party.

Typically, a report ended with a statement along these lines: "I hope the court finds this report useful. Enclosed please find a summary of my curriculum vitae which provides a statement of my qualifications for conducting this evaluation." The report concluded with a signature as well as a list of the persons to whom copies of the report were being sent. Most often these included the parents, the attorneys, and (when appointed) a guardian ad litem.

⚖ TEN
PROVIDING TESTIMONY
IN COURT

INTRODUCTION

Obviously, this chapter is pertinent to those who conduct evaluations in the context of litigation and is of little relevance to the mediation evaluation. In accordance with the principles laid out earlier in this book, I will use primarily the past tense because I am no longer accepting new cases in which litigation evaluations are involved. However, as mentioned in Chapter One, I am still fulfilling my commitments to those cases that were pending at the time of my June 15, 1988 decision. Accordingly, as I write this chapter (early 1989) I am still involved in court appearances, but at a diminishing frequency. I suspect that it will take two to three years before all prior commitments will be fulfilled. Nevertheless, I will use past tense when referring to my own experiences because that will be evermore the case after this book is printed. However, much will still be written in present tense because this is still a guide book for those who still choose to involve themselves in litigation evaluations.

Ideally, the impartial's report should be so convincing that the parties will agree not to proceed further with the litigation and will try to implement the recommendations. I have seen a number of situations in which the nonpreferred parent's attorney played an important role in convincing his (her) client of the judiciousness of the impartial's report. In addition, if the impartial has a good reputation with the court, if the judge has the highest respect for the impartial's recommendations, then the nonpreferred attorney may discourage the client from further litigation for that reason. Such "power" of the impartial is not without its drawbacks. Although it may be ego-enhancing for examiners, it places an extra heavy burden on them because of the powerful influence of their report. I generally had mixed feelings about being in such a position. On the one hand, I enjoyed the added prestige that it implied as well as the contribution of my report to the decision not to litigate. On the other hand, it concerned me that if I were indeed injudicious in my recommendations, my being placed in the position of final authority might perpetrate psychopathology. It was a genuine dilemma. All things considered, it is probably safest that the impartial's report not be looked upon as a document handed down from on high. Rather, it is *one opinion* that should be regarded with respect, but not as *the final word.* If the arguments in the report are so compelling that the unsupported attorney and client have reversed their positions then it is probably judicious and courtroom litigation can comfortably be avoided. If there is still significant disagreement then the parties have no choice but to subject themselves to the stresses and traumas of courtroom litigation. One of the advantages of the three-phase proposal described in Chapters One and Thirteen is that this problem is obviated at the arbitration and appeals panels levels by the decision being made by three people, rather than one.

FEAR OF PROVIDING COURTROOM TESTIMONY

One of the reasons mental health professionals hesitate to involve themselves in custody litigation is the fear of a court appearance. The prospect of being cross-examined on the witness stand is generally enough to chill the blood of most evaluators. Such dread is not necessary. The more thorough the investigation has been and the more familiar the examiner is with the family, the greater will be his (her) conviction for the recommendations made. And such conviction is the best allayer of these fears. Knowledge is a powerful weapon against fear. The more familiar we are with a situation, the more we know about it, the less likely we will fear it. Of course, courtroom experience also reduces such tensions.

Evaluators have heard stories about attorneys trying to compromise the credibility of the testifying expert by such methods as trickery and hair splitting. They have heard about attorneys becoming aggressive—to the point of being insulting and sarcastic. They know about lawyers who attempt to make them look like fools. They know about courtroom antics and histrionics. These are some of the reasons why examiners avoid getting involved in testifying if they possibly can. The evaluator may be honest, direct, and confident of having a valid position. He (she) may be trying to be of service to the family and may feel strongly that the testimony can be helpful. Yet the prospect of being involved in courtroom games whose main purpose is to degrade—professions of the "best interests of the child" notwithstanding—discourages significantly the involvement of many mental health professionals. In the section of this chapter devoted to the court appearance I will direct my attention to these courtroom antics and the ways in which the examiner can deal with them. The capacity to do so is also likely to assuage courtroom fears.

In my early years, I too was fearful of providing testimony in court. As my competence increased and as I became ever more confident of the value of my evaluations I became less fearful. Furthermore, as I became familiar with ways of dealing with the aforementioned courtroom antics I also found my fears reduced. By the time I decided to discontinue involvement in custody litigation, I actually enjoyed going to court. I reached the point where I compared providing courtroom testimony to a fencing match between the attorney and myself. However, it was not a fencing match between equals; rather it was a fencing match between a party with a short sword and poor protection (the testifier on the witness stand) and a party with a long, sharp sword and superior protection (the cross-examining attorney). Because I was entering the conflict at a disadvantage (or handicap) and because I was still required to play by rules in which I was viewed as an equal, the challenge became even greater and more enticing. Such an attitude, I believe, also played a role in reducing my fears of providing testimony in court.

THE BELATED ENGAGEMENT OF A "HIRED GUN" EXAMINER

It is not uncommon for the side (parent and attorney), whose position has not been supported by the impartial, to engage immediately the services of another mental health professional as an advocate. In fact, it is not uncommon for both sides to have a list of such individuals even prior to the revelation of the impartial examiner's findings. In spite of each side's initial professions of receptivity to the notion of giving serious consideration to the findings of an impartial, advocates are already being lined up for the courtroom battle. Of course, parents whose position has been supported are not likely to involve themselves in a further evaluation. This new evaluator is generally worthy of the epithet "hired gun." Such an individual is willing to come to court and testify on behalf of one side without interviewing the other. Accordingly, this new advocate comes to court at a distinct disadvantage. He (she) has not had the opportunity to evaluate both sides and this, in itself, is a serious compromise in the testimony. The attorney whose position is being supported by the original impartial is most likely to focus significantly on this deficiency. In addition, the new advocate is not likely to have the sanction of the court, and, in fact, will often be viewed disapprovingly by the judge as a statement of antagonism to the court's own appointee (the impartial examiner).

Unfortunately, such advocates are not hard to find. No matter how obvious the parent's deficiencies, they are willing to testify even that that parent is the preferable one — often without ever having seen the spouse. The examiner does well to appreciate, however, that the nonpreferred party has every *right* (under the rules of the adversary system) to enlist the aid of such individuals. Generally, the nonpreferred parent still believes that he (she) would be the preferable choice and that the impartial examiner has erred grievously. The nonpreferred parent's attorney may even believe (and not simply reflexively support) this position and therefore brings in such an advocate in the hope that it might help the cause. Sometimes, the attorney of the nonpreferred parent basically believes that the impartial evaluation and recommendation is judicious and that his (her) client should not have custody—but brings in such an advocate in the service of helping the client "win"—which is what litigation is all about anyway. We see here another example of how the best interests of the child are of lower priority than the wishes of the advocate parent. It is a strong argument for our utilizing mediation and, if necessary, the procedures outlined in Chapter One.

THE UPDATE CONFERENCE PRIOR
TO THE COURT APPEARANCE

In most litigation evaluations in which I was involved there was a six to twelve month gap between the time I presented my findings and recommendations to the clients and their attorneys and the time I went to court. Because this delay was psychologically detrimental to the parents and children, it generally entrenched the various kinds of psychopathology produced or intensified by involvement in custody litigation. Because of my appreciation that important things could happen during this period, things that might be pertinent to my testimony, I included in recent years a proviso in my provisions document that stipulated an update meeting, prior to my court appearance. My main purpose was to enable myself to provide the most up-to-date and therefore meaningful presentation in court, one that took into account factors that might not have been operative at the time of my evaluation. An extremely important fringe benefit of this meeting was that it placed me in a stronger position than other mental health examiners who did not conduct such a meeting and thereby bring themselves up-to-date on the custody conflict and other pertinent issues. Some of these examiners' reports, then, were one to two years old at the time of the litigation and this placed them at a serious disadvantage when providing testimony.

Generally, nonpreferred parents were unreceptive to this update meeting and were often discouraged from coming by their attorneys. However, the provisions document made it clear that even if only one party attended the meeting it would take place. Invariably the preferred party met with me because of the appreciation that the updated information could not but strengthen my testimony and put me at a significant advantage over adversarial examiners with out-of-date information. Parents who did not attend, whether or not as the result of their attorneys' advice, were generally making a mistake. They deprived themselves of the opportunity for input into issues that were generally crucial to my decision. For example, they could not comment on and even refute information provided by the parent who attended—information that might not have been accurate. Furthermore, they were depriving themselves of the chance to change my mind, a possibility that still existed even though it might have been remote. I cannot emphasize strongly enough the importance of such meetings and consider them crucial to the thorough evaluation.

PREPARATION FOR THE COURT APPEARANCE

Examiners should strongly request that their appearances be scheduled for a particular time on a particular day. Law courts are notorious for their lack of concern for witnesses' time and noncourt obligations. Witnesses can literally sit for days outside the courtroom waiting to be called. Whereas I recognize that one cannot know in advance how long a particular witness will be on the stand and that it is necessary to avoid a situation in which the court is available and there is no one standing by to be examined, the courts still show great insensitivity in this area. Although professional examiners are generally afforded a little more courtesy than parents and attorneys, they still do well to make every attempt to impress upon the lawyers their desire to appear at a particular time. As the reader may recall, in my list of provisos for involving myself in custody litigation, I specify that I will be paid completely for my time in court. There is no differentiation made between time on the stand and time waiting to testify. There were two reasons why my fee was higher for court appearances: 1) testifying is a more demanding experience than conducting a custody evaluation, and 2) it "helped the client remember" that I was in court and increased the motivation to get the attorney to put me on the stand as soon as possible. However, in spite of requests for consideration, the examiner will often wind up sitting in the courthouse for hours waiting to be called.

On the night prior to the court appearance, examiners should review all their material to the point where the major facts are easily recalled. In addition, they should have their notes well organized so that they can quickly refer to particular points. Impartials compromise their credibility if they have trouble recalling important data or if they cannot readily refer to the material in their notes on a particular issue. An examiner hunting through disorganized notes does both the supported client and the court a disservice. Ideally, the examiner should be so familiar with the material that little direct reference to written notes is necessary. The most impressive testimony is that which is verbally given, freely and spontaneously, by one who "has the facts at his (her) fingertips." A thorough grasp of the material is one of the best ways to reduce anxieties related to court appearances. And having the full conviction that one's position is valid and that one has compelling support—with material which can be readily conveyed—is the most predictable way to reduce fears of a court appearance.

One of the questions facing the examiner who is in full-time private practice is how many patients to cancel for a court appearance. One cannot know at the outset exactly how long he (she) will be required to remain in court. Generally, one can expect to stay longer than anticipated. The method I have found useful is to request that I be scheduled to appear as the first witness in the morning. In this way I lessen the likelihood that my appearance will be delayed by an unpredictably protracted testimony by someone appearing before me. Being the first person to testify makes it more likely that I will begin at an appointed time. I generally cancel all of my morning patients because my average time in court is two to three hours. About a week before, I tell all my afternoon patients that I am not certain whether or not I will be back in the office because I have to appear in court. I explain to them that I cannot know beforehand exactly when I will be able to return to the office. I advise them to call my office about one hour prior to the session time in order to learn from my secretary whether or not I will be back. During breaks in testimony I call my office and apprise my secretary of developments and the likelihood of the time of my return. In this way I protect myself from the loss of income that would be entailed if I were to cancel the full day and then find myself required to appear only in the morning.

THE COURT APPEARANCE

Introduction

It is important for impartial evaluators to appreciate that although they are viewed by the judge and attorneys as impartial, they must participate in the courtroom in accordance with fairly strict adversarial procedures. In fact, an observer who was not aware that the examiner was a court-appointed impartial, might not be able to perceive this to be the case from merely witnessing the trial. The impartial examiner becomes viewed as the advocate of the side whose position is supported and as the adversary of the side whose position is not supported. And all the procedural rules involving the providing of testimony operate within this format. These constraints notwithstanding, I have introduced certain practices that enabled me to maintain my individuality and make a statement that I was doing everything in my power to maintain my position as impartial examiner. Accordingly, when entering the courtroom, I would under no circumstances sit and converse with *either* party alone. There are some impartials who immediately join ranks with the supported party, sit next to that person during courtroom procedures, pass notes, whisper in the ear of the supported client and/or lawyer, and engage in all the little maneuvers of the adversarial examiner. In contrast, I sat in a neutral place and refused to speak to anyone, client or attorney, without the adversarial party being present. Furthermore, as will be discussed subsequently in this section, I unilaterally decided to invite both attorneys to talk with me—during breaks in testimony—if I felt that a cross-examining attorney's questions resulted in a misrepresentation of my position to the court.

Once in court the "friend of the court" may find fewer friends than anticipated. Certainly the parent who may lose the children because of the examiner's report is likely to be bitter and filled with rage. And that parent's attorney, even if secretly agreeing with the examiner, will often appear hostile—that, after all, is what the attorney is being paid for. Even the parent whose position the examiner supports may be dissatisfied. This parent may feel that the evaluator has not manifested the appropriate degree of hatred for the spouse and has not been properly appreciative of the partner's most obvious alienating characteristics. In addition, this supported parent may believe that the evaluator has not gone far enough in the recommendations—and this parent's attorney will often reflect these views. Although up until this time the impartial may have done everything possible to remain neutral and above the adversary proceedings, he (she) is now very much in the thick of it.

On the Witness Stand

Swearing In   When called to the stand, and throughout the court appearance, impartials should take a passive role in adhering to the structure of the court routine. They should make every attempt to follow court protocol and to comply with all reasonable requests. Evaluators should passively comply with the swearing-in rituals and with requests for such information as name, address, license to practice, and so on. (I generally refer to these as the "name, rank, and serial number" questions.)

The Evaluator's Credentials   Following this routine introduction, everything becomes pertinent and important—even though not appearing so. For example, at this point a question may be raised regarding the impartial's credentials—especially those which warrant testifying as an expert. This seems an innocuous enough question, but it can be quite loaded. Generally, the examiner will have been asked to provide a curriculum vitae and a list of publications to the court and to both attorneys. If the lawyers are well versed in the significance of these professional qualifications, they will try to find deficiencies in the examiner who supports their adversary's position. A common way of exposing such "defects" is to ask if the examiner has a qualification the lawyer knows full well is lacking. The attorney who can obtain a series of such negatives may be successful in lessening the court's respect for the examiner.

It is important for the evaluator to appreciate that there are generally no exact criteria for deciding what qualifications one needs to be an "expert." For example, within the field of psychiatry, being board certified would certainly increase the likelihood that the individual will be viewed as an expert. However, the attorney might point out that the evaluator's boards are in psychiatry in general and not in the subspecialty of child psychiatry, a qualification that would obviously enhance expertise in child custody litigation. But even if an evaluator has boards in child psychiatry, this does not necessarily mean that the individual would be viewed as an expert in custody litigation. I was once asked, in cross-examination, what my training was in doing custody evaluations. My response: "None!" I said this nonapologetically, but recognized that the judge was not too happy with my response. During a break I suggested that the attorney whose position I supported ask me to elaborate on that response. Accordingly, when back on the witness stand he asked me to elaborate on my statement that I had had no formal training in performing custody evaluations. My response: "During my residency training in the late 1950s custody/visitation litigation was extremely rare, to the point of being practically unknown. Accordingly, there was absolutely no reason to train anybody in this area. To criticize me in 1987 for not having had training in custody/litigation evaluations in 1957 is the same as criticizing in 1987 a physician who is giving testimony about AIDS for not having had training in the disorder during his residency in 1957 (when, obviously, the disease was unknown)."

On another occasion a cross-examining attorney said to me: "And who, may I ask, designated you an 'expert'?" My response: "People like yourself have often used this term when making reference to me. I myself do not use the term with regard to my qualifications." The important point here is that examiners do well to avoid referring to themselves as "experts." Rather, they should list their qualifications and experiences and let the attorneys and the court argue about whether their documentation warrants the label expert.

If the impartial examiner is extremely well qualified, then the attorney whose client this impartial is supporting will try to elicit the most detailed elaboration of this examiner's qualifications. The opposing lawyer may interrupt, even before the examiner has had a chance to begin, and say to the judge: "My client and I accept Dr. X's qualifications. Your honor, I suggest we proceed." At this point the well-qualified evaluator may not even have had the opportunity to tell the court that he successfully completed the first grade. Accordingly, the court will have been deprived of knowing the examiner's qualifications — information I believe the judge is not only entitled to have, but *should* have in order to weigh properly the testimony of conflicting experts. Following such an attempt to squelch the examiner's providing his (her) qualifications, the original lawyer (whose position the impartial is supporting) is likely to say to the judge: "I believe, your Honor, that it would be helpful to the court if Dr. X *were* to present his qualifications." While the judge and the two attorneys are trying to decide this question, the evaluator does well to sit quietly in accordance with my previous recommendation for taking a very passive role in following courtroom procedure. All would agree that the court has every right to know the qualifications of those who conduct custody evaluations. However, as the reader can well appreciate, this consideration may take second place to an attorney's attempt to lessen an examiner's credibility in order to enhance a client's position. So from the beginning of the trial the interests of the children become less important than the interests of the client in winning the case. My experience has been that most often judges did not allow an attorney to squelch the presentation of my qualifications. However, my guess would be that in 10 to 15 percent of cases the judge complied and instructed the attorneys to proceed.

If the witness does have the opportunity to present qualifications, it is preferable that the interrogating attorney ask questions for the examiner to answer. If the examiner is left alone to present the qualifications, there is a double risk. Examiners who present *too many* qualifications run the risk of being considered vain and boastful. In order to avoid creating such an impression, the examiner may present *too few* qualifications. Both of these risks can be avoided by the interrogating attorney's asking specific questions regarding college attended, medical school training, internship, residency training, psychoanalytic training, board certifications, publications, lectures, etc. Here too the attorney must be careful not to ask so many questions that an "overkill" results. Good attorneys will assess the situation and not overload the judge with too many qualifications. They know that a reasonable presentation of the most crucial and relevant is the best way to impress the judge. Of course, in many cases the court will have asked for the evaluator's curriculum vitae along with a report so that no new information is being provided during this part of the testimony. I often wonder, then, what a squelching attorney expects to accomplish in such situations, because the judge already knows what the expert's qualifications are.

Courtroom Antics   Although some witnesses are intimidated by a lawyer's pomposity and bombast, I generally welcomed such displays. I came to the court after having conducted an extensive and time-consuming evaluation. I had gathered an immense amount of information, was convinced of the validity of my conclusions, and was confident therefore when on the stand. I appreciated well that an attorney's histrionics and expressions of incredulity are maneuvers typical of lawyers whose positions are weak. Such displays may be for the benefit of clients and give the impression that the lawyers are working vigorously to earn their fees. One should take much more seriously attorneys who are well prepared and have logically and consistently thought out their arguments. There is a definite plan for the inquiry and the points logically follow one another. The people we should take most seriously in life are generally those who "speak softly and carry a big stick." But even here, if the impartial has done a solid evaluation, there is little to fear.

The impartial's testimony, as well, will gain or lose credibility in accordance with the same principles. The more volatility, the more sermonizing, the more harangues and histrionics, the less credibility will the evaluator have. And if the impartial becomes hostile, it suggests that a "sore point" or "soft spot" has been touched upon by the cross-examining attorney. Such overreaction and defensiveness will give an astute attorney a good "handle" for an effective refutation. The sensitive attorney recognizes that such emotional displays and defensiveness are compensations for basic deficiencies in the testifier's arguments and will exploit this knowledge to full advantage. At the point where the examiner has exhibited such defensiveness the lawyer will recognize the "soft spot" and "hammer away" relentlessly. These attorneys may not know exactly what they are looking for, but they recognize that a detailed inquiry into all aspects of this particular area is likely to prove useful for their position.

On occasion, the impartial will be confronted with an attorney who does not basically have conviction for his (her) client's position. As I have discussed, most attorneys will still accept a case and support a client's position even though they may not be in sympathy with it. (They are acting here in accordance with an ancient legal tradition.) Such attorneys are not likely to argue as strenuously or effectively as those who have a deeper commitment to their client's position. I recall an attorney who gave me much greater flexibility during cross-examination than I had ever been given before (or subsequently) and his granting me this was his way of helping his adversary, whose position I supported. He too was "going through the motions" in order to earn his fee and satisfy his client.

There are times when the examiner will have a strong impulse to respond with a joke or wisecrack. This is especially true when one is being interviewed by one of the wild types I have just described. Although the joke may be unusually clever and certain to make everyone in the courtroom laugh, the examiner does well to resist the impulse. The attorney is sure to ask the judge, in a very sanctimonious manner, to direct the examiner to observe courtroom decorum and to respect the dignity of the legal process. The judge will invariably honor this request, and the examiner's position will be compromised—the cleverness of the joke notwithstanding. For example, I recall on a couple of occasions being asked by a cross-examining attorney: "Are you being paid for your testimony, Dr. Gardner?" The implication of the question, of course, was that I was a "hired gun," even though I was brought in by both sides as an impartial. Of course, I had no choice but to answer "yes." My impulse was to say, "Aren't you?" or "Are you doing this for nothing?" I squelched these responses (even though one wisecrack usually deserves another), because the lawyer would have used it as an excuse to request of the judge that he quickly hit me over the head with his gavel (figuratively, of course) and require me to confine myself to simply answering the questions. I would not give him this opportunity to compromise me with the judge.

"Speak Softly and Carry a Big Stick"   It is important for the reader to appreciate that I am not suggesting that the impartial evaluator artificially "play it cool." Such advice implies that there may be strong underlying feelings that the evaluator does well to hide. Ideally, impartials should have such a full command of the material and such conviction for their position that they will be genuinely secure when testifying in court. Under such circumstances, the impartial will have few feelings to hide and will not have to create any false impressions of calmness. Nor am I suggesting that the evaluator ideally be free from tension. A cross-examination is an extremely difficult experience and one must be alert and "on top of it" at all times. Mental health professionals, especially, are in strange territory in the courtroom. They may be dealing with attorneys with years of experience in cross-examination who may be quite clever in utilizing maneuvers that attempt to make examiners look foolish, change their testimony frequently, get upset, or exhibit other qualities that will compromise credibility. The evaluator's best defense against such formidable adversaries is to have a firm and full grasp of his (her) position, to be clear on the issues, and to be able to state them as calmly and as concisely as possible. Also, the impartial can take solace from the appreciation that he (she) is more knowledgeable about the case than anyone else in the courtroom because only the impartial has had the opportunity to conduct the most extensive evaluation of all parties concerned.

I once had an experience in the courtroom that demonstrates well this principle. It also demonstrates other aspects of courtroom experience (especially judges' behavior) that may be useful for the reader. It was not long after I began testifying that it became apparent to me that the judge exhibited two personality qualities each of which is a serious deficiency. However, when they simultaneously exhibit themselves in the same individual they represent a formidable personality defect, and individuals who possess this combination cause much grief in the world. I am referring to the qualities of arrogance and ignorance. This man exuded arrogance. He was condescending toward everyone in the courtroom, the attorneys, the clients, the court reporters, the security guard and this examiner (last but certainly not least). Furthermore, I quickly appreciated that this man was ignorant. Whether he basically had a low IQ or whether he was effectively functioning at that level, I cannot know with certainty. Because he graduated from law school I suspect that the latter explanation was more probable, but there are certainly attorneys who fit into the former category with regard to their intellectual endowment.

As I sat there listening to some of the drivel that oozed from his mouth, I could not but think of the old poem:

> He who knows not and knows not he knows not, he is a fool, shun him.
> He who knows not and knows he knows not, he is simple, teach him.
> He who knows and knows not he knows, he is asleep, wake him.
> He who knows and knows he knows, he is wise, follow him.

There was no question that this judge was in category one. In this case I had submitted not one, but three reports. The first had been submitted one year previously, at the time of the completion of my original custody/visitation evaluation. However, there was a change in circumstances on the mother's side (which warranted an update) and then there was a change in circumstances on the father's side (which warranted a further update). Gradually, it became apparent to me that the judge had not read any of these reports. At the time of my testimony the case had literally been going on for five years. Early in my testimony it became clear that he had little knowledge of the details of the case. His ignorance resulted in his frequently interrupting the lawyers' interrogations of me to ask questions. It was clear that had he read the reports he would not have asked these questions. For example, at one point in my testimony I made reference to the mother's allegation of physical violence. At this point he interrupted the inquiry and, while snarling at me, said: "I don't know what you're talking about. What's all this about physical violence?" In response, I calmly stated, "In January 1985 Mrs. X claimed that her husband had physically abused her. In my report dated December 12, 1986 I discussed the results of my inquiry into this matter and stated therein my reasons for coming to the conclusion that there was no evidence that this allegation was valid. My main reasons for coming to this conclusion were. . ." At this point the judge grumbled incoherently and instructed the attorney to continue with his examination. My response was stated in a calm and methodical manner.

At another point, after I had elaborated on a question, he interrupted, looked at me in an angry and condescending way and said, "I don't have the faintest idea what you're talking about." I believe that my explanation was clear and straightforward and that everyone in the courtroom, including the security guard (who was listening intently), understood exactly what I had said. Accordingly, in a matter-of-fact way I simply repeated — this time more clearly and slowly — exactly what I had previously said. I then said to him, "Your Honor, I would be pleased to elaborate on anything that I have just said that may not be clear to you." He said nothing and angrily instructed the attorney to continue with his interrogation.

His favorite expressions to me were, "You're being illogical," "What you're saying is not logical," and "You're being extremely illogical." Again, I was convinced that what I said was consistent, logical, and readily understood by everyone else in the courtroom. When I would ask him if he could please be more specific regarding what was illogical, so I could elaborate, he never took me up on the invitation. I was convinced, however, that he just did not understand what I was saying and protected himself from awareness of his ignorance by attributing the problem to me. Again, although I found his interruptions and condescending attitudes mildly irritating, I remained completely calm, methodical, and direct.

At one point, he interrupted the proceedings with a little speech to everyone in which he proudly and sanctimoniously stated that he was above everything else concerned with the best interests of the children. He said this in an extremely self-righteous manner with the implication that everyone else in the courtroom was totally unconcerned with their welfare. He seemed not to appreciate that everyone waves that banner and that his little self-aggrandizing speech was a total waste of time. In the course of his self-serving diatribe about his concern for the children's welfare he stated that I had lost sight of this fundamental point. He did not give me the opportunity to ask him exactly how I was not serving their interests.

I was on the stand from 9:30 a.m. to 12:30 p.m., with only

one short break. Throughout that time he exhibited nothing but
the condescending attitude which did not succeed in hiding his
abysmal ignorance. And, throughout that time, I handled myself
with calm, never once letting on to the inner feelings that I had
about this man. Not once did he "get to me." Not once did I
exhibit any irritation. My main feelings were those of pity for
these poor people who had been sitting in his court for five years
and whose future lives depended upon his decisions. When I
returned at 1:30 p.m. there was more of the same. However, at
about 2:30 p.m. something happened that was quite dramatic.
Suddenly, all arrogance stopped. He adopted a most respectful
attitude toward me and began quoting my earlier comments as if
they were gospel. It was as if someone had suddenly put a
screwdriver in his head and turned a loose screw approximately
180 degrees. From then on, through him, my recommendations
were implemented. I believe that this judge ultimately allowed
himself to appreciate the judiciousness of what I was saying.
However, I do not think that such receptivity would have
occurred had I not handled myself with calm and dignity in spite
of the numerous provocations, insults, and condescending remarks directed toward me. The experience is an excellent example of the "speak softly and carry a big stick" principle.

The Heart of the Testimony   The evaluator does well to
bring to the courtroom extra copies of the written report, curriculum vitae, and the provisions document (if used). Although the
impartial has already sent copies of these materials to the court,
the attorneys, and the clients, these have a way of disappearing.
My experience had been that this was especially the case with
regard to the material sent to the court. In earlier years I thought
this related to my failure to have placed the docket number on the
first page of the report. My thoughts were that some clerk
misfiled my report because of this oversight. However, for many
years I routinely (and even compulsively) placed the docket
number on the first page of every report and addendum. Even
then my reports were often not on the judge's desk at the time of
the trial. I suspect that the main problem was the judge's lack of

interest in reading it and/or its being placed among thousands of pages of other documents pertinent to the case. I have been involved in cases in which people came to court with many suitcases filled with files or boxes that were carried in on their shoulders in caravan-like fashion. As a result, it was not uncommon for a judge to ask me if I had an extra copy of my report. If the examiner has only one copy to give the judge, then that copy will not be available for the examiner to use when giving testimony and, unfortunately, is not likely ever to be seen again. The copy given to the judge will be assigned an appropriate number and submitted as evidence. These documents have a way of disappearing into the bowels of the courthouse—never to be found again. Although the examiner might be reassured that the report will be readily available in the future, I had little faith that this would be the case. Rather, the more likely outcome would be the examiner's having to fill out forms, and go through various bureaucrats, and hope that then the files might be found. And I had similar experiences with copies of the provisions document. The easiest thing, then, is for evaluators to make copies of all documents that they believe might be taken by the judge during the course of the trial. A fringe benefit of having these available is that the examiner can, with a simple flourish, quickly hand the copy over to the judge. This makes a good impression and saves the judge the discomfort or embarrassment of searching around for his (her) copy.

The same flourish that the examiner utilizes when handing the judge a copy of an important report should also be used when responding to a cross-examining lawyer's request to peruse material from the evaluator's files. The chart material should be so well organized that a particular document can quickly be found. More important than the good impression that this makes is the examiner's state of total relaxation when providing it. One of the worst things an examiner can do is to be hesitant or defensive about providing certain material to a cross-examining attorney. Under these circumstances all the red bulbs in the attorney's head are likely to flash simultaneously and all the antennae that stick out of his head are likely to start buzzing. An attorney who senses that the examiner is tense about revealing a certain document is likely to focus on the acquisition of such, ask questions about why it is not available, and, when it is received, review it in great detail hoping to find some issue on which to embarrass or compromise the examiner. The best attitude the examiner can have is this: "Here's my chart in front of you. It's available to you in its entirety. Throughout the course of my evaluation any and all documents contained in the file are available for scrutiny by the parents. In fact, my instructions have been that they make copies for each other of one documents submitted to me. There is absolutely nothing in this chart that I fear you will see." If the examiner communicates this attitude the attorney is not likely to ask to look at any document at all. The rug is pulled out from under him and searches of this kind are decompressed from the outset. However, I am not suggesting that the examiner create a false impression here and hide tension over revelation. Rather, the evaluation should be so conducted that the examiner has full confidence that nothing compromising is contained in the file.

Early in the inquiry the impartial is generally asked to present the exact dates of the various interviews. The examiner should have such a list readily available to read to the court. It is obviously important that the court have this information. I usually list the dates of all interviews, as well as the parties interviewed, in the first few pages of my final report. I have read many evaluations in which there have been a total of one or two sessions from which the conclusions have been made. Such paucity of contact with the family is suggestive of a superficial evaluation. The greater the number of interviews the greater the likelihood the court will be receptive to the conclusions drawn from such contacts. Having this information readily available improves the evaluator's impression on the court. Last, lawyers like to dwell on minutiae of this kind. This is often done in the hope that there will be some slip-up on a minor point. An opposing lawyer may try to get much mileage from such an error—again in order to compromise the therapist's credibility.

As I emphasized earlier in this book, the strongest points in the final written recommendation are those based on the examiner's direct observations and direct quotations of the various parties involved. The same principles hold in the courtroom. For example, a strong statement in one's testimony might be: "During my interview with Mrs. X on July 14th, 1981 she stated, 'I never wanted to have children. I always found them a burden.'" The evaluator should avoid using any hearsay information. However, there may be times when it may be judicious to include such data in the report because it might be valid and contributory. To ignore it, in such cases, might very well result in an injudicious decision by the judge. Accordingly, I sometimes use hearsay information, but I am very careful when I do to label it as such and to present it with appropriate qualifications. For example, I might state in my report: "If the court substantiates Mrs. X's allegations that her husband has beaten the children on at least 15 occasions during the last year while in a state of inebriation, then I would consider this another reason to deprive him of custody." The reader should note that I leave it to the court to make the final decision regarding whether or not hearsay evidence is valid. No matter how credible it may appear, the examiner does well to avoid accepting it as truth. Evaluators who do so may be subject to justifiable criticism in court and may look foolish under cross-examination.

Throughout, the examiner should avoid, whenever possible, the use of psychological jargon. There are those who compensate for their feelings of professional inadequacy by using abstruse terminology. There is no concept in all of psychology and psychoanalysis that cannot be understood by the average child of twelve or thirteen. After all, we are talking only about human relations, not chemical and mathematical theories. Impartials who use an abundance of jargon compromise their credibility because the court may sense they are trying to hide ignorance with verbiage. In addition, they expose themselves to another common courtroom ploy. Suddenly, a lawyer may appear with a medical or psychiatric dictionary in hand. The attorney will ask the examiner (often in wise-guy fashion) to define a particular word that he (she) has used. No matter how experienced the evaluator may be regarding that particular word (possibly even more than the person who wrote the dictionary) it is not likely that the evaluator's definition will coincide with that in the dictionary. This is especially true in the field of psychiatry and psychology where concepts are often vague and ill-defined. The laymen's inordinate respect for the written word is such that the dictionary's opinion may be taken over that of the expert's. Or, the expert may not be familiar with some of the abstruse minutiae that the dictionary describes. It is rare that an evaluator will come out ahead in such a confrontation; therefore, one does best to avoid jargon. Again, we see here an example of how the court is used for the purpose of making an expert look foolish, rather than for its ostensible purpose of establishing what is best for the children.

It is not uncommon for cross-examining attorneys to preface their comments or questions with: "With all due respect, Doctor. . . ." When an attorney prefaces a question with "With all due respect," it generally means that there is no respect at that point. The attorney may have been questioning the examiner for many hours and, throughout the course of the interrogation, not once use this preface. Then suddenly, the attorney prefaces a statement with this introduction. Without exception the word is being used in the service of reaction formation. The attorney—at that point—has absolutely no respect at all for the evaluator's opinion and is now moving in to try to humiliate, expose deficits, or otherwise compromise the evaluator. The same introductory words are used toward the judge under similar circumstances. I have found it amazing that most attorneys do not appreciate this mechanism. In fact, I had two experiences in which attorneys actually said to me, after I explained to them what I considered to be going on, that such thoughts of denigration were "the last thing in the world" in their minds. My attempt to impress upon them that "the last thing in the world" is often "the first thing in the world" proved futile. Also, although the all-due-respect introductory phrase generally includes the word "Doctor," the way the lawyer says "Doctor" conveys even less of a feeling of admiration for the evaluator.

Most junior-high-school English teachers know that there

are certain words an instructor does well to avoid using in a classroom situation. A few of these are *mastication* (chewing), *formication* (an hallucination that insects are crawling under the skin), and *frigate* (a kind of boat). To use such words in the average junior-high-school classroom is to invite pandemonium. Similarly, there are certain words that the evaluator does well to strictly avoid using in the courtroom. Two examples are the words *always* and *never*. Such words are especially risky in court because of the likelihood that there will be exceptions. And a cross-examining attorney will attempt to get the examiner to agree that there are exceptions and thereby compromise him (her). Accordingly, examiners do well never to use the word *never* and always to avoid using the word *always*.

Another word that the examiner should studiously avoid is *speculate*. Although there is a significant amount of speculation in every evaluator's report, the speculations should not be labeled as such. Lawyer's love to jump on anyone who is foolish enough to use that word. They like to believe that their decisions are made on the basis of "hard facts" and "evidence." They like to believe that there is absolutely no place at all in the courtroom, or even in the legal process, for *speculations*. The reality is that most of the examiner's conclusions and recommendations are justifiably considered speculations. They involve extrapolations from present data to future events. They involve the hope that the conclusions derived from the present experiences will subsequently apply. However, one is not likely to have an opportunity to elaborate on this point in the courtroom. Even if the supporting attorney gives the examiner the opportunity to state what I just have regarding speculation, the evaluator's credibility will be compromised. The judge, and even the supporting attorney, has been deeply imbued with the idea that examiners who speculate in the courtroom are seriously compromised in their ability to provide meaningful testimony. So, if you want to have everyone in the courtroom jump down your throat just say, "It is my speculation. . ." or "I would speculate that. . . ."

As mentioned, impartial examiners do well not to use projective material in their evaluations. There is probably no other place where they are so vulnerable as in the interpretation of projective material. Our field has not reached the point where there is unanimity regarding the interpretation of any ink blot, figure drawing, self-created picture, dream, or fantasy. There is a wide variety of opinion regarding the meaning of such material and the less familiar the examiner is with the patient, the more likely his (her) opinion will diverge from that of another. Accordingly, no matter what interpretation the evaluator gives, the attorney is likely to be able to present an alternative that is equally credible to the court—which is often naive with regard to such matters. There are judges who routinely order psychological tests on parties embroiled in custody litigation and use the findings from projective tests as crucial determinants of their decisions. This is a grave mistake. It is very difficult, if not impossible, to differentiate the dreams of the normal person from those of the psychotic. Dreams may tell much about psychodynamics, but they tell very little about diagnostic status and even depth of pathology. In fact dreams, by the very nature of the logical (or, more correctly, illogical) processes they utilize, *are psychotic*. And material elicited in projective tests has the same drawbacks for the custody evaluator. Even the most highly maternal parent will have death wishes, on occasion, toward the children, and these may be symbolically represented in projected fantasies. It is therefore naive and injudicious on the part of courts to utilize such material in custody deliberations, and it is a disservice to the courts for evaluators to provide it.

A number of years ago there was an article in *The New York Times Magazine* in which the author presented *Rorschach Test* responses to a series of internationally famous experts on Rorschach interpretation. These experts claimed they could make accurate statements about the personalities of the respondents without clinical data or other identifying information. Accordingly, the author presented Rorschach protocols of famous individuals and invited the experts to make guesses regarding who the subject might be. The purpose of the article was to point out how far afield many of these *mavens* were. In fact, one was so far off that he begged the author not to reveal his name. I do not recall exactly the nature of his bizarre conclusion, but it was as if he had taken the protocol of Adolf Hitler and decided that the person was Mother Teresa. The author, out of pity for the "expert," complied with the request. Had I been the author I would not have done so. People who involve themselves in such a project should have the balls to allow their names to be revealed, whether or not the guesses were good ones. I often regretted that I never saved that article. I would have quoted it directly in publications. Unfortunately, *The New York Times* was unable to track down the original, so long ago had it appeared. (I believe it was in the mid-1970s.) I mention the article here because it is an excellent demonstration of the weakness of conclusions derived from projective tests, even conclusions made by world-famous "experts."

Most of the questions posed by the attorney whose position the impartial examiner supports will be open-ended and will thereby provide the examiner with the opportunity to elaborate on the findings and justify the conclusions and recommendations. For example, the lawyer may say, "Please state to the court your reasons for recommending that Mrs. X be designated the primary custodial parent." or "Can you tell us why Mr. X should not be designated the primary custodial parent?" The opposing lawyer, however, will generally pose most questions in such form that the therapist will have little opportunity to elaborate on the answers. They are so structured as to warrant, and even require, answers that are simple, short, and often yes or no. The questions are often so worded that evaluators may be required to provide responses that do not reflect their true intent or position. Evaluators do well to avoid such distortion of their position by not falling into the trap of answering yes or no when the issue is too complex to warrant such a response. The examiner, in such cases, should not hesitate to respond with "I cannot answer yes or no." One should be comfortable with answering in this way as many questions as the lawyer poses which warrant such a response. To do otherwise may result in the court's coming to oversimplified and even erroneous conclusions. In spite of these precautions, questions will be so worded and selective that the evaluator's true intent may be distorted or misrepresented. It is here that the impartial examiner sees most clearly how hypocritical is the attorney's claim to be "only interested in what is best for the child."

I have provided testimony in courts in various parts of the United States and have found there to be significant variation with regard to how stringent courts are to confining the examiner to yes-no questions. And even in the same geographical area there may be significant variation depending upon the judge and the attorneys conducting the trial. As mentioned, my primary problem with these questions is that they are designed to bring about a distortion, oversimplification, or compromise of the evaluator's position. Attorneys justify them under the procedural rules of the adversary system. Their use is one of the reasons (of the many presented in this book) why I will no longer have any part of this system of data collection. However, as the old saying goes, "When in Rome, do as the Romans do." Accordingly, evaluators who go into the courtroom must play by the rules of the lawyers' games. But like most rules, there is a certain amount of flexibility and they can be "bent" at times.

Bending rules around the yes-no questions presents the examiner with a conflict. If one subscribes strictly to the yes-no rules and responds accordingly in automaton-like fashion, one may create a good impression by virtue of this strict compliance with courtroom procedures. However, to do so may deprive the evaluator of the opportunity to "slip in" extra messages, while still working within the confines of the system. There are a variety of subtle ways of adding additional communications to the yes-no response. For example, one can say the word yes in such a way that it implies "Why that's obvious! How can you be so stupid as to ask such a foolish question?" Sometimes that message can be communicated by the examiner's looking incredulously at the attorney and saying, "Of course!" Sometimes additional messages can be communicated by substituting "Yep!" and "Correct!" These responses are provided in a very clipped way to imply: "I have absolutely no problem at all agreeing with you on that point." The implication is that the examiner has absolutely no embarrassment or hesitation agreeing and therefore his (her) position is not in any way being weakened by the yes response. This type of retort is especially useful when the attorney believes that the evaluator is unsure, or hesitant to provide, a strongly affirmative response. Sometimes the examiner may be able to stretch the yes answer further with such responses as "You're 100 percent correct" or "Absolutely true!" This can have the effect of taking the wind out of the sails of the cross-examiner, yet still appear to be in compliance with the courtroom procedure. I never had the experience of an attorney asking the judge to instruct me to change the intonation of my yes-no answers or to order me not to use the aforementioned kinds of substitute responses.

Similarly, one can often get across additional messages with "no" answers. For example, one can say no in such a firm way that one is transmitting the additional message: "There is absolutely no way in the world I could possibly consider an alternative response." This might be communicated by saying, "Absolutely not!" Such synonyms and minor alterations to the basic yes-no responses are generally allowed in the courtroom, even under the most stringent circumstances. However, there are times when I have found that I can "get away with more" and quickly insert a few extra words in order to protect myself from the inevitable distortions of my position that the attorney is trying to bring about with yes-no questions. For example, during one trial an attorney asked me a question about the mother that was clearly designed to give the impression that she was at the time of the trial a woman subject to frequent outbursts of hysterical rage. In actuality, that description was applicable at the time of my evaluation. However, by the time of the trial, one year later (a not uncommon hiatus), she was remarried, had quieted down, and that description was no longer applicable. I knew this from my direct observations of her during my update meeting one week before the trial. In the courtroom the attorney, holding my report in hand said, "Have you not stated that Mrs. X is a 'woman subject to frequent outbursts of hysterical rage'?" Instead of merely saying yes, the answer he expected, I, in a matter-of-fact way, responded, "Yes, at that point." Immediately, the judge interrupted me and asked me why I had said "at that point." Had he read my original report and the recent update, he would not have asked that question. He would have known from my update report that she no longer exhibited this symptom. I knew, from my earlier experiences on that day, that the judge had not read my reports (the usual case) and so I quickly added "at that point" in the hope that it would provide me with an entree to present the clarifying and more reliable data.

My general way of dealing with the dilemma regarding strictly adhering to yes-no questions (and thereby looking professional) and trying to "bend the rules," (and thereby risking one's professional status) was to carefully and gingerly test the waters regarding how much I could "get away with." All this is part of the fine art of the fencing match that I described previously. In short, I tried to get away with as much as I could without going so far that I compromised my credibility or status as a competent witness. The more I "got away with" the more satisfied I was that I was providing useful input to the court.

The examiner may feel quite frustrated on the stand when prohibited from elaborating on responses and clarifying the kinds of misleading conclusions that are often conveyed by the simple yes-no response. An evaluator who tries to elaborate will be interrupted by both the questioning attorney and the judge and instructed to strictly confine answers to the questions posed. With such questioning the attorney hopes to get the evaluator to selectively present and reveal items and material that will support his (her) client's position and withhold from the court that which will weaken the client's cause. Examiners do well to appreciate that most judges are well aware of the antics and are not so easily taken in by the cross-examining attorney's maneuvers. For example, I once served as an impartial examiner in a case in which I recommended that the mother have primary custody. One of my main reasons for coming to this conclusion was that the father was far more committed to his work than to his children. His wife and children viewed him as a "workaholic"—which he was. In the cross-examination the attorney asked: "To the best of your knowledge, Doctor, is Mr. X an alcoholic?" I answered no. He then repeated the same question with regard to drug addiction, wife beating, gambling, and philandering. Again, I had to answer that he was none of these things. He then continued and asked me questions about whether Mr. X had ever been in jail, committed to a mental institution, received electroshock therapy, or had attempted to kill himself. Again, I continually answered no to all of these questions. The attorney, of course, refrained from asking about any of the deficiencies that the client did have—deficiencies that contributed to my recommending custody to his wife. I suspected that the judge was not taken in by all of this game playing and that the inquiries were conducted for the sake of the client, who the attorney hoped would be impressed by the "brilliance" of this cross-examination. And his decision in favor of the mother supported my belief that he had not been taken in by the attorney's antics.

Another example of how the cross-examining attorney uses the yes-no answer to mislead the court is demonstrated by the case of Mr. X, a philanthropist, who was quite neglectful of his children. This was an important factor in my decision to recommend that his wife be given custody. The lawyer was able to elicit a long stream of yes answers from me regarding the various charities to which Mr. X had made generous contributions. He then asked, "You will agree that Mr. X is a very generous and giving person?" The lawyer here was obviously trying to get the court to generalize from Mr. X's social benevolence and conclude that he was equally benevolent to his children. Without hesitation I simply answered no—because the statement was not basically true. I could have answered, "I cannot answer yes or no." The attorney did not ask me to give the reasons *why* I answered no, because he suspected that I would use the question as an opportunity to make a comment along these lines: "In the area of public contributions, Mr. X is, without doubt, a generous man; however, when it comes to the care of his children, I do not consider him generous because. . . ." It is rare for an attorney to ask evaluators to elaborate on *why* they answered no or could not answer yes or no. To do so is to open the floodgates and to invite a barrage of responses that might compromise the client's position. At best, the attorney might try to rework the question in order to elicit a response that is more to his (her) liking. My general advice to examiners is that they provide as many "cannot answer yes or no" responses as they feel warranted, even if they provide 15, 20, or 30 in a row. Such perseverance gets across the message to the cross-examining attorney that the examiner is not going to be tricked into providing an over-simplified answer—an answer that will distort his (her) position.

The impartial examiner should also be aware of the simultaneous presentation of multiple questions presented as a single question for which a yes or no answer is requested. The lawyer here may be trying to sneak in a question that, if asked alone, would receive a different answer. The lawyer may have a question he knows the therapist will answer negatively. By mixing it in with a collection of questions he (she) knows the evaluator will answer positively, the lawyer hopes to get a yes answer for that particular question as well. If the examiner detects even one misstatement in a barrage of accurate facts, he (she) does well to answer no or state that he (she) cannot answer yes or no. Again the lawyer will usually not ask *why* the examiner has responded in this manner, because the attorney suspects that the examiner will use such an open question as an opportunity to focus on the single misleading statement hidden in the series of accurate ones.

On occasion an attorney will attempt to cause expert witnesses to lose their composure—and thereby compromise their credibility—by asking questions which suggest extremely abnormal behavior not picked up in the course of the evaluation. For example, under cross-examination I have been asked, "If you learned that Mr. X had a series of homosexual lovers during the course of his marriage, would that have changed your opinion?" "If you found out that Mrs. X had been hospitalized in a mental hospital prior to her marriage, would this have changed your opinion?" "If you learned that Mr. X would undress his 5-year-old daughter and ask her to dance naked in front of male friends, would this have affected your opinion?" These allegations were gross exaggerations and distortions of what had really gone on or were invented by the attorney and had absolutely no basis in reality. They were designed to get me flustered and seduce me into thinking that I had missed some extremely important points. The attorney here was trying to compromise me with such questions, and the examiner should be aware that this is occasionally done in the courtroom. Under these circumstances I generally tried to bend the rules a bit in my response in order to get across my parallel communications. Accordingly, I responded, "Yes, you're absolutely right! If I did *indeed* learn that Mr. X asked his daughter to dance naked in front of a group of his male friends I would *certainly* have reconsidered my conclusion!" The response was said in such a way that I communicated the message: "If indeed I have been so misled and if indeed he would engage in such a preposterous activity, I would have reconsidered my position. However, the absurdity of the allegation is so formidable that I am incredulous that such an activity ever took place." My understanding is that attorneys cannot frivolously bring in such hypothetical questions unless there is some nidus of truth, or unless there has been some previous testimony supporting the allegation. However, I have been in courtrooms in which such preliminary material was not presented and the attorneys were allowed to get away with this kind of horseplay.

At times a lawyer may bombard the examiner with a barrage of questions that appear to be irrelevant or only peripherally relevant to the issues at hand. In my experience, one of two things is going on in such a situation. The first, and less likely, is that the lawyer really has an important point to make which the impartial does not understand. The more likely alternative, in my experience, is that the attorney has no point in mind and is flooding the therapist with questions in the hope that some response might provide a useful issue to pursue. One would hope that the judge or the opposing lawyer would interrupt such inquiries very early; unfortunately, my experience has been that they may take considerable time before doing this. Courts traditionally allow wide latitude regarding the length and depth of cross-examination. The defendant, or weaker party, is thereby given the greatest opportunity to strengthen his (her) position. In such cross-examination (which can last hours and even days) the examiner should appreciate that the judge is generally not naive and will not be impressed by the lawyer's antics, misleading questions, attempts to deceive the court, etc.

As already described in this book, in earlier years I suffered significant frustration during court breaks when I could not communicate with the attorney whose position I supported. As an impartial examiner I suffered all the disadvantages of being an advocate and had none of the advantages. In more recent years I removed myself from such an impotent position. As mentioned, I circumvented this problem by making myself available to both attorneys, not only following the submission of my report, but right up through the trial—especially during the breaks in the course of the litigation. However, I strictly adhered to the position that I would not speak to one attorney without the other being invited to hear and contribute. This gave me the freedom to recommend lines of inquiry to either attorney. Of course, the attorney whose position I supported was generally quite receptive to my suggestions. As might be expected, the other attorney was generally interested in what I had to say, but not too happy that I was providing "ammunition" to the other side. I cannot recall this invitation ever having been declined. My status as impartial examiner was thereby preserved, and my moral obligation to do what was in the best interests of the children was thereby gratified.

CONCLUDING COMMENTS

Once the report has been submitted, the impartial examiner is basically serving as an advocate of one side against the other. Although the judge may still consider him (her) to be impartial, and although the examiner wishes to maintain this view, it is easy to get swept up emotionally in the adversary proceedings. There is often a thin line between serving the children dispassionately as an impartial and serving the children emotionally as an advocate. "Battle fever" tends to be contagious and generals rely upon it for the success of their campaigns. When one starts fighting, one generally fights hard. The risk here is that the impartial will be reduced to becoming one of the combatants who is "out to win." I consider this to be one of the occupational hazards of being an impartial evaluator. I would not, however, view such tendencies to be necessarily psychopathological or inappropriate. I consider them to be natural and would only warn the impartial not to let them get out of hand. To do so may very well compromise one's position; strong (not mild) emotionalism and objectivity do not go well together. And this is especially the case on the stand. Should the impartial be unable to place such feelings in proper perspective and control them to a reasonable degree, it is likely that psychopathological factors are operative.

For example, a male examiner who has fought for custody of his own children may overidentify with a father involved in such a dispute. He may even support inappropriately the father's position. This is a risk when serving as an impartial if one has been, or worse, *is* embroiled in a custody conflict oneself and at the same time is serving as an impartial examiner. Under such circumstances, the likelihood of maintaining full objectivity is almost at the zero level. Another example of the evaluator's inappropriate involvement might result from sexual-physical attraction. A male evaluator might be "turned on" by a young, seductive mother. This may not only contribute to his favoring her over the father but "fighting hard" for her cause. The evaluator who has significant problems in relating to either men or women has no business serving as an impartial evaluator. Such prejudicial attitudes toward one side over the other are bound to contaminate an impartial evaluation. In short, getting slightly swept up in the fray of custody litigation is probably normal. But when the evaluator harbors very strong feelings and preoccupations or fights very vigorously, the likelihood is that inappropriate and/or psychopathological elements are contributing. As is true in psychotherapy, such contaminations are a disservice to the parents and are signals to the examiner that such involvement should be reconsidered until the time these problems are resolved.

H. M. Fain (1977), an attorney, states:

>One must always bear in mind that the exercise of discretion by a judge is far less a product of his learning than of his personality and his temperament, his background and his interests, his biases and his prejudices, both conscious and unconscious.

The same caveat holds for mental health professionals. We, too, are not free from our prejudices and biases, and we should be aware of this when conducting custody evaluations. Awareness of our prejudices should make us more modest in conducting custody evaluations. Mental health professionals do well not to involve themselves in evaluations that might be contaminated by such prejudices. Although there are few who are noble enough to make such a decision, it is an ideal that is still valid.

◩ ELEVEN
RECOMMENDATIONS
FOR JUDGES

INTRODUCTION

One could argue that a chapter on judges interviewing children does not appropriately belong in this book. Designed as it is to deal with mediators, arbitrators, and those who are involved in adversary litigation as lawyers and mental health professionals, a chapter for judges may not seem warranted. However, judges are increasingly interviewing children in the course of adversary litigation. In fact, in my own state of New Jersey, they are required to do so. Furthermore, if my proposals regarding the three-phase program for custody dispute resolution are ultimately implemented, judges may very well be serving on such panels, especially at the appeals level. Accordingly, I believe that a chapter devoted to judges interviewing children is warranted.

**INTRINSIC WEAKNESSES OF
IN-CAMERA INTERVIEWS WITH CHILDREN**

It is important for judges to appreciate that when they interview children in their chambers they are doing so under significantly compromised circumstances. An appreciation of these compromises can help the judge place in proper perspective the information so gained.

Absence of Family Interviews

The court's primary question in custody/visitation litigation is this: Who would be a better parent for this *child* to live with, the *mother* or the *father?* This question is not likely to be answered reasonably unless data is collected from *all three parties* referred to in the question. Furthermore, the data-collection process will also be compromised if the parties are seen only alone and not in various combinations. Restricting oneself to interviewing only the child compromises the process significantly because it deprives the evaluator of obtaining data in joint interviews, which are often the most valuable part of the data-collection process. Family interviews also enable the interviewer to "smoke out" fabrications in which children traditionally say to each parent what they think that parent wants to hear at the moment. In custody evaluations, observing the parent-child relationship is the best source of information for ascertaining parental superiority. The present structure of courtroom proceedings generally precludes the court's conducting such parent-child and family interviews. It must rely on the information provided by mental health professionals who conduct these interviews elsewhere.

Absence of Multiple Interviews

Another compromise relates to the fact that interviewees, regardless of age and regardless of the circumstances, are more likely to reveal themselves to known parties than to strangers. And the longer and deeper the relationship with the interviewer, the greater the likelihood the interviewee will provide disclosures. And the greater the "dangers" of such revelations, the greater the likelihood that valid information will not be obtained in a short period. And the younger the interviewee, the greater the likelihood these impediments to obtaining valid data will be operative. Interviewing a child only once does not provide the court with the opportunity to develop the kind of relationship in which such divulgences are likely to be obtained. Judges rarely have the time for multiple interviews, which provide the optimum setting for the kinds of revelations the court is hoping to obtain. Furthermore, the child generally enters the judge's chambers in a state of fear. Although *in-camera* interviews are less frightening than courtroom testimony, the judge is still held in awesome regard by most children and many adults. The fear element is likely to compromise significantly the data-gathering process and this cannot but make the information so obtained of dubious value. Furthermore, without a series of interviews the judge is not in a position to observe the changes in the child's comments and preferences that are often observed in the course of intensive custody evaluations.

The Child's Cognitive Immaturity

The child's level of cognitive development is also an important consideration. Obviously, the younger the child, the less meaningful his (her) verbalizations will be. In the individual interview, the court does not have the opportunity to get "translations" from a parent who understands better the child's terminology, innuendoes, and gestures. Accordingly, judges must appreciate that the person they are interviewing is the one of the three who is least capable cognitively to provide data pertinent to the court's considerations.

The Child's Impaired Capacity to Differentiate Fact from Fantasy

The younger the child, the less the capability of differentiating fact from fantasy—a differentiation to which courts pay particular attention. In a recent case in Florida in which I was involved, during the *in-camera* interview (with the attorneys present), Florida law required that the interviewers first establish whether the four-year-old girl being questioned could "tell the difference between the truth and a lie." This interview was conducted with a child whose parents were litigating over her custody and whose father was brought up on charges of sexual abuse because the child had told her mother that "Daddy killed Santa Claus. . . .Daddy killed the Easter bunny. . .and Daddy put his finger in my 'gina.'" No one sent an expedition to the North Pole to see if Santa Claus was dead. No one sent out a search party to find out whether the body of the dead Easter bunny could be produced. But a horde of individuals descended upon this family in response to the third allegation. A four-year-old child who believes in the existence of Santa Claus and the Easter bunny *ipso facto* does not differentiate well between fact and fantasy. Yet all interviewers agreed that she could do so for the purpose of the sexual-abuse investigation and the inquiry continued. (Incidentally, I concluded that the third allegation was as much a fantasy as the first two.)

Learning "The Truth" from a Child

The purpose of the judge's interview is to find out what "the truth" is with regard to various aspects of the custody dispute. The assumption is made that the child knows what the truth is regarding a variety of issues pertinent to the allegation. All of us distort the truth somewhat in accordance with what our wishes are, and children even more so. Time generally blurs one's recollection of reality and the younger the person is when an event occurs, the greater the likelihood time will distort its recollection. By the time a judge sees a child in chambers, the events under consideration may have taken place months or even a few years previously. It is reasonable to say that for many of the events being discussed with the judge, many children no longer know the truth and could not tell what the truth was no matter how honest they were trying to be. The truth-versus-lie problem is further compounded when one considers that the child may indeed know the truth regarding certain simple issues, but not with regard to more complex ones. For example, judges are traditionally instructed to ascertain whether or not the child knows the truth by asking simple questions designed to assess the child's capacity to make the differentiation. For example, while pointing to something red, the child is told "this is green. Is that the truth or a lie?" Most children by three, or the latest four, will be able to say that the judge is lying. Similarly, the judge may point to the picture of a girl and say, "This is a girl. Is this a truth or a lie?" Again, most children, even at this low age range, will have little difficulty responding that the judge's statement is true. However, if the child is asked to talk about whether mother sleeps too much, father drinks too much, mother spends too much time on the telephone and is thereby neglectful, the child is not likely to provide reasonable answers even though the child is being honest.

Next, the ability to differentiate the truth from a lie should by no means lead the judge to conclude that the child will not lie. Criminals (many of whom are sociopathic) know quite well the difference between a truth and a lie, yet they have little if any hesitation lying (even under oath on the witness stand). Courts are well aware of this. Yet, an assumption is sometimes made that merely because a child will be able to differentiate between the truth and a lie that the child will therefore be honest. Some jurisdictions require the judge to proceed from the phase of establishing the child's ability to differentiate between the truth and a lie to extract from the child the promise that he (she) will tell the truth. This, I presume, is the equivalent of the oath an adult takes just prior to testimony.

I have never been involved in a custody case in which I have not directly observed libel, slander, and perjury. (Incidentally, I have also never observed anyone's being prosecuted for these crimes.) Courts certainly recognize that adults will most often and almost predictably lie in the context of custody disputes (after all, the stakes are high and this is indeed a situation in which most parents take the position that the end justifies the means). However, the assumption is somehow made that a child is more likely to adhere to the promise. For the court to believe this is an expression of naiveté. A number of studies demonstrate well how prone children are to lying. In fact, most people familiar with children consider it normal. D. Goleman (1988) describes a study conducted by M. Lewis, a psychiatrist at Rutgers Medical School.

Goleman quotes Lewis: "In one study we just completed with three year olds, we set up an attractive toy behind the child's back and tell him not to look at it while we leave the room." (The children are then observed through a one-way mirror.) "About ten percent don't peek while we're gone. Of the rest, a third will admit they peeked, a third will lie and say that they did not peek, and a third will refuse to say." With regard to the third group, Lewis states, "Those who won't answer seem to represent a transition group, who are in the process of learning to lie, but don't do it well yet. They are visibly the most nervous. Those who say they did not look – who lie – looked the most relaxed. They've learned to lie well. There seems to be a certain relief in knowing how to lie effectively." It is reasonable to conclude that the third who refuse to say (who invoke the fifth amendment or will not respond until consultation with their attorneys) are also consciously aware of the fact that they are lying. In short, two thirds of the children in this group lie and are consciously aware that they are lying.

As far back as 1911 J. Varendock demonstrated this point quite well in two classroom experiments. In one a group of 19 seven-year-olds were asked a question about a familiar teacher, namely, "What color is Mr. B's beard? " Sixteen replied that his beard was black and two did not provide an answer. The facts were that Mr. B had no beard. In another classroom experiment 27 eight-year-olds listened to a male teacher talk to the class for five minutes, after which he left. Each child was then asked, "In which hand did Mr. A hold his hat?" Seventeen children said that he held his hat in the right hand. Four stated that it was the left hand. And three stated that he wore no hat. The facts were that he wore no hat. In short, the vast majority of these seven- and eight-year-old children lied. The explanation is not difficult to understand. Children do not enter the world with knowledge of what is going on within it. They are constantly making speculations and guesses in an attempt to understand elements in their environment. They are constantly looking to adult authority to correct their distortions. When the seven-year-olds were asked "What color is Mr. B's beard?" it is reasonable to assume that many of their thought processes went along these lines: "I don't remember his having a beard. However, the question indicates that he had a beard. So I must have forgotten. I'm always distorting the real world anyway. I don't want to look stupid to the questioner. Therefore I'll guess and I hope that I'll get the right answer. Black is the most common color for a beard, so I might as well guess black. I hope I'm right." I would speculate also that a similar line of reasoning went through the minds of those who guessed in which hand Mr. A held his hat.

Children are constantly trying to ingratiate themselves to adults, especially to adults in authority like parents, teachers, and professionals such as physicians, lawyers, and judges. Like all of us, they want to be liked. If lying will serve this end, they are likely to do so. They also lie to avoid punishment. When caught fighting the vast majority of children under nine or ten are going to claim that the other child started. They lie also to make excuses for themselves, to rationalize inappropriate or unacceptable behavior. In divorce situations they predictably lie and say to each parent what that parent wants to hear, especially regarding criticisms of the other. This is the most common way they deal with the loyalty conflicts which emerge from divorce and especially from custody disputes. Children embroiled in a custody dispute know where their "bread is buttered." They know that when with parent A they express affection for parent B, they may alienate parent A. In contrast, if they join in with parent A, provide criticisms of parent B (new or more ammunition), they will ingratiate themselves to parent A. And the same procedure is used with parent B. It is only in joint interviews that these maneuvers may be "smoked out" and the judge's failure to employ them deprives him (her) of an important source of information about what is "the truth." Accordingly, when interviewing a child whose mother is outside the judge's chambers, the likelihood is that the child will say things that will ingratiate him (her) to the mother, because of the possibility that she might hear the proceedings or the judge might tell her what has transpired. Similarly, the child will lie in favor of father if he happens to be at close range (even though not in earshot).

Considering all these factors the judge does well to make the assumption that many of the things the child will be saying are going to be lies, distortions, and fabrications. And this is especially the case when one is going to touch directly on such tender issues as which parent would be preferable for the child to live with.

It is important for the judge to appreciate that by the time he (she) interviews the child in chambers there probably have been numerous earlier interrogations extending over many months and even a few years. Under such circumstances, children may no longer know what they want. So mind boggling have been the experiences with lawyers and mental health professionals that lying may have become a *modus vivendi.* Under these circumstances, many children operate on the principle that they will say whatever is most expeditious at that particular time, that which will ingratiate them to the person with whom they are speaking at that moment. The pattern has become so deeply ingrained that the bona fide preferences and opinions have long been suppressed and repressed from conscious awareness.

TECHNICAL CONSIDERATIONS

The Importance of Seeing Children Individually

On a number of occasions I have come across situations in which judges have interviewed two, and even three children at the same time. This is an error. Children should be interviewed one at a time. The judge does well to recognize that in a very high percentage of cases a younger child will mimic the statements of an older one. In a joint interview, then, one is basically getting the opinions of the older child. Even when the children are seen separately, this is likely to occur. However, when seen alone the younger child especially will not have the older one to provide clues and feed answers.

The Issue of Who Brings the Child to the Judge's Interview

The court also should recognize that the child's comments may be colored by individuals who are outside the judge's chambers during the course of the interview. Children embroiled in custody disputes suffer with terrible loyalty conflicts. They generally say to each parent that which will ingratiate them to that parent at that time, regardless of their true beliefs and regardless of the consequences of fabrications they may provide. This principle extends itself to the *in-camera* interview wherein the child is likely to support the parent who is close by. Moreover, the parent who brings the child and/or the parent who takes the child back home is also likely to have an influence on what is said in chambers. Furthermore, children have short memories. A father who brings the child to the court on Monday morning, after a weekend of fun activities, may very well be viewed as the preferable parent. And a mother who brings the child to court on Friday afternoon, after a difficult week in which the child was forced to do homework, chores, and was disciplined for normal childhood transgressions, is likely to be viewed with disfavor. Accordingly, the court should have both parents bring the child to the courthouse and both parents bring the child home or have a neutral third party accompany the child to the courthouse. But even under such circumstances the court does well to make inquiries regarding the aforementioned considerations of recent parental involvement.

The Issue of Confidentiality

Many judges will tell children, at the beginning of their interviews with them, that what the children say will be held strictly confidential and that their parents will never learn what they have revealed. Unless the court can be 100 percent certain that this promise will be fulfilled, it is a risky one to make. Generally, this reassurance is given under circumstances in which a transcriber is recording every word. The transcripts of the interview are usually sent to the attorneys who may or may not be instructed not to reveal their contents to the parents. It is but a short step to the child's learning as well that the judge has not kept the "secrets." Under these circumstances the child cannot but feel betrayed—especially by someone who is held in high esteem. It is yet another betrayal added to that of a parent's leaving home. Accordingly, I generally discourage courts from making such promises. Rather, judges should proceed without such a promise and hope that the child's needs to communicate important issues will override the fear that the parents may learn of the disclosures. If the child does ask about whether the divulgences will be revealed, the judge does well to tell the child that his (her) comments may be available to the parents or that the judge must be given the freedom to decide which information will be revealed and which will not.

Introductory "Basic Statistical Data" Questions

The court is advised to begin the interview by asking the child simple questions, which the child can answer with ease and freedom from anxiety, e.g., name, address, age, telephone number, etc. Each time the child gets the "right" answer, initial tensions and anxieties are reduced and it becomes easier for the child to answer the more anxiety-provoking questions that will inevitably follow. Other questions in this category would include the child's grade level, name of school, teacher(s), and names and ages of people in the family network (mother, father, stepmother, stepfather, siblings, stepsiblings, half-siblings, etc.). In the course of getting information about the names of these individuals, some useful information might be obtained. For example, the child might state: "My stepfather's name is Bob. I like to call him 'Daddy' and my real father 'Dad,' but my real father would get very angry at me if he ever knew." The response here indicates that the child's father is placing inappropriate demands upon the child.

The judge does well to appreciate that the basic information that one wants to obtain in the interview with the child relates to the manifestations of *parental* capacity, especially with regard to how one parent compares to the other. This is the basic data from which the court is going to make its decision. Similarly, the child's preference is also going to derive from this data. If the court approaches the question from the top (so to speak) with questions like "Which parent do you want to live with?" or "Which parent do you prefer?" meaningful answers are not likely to be forthcoming because of the child's loyalty conflicts. However, as will be described in detail below, the court can obtain information about basic parenting behavior (from which the child's preference is derived) without necessarily inducing tension or anxiety. Furthermore, the child's reasoning processes from which the conclusion may be derived may be faulty. For example, a child may say, "I want to live with my father. He's really good to me. When I see him every weekend he lets me watch television as much as I want and I don't have to do my homework. My mother is mean. She makes me go to sleep early, makes me do homework, and doesn't let me watch as much television as I want." In short, the judge should get the raw data relating to parenting capacity and use his (her) own reasoning processes.

"Blank Screen" Questions

After the initial period in which the judge simply asks "name, rank, and serial number" type questions the court does well to proceed in accordance with the principle that the best and most revealing responses are those which the child provides spontaneously, willingly, and without the awareness that important material is being revealed. The best way to obtain such information is to allow the child to talk about anything and hope that in the context of such conversation important material will be provided. My experience has been that information related to parental capacity is usually provided in such free discussions without the necessity to ask specific questions that the child appreciates may yield information about parental preference. Most children are deeply involved with their parents and are therefore likely to talk about them in the course of their conversations.

Along these lines, it is important for judges to appreciate the psychoanalytic principle of the "blank screen." The best way to learn about what is going on in the person's mind is to allow the individual to free-associate and talk as if his (her) thoughts and feelings are being projected on a blank screen, a screen that has no contaminations that might draw out a particular thought or fantasy. This is basically what is going on in the traditional psychoanalytic couch situation. The analyst sits behind the patient, unseen, and so few if any contaminating stimuli are brought to the attention of the patient, stimuli that might contaminate the free-associations. The *Thematic Apperception Test* (TAT) (Murray, 1936), an instrument that is widely used by psychologists in the course of their diagnostic evaluations, demonstrates this principle quite well. The patient is presented with a series of pictures, each of which depicts a scene in which there are vaguely depicted figures involved in some vague activity. The individuals can be distinguished from one another regarding sex and approximate age, but nothing else specific is indicated. In fact, the pictures are specially designed to be vague in order to approximate the blank screen phenomenon. The examinee is simply asked to tell a story about what is happening in the picture. One of the pictures, however, is completely blank. This picture is, at the same time, the most anxiety provoking and the most revealing. Because there are no stimuli on which to project fantasies, the individual may be a little anxious regarding what story to create. However, the same absence of stimuli will result in the least contaminated kind of story, i.e., a story that will be most revealing of the innermost and true processes operative in the mind of the storyteller.

The TAT is one of many *projective tests* used in psychology. The term *projective* refers to the process by which the examinee *projects* fantasies onto what is viewed as a blank screen. A good way to think about projective questions is to view them as a way of asking a person to select responses from a *universe* of possible answers. One does well to think of the total universe and so pose a question that the child is being asked to give a particular response that is self-selected from the universe of possible responses. This is the least contaminated response.

Although the aforementioned name, rank, and serial number type questions have a potential contaminant, it is generally miniscule. Any disadvantages of possible contamination from such questions are more than compensated for by the relaxation the child experiences when getting the "right" answers. Following this period of decompression of tension, the judge should attempt to elicit information with open-ended questions which facilitate the creation of the psychoanalytic blank-screen situation. A few examples: "So how are you doing?" "What would you like to talk to me about today?" "So what's on your mind?" The principles to utilize, when following through with the child's answers, are these: Extract from what the child says the information that is likely to shed light on the custody dispute. Use that material as a handle and point of departure for further inquiry. Maintain the posture of the "ignorant interrogator" (ignorant meaning not-knowing, rather than stupid) and continually ask questions. Ask for specifics; generalizations rarely provide useful material. Obtain clarifications that provide a visual image. When a boy, for example, says that his father is "mean" this may or may not be true. It is only by obtaining specific examples that the judge can determine with certainty whether the statement is valid. If the concrete, visualizable examples involve making the child do homework, turning off the television in order to go to sleep, or taking his clothes off the floor, the conclusions are very different from examples involving the father's humiliating, and denigrating the child. I cannot emphasize this point strongly enough. All too often interviewers, even mental health professionals, will come to conclusions on the basis of abstract statements made by patients. These may have absolutely no validity. It is only with specific examples, especially examples that one can visualize in a concrete way, that one is in a position to determine whether or not a statement is valid.

At this phase of the interview it is an error to ask the child the question: "Why are you here?" This may be anxiety provoking and may result in the child's tightening up and not providing useful information. Information given in a state of fear and anxiety is not likely to be useful. The child generally knows why he (she) is there, and to "rub the child's nose in it" may be counter-productive. Even the question, "What did your mother (father) tell you about your visit with me today?" may be anxiety provoking.

A six-year-old girl, for example, in response to one of these open-ended questions might show the judge a doll. This is the "handle." This is the point of departure from which the judge might then be able to obtain important information. Rather than shying away, running out of the room, or remaining mute the child is engaging the judge. At this point the judge might ask what the doll's name is. It would be an error for the judge to choose a name himself (herself) because that is a contaminant. Most dolls have a name. The judge might then ask where the name came from. The child might give a seemingly innocuous response like "I made up the name myself." However, the judge should not stop there, but should then ask "Where did you first hear about that name?" The child might then say, "My mommy thought it would be a good name for a doll." The response tells something about the child's relationship with the mother (and possibly about the father in comparison). Following this the judge might ask, "What is the doll doing?" or "I want to see how good you are at making up a story about your doll." Another example: a seven-year-old boy comes in with a model of a boat. When asked what he would like to talk about he proudly shows the judge the boat he built and says, "I built this boat myself, but my daddy helped me. He's a carpenter. He knows a lot about building things." The sense of pride the child has when exhibiting the boat as well as his pride in his father is important information regarding parental preference.

If children are allowed to talk about anything they wish, and although their comments may initially appear irrelevant to the court's purpose, there are times when useful information regarding parental capacity can be obtained. Such discussion might be introduced with questions such as "What would you like to talk about now?" and "So tell me something else." In response to such a question, a boy might start talking about his interest in baseball. In the context of his discussion he speaks with pride about his accomplishments in Little League and how proud he is that his father is one of the coaches. He expresses regret that the rules do not permit him to be on the team that his father is coaching. Or, a 14-year-old girl, again after professing to the judge that she does not want to state her parental preference, may start talking about the fact that she goes shopping with her mother, who is quite expert at selecting perfumes, lipstick and make-up and with whom she can discuss such personal matters as her period and her feelings about boys. Time does not generally permit the court to indulge itself to a significant degree in this kind of inquiry, but it does well to appreciate the value and recognize that its investigations are compromised without such questioning.

Other useful statements at this point might be "Tell me something about your mother" and "Tell me something about your father." Similar areas of inquiry might relate to other significant figures such as stepparents and new ongoing relationships that the parents may have. The statement is general enough to allow for a universe of possible responses within the confines of talking about a particular person. Other general statements that can provide useful specific responses are: "Tell me about the best thing that ever happened to you in your whole life" and "Tell me about the worst thing that ever happened to you in your whole life." Following general inquiries about each of the parents one can get a little more specific (yet still provide the opportunity for a universe of responses) with such statements as "No one is perfect. Everyone is a mixture of things that you like and things you don't like. I want you to tell me the things about your mother that you like, and the things about her that you don't like." And then one goes on to ask for similar information about the father, other parental surrogates such as stepparents, and new ongoing relationships that the parents may have. One should also ask for information about the child's relationships with extended family members such as grandparents, aunts, uncles, and cousins. Although one wants to direct one's attention primarily to the parent-child relationship, the commitment and availability of extended family members should play a role in the court's decision.

Self-created Stories

In the context of a self-created story family events are likely to be depicted. Here the child will utilize the process of projection (similar to that used when creating stories around TAT cards). It is much easier for all people (children and adults as well) to talk about third parties, fantasy figures, and others than to talk directly about themselves—especially when the depicted events are guilt evoking or anxiety producing. The self-created story serves as a disguise, as a vehicle for expressing unacceptable thoughts and feelings without the child's consciously realizing that the forbidden material is being revealed. How the children in the child's story interact with the parents can provide the judge with useful information about the child's own interactions with parents.

"Yes-No" and "True-False" Questions

The court should avoid questions that could be answered by either yes or no. Of course, this is just the opposite of what is done in cross-examination, where the yes-no question has a deep-seated heritage. Although this form of inquiry may be useful in "nailing down the facts," I do not hold it in as high regard as my legal colleagues. When one asks a question that could be answered with either yes or no, one does not really know whether the response is valid. A quick answer of yes or no may be an easy way for the responder to "get off the hook" without providing a meaningful answer. Much more valid material is obtained with questions that elicit sentences and descriptions that are self-derived by the respondent. For example, if one asks a boy whether he loves his mother, one is likely to get a yes answer—even if she has been brought up on charges of physical abuse. Or, if a child says no, one still has very little information. However, if one asks questions like, "Tell me about your mother" or "I'd like you to tell me the things about your mother you like and the things about her that you don't like," the responses are likely to be far more revealing. A similar principle holds for true-false questions. There is little if any place for them in such interviews.

"When" Questions

The court does well to avoid questions relating to *time*. To ask children about *when* a particular event took place is not likely to produce meaningful data. The younger the children, the less appreciative they are of the passage of time and the less capable they are of pinpointing the exact time that a particular event occurred. Time questions only invite fantasized answers, which only compromise the data-collection process. The court should ask questions that begin with *what, where, who, and how.* These help "nail down" the facts. The court should get specific details about each item described. One wants the child to verbalize from concrete imagery that is being visualized.

"How Did You Feel. . .?" Questions

Most mental health professionals are very enthusiastic about the "How did you feel. . .?" question. This question, borrowed by presumably sophisticated laymen from the psychiatric inquiry, is supposed to help a person express feelings and thereby feel better. In recent years radio and television reporters have been using the question with the implication that learning about the interviewee's *feelings* about a particular event enriches our understanding of what has gone on. Questions from these public media interviewers usually go like this: "How did you feel when you learned that you lost the election?" "How did you feel when you first saw your son after his release from three years in a prisoner-of-war camp?" The correct answer to these and all similar questions is identical: "How do you think I felt you idiot? Get out of here before I hit you." Unfortunately, most people are not free enough to express this on nationwide television and so provide either the obvious answer or formulate the response that they consider will be the most acceptable to the audience.

I cannot be too critical of laypeople (including judges) for using this form of inquiry. They have been taught by experts in the field of psychiatry and psychology that it is a most valuable question. There is hardly a trainee in psychotherapy who is not repeatedly advised by supervisors to "get out the patient's feelings" and that a good way to do this is to ask, "How did that make you feel?" With rare exceptions, the question is absurd. People who know how they feel can only consider the question naive, simplistic, extraneous, or an affront. People who are so repressed that they indeed have no conscious awareness of their emotions are not likely to get in touch with their feelings by such a question. Rather, they are likely to respond with puzzlement, denial of feelings, rationalization, or what they think the interviewer wants to hear. Eight-year-old Sarah, then, who is afraid to express the anger she feels over Gail's having broken her doll, is asked by her mother, "How did you feel when Gail broke your doll?" Mother would do far better for Sarah's inhibitions to say, "Even though you're not showing it, I know that deep-down you're very angry at Gail. And I don't blame you. I'd be angry as well. Now what do you think you can do about this? If you don't do anything it might happen again." This comment not only communicates to the child that anger is the expected and socially acceptable response, but structures the situation in such a way that it is clear to the child that she must effectively express her anger if she is to avoid a repetition of the situation that provoked it. Such structuring can be far more effective than merely encouraging a child (or anyone else) to *act* in a desired fashion. Accordingly, judges do well to stay away from "How did you feel. . .?" questions. Elsewhere (1973a, 1986b, 1988a) I discuss in detail the techniques therapists should use in order to elicit feelings from repressed patients, techniques that do not rely on this type of question.

"Grandma's Criteria"

When providing examiners with guidelines for the kinds of questions to ask children involved in custody conflicts, I generally recommend that they use what I refer to as "grandma's criteria." These are the parental manifestations that grandma's ghost would consider if it were free to roam the house and then report its findings to the court. If she is like most grandmas, she does not have an M.D. or Ph.D. and has very little formal so-called "psychological sophistication." She would observe the children from the time they get up in the morning until they went to sleep, and sometimes even in the middle of the night. She would determine who wakes the children in the morning and who gives them breakfast and prepares them for school. Of course, if father's work requires him to leave so early that he cannot involve himself in these activities, this cannot be considered a deficiency on his part. This is similarly the case for spending lunch time with the children and being available after school. It is during the after-work hours, when both parents traditionally are home, that grandma would get her most useful information. She would want to observe who helps the children with their homework and if this is done smoothly or whether there are typically power struggles, tears, fits, tantrums, threats, impatience, and other manifestations of a poor parent-child relationship. She would observe disciplinary measures, especially whether they are humane, consistent and benevolently administered. She would pay close attention to the bedtime scene. Are bedtime stories read? Are the children lulled into sleep in a loving manner or is it typically a time of threats and punishments? What happens during the night may also be important. Who gets up to change the diapers? To whom does the child turn for consolation after nightmares? Which parent has traditionally taken the child to the emergency room or the doctor's office when there have been evening and nighttime accidents and/or other medical emergencies? She would be particularly concerned with which parent is willing to make the most sacrifices on the child's behalf.

The judge does well to get information in these areas by discussing directly with the child the day's events, from arising in the morning to going to sleep at night, and finding out who are the adults involved in these various activities. Again, the best way to get information about this is to ask general questions. One might start: "Tell me about your day from the time you get up in the morning to the time you go to sleep at night." One can narrow down on specifics (again with questions posed in a general way to allow a universe of possible responses), for example: "Tell me what happens at breakfast time." "What happens in your house after supper?" "What does your mother do when you're bad?" "What does your father do when you're bad?" One is especially concerned here with how humane are the disciplinary and punitive measures.

Parental Involvement with School Activities

Another important area of inquiry is parental attendance at school activities, both curricular and extracurricular. The court should find out who attends teacher conferences and what the parental reactions are to report cards. Is there pride and/or emotional reaction or complete indifference? Who attends various plays, concerts, recitals, and open-school activities? These are among the most valuable criteria for ascertaining parental capacity and the nature of the parent-child relationship.

Inquiries into Visitation

The court may learn much by asking the child about the details of the visitations: what was done, who was present, where did they go, etc. When inquiring about visitation it is useful to use open-ended statements and questions such as "Tell me about your visits with your father." It is not a good idea to ask questions which can be answered by yes or no, questions such as "Did you have a good time when you visited with your father?" Whether the child answers yes or no, one does not really know if the child had a good time. He may have had a terrible time and "gotten off the hook" with regard to criticizing his father by simply saying yes. The child may recognize, as well, that the no answer will be responded to with further inquiry, and this the child may wish to avoid. When asking a general question about visitation, a child, for example, might describe a father who brings along every transient date, thereby fulfilling two obligations at the same time.

Some children describe visiting parents' dropping them off at the home of third parties (aunts, grandparents, and an assortment of other individuals) and then pursuing their own interests. Many children describe the visiting parent's cross-examination of them on visitation days to extract information that might be useful in litigation. Other children go on a round of circuses, rodeos, zoos, etc. Although such overindulgence may serve the purpose of guilt assuagement or rivalry with the custodial parent, in excess it is a parental deficit. In the course of conversations about visitation one is likely to get information about whether the visiting parent involves the child with homework and includes in the visitation time activities that are somewhat less pleasurable, but possibly more important. One should try to ascertain whether the child spends long periods propped up in front of a television set.

Sometimes, in the course of a description of a visitation, the child provides very valuable information without realizing the importance of what is being revealed. For example, a child whose father was litigating for a significant reduction in support payments, because of professed inability to pay, told me when discussing visitation with his father "We had a great day last Sunday. We went out with my dad's new girlfriend Barbara. Boy is she great. And you should see the ring my dad gave her. It's the biggest diamond I ever saw in my whole life. Jane said it cost $5,000.00." This is the best kind of information to obtain. It is given naively and openly without the child's realizing its implications for the judge's considerations. Another response in this category, told by a child who was simply asked how his week went: "I had a great week. Since Mike's moved into the house everything's been great. Because he doesn't work, he's home when I come home from school. He used to be a basketball player and he's taught me a lot of good shots." This occurred at a time when this boy's mother was asking for an increase in her support and alimony allotments.

In the course of a description of a visitation one might learn that the father is unreceptive to allowing friends in the home because of the potential damage. Committed parents recognize and tolerate these potential "dangers" of having friends in the home and appreciate that good relationships with friends are more important than intact furniture. Or, the child may not be allowed to run in the back yard because it interferes with the growth of the grass. Of course, primary custodial parents can also exhibit these manifestations of parental deficit and the examiner must be alerted to their presence in either home.

Inquiry into the Reasons for the Divorce

Sometimes questions about the reasons for the divorce may provide the court with useful information. The child's description of the nature of the marital conflict may include information about parental capacity. For example: "My mother couldn't stand my father's drinking anymore. I used to help her find the bottles that he would hide." One can ask about each parent's receptivity to friends' visiting the home and the parental tolerance of the noise, rambunctiousness, horseplay, and the minor damage that inevitably occurs when children are in the home. Do the child's friends like each of the parents? Is the parent receptive to the child's visiting other homes? Although none of the aforementioned questions are in the category: "Who do you want to live with, your mother or your father?" they clearly provide useful information for the court's making its decision regarding parental preference.

Closing the Interview

Before closing the interview the court does well to ask the child a final question such as: "Is there anything else you'd like to talk to me about that you haven't mentioned." It is an open-ended question that will give the child the opportunity for final input. The court does well to make the assumption that the child wants to get across information to the judge about parental preference and needs to do it in such a way as to not feel disloyal. A comment here—just before parting ways—gives the child the opportunity for final input. The child might say, "My brother wants to live with my mother. He says he loves her very much. My brother and I are very good friends and I would never want to live in a different place." Or the child may say, "Don't make me live with someone who doesn't like to play baseball." I am not claiming that the wisdom of these final comments, or the criteria upon which parental preference is based, are necessarily the most judicious. I am only stating that the opportunity to provide a final comment before parting may provide the judge with useful information, not previously mentioned.

Last, judges who, at the beginning of the interview, felt the need (sometimes by legislative mandate) to extract a promise from the child to tell the truth may end the interview by asking if the child has told the truth. Like the request for the initial oath, the request for a final vow is not useful. No matter how psychopathic the child, no matter how many lies may have been perpetrated upon the court, it is extremely unlikely that the child will confess to having provided the court with fabrications.

INTERVIEWING CHILDREN WITH PARENTAL ALIENATION SYNDROME

Children suffering with a parental alienation syndrome (discussed in detail in Chapter Six) may present the judge with a convincing picture. By the time such children reach the judge, they have developed a well-rehearsed litany of complaints against the presumably hated parent. This can be quite convincing, especially because the script has probably been rehearsed many times over with the allegedly preferred parent. Also, by this time, children have probably presented the scenario to a parade of attorneys and mental health professionals. This has given such children the opportunity to practice and sharpen their speeches. I have been involved in many cases in which judges have been completely taken in by parental alienation syndrome children, and have not appreciated that they were being handed a "bill of goods." These children have a way of "snow balling" even experienced psychologists and psychiatrists, so I cannot be too critical of these judges.

I present below a series of questions that judges should find useful when interviewing these children. It is important to appreciate that the questions provided here relate to the more common situation, the one in which the father is the allegedly hated parent and the mother the professed loved one. However, when the situation is reversed (the mother the hated one and the father the loved one) I obviously reverse the questions.

Describe Your Mother to Me   Children with parental alienation syndrome typically provide only positive responses. If any negatives are provided, they will usually be minimal. If asked to elaborate upon the negatives, only inconsequential criticisms will be provided. Children who suffer with other kinds of psychiatric disturbances or are "normal" will generally be able to list both positives and negatives about each parent. The complete idealization of a parent is a clue to the presence of this disorder.

Describe Your Father to Me   The child with parental alienation syndrome will enumerate various criticisms at great length. These will be both present and past. Often the past indignities will be about experiences that other children would consider normal or would have forgotten long ago. Sometimes a complaint will be about an event which the child has not actually observed but which the mother has described. The child will accept as valid the mother's rendition and not give any credibility to the father's refutation. If the judge points out to the child that the mother's rendition is being given preference over the father's, the child is likely to respond, "My mother would never lie to me." An attempt to confront the child with the inegalitarianism and bias of such a response will generally prove futile. But this prejudice provides the judge with data nevertheless because it confirms the presence of a parental alienation syndrome.

When it is pointed out to the child that few if any positives about the father have been described, the child will claim flatly that there are none. Inquiries into past good times between the child and the father will be denied as nonexistent or the child will claim that these events were painful and the child's professed enjoyment of them stemmed from the fear of punishment for not doing so. It is this complete one-sidedness of the response, the total absence of normal ambivalence, that should alert the interviewer to the fact that one is probably dealing with a child suffering with parental alienation syndrome.

What Do You Think About Your Father's Family? The child with a parental alienation syndrome will generally respond that all members of the father's extended family, even the child's own grandparents and previously loved aunts, uncles and cousins, are somehow obnoxious and vile. When asked for specific reasons why there is absolutely no contact at all with any of these individuals, no compelling reasons are provided. Often inconsequential reasons are given. Attempts to impress upon the child how important it is to have relationships with these loving relatives prove futile. The child extends the view of the father as noxious to the father's extended family. The child will describe no sense of loss or loneliness over this self-imposed removal from the father's extended family. If a potential or actual stepmother is involved with the father, this hatred will extend to her and her extended family as well.

Does Your Mother Interfere with Your Visiting with Your Father? Generally the child will describe absolutely no interference on the mother's part. Often the child will proudly describe the mother's neutrality and state that the decision is completely his (her) own.

Why Then Don't You Want to Visit with Your Father? The child may give very vague reasons. When asked to give *specific* reasons, these children may describe horrible abuses in a very convincing way. In addition, they often provide gross exaggerations of inconsequential complaints. They make "mountains out of mole hills" and will dwell on frivolous reasons for not visiting. Often they will claim that they want absolutely no contact at all with the father for the rest of their lives, or at least not before they are adults. When it is pointed out to these children that the vast majority of other children would not cut their fathers off entirely, forever, for such "indignities," they insist that their total rejection is justified.

Does Your Mother Harass You?   Healthy children generally will give some examples of "harassment" such as being made to turn off the television, do homework, or go to bed earlier than they want. Children with parental alienation syndrome describe no such harassments. They often will describe their mother as being perfect and as never asking them to do things they don't want. This is obviously a fabrication and is a manifestation of the whitewash of the mother. I use the word *harassment* with these children because it is a common expression utilized by mothers of parental alienation syndrome children. The father's overtures for involvement with the child are generally referred to as harassment by the mother. If the child is unfamiliar with the word harassment, I substitute "bother you a lot."

Does Your Father Harass You?   These children are likely to describe in great detail the father's "harassments." Generally, they involve attempts on his part to gain contact with the children. Letters, telephone calls, and legal attempts to gain visitation are all clumped under the term "harassments." Although the father's initial overtures may have been spaced reasonably, with mounting frustration over rejection and alienation, the father's overtures increase in frequency and intensity. The love and affection that is at the foundation of these overtures is denied completely by both the mother and the parental alienation syndrome child. Rather, they are viewed simply as onerous harassments.

The above questions are general ones. The judge does well to ask more specific questions pertinent to the particular case. These might include questions regarding why the child wants to change his (her) name back to the mother's maiden name, why the father's Christmas presents were thrown in the garbage (usually in the mother's presence), why the child wants to have the father still contribute to his (her) education even though he (she) never wants to see the father again, what the siblings' reasons are for not wanting to see the father (these too often prove inconsequential), and so forth. When speaking to the parental alienation syndrome child it is also important to make a sharp differentiation between the child's words and the associated emotional tone and gestures. The child who describes hatred of the father may do so while smiling and may present a list of alleged indignities suffered at his hands in such a way that one gets the feeling that there was absolutely no pain involved. This is an important clue regarding whether or not one takes these complaints seriously.

Judges who interview children in chambers must appreciate that these children may be very convincing. Judges may be taken in by the litany of complaints and give such great weight to the child's statements that they may go along with the child's stated preference. Judges must be alerted to the primary manifestations of this disorder, especially the complete lack of ambivalence, the dwelling on frivolous and inconsequential "indignities," the total removal from the extended family of the hated parent, the absolute denial of any positive input on the hated parent's part at any time in the child's life, and the definite statement that the child wishes *never* to see the hated parent again. It is hoped that judges will increasingly appreciate what is occurring when they see such children and rectify the situation in accordance with the guidelines to be presented in the following section.

GUIDELINES FOR JUDGES FOR MAKING CUSTODY DECISIONS

As discussed in detail in Chapter Nine I believe that mental health professionals as well as the courts do well to make custody decisions on the basis of what I refer to as the *stronger, healthy psychological bond presumption*. Implementation of this presumption is a three-step process:

> 1) Preference (but not automatic assignment) should be given to that parent (regardless of sex) with whom the child has established *over time* the stronger, *healthy* psychological bond.

2) That parent (regardless of sex) who was the primary caretaker during the earliest years of the child's life is the one with whom the child is more likely to have established the stronger bond. Residua of that early bonding are likely to influence strongly subsequent bonding experiences with the parents.

3) The longer the gap between the early bonding and the time of the dispute, the greater the likelihood other experiences will affect the strength of the bond. Whether or not these have resulted in the formation of an even stronger bond with the parent who was not the primary caretaker during the earliest years has to be assessed in the course of the evaluative process.

I believe courts have not been paying enough attention to the formidable early life influences on the child's subsequent psychological status. Early life influences play an important role in the formation of the child's psychological bond to the parent who was the primary caretaker during the earliest years. Courts have been giving too much weight to recent and present-day involvement and ignoring the residual contributions of early bonding to present experiences. Mothers have been much more often the primary custodial parents during the early child-rearing process. This produces a bond between the two that results in strong attachment cravings when there is a rupture of the relationship. Accordingly, when there is a threatened disruption of this relationship by a sex-blind judge or joint-custodial mandate, mother and child fight it vigorously. Commonly, the mother brainwashes the child and uses him (her) as a weapon to sabotage the father's attempts to gain primary custody. The children develop their own scenarios, as well, in an attempt to preserve this bond. I believe that residua of the early influences are playing an important role in the attempts on the part of both parties to maintain the attachment bond.

The implementation of the presumption that children do best when placed with the parent who is most involved in child rearing, especially during the formative years, would reduce significantly the custody litigation that we are presently witnessing. It would result in many mothers' being automatically awarded custody. It would not preclude, however, fathers' obtaining custody because there would be some fathers who would satisfy easily this important criterion for primary custodial assignment. The implementation of this presumption would still allow those parents (whether male or female) who were only secondarily involved in the child's rearing to have the opportunity to seek and gain custody. They would, however, have to provide compelling evidence that the primary custodial parent's child-rearing input was significantly compromised and their own contributions so formidable that they should more justifiably be designated primary custodial parents.

I believe that the implementation of these guidelines will reduce significantly the likelihood that mothers will brainwash their children and that parental alienation syndromes will develop. Furthermore, it will reduce the likelihood of injudicious decisions regarding custodial placement and prevent, thereby, the wide variety of psychopathological processes that can develop therefrom.

Last, I recommend that we replace the best interests of the child presumption with the *best interests of the family presumption.* The best interests of the child presumption is somewhat narrow. It does not take into consideration the psychological effects on the parents of the child's placement and the effects of the resultant feedback on the child's welfare. As mentioned, the strong bond that forms in early life between the child and the primary caretaker produces immensely strong cravings for one another when there is threatened disruption of the relationship. Just as the child suffers psychologically from removal from the adult, so is the adult traumatized by removal from the child. The psychological trauma to the adult caused by such disruption can be immense, so much so that parenting capacity may be compromised. This negative feedback, of course, is not in the best interests of the child. But we are not dealing here simply with the question of placing the child with a parent in order to protect that parent from feeling upset about the child's being placed with another parent. Rather, we are considering the ultimate negative impact on the child of the disruption of the bond with the primary caretaker. Accordingly, I am recommending that courts assign primary custody in accordance with the presumption that the *family's* best interests will be served by the child's being placed with that parent who was the primary caretaker during the formative years. Furthermore, the longer that parent continued to be primary caretaker, the greater likelihood the *family's* interests will be served by placement with that parent. The implementation of this presumption will, I believe, also serve as a form of preventive psychiatry in that it will not only reduce significantly custody litigation but serve to obviate the terrible psychological problems attendant to such litigation.

THE ROLE OF THE JUDICIARY IN DEALING OPTIMALLY WITH PARENTAL ALIENATION SYNDROME CHILDREN AND THEIR PARENTS

I believe that the courts can play a crucial role in helping families in which a child manifests a parental alienation syndrome. The courts have the power to make custodial assignments that can be quite therapeutic—a power that therapists do not have. I would go further and state that without the court's utilization of its powers in many cases, it would be extremely unlikely, if not impossible, to treat certain children in this category.

In Chapter Nine I have discussed in detail the categories of mothers who contribute to their children's parental alienation syndrome. The recommendations I made for mental health professionals there are applicable to the judiciary. Whereas the mental health professional can only make recommendations, the courts have the power to effect the kinds of transfers (parent and/or child) that are warranted. I will, however, review here (for judges) certain aspects of my recommendations made in Chapter Nine for mental health professionals.

It is important for judges to ascertain in which category the parental alienation syndrome lies: severe, moderate, or mild. This differentiation is crucial if the court is to make proper rulings. Without the court's providing proper placement of the children the therapist may be left impotent. I will present here the approaches courts do well to utilize for each of the three types of parental alienation syndrome.

Severe Cases of the Parental
Alienation Syndrome

The mothers of children in this category are often fanatic. In many cases they are paranoid. Court-ordered treatment is likely to prove futile, so little is their insight into their psychopathology. Rage and vengeance against the husband for having been abandoned are often present, but less important than the paranoid mechanism. Some were paranoid before the litigation; most were pre-paranoid and exhibited paranoid deterioration as a result of the litigation (1986a). The children join the mother in a folie à deux relationship and may harbor the same delusions about the father that their mother exhibits.

Therapy of these children is often not possible while they are still living in the mother's home. There is a sick psychological bond between the children and the mother that is not going to be changed by therapy as long as they remain in her home. While still there they are going to be exposed continually to the bombardment of denigration of the father that contributes to the perpetuation of the parental alienation syndrome. The only hope for these children, therefore, is court-ordered removal to the home of the father, the allegedly hated parent. Often, this is not accomplished easily and the court might have to threaten sanctions and even jail if the mother does not comply. Following the transfer there must be a period of decompression in which the mother has no opportunity at all for input to the children. This is the only possible way they can re-establish the former relationship with the father and protect them from the reindoctrinations of the mother. Even telephone calls must be strictly prohibited for at least a few weeks, and perhaps longer. Then, according to the therapist's judgment, slowly increasing contacts with the mother may be initiated, starting with monitored telephone calls. There is still a danger here that these telephone calls will be used as opportunities for programming the children.

It is important that the therapist be court ordered, and that *one* therapist serve the whole family, separated or divorced status notwithstanding. Ordering separate therapists will only fractionate the family more and contribute to the perpetuation of the parental alienation syndrome. Although, as mentioned, the mothers in this category are not candidates for meaningful insight therapy, they can still be required to comply with the court-appointed therapist's instructions in the child's treatment. The therapist must be given certain powers through the court. Obviously, the judge cannot delegate his (her) authority directly to the therapist. However, the therapist can have an open line to the court either directly or through a child advocate or guardian ad litem.

If the father had established a good and reasonably healthy psychological bond with the children prior to the litigation (the more common situation) then they are likely to exhibit such manifestations of affection once separated from the programming mother. At that point *carefully monitored* visits with the mother may be possible. The determinant of how much contact they will have with the mother should be made by the therapist. The main criterion for deciding how much time the children will spend with the mother should be determined by the amount of programming by the mother and the degree of complying scenarios manifested by the children. For most cases in this category permanent transfer to the father is the best course of action for the court to take. The mother's psychological bond with the children is often quite sick, whereas that with the father is more likely to be a healthier one. Transfer back to the home of the mother may result in lifelong alienation from the father. The degree of contact with the mother, during visitation, depends upon the mother's degree of programming. And, as mentioned, this is determined by the therapist with monitoring and input by the court.

Moderate Cases of the Parental Alienation Syndrome

The mothers of children in this category are not as fanatic as those in the severe category and are less likely to be paranoid. Most often they have established a healthy psychological bond with the children prior to the custody litigation. They are, however, programming their children against the father, but to a lesser degree than mothers in category one. Such programming relates to vengeance maneuvers and the desire to maintain the healthy psychological bond. These mothers may be in therapy, but often with a therapist (more often a woman than a man) who supports the antagonism toward the father. The court's ordering a discontinuation of such therapy often proves futile in that the mother is likely to find another therapist who will support her in her animosity toward the father. Accordingly, here again, the mother should be ordered to attend sessions with a court-ordered therapist who sees the whole family, the parents' separated or divorced status notwithstanding.

Here the children can continue living with the mother, but the therapist needs the court's power to require the mother to cooperate in the visitation and not to obstruct it. This may involve the utilization of neutral parties at transfer points, or transfers taking place in the therapist's office. Whereas the therapist in the severe category of mothers needs the court's support for monitoring visitation from the father's house to the mother's, here the court's power is necessary to enforce implementation of visitation from the mother's house to the father's. The court may also have to threaten sanctions, removal of custody, and even jail in order to get such mothers to cooperate in facilitating visitation.

Mild Cases of the Parental Alienation Syndrome

The mothers in this category also have established a healthy psychological bond with their children prior to the onset of the custody litigation. They are less enraged than mothers in the moderate category, but there is some anger, especially regarding the misguided egalitarianism of recent legislation—which does not give proper respect to the importance of the parent with whom the child has developed the stronger psychological bond (most often the mother). The children's scenarios of denigration of the father are created in an attempt to maintain the stronger bond with the mother. The symptoms, in both mother and children, are likely to disappear (most often dramatically) as soon as the court makes a final decision that the children shall remain permanently with the mother. From that point on the symptoms serve no purpose and can be allowed to evaporate. Here again, the judge can do much more than even the most skilled therapist. To attempt therapy while the parents are still litigating for custody—when there is still the threat that the children might be ordered to reside permanently with the father—is not likely to be effective.

CONCLUDING COMMENTS

This book has been written primarily for mental health professionals. However, members of the legal profession have certainly been in mind in the course of its writing. And this is especially the case for the material in this chapter. It has been written primarily for judges in order to provide them with optimum interviewing techniques for in-camera interviews with children. It has been written, as well, for attorneys to enable them to make judicious recommendations to the court. And it has been written for mental health professionals to provide guidelines for their recommendations to attorneys and the courts.

The material describing the healthy psychological bond presumption for making custody decisions is crucial. Its implementation by the courts could result in a reduction and prevention of significant psychopathology. The material on judges' interviewing and dealing with parental alienation syndrome families is also extremely important. Proper placement of these children by the court is central to the therapeutic process. The legal and psychotherapeutic handling of these children provides an excellent example of how the courts and the mental professional must work hand-in-hand if there is to be any hope for alleviation of these children's problems. Without the combined efforts of both, the likelihood of these children being helped is quite small.

⚖️ TWELVE
MEDIATION AND THE
CUSTODY EVALUATION

INTRODUCTION

I believe that mediation is the most judicious option for parents to utilize when they are unable themselves to resolve a dispute over child custody. We are living at a time when there is good reason to believe that mediation will ultimately replace adversary litigation as the primary mode of resolution of child custody disputes. Although it may appear to be a "new" way to resolve such conflicts, actually it is ancient. Furthermore, it is important to understand that we Americans live in a litigious society, possibly the most litigious on earth (J. K. Lieberman, 1983). In other countries people are far less committed to adversary litigation as a way of resolving disputes, whether in child custody or in other areas.

J. Folberg and A. Taylor in their comprehensive book on mediation (1984) state that mediation is an ancient tradition that is still viewed as the preferable method for dispute resolution in many parts of the world. In China, for example, from ancient times to the present, mediation and self-determination are the preferred methods for dealing with disputes. In Japan, as well, the tradition is so deep that there are relatively few attorneys (1 per 10,000 population) as compared to the United States (1 per 340 population). L.L. Riskin (1982) points out: "In parts of the Orient litigation is seen as a shameful last resort, the use of which signifies embarrassing failure to settle the matter amicably." Many African tribes traditionally engage the services of mediators. Since ancient times religious organizations have considered mediation to be an important aspect of their leaders' role. The Bible, for example, contains numerous references to conflicting parties seeking the counsel of a prophet, seer, or wise man. And King Solomon's decision, regarding two women, each of whom claimed to be an infant's mother, is not only one of the most famous examples, but is particularly relevant to this book.

Up until the last few years the legal profession was generally unsympathetic to mediation and even considered it unethical on the grounds that an attorney serving as a mediator might be biased. The same argument, however, was not utilized when attorneys were invited to serve as mediators in labor and commercial disputes. Two partners who wanted to dissolve their business contract could engage the services of an attorney to mediate their problems and the lawyers did not risk being considered unethical. Yet two marital partners who wanted to engage the services of an attorney to mediate the dissolution of their marriage contract had little opportunity to do so—so great was the resistance of the legal profession. Furthermore, the same attorneys who would view mediation as unethical did not have any conflicts accepting appointments as judges. Somehow, bias at the level of divorce mediation was considered a high risk, but bias at the level of the judge's ruling was not considered to be so.

In recent years, however, this resistance has been reduced significantly, especially by mediation procedures that incorporate independent attorneys as reviewers of the mediation agreement and encourage active communication between the mediator and each party's independent counselor. Whereas older attorneys, those more deeply committed to the adversary system, have generally shown resistance to mediation, younger lawyers are more receptive. These changes have been reflected in the recent organization of a committee that deals specifically with mediation issues by the Family Law Section of the American Bar Association. Setting up such a committee is a clear statement of approval by the Bar Association of the mediation procedure and the recognition that it is an acceptable option for an attorney. One of the committee's obligations will be to set up guidelines for attorneys when they serve in this capacity.

DEFINITIONS OF MEDIATION, NEGOTIATION, ARBITRATION, AND THE CUSTODY EVALUATION

The word *mediation* is derived from the Latin word *mediare,* which means *to be in the middle.* Mediators are individuals who place themselves between two parties for the purpose of helping them resolve their differences. Traditionally, the mediator has been someone who was viewed as neutral by both parties and whose opinion is mutually respected. In divorce mediation, as it is practiced today, the mediator is generally viewed as a *facilitator* of communication between the parties. The mediator attempts to *catalyze* the parties' expressing their views. The goal is for the parties themselves to play the primary role in bringing about a resolution of their differences. Mediation is differentiated from *arbitration* in that in arbitration the neutral party is asked to come forth with one or more specific recommendations. Of course, the differentiation in some cases becomes blurred if the mediator becomes too active and provides specific courses of action or the arbitrator becomes too passive in contributing significant conclusions and recommendations.

J. Folberg (1983) defines mediation as "a nontherapeutic process by which the parties, together with the help of a neutral person or persons, systematically isolate points of agreement and disagreement, explore alternatives, and consider compromises to reach an agreeable settlement." J. Folberg and A. Taylor (1984) define mediation as ". . .the process by which the participants, together with the assistance of a neutral person or persons, systematically isolate disputed issues in order to develop options, consider alternatives, and reach a consensual settlement that will

accommodate their needs. Mediation is the process that emphasizes the participants' own responsibility for making decisions
that affect their lives. It is therefore a self-empowering process."
They also state "unlike the adjudicatory process, the emphasis is
not on who is right or wrong, or who wins and who loses, but
rather upon establishing a workable solution that meets the
participants' unique needs. Mediation is a win/win process."

One of the important functions of the mediator in custody
disputes is to help the parties focus on the important issues and
not get sidetracked into irrelevant areas of conflict or dead-end
streets. The mediator tries to discourage parents from getting
involved in arguments about past indignities and issues irrelevant
to the topics under consideration. People involved in such
disputes are likely to contaminate the mediation process with
heated digressions. Good mediators use their authority to interrupt time-wasting discussions and bring the parties back to the
crucial issues. Effective mediators do this, but still do not impose
decisions upon the parties. They structure the process so that the
clients themselves may more efficiently bring about a resolution
of their difficulties.

Mediation is not, strictly speaking, a form of therapy. In
therapy, or at least in psychotherapy, the therapist tries to
understand the motivation of the patients and help them gain
insight into the factors that underlie their thoughts, feelings, and
actions. In mediation, these are not the primary purposes. The
aim is to bring about resolution of the conflict with compromise,
with little direct inquiry into underlying psychodynamics. I am
not suggesting that in mediation no reference or attention should
be given at all to these underlying processes. It is, however, not
the aim to bring about therapeutic change in individuals through
insight, but rather to bring about some kind of resolution of their
problems. I am not stating that mediation is entirely different
from therapy, only that the emphasis on insight is far less than
one would rely upon in a purely therapeutic process. Although
mediation may not be therapy per se, there is no question that it
can be therapeutic. When effective, it can interrupt psychopathological processes. And it is the most powerful vehicle for prevent-

ing the kinds of psychopathology that result from adversarial litigation. Elsewhere (1986a) I have described in detail the most common examples of such psychiatric disorders.

Mediation should be differentiated from *negotiation*. Negotiating is often referred to as "horse trading" or "this-for-that" exchanges. Negotiating is like economic bargaining. It involves tradeoffs. A basic principle is "I'll give *you* what you want most, if you give me what *I* want most" or "What is it worth to you to have X?" An example of this would be a mother who would be willing to take a smaller cash settlement if the father would be willing to send their daughter to college. Sometimes competitive negotiations work. At other times they don't, and it is the role of the mediator to move the participants from competitive negotiations to cooperative problem solving. Negotiation, then, is the traditional bargaining encounter in which proposals and counter-proposals are presented, and an agreement may be obtained.

Sometimes individuals negotiate themselves or they may use representatives. The representatives, sometimes attorneys, "sound out" each other and bring about some kind of compromise, often in a piecemeal fashion. By using representatives, the parties may protect themselves from the animosity they would suffer in a direct confrontation. In addition, the representative, being emotionally uninvolved, may be more effective. In some situations the individual lacks the expertise or knowledge to bargain effectively and recognizes that the use of a negotiator may bring about a much more favorable settlement. Generally, negotiation does not take place in the presence of a third party such as a mediator or a judge. However, some of the interchanges that take place between the parties in the mediation process can certainly be referred to as negotiations. Although there is some overlap between mediation and negotiation, the differences should be recognized.

Arbitration differs from mediation in that in arbitration the neutral party is asked to come forth with specific recommendations. In "pure" mediation the parties themselves work out their own resolutions. In "pure" arbitration the arbitrator, after hearing all pertinent information, comes forth with one or more recommendations. I have placed the word *pure* in quotes because in actual practice the differentiation between these two processes often becomes blurred.

There are two kinds of arbitration, *binding* and *nonbinding.* In binding arbitration, the parties agree beforehand that they will accept the recommendations of the arbitrator and appreciate that such acceptance may involve discomforts and frustrations. In nonbinding arbitration, the parties generally agree to give serious consideration to the arbitrator's recommendations but do not commit themselves in advance to automatically accept them. Another term for nonbinding arbitration is *advisory arbitration.* Nonbinding arbitration is closer to mediation because both allow for rejection of the final recommendations. Binding arbitration, in contrast, is close to what takes place in court. The judge is essentially a binding arbitrator. However, the judge is not chosen by the parties and the binding arbitrator generally is. In addition, the setting of binding arbitration is much more flexible than the courtroom and there is greater opportunity to provide the arbitrator with all pertinent information.

Mediation is preferable to arbitration because the decision is still in the hands of the parties in conflict. This difference is particularly important when the conflict is over child custody in that parents who cannot mediate their differences regarding their children's custody will be placing the decision in the hands of someone else if they need to resort to arbitration or, worse, courtroom litigation. No matter how skilled and brilliant the arbitrator, no matter how dedicated to the task, the arbitrator cannot be more knowledgeable about what is best for the parties than they are themselves. The arbitrator does not have to live with the agreement; the parties do.

As stated, arbitration differs from courtroom litigation in that it is a looser and more flexible arrangement. In arbitration one has greater control over the amount of time spent in the process because one is generally paying the arbitrator. One does not have the stultifying and paralyzing restrictions of the courtroom setting. One is not subjected to the indignities and frustrations of cross-examination and the suppressing of important information

often entailed in such examination. This informality makes arbitration a more humane and civilized arrangement. In recent years
some retired judges have worked part time as arbitrators. Also,
The American Arbitration Association has become increasingly
involved in the arbitration of marital disputes.

Many mediation centers are now providing arbitration services when the mediation breaks down and the clients are
receptive to this option. Meaningful mediation and arbitration
presupposes a willingness to be honest and to divulge all pertinent information. Individuals who are not willing to divulge
completely their financial situations are not candidates for either
of these two processes. The revelation of such information is
generally referred to as *disclosure*. People who will only disclose
such data after court order are not candidates for either mediation
or arbitration. Rather, they doom both themselves and their
families to the horrendous psychological traumas attendant to
adversary litigation.

THE CUSTODY EVALUATION WITHIN
THE CONTEXT OF MEDIATION

The intensive custody evaluation described in this book is the
kind that a mediator or mental health professional might conduct
for parents who are embroiled in a custody dispute. Mediation is
a relatively superficial process compared to the custody evaluation conducted by a mediator. When the parents' problems are
relatively superficial they might very well be resolved by the
traditional mediation process. However, when the problems are
complex and the parties still wish to mediate their difficulties,
they do well to consult a mediator who is qualified to conduct the
kind of in-depth evaluation I have described at length in this
book. Whereas mediation is basically catalytic, in the custody
evaluation the examiner conducts a detailed inquiry into the
factors that must be considered before making a recommendation. Furthermore, after conducting the custody evaluation, the
examiner comes forth with recommendations derived from the
data provided by the parents and children. One might argue then

that the procedure should justifiably be called arbitration. I prefer not to use that term because the parents have significant input into the procedure and have the opportunity to change my mind and/or reject my proposals. Rather than view the recommendation as being "handed down from above," I prefer to view it as being "hammered out together." The "hammering out" process takes place at the time when I first present my findings and recommendations to the parents. Previously, when I worked as a court-appointed impartial examiner, this was the point at which I presented my findings and recommendations to the clients and the attorneys. In that conference they had the opportunity to change my opinions and contribute to the modification of my recommendations. At the same point in the custody evaluations conducted in the context of mediation, no attorneys are present but the parents have the same opportunities for input.

THE ADVANTAGES OF MEDIATION

One of the most important advantages of mediation over court-room litigation is that it places control in the hands of the parties in conflict. They themselves are the ones making the decisions. They are not putting themselves in the hands of a nonbinding arbitrator or a judge over whom they will have no control. People who go to court place themselves at the mercy of the judge and the laws governing child and spouse support, alimony, property division, and child custody. These laws are subject to differences in interpretation, even by the same judge at different times. Thus, there is little predictability regarding what the outcome might be. In mediation one makes one's own laws. This does not preclude considerations of law entirely. The individuals must satisfy state requirements regarding property division, equitable distribution, inheritance, child support, and so forth. The participants in mediation, however, have great flexibility within the confines of the laws. It is the mediator's role to define what these restrictions are and to help the parties work within the legal requirements. There is far less risk in mediation; therefore, people who generally avoid or fear risk are attracted to mediation. Some may find risk intolerable. Whether or not the risk avoidance factor in the mediation selection is pathological, the choice is still a healthy one.

Adversary litigation is invariably an ego-debasing process. Even those who "win" really lose in that the psychological toll attendant to such winning is generally formidable. In adversary litigation one disputant wins and the other loses. And this can be ego-debasing. In mediation no one wins and no one loses. Mediation not only protects individuals from suffering with the ego-degrading aspects of courtroom litigation but can be ego-enhancing in its own right. Mediation is psychologically healthy because it encourages independence and control over one's fate. The adversary system does just the opposite; the clients often become extremely dependent on their attorneys and suffer with a deep sense of impotence regarding their fates. The sense of impotent rage cannot but be ego-degrading. In mediation one does not place oneself in such a vulnerable position. In successful mediation the parties resolve their differences amicably.

The adversary system focuses to a significant degree on monetary issues. L.L. Riskin (1982), an attorney, points out that nonmaterial values such as honor, respect, dignity, security, and love are generally not taken into consideration. In mediation these factors are definitely considered, and mediation thereby enables individuals to respect these important human factors while resolving their differences.

In the process of mediation a weaker party may learn some techniques for negotiating better with the more powerful spouse. Mediation thereby protects the weaker party from possible future indignities. This can be an ego-enhancing outcome of the mediation process. Divorce mediation can also be creative. The process by which the parents work out the final resolution of their problems is a creative one that can be ego-enhancing as well.

Mediation is generally far less expensive than courtroom litigation, especially if the litigation is protracted. The drainage of finances attendant to prolonged litigation is one of the more devastating psychological drawbacks of protracted litigation. Furthermore, mediation ultimately serves the public benefit as well;

courtrooms have less pressure on them to hear divorce trials and the judges' time can be devoted to other kinds of cases.

One of the great advantages of the mediation process is that it allows for empirical determinations of what might be the best solutions for the wide variety of problems with which divorcing couples are confronted. In litigation the judge often comes down with a decision regarding many issues and these must be adhered to by both parties. Even the most brilliant judges cannot know with certainty whether or not their rulings will ultimately prove judicious. The decisions often appear to be "pulled down from the sky," having little if any relevance to the parties' actual situation. Although a judge's rulings may be based on specific legal guidelines, these cannot predict relevance to a particular family. In mediation one can empirically try a particular plan and then see how it works out. For example, if a support and alimony payment appears reasonable, the parties try it out for a month or two and then discuss it again in a subsequent mediation session. In this way they can determine through actual experience—before a final decision is made—exactly what program best fits their needs. The final agreement, then, will reflect *afterwards* what they have previously found to be a reasonable program. This is clearly one of the major benefits available to couples who are judicious enough to mediate their differences.

Mediation is likely to reduce hostility between the participants. It does this by resolving the areas of conflict one at a time. It encourages direct communication and cooperation, the absence of which often contributes significantly to animosity. Adversary litigation, as described extensively earlier in this book, does just the opposite. It predictably intensifies hostility. It brings hostility to pathological proportions, and this contributes to the development of psychopathology.

Another advantage of mediation is that it is private. If the divorce is held in a courtroom, the proceedings are generally public record. Of course, most divorces do not attract widespread attention and there are few visitors to the courtroom. However, in most jurisdictions the public is entitled to witness divorce litigation. Furthermore, the proceedings may become part of the public record. Most divorces involve personal matters which the individuals would prefer to be kept private. The divulgence of such information can be ego-debasing. And even when not disclosed, the knowledge of the potential for such divulgence also produces unnecessary fears and tensions. Mediation provides protection from such publicity. And if one or both of the participants are well-known, then the likelihood of public interest may be great, and the privacy that mediation can offer is thereby even more desirable.

Our courts present themselves as providing justice. At this point, I have been involved actively in forensic psychiatry for about 30 years. I am convinced that many, if not most, judicial decisions in divorce cases are capricious and hastily made and that individuals who *voluntarily* allow judges and attorneys to play an active role in deciding what is just and fair for them are taking a big risk. It is like leaving these decisions to chance or to other forces over which one has no control. J.J. Shapiro and M.S. Caplan (1983) hold that the utilization of litigation as a method for deciding custodial preference is "little more than an expensive roll of the dice." Accordingly, I do not believe that the courtroom is a place to look for justice to a predictable degree. Judges have overloaded calendars and cannot give as much time to any case as is justified. With the limited information presented, they are as likely as not to make injudicious decisions. And the adversary system lessens the likelihood that all the pertinent information will be presented to them in a balanced way, its professions of such balance notwithstanding. Mediation allows for a much more efficient data-gathering process, and the custody evaluation provides parents with an even greater opportunity for a detailed investigation into the factors that are important to understand if one is to make a wise decision in a custody dispute. More data is likely to be collected in a specific period and, with more information, it is more likely that judicious decisions will emerge. Much time in the courtroom is wasted on irrelevancies and digressions. This is less likely to happen in the mediation process.

Mediation can have the fringe benefit of helping the disputants learn how to work together. It can provide them with the living experience that they have much more to gain than to lose by cooperation. It has the potential for helping people learn the process of dispute resolution. Aside from the substantive issues that may be resolved, it also provides guidelines and experience with a general method for dispute resolution in many other areas. This benefit of mediation may not only be of use to the couple in resolving future differences between themselves, but in resolving disputes they may have with others as well.

There is good reason to believe that the agreements that emerge from mediated disputes are more likely to be adhered to than those that have been adjudicated. Having played a role themselves in bringing about the resolutions, the parties may be more committed to the solutions. This view is supported by the studies of J. Pearson and N. Thoennes (1982) and C. McEwen and R. Maiman (1981). J. Folberg (1983) is also in agreement: "Concerns that mediated agreements will haunt the court with motions to set aside or modify are unfounded. The opposite appears to be true." This is in contrast to court-ordered decisions for which both parties may have little if any conviction. As a result the spouses are less likely to adhere to the final decision and are much more likely to abrogate responsibilities, defy the court order, or return to court.

Mediation makes it relatively easy for couples to *come back and re-evaluate* their agreement if new situations arise that warrant such re-evaluation. This is one of the other great benefits of mediation. This is not the case for couples who are committed to adversary litigation. Generally, if a situation arises that warrants revision, the individuals will have to start the whole trial process over again—an extremely lengthy and expensive procedure. Many individuals suffer with injudicious decisions rather than expose themselves once again to the terrible psychological traumas of further litigation. Happily, couples who have been divorced in the traditional manner may now utilize mediation to re-evaluate their agreement. Sometimes there are couples whose original divorce took place at a time when mediation was not generally available. For such individuals to forego the mediation option and return once again to the bloodbath of courtroom litigation is clearly a pathological choice.

THE DISADVANTAGES OF MEDIATION

Mediation, like everything else that's good in this world, is not perfect. It too has its risks and drawbacks. However, I am convinced that its risks are small compared to its advantages. Judicious parents should be aware of these drawbacks and do whatever is possible to avoid or circumvent them. One criticism directed against mediation is that it creates a potential for the more dominant and coercive party to subjugate the more passive. This danger can be obviated by the mediator's taking a more active role and protecting the more passive partner from readily agreeing to what might be unreasonable demands by the more active party. Another criticism is that two well-meaning people may come to a compromise that may be severely detrimental to one of them. Again, a knowledgeable mediator will not only apprise the parties of the injudiciousness of such a compromise but will even refuse to draw up an agreement that supports such an inequitable resolution.

Another criticism directed against mediation is that it may enable individuals to agree to inappropriate and self-destructive terms because of psychopathological processes. For example, a father who is excessively guilty over the divorce may, in order to assuage his guilt, offer concessions that are basically exploitive of him. Individuals who have strong masochistic and self-destructive tendencies are also likely to agree readily to terms that will cause them pain and suffering. Impulsive individuals, and those who cannot tolerate prolonged discussions and detailed inquiries, may agree to an unfair arrangement in order to shorten the mediation process. Again, sensitive mediators should be aware of those possibilities and should use their influence to protect the clients from inappropriate agreements. Clearly, it is in this area that the mental health professional can be particularly useful as part of the mediation team or as a consultant to an attorney mediator.

In adversary litigation divorce lawyers may sometimes serve a broader role beyond that of drafting documents, negotiating, and litigating. They may also serve to provide consolation, commiseration, and psychological support. A.G. Berg (1983) points out that mediation deprives clients of the opportunity for this second function of the attorney. The presence of a spouse tends to preclude the kind of privacy and intimacy that allows the attorneys to provide psychological support. In addition, because mediation is a much shorter process, the opportunities for such relationships evolving are also lessened. Because its primary purpose is to focus in quickly on the crucial areas, the clients may not have the opportunity to unburden themselves, and this decreases the likelihood that this type of supportive relationship will develop. Although Berg's comments are certainly applicable in some situations, there are mediation procedures and custody evaluations in which both parties develop a good relationship with the evaluator who can then provide the kind of psychological support described by Berg.

Those who criticize mediation because it does not provide for this kind of opportunity imply that such support is always positive. Specifically, the implication is that attorneys' providing such psychological support is a definite advantage. I am not in agreement here. Such psychological support is best done by someone who has training as a mental health professional; because attorneys do not generally have such training, the psychological input that attorneys provide may be injudicious, inappropriate, and sometimes destructive. For example, many attorneys still believe that during the first interview it is both ethical and psychologically beneficial for them to discourage clients from getting a divorce. This approach is only seemingly benevolent. It may have taken the client years to reach the point of coming to an attorney to seek a divorce, and the attorney's reflex discouragement may drive the client back into further years of grief and misery.

Many women turn to their attorneys as substitutes for the

lost husband. Although benefits can certainly be derived from this aspect of the lawyer-client relationship, it may also serve to reduce the likelihood that such women will turn to more suitable partners with whom there might be a future relationship. (Of course, if the attorney is indeed going to provide such a relationship, then this risk is not valid.) Attorneys' having affairs with their clients under these circumstances is not unknown. Obviously, statistics on this subject would be impossible to obtain. Clearly, whatever gratifications both parties may derive from this relationship, it is likely to compromise the attorney's objectivity with regard to handling the client's case. Obviously, in the mediation situation, when both spouses are present together throughout the course of the mediation, this is far less likely to occur. In short, I believe that the criticism that mediation does not as readily allow for an intimate, supportive relationship with the lawyer has some validity for some clients. However, as I hope the reader can appreciate, the opportunity for the psychologically supportive relationship between the attorney and the client is not without its risks and drawbacks.

Another criticism directed at mediation is that there is a risk of unfairness because only one professional party is involved in the decision-making process. Specifically, there is the risk that the mediator, no matter how neutral and impartial, is still likely to be subjective and prejudicial. I cannot deny the validity of this criticism. However, it also cannot be denied that the judicial process—especially adversary litigation—is not famous for the fairness of the decisions that emerge from it. I believe that if one compares the fairness of divorce arrangements that have resulted from adversary litigation and judicial decree with those that have evolved from mediation, there would be much more fairness in the mediation group. In the courtroom the clients have little opportunity to express freely their wishes in a relaxed and nonrestrictive setting. Only a small fraction of all pertinent data is presented to the presiding judge and even then under very stringent and restricted conditions. In mediation there is generally more time for the presentation of facts. The parties have much more opportunity for input as to what each considers to be fair, and this is probably the most important reason mediated agreements are more likely to be fair. Furthermore, if the parties suspect that a judge is not being fair, there is little if anything that they can do. They must sit silently and suffer impotent rage as they watch the judge act in a way that they consider capricious, irrational, and even insane. In mediation, they can remove themselves completely and instantaneously from an individual who is seen to be behaving in this way (whether the perception is justifiable or not). Both parties are then free to seek the services of someone whom *they* view to be fair and judicious. Although we have no good statistics on such a subjective matter as fairness (and we may never be able to gather them), I am convinced that there is far greater likelihood of fairness emerging from mediation than adversary litigation.

WHO IS BEST QUALIFIED TO SERVE AS MEDIATOR

The Attorney as Mediator

Up until the last few years, the members of the legal profession were strongly opposed to mediation. The opposition was often vehement. One argument given was that mediators were not serving within the confines of the adversary system, and this was enough to justify reluctance by the legal profession for lawyers serving in this capacity. Many attorneys were (and many still are) blindly committed to the adversary system as an institution that is not to be questioned. Others claimed that mediation was risky because of the possibility of partiality on the part of the mediator. These arguments, I believe, were often thin rationalizations for the basic fact that adversary litigation, especially when protracted, earns lawyers far more money than mediation. Mediation is not simply a threat to lawyers with regard to the divorce/custody issue. It can cause lawyers to lose income from future cases. Clients who use mediation for a divorce may then do so for the resolution of other disputes. Thus the attorney gets "shelved" for these future disputes as well.

The attitude of the legal profession toward mediation has changed in recent years. One does not hear lawyers talking as frequently about commitment to the adversary system as if it were the perfect system against which all other modes of dispute resolution must be judged. This has certainly been the case among younger lawyers who are showing much greater flexibility. Recently the family law section of the American Bar Association has set up a mediation division, The Family Mediation Institute. This gives the full sanction of the association to the process and represents a great step forward. This step clearly indicates that mediation is very much with us and "here to stay." It has reached the point of no return. The reasons for this change, however, are not simply benevolence and enlightenment on the part of the legal profession. Less noble factors were operative in bringing about the new receptivity. Attorneys came to appreciate that if they did not sanction mediation for their members, they might lose their "piece of the pie" to other professionals who were swarming into the field.

Many attorneys fear that support of mediation will result in a loss of money. However, their loss may not be that great. Many of the clients involved in protracted litigation become depleted of funds and never pay all their legal bills anyway. It is often difficult for attorneys to remove themselves from cases, even when the client can no longer pay. Furthermore, mediators often refer clients back to the originally referring nonmediator attorney for other legal services which they cannot ethically provide. So the mediator may become a new referral source for attorneys who do not involve themselves as mediators and vice versa.

Many attorneys hold that only lawyers should be mediators because the divorce process is basically one of dissolving a legal contract. Many mental health professionals, however, hold that extensive legal training is not necessary to conduct meaningful and successful mediation and that all one needs to learn are those aspects of the law that are directly relevant to the divorce process. A.G. Berg is a strong supporter of the view that the attorney's legal skills are more fundamental to the mediation process than are those of the mental health professional. I believe that for the more complex cases—those in which there are complicated legal and/or financial considerations—the lawyer is the preferable mediator. I do not believe, however, that *any* lawyer will do. Rather, the lawyer should be someone who has *specific training in marital/divorce law* and who, in addition, views mediation rather than adversary litigation as the preferable mode of resolving divorce disputes. It is important that the attorney have the deep conviction that mediation is the *preferable* course. Because mediation was not in vogue until the last few years, the ideal mediator would have to be someone who was trained in divorce and marital law in the traditional way and gradually shifted orientation.

It is important for the reader to appreciate that attorneys are not automatically knowledgeable enough to serve as a divorce mediator. Financial planning and tax law (so important to know about if one is to be a mediator) are not required courses in law schools. Clearly, one must know about these areas to serve as a divorce mediator. Furthermore, law schools do not generally require a course in family law. Obviously, one must know about family law if one is to mediate divorces. All of these courses are generally electives. Lawyers, however, are trained in basic legal principles and are in a better position to gain expertise in these areas than those who have had no such training. This is one of the reasons why I consider the lawyer to be the preferable mediator.

I believe that for the less complex cases a mental health professional, or other person who is specially trained, may serve as mediator. Such individuals, however, should still be oriented toward bringing in the services of an attorney when warranted. Furthermore, most agree that whoever does the mediation, the final documents have to be drawn up by attorneys if they are to satisfy the requirements of the courts and the law.

However, when the primary dispute relates to custody, I believe that mental health professionals serve better as mediators. The training of lawyers generally does not provide the kind of background necessary to mediate properly a custody dispute. As I stated above, not any lawyer can serve as a mediator; similarly, not any mental health professional can do so either. The individual must have special expertise in child psychology and psychiatry as well as family psychodynamics. Preferably, the individual should have had formal training in mediating custody/visitation disputes. Unfortunately, I know of few training programs for mental health professionals that provide formal courses in this area. Accordingly, mental health professionals still need to acquire for themselves "on the job training."

The Mental Health Professional as Mediator

In the early 1980s mediation became increasingly popular. At that time it appeared to be growing rapidly to the point where I had the feeling that the idea was "sweeping the nation." Mediation programs were set up all over the country. In such a climate, practitioners of all persuasions wanted to get in on "the action." During that period (1983) J. Folberg wrote: "Tight economic times may draw marginal practitioners of all types to what is viewed as a growth industry. No one has satisfactorily answered questions of certification, licensure, and standards." I believe that some of the "marginal practitioners" referred to by Folberg are mental health professionals. As mentioned, I do not believe that we in the mental health professions should be serving as primary mediators in complicated divorce/custody mediation. Rather, we may be able to serve in simple cases, but even here we should be under the supervision of attorneys particularly knowledgeable about mediation. Furthermore, I believe that we can perform a valuable service as *consultants* to attorneys who are serving as primary mediators. It is in this area that we can make our greatest contributions.

The mental health professional is sensitive to many of the psychological nuances that may be operating to impede the mediation process. For example, the mental health professional may be sensitive to a husband's giving away too much in order to assuage guilt over leaving his wife. Although the maneuver may momentarily ease his guilt, it is likely to produce chronic dissatisfaction with and resentment about the agreement and this may ultimately bring about its breakdown. Masochistic individuals, as well, may be too benevolent in what they offer in the service of causing themselves subsequent pain. Mental health professionals are trained to appreciate that in divorce disputes the conflict may be present at two levels: the manifest and the latent. What are ostensibly presented as the problems may only be the tip of the iceberg and there is often a hidden agenda. A husband and wife, for example, may seem to be fighting over money. However, they may be unable to resolve their differences or come to compromises because each one is unconsciously fighting for something else, such as power, security, or proof of affection. If there is no resolution of these underlying (sometimes unconscious) factors, there is not likely to be a successful resolution of the ostensible conflict.

Attorneys are particularly weak in the joint interview situation. The adversary system often precludes their conducting joint interviews in which each side has the opportunity to present its position in a relaxed and noncontrived setting. In fact, strict adherence to the rules of adjudication often precludes such joint interviews. Certainly in the courtroom this does not occur. Mental health professionals, especially those who work closely with families and do marital counseling, are particularly skilled in this kind of interview. They recognize that direct confrontations between the parties often brings out more information than is possible to obtain by single interviews. They know well that the joint interview is a far better way of learning "the truth" than the adversary system. They are trained to pick up the subtle nuances, gestures, intonations, or slips of the tongue that are often valuable sources of information. They recognize that the "whole is greater than the sum of the parts" insofar as the knowledge that can be obtained in these kinds of sessions. Because of this particular advantage over attorneys, the mental health professional can play a vital role in the mediation process.

Attorneys are taught that they should be unemotional in their dealings with their clients. In fact, they generally view emotions as compromising objectivity. Mental health professionals, in contrast, are very respectful of emotions and consider them to be valuable sources of information, not only about their patients, but themselves as well. With the exception of some with a strong commitment to the classical psychoanalytic theory, most mental health professionals appreciate that their own emotional responses can be valuable sources of information in their work with patients. The skilled therapist knows how to use these emotions judiciously and sensitively. This difference too places the mental health professional at an advantage when dealing with some of the special psychological problems that inevitably affect the mediation process.

Mental health professionals can help reduce animosities and this can make the mediation smoother and increase the likelihood that the parties will be willing to make the necessary compromises. For example, the mental health professional can help the parents understand that the children will commonly lie to them in order to ingratiate themselves to the parent to whom they are speaking at that particular time. Parents in the midst of divorce proceedings may injudiciously believe these fabrications to be truths. The mediator can help them appreciate what is going on. This reduces their anger and makes it more likely they will cooperate in the mediation process. The mental health professional can help a father whose child is being "brainwashed" by a mother appreciate that part of the scenario of deprecation has originated within the child himself (herself) and the alienation is not entirely due to the mother's programming. This too can lessen animosity. When this problem becomes severe, the child may develop a parental alienation syndrome (Chapter Six). Its etiology and pathogenesis are important to understand if one is to reduce the family problems that result, e.g., difficulties resolving a custody dispute. Here special therapeutic and legal approaches may be necessary (Chapter Nine) to alleviate this disorder.

The mental health professional can help a mother who is so blinded with rage at her husband that she wishes to cut off visitation. She has to be helped to realize that this will harm her children. Similarly, the father who is withholding money as a manifestation of anger and as a vengeance weapon also has to be helped to appreciate that he is hurting his children by this maneuver. A father who is not particularly involved with his children prior to the separation may propose to the mediator a heavy visitation program that involves frequent visits to the home. Sometimes this is a maneuver to effect a reconciliation, and the mediator has to recognize this as a specious motivation for frequent visitation. Supporting this frequency may be a disservice to the wife who wants a psychological as well as a physical separation from her husband.

D. T. Saposnek (1983) reports about a four-year-old girl who told her father during visitation that there was no food in the house and that he should please come over and put some peanut butter and jelly sandwiches in the refrigerator. The father, whose objectivity was blinded by his rage at the mother, believed that the girl was being deprived of food by the mother and initiated a petition for sole custody of the child. The mother, in response, counterpetitioned for reduction of visitation times as a retaliatory maneuver and as a bargaining chip in subsequent litigation. Neither saw that the girl was trying to effect some kind of reconciliation by so structuring events that it would behoove her father to come to the house. The mediator's help in enlightening these parents brought about significant decompression of the situation.

In the early to mid-1980s there were hundred of courses throughout the United States which provided short training programs in mediation for attorneys and mental health professionals. Unfortunately, many others, outside of these two professional areas, were also trained. Most often the courses were organized by attorneys and mental health professionals. The organizers claimed that the amount of legal knowledge necessary to be an effective mediator could be learned in a relatively short time, and that mental health professionals could easily master the legal and financial knowledge necessary for effective mediation. I was and still am in disagreement. I believe that some of these "trainers" did not appreciate that their expertise had come after many years of experience, and what seemed obvious and simple to them is not so to the novice. This is one of the manifestations of the expert. He (she) sees things extremely quickly, almost by reflex. But such learning does not generally take place overnight.

It took long years of training, knowledge, collection of data, and *experience*. There is no reason to believe that one can impart all this very quickly to the novice.

This is not to say that the people who are now functioning as mediators are not properly trained. Many of them are training themselves, many others are pioneers, but there are also many who have jumped on the bandwagon who are inadequate and incompetent. I never had formal training in custody litigation, and yet I am generally considered to be an expert in this area. I have never taken a course in custody litigation, rather I have learned on my own. I am sure that there are many others in the same position. And I am sure, as well, that there are many who present themselves as experts who are grossly incompetent.

As mentioned, I believe that the mental health professional is ill equipped to serve as a mediator in any divorce in which there is a significant amount of money and/or property. To give the reader an idea of the complexity of the financial issues that often have to be dealt with in such cases, I have itemized below a list of the topics "taught" in a few hours in one of the better divorce-mediation training programs.

> Child support and alimony
> Factors determining amount and duration of alimony
> Permanent vs. temporary alimony
> Child support as function of ability to pay
> "Industry" standards vs. real need
> Tax consequences of child support and alimony
> Adjustment to new living standards
> Income shortage
> Developing, verifying, and reducing budgets
> Cost accounting
> Treating short- and long-term debt
> Long-term financial planning
> Tax-saving strategies
> Handling life and medical insurance
> Cost-of-living increases
> Tax exemptions and tax return issues
> Doctrine of equitable distribution
> Assets to be included

Co-mingled property

Non-economic contributions

Problems of valuation in pensions, business, closely-held corporations, professional practices, tax shelters

Evaluating sale of marital home

Equitable distribution in conjunction with support

Revision of wills

Distribution of pension plans, stocks, bonds, and other securities

My hope is that the reader will view the list as mind-boggling. Furthermore, most of the aforementioned are not taught as required courses in the vast majority of law schools. Thus we can appreciate even more how naive it is for a mental health professional to mediate these issues. We must remember, as well, that all of the above relate to the financial aspects of the separation. Legal considerations can be equally mind-boggling, especially as they overlap with the financial.

At the time I am writing this (early 1989), the enthusiasm for mediation has leveled off somewhat. Many of the people trained in the aforementioned crash programs were never able to make a living doing mediation. This resulted in part from general dissatisfaction (among lay people as well as among legal and mental health professionals) with the results of mediation conducted by ill-trained individuals. As a result of this leveling, fewer people are entering the field; but higher quality people are being trained. There is now slow and steady growth, but there are few good formal training programs. Most people have "on the job training" or have taken the kinds of courses conducted under private auspices by people who set up their own mediation training centers. Also, many courts now utilize clinics and private mediation centers in a kind of liaison operation.

When the mediator is a mental health professional with a classical psychoanalytic orientation, this may compromise the mediation process. Such individuals often take a passive approach to the mediation process and they view their role as being primarily catalytic. This can unnecessarily prolong the process and even contribute to its failure. Mediation is not a place for wishy-washy neutrality. Rather, I consider the preferable mediator to be someone who is reasonably authoritarian, but not dictatorial. One should be interrupting and discouraging irrelevant digressions. One should be active and confrontational, but always in a benevolent fashion. I have often said that "Benevolent despotism is the best system of government for children and other primitive peoples." I believe this principle holds for the mediation process. D. T. Saposnek (1983) emphasizes this point. He states: "When the mediator's presence and style are confident and authoritative, the spouses will be respectful. When the mediator's style is ambivalent and weak, the spouses' attempts at power and assertions and intimidation will be excessive. In many ways the mediator must present himself or herself as a strong confident parent figure to the parents, since their struggle is often not unlike those of siblings squabbling over and competing for mutual possessions."

Mediators who come from the mental health professions make a grave mistake if they believe they can combine mediation with psychotherapy. This is an extremely risky combination, and it is likely to compromise both the mediation and the therapy. There are mediators who act as therapists during the mediation by interrupting the proceedings and then switching into the role of therapist for one or even both of the parties. They will justify this interruption with the rationalization that the mediation has bogged down and that one or both of the parties need some individual therapy before the mediation can proceed. This compromises both processes. If the mediator interrupts the mediation for private sessions with one of the parties for alleged therapeutic purposes, it is bound to compromise the relationship with the noninvolved party. The nontreated party is likely to resent the special relationship that has developed between the spouse and the mediator (now serving as therapist). In addition, transferential reactions, which are central to therapy, are likely to evolve. The feelings attendant to this process cannot but compromise the mediation for the patient and possibly even for the therapist because of his (her) own countertransferential feelings (that also arise quite often in treatment).

Therapy involves exploration into unconscious processes to a significant degree and this, if done properly, can be time consuming. The mediation process is designed to be short. Also, successful therapy requires a confidential relationship with the patient. Successful mediation requires open communication of all issues between both parties. There is a direct contradiction here. If the therapeutic confidential relationship precludes revelations to the other spouse, then the mediation is completely sabotaged. Furthermore, the mediator who brings the client into therapy might justifiably be criticized for using the mediation process in the service of earning extra money. This is likely to reduce referrals for the mediator. And, if the mediator treats one of the parties afterwards, it would be a good argument for bringing the whole mediation agreement into question in subsequent litigation in that the mediator could be accused of having used the process to attract clients for treatment.

Some family therapists believe that they can serve as divorce mediators after their relationship has been one of therapist. This too is injudicious. If the mediation breaks down, at least one of the parties has had to be dissatisfied with the mediation. That party cannot continue meaningful therapy with a therapist toward whom he (she) has these negative feelings and criticisms. The patient cannot separate the two functions and say I dislike him (her) as a mediator but have confidence in him (her) as a therapist. Associated with dissatisfaction are loss of trust and respect and these feelings will inevitably spill over into the therapeutic relationship in a compromising way.

Choosing the Mediator

This may be very difficult. At the present time there are no formal requirements and no state certifications. It is legal for any individual to go into the business of mediation and mediation is still a "growth industry." My advice to people is this: If the family is reasonably well off and there are significant holdings (investments, retirement funds, property, etc.) then the divorcing parties *must* utilize the services of one or more individuals who are highly competent in both the law and finance. The ideal person for this would be an attorney who has experience both in marriage and divorce law and in the financial issues attendant to divorce. If there is any question about the attorney's competence in the financial realm, then an expert in this area should be brought in as a co-mediator or, at least, as a consultant to the attorney. For individuals with minimal holdings the mediator might well be a person such as a mental health professional. However, this individual must consult an attorney to draw up the final mediation agreement. The fact that the mental health professional has taken a course in mediation may not provide very much information regarding the individual's training and experience. Many of these courses are "fly by night" arrangements that are open to anyone who is willing to pay the fee (roughly $1000). If, however, the mental health professional mediator can demonstrate significant experience (and this may be difficult because the field is a young one) then one is justified in having more confidence in him (her). If a person has been actively involved in teaching mediation, it is more likely that the person is competent. In recent years a few graduate schools have instituted programs in mediation. A graduate of such a program is probably qualified. Furthermore, law schools now are starting to give courses in mediation, and an attorney who has taken such a course is likely to be qualified.

Because no generally recognized formal criteria have yet been set up for certification as a mediator, the public is in a very precarious position. I hope that this will be a temporary situation and that formal training requirements will be set up soon. Until that time the general public are very much guinea pigs from whom many aspiring experts are learning. However, the situation here is no different from most other new fields. The first subjects often serve in the guinea pig role and may have little choice other than to do so because the future experts are still in the early phases of their development. In spite of this drawback, mediation still offers the best hope for separating couples to resolve their problems in a civilized way.

WHO SHOULD RECEIVE MEDIATION

People Who Are Candidates for Mediation

Not every divorcing couple is a candidate for mediation. Both parties (and I emphasize *both*) must satisfy certain criteria if the mediation is to be successful. If only one of the parties satisfies the prerequisites I describe here, there is little if any chance that the mediation will be successful. In fact, in such situations the ethical mediator will interrupt the process and refuse further services to both clients, even though only one may lack the qualifications for the procedure.

Receptivity to Full Disclosure   A crucial prerequisite for successful mediation is that both parties be willing to disclose *all* pertinent information. Litigating spouses will often have to resort to court-ordered disclosure in order to obtain information about the other party's financial situation. Court-ordered disclosure and mediation do not go together. In mediation each party must be willing to divulge freely and openly all pertinent information. Related to the willingness to disclose are feelings of mutual trust. And this trust must exist not only throughout the course of the mediation but *following* the process if the compromises and resolutions are to be effectively implemented. The ultimate success of the mediation depends upon each individual's trust that the other will fulfill the commitments of the agreement. This relates not only to financial obligations but to adhering to visitation schedules, commitment to the children's welfare, and a variety of other matters that involve mutual commitments following the divorce.

Ability to Compromise   To be successful candidates for mediation the parties must be willing to *compromise*, rather than be bent on winning. They must appreciate that "half a loaf is better than none" and that there is no perfect solution to most of the conflicts with which they are dealing. Rather, a whole series of compromises will be necessary if there is to be a relatively peaceful and equitable solution to the problems they are facing. Furthermore, they must be able to consider as possibly valid the other party's position, in spite of the fact that they are filled with a variety of painful emotions attendant to the divorce process. This may be particularly difficult at that time. It involves a conscious suppression of emotional reactions in order to allow reasonable and logical thought processes to emerge. The parties must be able to appreciate that most of their solutions will involve selecting what is the least painful of a variety of painful options. This is an extremely important point. There is hardly a conflictual issue in divorce that does not involve this principle. There is *no* happy solution for most of the problems; rather the two parties hope to suffer as little grief as possible by selecting the least painful of various grievous choices.

Capacity to Communicate   People involved in mediation must be able to communicate well. It is important that the mediators themselves serve as models for good communication. If the mediator does not communicate well, it is likely that he (she) will compromise the communication capacity of the participants. They must be able to comply with the mediator's interruptions when communication is faulty and to be receptive to the mediator's comments that are designed to enhance accurate communication. The parents must appreciate that the best kind of communication takes place when the parties focus on substantive concrete issues and avoid generalities. Furthermore, they must appreciate that their communication is likely to be impaired if they are overwhelmed by a wide range of emotions related to the divorce: feelings of grief, despair, rage, and so on. It is in this area that the services of the mental health professional may prove useful. If the individuals deal better with their emotional reactions they are more likely to be logical in their thinking and thereby communicate better. The mediation process may improve communication between the parties and this improvement may persist beyond the termination of the formal mediation procedure. This enhanced communication capacity may be viewed as one of the potential fringe benefits of mediation. As mentioned, adversary litigation does just the opposite. From the outset, communication between the parties is compromised significantly, especially when messages are transmitted through attorneys and other intermediaries.

Capacity to Cooperate   People who are to be successful candidates for mediation must have a reasonable capacity to cooperate in the mediation proceedings. Clearly, if they could cooperate to a significant degree, they might not have separated. We are dealing here with a situation in which there has been lack of cooperation in many areas, and yet the individuals must still have preserved enough capacity to cooperate to involve themselves meaningfully in the mediation process. The separation between these two areas is possible for some and not for others. Sometimes the mediation process improves cooperation and provides the participants with an experience that lays the groundwork for more effective cooperation in the future. This is another potential fringe benefit of mediation. Clearly, adversary litigation does just the opposite. It is extremely unlikely, if not impossible, for litigation to improve the individuals' capacity to cooperate.

People Who Are Not Candidates for Mediation

Reluctance to Disclose Finances   Conflicts over money are at the root of a vast majority of divorce conflicts. With the goal of getting as much money as possible, or paying as little as possible, individuals will often hide money from one another and sequester assets. People who do this are not candidates for mediation. Without openness and honesty the mediation becomes a farce. Accordingly, individuals who anticipate hiding such information should not waste their time on a mediator. For these individuals mediation is absurd, and ethical mediators will remove themselves from the mediation process as soon as they suspect what is going on. Such individuals have little choice but to resort to adversary litigation, because the party from whom the information is being withheld is likely to engage the services of an attorney in order to obtain the information. This generally is quite expensive: it requires court orders to bring in accountants (sometimes in teams, if the person is rich enough).

In the legal profession, the word *discovery* refers to the process by which one party gains information from the other, especially about financial matters. Obviously, discovery is extremely time consuming, may cost tens of thousands of dollars, and may last for years. That this is a crazy thing to do is obvious. However, some individuals are so enamored of money and/or the desire to wreak vengeance on a spouse that they blind themselves to the fact that they are probably giving more money to strangers (lawyers and accountants) than to the spouse (if they were to have agreed to give higher payments at the outset). Furthermore, one cannot translate into dollars the psychological toll and stress involved in such maneuvers. Last, one must add psychiatric bills to the money that is spent in many cases as a result of such a foolhardy approach to divorce. Because money and custody issues are often so intertwined, the inability of divorcing parties to utilize mediation for resolving financial conflicts generally precludes its use in custody conflicts. In selected cases, however, it may be possible.

Specious Motivations for Seeking Custody   Individuals in conflict over their children may be candidates for mediation if they genuinely have deep love and affection for them. However, those who utilize specious motivations are not candidates for mediation of their custody conflicts. Rather than love and affection for their children, they are using psychopathological reasons for attempting to gain custody. And this is the area where the expertise of the mental health professional may be helpful.

Vengeance   One common reason is vengeance. There is no better way to wreak vengeance on a hated spouse than to try to wrest away the partner's most treasured possessions: the children. The most extreme form of vengeful anger occurs when a spouse has been left for another party. There is much wisdom to the old saying, "Hell hath no fury like a woman scorned," and spouses in such situations, in their futility and rage, may use the children as weapons in their war of vengeance. They are so blinded by their rage that they may not be able to involve themselves in the kinds of compromises crucial to a successful mediation process.

"Going Through the Motions"   Another example of specious motivation that compromises mediation is the situation in which a parent basically does not want to have custody but "goes through the motions" of requesting it in order to assuage guilt over that fact. In our society there is no stigma for a man to say publicly that he recognizes that his former wife would make a better custodial parent for the children, and he therefore did not seek primary custody. Women who make such statements are generally viewed with distrust and their maternal capacity questioned. Many women who recognize that their husbands would make better custodial parents will attempt to gain custody without genuinely desiring it. Some of these women may actually litigate, but do so with the underlying hope that they will lose. Then they can blame the loss of the children on the judge or mental health professional who recommended that their husbands be the primary custodial parents. Some may go to mediation for this purpose. In the mediation process they will typically be "flexible" and will readily "compromise." A skilled mediator will recognize such spurious motivation and appreciate that such a woman needs to use the mediator as someone she can blame for having "twisted her arm" into agreeing that the husband should be the primary custodial parent. There are fathers who will also "go through the motions" for custody, hoping secretly to lose. This has been especially true in recent years since joint custody has come into vogue. Mediators do well, therefore, to look for these hidden agendas when mediating custody disputes. Some people need to go to court, and lose, and then be able vociferously to blame the judge for his "idiotic decision." Others save money and time by using a mediator for this same purpose. In such cases the mediator may have to take a more forceful and less catalytic role in order to provide these individuals with the excuse that they were "railroaded" into the decision by a shrewd and

coercive mediator. However, under those circumstances, the mediator need not fear that such parties will complain to ethics committees or institute malpractice suits. Rather, they are secretly pleased with the decision and are thankful that the mediator has "imposed" it on them.

Need for a "Bargaining Chip"   Some individuals will use their attempts to gain custody as a "bargaining chip" in the divorce negotiations. These parents blind themselves to the psychologically detrimental effects of using their children for this purpose. Here the money issue can again compromise the mediation. There is a tradition that the children stay with the house because of the general recognition that they are less capable of tolerating changes in neighborhood, friendships, and schooling. At the time when mothers traditionally got custody, the children, the house, and the mother went together as a package. Now that fathers have a greater likelihood than before of gaining custody, they know well that, in that instance, it will be the mother who will probably have to leave the home and they will be able to remain in it with the children. It will be the mother then who will have to adjust to the new neighborhood and the other changes attendant to moving out of the home. Furthermore, living with children is less expensive than supporting them from another domicile. People who are seeking custody primarily because of the desire to avoid these anxieties and tensions may not be good candidates for mediation. Their motives for wanting the children are specious, and they are less likely to be receptive to the compromises that mediation inevitably entails.

These spurious motivations need not preclude the possibility of meaningful mediation. Rather, they are potential contaminants — which might be worked through if the mediator has been alerted to them and if the parties are willing to face squarely their existence. Once they are "out on the table" there is a greater possibility of their being resolved. If they remain hidden, they inevitably compromise the mediation process.

Presence of Significant Psychopathology   People with serious psychological problems are not generally candidates for mediation. They do not have the stability and psychological capacity to involve themselves meaningfully in the process. They may not be able to bring their emotions under control enough to consider logically their various options. In this category are people who are psychologically weak and who therefore may not be as receptive to mediation as those who are psychologically stronger. The weaker person, from feelings of impotence, may need an attorney to provide the support and strength to tolerate divorce negotiations. Psychologically stronger people have greater confidence in their own capacity to mediate successfully. They have confidence in their ability to control their own fates. People with severe psychological disturbance do not have such self-confidence.

Where physical abuse and physical intimidation are taking place in a marriage, the divorcing parties are not generally candidates for mediation. If a wife, for example, fears that her husband's dissatisfaction with the arrangement might result in his beating her, she may very well agree to an injudicious arrangement. Skilled mediators, of course, will recognize this situation and not agree to the unfavorable "compromise." In some cases the mediator may not be aware of the wife's fear of beatings if she divulges the fact that she is so abused. The ethical mediator will not agree to the inequitable terms which such a wife might be willing to accept.

When the mediator detects psychopathological processes interfering with the smooth flow of the mediation, he (she) should bring in a mental health professional to assess the situation. Although therapy may be recommended, only the naive mediator will try to coerce a participant into treatment. Treatment is not likely to be effective under such circumstances. It is relatively rare for a person who is forced into treatment to profit from it. It is inappropriate for the mediator to say, "If you don't go into treatment, I won't continue the mediation." The mediator's position should be: "If you wish to have treatment, you might find that you might benefit from it. You might then find yourself in a better position to profit from mediation. Right now I don't think mediation can be successful. If you decide to go into treatment and if, after that, you think you're in a better position to profit from mediation, I'll be happy to see you again and reassess the situation." This approach places the burden on the client, is noncoercive, and is more likely to bring about results. The mediator is basically saying to the client: "If *you* want to profit from mediation, you'll have to do something to change yourself." I refer to this as the *ball-is-in-your-court-baby principle* (1986b). I find it a useful tactic in psychotherapy and I recommend it highly. Last, for the many reasons already mentioned, it is inappropriate for the mediator to serve as the therapist for one of the parties in that this will compromise significantly the mediation process.

Presence of Child Abuse   Another group of parents who are not candidates for mediation are those whose physical or psychological abuse of the children is so formidable that it behooves the mediator to report the parent(s) to the proper community authorities. This break in confidentiality, which is required by law, may serve the interests of the children and the protection that it thereby provides them; however, it is likely to destroy the mediation because the divulgence has destroyed the confidentiality. Furthermore, it cannot but produce distrust of the mediator and significant resentment. Without trust there can be no mediation and with significant hostility toward the mediator there can be no mediation that can be considered meaningful. J. Folberg and A. Taylor (1984) advise mediators to include in their stipulations in the initial agreement that the parents recognize that if child abuse becomes apparent the mediator will report it to the proper authorities. Although this may reduce the distrust element, I believe that reporting abuse would still compromise significantly the mediation procedure, especially because of the hostility that such referral would engender. Accordingly, my final view on this is that child-abusing parents are not likely to be candidates for meaningful mediation.

People Who Play "Chicken"   R. H. Mnookin and L. Korn-hauser (1979) describe a type of couple who are not candidates for mediation to be those who are heavily involved in "calling the bluff" of the other party. Each feels that giving in represents cowardice. They are like the teenagers who play the game of "Chicken," in which they set their cars on a collision course to see who veers off first. Clearly, this is an extremely dangerous game and many deaths result from it. Similarly, parents involved in custody disputes may play "Chicken" and end up in court destroying each other.

The Excessively Confident   Mnookin and Kornhauser describe another group who are not candidates for mediation: individuals who overestimate their chances of winning in litigation. They are so confident that their cause is a worthy one, and so sure that the judge will award them custody, that they are not interested in mediation. Attorneys, also, are likely to support these expectations—especially because they do not have the opportunity to get full information from the other side. As one who has served as an impartial examiner to courts for many years, I have witnessed this phenomenon many times. Some attorneys will gladly enlist my aid as an impartial examiner, so sure are they that their client's position is faultless and unassailable. Many are struck with amazement when my final report demonstrates how misguided they were. These attorneys have been completely taken in by their clients. Not having gotten direct input from the other side they have been "led down the garden path." And this is just one of my many criticisms of the adversary system and one of its drawbacks when utilized in divorce and custody disputes.

Stallers   People who use stalling in order to gain certain advantages in the divorce settlement procedure are not candidates for mediation. Mediation is designed to be a short process, in order to help people "get it over with quickly." People who believe they have something to gain by stalling are not going to commit themselves to mediation in a meaningful way. Generally, in a custody dispute, the parent with whom the children are living recognizes that the longer the children stay, the greater the likelihood they will opt to remain residing in the same household. This parent is not likely to mediate meaningfully the custody aspect of the separation. Or, a mother may recognize that if her husband meets a new woman and wants to marry her, she will have more leverage with regard to support and alimony payments because of his eagerness to dissolve the marriage and marry the new woman. She too is likely to stall and not make meaningful use of mediation.

People Who Thrive on Conflict   In order for mediation to be successful, *both* participants must have the desire to end the conflict. This is not invariably the case. There are some individuals who thrive on conflict; in fact, it may fill up the vacuum of their lives. This is often the case with women whose husbands have left them and who have not involved themselves in a new relationship. The ongoing conflict can serve as a way for them to remain involved with their former husbands. They work on the principle that it is preferable to fight him for the rest of their lives than to be lonely indefinitely. There are men also who do not let go, whose lives are left empty by the divorce, and who use the ongoing litigation as a vehicle for giving their lives purpose. Court-ordered mediation (to be discussed below) does not give proper respect to this factor. People who want to continue the conflict are not likely to be successful with mediation. Rather, they litigate for years, clog the courts, and enrich the attorneys.

Client Disparity   If there is a significant disparity in the financial sophistication of the two parties, the individuals may not be meaningful candidates for mediation. Sometimes this is related to lower intelligence on the part of one participant; on other occasions it merely relates to education and experiences with finances. One role of the mediator is to help the less sophisticated party appreciate some of the subtle nuances of the financial arrangement. The party who is significantly incapable of grasping such matters is generally not a candidate for mediation because that person cannot make meaningful decisions. This is especially the case when the financial issues are quite complex.

Power-Hungry Individuals People with an inordinate need to gain power over other individuals are not likely to be good candidates for mediation. And the struggle for power underlies many divorce conflicts. In fact, it may have been one of the factors contributing to the divorce. This element then becomes played out in the divorce proceedings, whether in mediation or adversary litigation. To such individuals power is viewed as esteem enhancing and being overpowered by others is considered to be one of the greatest sources of humiliation—something that should be avoided under any circumstances. Such people may even view a *compromise* as a humiliation. Power-hungry individuals may attempt to gain power over the mediator, so great is the drive. In such cases there is the possibility that the mediation may be salvaged by the intervention of the skilled mental health professional. If this fails, the mediation may not be possible.

Veterans of Protracted Litigation Couples who have been involved for lengthy periods in adversary litigation are not likely candidates for mediation. Some people can switch from adversary proceedings into mediation. Sometimes even attorneys sympathetic to mediation will advise their clients to interrupt the adversarial proceedings and try to mediate their problems. However, some people in this category have been so swept up in the adversary litigation that they have become obsessed with "winning." And their attorneys, as well, may lose sight of what is going on, so drawn up are they in the "war." Clearly, such people are not candidates for mediation. They might have been had they not involved themselves initially in adversary proceedings.

The Question of Third Party (Nonspouse) Involvement J. Pearson and N. Thoennes (1982) state that mediation is not applicable when the dispute involves third parties such as grandparents, lovers, or new spouses. I do not agree. These parties can be brought into the mediation process. In fact, I can think of no better way to resolve such disputes than to bring them in. I am not claiming that one will be successful in a high percentage of cases. I am only claiming that of the various ways of reducing disputes when third parties are involved the best is to bring them together in the same room. In mediation votes are often taken. This does not involve formal balloting, but merely each of the parties stating an opinion. Usually this involves three people, the two parents and the mediator. Often, the mediator does not vote. Accordingly, the "vote" is often a "tie." When other parties are brought in, there is a greater likelihood that there will be a majority and that the person who "loses" in the balloting may consider the possibility that his (her) position was injudicious. Furthermore, and of more importance, these individuals can often provide data previously unavailable to the mediator. They have been there; they have been observers to various events under dispute, and they may be in a far better position than the mediator to come to conclusions regarding a wide variety of incidents brought into the mediation. Chapter Eight provides some excellent examples of the use of these outside parties in the custody evaluation.

The Question of Passive Individuals   Those who criticize mediation frequently claim that it is particularly risky for passive individuals who may succumb to an overbearing spouse. The most common example provided is that of the passive-dependent woman who will be subjugated by her more aggressive, overbearing husband and will thereby agree to a series of compromises that are much to her disadvantage. Feminists especially who criticize mediation point out this risk for women. I am not in agreement with those who hold this criticism. It is the role of the mediator to be aware of such imbalances in the mediating parties and to ensure that a weaker party is protected under these circumstances. Serving as a catalyst or facilitator does not necessarily mean that the individual passively and uncritically accepts every compromise. If this were the case, then the mediator would not need any training or any capacity to assess the judiciousness of each of the compromises. Furthermore, the memorandum of agreement is often reviewed by attorneys who represent each of the parents. It is the role of these individuals to review the agreement, especially with an eye to protecting his (her) client from such exploitation. These independent counselors, as well, generally have input to the mediator in order to help resolve such inequities. My experience has been that this criticism often serves as a rationalization for those who object to mediation on other grounds, especially the grounds that mediation earns lawyers much less money than protracted litigation.

Mandatory Mediation

Many states have instituted mandatory mediation. Like most things, there are both advantages and disadvantages to this policy. It certainly has the advantage of using court influence to bring individuals who might not have otherwise availed themselves of it into the mediation process. And there is no question that some of these people derive a benefit that they might not have otherwise enjoyed. In most states at this time, one must make private arrangements for mediation. It is not provided as a public service. In California, however, it is provided as a public service. H. McIsaac (1983) describes the mandatory mediation program in California. Briefly, the mediator first meets with the attorneys to gain information about the parties. The clients receive an orientation that includes a film describing the effects of divorce on children. The mediator then meets with the parents both separately and together and, if the mediator considers it necessary, interviews the children as well. The mediator may also interview significant others, such as stepparents, grandparents, or anyone else who has significant involvement with the children. McIsaac is a strong adherent to the view that "anyone left out of the negotiation who has an interest in its outcome may sabotage the agreement." I am in full support of his position and actively involve these other people in my attempts to resolve custody conflicts. In Los Angeles (where McIsaac is director of the county mediation program), the mediation generally takes four to five hours, the agreement is sent to the court and copies are then made available to the attorneys (who have ten days to respond). If the mediation proves successful, the agreement is incorporated into the divorce decree. The mediator is available for future consultation to work out subsequent problems. If there is no agreement, then no report is sent to the court. The parents then proceed along the adversarial track.

The courts and legislators recognize that one cannot expect to be 100 percent successful with mandatory mediation. There will always be some individuals who will not be candidates for mediation, under any circumstances. Fifteen to twenty years ago I was very unsympathetic to the concept of mandatory mediation. This was primarily the result of my psychoanalytic training wherein coercive techniques were generally considered antitherapeutic and likely to cause more harm than good. Over the years I have changed my position. I have come to appreciate that certain individuals can ultimately profit from a therapeutic arrangement that may have initially been coerced. Courts have the power to provide such coercion; others generally do not. I have known situations in which the judge has ordered both clients and both attorneys to sequester themselves in a room in the courthouse and not come out until they have hammered out a mediated program. In such marathon negotiations the individuals have sometimes been successful in resolving their disputes. Often they reach the point of such weariness that they agree to compromises they would not have previously considered reasonable. Although their weariness may have certainly played a role in their receptivity to compromise, the parties have still had the input and supervision of their attorneys to help ensure that none of the compromises were injudicious.

THE MEDIATION PROCESS

The Various Mediation Models

Mediation Followed by Independent Representation   As mentioned, mediation is very much in its infancy. There is much we have yet to learn regarding which models will be most effective and which will prove ineffective and even detrimental. The model that I prefer at this time is one in which the parents consult with the mediator at the outset, *before* consulting individual attorneys. If the mediation is successful, then a *Memorandum of Agreement* is drawn up and the parties have this reviewed by their independent attorneys. However, it is important that the attorneys chosen for this role be individuals who are sympathetic to the mediation process and/or serve themselves as mediators for other clients. The independent attorneys review the agreement in order to ensure that their clients have been dealt with fairly in the mediation process. The attorneys should be willing to talk with and even meet with the mediator in order to resolve any difficulties that may still be present. When all further problems have been resolved, then the parties can go to court for an uncontested divorce. In this model the mediating attorneys are not serving as attorneys; rather, they are serving as mediators. Accordingly, the mediator cannot be considered to be doing anything unethical such as representing both parties simultaneously. This structure is generally acceptable in most states, even those in which mediation has not yet enjoyed much popularity among lawyers and judges. I say *not yet* because I am certain that mediation is the wave of the future, is here to stay, and all 50 states will ultimately be utilizing it. The reader will note that when introducing this model I presented it as the one that I prefer "at this time." By those words I was referring to mediation within a society that still subscribes strongly to the adversary system. As I described in Chapter One (and as I will discuss further in Chapter Thirteen), the three-phase program that I am proposing also involves mediation, but completely removed from the possibility of adversarial proceedings.

Co-mediation   Another model is that of co-mediation. Here there are two mediators instead of one, working together with the couple. Generally, one of the mediators is an attorney and the other a mental health professional. The rationale for this approach is that many of the issues involved relate to psychological difficulties and a mental health professional being available throughout the course of the mediation increases the likelihood of its success. This model can also serve to circumvent one of the problems inherent in the model in which there is only one mediator. In that model a parent of the sex opposite to that of the mediator may feel that the mediator is biased. Co-mediation can avoid this problem when one of the mediators is male and the other is female. Co-mediation, of course, is likely to cost more than mediation by a single individual. However, it lessens the likelihood of the mediator's need to bring in a consultant.

I believe that there are many situations in which co-mediation is unnecessarily utilized. This is particularly true of cases in which the mental health professional is brought in when there is little real need for the services of such a person. As mentioned, the issues over which there is conflict most often are property, finances, and legal rights. To routinely bring mental health professionals into mediation is sometimes exploitive of the client. I am certain that some mental health professionals who involve themselves in this arrangement do so because mediation is a "growth industry" and in many areas there is a paucity of patients and keen competition for them. There are, however, cases in which psychological problems are obviously interfering with the smooth progress of the mediation. In such cases co-mediation may very well be the preferable modality.

A mediation model that I have not seen referred to in the literature is one in which the couple uses a mediation team consisting of the family attorney and the family accountant. This can be especially useful if the attorney has been involved intimately in the family's estate planning and will revisions. Both of these individuals are clearly knowledgeable about the couple's financial situation and need not "start from scratch" as others would who might be brought in to serve their functions. Obviously, one of the advantages of this program is that there can be no question about honest disclosure of finances. Each party is completely certain that all information in this area is being disclosed. These two individuals then can draw up the *Memorandum of Agreement* for submission to review by independent counselors. If this arrangement is to work, both parties must have confidence in these two professionals and believe that they will remain impartial. One risk of this form of mediation is that the mediators were not (and are not likely to be) strangers to the parents. They may bring to the mediation biases that antedated the separation and, in their desire to maintain good relationships with both parties, may compromise their objectivity. Although this is a rare form of co-mediation, I have had some experience with it (admittedly limited) and my initial reactions are quite positive. I recommend it strongly for consideration in selected cases.

Litigation Followed by Mediation Another mediation model that has been proposed is one in which the clients begin in the traditional adversary way with each party represented by an independent attorney. Then, they engage the services of a mediator to whom both attorneys have input. After a *Memorandum of Agreement* is drawn up, the document is reviewed by the independent counselors. I am not in favor of this model. The main risk is that the clients will get so swept up in the early adversary proceedings that they will not then have the capacity to involve themselves meaningfully in the mediation. As discussed in previous chapters, adversary proceedings have a way of developing a life of their own, independent of the original conflict which brought the clients to seek legal representation. The parties become so embroiled in the conflict that they are not likely to "switch tracks" and proceed calmly and meaningfully on a more neutral course. Furthermore, this model introduces three attorneys from the outset and is therefore likely to be more expensive. It has not gained widespread utilization and I am not sorry about this.

Shuttle Mediation Another mediation option is sometimes referred to as shuttle mediation. Here, the mediator meets alternately with the husband and wife. This model is based on labor mediation in which the shuttle approach is frequently used. When applied to couples it is often most applicable to people who become so enraged or otherwise emotionally involved with one another, when in the same room together, that they require a shuttle approach. One of the disadvantages of this approach is that it does not provide the couple with the opportunity to experience good communication and cooperation or to have an experience that attempts to help them reach this goal. Good mediation provides this fringe benefit. Furthermore, I believe distrust is engendered by this method. Each party cannot but wonder what is said in privacy about him (her). The mediator is viewed as someone who has "secrets" which are not to be divulged but which are pertinent and relevant. So a triangle of distrust is created, each party with the mediator and the parties with one another.

I recognize that people who are prone to be violent with one another or so enraged that they cannot negotiate meaningfully may have to be separated. In such cases I would recommend that these people be referred for separate counseling by a mental health professional in order to attempt to reduce the rage. Then they might be candidates for mediation. I recognize, however, that the shuttle approach, in spite of its disadvantages, is still better than courtroom adjudication. J. Folberg and A. Taylor (1984) are also dubious about the use of private caucuses in mediation. They believe that there is a danger that the participants might use the private sessions to manipulate the mediator. Without the other party being present, there is a definite likelihood that this may take place. The mediator may not even realize that he (she) is being so manipulated. The parents know one another far better than the mediator and may easily pick up maneuvers that the mediator may be blind to. Just as good therapy requires a trusting relationship with the therapist, mediation is not likely to be successful when there is distrust of the mediator. And the shuttle mediation approach is likely to engender distrust and thereby compromise significantly a central element in the successful mediation process.

The Initial Meeting with the Mediator

Most mediators agree that it is highly desirable for the mediator to meet with both parties together at the outset. In fact, most agree that it is highly desirable that both parties are seen together throughout the full course of the mediation. Private sessions tend to engender distrust. There are mediators who will meet with one party and then the other at the outset. I am in strong disagreement with this practice. Although the mediation may ultimately be successful, it is a poor start and lessens the likelihood of success. The party who is seen second cannot but wonder what the first party told the mediator, what distortions were presented, and what corrections need to be made in order to "get the record straight." And, after the second party has met with the mediator, the first party is likely to have similar concerns. These unnecessary worries and preoccupations can be obviated easily by seeing both parties alone at the outset and strictly avoiding private meetings throughout the course of the mediation.

In the initial meeting the mediator should outline some of the advantages of mediation over adversary litigation. This may help motivate the clients to mediate. In the context of such a discussion the mediator points out the costs of mediation vs. adversary litigation and apprises the clients at that time of the exact mediation fee and the method of payment.

Most mediators have a document that they review with the parties at that point. This document is generally referred to as the *Agreement to Mediate* or the *Preliminary Statement.* It is generally read over carefully with the parties and they are asked to sign it—signifying their commitment to uphold its stipulations.

The document usually designates the mediator by name and indicates the agreement by the parties to retain the mediator's services. It generally states clearly that the mediator is not serving as an attorney to represent either the husband or the wife. It confirms what the mediator has stated verbally, namely, that the parties have been advised to engage the services of independent counsel to review the final agreement document. The parties agree to divulge all matters regarding property, finances, and so forth, and to be willing to submit statements regarding these matters to the mediator and other experts whom the mediator may retain. A statement is made about the neutrality of such consultants, and the parties agree that their services will be enlisted when necessary.

Some comments are generally made about the final *Memorandum of Agreement*. For example, it may not only state the areas in which agreement was made but also list areas in which there are still unresolved problems. The parties agree that the mediator shall send copies of the memorandum to their independent attorneys.

The *Preliminary Statement* usually provides a provision that either party may withdraw unilaterally from the mediation at any time and that the mediator may discontinue the mediation if he (she) believes that one or both of the parties are not candidates for involving themselves in the process in a meaningful way. The most common reason for the mediator's withdrawal is the recognition that one or both of the parties are not providing full disclosure of all financial assets. An important point in this initial *Agreement to Mediate* is the agreement of the clients that the mediator shall not be brought into court in any subsequent adversarial proceedings and that any of the information obtained in the mediation process is not admissible in court.

Appendix II is the document I require parents to sign when I mediate a custody dispute. Its primary purpose is to ensure that I am never brought into adversarial proceedings, either directly or indirectly. When I first drew up this document, about ten years ago, I was concerned that some judge might tear it up and subpoena me into court to provide testimony. This has never happened. I have, however, received letters from attorneys requesting information. Most often the letter has been accompanied by a release signed by the parent who is presumably releasing me to provide the information. In these cases I have made a photocopy of this document, and written on the bottom a note along these lines: "In response to your letter of (date) please see above." I then sign my name. This has worked so far. Over the years I have become increasingly secure that documents like this will work even in vicious adversarial proceedings. Courts are becoming increasingly respectful of mediators and increasingly appreciative of their value in reducing court pressures and diverting an ever increasing percentage of potential litigants from adversarial litigation. Not to recognize such documents reduces the likelihood that clients will take the mediation path and ease thereby the pressure on the courts. This is a situation where the judges and the attorneys have different views. The attorneys are generally happy to litigate because of the increased money it provides them. In contrast, judges, under the pressure of very heavy court calendars, are more appreciative and supportive of the mediation option. To date I have not found it necessary to spell out in detail all the other issues delineated in my provisions document for doing a custody evaluation (Appendix I). Merely discussing these in the initial meeting has sufficed. The reason for this difference is that the provisions document grew over the years in the context of adversarial litigation wherein attorneys were ever finding loopholes and ways of circumventing the agreement. Parties who come for mediation are oriented toward resolving their problems and are not being wound up and "counseled" by attorneys who, in many situations, have done them more harm than good.

Stages in the Mediation Process

A. G. Berg, an attorney mediator, describes mediation as a five-step process. In the first meeting the mediator describes the process and reviews with the clients a typical *Memorandum of Agreement*. They are told the steps by which this agreement can be converted into a divorce. The rules of confidentiality are reviewed, especially with regard to the understanding that what is revealed in the mediation may not subsequently be brought into court, if adversary litigation becomes necessary. Berg places particular emphasis on disclosure of financial material with special regard to how vital it is in successful mediation. Discussion of fees also takes place during this first step. Berg does not meet with the parties separately as she believes that so doing can engender distress and distrust.

In the second step the clients sign the initial contract which defines in writing the issues discussed in the first step.

In the third step the actual mediation process takes place. (Details of this phase will be described below.) Berg states that the average length of mediation for her clients is about ten sessions. It is in this phase that other consultants may be brought in. Berg considers it preferable that the mediator have significant experience in financial planning. If not, such a expert should be brought in. Berg herself appears to be an experienced financial planner and uses computers to a significant degree in her mediation process. She states: "Our office can do financial planning for divorcing clients only because we have developed computer software that can show cash flow, budget, repositioning of existing assets, and tax savings that allow the divorcing couple to reach their goal. Moreover, our software includes a transition program that explains to the clients what will happen immediately after the separation when they have two overheads, and it can give them dollars-and-cents examples of the various solutions that they can choose in their separation agreement."

In step four the contract is prepared in legal terms and sent out to the clients to be read privately. She then meets with the clients again in order to discuss the agreement. At this point they are encouraged to obtain the services of independent counselors to represent them.

In step five the couples sign the agreement. Some mediators do not require a signature. The rationale for this is that it makes the document less "legal" and more "voluntary." It also serves the purpose of absolving the attorney of any criticism of having represented both parties simultaneously. I personally do not ask the parents to sign anything at the completion of custody mediation. Having them sign such a document would be contrary to the statements made in the aforementioned agreement of mine (Appendix II) in which I say that no reports of the mediation will be prepared. The parents have, however, written down carefully the recommendations I have verbally provided, especially when both parties have agreed to them. In this way, there is less likelihood that distortions will creep into the renditions that they provide their attorneys for ultimate incorporation into the divorce agreement.

Important Considerations in the Mediation Process

Mediators try to serve as catalysts. They attempt to facilitate the parties' coming to their own resolutions. This is the ideal situation. In practice, however, the mediation process is generally a more active one. But if such activity by the mediator reaches the point of imposing solutions on the parties, then the process cannot properly be referred to as mediation. The mediator attempts to define the specific issues and clear away contaminating considerations. This is an important aspect of the mediation process. Couples involved in the throes of a divorce are likely to be bringing in a barrage of extraneous and unrelated complaints that becloud the mediation and distract the parties from the central issues under consideration. In a piecemeal fashion each particular area of conflict is delineated and each side's position clarified. This process is central to successful mediation. Areas in which agreement has been made are defined as well as those in which agreement has not been made. The final *Memorandum of Agreement* will specify these two areas.

The Issue of the Mediator's Values   Some mediators would like to believe that they are neutral, nonjudgmental, and do not impose their values on their clients. Mediators who genuinely believe this are blind to what they are doing. There is absolutely no transaction I can imagine in the mediation process that does not involve the values of the mediator. Even silence is a communication; it says, "I agree with what is going on and no intervention on my part is warranted." Silence is ostensibly a neutral position, but neutrality is no less a position than being on either side of the fence. Mediators are generally concerned with what is "fair." This is just another way of saying that mediators concern themselves with what *in their opinion* is "good" or "bad," and this obviously involves value judgments. The mediator supplies both parties with information, among which are the legal issues involved. Laws necessarily involve value judgments by clarifying what is "legal" and what is "illegal." These are also values. It is the mediator's role to make reasonable attempts to ensure that a weak, passive party is not intimidated by a more powerful and knowledgeable party. Again, such efforts involve the attempt to impose the mediator's values on the clients. A mediator without values would sit by and allow the parties to come to a resolution or compromise which might be to the disadvantage of the weaker party. It is unethical for the mediator not to "pass judgment" on such a resolution.

The fact that the mediator is willing to serve in this capacity is in itself a statement of his (her) values. There are people who consider divorce wrong and sinful. A mediator is clearly not an adherent to this value; otherwise he (she) would not serve as a mediator—whose function it is to facilitate divorce. Accordingly, before the parties enter the office the mediator has already communicated an important aspect of his (her) value system. Yet many leaders in the field of mediation education subscribe to the notion that mediators should not impose their values on the clients and teach this to their students. This is unfortunate. What we have to hope for is that the values that mediators impose upon their clients will serve them well.

The Issue of What Is "Fair"   Mediators work on the principle that they should do everything that is fair. *Fair*, of course, involves a heavy loading of value judgment. Adversary litigators, in contrast, are less concerned with what is fair than with whether or not their clients can "do better." The ethical mediator asks, "Is it fair?" The attorney who is strongly committed to the adversary system asks, "Can I do better for my client?" The litigator believes (or professes) that fairness ultimately comes about when each attorney tries to do better for his (her) client because the compromises that result from such adversary proceedings are likely to be fair. Although this may sometimes be the case, I believe that there is a heavy price paid, both financial and psychological, for such fairness. I doubt whether mediation is significantly less fair and I suspect that it is more fair, in part because it is more efficient. There is less time and energy wasted; there is more time spent in meaningful data collection than in courtroom antics and in legal hair-splitting. At this point I have been involved actively in custody litigation for over 25 years. I have not been impressed with the so-called fairness of the adversary system. Many of the decisions that have come down have been unconscionably unfair. Although my experience with mediated resolutions is more limited, I am definitely of the opinion that these agreements have been far more fair.

Furthermore, what is fair to one mediator may not be to another. Individuals who are involved in labor/management negotiations often take the position that their main goal is to provide *peace*, and they do not concern themselves with what is *fair*. What they want to do is to get the workers back into the factory to produce goods once again. They want peace. The agreement that results in peace may be viewed as unfair by one or even both parties. In mediation, however, most agree that it is not simply compromise and peace that one wants; one wants a *fair peace*. And this is where value judgments contribute to a significant degree. Similarly, the independent attorneys who review the *Memorandum of Agreement* are also making judgments with regard to whether it is fair. Last, the presiding judge will also review it with this end in mind.

Discussing the Past   Some mediators have a hard and fast rule that the past shall not be discussed, especially the past indignities the spouses have suffered at one another's hands. Their justification here is that no one could possibly solve these problems or untangle the mess. They claim that dwelling on these horrendously emotionally charged issues just increases the likelihood that the couple will involve themselves in various kinds of smoke screens, distractions, and the introduction of irrelevant issues. Furthermore, they claim that most people (even mental health professionals) cannot understand these problems well because they are so complex. I agree with all these drawbacks to going into the past. However, I still believe that the mediator does well to spend some time learning about the nature of the marital problems that contributed to the separation. This information puts the mediator in a better position to *mediate* by discovering "where the people are coming from" and something about their personality patterns. There is the general principle in therapy (as in life) that the more information one has about a situation, the greater the likelihood one will be able to solve a problem. I am not suggesting here that the mediator spend many hours discussing all the details of past problems. Rather, I am only suggesting that mediators acquaint themselves with the basic marital problems and not subscribe to a strict rule that the past should never be mentioned. Such inquiry also helps the mediator detect the presence of specious motives for mediation that were discussed previously.

In order to prevent individuals from digressing into irrelevancies and past indignities which provide little new information, the mediator must be somewhat active and even dictatorial at times. Furthermore, the mediator must serve as a good model for communication. As mentioned, successful mediation helps the parties cooperate and communicate better. The mediator should therefore be proficient in focusing on core issues, while sweeping away smoke-screen communications and irrelevant digressions. Good mediators, like good therapists, do not involve themselves in discussions on abstract issues. Rather, they focus on concrete and factual issues. These provide much more accurate information, and such focus is more likely to speed up the mediation process. When the mediator observes a participant to be vague and noncommunicative, it is the mediator's obligation to point this out to the person and to encourage accuracy of communication. The good mediator also discourages the use of catch phrases and clichés that may not provide accurate information.

Inquiry into the past may provide the mediator with important information about how the parties are likely to conduct themselves in the mediation process. For example, the same power patterns that contributed to the marital difficulties are likely to exhibit themselves in the mediation process. Patterns of domination/submission, interpersonal competition, dependence/ independence, and competence/incompetence are some of the more common ones. The effective mediator appreciates that in the context of such struggles one of the parties may be at an advantage over the other and coerce an injudicious agreement on the weaker party. It is the mediator's role to be alert to this possibility and to prevent the occurrence of such inequities. An inquiry into the past places the mediator in a better position to do this.

Discussing the Mediation with Other Parties   J. J. Shapiro and M. S. Caplan (1983) recommend that the couple not discuss with outside parties the details of their mediation during the mediation process. They believe that this may complicate matters because input provided by well-meaning friends and relatives can cause much friction and animosity. They recommend that the mediation not be discussed with these parties until the final agreement has been formulated. I am dubious about both the wisdom and practicality of this recommendation. A moratorium on such communication may deprive the couple of useful input from these outside parties. I am not referring here simply to information but the psychological benefits that may be derived from such conversations. As mentioned (especially in Chapter Eight) the third parties can often provide useful input and I frequently involve them directly in my custody evaluations. Last, I am dubious about the capacity of most couples involved in divorce proceedings to refrain strictly from discussing their problems with their friends and relatives. For most people this is an impossible restriction. In other words, even if there were a good rationale for such a moratorium, in practice it could not be realized in the vast majority of cases.

Empirical Learning   The mediator has the opportunity to help the clients learn *empirically* what is in their best interests. Court decisions that are handed down after litigation often appear to be "pulled down from the sky" by the judge, and the parents have little choice but to live with what might prove to be an extremely injudicious ruling. In mediation the couple has the opportunity to try a particular arrangement regarding financial payments and visitation/custody and *see how it works*. In this way they are more likely to bring about a reasonable arrangement. I consider this to be one of the most important benefits of the mediation process. Individuals who involve themselves in adversary litigation may often be forced to "live with" an extremely injudicious and ill-conceived decision. The only way to change it is to go through another exhaustive and expensive process of litigation. In many cases the family's funds have been so depleted that this is impossible. As a result, they suffer unnecessary further psychological trauma, and they have to live with the unwise and even injurious decision.

Involvement of the Children in the Mediation Mediators disagree regarding whether the children should be participants in the mediation. J. M. Haynes (1981) and O. J. Coogler (1978), two prominent mediators who could generally be viewed as pathfinders, hold that children should not be part of the mediation. I am in disagreement. I believe that they should have input and that the older the children the more weight should be given to their opinions. But I am not simply recommending children's participation for their direct contribution regarding parental preference; rather, I recommend their participation for the wide variety of reasons described in earlier sections of this book (especially Chapter Seven). The mediator must be familiar with the parental alienation syndrome, discussed in detail in Chapter Six. Otherwise the mediator may very well take at face value a child's parental preference, and this might result in an injudicious recommendation. As mentioned, the mediator does well to try to separate specific issues and focus on their particulars one at a time. Although this process is a desirable one, there are times when it is less so. For example, child custody issues cannot be easily separated from financial considerations. Supporting two children in one's own home is generally less expensive than supporting them in the former spouse's household. Furthermore, property considerations may also contaminate the custody conflict. Generally, the parent who is awarded custody of the children remains living in the marital home. This parent then does not have to suffer the adjustment problems attendant to moving into a new home and neighborhood.

Advice Commonly Provided
in the Mediation Process

Introductory Comments Parents mediating for custody of
their children should understand that there will be absolutely no
perfect solution to their conflicts. They have to be helped to
appreciate that there are many possible solutions to their problems regarding custody and that each one has both advantages
and disadvantages. They have to try to select from the various
options the one (or those) that will involve the least amount of
pain and the greatest benefits for themselves and their children.
And, if they believe that the adversary system is going to increase
the likelihood that the best or most judicious solution will be
found, they are naive, misguided, and have to deny the experiences of the millions who have chosen this route for the solution
to their custody/visitation disputes. They have to delude themselves into believing that hired guns, arguing before judges
unknown to them (of varying degrees of commitment, intelligence, intent, availability, etc.), will provide better solutions than
they. Parents have to be helped to subscribe to the ancient
wisdom that "half a loaf is better than none." They may believe
that the legal system actually enables them to get the full loaf.
Even when this occurs, it may not necessarily be in the best
interests of all the family members—especially the children.

Parents should appreciate that prior to the court's decision,
they have it within their *own* power to make whatever compromises are necessary to resolve their disputes and that they have
complete control over the living and visitation arrangements of
their children—if they wish to exercise such control. They can
voluntarily choose to place power in the hands of others (lawyers,
and ultimately judges) if they so wish. They do well to appreciate
that voluntarily giving control of their children's lives over to
others is likely to produce extreme frustration for both themselves
and their children and is not likely to result in an arrangement
that would be better than one they could probably devise for
themselves. Parents should appreciate that, once they embark on
the litigation route, it may be very difficult if not impossible for

them to change their course because they may become so embroiled in the conflict that they will blind themselves to the fact that a turnaround is possible. All know that little skirmishes have a way of escalating into full-blown wars as individuals become swept up in the battle. Winning then becomes an end in itself, with little appreciation that the victory will inevitably be Pyrrhic.

One of the mediator's roles is that of helping parents consider options that they may not previously have thought about. A mediator should expand the parents' horizons and provide them with more choices. Often they have not considered alternatives that may be preferable to the ones they have previously deliberated over.

Advice Relating to the Choice and Utilization of Attorneys

If the mediation occurs prior to the time the parents have chosen an attorney, I will generally advise them to wait until the mediation is completed before selecting a lawyer. If, however, they decide to seek independent counsel at the outset, I will generally advise each to select a lawyer who is sympathetic to the mediation process and receptive to conferences with his (her) adversary in which all four parties are present, namely, both parents and both attorneys. I will further advise them to be sure to select an attorney who has a reputation for returning telephone calls. This may seem like an inconsequential point, but readers who have had experiences with attorneys who do not return calls know well the extra stress that such a practice can cause them. Unfortunately, the vast majority of attorneys (in my experience) do not return telephone calls. Secretaries repeatedly tell clients that the attorney is "in conference" or "in court." These ladies and gentlemen seem always to be in conference or in court and never appear to be spending their time elsewhere. Clients should emphasize in the initial consultation with an attorney that they are willing to pay for telephone time and expect to be charged. It is hoped that the attorney will be honest in this regard (also rare), but that if a promise cannot be made, the client will seek the services of another lawyer. One is also entitled to an itemized bill indicating the time and the duration of telephone calls in that attorneys are notorious for padding their bills in the area of time expenditures.

It is important also to find out at the outset whether the attorney will be doing the work himself (herself) or assigning the work to an associate. It is a common practice for a well-known attorney to give clients the impression that he (she) will be doing the actual work and then the client (after providing a large retainer) will learn that most (if not all) of the work is being done by a junior associate with far less experience. This is just another one of the unconscionable practices that people are subjected to when they choose to involve adversarial attorneys to resolve custody/visitation disputes. Failure to return telephone calls, and assignment of the case to a junior colleague, are just two of the many deplorable practices that contribute to my belief that many attorneys do their clients more damage than the spouses against whom they are litigating.

Parents should appreciate that their attorneys are not their masters but their employees and advisors. Parents pay the bills and are entitled to the services. They should find out whether the attorney has had significant experience in marriage and divorce law or only occasionally handles such matters. One wouldn't want a brain surgeon who only occasionally practices brain surgery. Similarly, in matters such as custody, one does well to engage the services of someone with specific expertise.

It is preferable, however, for the clients to hold off involving themselves with attorneys (at least for the custody issue) until the end of the mediation. The more actively attorneys are involved during the course of the mediation, the greater the likelihood it will be compromised.

Advice Relating to Providing New Information and the Correction of Distortions   It behooves the mediator to comment on whether a proposed program is reasonable. For example, a mother may be so blinded by her rage over the separation that she may want to include as one of the provisions in the agreement that her husband not take up residence in the same community. Although the mediator might express appreciation that his living there may cause her some distress, she has to be helped to appreciate that his proximity may be extremely beneficial to their children—especially if they are younger. I will often describe to the parents what I consider to be the optimum living situation for divorced people, namely, that they live approximately four to six blocks from one another. Under these circumstances, they live far enough away from one another that encounters will be infrequent; yet they will be close enough for the children to enjoy the benefits of the easy availability of both parents. One benefit of such proximity is that it obviates the problems attendant to the need for two sets of friends. The farther the parents live from one another, the greater the likelihood that two sets of friends will be necessary. Obviously, when the children have the opportunity to move freely back and forth between the two homes, and their friends can also do so, there is a greater likelihood that there will be continuity of friendships and this cannot but be salutary. The arrangement has other benefits. It reduces the wear and tear of visitation travel for both parents and children. It most often ensures that both parents will be optimally available for school carpooling and attendance at school activities. The parents may have assumed that living farther apart from one another—even in separate communities—is optimum. The four-to-six block option may never have been considered. Advising its serious consideration may result in their agreeing to implement what I consider to be this optimum residential arrangement.

A parent, for example, may strongly resist a visitation arrangement that involves the children's frequent shuttling back and forth between the two homes. Although there is no question that it is preferable for a child, especially a younger one, to have continuity, there is also no question that a healthy custodial arrangement *must* involve a certain amount of shuttling. When trying to devise an optimum arrangement, parents will often ask the mediator for the minimal age at which children can tolerate such alternation without detrimental effects. In discussions of this question, parents (and often attorneys and judges) may lose sight of the fact that it is not simply the place where the children are at a particular point that is going to determine whether they are going to be confused or otherwise suffer but the *quality* of the caretaking individuals in that particular place. Generally, it is not the transportation per se that causes difficulty, but impairments in caretaking in one or both homes. In fact, I would go further and state that infants under the age of one, who are not breast-feeding, could tolerate frequent shuttling back and forth if each of the parents were strongly nurturing and providing optimum care. (Of course, when breast-feeding is taking place, such frequent shuttling is obviously not possible.) In short, problems associated with transportation and change of location are minor compared with those attendant to poor quality parenting.

When one of the parents has to live at a significant distance from the other, the mediator's advice regarding maintenance of continuity can sometimes be helpful, and this may reduce or even obviate one of the problems that may come up in a custody conflict. The parent who lives at a significant distance from the children can be advised to maintain certain kinds of contact that may not have been previously practiced. For example, this parent can make frequent telephone calls, write many letters, and make sure that there is ongoing interest in all the details of the child's life: school, playmates, exciting experiences, and so on. It has been a source of amazement to me that there are many parents who do not recognize these obvious ways of ensuring ongoing contact from a distance.

A practice that I have found particularly useful when a parent travels extensively and cannot be sure of mail predictabil-ity is to write the letters beforehand with the appropriate future dates. These are given to the custodial parent—before the day of departure—and each day the custodial parent opens up the letter written by the absent parent. The younger child will generally not realize what is going on and may benefit immensely from the letters that predictably arrive every day from "Africa," "Asia," or "South America." I have absolutely no guilt over recommending this kind of ruse. To be completely honest under such a situation requires one to be dependent on mail services for punctual delivery. People who harbor such a delusion will not be able to provide their children with a useful form of contact with the traveling parent.

A common problem occurs in the situation in which the father is the breadwinner and the mother is the homemaker. The father, in the desire to prevail in a custodial conflict, will propose a series of caretakers for the children until he becomes available after work. He may naively believe that these individuals will do as good a job as his wife. Generally, his anger has so blinded him at that point that he does not appreciate that they are not as likely to provide the continuity that his wife can offer, as well as the dedication of care she can provide. (Of course, there *are* situations in which the wife indeed cannot provide this continuity and quality of care; in such circumstances this advice does not hold.) If my arguments are not convincing I might say to the father something along these lines: "If I were involved in this case as a court-appointed impartial examiner, there is no question that I would describe your program as impractical and not in the children's best interests. It would be a strong argument in favor of your wife's gaining primary custody." Sometimes a statement such as this can help the father appreciate the impracticality of his proposal.

At times, when there is the threat that the mediation might break down, I have found it useful to remind the parents that they do far better for themselves and their children to keep the money in the family rather than give it to strange lawyers. Fathers, who are more often the ones paying the most for the litigation, are often so embroiled in the conflict that they don't even realize they do better for themselves and their children by giving their money to their ex-wives rather than to attorneys. After all, the more money their ex-wives have, the easier it is going to be for the children. Also, a father giving money to his former wife is likely to have much less psychological stress than one giving it to an attorney. Fathers must be helped to see through their rage and appreciate this obvious advice.

Advice Relating to the Naming of the Custodial Arrangement Another area in which relatively simple advice can prevent much expense, grief, and psychological stress relates to the terminology so often utilized in custody disputes. At this time the *joint custodial concept* is very much in vogue. However, it is variously defined, and this can produce much unnecessary psychological trauma. Often the individuals utilizing the term are thinking of entirely different concepts and such communication errors complicate what is already a complex issue. Hours of time and thousands of dollars may be spent defining the term, and arguments over what it really means divert the involved parties from the crucial issues. Time may be wasted on arguing about whether a particular arrangement should be called *joint custody* or something else. References to precedents in which the joint custodial arrangement was utilized may also occupy the time of the attorneys. And, of course, the more time the attorney spends on such deliberations, the greater the cost to the client.

Mediators do well to circumvent all these irrelevant deliberations by focusing specifically on the *substantive* issues involved, namely, where the children shall be living at any given time, whether or not a scheduled arrangement is necessary (this will be dependent on the parents' capacity for cooperation and communication), and what the decision-making powers of each parent shall be with regard to each of the various issues over which decisions must be made. These issues must be kept in focus and are most important for the children. It does not matter to the children what the arrangement is called; what matters to them is *where* they shall be living at any particular point (whether in accordance with a schedule or not) and the quality of the caretaking they are receiving at that time. Advising the parents to focus on these issues can be salutary. (In Chapter Nine I have discussed in greater detail the issue of custodial arrangements and terminology.)

Advice Regarding the Children's Credibility   Another problem that can both engender and perpetuate custody litigation is parents' automatically believing what their children tell them in the course of the custody dispute. Children want to ingratiate themselves to adults and children of divorce have a significant loyalty conflict. In the divorce situation they most often have little guilt over saying to each parent what they believe that parent wishes to hear, even to the point of providing fabrications designed to win favor. These lies tend to foment the hostilities and are often utilized by attorneys in the course of a litigation. The parents are so blinded by rage and so eagerly welcome any support for their positions that they fail to see that they are being deceived by their children. And, if the parents are not speaking with one another, such fabrications will not be exposed, and the troubles they cause will persist and polarize the parents even further. I have even seen situations in which parents have initiated custody litigation because their children were telling each one that they wanted to live with that one and not the other. Mediators who work with parents in these circumstances should try to help them appreciate this common process and not to automatically accept as valid children's support of one parent and criticism of the other. Parents who come to appreciate this almost universal phenomenon are likely to save themselves much grief and avoid significant strife.

Advice Regarding Involvement with a Lover   A common situation that may initiate custody litigation is the one in which a parent becomes involved with a lover. A mother, for example, may have had no problem with a traditional visitation schedule, one that involves the children's sleeping over at the father's home every other weekend and enjoying a midweek dinner visitation with him. However, when the father becomes involved with a new woman and the relationship reaches the point where she may be sleeping over at the father's home during visitation, the mother may become extremely moralistic and withhold visitation on the grounds that the children are now being exposed to the father's depravity and immorality. Some of these mothers were not particularly religious beforehand, but now start invoking claims of sin and moral turpitude. They are often responding less to morality than to jealously. In fact, were the situation reversed, and it was they who had the lover, they would be doing the same as the father. Fathers may similarly react when jealous over a mother's new lover.

Mediators should help such parents separate jealously from morality and help them appreciate that there is nothing intrinsically detrimental (from the psychological point of view) to children's visiting a home in which a parent is sleeping with a lover with whom there is an ongoing relationship. (Obviously, I am not referring here to situations in which the children are directly exposed to sexual activities or to a parade of sexual partners.) Hamlet's wisdom is applicable here: "There's nothing either good or bad but thinking makes it so." If the parents view such activities as detrimental to the children, they will become so. In contrast, if they take a matter-of-fact attitude and appreciate that sleeping over is part of a normal, healthy human relationship, the children will come to view it similarly. If mediators can be successful in this regard, they may be helpful in preventing parents' litigating over this issue.

Consultants   Mention has already been made of the important role of consultants in the mediation process. Mediators who are attorneys may very well want to bring in a mental health professional if the situation warrants it. As mentioned, one of my objections to the routine use of co-mediation teams consisting of an attorney and a mental health professional is that all mediations do not require the services (and additional cost) of a mental health professional. All do, however, require the involvement of an attorney, at some level. I say at some level because the primary mediator may very well be a mental health professional, but that mediator should still involve an attorney for supervision, review of the mediation agreement, and writing it in proper legal form.

Law schools do not generally train attorneys in the kinds of sophisticated financial issues necessary for mediation of cases where the financial holdings of the parties are significant. Most attorneys are self-trained in this area. Few mental health professionals are. The services of an accountant mediator in these cases is often desirable. If both parties agree, the accountant may be the person who has served the couple prior to the separation. It is hoped that both parties will view this accountant as someone who will maintain impartiality throughout the course of the mediation. This accountant comes in with a vast amount of information about the parents and can generally work quite rapidly in supplying the mediator with useful advice. In contrast, an accountant who has had no previous familiarity with the clients is likely to cost more money because of the extra time required to gain familiarity with the particular financial situation of the clients. A real estate appraisal may sometimes be necessary. Sometimes the couple may prefer to bring in two independent real estate appraisers and the averaged value is then taken as the working figure. The mediation may require the services of someone who can appraise the value of a business or other types of property. Again, it is common to get two such appraisals and use the average figure.

The couple may have used the services of an attorney who has become a friend and advisor to both. It may be risky to use this attorney as the primary mediator, but he (she) may serve well as a consultant who has important information to provide. This attorney may have been involved in the couple's estate planning and will revisions over the years and is therefore knowledgeable about the personalities of the clients as well as the details of this aspect of their financial situation. Again, both clients must have the confidence that this attorney will continue to be impartial, even though the couple has separated. Because such an attorney may have some partiality, it may be wiser to use him (her) as a consultant rather than as the primary mediator.

The Final Steps

When all the contested issues have been discussed in full and when as many as possible have been resolved, the mediator generally draws up what is referred to as the *Memorandum of Agreement*. Other names used for this document are *Marital Settlement Agreement, Mediation Plan,* and *Memorandum of Understanding*. In this document the areas in which agreement has been reached are defined and the particular resolutions spelled out. It is hoped that all contested areas will be resolved and that the divorce can then run smoothly without the necessity of resorting to adversary litigation. If, however, the parties are unable to resolve certain issues, these should also be stated in the *Memorandum of Agreement*.

The next step is for the parties to review the document at their leisure and then bring it for review to independent counselors. It is extremely important that the parties not select attorneys who have reputations for being vicious litigators. Such attorneys are generally antagonistic to the mediation process and will most often find reasons for discouraging their clients from agreement to the document. Because of the vagueness of many of the guidelines for deciding the various contested issues involving divorce, it is easy for an attorney to say that the client would probably do better to litigate. There is no mediation document that does not lend itself to some warning about future consequences or some potential loophole. The clients should select attorneys who themselves are mediators and who have established for themselves reputations for working closely with mediators when they serve as adversary reviewers of the *Memorandum of Agreement*. Sometimes a few telephone conversations among the three attorneys (the mediator and the two adversary attorneys) may be enough to resolve the remaining conflictive areas. Sometimes a meeting of the five parties may be necessary. If this is successful in resolving any remaining conflict, the final *Memorandum of Agreement* should be formulated.

There are some individuals who view the mediation process as an endpoint in itself. They are unreceptive to seeking the services of an independent attorney for review of the *Memorandum of Agreement*. From a purely practical point of view this is an error. Like all human beings, mediators are prone to bias, and the independent counselors can serve as checks. In the initial interview the mediator should discourage the client(s) from this view of the mediation process. Signing the initial document that outlines the terms of the mediation lessens the likelihood that the person will not then seek an independent counselor. However, there are some individuals who, although they signed a statement in which they have agreed to seek the services of an independent counselor, will then have second thoughts on this matter. If this client has a good relationship with and respect for the mediator, then he (she) will be more likely to follow the mediator's advice and seek the review of an independent counselor. If the mediator's advice fails, however, the couple may have difficulty obtaining a divorce in most states in that the legal process is still unreceptive to granting divorces to individuals who do not have separate attorneys.

The final step in the process generally involves the incorporation of the *Memorandum of Agreement* into the divorce decree. The divorcing couple and the attorneys go to court. There is still a plaintiff and a defendant, the plaintiff being the one who has initially requested the divorce, and the defendant being the one who has agreed to the divorce. In this situation the divorce is viewed by the court as noncontested. The procedure is relatively short. Each party takes the stand and swears under oath that he (she) has agreed to the terms of the *Memorandum of Agreement* and has not been coerced into agreeing to any of the stipulations. The attorneys generally make statements indicating that they have reviewed the agreement and have informed their clients that they think it is fair and just. The clients are asked to make statements that this was indeed the case. The judge may ask a few questions to ensure that everything that has been said is valid. The judge then issues a divorce decree in which the *Memorandum of Agreement* is incorporated.

For couples contemplating mediation, I would recommend Shapiro and Caplan's book, *Parting Sense: A Couple's Guide to Divorce Mediation* (1983). It provides a useful introduction to the mediation process and practical advice regarding the psychological as well as the financial aspects of mediation. It is also a valuable guide to the complex financial operations that are often attendant to the mediation process.

CLINICAL EXAMPLES

The examples presented here demonstrate the value of mediation for resolving custody disputes. These cases did not involve a significant amount of evaluation such as is often necessary when the parents are litigating. In a sense, one could consider these to be examples of "pure" mediation of custody disputes. The more complex the issues the greater the likelihood the mediator may have to conduct the more intense kind of custody evaluation described earlier in this book. But, as mentioned, even this kind of intensive evaluation is best done in the context of mediation, rather than adversarial litigation.

Tom and Hilda

Tom was born in Australia and Hilda in Denmark. They had both come to the United States as exchange students and met while studying at the same university. Both had fully intended to return to their native countries after completion of their studies. Both had extensive family networks in their native countries and were deeply involved with their relatives back home. However, they immediately developed a strong attachment to one another, attachments that they later appreciated stemmed partly from the loneliness each felt so far away from home. After the first year of a tempestuous love affair, they began living together and married after they had known one another for two years. At that time, although still deeply tied to their relatives and friends in their respective homelands, they decided to remain living in the United States. They believed that their strong loving feelings would overcome their homesickness. The option of their both settling in either Australia or Denmark was not considered because this would take one of them even farther away from contacts with his (her) native country.

A few years later they had two children, Fred and Grace. As the years passed they found that their homesickness did not diminish. Now they had a new problem. Whereas prior to the birth of the children, a marital separation because of homesickness would involve a painful disruption of what was otherwise a good marriage, a divorce now presented a new source of grief and dilemma, namely, what to do with the children. This is the problem they presented me with when I first saw them for mediating. At that time Fred was ten and Grace was eight years old.

In my initial interviews I tried to ascertain whether psychopathological factors were operative in Tom and Hilda's dilemma.

Basically, I found the marriage to be a good one and did not conclude that their homesickness was significantly pathological. Some people who emigrate to the United States and then express ambivalence with regard to remaining here sometimes do so because of psychological problems that interfere with their adjusting. Other emigrées, however, may have justifiable reasons for preferring to return to their native countries. Those who counsel such immigrants must overcome feelings of chauvinism and even grandiosity that they may have about the United States. They have to recognize that this country, like all others in the world, has both advantages and disadvantages for those who live within it. There are some people who will blame their inability to adjust on real factors in this country that are causing them difficulty. Some of these individuals may be still externalizing the problem and blaming reality events in order to rationalize their own impairments. Others, however, have bona fide feelings of disappointment and disgruntlement, and their returning to their native countries cannot be considered a manifestation of psychopathology.

In Tom and Hilda's case I concluded that their extended family ties were formidable and that their involvement with the United States had been nonexistent prior to their coming here. Therefore, there were no particular symptoms to treat and mediating had to deal with consideration of the various options, with the full recognition that no option was going to be free from grief. We discussed the various options and each knew that there was absolutely no solution which would not be without its attendant psychological pain.

One possibility would be for both children to go back to Denmark with Hilda. This option, obviously, was particularly painful to Tom because he would be completely removed from his children's upbringing and, because of the financial situation, there would be only rare opportunities to actually see his children. The second option was for both children to return to Australia with Tom. And this, of course, was extremely painful for Hilda. The third option was to split the children. Here, too, each recognized that this would result in not only the loss of a child by a parent but also the loss of sibling for each of the children. The fourth option was only mentioned to cover all possibilities, but was dismissed immediately because it was not even momentarily given any serious consideration. In this plan both children would remain together in the United States with other parties, and the parents would return alone to their native countries. This was an unthinkable option and was not discussed further.

In the process of exploring the relative advantages and disadvantages of each of the first three options, the parents agreed that the third would be the least painful. The question then arose as to which child would go with which parent. It was finally decided that Fred would go with Tom and Grace with Hilda. Although both parents had close relationships with both children, Fred was very much involved in father-son activities with Tom and Grace was significantly involved with mother-daughter activities with Hilda. It was agreed, as well, that everything reasonable would be done to keep up contact between the children and the parents. They planned frequent letter writing, the sending of gifts, and periodic telephone calls. Although both hoped that this would provide ongoing continuity, both recognized the strong possibility that the immense distances between the parties might result in a gradual diminution in the relationships, to the point where there might be no relationships at all.

Tom and Hilda's case demonstrates a number of important points. First, it is testimony to their wisdom in that they did not reflexly resort to litigation in the attempt to resolve their problems. Even though they came at a time when divorce litigation was the routine method in such disputes, they recognized the self-destructiveness of such a course and sought a more rational and humane method out of their dilemma. They came in part with the hope that I might somehow come up with a recommendation that would not be particularly painful although they could not think of one themselves. In my consultations with them I helped them resign themselves to the reality that there was absolutely no solution that would not be associated with grief.

The case also demonstrates another important point with regard to romantic love. Like many other phenomena, it often includes psychopathological processes. When under its influence individuals often show poor judgment. In Tom and Hilda's case an important contributing element to the romantic loving feelings was their sense of loneliness from friends and relatives in their homelands. They became completely wrapped up in one another and were so desirous of maintaining their state of ecstasy they did not allow themselves to think of important future consider-ations—such as whether they could remain living in the United States indefinitely and what would happen if they did get divorced after they had children. Such practical considerations often put a damper on romantic loving feelings and are therefore dissociated from conscious awareness in order not to disrupt the euphoria. Had Tom and Hilda come for counseling at that time (extremely unlikely because romantic love is generally considered normal and healthy), I might have introduced such consider-ations, even at the risk of being considered disrespectful of romance.

Jeffrey and Denise

Jeffrey and Denise separated after 13 years of marriage. At the time of the separation they had two children, Gail, age seven and Bill, age nine. The family lived in a town which I will call Springfield. Denise initiated the separation, giving as her reason: "A year before we were married I got pregnant. Jeff insisted that I get an abortion. I was brought up in a very religious Catholic home. Having sexual intercourse before marriage was a terrible burden for me, but having an abortion was completely out of my scheme of things. I considered it to be a sin against God. However, Jeff pounded away at me and hounded me day and night, until I finally got the abortion. I never got over that. I still feel guilty about it to this day—even though it happened over 14 years ago. Even confession hasn't helped. I'm still angry at him for it and it's one of the reasons I got divorced."

Jeffrey, however, gave a very different story. He stated, "I think my wife has a big hang-up over that abortion. I think she uses it as an excuse to explain many other things. She's never let me forget the abortion and she's never let herself forget it. Actually, she wasn't that religious when I met her, or else we wouldn't have had intercourse. And she certainly hasn't been that religious since, in that we don't go to church that often. Besides, I'm Protestant and if she were that religious she wouldn't ever have married me. I think she's always been a very uptight woman and we've had a serious communication problem. I never know what's on her mind. Sometimes when I ask her what she's thinking, she'll tell me that it's about the abortion. I think that's a lot of bullshit. I think she's giving me that answer in order to avoid telling me what's really on her mind. I think one of the things she was thinking of was her boyfriend Gary. Although she denies it, I believe she was having an affair with Gary before we split, and she uses this abortion bullshit excuse to cover up what was really going on. She said she left the house because I made her get the abortion. She immediately rented a house in the next town, Linden Gardens. I think she got out of the house in order to be with Gary. Within two weeks after her leaving, Gary was already sleeping over. I know that from friends of mine who live in the neighborhood."

Jeffrey and Denise had been referred by their lawyers because they strongly suspected that psychopathological problems were interfering with their ability to make some decisions regarding the children's custody and visitation programs. At the time I saw them, the children were living with the father in the marital home and, of course, continuing school in Springfield. They were, however, visiting frequently with their mother in Linden Gardens, in what was basically a very flexible visitation arrangement. Their mother, however, insisted that she wanted the children to move in with her and that she should be the primary custodial parent. When I asked her main reason for this, she stated: "Well, he got his way about the abortion, so I think I should get my way on this one. Also Jeff wants me to move back to Springfield so I can be closer to the children and they can still attend the same school. I think that would be a bad idea because of the rage he feels toward my boyfriend Gary. If I live in Springfield, he's more likely to see Gary and he told me that he feels like killing him."

To this Jeffrey replied, "There you see, Doctor, she's still using this old abortion thing. She uses it as an excuse for everything and anything. Now she's using it to play a game of 'even Steven.' She left me for Gary and now she wants to take the kids with her. We're doing quite well with the present arrangement. Sure I'm angry at Gary. That guy was screwing my wife while we were still married. What do you expect? Does she think I'm going to be his friend? Yes, I did say I *feel* like killing him, but that doesn't mean that I *will* kill him. If I wanted to kill him, I know exactly where to find him, namely, in her bed. I may have many faults, but being a murderer is not one of them. She's just using that as an excuse not to move back to Springfield so the kids can remain in the same school and have a good visitation arrangement with her. She wants everything, her lover, her kids, and complete removal of me from the scene. I don't want her to be living very close. I don't want to see her around and I certainly don't want to see Gary. However, I want her to live close enough so the children will have easy access to her house. There's a house for sale about six blocks away. I've encouraged her to buy it. Together we have enough money to buy it."

In the ensuing session I was successful in helping Denise appreciate that she was using the abortion experience in the service of a series of rationalizations, the latest of which was going to be disruptive to her children. She came to realize that the plan that made most sense was for her to move into the house in Springfield that was six blocks from the marital home. There the children would have free access to both homes and could truly enjoy a joint custodial arrangement without a fixed schedule. I also pointed out to her how advantageous this would be with regard to the children's keeping their present friends without having to form a second set of friends in Linden Gardens. I helped her appreciate that she had the opportunity for what I considered to be the optimum living arrangement for separated and divorced parents. I helped her appreciate that her use of the abortion experience to justify her husband's now giving in on her custody demands was irrational and that it served other purposes, especially her desire to leave the home, abandon her husband, live with a lover, and now have her children as well. I helped her to understand that she didn't need the "even Steven" rationalization and that she could live with her lover, live with her children half the time, and have access to them on a frequent basis if she were to return to Springfield. I also helped her appreciate that there was little evidence that her husband would try to murder Gary and that this too was being used as a rationalization for promulgating the children's moving to Linden Gardens. Fortunately, she was receptive to my advice. She gained insight into what she was doing and agreed to move into the new house in Springfield. Although this caused some economic privation for both her and Jeff, both agreed that it was a small price to pay for the benefits the children would derive from the arrangement. It is a credit to Denise that she was able to gain insight into and work toward alleviating the psychopathological processes contributing to her custody/visitation problems. And it is a credit to their attorneys that they recognized that psychotherapy and mediation might be the more judicious and humane route to the resolution of their clients' problems.

Bea and Tom

The case of Bea and Tom demonstrates how mediation of a custody dispute may not run too smoothly, but may still work to benefit the children. It was Bea, an interior decorator, who first called me and stated that she would like to try to mediate the visitation difficulties she was having with her former husband, but that he was refusing to participate. She stated that if mediation was not possible she was planning to litigate for custody of the children, in order to protect them from a series of detrimental influences to which she believed her husband was exposing them. I advised her that if she wished to see me she would have to make a choice regarding whether she wanted me to serve as a mediator or as a court-ordered impartial examiner, and that this decision would have to be made *prior* to the first interview. I told her that I would be willing to serve in either capacity, but that I could not switch tracks after one route had been chosen. I advised her that she would have to sign an appropriate document, whichever course she chose, which would prevent both of us from changing the decision. (Obviously, this case was referred to me in the days when I still conducted custody evaluations in the context of adversarial proceedings.) Accordingly, she decided to engage my services in the mediation role and the initial appointment was made. It was understood on the telephone that in that first session high priority would be given to exploring the possibilities of engaging her husband in the mediation. It is not my usual practice to see only one party at the beginning of a mediation program. On occasion, I have departed from this rule when I considered the situation to warrant it, as in Bea's case.

In the initial interview, she informed me that she had three children, a nine-year-old boy, a six-year-old girl, and a four-year-old boy. She and her former husband had been separated three years and divorced one-and-a-half years. It was she who had initiated the separation after learning that her husband had a lover with whom he refused to break up. When I asked her what problems there might have been in the marriage that may have contributed to his involving himself with a lover, she denied that she knew of any and considered the relationship to have been a good one. She also denied recalling any particular criticisms her husband made of her that warranted his leaving her for this other woman. She stated that her husband was living with his lover and planned to marry her. She was quite sure that the lovers were indiscreet with regard to their lovemaking, but she could not provide me with specific examples of such indiscretions.

Bea had a variety of other complaints about her former husband. She claimed that he had always been somewhat neglectful of the children and that during visitations her husband and his woman friend, Sandy, would leave the three children alone, often for many hours. On other occasions, they would leave them overnight with her husband's mother—whom she described as overindulgent of the children, who did not properly discipline or provide limits, and who fed them "junk foods." She claimed that when the children came back from visitation it was clear that they had been neglected and that they were tired, withdrawn, irritable, and had many complaints about their visitation. She claimed that it would often take her two or three hours of discussion with them in order to calm them down after visits with their father.

Bea claimed that her former husband, Tom, refused to mediate with her because he considered their situation "hopeless." She was not able to provide me with any further information regarding Tom's refusal to mediate. We then discussed the possible ways of bringing Tom into mediation. She first proposed, somewhat naively, that I call him myself. I informed her that I considered this both unethical and antitherapeutic and that I have never initiated contact with a patient prior to the first interview. I explained to her that he might consider my invitation a solicitation of business and could justifiably make a complaint about me to the ethics committee of my medical society. I also explained that from the therapeutic position, soliciting a new patient's involvement can compromise the treatment from the outset, and thereby lessen the likelihood of success. She then suggested that she might ask her therapist to call her husband's therapist (both were in treatment). I advised her that I did not consider this the optimum approach to the problem. Although it was conceivably a viable option, it ran the risk of both therapists' being used as tools and/or messenger boys in bringing her former husband into mediation. I suggested that she speak to Tom herself, and tell him what had transpired during our interview. My hope was that, although he had previously refused to meet with me, some information about the interview might change his mind.

About three days later I received a telephone call from Tom, saying that he would like to discuss mediation with me. When I asked whether he would prefer to have a joint interview with Bea or to see me alone, he stated that he definitely wanted to see me alone. In fact, he stated that this would be the only way he would be willing to come to see me, that he wasn't certain he wanted mediation, but he was certain that he was not going to discuss the issue of his involvement in Bea's presence. Accordingly, I made an appointment to meet with him alone.

In the interview Tom told me that he considered Bea to be a "pathological liar" and "mildly paranoid." He stated: "She makes mountains out of molehills. She takes the smallest things and builds them up into big deals. She has a very vivid imagination. She probably told you that Sandy and I were exposing the children to sexual activities. That's absurd. We're very affectionate people, but we're also very discreet. I'll put my hand around her waist once in a while or hold her hand. I'll even give her a peck on the cheek from time to time. She grills the kids when they come home and tries to extract from them evidence that they've been exposed to much more. Doctor, they haven't been. If you ask her for specifics, she can't give them. It's all in her head. She also complains that Sandy and I leave the kids alone for long periods of time. That's also a lie. I'll send our nine-year-old on errands alone to places where I know he's capable of going safely. The three kids will sometimes go to the home of a friend down the block. I can trust them to go as a pack without going into the street. She calls that neglect. She's not helping them to become independent."

Tom continued, "She's always complaining to me about how terrible the kids look when they come back from visitations with me. She tells me they're sad, upset, and irritable. She's right, but it's not because of anything that's happened with me. They dread returning to her. They start getting that way about an hour before they know they have to go back. They know that they'll be exposed to her cross-examinations. I think the main thing that's going on is that she's jealous that I have a new woman friend and that she has no one. Her inquisitions are designed to get information about me and Sandy. She's obsessed with the details of our sex life. She sometimes says to me that she's going to go to court to reduce visitations even further. In fact, sometimes she's threatened to try to cut visitations out entirely. I don't think she'll do this because then she won't be able to use them to get information about us."

I then asked Tom why he had refused to join Bea at the time of the first interview. He stated that he feared that if he were to confront me with his opinions about what was going on with Bea, that she might retaliate by unilaterally withholding the children, without even going to the court. He described her as being unpredictable, volatile, and vengeful. He stated that she had already cut down the visitation schedule below what was in the court order and that he had neither the money nor the gumption to try to litigate for a resumption of the previous schedule. I informed Tom that Bea had indeed told me that she was planning further restrictions and his best hope to prevent them was to participate directly in mediation. I told him that I thought Bea had respect for my opinions and that she wanted him to participate in the mediation. I informed him that if he did not participate, the likelihood would be that the present situation would get worse, the visitations would probably be reduced, and his only recourse then would be to go to court. Tom reluctantly agreed to begin the mediation, starting somewhat sadly, "I guess I have no choice. I hope you're right, Doctor, that this won't make it worse."

The ensuing sessions were difficult. Tom's description of Bea was quite accurate. She was volatile, vindictive, tended to "make mountains out of molehills," and was "mildly paranoid." In spite of these difficulties, Bea was able to develop some insight into the fact that she tended to distort. We discussed in detail her various allegations and over a period of about five sessions, during which time she became more trustful of me and more receptive to what I had to say, she reluctantly agreed to resume the previous visitation schedule ordered by the court. She predicted, however, that I would finally come to see that she was right after all and that one of her reasons for agreeing to the expanded visitation program was to provide Tom with more opportunity to expose the children to the various indignities she had previously described. After a few more sessions, it became apparent that the children were adjusting well on the old schedule. Bea's predictions did not come to pass.

Unfortunately, instead of being pleased over this turn of events, Bea became increasingly hostile toward me. I did not have the opportunity to explore all that was going on in that she discontinued the mediation one day by storming out of the office in the middle of a session. This occurred just after Tom expressed his opinion that Bea was jealous of his relationship with Sandy and that if she had a new man friend in her life, many of the problems they were having with the children would not be occurring. Leaving at that point was, of course, confirmation of the validity of Tom's statement. Although I never saw them again, the counseling did have the effect of Bea's allowing the children to spend more time with Tom and reducing her cross-examination of them. Two months later I received a telephone call from Tom informing me that things were status quo, namely the children were still visiting him at the expanded level and that Bea was maintaining a stance of antagonism toward him. He also stated that she had many unkind things to say about me. As mentioned, I cannot claim that this was one of my more successful experiences in helping a couple mediate their differences. However, Bea's animosity notwithstanding, the general situation was indeed improved by the treatment, and courtroom litigation was avoided.

Juanita and Dan

Gloria was two when her parents separated. When she was eight years old her parents came to me for my assistance in helping them resolve a custody/visitation problem. They recognized how vicious courtroom litigation could be and wanted to do everything possible to avoid the psychological traumas of such a course of action. Juanita was born and raised in Rio de Janeiro. Dan was born in San Francisco and raised in Portland, Oregon. He was serving in the diplomatic service when he met Juanita in Rio de Janeiro. At the time, she was living under very stressful conditions in that she felt oppressed by her large family network and the crowded conditions of her home, where she lived with her parents and five siblings. Her family was not particularly poor, but they were of modest means and could not afford more spacious quarters. In addition, her father was an extremely authoritarian man, who "ruled with an iron fist" and insisted that the whole family move en bloc regarding participation in family functions. Furthermore, her parents' very rigid values regarding dating required her to have a chaperone until the time of her marriage. Under these circumstances she welcomed the overtures of this young American diplomat who promised her a much freer lifestyle if she would marry him and come to the United States.

Back in America, things went well for the first few years of their marriage. However, her husband developed a drinking problem which necessitated his being asked to leave the diplomatic corps. During the next few years he had difficulty finding and keeping jobs and adjusting, and it was during this period that Gloria was born. Soon after her birth Gloria's mother became involved with another man and this resulted in a separation when Gloria was two and a divorce when she was three-and-a-half.

During subsequent years, with the help of Alcoholics Anonymous and therapy, Dan became more stable and entered into a business which rapidly became quite successful. Although during the year following the separation he was not particularly attentive to the needs of his daughter, he progressively became more involved. By the time I saw them (when Gloria was eight) I viewed him to be a reasonably dedicated father. During this period Gloria remained living with her mother who had a part-time job during the child's school hours. However, Juanita was quickly becoming dissatisfied with living in the United States. At the time I saw them in consultation they were living in New York City and she found conditions there to be oppressive. She complained about the violence, muggings, and rape that characterizes city life. She no longer wanted to continue bringing Gloria up in an atmosphere where she was constantly vigilant to these dangers. She complained about the materialism of the children in Gloria's private school and the general unfriendliness of the people in the city. Then she became increasingly lonesome for her life back in Rio de Janeiro. She had made a number of trips there and recognized that she did not have to submerge herself as deeply in family life as her father wished, that she was now an adult with a child, and that she could participate as little or as much as she desired. She believed that it was important for Gloria to have stronger family ties and this could only be accomplished in Rio de Janeiro, especially because her husband's family was primarily on the West Coast and even when there was contact with them they did not have the same strong sense of family involvement that her family had.

At the time of the consultation Juanita had decided with 100 percent certainty to move to Rio de Janeiro and wanted to do everything possible to make the best arrangements under the circumstances for her daughter Gloria. She recognized that such a move would by necessity compromise Gloria's relationship with her father, but she believed that this drawback would be more than compensated for by the benefits to be derived from the extended family involvement in South America. Dan's primary hope was that the consultation would result in my persuading his wife not to make the move. If that were not possible, he hoped that I would support his contention that Gloria would do best living with him. One of the arguments he gave in favor of his position was that Gloria was born and raised in the United States, was well adjusted to American society, and that the move to Rio de Janeiro would involve a "culture shock" and a dramatic psychological reorganization if she were to adjust properly. He also stated that he was now involved with another woman who would serve as a good mother surrogate if he were to marry her. However, he was not certain at that point whether he was going to remarry.

In conflicts of this kind I give the greatest amount of attention to the personality qualities of the parents, especially with regard to parenting capacities. I also give serious consideration to availability for parenting involvement. Other factors are certainly considered, as described in detail in this book. On the basis of my evaluation I concluded that Juanita was indeed the preferable parent with regard to parenting qualities. She clearly had a stronger bond with Gloria than had her father. The fact that her father had been somewhat neglectful of her in the year following his departure from the home was a definite parental compromise. However, it was a past compromise and was not given as much weight as I would have given such removal at the time of the mediation. Juanita was the one who had most frequently taken Gloria to the pediatrician when she was ill, even at night when both were equally available. She had been more involved in teacher conferences, PTA meetings, and attendance at school plays and recitals. Furthermore, she was more available at the time of the mediation because of her part-time job, whereas her husband worked full-time. However, his business did allow him great flexibility, which he had not at that point availed himself of. I also took into account the fact that if Juanita went to Rio de Janeiro alone, Gloria would be deprived of a significant family network. This would not be the case if Gloria accompanied her mother to South America.

It was these and other considerations that led me to recommend that Gloria accompany her mother and that arrangements be made for the most frequent possible contacts between Gloria and her father. The father was advised to make as many trips as possible to South America and to bring Gloria up to the United States as much as possible. They agreed that her school program would allow her to come north for a one-month period in January and July. Furthermore, Dan considered it possible for him to travel down to South America twice a year during the intervening periods. They agreed that they would speak on the phone at least once and preferably twice a week and that frequent letters would also be exchanged. Although Dan was certainly unhappy about this proposal, I was able to convince him that it was best for Gloria considering the other options. I also advised the family to keep in touch with me and to consult with me periodically if they had any further problems. There were two follow-up visits, one and two years following the move and things appeared to be progressing well. My interview with Gloria revealed that she was suffering no untoward effects from this arrangement.

CONCLUDING COMMENTS

The primary focus in this chapter has been on the mediation process in general. I have focused on the larger format of mediation, which includes attempts to resolve the variety of disputes divorcing individuals are often embroiled in. These include disputes over finances, property, as well as custody (including visitation and decision-making powers). When a custody evaluation is conducted in the context of mediation, it generally takes much less time than when the same evaluation is conducted in the context of custody litigation. There are a number of reasons for this. The clients are generally more honest when mediating and so less time need be spent "smoking out" the various fabrications that are inevitably provided the examiner. When custody litigation is taking place, the clients are generally "wound up" by their attorneys and so the animosity is much higher and the cooperation much less. Communication is also impeded by adversarial proceedings. Often the attorneys have briefed their clients regarding what they should admit to me and what they should not and this cannot but make the evaluation more difficult. The children, as well, are more likely to exhibit signs of the parental alienation syndrome, which makes it more difficult for the examiner to know which of their allegations are valid and which are fabrications.

⚖️ THIRTEEN
RECOMMENDATIONS
FOR THE FUTURE

THE EDUCATION OF LAWYERS

If the recommendations made in this book are to be brought about, it is crucial that significant changes be made in the education of attorneys. If law schools continue to churn out graduates who are as committed to the adversary system as have been those of past years, then it is unlikely that many of the proposed reforms will be realized. At this time there is good evidence that many law schools are beginning to make such changes. Some schools have introduced courses in mediation and other alternative methods of dispute resolution. However, the schools still have a long way to go. In this section I will focus on both what is starting to be done and what still needs to be done.

Law School Admissions Procedures

Most of the major law schools with which I am familiar do not interview students who are being screened for admission. Rather, the criteria upon which the decision is made are mainly class standing, grade point average, the academic prestige of the institution(s) from which the student has graduated, letters of recommendation, and last (but certainly not least) the applicant's score on the Law School Aptitude Test (LSAT). This information is fed into a computer and a decision is often made without human intervention. A school will often grant an interview if an applicant requests it, but this aspect of the admissions procedure is not well publicized or encouraged. The faculty generally prefers to use the above criteria to determine suitability for admission rather than devote significant time to interviewing the sea of applicants who apply to the best law schools. At the time of this writing (early 1989) law schools are enjoying an unprecedented record number of applicants, surpassing even the peaks of recent years. Some of these applicants have been discouraged from applying to medical school because of the glut of physicians in densely populated areas and because of the AIDS epidemic. I believe that the failure to interview applicants is an unfortunate practice. Medical schools also receive floods of applicants (recent drops notwithstanding) and yet routinely interview those among the highly qualified group who are under serious consideration for admission. Medical school admissions committees consider themselves to have an obligation to both the school and society to learn something about the morals, ethics, values, and psychological stability of potential candidates. Although the law schools claim that such information will be found in the undergraduate school's letter of recommendation, there is no question that colleges try to portray candidates to graduate school in the best possible terms. The more prestigious the school their graduates enter, the more prestige the undergraduate school will enjoy. Under these circumstances, hyperbole characterizes the letters of recommendation because even a hint of impairment is likely to doom the candidate—*especially* at the more prestigious law schools.

Such admission policy contributes to the development and continuation of some of the problems described in this book. Specifically, those lawyers who perpetrate the evils described herein must have certain personality defects in order to operate in the way they do. They must have significant impairments in their sensitivity to the feelings of others and be capable of blinding themselves to the psychological damage they are inflicting on clients—both their own and those of their adversaries. They must be people with little sense of guilt concerning their actions. In extreme cases such individuals are called *psychopaths*. Psychopaths, by definition, are people who have little guilt or remorse over the pains and suffering they cause others. They have little capacity to place themselves in the positions of those whom they are exploiting or traumatizing. The primary deterrent to their exploitive behavior is the immediate threat of punishment or retribution from external sources. They have little, if any, internal mechanisms to deter them from their heinous activities. Psychopathic types can be very convincing and ingratiating; they are often master manipulators. They may do quite well for themselves at the undergraduate level, demonstrating their brilliance to professors and convincing school administrators and faculty that they are major contributors to their academic institutions. Such individuals often receive the most laudatory letters of recommendation to law schools and other graduate institutions. It is important for the reader to appreciate that I am not by any means claiming that all lawyers who engage in protracted custody litigation are psychopaths or psychopathic types. I am only claiming that law school admissions procedures are not well designed to screen such people, and the legal educational process intensifies such tendencies when they exist.

It is important for the reader to appreciate that the terms *psychopath* and *psychopathic type*, do not refer to clearly defined categories. There is a continuum from the normal to the psychopathic type to the extreme psychopath—with varying gradations of impairment. When I use the term psychopath I am referring to the people at the upper end of the continuum. Psychopathic types are found lower down on the continuum, but they still exhibit occasional psychopathic traits. Individuals in both of these categories may very well gain acceptance into law school, especially if no interview is required. I am not claiming that interviewers would routinely detect such individuals, only that astute interviewers should be alerted to their existence. Interviewers who screen applicants for medical schools are generally concerned with such types. Although medical school interviewers may certainly be fooled by psychopaths, they are less likely to be duped than computers.

It is also important for the reader to appreciate that this negative comparison between medical school and law school admissions procedures is not a statement on my part that we do not have psychopathic types in medicine. Rather, I believe that we have too many and that admissions screening procedures are not stringent enough and interviewers not astute enough always to detect such individuals at that point. I do believe, however, that there are fewer psychopaths in medicine than in law, partly due to admissions interviews. Moreover, I fully appreciate that we in medicine have our own brands of psychopathology and personality disorder, as does every field. I am not whitewashing medicine here; I am only pointing out certain differences in admissions procedures relevant to the issues in this chapter.

Another category of psychopathology likely to be found among members of the legal profession is *paranoia*. A paranoid individual is generally defined as someone who has delusions of persecution. Specifically, paranoids believe that others are persecuting, plotting against, exploiting, and engaging in a variety of other harmful acts against them when there is no evidence for such. These individuals may be always on the defensive and may seize upon every opportunity to "fight back." *Paranoid types* are individuals who have paranoid tendencies, but are not grossly paranoid. They are at a point along the continuum between normal and paranoid, but closer to the paranoid end. Paranoid tendencies and the practice of law go well together. These individuals may view legal education as a vehicle for providing themselves with ammunition for protection against their persecutors. Again, we certainly have our share of paranoids in medical school; however, because our admission procedures lessen the likelihood that paranoids will gain admission, I believe that there is a higher percentage in the legal profession. Paranoids are very likely to encourage litigation, whether it be custody litigation or any other type. And they thereby contribute to the grief of parents involved in custody/visitation conflicts. Of particular pertinence to this book is the paranoid type or paranoid lawyer who does not appreciate that a mother in the severe category of parental alienation syndrome parents may be basically paranoid. Such an attorney is more likely to support her delusions, much to the grief and detriment of all concerned. And if the judge as well has such tendencies (not a remote possibility considering judges are generally drawn from the pool of lawyers) then the mother's paranoia may be even more harmful. In short, when a paranoid mother is supported by a paranoid lawyer and presents her case before a paranoid judge, the likelihood of family devastation approaches the 100 percent level.

Then, there is the plethora of lawyers being graduated by the law schools. At this time the best estimates are that there is approximately one lawyer for every 340 people in the United States. The ratio in Japan is one to 10,000. Although we live in the most litigious society in the world even we cannot use so many lawyers. In such a situation there are many "hungry" lawyers willing to take on any clients who are simpleminded or sick enough to engage their services. The lawyer and client work together as a team. Both must commit themselves to the "cause." The client who is foolish and gullible enough to believe that adversary litigation is the best first step toward resolving a custody/visitation dispute then teams up with an attorney who is hungry enough to exploit such a client and we have a "team."

The cure for this problem, obviously, is to reduce the number of people entering law school. This is not going to be accomplished easily. Many schools (including law schools) are money-making propositions. There is no medical school in the United States that earns money on each medical student, regardless of how high the tuition. Hospitals, laboratories, faculty in twenty or more specialities, and extremely expensive equipment make the cost of medical education extremely high. By comparison, legal education is relatively inexpensive. There are no laboratories and expensive equipment such as is necessary in departments of chemistry, psychology, physics, biology, engineering, and other scientific disciplines. Of course, a law library is necessary; otherwise all that is required are classroom facilities.

Legal training, then, may be a "money-making proposition" and may help to offset the costs of the more expensive departments within a university (such as medical schools). So there is little likelihood that universities are going to curb law school admissions.

Imposing restrictions on the number of people entering the legal profession would generally be viewed as undemocratic. In this "land of opportunity" we believe that everybody should have the chance to pursue any reasonable goal. But every single discipline and trade has restrictions on membership. Certainly the maintenance of standards of competence is a factor. Also, many disciplines restrict the number of trainees because they want to maintain a high earning power for those who have gained admission. Unions do this routinely; in fact, nepotism is the rule among many trade unions. Although considered undemocratic, the practice is widespread. As long as there is a sea of lawyers, many of whom are hungry, there will be too many attorneys available to perpetuate the kinds of family psychopathology described in this book.

Teaching Law Students About the Deficiencies of the Adversary System

Prevention is best accomplished if one's attention is directed to the earliest manifestations of the processes that bring about a disorder. With regard to the prevention of the parental alienation syndrome and other disorders that arise from protracted adversarial proceedings, one does well to start at the law-school level, where lawyers first learn the system. Although all law schools teach that the adversary system is not perfect, most professors teach their students that it is the best we have for ascertaining the truth when such determination is crucial to resolve a dispute. Law students are taught that the system has evolved over centuries and that it is the best method yet devised for determining whether or not a defendant has indeed committed an alleged crime. It is based on the assumption that the best way of finding out who is telling the truth in such conflicts is for the accused and the accuser each to present to an impartial body (a judge or jury) his (her) argument, in accordance with certain rules and guidelines of presentation. More specifically, each side is permitted to present any information that supports its position and to withhold (within certain guidelines) information that would weaken its arguments. Out of this conflict of opposing positions, the impartial body is presumably in the best position to ascertain the truth.

Many in the legal profession have never given serious consideration to the system's weaknesses and blindly adhere to its tenets. Essential to the system is the principle that the impartial body attempts to rule on and/or resolve the dispute through the application of some general rule of law. Although this certainly serves to protect individuals from misguided justice, it produces in many legal professionals what I consider to be an exaggerated deference to "the law." This may result in a blind adherence to legal precedents, statutes, and laws—often with little consideration to whether they are just, honorable, or fair. I would like to focus in this section on what I consider to be some of the grievous weaknesses of the adversary system, weaknesses that directly contribute to the kinds of family psychopathology already described.

Lies of Omission and Lies of Commission   Lies can be divided into two categories: lies of omission and lies of commission. A merchant who sells a piece of glass while claiming it is a diamond is lying by commission (a lie has been committed). A pregnant woman who does not tell her husband that he is not the father of the child she is carrying is lying by omission (she has omitted telling him the truth). In both cases someone is being deceived. The adversary system basically encourages lies of omission. It encourages withholding information that might compromise a client's position. This is lying. The same attorneys who routinely justify such omissions in their own work would not hesitate suing a physician for malpractice for the omission of information that could be detrimental to a patient. Many lawyers get defensive when one tries to point out that lies of omission are still lies, and that teaching law students to utilize them is to teach deceit. The argument that this is how the adversary system works is not a justifiable one. It is a rationalization. Psychiatrists, and physicians in general, work on the principle that all pertinent information must be brought to their attention if they are to make the most judicious decisions regarding treatment. The same principle holds with regard to the solution of other problems in life. The more information one has, the better is one's capacity to deal with a problem. The adversary system encourages the withholding and covering up of information. The argument that the other side is very likely to bring out what is withheld by the first is not a valid one. The other side may not be aware that such information exists. Furthermore, the procedure encourages nit-picking and other time-wasting maneuvers, delays, and interrogatory procedures that usually impede rather than foster the divulgence of information. These time-wasting elements in the procedure often so becloud an issue that important facts get lost or are not given proper attention. Furthermore, only the wealthiest can afford a trial that attempts to ensure that all the pertinent information will ultimately be brought forth.

It is unreasonable to expect that one can teach law students how to lie in one area and not to do so in others. These practices tend to become generalized. Attorneys have been known to say to clients, "Don't tell me. It's better that I don't know." The next step, after a client has unwittingly provided the compromising information, is for the attorney to say, "Forget you told me that" or "Never tell anyone you said that to me." And the next step is for the attorney to say, "You know it and I know it, but that is very different from their *proving* it." This "deal" is, by legal definition, collusion: an agreement between the lawyer and the client that they will work together to deceive the other side. Like chess, it is a game whose object is to trick and entrap the opponent.

Professors at many law schools may respond that such criticism does not give proper credit to or demonstrate respect for the "higher" principles taught at their institutions. They claim that their students are imbued with the highest ethical and moral values known to humankind. Although they may actually believe what they are saying, my experience has been that the graduates of these same institutions are still prone to involve themselves in the aforementioned kinds of deceitful maneuvers with their clients. Moreover, even these institutions teach the adversary system. When one begins with a system that is intrinsically deceitful, one cannot expect those who implement it to use it in an honest manner. To use it is to deceive and to risk an expansion of deceit into other areas. If one teaches a child to steal pennies and only pennies, one should not be surprised when the child starts stealing nickels. To say I only taught the youngster how to steal pennies is no defense. If one teaches a child to lie to the butcher but not to the baker, one should not be surprised when the child lies to the baker as well. After years of involvement with adversarial deceit in the professional realm, many attorneys no longer appreciate how deep-seated has become their tendency to fabricate. Cover-ups and lies of omission become incorporated into their personality and lifestyle. Many reach the point where they no longer appreciate that they have been corrupted by the system within which they earn their livelihood.

The Failure to Allow Direct Confrontation Between the Accused and the Accuser   It amazes me that after centuries of utilization, adherents of the adversary system do not appreciate that they are depriving themselves of one of the most valuable and predictable ways of learning the truth. I am referring here to the placing of the accused and the accuser together in the same room in direct confrontation. Proponents of the system will immediately take issue with me on this point. They will claim that one of the reasons for the development of the adversary system was the appreciation that the system's predecessor, the inquisitorial system, left accused parties feeling helpless. During the early use of the inquisitorial system, accused individuals were not permitted direct confrontation with their accusers, and frequently did not even know who they were. This insistence upon the right of accused individuals to face their accusers is considered to be one of the strongest arguments for perpetuating the adversary system. Unfortunately, many of the system's proponents fail to appreciate that the confrontations insisted upon are not as free and open as they would like to believe. When referring to this practice, the general assumption is that the confrontation will take place in an open courtroom. This too is considered an advance over inquisitorial procedures in which the proceedings were often held in secret. On the one hand, this is an advance because there are many witnesses to the confrontation: a judge, a jury, and often observers in the audience. On the other hand, the confrontation is extremely constrained by rites of courtroom procedure, and both parties are required to work under very confining circumstances. They are rarely allowed direct communication with one another; rather, communication is usually through their attorneys. These elements significantly compromise the benefits that are presumably obtained from the confrontation. In short, the principle of direct confrontation between accused and accuser is certainly a good one, but its implementation in the adversary system has reduced its efficacy enormously.

The central problem with the adversarial courtroom confrontation is that the two individuals are not permitted to speak directly to one another. The argument that in more volatile situations they might cause one another physical harm is no justification for such formidable constraints. The litigants could, if necessary, be provided with some kind of physical barrier such as a perforated steel screen (through which they could still converse). The argument that the accused and the accuser are still better off having representatives is, I believe, a residuum of the medieval practice of trial by champion. No matter how brilliant the lawyer and the judge, no matter how obsessive they are with regard to getting the details of the alleged incident, no matter how devoted they are to the collection of their data, the fact is that *they were not present as observers of the alleged incident.* The accused and the accuser know better than anyone else whether or not the events actually occurred. Similarly, they often know each other better than any of the other parties involved in the litigation. If the system were to allow the two to talk directly to each other, and confront each other with their opinions of one another's statements, much more "truth" would be obtained. Of course, less money would be made by the "middle men." In some cases their "services" could be dispensed with entirely. In other cases attorneys would still be necessary because of their knowledge of the law and other genuine services that they could provide their clients.

These factors are especially valid for custody litigation. The litigants know one another "inside out." Each knows better than anyone else when the other party is fabricating. Each knows the signs and symptoms of the other's lying: stuttering, the hesitations, the embarrassed facial expressions, and the wide variety of other manifestations of duplicity. The adversary system does not give individuals the opportunity for an "eyeball to eyeball" confrontation. I am convinced that this is one of the best ways of finding out who is telling the truth, and I am astounded that after all these years, the system still deprives itself of using this valuable source of information.

It is for this reason that I make joint sessions mandatory in my custody evaluations (1982a, 1986a). In such meetings the parents can immediately "smoke out" one another's lies in a way far superior to the procedures used in the courtroom. Furthermore, in joint interviews the examiner has the immediate opportunity to telephone other individuals who might be able to provide important information regarding which parent is telling the truth. The judge cannot do this; an impartial evaluator can do so readily. It might take weeks or months to bring in a third party to provide testimony and even then one might not be successful because of the reluctance on the part of the person to "get involved." However, a telephone call made by one of the spouses is much more likely to elicit the third party's comments during a brief conversation over the telephone. Such participation is very different from appearing on a witness stand in a courtroom. And the spouse who lies and risks being exposed by such a call is not likely to resist strongly because of the knowledge that such resistance implies guilt, shame, or some kind of cover-up that will compromise the resistor's position in the custody evaluation. There is no lawyer involved to "protect" the client's rights and to justify thereby cover-ups and the perpetuation of the fabrication. There is no time lag to allow the individual to "prepare a response" and thereby selectively withhold information or even introduce fabrications.

Accordingly, when I conducted custody evaluations under the aegis of the court I did so with the proviso that I would be free to bring the involved parties together in the same room at the same time. And I now continue this pattern in custody evaluations conducted in the context of mediation. Obviously, this pertains to the parents who are mediating, but also I obtain their agreement to invite other parties to participate as warranted. Any reluctance is viewed as an obstruction to the mediation process and results in my considering whether the parties are indeed candidates for mediation. And the same considerations hold when I am asked to conduct other kinds of evaluations, such as sex-abuse evaluations (1987a). Here, again, I am surprised that the tradition is for the courts to send a child to examiners such as myself and ask us to evaluate the child alone to find out whether or not there has been sex abuse. When I have asked for the opportunity to bring the alleged abuser and the child into the same room at the same time (at my discretion), I was often met with an incredulous response. This too amazes me. Admittedly, there are extra complicating factors in such situations, such as the child's fear of the confrontation and the repercussions of the disclosures. However, these drawbacks notwithstanding (there is no situation in which there are no drawbacks), not including such joint interviews seriously compromises the evaluation.

The Issue of Conviction for the Client's Position   Most lawyers believe that they can be as successful helping a client whose cause they may not be particularly in sympathy with as they can with one whose position they strongly support. From their early days in law school, they are imbued with the idea that their obligations as lawyers is to serve the client and work as zealously as possible in support of his (her) position. They are taught that they must do this even though they may not be in sympathy with the client's position and even though they might prefer to be on the opponent's side. This is another weakness of the adversary system. It assumes that attorneys can argue just as effectively when they have no commitment to the client's position as when they do.

In most law schools students are required to involve themselves in "moot court" experiences in which they are assigned a position in a case. The assignment is generally made on a random basis and is independent of the student's own conviction on the particular issue. In fact, it is often considered preferable that the assignment be made in such a way that students must argue in support of the position for which they have less conviction. On other occasions, the student may be asked to present arguments for both sides. Obviously, such experiences can be educationally beneficial. We can all learn from and become more flexible by being required to view a situation from the opposite vantage point. However, I believe that those attorneys who hold that one can argue just as effectively without conviction as one can if one has conviction are naive. Noncommitted attorneys are going to serve less effectively in most cases. Accordingly, before they enter the courtroom, their clients are in a weakened position. Most (but not all) attorneys are not likely to turn away a client whose position they secretly do not support. (One doesn't turn away a paying customer so quickly.) Accordingly, it would be very difficult for a client to find a lawyer who is going to admit openly to a lack of conviction for the client's position.

I recall a situation in which I had good reason to believe that an attorney was basically not supporting his client, the father in a custody case, and that his lack of conviction contributed to his poor performance in the courtroom. In this particular case I served as an impartial examiner and concluded that the mother's position warranted my support. However, once in the courtroom, I was treated as an advocate of the mother (the usual situation). Early in the trial the guardian ad litem suggested that I, as the impartial examiner, be invited into the courtroom to observe the testimony of a psychiatrist who had been brought in as an advocate for the father's side. The father's attorney agreed to this, which surprised me because I did not see what he had to gain by my having direct opportunity to observe (and potentially criticize) his client's expert. I thought that there would be more to lose than gain for this attorney because his own expert's testimony would be likely to provide me with more "ammunition" for the mother.

While the advocate expert testified, I took notes and, as was expected, the father's attorney provided him ample time to elaborate on his various points. When I took the stand, I was first questioned by the mother's attorney, the attorney whose position I supported. He, in turn, gave me great flexibility with regard to my opportunities for answering his questions. Then the father's attorney began to question me. To my amazement, he allowed me to elaborate on points on which I disagreed with him. At no point did he confine me to the traditional yes-no answers that are designed to weaken and distort testimony. He persistently gave me the opportunity for elaboration and naturally, I took advantage of it.

During a break in the proceedings, when the judge and attorneys were conferring at the bench, I heard the judge ask him, "Why are you letting Gardner talk so much?" I suspect this was an inappropriate statement for the judge to make, but it confirms how atypical and seemingly inexplicable was the attorney's examination of me. The lawyer shrugged his shoulders, said nothing, and on my return to the stand continued to allow me great flexibility in my answers. I had every reason to believe that he was a bright man and "knew better." I had no doubt that he did not routinely proceed in this way. To me, this attorney's apparently inexplicable behavior was most likely motivated by the desire (either conscious or unconscious) that his own client lose custody because of his recognition that the mother was the preferable parent. He "went through the motions" of supporting his client, but did so in such a way that he basically helped the other side win the case.

Therapists, in contrast, generally work in accordance with the principle that if they have no conviction for what they are doing with their patients, the chances of success in the treatment are likely to be reduced significantly—even to the point of there being no chance of success at all. If, for example, the therapist's feelings for the patient are not strong, if there is no basic sympathy for the patient's situation, if the relationship is not a good one, or if the therapist is not convinced that the patient's goals in therapy are valid, the likelihood of the patient's being helped is small. Without such conviction the therapy becomes boring and sterile—with little chance of any constructive results.

A. S. Watson (1969), an attorney, encourages lawyers to refuse to support a client's attempts to gain custody when the attorney does not consider the client to be the preferable parent. He considers such support to be basically unethical because one is likely to be less successful with a client for whose position one does not have conviction. This is a noble attitude on this attorney's part. Unfortunately, far too few lawyers subscribe to this advice, and most succumb to the more practical consideration that if they do not support their client's position, they will lose that client and the attendant fee.

The Issue of Emotions and Objectivity   Attorneys are taught in law school that emotions compromise objectivity. They use the word *objectivity* to refer to the ability to "stay cool," think clearly, and thereby handle a situation in the most judicious and "clear-headed" way. Emotions are viewed as contaminants to such clear thinking, i.e., they are *subjective*. Objectivity is equated with the ability to deal with a situation in the most judicious way. And this is the concept of the word that I will utilize here. Accordingly, they are taught that if one gets emotional in a legal situation, one's clients may suffer. This polarization between emotions and objectivity is an oversimplification and compromises thereby many attorneys' capacity to represent optimally their clients. I believe there is a continuum between objectivity and emotions. To set up a dichotomy is not consistent with the realities of the world. An emotion in fact *exists*. That one cannot measure it or weigh it does not negate its existence. To say that a thought is objective and a feeling is not is to make an artificial distinction between two types of mental processes. Emotions have many more concomitant physiological responses outside the brain than do thoughts, but this does not mean that emotions are thereby "not real" (the implication of the word *subjective*). At one end of the continuum are thoughts with little if any emotional concomitants. At the other end are emotions with little if any associated thoughts. As one moves along from the cognitive (thoughts) end toward the affective (emotional) end, the percentage of thoughts decreases and the percentage of emotions increases. At some point along this continuum, closer to the affective end, are *mild* emotions. As I will discuss in detail below, I believe that extremely strong emotions generally will compromise objectivity, but mild ones are likely to *increase* objectivity – if used judiciously. Again, I use the word *objectivity* here to refer to the capacity to handle a situation in the most effective way.

Attorneys generally do not differentiate between strong and mild emotions; they simply view all emotions as potentially contaminating attempts to learn the truth. *Both mild and strong emotions are sources of information.* When a psychotherapist, while working with a patient, exhibits emotions, he (she) does well to determine whether or not they are in the mild or severe category. The therapist has to differentiate between emotions that will compromise objectivity and those that will enhance it. If a therapist experiences mild emotions – which are engendered by the patient's behavior and are similar to emotions that the vast majority of individuals are likely to have in that situation – then the expression of such emotions to the patient can prove therapeutic. For example, if a therapist becomes irritated because the patient is not fulfilling financial obligations, the therapist does well not only to confront the patient with the default but also to express the frustration and irritation thereby engendered. After all, if a psychotherapist is not going to be open and honest with the patient about his (her) *own* emotional reactions, how can the therapist expect the patient to be so. Also, one of the services for which the patient is paying is the therapist's honest responses. Such expression of feelings by the therapist is a good example of the proper use of a mild emotion in the therapeutic process. It enhances the efficacy of the treatment. I am therefore in sharp disagreement with those who consider the presence of such emotions in the therapist to be necessarily inappropriate, injudicious, psychopathological, or a manifestation of a lack of objectivity.

Now to the issue of very strong emotions. These may be useful or not useful, therapeutic or antitherapeutic, in the treatment process. Because the therapeutic process is another "slice of life" in which the same general principles of living are applicable, my comments on the roles of emotions in treatment apply to their role in handling situations elsewhere. First, an example of a severe emotion in the therapeutic process. If a patient threatens to kill a psychotherapist, the therapist is likely to be frightened and/or extremely angry. And such feelings may be very powerful. If these feelings are used judiciously, the therapist may save his (her) life and may even protect the lives of others. We see here how a strong emotion may be useful and not necessarily becloud objectivity. If the therapist, however, fears for his (her) life when there is no actual threat, then he (she) is likely to be delusional and is clearly compromised in the capacity to help the patient. Here inappropriate, strong emotions are operative in reducing the therapist's objectivity.

Now to a more common situation. If a therapist overreacts because of neurotic reactions to what the patient is saying, he (she) becomes compromised as a therapist, e.g., getting angry at a patient for leaving treatment or having sex with a patient. Such overreaction results in injudicious, antitherapeutic, or unethical handling of the matter—again reducing the therapist's objectivity. In short, emotions per se do not compromise objectivity; they may or they may not. When mild they are less likely to; when severe they are more likely to. Even severe emotions, used judiciously, can enhance one's efficacy (and thereby objectivity) in dealing with a situation.

Accordingly, lawyers have to appreciate that the traditional advice that they should be unemotional is injudicious. They should try to be sensitive to their emotions and make the kinds of discriminations I have just described. They should recognize that emotional reactions are not necessarily a hindrance to their work and do not necessarily interfere with objectivity. Lawyers should use their emotions to help their clients; they should not deny their emotions and conclude that their expression will be a disservice to their clients. It is better for them to recognize that mild emotional reactions can often enhance their efficacy. We fight harder when we are angry to a reasonable degree. We lose our efficiency in fighting when our anger deranges us and we enter into states of rage and fury. We flee harder when we are frightened. However, if the fear becomes overwhelming, we may become paralyzed with our fear.

The failure of attorneys to appreciate these principles relating to emotions and objectivity has caused me difficulty on a number of occasions in the course of adversary litigation. By the time of my courtroom appearance I generally felt deep conviction for a particular client's position. This was often an outgrowth of my having committed myself strongly to the custody evaluation, worked assiduously at the task, and come to the point where I could firmly support one client's position over the other. In the course of the litigation I had expressed feelings—sympathy, irritation, frustration, and a variety of other emotions. Some lawyers seized upon my admission of such feelings as a justification for discrediting me as being compromised in my objectivity. My attempts to explain that these emotions were engendered by the reality of the situation, and that I was reacting like any other human being, often proved futile. My efforts to impress upon the attorneys that such emotions have an objectivity of their own and could enhance my understanding of the case were met with incredulity and distrust. And even presiding judges usually agreed with the attorneys that it was inappropriate of me to have these emotions. Because of this prevailing notion among members of the legal profession, I came to consider it injudicious to express my emotions and to be much more cautious about revealing them—so as not to compromise the position of the client whom I was supporting.

This is an unfortunate situation. On the one hand, I would have preferred to state, with a reasonable degree of emotion, the position I held and then explain that these attendant emotions did not necessarily compromise my objectivity. On the other hand, to have done so just invited refutation. It would give an adversary attorney "ammunition," even if unjustifiable. At the point when I discontinued involvement in adversarial custody proceedings, I was following primarily the judicious course of not revealing the emotional factors that played a role in the decision-making process. My hope is that attorneys will become more sophisticated regarding this issue, so that evaluators might ultimately be able to provide more complete and honest testimony. My hope also is that the comments I have made here will play a role (admittedly small) in bringing about some elucidation in the legal profession on this point.

Concluding Comments   L. L. Riskin, a law professor who is very critical of the adversary system and the educational system that emphasizes it inordinately, states (1982):

> Nearly all courses at most law schools are presented from the viewpoint of the practicing attorney who is working in an adversary system. . . .There is, to be sure, scattered attention to the lawyer as planner, policy maker, and public servant, but 90 percent of what goes on in law school is based on a model of the lawyer working in or against a background of litigation of disputes that can be resolved by the application of a rule by a third party. The teachers were trained with this model in mind. The students get a rough image with them; it gets sharpened quickly. This model defines and limits the likely career possibilities envisioned by most law students.

In further criticism of the narrowness of the adversary system he states:

> When one party wins, in this vision, usually the other party loses, and, most often, the victory is reduced to a money judgment. This "reduction" of nonmaterial values—such as honor, respect, dignity, security, and love—to amount of money, can have one of two effects. In some cases, these values are excluded from the decision makers' considerations, and thus the consciousness of the lawyers, as irrelevant. In others, they are present by transmutation into something else—a justification for money damages.

These "irrelevant" issues—"honor, respect, dignity, security, and love" are certainly professed by attorneys involved in custody litigation, especially when they wave the banner of the best interests of the child philosophy. In reality the children are often merely the objects that are "won." Often there may be a trade-off of the children with monetary awards. Children become chattel, objects, or booty—with only lip service paid to the emotional consequences of the litigation. The adversary system and the legal education that promulgates the method program attorneys in their earliest phases of development to ignore these crucial elements in their work.

Other Changes in Law School Education That Would Benefit Attorneys and Their Clients

Medical schools require certain courses be taken at the premedical level, courses that serve as foundations for medical education. It is generally recognized that certain science courses at the undergraduate level, especially chemistry, biology, and physics, are so useful at the medical school level that a candidate who has not proven significant efficiency in them would not be considered for admission. Law schools generally do not have any prescribed prelaw curriculum. Most require only three or four years of college. It matters not whether one studied engineering, political science, anthropology, biology, psychology, or anything else. This is unfortunate. I believe more serious attention should be given to this issue. Obviously, if one is going into patent law, one does well to acquire some training in the sciences and engineering. If one is going to use the law as a vehicle to politics, then one should have some background in political science, sociology, and psychology. If one is going to go into family law and involve oneself in divorce litigation then one should certainly have some background in normal and abnormal psychology as well as child development. And students who are not sure which aspect of the law they wish to enter should be required to take such courses subsequently.

It is unfortunate (to say the least) that attorneys have been so slow to recognize the importance of postgraduate specialization. Most lawyers are viewed by the public as "jacks of all trades" and even "masters of all trades" within the law. People go to "a lawyer," whether the problem be divorce, preparation of a will, or getting a mortgage on a house. The assumption is that good lawyers are trained in all of these areas. Actually, they are trained in very few of them. Most attorneys learn from their experiences over the years. These same individuals will, however, go to an orthopedist, gynecologist, surgeon, etc. Most people recognize that the general medical practitioner is a "jack of all trades, but a master of *none*." The arguments given by attorneys for not setting up rigorous programs of specializations are not, in my opinion, valid. They will argue that it is very difficult to decide what the criteria should be for certifying someone in a particular legal specialty and they question who should be doing the examining. Medicine seems to have worked out these problems. No one is claiming that the specialization system is perfect, but most physicians agree that it is better than having no system for specialty training and certification at all.

Accordingly, some of the damage done to clients in the course of custody litigation would be reduced if people planning to go into family law were required to include courses in clinical psychology (normal and abnormal) in their undergraduate training. Furthermore, there should be a postgraduate discipline, involving one or two years of further study, in which there would be specific preparation and experience in family law. During such training many of the issues raised here would be taught—issues such as the drawbacks of the adversary system in general, the disadvantages of the adversary system as it applies to custody litigation, and psychopathological disorders that result from protracted custody litigation. Moreover, I would include such topics as ethics and values in the law, sensitivity to the feelings of clients, psychopathy and paranoia among lawyers, and how these conditions harm clients. Again, I recognize fully that we in medicine are not free from our share of psychopaths and paranoids, nor from incompetence, but we in medicine do much more to screen such individuals at every level of training.

THE EDUCATION AND TRAINING OF
NONLEGAL PROFESSIONALS

On a few occasions I have been asked, when presenting my credentials to testify in court, what my formal training has been in custody litigation. My answer has been simply: "none." The questioning attorney has generally been quite aware that I had no formal training in this area because there was no such training in the late 1950s when I was in my residency. The attempt here was to compromise my credibility by attempting to demonstrate to the court that I was not qualified to testify on child custody matters. Asking me that question is the same as asking an internist, who like myself attended medical school in the mid-1950s, to state what education he had at that time on the subject of AIDS. (Obviously, this question was not asked by the attorney whose position I supported.) Unfortunately, there are young people today who are asked the same question and must also provide the same answer. Considering the widespread epidemic of custody litigation that now prevails, the failure to provide training in this area at the present time represents a significant deficiency in the education and training of professionals doing such evaluations. Most people, like myself, have "learned from experience." Some have learned well and some have not. Accordingly, I would consider it mandatory that all child therapy programs in psychology, psychiatry, social work, and related disciplines require training and experience in custody litigation.

I would emphasize in such programs the point that having professionals automatically serving as advocates ("hired guns") in child custody litigation is a reprehensible practice and a terrible disservice to the family, the legal profession, and the mental health professions as well. The attempt here would be to bring about a situation in which attorneys looking for hired guns would not be able to find any mental health professional who would allow himself (herself) to be so utilized. Although I believe that this is an ideal that will never be reached, it still cannot hurt to have the principle promulgated at the earliest levels of education and training. It is my hope that this principle would be incorporated into the ethical standards of the various professional societies. A strong statement that such advocacy is unethical would certainly help protect and discourage mental health professionals from prostitution of their talents and skills. Such refusal could be considered to be a kind of preventive psychiatry in that it would remove us from contributing to legal maneuvers that play a role in bringing about the parental alienation syndrome and other disorders that result from protracted divorce/custody litigation. Such training would also involve impressing upon the trainees the importance of their doing everything possible to discourage their patients from involving themselves in such litigation and to point out the variety of psychopathological reactions that can result. Elsewhere (1986a), I have described many of these in detail. In addition, trainees should be advised to encourage their patients to involve themselves in mediation as a first step toward resolving divorce/custody disputes. They should be helped to appreciate that adversary litigation should be the parents' very last resort, after all civilized attempts at resolution have failed.

At the present time mediation is very much a "growth industry." Lawyers and mental health professionals are the primary individuals attracted to the field (O. J. Coogler, 1978; J. M. Haynes, 1981; R. Fisher and W. Ury, 1981; J. Folberg and A. Taylor, 1984). However, there are many others with little if any training or experience in these areas. At the present time there are no standards with regard to training requirements. These will inevitably have to be set up, and I believe that they should be set up soon. At the time of this writing, mediation has been popular for about ten years. This might be considered too short a period to give us enough information to decide what the standards should be. Still, I think sufficient time has elapsed to enable us to propose guidelines for a training program. My own view is that it should take place at the graduate level. I would consider two years of course work and a year of practical work under the supervision of experienced mediators to be optimum. During the first two years the program should provide courses in both law and psychology. There should be courses in basic law as well as marriage and divorce law. Courses in finance should cover the kinds of financial problems that divorcing people are likely to encounter. In the mental health area there should be basic courses in child development, child psychopathology, family psychodynamics, and interviewing techniques. Furthermore, there should be courses in mediation techniques and conflict resolution. This academic material would serve as a foundation for the clinical work in the third year.

At this time universities in the United States do not appear to be particularly enthusiastic about setting up such programs. My hope is that they will become more appreciative of the need for these in the near future. In addition, I believe that graduate programs in psychology, social work, and residency training programs would also do well to incorporate mediation training as part of their general curricula. However, training at these levels cannot provide the same kind of in-depth experience that one gets from a full two- or three-year program of the aforementioned type.

CHILD ABUSE REPORTING LAWS

At this time, an increasing number of states are requiring all persons, professional and nonprofessional, to report immediately all cases of suspected child abuse (especially sex abuse). The most flimsy and preposterous suggestions of abuse are being reported. Many lives and careers have been destroyed as a result of such allegations. Innocent individuals have been wiped out financially in the attempt to prove themselves innocent. One may never get back to the same career level—even when completely innocent—because one's reputation may be marred permanently. Who would want to bring a child to a pediatrician charged with sexual molestation of a child? Who would bring a child to a psychotherapist who has been similarly accused? Who would want one's child to play at the home of a divorced father who is up on charges of having sexually molested his child? After months and even years of litigation the individual may be considered not guilty because "there wasn't enough evidence." This still leaves doubt in those who would have their children associate with the alleged abuser. A dramatic account of such a nightmare is described by L. D. Spiegel (1986). His is only one example of many such tragedies innocent individuals have suffered.

Mental health professionals are faced with a terrible dilemma regarding such reporting. If they do report the abuse, they will generally destroy the therapeutic relationship they have with the child and/or at least one of the parents. In addition, such reporting can easily be considered an illegal, immoral, and unconscionable divulgence of confidential material. Not to report the abuse may result in criminal action against the therapist. The courts and the law appear to be oblivious to the implications of such divulgence to therapy. They give the therapist little option, little room to decide whether or not the allegation is indeed bona fide or fabricated. Laws requiring such automatic reporting are often based on the principle that if the child makes the allegation, the therapist should report it. The statutes appear to be based on the premise that children rarely if ever lie about sex abuse. They were formulated, I believe, at a time a few years ago when many sex-abuse workers were of that conviction. Unfortunately, at the time of this writing there are still many sex-abuse workers who still hold that children do not, under any circumstances, fabricate sex abuse. However, there is no question that sex-abuse investigators are becoming increasingly appreciative of the epidemic of fabricated allegations we are now witnessing, especially those that emerged from custody disputes and litigation.

Generally, the statutes take the position that the therapist *must* report the allegation and leave it to community authorities to investigate and decide whether or not the allegation is true. The general presumption, however, is that the allegation is likely to be true, and the lawmakers appear to have been completely oblivious to the implications on the life of the alleged perpetrator, even if proven innocent. L. Denton (1987) reports the experience of a psychologist, Arne Gray, who was treating parents who were disciplining their two adopted children with "time outs" in the basement. The psychologist did not consider the disciplinary measures to be excessive enough to be considered reportable abuse or neglect. However, someone in the community reported the parents to the local Department of Social Services, because of the possibility that the parents were abusing the children. The psychologist testified in court that he saw no evidence for reportable abuse or neglect and considered the parents to be highly motivated for treatment, which he considered to be going well. Denton then states, "But the next day the judge issued two warrants for Gray's arrest for failure to report suspected abuse and neglect."

As a result of these laws, we are now witnessing an avalanche of reports of sex abuse by therapists to child protection agencies. Many therapists are taking the position that it is better to protect themselves and to hell with confidentiality, the therapist-patient relationship, and professional ethics. Child protection agencies are being glutted with these cases and cannot possibly deal with them adequately. Another problem for therapists relates to the threat of malpractice suits for the grief and psychological trauma that may ensue when a family member is so reported. This is especially the case if the allegation proves to be fabricated. As a practitioner myself I am certainly not in support of widespread malpractice litigation. However, I am sympathetic with anyone who sues for malpractice after having been reported to a child protection agency when there has been a false allegation of sex abuse. To the best of my knowledge, reporting laws provide immunity from civil or criminal liability to those who report such abuse if they can demonstrate that they did so in good faith. Whether such protection will hold up in the future remains to be seen. It will certainly not prevent many from initiating malpractice litigation, which is psychologically traumatic even if one "wins." Another problem that results from such laws is that many families in which sex abuse has taken place now justifiably avoid therapy because they recognize that the therapist will be required to report the abuse, even at the time of the first session. Many therapists are now telling families at the beginning of the first interview that they will be required by law to report any abuse of the child. Obviously, many are either turned away by such a statement or withhold any information that might even suggest the abuse. Under these circumstances the therapy for the abuse will be futile.

According to Denton (1987) most statutes require that the reporter have "reasonable suspicion" before being required to report the abuse. The word *reasonable* here is the point of difficulty. What may be reasonable to one therapist may be unreasonable to another. Therapists who believe that there is no such thing as fabricated sex abuse are likely to report every fantasy, no matter how absurd. And those who hold that fabrication is common, especially in the context of custody cases, will be less likely to report and will argue that there was no reasonable suspicion.

My own position on this issue is that therapists should *not be required* to report abuse, whether fabricated or genuine. In this way they will be allowed to work with these families and assist in the rectification of the problem. After all, families coming to therapists are already on the road to alleviation of their difficulties because they have recognized that there are problems for which they are seeking help. Requiring the therapist to report the sex abuse will destroy the treatment and will only increase the likelihood that the abuse will continue. However, if the therapist finds that the therapy is not successful and that there is no therapeutic relationship to be lost, because there was no relationship in the first place, then he (she) should not only be permitted to report, but should be protected from prosecution or malpractice suits for having done so. Therapists should only report cases of abuse when they believe that they can no longer be of assistance and that outside agencies may be able to help where they cannot. Child protection agencies then can work closely with the family and have more power to interrupt the abuse.

Those who make allegations of abuse should be required to stand up to their accusation and suffer some penalty if the accusation proves to be false, maliciously motivated, or frivolous. I recognize that laws requiring such potential repercussions are not without their difficulties. However, there is no question that the threat of such consequences will vastly reduce the number of false accusations. It may also reduce the number of bona fide accusations, but more will be gained than lost by such a policy. Such laws would certainly make many brainwashing parents think twice about initiating and/or promulgating a sex-abuse allegation in the context of a child custody dispute. At the present time there are no consequences for such maliciousness and slander. If the allegation is proven false, the only thing the fabricating parent loses is one important bit of ammunition in the custody fight. There are no other consequences for the parent who fabricates the abuse, whereas the parent who has been so charged may never live down the humiliation and public disgrace.

THE STRONGER, HEALTHY PSYCHOLOGICAL BOND PRESUMPTION

As discussed previously in this book (especially Chapter Nine) I believe that the best interests of the child doctrine, the principle that has been used as a primary guideline in custody litigation for the last 15 years, is far too general to be of value. Furthermore, the belief that sex-blind custody evaluations serve the best interests of children is, I believe, misguided egalitarianism. Courts would do well to utilize what I refer to as *The Stronger, Healthy Psychological Bond Presumption.* This is a three-step principle:

> 1) Preference should be given to that parent (regardless of sex) with whom the child has developed the stronger, healthy psychological bond;
> 2) That parent (regardless of sex) who was the primary caretaker during the earliest years of the child's life is the one most likely to have developed the stronger, healthy psychological bond; and,
> 3) The longer the time gap between the infancy period and the time of the custody evaluation, the greater the likelihood that other factors will operate to affect each parent's psychological bond with the child.

This presumption is sympathetic to present-day emphasis on sexual egalitarianism but gives priority to the more important consideration, namely, the strength of the psychological bond that the child has with each of the parents. In accordance with the third principle, a parent who might have been viewed as preferable during the infancy period might not be viewed as such in the adolescent period because during the many years that have intervened other factors may have been introduced that tipped the balance away from the parent with whom the stronger, healthy psychological bond originally existed. The reader should note, as well, the use of the word "healthy" in these principles. It is not a situation in which any psychological bond will serve. Clearly, if a parent has a sick psychological bond with a child, that is a serious compromise and evaluators must give consideration to transfer of custody to the parent with whom the child has the healthier psychological bond, even though that parent may not have been the primary caretaker during the earliest years of the child's life.

I believe that legislators would do well to give serious consideration to these principles with an eye toward substituting them for the present best interests of the child philosophy. I believe that this would reduce significantly the incidence of the development of the parental alienation syndromes as well as the false allegations of sex abuse that so often arise in the context of this disorder.

THE REMOVAL OF CUSTODY DISPUTES
FROM ADVERSARIAL PROCEEDINGS

In Chapter One I presented my three-phase proposal for dealing with child custody disputes. As outlined there, this three-phase system (mediation, arbitration panel, and appeals panel) would be the *only* route for dealing with custody disputes. Parents would have absolutely no other option. As mentioned also in Chapter One, the proposal does not deprive any individual of rights of due process as defined in the Constitution of the United States. Their right to representation by an attorney is still preserved; however, the attorney is not permitted to utilize traditional courtroom procedures of cross-examination (which are nowhere mandated in the Constitution). The ability to confront one's adversary in an open courtroom is still preserved, as is the opportunity to plead one's case before a judge (in this case a tribunal). In this system, however, the individuals choose their own judges, rather than submit themselves to individuals assigned by the community. Most important, this system would protect parents disputing for custody from becoming embroiled in adversary litigation and protect them, thereby, from the wide variety of psychiatric disturbances that derive from such involvement. It would be a far less costly procedure, far less time consuming, and protect parents from the sense of impotency that they inevitably suffer when involved in traditional adversarial methods for resolving custody disputes.

The system can be instituted in the structure of the present legal system. Although it does not require any constitutional changes, it would require new legislation. But there is no element in the proposal that is not viable and reasonably possible to implement. Although changing state statutes would be difficult, it would be far less difficult than dealing with the problem of training individuals to serve at the various levels of my proposal. We need mental health professionals and lawyers who have received more training in mediation, because such training is crucial at all three levels. We need more mental health professionals who are trained to conduct the kind of intensive custody evaluation described in this book. Traditional mediation training does not generally involve experiences with such exhaustive investigations. Rather, mediators traditionally work at a more superficial level and attempt to resolve the dispute by negotiation and compromise. However, this is all many couples require. It is for the more complex problems that the more intensive kind of custody evaluation described in this book is often necessary.

At this point there are certainly many people who have enough experience to serve at the mediation level. However, we have to set up standards of certification so that parents will be protected from involving themselves with mediators who are not competent to handle a custody dispute. Furthermore, standards have to be set up for individuals functioning at the arbitration panel and appeals panel levels. The primary consideration for such appointments should be knowledge and experience. People who have served for prescribed periods of time at the mediation level would qualify for consideration to serve at the higher levels. At this time a "grandfather clause" would probably have to be utilized in order to allow people who are presently experienced to serve at these levels. In the future, very specific requirements need to be set up in order to decide which individuals would qualify for service at the higher levels.

The three-phase proposal has been designed to deal with custody disputes. However, at this time, false-allegations of sex abuse often have to be dealt with in the context of custody disputes because of the common problem of such allegations in these conflicts. This is especially the case when a parental alienation syndrome is present. Because sex abuse is a crime, it cannot be dealt with simply in a civil proceeding, such as the above three-phase proposal. At this time, individuals who are accused of sex abuse in the context of a custody dispute must involve themselves in two parallel legal procedures: the civil and the criminal. This often involves a double trial, and even two attorneys. The information from one trial, however, may become available to the court conducting the other. I believe that my proposal would still be applicable in sex-abuse cases if one dispensed with the mediation level. If such cases went directly to the arbitration level, they would be dealt with directly under the aegis of the court. Both the civil and the criminal proceedings could be done simultaneously, with the panel having the power to sentence individuals found guilty. The same panel would make the recommendations regarding custody. The accused would still have the right to appeal to the appeals panel who could deal with the problem in the very flexible manner described in Chapter One.

CONCLUDING COMMENTS

As mentioned in Chapter One (*Where Do I Go From Here?*), my decision no longer to involve myself directly in adversarial proceedings associated with custody litigation does not mean that I am removing myself entirely from the field. Rather, I will be continuing to serve as a mediator for couples involved in such disputes (something I have done for many years). However, such mediation will only be done with the understanding (verified by a signed contract) that I will in no way be involved in subsequent custody litigation should the mediation not prove successful.

In addition, I will attempt to promulgate (through lectures and writing) the aforementioned *stronger, healthy psychological bond presumption* to serve as a guideline for courts and mental health professionals when dealing with custody disputes. Furthermore, I will also attempt to call attention to the aforementioned three-phase system that I have proposed for dealing with custody disputes within the legal system, but without the utilization of traditional adversarial proceedings. I have already started, and I plan to continue, promulgating these ideas in my lectures to mental health and legal professionals and to publish my views in journals in both disciplines. At this time (early 1989) three such publications are already in press (1989a, 1989b, 1989c). At this point I am also scheduled to present these proposals to conferences in both the legal and mental health professions in 1989 and thereafter. Last, it is my hope that this book will also play a role in implementing the changes that I believe are crucial if we are to protect people from the psychological ravages of custody litigation.

I appreciate that my efforts will probably prove futile and that the chances of these changes being brought about are extremely small. As described in detail elsewhere (1986a, 1987a) the United States is probably the most litigious society that has ever existed in the history of the human race. J. K. Lieberman (1983) describes in detail the reasons for this phenomenon. It may be that a total reorientation of society is necessary before my proposals could be implemented. We are a country obsessed with litigation. People sue one another for the most frivolous reasons. Protracted adversarial proceedings are an immense source of income for members of the legal profession who do not welcome shorter and less expensive methods of dispute resolution. And the people in the legislatures, to whom I am appealing with my proposals, are most often members of the legal profession. Accordingly, it is unrealistic to expect them to enact legislation that will lose income for themselves and/or their legal associates. Furthermore, there is an army of mental health professionals out there who are also eager to serve as hired guns for attorneys involved in custody litigation. There are psychiatrists, psychologists, social workers, pastoral counselors, family counselors, and a variety of other types of therapists who are eager to enjoy the benefits to be derived from involvement in custody litigation. Therefore, I do not consider it likely that many of my colleagues in the mental health professions will take the course that I have and remove themselves from such involvement.

On the positive side, judges appear to be sympathetic to my proposals because implementation might very well lessen their burden and reduce their overloaded schedules. It may be that help will come from the malpractice insurance companies. Inevitably, they will come to appreciate that people who involve themselves in custody litigation are more likely to be sued for malpractice. Traditionally, high-risk groups pay higher premiums. The implementation of such higher premiums is likely to work much faster toward discouraging mental health professionals from involving themselves in such litigation than anything I could possibly say, and anything I could possibly write.

APPENDIX I

RICHARD A. GARDNER, M.D.
P.O. BOX R
CRESSKILL, N.J. 07626-0317

PROVISIONS FOR ACCEPTING AN
INVITATION TO SERVE AS AN IMPARTIAL
EXAMINER IN CUSTODY LITIGATION

Whenever possible, I make every reasonable attempt to serve as a court-appointed impartial examiner, rather than as an advocate, in custody/visitation litigation. In order to serve optimally in this capacity I must be free to avail myself of any and all information, from any source, that I consider pertinent and reasonable to have. In this way, I believe I can serve best the interests of children and parents involved in such conflicts. Accordingly, before agreeing to serve in this capacity, the following conditions must be agreed upon by both parents and both attorneys:

1) The presiding judge will agree to appoint me impartial examiner to conduct an evaluation of the concerned parties.

2) I will have available to interview all members of the immediate family--that is, the mother, father, and children--for as many interviews (individual and in any combination) as I consider warranted. In addition, I will have the freedom to invite any and all other parties whom I would consider possible sources of useful information. Generally, these will include such persons as present or prospective parental surrogates with whom either parent may be involved and the housekeeper.

Usually, I do not interview a series of friends and relatives each of whom, from the outset, is particularly partial to one of the parents (but I reserve the right to invite such parties if I consider it warranted). The decision to interview such additional parties will be based solely on the potential value of their contributions to the data-collection process and not on whether one parent is represented by more such people than the other.

3) Information will be gathered primarily from the aforementioned clinical interviews. Although I do not routinely use formal psychological tests, in some

evaluations I have found certain psychological tests to be useful. Accordingly, the parents shall agree to take any and all psychological tests that I consider helpful. In addition, they will agree to have one or more of the children take such tests if I consider them warranted. Some of these tests will be administered by me, but others by a psychologist of my choosing if I do not consider myself qualified to administer a particular psychological test.

4) In order to allow me the freedom of inquiry necessary for serving optimally families involved in custody/visitation litigation, the parents shall agree to a modification of the traditional rules of confidentiality. Specifically, I must be given the freedom to reveal to one party what has been told to me by the other (at my discretion) so that I will have full opportunity to explore all pertinent points with both parties. This does not mean that I will not respect certain privacies or that I will automatically reveal all information provided me--only that I reserve the right to make such revelations if I consider them warranted for the purpose of collecting the most meaningful data.

5) The parties shall agree to sign any and all releases necessary for me to obtain reports from others, e.g. psychiatrists, psychologists, social workers, teachers, school officials, pediatricians, hospitals (general and psychiatric), etc. This includes past records as well as reports from professionals who may be involved with any of the parties at the time of the litigation. Although I may choose not to request a particular report, I must have the freedom to request any and all such reports if I consider them useful sources of information.

6) My fee for conducting a custody evaluation is $150 per hour of my time. Time spent in interviewing as well as time expended in report preparation, dictation, telephone conversations, responses to letters (regardless of which side submits them), court preparation, and any

other time invested in association with the evaluation will also be billed at the $150 per hour rate. My fee for court and deposition appearances is $200 per hour while in court and $120 per hour travel time to and from my office. During the data-collection phase of the evaluation, payments shall be made at the time services are rendered. Payments for the final conference at which my findings and recommendations are presented (item #9 below), the court report, and my court appearance shall be made in advance--in accordance with estimates provided prior to the rendering of these services.

Prior to the initial interview (with both parents together) the payer(s) will deposit with me a check (in my name) for $2,500. This shall be deposited in the Northern Valley-Englewood Savings and Loan Association branch in Cresskill, New Jersey, in my name, in a day-to-day interest bearing account. This money, with accrued interest (taxable to the payer), shall be returned _after_ a final decision has been made regarding custody/visitation and after I have received a letter from _both_ of the attorneys that my services are no longer being enlisted.

This payment is a security deposit. It will not serve as an advance retainer, in that the aforementioned fees will not be drawn against it, unless there has been a failure to pay my fees. It also serves to reassure the nonpayer that my objectivity will not be compromised by the fear that if I do not support the paying party, my fee will not be paid.

The average total cost for an evaluation is generally in the $3,000-$6,000 range. Although this figure may initially appear high, it is generally far less costly than protracted litigation. If as a result of the evaluation the litigation is shortened (often the case) or the parties decide not to litigate further over custody/visitation (also a common occurrence), then the net savings may be significant. It is very difficult, if not impossible, to predict the cost of a particular evaluation because I cannot know beforehand how many interviews will be warranted and whether or not I will be asked to testify in court.

On occasion, I am invited to conduct evaluations in cities at varying distances from Cresskill, New Jersey. This generally entails situations in which there is a choice between my travelling to the family's location and all interviewees travelling to New Jersey and acquiring temporary accomodations in the area of my office. Although I prefer that the evaluation take place in my office, I have on occasion agreed to conduct the evaluation elsewhere. However, my fees for such evaluations are higher than for those conducted in my office and are determined by the distance I have to travel and the time I am being asked to be away from my office. My fee schedule for such distant evaluations is available on request.

7) Both attorneys are invited to send to me any material that they consider useful to me.

8) After receiving 1) the court order signed by the presiding judge, 2) the signed statements (page 8) from both parties signifying agreement to the conditions of the evaluation, and 3) the $2,500 deposit, I will notify both parties that I am available to proceed with the evaluation as rapidly as is feasible. I generally cannot promise to meet a specific deadline because I cannot know in advance how many interviews will be required, nor can I predict how flexible the parties will be regarding availability for appointments I offer.

9) Upon completion of my evaluation--and prior to the preparation of my final report--I generally meet with both parents together and present them my findings and recommendations. This gives them the opportunity to correct any distortions they believe I may have and/or alter my opinion before it becomes finalized in my report. In addition, it saves the parents from the

unnecessary and prolonged tension associated with wondering what my findings are.

Both attorneys are invited to attend this conference. However, this invitation should be considered withdrawn if only one attorney wishes to attend because the presence of only one attorney would obviously place the nonrepresented parent in a compromised position. When a guardian ad litem has been appointed by the court, he or she will also be invited to attend this conference. Before accepting this invitation attorneys should appreciate that the discussion will be completely free and open. Accordingly, during this conference it would be improper for an attorney in any way whatsoever to restrict or discourage the client from answering questions or participating in the discussion. On occasion, the litigants have used this conference as a forum for resolving their custody/visitation dispute and avoiding thereby the formidable expense and psychological trauma of courtroom litigation. After this conference the final report is prepared and sent simultaneously to the court, attorneys, and parents.

10) After this conference I strictly refrain from any further communication with either parent or any other party involved in the evaluation. However, I am willing to discuss any aspect of the case with <u>both</u> attorneys at the same time, either personally or by conference telephone call. Such communication may occur at any time from the end of the aforementioned conference to the end of the trial. This practice enables me to continue to provide input to the attorneys regarding what I consider to be in the children's best interests. And this may be especially important during the trial. At that time, in order to preserve my status as impartial, any discussions I may have with an attorney and/or parent is only conducted under circumstances in which the adversary attorney and/or parent is invited to participate.

11) When there has been a significant passage of time between the submission of my report and the trial date, I will generally invite the primary participating parties for an interview update prior to my court appearance. This conference enables me to acquaint myself with developments that succeeded my report and ensures that my presentation in court will include the most recent information. All significant adult participants will be invited to this meeting and on occasion one or more of the children (especially teenagers). This conference will be held as long as at least one party wishes to attend.

My experience has been that conducting the evaluation in the manner described above provides me with the optimum conditions for providing the court with a thorough and objective recommendation.

12) Often one party will invite my services as an impartial examiner and the other will refuse to participate voluntarily. On occasion, the inviting party has then requested that the court appoint me impartial examiner and order the reluctant side to participate. Generally, there are three ways in which courts respond to this request:

A. The court responds affirmatively and appoints me the impartial examiner. In such cases I then proceed in accordance with the above provisions (#1-#11).

B. The court is not willing to formally designate me its appointed impartial examiner, but rather orders the reluctant side to cooperate in interviews with me as if I were the advocate of the initiator. (This usually occurs when the presiding judge orders both parents to be evaluated by each one's selected adversary examiner.) In such cases, I still do not view myself to be serving automatically as the advocate of the initiating party. Rather, I make it understood to all concerned that I will proceed as closely as possible with the type of evaluation I conduct when serving as impartial examiner--even to the point of testifying in court as an advocate of the initially reluctant party. In that eventuality, if the initially reluctant party requests a court appearance, that party will be responsible for my fees (item 6) beyond the point at which my final report has been sent to the court, attorneys, and the clients. The party who initially invited me, however, will still have the obligation to pay for my report, whether or not it supports that party's position. I believe that this plan insures my input to the court regarding what I consider to be in the children's best interests and precludes my serving merely as a hired advocate.

C. The court refuses to order my participation, but recognizes the right of the inviting party to enlist my involvement as an advocate. In such cases I proceed in accordance with provision 13.

SERVING AS AN ADVOCATE

13A) On occasion, I am willing to consider serving as an advocate in custody/visitation litigation. However, such participation will only be considered after evidence has been submitted to me that: 1) the nonparticipating side has been invited to participate and has refused and 2) the court has refused to order such involvement. If I do then suspect that the participating party's position merits my consideration, I would be willing to interview that party with no promise beforehand that I will support his or her position. On occasion I have seen fit to support the participating party's position, because it was obvious to me that the children's needs would be served best by my advocacy and/or not to do so would have deprived them of sorely needed assistance. On other occasions I have concluded that I could not serve with conviction as an advocate of the requesting party and so have refused further services to the client.

B)   If I do decide to serve as an advocate, I ask for the standard $2500 security deposit, which is dealt with as described in item #6. Furthermore, if in the course of my evaluation in which I am serving as an advocate, the nonparticipating party decides belatedly to participate I will, at that point, no longer consider myself automatically committed to serve as an advocate for the original party. Rather, I will conduct the evaluation, as far as possible, in accordance with the provisions for my serving as an impartial examiner--even to the point of testifying in support of the belated participant. Before interviewing the belated participant, however, all parties will have to agree upon any possible modifications of the fee-paying arrangement that may be warranted.

Richard A. Gardner, M.D.

I have read the above, discussed the provisions with my attorney, and agree to participate in the evaluation procedures delineated above. I agree to pay _____% of the $2,500 advance security deposit and _____% of the fees in accordance with the aforementioned payment schedules. I recognize the possibility that Dr. Gardner may not ultimately support my position in the litigation. Nevertheless, I will still fulfill my obligation to pay _____% of his fees. I appreciate that this may entail the payment of fees associated with his preparing reports that do not support my position and even testifying in court in support of my adversary (with the exception of the situation in which items 12B and 13B are operative).

Date: _____   _____
                                        Parent's Signature

Revision No. 36

626

APPENDIX II

RICHARD A. GARDNER, M.D.
P.O. BOX R
CRESSKILL, NEW JERSEY 07626-0317
201-567-8989

PROVISIONS FOR MEDIATING
A CUSTODY DISPUTE

When parties involved in a custody conflict wish to resolve their differences by mediation, rather than litigation, it is crucial that I have every reassurance that there will be absolutely no involvement on my part in ensuing litigation--should the mediation not prove successful in resolving the dispute. This is best accomplished by both parties signing this statement:

We wish to enlist Dr. Richard A. Gardner's services in helping resolve our custody conflict. Accordingly, we agree to participate in Dr. Gardner's custody evaluation and mediation procedures. We recognize that such mediation will be compromised if information revealed therein may subsequently be brought to the attention of the court by Dr. Gardner in any ensuing litigation.

Accordingly, we enter the mediation with the mutual pledge that we will neither individually nor jointly involve Dr. Gardner in any way in ensuing litigation if the mediation does not prove successful in resolving our conflict. We will neither request nor require that Dr. Gardner provide written reports of the custody evaluation or mediation, because such documents might ultimately be used in the litigation. We will not permit Dr. Gardner to communicate with either of our attorneys in any manner, either verbally or in written form. In short, we will strictly refrain from involving Dr. Gardner in any ensuing litigation--in any way whatsoever--either directly or indirectly.

If the services of a mental health professional are considered desirable for the purposes of litigating our custody dispute, either as an advocate or as an impartial, the services of another person--other than Dr. Richard A. Gardner--will be enlisted.

We have read the above and agree to proceed with the mediation.

_____   _____
Signature   Signature

_____   _____
Address   Address

_____   _____
Date   Date

APPENDIX III

RICHARD A. GARDNER, M. D.
P. O. BOX R
CRESSKILL, N. J. 07626
TELEPHONE 201 - 567-8989

PROVISIONS FOR SERVING AS A CHILD THERAPIST FOR LITIGATING PARENTS

When separating and/or divorced parents--who are involved in litigation--bring their child for treatment, a special risk situation exists regarding the child's therapy. Specifically, if the therapist is asked to participate in any way in the litigation, the therapy may be seriously compromised. Effective child psychotherapy is best accomplished when both parents have a good relationship with the therapist. Information that the therapist provides the court is likely to benefit one parent at the expense of the other. The parent whose position has been weakened by this information cannot but harbor animosity toward the therapist. And such hostility toward the therapist is likely to compromise significantly the child's treatment. In order to prevent such deterioration of the child's therapy it is crucial that I have every reassurance that there will be absolutely no involvement on my part in the litigation between the parents. This is best accomplished by both parents signing this statement:

> We wish to enlist Dr. Richard A. Gardner's services in the treatment of our child. We recognize that such treatment will be compromised if information revealed therein may subsequently be brought to the attention of the court in the course of litigation.

> Accordingly, we mutually pledge that we will neither individually nor jointly involve Dr. Gardner in any way in our litigation. We will neither request nor require that Dr. Gardner provide testimony in court, either as an advocate or as an impartial. We will neither request nor require that Dr. Gardner provide written reports of the treatment, because such documents might ultimately be used in the litigation. We will not permit Dr. Gardner to communicate with either of our attorneys in any manner, either verbally or in written form. In short, we will strictly refrain from involving Dr. Gardner in any litigation--in any way whatsoever, either directly or indirectly.

> If the services of a mental health professional are considered desirable for the purposes of litigation, either as an advocate or as an impartial, the services of another person other than Dr. Richard A. Gardner will be enlisted.

628

-2-

We have read the above, discussed these provisions with our
attorneys, and agree to proceed with the therapy.

_____   _____
        Date   Signature

_____   _____
        Date   Signature

629

APPENDIX IV

RICHARD A. GARDNER, M.D.
155 COUNTY ROAD
P.O. BOX R
CRESSKILL, NEW JERSEY 07626-0317
201-567-8989

PROVISIONS FOR PROVIDING ANSWERS
TO HYPOTHETICAL QUESTIONS IN
COURTROOM TESTIMONY

I am willing to answer hypothetical questions in court only if the following conditions are met:

    1) The inviting attorney will ask the adversary attorney to join him (her) in asking the court to appoint me as an impartial witness for the purposes of answering hypothetical questions. If the other side responds in the affirmative, then the proper court order will be drawn and signed by the presiding judge. Upon receipt of such order I will proceed with arrangements for my appearance.

    2) If the opposing side does not wish to engage my services for answering hypothetical questions then the presiding judge will be asked to appoint me to such capacity--over the objections of the reluctant side. In such cases the proper court order is drawn, signed by the presiding judge, and arrangements are made for my appearance.

    3) On occasion the guardian ad litem or child advocate wishes to engage my services for answering hypothetical questions. In such cases that person shall draw up the court order for the signature of the presiding judge.

If the presiding judge refuses to sign a court order in any of the aforementioned situations then I will not be willing to involve myself in the litigation in any way whatsoever. If such a document is signed by the presiding judge then I will proceed with arrangements for my court appearance. In order to preserve my status as an impartial, I will not communicate with the clients, but I will be willing to communicate with the attorneys under circumstances in which I can speak with <u>both</u> together (generally via conference telephone call). If a <u>guardian ad litem</u> or child advocate is involved, I generally communicate only with him (her) prior to my court appearance.

My fee for answering hypothetical questions in court in the Greater New York City area is $300/hr. while in court and

$150/hr. travel time to and from my office.   I also request   a prepayment that approximates the cost of such an appearance.   My fee schedule for providing testimony that involves my traveling to points beyond the Greater New York City area is available on request.

Sincerely,

Richard A. Gardner, M.D.
Clinical Professor of
    Child Psychiatry
Columbia University,
College of Physicians
    and Surgeons

RAG/dll

631

APPENDIX V

RICHARD A. GARDNER, M.D.
P.O. BOX R
CRESSKILL, N.J. 07626-0317
201-567-8989

FEE SCHEDULE FOR EVALUATIONS
WARRANTING TRAVEL TO LOCATIONS
BEYOND THE GREATER NEW YORK CITY AREA

This fee schedule is generally operative when the inviting parties consider it more expeditious (and possibly less expensive) for me to travel to the family's location then for all interviewees to travel to and find temporary accomodations in the area of my office. My basic foundation fee for conducting such evaluations is $100.00 per hour (or $2,400 per day) from the time of departure from my home or office until the time of return. In addition, I bill my usual fee of $150.00 per hour. As described in my provisions document, this not only includes interviewing time, but time spent in preparation of the presentation of my findings, preparation and review of my report, telephone communications, and any other time expended in association with the evaluation. Last, I ask for reimbursement of travel and lodging expenses.

A few weeks prior to my departure, I will submit an itemized statement of the approximate cost of the segment of the evaluation to be conducted during that particular trip. Such payment will be due, in the form of a certified or bank check, no later than two weeks prior to my departure. On my return, I will submit a final statement of fees and expenses with a reimbursement or request for further payment, as warranted.

If testimony in court is requested, either during the same trip (for a variety of reasons, extremely unlikely) or during a subsequent trip, the same fee schedule holds--with the exception that I ask for $200.00 per hour from the time I arrive in court until the time I leave, again in addition to the $2,400.00 per day basic foundation fee and travel and lodging reimbursement.

I have read the above, discussed the provisions with my attorney, and agree to pay _____ % of the aforementioned fees. I

632

recognize the possibility that Dr. Gardner may <u>not</u> ultimately support my position in the litigation. Nevertheless, I will still fulfill my obligation to pay ____% of his fees. I appreciate that this may entail the payment of fees associated with his preparing a report that does not support my position and even testifying in court in support of my adversary.

Date _____   _____
                                        Parent's Signature

APPENDIX VI
Request for Information—Sample Letter

RICHARD A. GARDNER, M.D.
155 COUNTY ROAD
P.O. BOX R
CRESSKILL, NEW JERSEY 07626-0317
201-567-8989

February 13, 1988

John Smith, Ph.D.
100 Pine Street
Dumont, N.J. 07628

Re: Jones vs. Jones

Dear Dr. Smith:

Judge Alexander Burns, Superior Court of New Jersey, Bergen County, has invited me to serve as court-appointed impartial psychiatrist to render the court my recommendations regarding the custody/visitation conflict between Mrs. Alice Jones and Mr. Robert Jones.

Mr. and Mrs. Jones inform me that you saw their daughter Cindy in treatment and that there were contacts with the parents as well. They stated that such treatment took place between January 1987 and June 1987. I would be most appreciative if you would send me a report of your findings and recommendations. I am particularly interested in any statements you can make regarding their parental capacity and any other comments you may have that may be of help to me in making a recommendation about their children's custody and visitation arrangements.

For the purposes of the litigation it is important that this information be provided in written form rather than verbally. Enclosed please find signed releases granting you permission to provide me with this information. In order not to slow this matter unnecessarily, I would be most appreciative if you would send me your report as soon as possible.

Sincerely,

Richard A. Gardner, M.D.
Clinical Professor of
  Child Psychiatry-
Columbia University,
College of Physicians
  and Surgeons

APPENDIX VII
Parent Questionnaire

RICHARD A. GARDNER, M. D.
155 COUNTY ROAD
CRESSKILL, N. J. 07626

TELEPHONE 201 - 567-8989

PLEASE BRING THIS COMPLETED FORM WITH YOU AT THE TIME OF YOUR FIRST APPOINT-

MENT ON_____AT_____

IT IS PREFERABLE THAT BOTH PARENTS ACCOMPANY THE CHILD TO THE CONSULTATION.

Child's name_____ Birth date_____ Age___ Sex_____
           last   first   middle
Home address_____
         street   city   state   zip
Home telephone number_____
               area code   number
Child's school_____
           name   address   **grade**
Present placement of child (place check in appropriate bracket):

	Column A Adults with whom child is living	Column B Non-residential adults involved with child
Natural mother	( )___	( )___
Natural father	( )___	( )___
Stepmother	( )___	( )___
Stepfather	( )___	( )___
Adoptive mother	( )___	( )___
Adoptive father	( )___	( )___
Foster mother	( )___	( )___
Foster father	( )___	( )___
Other (specify)	___ ___	___ ___

Place the number 1 or 2 next to each check in Column A and provide the following information about each person:

1. Name_____Occupation_____
      last   first
  'Business name_____Business address_____

_____Business tel. No._( )_____

2. Name_____Occupation_____
      last   first
  Business name_____Business address_____

_____Business tel. No._( )_____

Place the number 3 next to the person checked in Column B who is most involved with the child and provide the following information:

3. Name_____Home address_____
                               street
_____Home tel. No._( )_____
  city   state   zip
Occupation_____Business name_____

Business address_____Bus. Tel. No. ( )_____

Source of referral: Name_____Address_____

_____Tel. No. ( )_____ _____

Purpose of consultation (brief summary of the main problems):_____ _____

_____

_____

_____

_____

PREGNANCY
  Complications:
    Excessive vomiting_____hospitalization required_____

    Excessive staining or blood loss_____

    Threatened miscarriage_____

    Infection(s) (specify)_____

    Toxemia_____

    Operation(s) (specify)_____

    Other illness(es) (specify)_____

  Smoking during pregnancy_____average number of cigarettes per day_____

  Alcoholic consumption during pregnancy_____describe, if beyond an occa-

    sional drink_____

  Medications taken during pregnancy_____

  X-ray studies during pregnancy_____

  Duration_____weeks

DELIVERY
  Type of labor: Spontaneous_____Induced_____
  Forceps: high_____mid_____low_____
  Duration of labor_____hours

  Type of delivery: Vertex (normal)_____breech_____Caesarean_____

  Complications:
    cord around neck_____

    cord presented first_____

    hemorrhage_____

636

3--

infant injured during delivery_____

other (specify)_____

Birth Weight_____
  Appropriate for gestational age (AGA)_____
  Small for gestational age (SGA)_____

POST-DELIVERY PERIOD (while in the hospital)
Respiration: immediate_____delayed (if so, how long)_____

Cry: immediate_____delayed (if so, how long)_____

Mucus accumulation_____

Apgar score (if known)_____

Jaundice_____

Rh factor_____transfusion_____

Cyanosis (turned blue)_____

Incubator care_____number of days_____

Suck: strong_____weak_____

Infection (specify)_____

Vomiting_____diarrhea_____

Birth defects (specify)_____

Total number of days baby was in the hospital after the delivery_____

INFANCY-TODDLER PERIOD
Were any of the following present--to a significant degree--during the
first few years of life? If so, describe.

  Did not enjoy cuddling _____

  Was not calmed by being held and/or stroked _____

  Colic_____

  Excessive restlessness _____

  Diminished sleep because of restlessness and easy arousal _____

  Frequent headbanging_____

  Constantly into everything_____

  Excessive number of accidents compared to other children_____

DEVELOPMENTAL MILESTONES
  If you can recall, record the age at which your child reached the following developmental milestones. If you cannot recall, check item at right.

	age	I cannot recall exactly, but to the best of my recollection it occurred		
		early	at the normal time	late
Smiled				
Sat without support				
Crawled				
Stood without support				
Walked without assistance				
Spoke first words besides "ma-ma" and "da-da"				
Said phrases				
Said sentences				
Bowel trained, day				
Bowel trained, night				
Bladder trained, day				
Bladder trained, night				
Rode tricycle				
Rode bicycle (without training wheels)				
Buttoned clothing				
Tied shoelaces				
Named colors				
Named coins				
Said alphabet in order				
Began to read				

COORDINATION
  Rate your child on the following skills:

	Good	Average	Poor
	---	---	---
Walking			
Running			
Throwing			
Catching			
Shoelace tying			
Buttoning			
Writing			
Athletic abilities			

COMPREHENSION AND UNDERSTANDING
Do you consider your child to understand directions and situations as well as other children his or her age?_____If not, why not?_____

_____

How would you rate your child's overall level of intelligence compared to other children? Below average_____Average_____Above average_____

SCHOOL
Rate your child's school experiences related to academic learning:

	Good	Average	Poor
Nursery school			
Kindergarten			
Current grade			

To the best of your knowledge, at what grade level is your child function-

ing: reading_____spelling_____arithmetic_____

Has your child ever had to repeat a grade? If so, when_____

Present class placement: regular class_____special class (if so, specify)

_____

Kinds of special therapy or remedial work your child is currently receiving

_____

Describe briefly any academic school problems_____

_____

_____

Rate your child's school experience related to behavior:

	Good	Average	Poor
Nursery school			
Kindergarten			
Current grade			

Does your child's teacher describe any of the following as significant classroom problems?

Doesn't sit still in his or her seat_____

Frequently gets up and walks around the classroom_____

Shouts out. Doesn't wait to be called upon _____

Won't wait his or her turn_____

Does not cooperate well in group activities_____

Typically does better in a one-to-one relationship_____

Doesn't respect the rights of others_____

Doesn't pay attention during storytelling_____

Describe briefly any <u>other</u> classroom behavioral problems_____

_____

_____

PEER RELATIONSHIPS

Does your child seek friendships with peers?_____

Is your child sought by peers for friendship?_____

Does your child play primarily with children his or her own age?_____

    younger_____older_____

Describe briefly any problems your child may have with peers_____

_____

_____

HOME BEHAVIOR

All children exhibit, to some degree, the kinds of behavior listed below. Check those that you believe your child exhibits to an excessive or exaggerated degree when compared to other children his or her age.

Hyperactivity (high activity level)_____

Poor attention span_____

Impulsivity (poor self control)_____

Low frustration threshold_____

Temper outbursts_____

Sloppy table manners_____

Interrupts frequently_____

Doesn't listen when being spoken to_____

Sudden outbursts of physical abuse of other children_____

Acts like he or she is driven by a motor_____

Wears out shoes more frequently than siblings_____

Heedless to danger_____

Excessive number of accidents_____

Doesn't learn from experience_____

Poor memory_____

More active than siblings_____

640

INTERESTS AND ACCOMPLISHMENTS
What are your child's main hobbies and interests?_____

_____

What are your child's areas of greatest accomplishment?_____

_____

What does your child enjoy doing most?_____

_____

What does your child dislike doing most?_____

_____

MEDICAL HISTORY
If your child's medical history includes any of the following, please note
the age when the incident or illness occurred and any other pertinent information.

Childhood diseases (describe any complications)_____

_____

Operations_____

_____

Hospitalizations for illness(es) other than operations_____

_____

Head injuries_____

_____with unconsciousness_____without unconsciousness_____

Convulsions_____

_____with fever_____without fever_____

Coma_____

Meningitis or encephalitis_____

Immunization reactions_____

Persistent high fevers_____highest temperature ever recorded_____

eye problems_____

ear problems_____

poisoning_____

PRESENT MEDICAL STATUS

Present height_____Present weight_____

Present illness(es) for which child is being treated_____

_____

Medications child is taking on an ongoing basis_____

_____

FAMILY HISTORY - MOTHER

Age_____ Age at time of pregnancy with patient_____

Number of previous pregnancies_____Number of spontaneous abortions

(miscarriages)_____Number of induced abortions_____

Sterility problems (specify)_____

School: Highest grade completed_____

  Learning problems (specify)_____grade repeat_____

  Behavior problems (specify)_____

Medical problems (specify)_____

Have any of your blood relatives (not including patient and siblings) ever

had problems similar to those your child has? If so, describe_____

_____

_____

FAMILY HISTORY - FATHER

Age_____Age at the time of the patient's conception _____

Sterility problems (specify)_____

School: Highest grade completed_____

  Learning problems (specify)_____grade repeat_____

  Behavior problems (specify)_____

Medical problems (specify)_____

Have any of your blood relatives (not including patient and siblings) ever

had problems similar to those your child has? If so, describe_____

_____

Most children exhibit, at one time or another, one or more of the symptoms listed below. Place a P next to those that your child has exhibited in the PAST and an N next to those that your child exhibits NOW. Only mark those symptoms that have been or are present to a significant degree over a period of time. Only check as problems behavior that you suspect is unusual or atypical when compared to what you consider to be the normal for your child's age. Then, on page 12, list the symptoms checked off on pages 9-12 and write a brief description including age of onset, duration, and any other pertinent information.

Thumb-sucking ___	Preoccupied with food--what to eat and what not to eat ___	Frequently likes to wear clothing of the opposite sex ___
Baby talk ___		
Overly dependent for age ___	Preoccupation with bowel movements ___	Exhibits gestures and intonations of the opposite sex ___
Frequent temper tantrums ___	Constipation ___	
Excessive silliness and clowning ___	Encopresis (soiling) ___	Frequent headaches ___
Excessive demands for attention ___	Insomnia (difficulty sleeping) ___	Frequent stomach cramps ___
Cries easily and frequently ___	Enuresis (bed wetting) ___	Frequent nausea and vomiting ___
Generally immature ___	Frequent nightmares ___	Often complains of bodily aches and pains ___
Eats non-edible substances ___	Night terrors (terrifying night-time outbursts) ___	Worries over bodily illness ___
Overeating with overweight ___	Sleepwalking ___	Poor motivation ___
Eating binges with overweight ___	Excessive sexual interest and pre-occupation ___	Apathy ___
Undereating with underweight ___	Frequent sex play with other children ___	Takes path of least resistance ___
Long periods of dieting and food abstinence with underweight ___	Excessive masturbation ___	Ever trying to avoid responsibility ___

643

Poor follow-through ___

Low Curiosity ___

Open defiance of authority ___

Blatently uncooperative ___

Persistant lying ___

Frequent use of profanity to parents, teachers, and other authorities ___

Truancy from school ___

Runs away from home ___

Violent outbursts of rage ___

Stealing ___

Cruelty to animals, children, and others ___

Destruction of property ___

Criminal and/or dangerous acts ___

Trouble with the police ___

Violent assault ___

Fire setting ___

Little, if any, guilt over behavior that causes others pain and discomfort ___

Little, if any, response to punishment for anti-social behavior ___

Few, if any, friends ___

Doesn't seek friendships ___

Rarely sought by peers ___

Not accepted by peer group ___

Selfish ___

Doesn't respect the rights of others ___

Wants things own way with exaggerated reaction if thwarted ___

Trouble putting self in other person's position ___

Egocentric (self-centered) ___

Frequently hits other children ___

Argumentative ___

Excessively critical of others ___

Excessively taunts other children ___

Ever complaining ___

Is often picked on and easily bullied by other children ___

Suspicious, distrustful ___

Aloof ___

"Wise-guy" or smart aleck attitude ___

Brags or boasts ___

Bribes other children ___

Excessively competitive ___

Often cheats when playing games ___

"Sore loser" ___

"Doesn't know when to stop" ___

Poor common sense in social situations ___

Often feels cheated or gypped ___

Feels others are persecuting him when there is no evidence for such ___

Typically wants his or her own way ___

Very stubborn ___

Obstruction-istic ___

Negativistic (does just the opposite of what is requested) ___

644

Quietly, or often silently, defiant of authority ___

Feigns or verbalizes compliance or cooperation but doesn't comply with requests ___

Drug abuse ___

Alcohol abuse ___

Very tense ___

Nail biting ___

Chews on clothes, blankets, etc. ___

Head banging ___

Hair pulling ___

Picks on skin ___

Speaks rapidly and under pressure ___

Irritability, easily "flies off the handle" ___

Fears
dark ___
new situations ___
strangers ___
being alone ___
death ___
separation from parent ___
school ___
visiting other children's homes ___
going away to camp ___
animals ___
other fears (name)

_____ ___

_____ ___

Anxiety attacks with palpatations (heart pounding), shortness of breath, sweating, etc. ___

Disorganized ___

Tics such as eye-blinking, grimacing, or other spasmodic repetitious movements ___

Involuntary grunts, vocalizations (understandable or not) ___

Stuttering ___

Depression ___

Frequent crying spells ___

Excessive worrying over minor things ___

Suicidal preoccupation, gestures, or attempts ___

Excessive desire to please authority ___

"Too good" ___

Often appears insincere and/or artificial ___

Too mature, frequently acts older than actual age ___

Excessive guilt over minor indiscretions ___

Asks to be punished ___

Low self-esteem ___

Excessive self-criticism ___

Very poor toleration of criticism ___

Feelings easily hurt ___

Dissatisfaction with appearance or body part(s) ___

Excessive modesty over bodily exposure ___

Perfectionistic, rarely satisfied with performance ___

Frequently blames others as a cover-up for own shortcomings ___

Little concern for personal appearance or hygiene ___

Little concern for or pride in personal property ___

"Gets hooked" on certain ideas and remains preoccupied ___

Compulsive repetition of seemingly meaningless physical acts ___

Shy ___

Inhibited self-expression in dancing, singing, laughing, etc. ___

Recoils from affectionate physical contact ___

Withdrawn ___

Fears asserting
self ___

Inhibits open
expression of
anger ___

Allows self to be
easily taken
advantage of ___

Frequently pouts
and/or sulks ___

Mute (refuses to
speak) but can ___

Gullible and/or
naive ___

Passive and
easily led ___

Excessive fan-
tasizing,
"lives in his
(her) own
world" ___

Flat emotional
tone ___

Speech non-
communicative or
poorly communica-
tive ___

Hears voices ___

Sees visions ___

   As requested above, please first list below symptoms marked with the
letter P and next to each symptom give descriptive information such as age
of onset, age of termination, and other important data. Then list symptoms
marked with an N and provide similar information.

P or N   Symptom   Brief Description

_____   _____   _____

_____   _____   _____

_____   _____   _____

_____   _____   _____

_____   _____   _____

_____   _____   _____

_____   _____   _____

_____   _____   _____

_____   _____   _____

_____   _____   _____

_____   _____   _____

_____   _____   _____

_____   _____   _____

_____   _____   _____

_____   _____   _____

_____   _____   _____

_____   _____   _____

_____   _____   _____

SIBLINGS

	Name	Age	Medical, social, or academic problems
1.			
2.			
3.			
4.			
5.			

LIST NAMES AND ADDRESSES OF ANY OTHER PROFESSIONALS CONSULTED

1. _____
2. _____
3. _____
4. _____

ADDITIONAL REMARKS

Please use the remainder of this page to write any additional comments you wish to make regarding your child's difficulties.

APPENDIX VIII

Typical Child Behavior Problems

ONE OF THE THINGS WE'RE INTERESTED IN IS HOW YOU HANDLE _____ WHEN S/HE MISBEHAVES. I AM GOING TO DESCRIBE SOME DIFFERENT WAYS IN WHICH CHILDREN DISOBEY THEIR PARENTS. I WOULD LIKE YOU TO IMAGINE YOUR CHILD IN EACH SITUATION AND TELL ME HOW YOU WOULD DEAL WITH HIM/HER.

1. You need to take _____ out for an errand and you don't have much time. You call out for him, but he does not answer. After calling a few more times, you begin to look for him. Soon you become worried, but then find out that he has been hiding from you.

First method: What would you do?

Second method: What if he did it again the next day? What would you do then?

Third method: What would you probably do if he did it once again?

2. You're shopping in a store and _____ is with you. He sees something that he likes and asks you if he can have it. You tell him "NO," but he demands to have it and starts crying and screaming.

First: What would you do?

Second: What if she continues crying and screaming? What would you do?

Third: What if she did it once again?

3. You're busy cooking in the kitchen and you tell _____ to stay out for a while. Instead he climbs up on a table and knocks over a bowl, spilling all of the food on the floor.

First: What would you do?

Second: What if she came back into the kitchen and climbed back onto the table?

Third: What if she did it once again?

4. You and your family are in a strange area with lots of people and you tell _____ not to go too far away. However, he soon wanders off and you have to go looking all over the place for him.

First: What would you do when you found him?

Second: What if he wanders off again and you had to go looking for him again? What would you do when you found him?

Third: What if it happened again? What would you do when you found him?

5. _____ and a neighbor's child are playing together in your living room. _____ asks to play with a toy, but the other child refuses. _____ gets angry, hits his playmate, and takes the toy.

First: What would you do?

Second: What if she did it again? What would you do?

Third: What if the next day, she did it again? What would you do?

6. After being told many times not to go into your closet, you come home to find
   that _____ has be playing there for a while and has made a big mess.

First: What would you do?

Second: What if later that same day you found him in your closet once again making
   a mess? What would you do?

Third: What if it happened again?

7. While playing in another room, _____ accidently breaks a lamp, but does not come
   and tell you. You know that he has done it.

First: What would you do?

Second: What if the next time he broke something, he didn't tell you? What would
   you do?

Third: What if it happened again?

8. _____ is especially rude to one **of** the grandparents.

First: What would you do?

Second: What if later that day, it happened again? What would you do?

Third: What if it happened again that same day?

9. _____ "acts up" by running around and making a lot of noise while a neighbor or
   casual acquaintance is visiting and talking with you.

First: What would you do?

Second: What if he continues to distract the two of you by making lost of noise?
   What would you do?

Third: What if it happened the next day? What would you do?

10. _____ has broken a very important possession of yours. When you ask him for
   an explanation, he denies having done it. You know he is lying.

First: What would you do?

Second: What if he continues to lie? What would you do?

Third: What if a similar thing happens the next day? What would you do? (Depending
   on the type of punishment described, could be replaced with: What if he still
   continues to lie?)

11. _____ refuses to go to bed when you tell him to.

First: What would you do?

649

Second: What if he still refuses to go to bed? What would you do then?

Third: What if the same thing happens the next night? What would you do?

12. Instead of eating his dinner, _____ plays with his food and then starts throwing
     it.

First: What would you do?

Second: What if he continues to throw his food? What would you do?

Third: What if he did the same thing at the next meal? What would you do?

13. You are busy in the kitchen, and you ask him to do you a favor by answering
     the door. Instead of helping out, he just says "No."

First: What would you do?

Second: What if he still refused? What would you do then?

Third: What if later that same day, you asked him to do you another small favor,
     and he refused? What would you do?

14. You and your family are outside. When you are not looking he runs into a busy
     street, falls down and starts crying and calling for you. You pick him up
     and see that he doesn't seem to be hurt.

First: What would you do?

Second: What if later that day, it happens again? What would you do?

Third: What if the next day, it happens again? What would you do?

15. You're very tired and _____ has been pestering you. You have told him to stop,
     but he continues to bother you.

First: What would you do?

Second: What if he continues to pester you? What would you do?

Third: What if later that day, he bagan to bother you again? What would you do?

16. You are in a store. _____ reaches up on the counter, takes something, hides
     it in his pocket and walks away.

First: What would you do?

Second: What if he refused to give it back? What would you do?

Third: What if the next day, he did the same thing in a store? What would you do?

APPENDIX IX
Mediation Letter to Parents

RICHARD A. GARDNER, M.D.
P.O. BOX R
CRESSKILL, NEW JERSEY 07626-0317
201-567-8989

Dear

This is in response to your request for my services in association with your custody/visitation litigation.

In June 1988, after many years of involvement in such litigation--and after giving the matter serious and careful consideration--I decided that I would no longer provide custody/visitation evaluations within the context of adversarial proceedings. Many considerations went into this very difficult decision, only one of which is my belief that adversary proceedings are just about the worst way of resolving such disputes and should only be used as a last resort--after all attempts at mediation have failed. Custody/visitation litigation inevitably causes significant psychological trauma to both parents and children. Mediation is much more likely to protect families from such grief. Custody/visitation litigation is enormously expensive, and this adds to the family's psychological trauma. In contrast, the cost of mediation is generally a small fraction of the usual cost of custody/visitation litigation.

Although no longer willing to serve litigating parents in adversarial proceedings, I will be quite pleased to serve as a mediator to help resolve custody/visitation disputes. Such mediation will focus exclusively on the custody/visitation dispute (my area of expertise) and not consider other conflicts that may be unresolved at the time, e.g., legal and financial. These will have to be dealt with by attorneys, accountants, etc. (in accordance with their expertise).

Before agreeing to serve in the capacity of mediator I request parents sign a statement (attached) that precludes my involvement--in any way whatsoever--in their litigation. They must agree that I will have absolutely no contact with their attorneys or the court--in either written or oral form. My findings and recommendations will be provided verbally and I will not be asked to write any written report, either at the time of the mediation or subsequently. The parents, of course, are free to take my advice or reject it. If they agree to accept my findings they can verbally communicate these to their attorneys for incorporation into the proper legal documents. If one or both rejects them they need not fear that what transpired during our meetings will be revealed by me in their adversarial proceedings. In this way both parties can be assured that the mediation will not be contaminated by the flow of data into the adversarial process.

I recognize that most parents--in the litigious society in which we live--will not be receptive to this approach. They are too committed to the notion that mental health professionals can provide powerful weapons in their custody/visitation disputes. Parents who recognize that mediation is the more humane and civilized approach to the resolution of their custody/visitation dispute not only protect themselves and their children from unnecessary psychological trauma, but are likely to save themselves significant expense as well.

My fee for mediation in my office in Cresskill, New Jersey is $150 per hour. Time spent in interviewing as well as time expended in reviewing submitted documents, lengthy telephone calls, or any other time invested in association with the mediation is billed at the $150 per hour rate. I also require a $1000 advance security deposit. This money, with accrued interest (taxable to the payer), will be returned when the mediation is terminated. Providing mediation outside my office is more costly and the fee schedule for such services is available on request.

Please know that if you and your spouse decide to enlist my services as a mediator for your custody/visitation dispute I will do my utmost to provide you with a thorough evaluation and humane and reasonable recommendations.

Sincerely,

Richard A. Gardner, M.D.
Clinical Professor of
   Child Psychiatry
Columbia University,
College of Physicians
   and Surgeons

RAG/dll

652

APPENDIX X
Mediation Letter to Attorneys

RICHARD A. GARDNER, M.D.
P.O. BOX R
CRESSKILL, NEW JERSEY 07626-0317
201-567-8989

Dear

This is in response to your request for my services in association with your client's custody/visitation litigation.

In June 1988, after many years of involvement in such litigation--and after giving the matter serious and careful consideration--I decided that I would no longer provide custody/visitation evaluations within the context of adversarial proceedings. Many considerations went into this very difficult decision, only one of which is my belief that adversary proceedings are just about the worst way of resolving such disputes and should only be used as a last resort--after all attempts at mediation have failed. Custody/visitation litigation inevitably causes significant psychological trauma to both parents and children. Mediation is much more likely to protect families from such grief. Custody/visitation litigation is enormously expensive, and this adds to the family's psychological trauma. In contrast, the cost of mediation is generally a small fraction of the usual cost of custody/visitation litigation.

Although no longer willing to serve litigating parents in adversarial proceedings, I will be quite pleased to serve as a mediator to help resolve custody/visitation disputes. Such mediation will focus exclusively on the custody/visitation dispute (my area of expertise) and not consider other conflicts that may be unresolved at the time, e.g., legal and financial. These will have to be dealt with by attorneys, accountants, etc. (in accordance with their expertise).

Before agreeing to serve in the capacity of mediator I request parents sign a statement (attached) that precludes my involvement--in any way whatsoever--in their litigation. They must agree that I will have absolutely no contact with their attorneys or the court--in either written or oral form. My findings and recommendations will be provided verbally and I will not be asked to write any written report, either at the time of the mediation or subsequently. The parents, of course, are free to take my advice or reject it. If they agree to accept my findings they can verbally communicate these to their attorneys for incorporation into the proper legal documents. If one or both rejects them they need not fear that what transpired during our meetings will be revealed by me in their adversarial proceedings. In this way both parties can be assured that the mediation will not be contaminated by the flow of data into the adversarial process..

I recognize that most parents and, unfortunately, many attorneys--in the litigious society in which we live--will not be receptive to this approach. They are too committed to the notion that mental health professionals can provide powerful weapons in their custody/visitation disputes. Parents who recognize that mediation is the more humane and civilized approach to the resolution of their custody/visitation dispute not only protect themselves and their children from unnecessary psychological trauma, but are likely to save themselves significant expense as well.

My fee for mediation in my office in Cresskill, New Jersey is $150 per hour. Time spent in interviewing as well as time expended in reviewing submitted documents, lengthy telephone calls, or any other time invested in association with the mediation is billed at the $150 per hour rate. I also require a $1000 advance security deposit. This money, with accrued interest (taxable to the payer), will be returned when the mediation is terminated. Providing mediation outside my office is more costly and the fee schedule for such services is available on request.

Please know that if your client and his/her spouse decide to enlist my services as a mediator for their custody/visitation dispute I will do my utmost to provide them with a thorough evaluation and humane and reasonable recommendations.

Sincerely,

Richard A. Gardner, M.D.
Clinical Professor of
Child Psychiatry
Columbia University,
College of Physicians
and Surgeons

RAG/dll

654

REFERENCES

Abrahms, S. (1979), The joint-custody controversy. *New York*, June 18, 1979.

American Bar Association (1988), *Membership Report, 1788e/5*. Chicago, Illinois: American Bar Association.

American Psychiatric Association (1987), Diagnostic and Statistical Manual of Mental Disorders, Third Edition, Revised (DSM-III-R). Washington, D.C.: American Psychiatric Association.

Association of Family Conciliation Courts (1979), *Joint Custody: A Handbook for Judges, Lawyers, and Counselors*. Portland, Oregon: Association for Family Conciliation Courts.

Bazelon, D. L. (1974), The perils of wizardry. *The American Journal of Psychiatry*, 131:1317-1322.

Beck, P. W. (1977), The law of child custody. *The Journal of Legal Medicine*, January, 1977, pp. 8CC-8FF.

Bellak, L. and Bellak, S. S. (1949), *The Children's Apperception Test*. New York: The Psychological Corp.

Benedek, E. P. (1972), Child custody laws: their psychiatric implications. *The American Journal of Psychiatry*, 136(12):1540-1544.

_____ and Benedek, R. S. (1979), Joint custody: solution or illusion? *American Journal of Psychiatry*, 136(12):1540-1544.

Berg, A. G. (1983), The attorney as divorce mediator. In: *Successful Techniques for Mediating Family Breakup*, ed. J. A. Lemmon, *Mediation Quarterly*, No. 2, pp. 21-28. San Francisco: Jossey-Bass Publishers.

Buck, J. N. (1946), *The House-Tree-Person Test*. Los Angeles, California:

Western Psychological Services.

Cardozo, B. (1925), Finlay v. Finlay. 148 N.E. p. 626.

Cantor, D.W. and Drake, E.A. (1983), *Divorced Parents and Their Children: A Guide for Mental Health Professionals.* New York: Springer Publishing Co.

Coogler, O. J. (1977), Changing the lawyer's role in matrimonial practice. *Conciliation Courts Review,* 15(1):1-7.

————— (1978), *Structured Mediation in Divorce Settlement.* Lexington, Massachusetts: Lexington Books (D.C. Heath and Co.).

Denton, L. (1987), Child abuse reporting laws: are they a barrier to helping troubled families? *The American Psychological Association Monitor,* 18(6):1ff.

Derdeyn, A. P. (1975), Child custody consultation. *American Journal of Orthopsychiatry,* 45(5):791-801.

————— (1976), A consideration of legal issues in child custody contests. *Archives of General Psychiatry,* 33:165-171.

Despert, L. (1953), *Children of Divorce.* Garden City, New York: Dolphin Books (Doubleday and Co., Inc.).

Eder, V. (1979), Shared custody—an idea whose time has come. *Joint Custody: A Handbook for Judges, Lawyers, and Counselors,* pp. B22-B23. Portland, Oregon: The Association of Family Conciliation Courts.

Fain, H.M. (1977), Family Law—"whither now?" *Journal of Divorce,* 1(1):31-42.

Fisher, R. and Ury, W. (1981), *Getting to Yes.* Boston: Houghton Mifflin Co.

Folberg, J. (1983), Divorce mediation: promises and pitfalls. *The Family Advocate,* 4:4-7.

————— (1984), *Joint Custody and Shared Parenting.* Portland, Oregon: The Association of Family Conciliation Courts.

————— and Taylor, A. (1984), *Mediation: A Comprehensive Guide to Resolving Conflicts Without Litigation.* San Francisco: Jossey-Bass Publishers.

Foster, H. H. and Freed, D. J. (1978), Life with Father: 1978. *The Family Law Quarterly,* 11:321-362.

Freud, A. and Burlingham, D. T. (1944a), *War and Children.* New York: International Universities Press.

————— (1944b), *Infants Without Families.* New York: International Universities Press.

Freud, S. (1905), Three Contributions to the Theory of Sex: II—Infantile Sexuality. In *The Basic Writings of Sigmund Freud,* ed. A. A. Brill, pp. 592-593. New York: Random House, Inc. (The Modern Library), 1938.

Gardner, A. K., Scarr, S., and Schwarz, C. (1980), Maternal discipline techniques—questionnaire. (unpublished manuscript)

Gardner, R. A. (1968) The mutual storytelling technique—use in alleviating childhood oedipal problems. *Contemporary Psychoanalysis*, 4:161-177.

_____ (1970), The use of guilt as a defense against anxiety. *The Psychoanalytic Review*, 57:124-136.

_____ (1971), *Therapeutic Communication with Children: The Mutual Storytelling Technique*. Northvale, New Jersey: Jason Aronson, Inc.

_____ (1973a), *Understanding Children: A Parents Guide to Child Rearing*. Cresskill, New Jersey: Creative Therapeutics.

_____ (1973b), *The Talking, Feeling, and Doing Game*. Cresskill, New Jersey: Creative Therapeutics.

_____ (1974), *Fairy Tales for Today's Children*. Cresskill, New Jersey: Creative Therapeutics.

_____ (1976), *Psychotherapy with Children of Divorce*. Northvale, New Jersey: Jason Aronson, Inc.

_____ (1977a), *Modern Fairy Tales*. Cresskill, New Jersey: Creative Therapeutics.

_____ (1977b), *The Parents Book About Divorce*. Garden City, New York: Doubleday and Co., Inc.

_____ (1979a), Death of a parent. In: *Basic Handbook of Child Psychiatry*, ed. J. D. Noshpitz, vol. IV, pp. 270-283. New York: Basic Books, Inc.

_____ (1979b), *The Parents Book About Divorce*. New York: Bantam Books, Inc.

_____ (1979c), Intergenerational sexual tensions in second marriages. *Medical Aspects of Human Sexuality*, 13(8):77ff.

_____ (1980), *Dorothy and the Lizard of Oz*. Cresskill, New Jersey: Creative Therapeutics.

_____ (1982a), *Family Evaluation in Child Custody Litigation*. Cresskill, New Jersey: Creative Therapeutics.

_____ (1982b), Joint custody is not for everyone. *Family Advocate*, 5(2):7ff.

_____ (1984), Counseling children in stepfamilies. *Elementary School Guidance and Counseling*, 19(1):40-49.

_____ (1985), Recent trends in divorce and custody litigation. *The Academy Forum*, 29(2):3-7. New York: The American Academy of Psychoanalysis.

_____ (1986a), *Child Custody Litigation: A Guide for Parents and Mental Health Professionals*. Cresskill, New Jersey: Creative Therapeutics.

_____ (1986b), *The Psychotherapeutic Techniques of Richard A. Gardner*. Cresskill, New Jersey: Creative Therapeutics.

_____ (1987a), *The Parental Alienation Syndrome and the Differentiation Between Fabricated and Genuine Child Sex Abuse*. Cresskill, New Jersey: Creative Therapeutics.

_____ (1987b), Judges Interviewing Children in Custody/Visitation Litigation. *New Jersey Family Lawyer*, 7(2):26ff.

_____ (1988a), *Psychotherapy with Adolescents.* Cresskill, New Jersey: Creative Therapeutics.

_____ (1988b), *The Storytelling Card Game.* Cresskill, New Jersey: Creative Therapeutics.

_____ (1989a), A psychiatrist's opinion of the adversary system, especially as utilized in custody disputes. *The New Jersey Family Lawyer.* (in press)

_____ (1989b), My involvement in child custody litigation: past, present, and future. *Conciliation Courts Review*, 27(2): (in press)

_____ (1989c), A proposal for lawyers and mental health professionals for resolving child custody disputes without the utilization of adversarial proceedings. *The New Jersey Family Lawyer.* (in press)

_____ (1990), *Psychotherapy of Psychogenic Learning Disabilities.* Cresskill, New Jersey: Creative Therapeutics. (in press)

Goldstein, J., Freud, A., and Solnit, A. J. (1973), *Beyond the Best Interests of the Child.* New York: The Free Press (Macmillan Publishing Co., Inc.).

Goldzband, M. G. (1980), *Custody Cases and Expert Witnesses: A Manual for Attorneys.* New York: Harcourt Brace Jovanovich.

_____ (1982), *Consulting in Child Custody: An Introduction to the Ugliest Litigation for Mental Health Professionals.* Lexington, Massachusetts: D.C. Heath & Co.

Goleman, D. (1988), Lies can point to mental disorders or signal normal growth. *The New York Times*, May 17, 1988, pp C1,C6.

Group for the Advancement of Psychiatry (1980), *Divorce, Child Custody and the Family.* New York: Mental Health Materials Center.

Haynes, J. M. (1981), *Divorce Mediation: A Practical Guide for Therapists and Counselors.* New York: Springer Publishing Co.

Holsopple, J. Q. and Miale, F. R. (1954), *Sentence Completion: A Projective Method for the Study of Personality.* Springfield, Illinois: Charles C. Thomas.

Isaacs, M.B., Montalvo, B., and Abelsohn, D. (1986), *The Difficult Divorce.* New York: Basic Books, Inc.

Isaacs, M.B. (1988), The visitation schedule and child adjustment: A three-year study. *Family Process*, 27:251-256.

James, R. J. (1978), Psychiatry and the family law bill. *Australian and New Zealand Journal of Psychiatry*, 12:119-122.

Kestenbaum, C. and Underwood, S.(1979), *Mental Health Assessment Form, Addendum: Maternal Attitudes and Adaptation*, New York: St. Luke's Hospital Center.

Kritzberg, N. (1966), A new verbal projective test for the expansion of the projective aspects of the clinical interview. *Acta Paedopsychiatrica*,

33(2):48-62.

Kubie, L. S. (1964), Provisions for the care of divorced parents: a new legal instrument. *Yale Law Journal,* 73:1197-1200.

Lambuth, D. (1923), *The Golden Book on Writing.* Hanover, New Hampshire: Dartmouth College Press.

Lewis, M. (1974), The latency child in a custody conflict. *Journal of the American Academy of Child Psychiatry,* 13:635-547.

Lieberman, J.K. (1983), *The Litigious Society.* New York: Basic Books, Inc.

Mackover, K. (1949), *Personality Projection in the Drawing of the Human Figure: A Method of Personality Investigation.* Springfield, Illinois: Charles C. Thomas.

McEwen, C. and Maiman, R. (1981), Small claims mediation in Maine: an empirical assessment. *Maine Law Review,* 33:237-263.

McGarry, A.L. (1986), Child Custody. In *Forensic Psychiatry and Psychology,* ed. W.J. Curran, A.L. McGarry, and S.S. Shah. pp. 247-261. Philadelphia: F.A. Davis Co.

McIsaac, H. (1983), Court connected mediation. *Conciliation Courts Review,* 21(2):49-56.

_____ (1984), *Family Mediation and Conciliation Service: Standards and Procedures.* Los Angeles, California: The Conciliation Court of the Los Angeles Superior Court.

Mnookin, R. H. and Kornhauser, L. (1979), Bargaining in the shadow of the law: the case of divorce. *The Yale Law Journal,* 88:950-997.

Murray, H. (1936), *The Thematic Apperception Test,* New York: The Psychological Corp.

Parental Kidnapping Prevention Act (Public Law 96-611, 1980). *Statutes at Large,* 94:3568.

Pearson, J. and Thoennes, N. (1982), Divorce mediation: strengths and weaknesses over time. In: *Alternative Means of Family Dispute Resolution,* ed. H. Davidson, L. Ray, and R. Horowitz. Washington, D.C.: American Bar Association.

Ricci, I. (1980), *Mom's House, Dad's House.* New York: Macmillan Publishing Co., Inc.

Riskin, L. L. (1982), Mediation and lawyers. *Ohio State Law Journal,* 43:29-60.

Rorschach, H. (1921), *The Rorschach Test.* New York: The Psychological Corp.

Salius, A. (1979), Joint Custody. *Joint Custody: A Handbook for Judges, Lawyers, and Counselors,* pp. B16-B19. Portland, Oregon: The Association of Family Conciliation Courts.

Saposnek, D. T. (1983), *Mediating Child Custody Disputes: A Systematic Guide for Family Therapists, Court Counselors, Attorneys, and Judges.* San Francisco: Jossey-Bass Publishers.

Saxe, D. B. (1975), Some reflections on the interface of law and psychiatry in child custody cases. *Journal of Psychiatry and Law,* 3(4):501-514.

Schneidman, E. S. (1948), *Make-A-Picture Story Test.* New York: The Psychological Corp.

Selby, D. M. (1973), Custody of children and the law. *The Medical Journal of Australia,* 2:896-898.

Shapiro, J.J. and Caplan, M.S. (1983), *Parting Sense: A Couple's Guide to Mediation.* Lutherville, Maryland: Greenspring Publications.

Siegel, D. M. and Hurley, S. (1977), The role of the child's preference in custody proceedings. *Family Law Quarterly,* 11(1):1-58.

Slosson, R. L. (1961), *Slosson Intelligence Test.* East Aurora, New York: Slosson Educational Publications, Inc.

Solow, R. A and Adams, P. L. (1977), Custody by agreement: child psychiatrist as child advocate. *The Journal of Psychiatry and Law,* 5(1):77-100.

Spiegel, L. D. (1986), *The False Accusation Syndrome: A Question of Innocence: A True Story of False Accusations.* Parsippany, New Jersey: Unicorn Publishing House.

Thompson, C. (1959), The interpersonal approach to the clinical problems of masochism. In: *Individual and Family Dynamics,* ed. J. Masserman. New York: Grune & Stratton.

United States Census Bureau (1988), *Current Population Reports,* Series P-25, No. 1024. Washington, D.C.: U.S. Census Bureau.

Varendock, J. (1911), Les teroignages d'enfants dans un proces retenissant. *Archives of Psychology,* 11:129.

Wallerstein, J. S. and Kelly, J. B. (1980), *Surviving the Breakup: How Parents and Children Cope with Divorce.* New York: Basic Books, Inc.

Wallerstein, J.S. and Blakeslee, S. (1989a), Children After Divorce: Wounds That Don't Heal. *The New York Times Magazine,* January 22, 1989, pp. 19 ff.

_____ (1989b), *Second Chances: Men, Women & Children a Decade After Divorce.* New York: Ticknor & Fields.

Watson, A. S. (1969), The children of Armageddon: problems of custody following divorce, *Syracuse Law Review,* 21:55-86

Watts vs. *Watts,* 350 NYS 2d 285, 1973.

Wechsler, D. (1974), *Wechsler Intelligence Scale for Children-Revised.* New York: The Psychological Corp.

AUTHOR INDEX

661

SUBJECT INDEX